WHO'S WHO
IN
BLACK CANADA

BLACK SUCCESS AND BLACK EXCELLENCE IN CANADA

A CONTEMPORARY DIRECTORY

2002

Dawn P. Williams

© Dawn P. Williams, 2002
All rights reserved

Published by:
d.p.williams & associates
3 Massey Sq., Unit 1706, Toronto, ON M4C 5L5

Copy editor: Kate George

Graphic design and layout:
Ofelia Infante and Juan Escareño, ARTiFACT graphic design

National Library of Canada Cataloguing in Publication

Williams, Dawn, 1961-
    Who's who in Black Canada: Black success and Black excellence in Canada: a contemporary
    directory / Dawn Williams.

Includes some text in French.
ISBN 0-9731384-0-8 (bound).—ISBN 0-9731384-1-6 (pbk.)

1. Black Canadians—Biography—Dictionaries. 2. Blacks—Canada—Biography—Dictionaries. I. Title.

FC106.B6W54 2002   920'.009296071   C2002-904204-6
F1035.N3W54 2002

Logo: courtesy of Logos Inc.

Printed by:
University of Toronto Press Inc.

Table of Contents

To those who went before:
it is on your shoulders that we stand;
it is in your footsteps that we tread.

UNKNOWN

Acknowledgements

A work like **Who's Who in Black Canada** (WWIBC) is the result of many helping hands and generous individuals. My apologies beforehand to those whose names have been unintentionally left off this list. First, thanks to my parents, Daphne & Leslie Williams, who, once I had exhausted all my savings, lent me some of theirs so that I could continue working on this project. Special thanks go to Raymond Cohen and Colin Rickards: Ray, editor/publisher of *Abilities* Magazine, who supported me throughout the entire process answering questions and providing advice, and who never once said he regretted uttering those fateful words: "great idea! If you decide to go for it, let me know what I can do to help."; Colin, who spent hours providing names of contacts and likely candidates from his extensive lists of journalistic sources, and who generously shared books and other reference material relevant to this compilation. Special thanks also go to: CWO Cy Clayton, from Halifax, one of the first to call after reading an article about WWIBC in the *Halifax Herald* and who was invaluable in providing me with names and contacts of people who were serving or who had served with the Canadian Forces; Rustum Southwell (and staff) of the Black Business Initiative (BBI) in Halifax who encouraged me to attend their Summit 2001, and provided many valuable leads and much support throughout this exercise; MP Jean Augustine who also facilitated my attendance at the BBI Summit; Dorothy Williams, in Montreal, who, over a period of several weeks, spent hours with me on the phone, providing contact names for likely candidates in Quebec; Dr. Dorothy Wills, who provided many valuable contacts from the world of academia; Dr. Okechukwu Ikejiani, who not only provided contact information for likely candidates from across the country but who also contacted each one beforehand so that they knew to expect my call; Flora Blizzard Francis who generously identified many candidates in the Guelph, Kitchener/Waterloo area; Winsom, who put me in touch with many artists and poets; Donna Nurse, who provided the names of a number of writers and painters in Ontario and Quebec; Roger McTair, who provided an extensive list of contacts from a variety of sectors; Rosemary Sadlier, who generously provided contacts from across Ontario; Wofa Yaw and Oni Vincent welcomed me into the African Heritage Family and gave me invaluable contacts from the Nigerian and Ghanaian populations; Sharon Headley, who discovered my website by accident and who, being the coordinator of the Black Achievement Awards Society of Alberta, provided me with a number of Western candidates; Pastor John Adams, who gave me the names of individuals from his current and previous congregations, whom otherwise I might have missed; Michelle-Lee Williams, editor of *The Afro News,* provided several contacts from BC; Norman Alexander provided contacts, and engaged me in several amusing and thought-provoking e-mail discussions; Hutton Archer, provided contacts for Canadians no longer living in Canada, and contacts in the Canadian Guyanese population. My thanks to members of the Advisory Group for attending meetings and providing advice; the Patrons, for lending their names, in particular, Dr. George Elliott Clarke for his enthusiasm and words of encouragement, and Senator Donald Oliver, for his support throughout and leads for potential advertisers; and, to members of the Review and Selection Committee as well as those from the Reading Committee for their valuable assistance and feedback. Many others provided names of candidates or contacts or general assistance. They include: Archie Alleyne; Kemeel Azan; Cliff Bailey; Dr. George Bancroft; Ned Blair; Theresa Gayle-Benedek; George Borden; Rella Braithwaite; Chloe Callender; Sister Hazel Campayne; Donald Carty; Victor Chandler; Austin Clarke; Lucille Vaughan Cuevas; Lauris DaCosta; Judge Daniel Dortelus; Dr. Emerson Douyon; Prof. Gervan Fearon; Margaret Gittens; Dr. Donald K. Gordon; Amy Grant (so nice to have re-connected again after nearly 20 years); Hector Gray, JCA; Judge Stanley Grizzle; Marilyn Gurney, Maritime Command Museum; Frankie Halls; Patricia Holas; Peter Anthony Holder; Dr. Renn Holness; Sarah Hood; Dr. Jude Igwemezie; Prof. Carl James; Dr. June James; Stanley Julien; Jude Kelly; Delores Lawrence; Coach Gary Lubin; Howard Matthews; Donald McLeod; Kathleen Nelson; Dr. Sharon Oliver; Jean Parris; Pat Patterson; Kim Roberts; Sandi Ross (who got us the logo); Judge Vibert Rosemay; Itah Sadu; Sandy Sabharwal; Warren Salmon; Dr. Keith

A.P. Sandiford; Frank Saptel; Mairuth Sarsfield; Sylvia Searles; Dr. George Sewell; Herman Silochan; Denis Simpson; Craig Smith; Janet Somerville; Jadro Subic; Dr. Sheldon Taylor; Sandy Thomas; Harold Usher; June Veecock; Ewart Walters.

About the advertisers: my sincere thanks to the advertisers who deemed it appropriate to support the first edition of this publication. They are: TD Bank Financial Group; CIBC; Business Development Bank of Canada (BDC); the National Film Board of Canada (NFB); the Ontario Provincial Police (OPP); and, the Black Business Initiative (BBI). Quite a few public, private, consular, and post-secondary educational institutions were contacted some have even promised support for future editions. Thanks to the support of those listed, the possibility of future editions is closer to becoming a reality.

I am also grateful to Rella Braithwaite, Craig Smith, Dorothy Williams, Patricia Holas, and the JCA/Toronto for their publications, which were extremely helpful in the preparation of this publication (see Bibliography). In addition, a lot of information was found on the Internet and used to supplement information provided by a number of the people included in this publication. Technical assistance: Mark Dininio, of A4S/SMART Toronto, was invaluable in walking me through the design and the publishing of my web site; Philip Hartwick designed my database; Kate George provided very capable editing with great flexibility and respected my always too-tight deadlines; Ofelia Infante and Juan Escareño did the layout and graphic design at way below cost and with a great deal of patience; Don Alland, University of Toronto Press, was extremely helpful and patient with this first-time publisher; invaluable assistance for translating came from Jean de Dieu N'djore-Acka, Karine Morin, and Jacqueline Jean-Baptiste. The biggest thanks of all goes to God for giving me the strength to complete this project, who carried me when my energy waned and reassured me when my courage wavered, and who kept me believing that this was a good thing, a necessary thing and had to be completed.

Of course, despite all the assistance and input from others, there may be oversights and mistakes, those are my own but certainly unintentional. The 2nd edition of **Who's Who in Black Canada** will be available in 2005, do let me know how we can make it better.

DAWN WILLIAMS

Preface

I t is common practice to invite one person to write the preface for a publication. However, given the cross-section of people, sectors, and regions contained in this book, I considered it appropriate to invite submissions for the preface from a number of people from across the country, in order to capture some of the many different voices. In their own words, here is what they wrote:

Who's Who In Black Canada *is an undertaking that I am proud to support. It will be a valuable resource for Canadian businesses, media and educational institutions, as well as an educational resource for many young people.*

Through the use of this new directory, Canadians will be able to gain a better understanding of the contributions and achievements of some Black Canadians who have made great contributions to making Canada the best country in the world to live.

It will serve as a useful resource of talented people whose skills and abilities will be of great benefit to Canada in the future. It will also highlight our diversity.

Who's Who In Black Canada *will contribute to a better understanding of the need for an end to racism and employment discrimination. Ending discrimination is a task that can only be completed through education and understanding.*

The individuals found within the directory will serve as powerful examples of hard work and dedication, regardless of race or ethnicity. Their achievements will motivate others to follow their example and to help erode the barriers of intolerance.

*I wish **Who's Who In Black Canada** great success.*

THE HON. LINCOLN M. ALEXANDER
Former Lieutenant-Governor of Ontario

What's What with the Who's Who?

By GEORGE ELLIOTT CLARKE

*Identity. Black identity. Black Canadian identity. African-Canadian identity.
What is it? Do you got it? Do you want it? Do you need it?
I want it. Gotta, gotta have it. I need it.*

*I gotta know if there's anyone else out there
who look like me, talk like me, act like me....
Who's out there in this cold, big-up land
to gimme some community?*

*What about you? Are you all alone? Do you got it goin' on?
Is you in the book?*

I wanna know. Said, I wanna know.

What's what? Who's who?

Do you identify?

*The **Who's Who in Black Canada** directory is an undertaking that is long overdue. This will be an invaluable resource to Canada's multicultural community. This new directory will serve multiple purposes. Canadians will gain a better understanding of various career opportunities that are available to them. It will provide young black children with role models whose examples they will be able to follow.*

*The directory will also serve as a powerful instrument for networking. Through the use of **Who's Who in Black Canada,** businesses, search firms and the media will possess a resource that will aid them in their search for skilled black professionals, artists and leaders.*

Finally, and perhaps most importantly, the directory will be a great symbol of achievement and success of and for Canada's Black community. It will allow the greater Canadian population to see first-hand, (and perhaps for the first time) the efforts and contributions of black Canadians to the country's multicultural heritage.

*I wish **Who's Who In Black Canada** great success in the future. It is a project that I am proud to support.*

SENATOR DONALD H. OLIVER, Q.C.

*Un outil de référence, une collection bibliographique...plus que ça!! Cet ouvrage **Qui est qui au Canada noir** est un récit historique sur la présence des Noirs au Canada et leur contribution socioéconomique et politique au pays.*

Ce travail 'de moine' se veut une mémoire collective : il renseigne sur les Noirs au Canada, leur cheminement personnel, leurs accomplissements, leurs succès. Cet ouvrage leur rend hommage et sert de modèle pour les générations montantes. Il permet la création d'un réseau de contacts, instaurant ainsi une nouvelle solidarité inter-culturelle.

Je me suis associée à cet ouvrage tout modestement, croyant que ma contribution aiderait à faire valoir notre présence en tant que Noirs, membres isolés de la grande communauté que nous sommes.

Je félicite Dawn Williams et ses collaborateurs pour cette belle iniative qui aura le mérite d'être un point d'ancrage pour nous et tous les utilisateurs de ce livre.

HÉLÈNE WAVROCH, Présidente
Conseil des aînés

In a just society **Who's Who in Black Canada** *would not be necessary. The publication of this biographical directory is important because it gives a representative cross section of people of colour who, while finding self-satisfaction in their own chosen fields, are contributing vitally in a variety of ways to Canadian society and its betterment. Too often do the popular media focus on what is negative and unflattering.* **WWIBC,** *by publishing informational data on some of the many individuals who have excelled, at times overcoming great obstacles put in their way, is a source of encouragement to blacks, particularly younger ones, some of whom are already deservedly included here.*

Although Africa is the cradle of civilization in general, and of Blacks in particular, **WWIBC** *is exemplary and elucidative in its inclusiveness, there being among its pages Blacks whose recent geographic origin are, inter alia, Africa, the Caribbean, the United States, Canada. It helps expose the fallacy of Black Canadians being asked where they are from; it compels one to reflect on the vast extent to which Caribbeanites are contributing through their expertise to Canada, and on the inestimable loss to the Caribbean where more ought to be done to retain or attract its sons and daughters whose educational roots are in the Caribbean.*

WWIBC *presents many people who have excelled academically, many who have excelled in athletics, and many both ways, demonstrating the efficacy of the Latin phrase, "mens sana in corpore sano" (a sound mind in a sound body). Many of the biographees make time for, and find pleasure in community work. Among the selectees are some who have been granted honours and awards for their professional and/or community contributions.*

This publication will help some teachers and school counsellors resist the presumptive urge to channel Blacks into what they call "the vocational stream," important though the latter is. It is no paradox to aver that this worthy biographical directory should help eliminate offensive concepts like "visible minorities," and "affirmative action," more honoured in the breach than anything else. In our educational system there have been justified complaints about a Eurocentric emphasis, which causes myopia with respect to figures like Sojourner Truth, Madame C.J. Walker, Elijah McCoy, Dr. Daniel Hale Williams.

*Ms. Dawn Williams by conceiving the idea, and her editorial board by helping to make the publication of **WWIBC** a reality, are ensuring that in the early years of the 21st century, Black achievers in Canada are recognized. School and library personnel, employers, general readers, will find much information, and inspiration, in a requisite **Who's Who in Black Canada.***

PROF. DONALD K. GORDON (Ret.)
University of Manitoba

This public record is long overdue. It portrays the versatility of our race throughout the spectrum of everyday life. The contributions made by Canadian Blacks to our country's military is a work of several volumes in itself. From Samuel de Champlain's interpreter, Mathieu Da Costa in 1604, at Port Royal, NS to the tragic death of Corporal Ainsworth Dyer of Montreal on April 2nd, 2002 in Afghanistan, along with fellow comrades Sgt. Leger, Cpl. Smith and Pte. Green.

We as a race want no freebees; we want to be judged on our merit and ability, not the colour of our culture. We are proud Canadians. We as a race owe an expression of gratitude to all those involved in this project...

CYRIL A. CLAYTON, MMM, CD
Chief Warrant Officer (Ret.)

This first edition of **Who's Who in Black Canada** *provides detailed profiles of Canada's Black leaders as well as the other Blacks that are prominent among those the nation is depending on to guide her to a new era of greatness and prosperity. It is an indisputable fact that Canada is blessed with teeming and trained Black human resources. This first edition stands out as the most comprehensive, authoritative and up-to-date biographical encyclopedia ever published on Black Canadians.*

It is expected to serve as a standard ready reference source of information on Black Canadian men and women of accomplishments, Blacks in commerce and industry, academia, administration, scientists, lawyers, physicians, etc. It contains a mine of essential information. As you explore it, you are likely to discover a deep well of information on persons you have heard or have not heard something about but who have quietly carved a niche for themselves. You will also discover something you did not know about the Black people in Canada.

The liberalization of discriminatory policies in 1962 and the subsequent increase of immigrants from third world countries, which since the 1970s have become one of the leading sources of immigrants, helped in the presence of many of the Black Canadians in this edition. As one of them, I welcome this edition of **Who's Who in Black Canada**.

OKECHUKWU IKEJIANI, MD, FRC Path., CON

One of the most interesting things about the life of Blacks in Canada is that, by and large, we don't know each other. It wasn't until I travelled the country with Almeta Speaks, producer of the four-hour Black history documentary series Hymn To Freedom, *that I got a sense of how many of us have been living successful lives in mainstream Canada. In big cities and small towns, from Saltspring, where a graveyard holds five generations of Blacks, to Pictou, where the first Black battalion was demobilized, we are mayors, judges, educators, doctors and entrepreneurs, quietly going about our business.*

Those of us who were born here, some with many generations behind us, tend not to trumpet our achievements. We have, of course, had to leap hurdles of discrimination and marginalization, and we have done so as a matter of course. And we persevere. One of the most useful things this book will do is introduce us to each other. I think we will have much to say to each other, and I look forward to those conversations.

FELIX (FIL) BLACHE FRASER, CM
Broadcaster/writer

*The launching of **Who's Who in Black Canada** is a significant reflection of the breadth and depth of the Black presence in this country. Blacks have been in Canada for over 300 years yet never before has there been a publication of this magnitude affirming the diverse skills and work experiences of the nation's Black residents. This compilation should be a welcome reference in any library, particularly in areas of the country with significant Black populations. **Who's Who in Black Canada** is a current biographical dictionary and offers a glimpse of one of Canada's hidden resources— its Black politicians and entrepreneurs, its dreamers and inventors, artists, poets and educators. Think of it as a directory of achievers and in ten or fifteen years, **Who's Who in Black Canada** will become an indispensable part of the historical record of Blacks at the turn of the 21st century in Canada. It is a record of which all Canadians can be proud.*

DOROTHY W. WILLIAMS, Historian

Introduction

F rustration can be a wonderful catalyst for evoking change. The idea for this directory, this **Who's Who in Black Canada,** grew out of my frustration in seeing very few representatives of the various ethno-racial groups in Canada reflected in trade publications and some public media events. It concerned me that examples of success in business rarely portrayed those who were not from the mainstream culture, meaning White-Anglo-Saxon-and usually male. Yet, my reality was different; living in Toronto and seeing the ethnic diversity in this city as well as other Canadian urban centres such as Halifax, Montreal, and Vancouver I knew there had to be successful Asians, Aboriginals, East Indians, Arabs, and Blacks. It occurred to me that either their exclusion was deliberate, or those compiling and disseminating information lacked the means necessary to identify contacts within these various ethno-cultural groups. After all, what is the politically correct way of asking "who are the leading Chinese chemical engineers? Arab scientists? Black neurosurgeons?" Then, a chance discussion with Gaylene Gould about informing more people from the Black population about the Planet Africa category of the Toronto International Film Festival (which she programs), led to the realization that a listing of "who's doing what where among Blacks across Canada," could be a useful tool, not just for Blacks but also for the larger population. It soon became apparent that many needs and interests would be served through such a resource: it would be a source of reference for members of the media looking for "experts" or spokespeople from various sectors; executive search firms looking for capable individuals who could also help them meet a growing number of corporate clients' requests for "diversity" in their ranks; a mentoring tool for youth, through their educators, social workers, parents, etc.; **Who's Who in Black Canada** would facilitate networking and provide members of the Black population with a big picture view of our activities and accomplishments across the country; and, it would be a snap-shot of our place in contemporary history.

How was the compilation of this directory accomplished? First, I met with Gillian Holmes of *Who's Who of Canadian Women,* who generously explained the basics of how they prepare their publication. I then identified people for the Advisory Group who could provide technical advice, and people who would be Patrons, lending their names in support of this initiative. As this would be a contemporary directory, candidates had to be living; it was open to all sectors (e.g. business, education, the arts, religion, the military, sports, volunteerism, labour, etc.), and to all ages. Individuals selected belonged to one or more of the following categories: pioneers or trailblazers; those occupying senior positions; those making a difference in their communities; those being innovative and creating a niche for themselves or others. Selection for inclusion was based upon actual accomplishments; academic success alone did not ensure inclusion. People could self-nominate or nominate others. Initially, close to 200 ethno-cultural organizations, professional associations, and unions across the country were contacted and invited to inform their members that candidates were being sought for this initiative. Next, individuals were contacted and asked for leads. I attended conferences and began spreading the word. As a result of our press release in April 2001, I had a number of radio interviews and articles appeared in the printed press. People began calling because they had either read an article or heard an interview and wanted to learn more. Some made contact through the website, which they had either heard about or had come across accidentally. Each person proposed as a likely candidate was contacted and invited to make a submission. And, each nominee was asked to propose other candidates. In the end, over 1,400 individuals were contacted and invited to make submissions for this first edition; many were well known, others less so, most were very accomplished in their respective fields. In the end, about 60 per cent of those contacted responded favourably by making submissions. Some declined from the outset. A large number simply never responded to the phone messages, e-mails or mailings sent. The reasons given by those who declined ranged from: "I like to keep a low profile; I'm shy/modest; I don't believe in those things (too elitist); it will just be filled with 'the usual suspects'; I like to think of myself as a (*fill-in-the-blank professional*), not as a Black (*fill-in-the-blank professional*); to, I don't like the idea of someone determining if I qualify or not…" Many will be surprised that some well-known figures are not included in this first edition, and while undoubtedly we missed some individuals, it should not be presumed that those not included were not asked. Beyond the reasons already stated, I can only speculate as to why some others might have chosen not to participate: some people are wary of anything new and want to see how it will look and be received before becoming involved; some believe that if we (Blacks) keep a low profile and just do a good job, all will be rewarded; others have been sniped at too many times and no longer wish to expose themselves to the possibility of further criticism. Obviously we needed consent so only those who clearly gave authorization and approved the final version of the biographical profile prepared were included. Some initially gave consent but did not return the proof; and, some withdrew towards the end for personal reasons. Regardless, our focus should be with this group of 705, who had the courage to stand up and be counted; who believed me (or trusted me) when I said that what they are doing is important and who accepted to be some of the many examples of "Black success and Black excellence" in Canada.

The purpose of **Who's Who in Black Canada** then is to inform, educate, and celebrate; celebrate the men and women in the various provinces in the various sectors who are contributing to their professions and to their communities. I hope that you will be as inspired as I was when I had the pleasure of learning about these individuals and their various activities. There is truly a wealth of talent in our cultural mosaic, and this publication helps to focus attention on at least one group. One day, a publication such as this will no longer be necessary. Until that happy day arrives, it is my hope that by recognizing and embracing this diversity, we will become a richer, more inclusive society, all the stronger, and all the more capable for capitalizing on the human resources which exist within our midst.

Aux lecteurs francophones : A mon avis, c'était impératif de solliciter les soumissions de biographies dans les deux langues officielles du pays. Ceci, afin de ne pas perpétuer l'exclusion que plusieurs parmi nous ont déjà expérimentée.

Par ailleurs, j'implore d'emblée votre indulgence sur des erreurs et ou omissions susceptibles de s'être glissées dans ce premier effort. Je vous invite à m'en faire part, si tel est le cas, en me faisant parvenir vos commentaires. Ceci nous permettra, ensemble, de parfaire ce livre de nos succès, que nous souhaitons léguer aux générations futures. Elles verront ainsi, que la lutte pour l'égalité à commencer bien avant elles, en plus de leur enseigner qu'elles sont issues d'une race forte et capable, et que leur responsabilité est de prendre courage, et de continuer à faire des contributions dont tout le Canada pourrait être fière.

Toronto, September 2002

PATRONS

Dr. Jean Augustine, MP
Etobicoke-Lakeshore, Govt. of Canada

Dr. Rosemary Brown, PC
MLA (Ret.), BC Govt.

Dr. George Elliott Clarke
University of Toronto

Hugh Graham
Black Business & Professional Assn.

Me Irma Lapommeray
Assn. des Avocat(e)s et Notaires Noirs du Québec

Senator Donald H. Oliver, QC
Senate of Canada

ADVISORY GROUP

Raymond Cohen
Canadian Abilities Foundation

Francis Jeffers
Visions of Science

Boris Masip
Urban Financial Services Coalition

Erica J. Phillips
Black Business & Professional Assn.

Joan Pierre
Events Specialist

Colin Rickards
Journalist

Dr. David Trotman
York University

SELECTION & REVIEW COMMITTEE MEMBERS

Dr. George Bancroft

Judge Stanley Grizzle

Frankie Halls

Prof. Carl James

Francis Jeffers

Jude Kelly

Edward Ndububa

Dr. Odida Quamina

Winsom

READING COMMITTEE

Neil Armstrong

Kim Gallant

Amy Grant

Carl Ramsay

Carla Moore

ADVERTISERS

TD Bank Financial Group

CIBC

Business Development Bank of Canada (BDC)

National Film Board of Canada (NFB)

Ontario Provincial Police (OPP)

Black Business Initiative (BBI)

Acronyms & Abbreviations

ACRONYMS

AABHS	Association for the Advancement of Blacks in Health Sciences
AACP	Association for the Advancement of Coloured People (in NS, NB, ON, and BC)
ABLE	Association of Black Law Enforcers
ACAA	African Canadian Achievement Awards/*Pride* Newspaper
ACAM	Afro-Caribbean Association of Manitoba
ACLC	African Canadian Legal Clinic
ACS	American College of Surgeons
ACTRA	Alliance of Canadian Cinema, Television and Radio Artists
AG	Attorney General
AMSSA	Affiliation of Multicultural Societies & Service Agencies (of BC)
ANC	African National Congress
ARCT	Associate, Royal Conservatory of Music
ARDMS	American Registry of Diagnostic Medical Sonographers
B.Comm	Bachelor of Commerce
BAA	Bachelor of Applied Arts
BAASA	Black Achievement Awards Society of Alberta
BADC	Black Action Defense Committee
BBI	Black Business Initiative (NS)
BBPA	Black Business & Professional Association
BCC NS	Black Cultural Centre for Nova Scotia
BET	Black Entertainment Television
BFVN	Black Film & Video Network
BHM	Black History Month
BLAC	Black Learners Advisory Committee
BLS	Bachelor of Library Sciences
BME	British Methodist Episcopal Church
BN	Bachelor of Nursing
BSCP	Brotherhood of Sleeping Car Porters
BSP	Bachelor of Science in Pharmacy
BTC	Black Theatre Canada (Toronto)
B.Th	Bachelor of Theology
BTW	Black Theatre Workshop (Montreal)
BUF	Black United Front
CABJ	Canadian Association of Black Journalists
CABL	Canadian Association of Black Lawyers
CACE	Council on African Canadian Education
CAMH	Centre for Addiction and Mental Health
CAN: BAIA	Canadian Artists Network: Black Artists in Action
CANACT	Canadian African Newcomer Aid Centre of Toronto
CAS	Children's Aid Society
CAW	Canadian Auto Workers (union)
CBTU	Coalition of Black Trade Unionists
CC	Companion, Order of Canada
CCMD	Canadian Centre for Management Development
CD	Canadian Forces Decoration
CD(JM)	Commander, Order of Distinction, Jamaica
CAN J W & L	*Canadian Journal of Women & the Law*
CEC	Canadian Ethnocultural Council
CED	Community Economic Development
CF	Canadian Forces
CFB	Canadian Forces Base
CFL	Canadian Football League
CFO	Chief Financial Officer
CIDA	Canadian International Development Agency
CLC	Canadian Labour Congress
CM	Member, Order of Canada
CMAJ	*Canadian Medical Association Journal*
CNR	Canadian National Railway
CONCACAF	Confederation of North, Central American and Caribbean Association Football
CPR	Canadian Pacific Railway
CQ	Chevalier de l'ordre national du Québec/Order of Quebec
CRRF	Canadian Race Relations Foundation
CRTC	Canadian Radio-television and Telecommunications Commission
CSIRO	Commonwealth Scientific & Industrial Research Organisation (Australia)
CSPQ	Certified Specialist Province of Quebec
CUM	Communauté Urbaine de Montréal
CUPE	Canadian Union of Public Employees
CWO	Chief Warrant Officer
D.Litt.	Doctor of Literature
DABNS	Diplomat, American Board of Neurological Surgery
DTM	Distinguished Toastmaster
DVM	Doctor of Veterinary Medicine
EEO	Equal Employment Opportunity
ENOWAH	Ecumenical Network of Women of African Heritage
ESL	English as a Second Language
EU	Etats-Unis
FAAP	Fellow, American Academy of Pediatrics
FACOG	Fellow, American College of Obstetricians and Gynecologists
FACS	Fellow, American College of Surgeons
FCCRS/C	Fellow, College of Chiropractic Rehabilitation Science/Canada
FIFA	Fédération Internationale de Football Association
FMCP	Fellow, Nigerian Postgraduate Medical College (Physics)

FRCPS	Fellow, Royal College of Physicians and Surgeons
FTCL	Fellow of Trinity College of Music, London (England)
FWACP	Fellow, West African College of Physicians
GAA	Goals Against Average (hockey)
GG	Governor-General
GG 125th	Governor-General 125th Anniversary Commemorative Medal
GM	General Motors/General Manager
GNWT	Government of the North West Territories
GTA	Greater Toronto Area
HRC	Human Rights Commission
HSC	Health Sciences Centre
IAAF	International Association of Athletics Federations (since 2001 – formerly International Amateur Athletic Federation)
ICAO	International Civil Aviation Organization
IDRC	International Development Research Centre
ILO	International Labour Organization
JCA	Jamaican Canadian Association
LEAF	Women's Legal Education and Action Fund
LLD	Doctor of Law
LRSM	Licentiate of the Royal Schools of Music
LSUC	Law Society of Upper Canada
LTCL	Licentiate of Trinity College of Music, London (England)
MAARS	Metro Addiction Assessment Referral Service
MABBP	Montreal Association of Black Business Persons and Professionals
MAS	Mouvement Haïtien de Solidarité
MB BS	Bachelor of Medicine & Bachelor of Science (MD equiv.)
MB Ch.B	Bachelor of Medicine & Bachelor of Surgery (MD equiv.)
MBE	Member of the Order of the British Empire
MES	Master of Environmental Studies
MHN	Mois de l'Histoire des Noirs
MLA	Member of the Legislative Assembly
MLS	Master of Library Sciences
MP	Member of Parliament
MPP	Member of Provincial Parliament
MSVU	Mount Saint Vincent University
MTS	Master of Theological Studies
NA	North America
NACE	National Association of Corrosion Engineers
NAUB	National Association of Urban Bankers
NBC	National Ballet of Canada
NCAA	National Collegiate Athletic Association
NCC	Negro Coloured Centre (Montreal)
NCCP	National Coaching Certification Program
NCO	Non-commissioned Officer
NCVM	National Council of Visible Minorities

NDG	Notre-Dame-de-Grace
NFB	National Film Board of Canada
NS AACP	Nova Scotia Association for the Advancement of Coloured People
NSERC	Natural Sciences and Engineering Research Council of Canada
NWT	Northwest Territories
O.Ont./O.ON	Order of Ontario
OBHS	Ontario Black History Society
OC	Officer, Order of Canada
OCA/OCAD	Ontario College of Art and Design
OD(JM)	Officer, Order of Distinction, Jamaica
ODA	Ontario Dental Association
OFL	Ontario Federation of Labour
OIC	Order-in-Council
OISE	Ontario Institute for Studies in Education
OM	Order of Merit, Jamaica
OPS	Ontario Public Service
OSSTF	Ontario Secondary School Teachers' Federation
PACE	Projects for the Advancement of Childhood Education in Jamaica & Canada
Pan Am	Pan American Games
PRUDE	Pride of Race, Unity and Dignity through Education/NB
PS	Public School
PSA	Public Service Announcement
RCAF/CF	Royal Canadian Air/Armed Forces/ now Canadian Forces
RCDSO	Royal College of Dental Surgeons of Ontario
RCM	Royal Conservatory of Music
RCPS	Royal College of Physicians and Surgeons
RCSC	Royal College of Physicians and Surgeons/ Canada
RDI	Radio Canada Internationale
RFI	Radio France Internationale
SAPACCY	Substance Abuse Program for African Canadian and Caribbean Youth
ScD	Doctor of Science
SDA	Seventh-day Adventist Church
SFU	Simon Fraser University
SGWU	Sir George Williams University (now Concordia)
SMU	Saint Mary's University
SOCAN	Society of Composers, Authors and Music Publishers of Canada
SRC	Société Radio Canada
SSHRC	Social Sciences and Humanities Research Council of Canada
TCDSB	Toronto Catholic District School Board
TDSB	Toronto District School Board
TIFF	Toronto International Film Festival
TPS	Toronto Police Service
TUNS	Technical University of Nova Scotia
TVO	TVOntario

24

U de T	Université de Toronto
U of T	University of Toronto
UBC	University of British Columbia
UCLA	University of California at Los Angeles
UFSC	Urban Financial Services Coalition
UGRR	Underground Railroad
UMAC	Urban Music Association of Canada
UNIA	Universal Negro Improvement Association
UNWCAR	UN World Conference Against Racism (S. Africa, 2001)
UQAM	Université de Québec à Montréal
UTCWI	United Theological College of the West Indies
UUC	Union United Church
UWI	University of the West Indies
VON	Victorian Order of Nurses
WADE	Watershed Association Development Enterprises
WHO	World Health Organization
WLU	Wilfrid Laurier University
WTN	Women's Television Network (now W Network)
WWCB	Who's Who in Canadian Business
WWCW	Who's Who of Canadian Women
WWIC	Who's Who in Canada

WORKING ABBREVIATIONS

a.k.a.	also known as
Admin.	Administration/ Administrative/ Administrator
Affil/Mbrshp	Affiliations/Memberships
Assn.	Association
Assoc.	Associate
Asst.	Assistant
b.	born
CA	Chartered Accountant
Can/Cdn	Canadian
Cert.	Certificate
Cmtee	Committee
Co.	Company
Comm'y	Community
d.	died
Dipl.	Diploma
Dir.	Director
Dist.	District
Div.	Division
EA	Executive Assistant
ED	Executive Director
ed.	editor/edited/editorial
Ed.	Education
esp.	especially
Exec.Dir.	Executive Director
Fdn.	Foundation
GG	Governor General
Gouv.	Gouvernement
Govt.	Government
Hons.	Honours
incl.	including
Int'l	International
J	Journal
Lt.-Gov.	Lieutenant-Governor
mngmt.	management
Mtl	Montreal
Nat'l	National
Org.	Organization
Prof.	Professor/Professeur
Rev.	Revue/Review
Sch.	School
Sec.	Secretary
U.	University
VP	Vice President/Vice-President
WW	Who's Who

Symbols

 Academia: post-secondary; educators; administrators

 Acting: actors; educators; administrators

 Activism: activists; members of unions, community organizations, government related agencies

 Athletics: athletes; coaches; administrators

 Business: entrepreneurs; owners; business professionals; administrators

 Community: associations; national & international organizations; volunteers; administrators

 Dance: dancers; educators; administrators

 Education: primary; secondary; educators; administrators

 Film: filmmakers, producers, directors, critics

 Government: elected officials, appointees, administrators

 History: historians; curators; administrators

 International: government appointees; representatives; administrators

 Law: lawyers; judges; administrators

 Media: radio; TV; print; writers; producers; directors, presenters

 Medicine: doctors; dentists; chiropractors; researchers; administrators

 Military: veterans; officers; administrators

 Music: performers, producers, composers, administrators

 Natural Resources: forestry; soil; agriculture; administrators

 Nursing: nurses; administrators; educators

 Philanthropy: donors; foundations; related agencies

 Photography: photographers

 Police: officers; administrators

 Religion: ministers; pastors; educators; administrators

 Science: scientists; researchers

 Science & Technology: researchers; engineers; technicians, administrators

 Visual arts: painters, sculptors, designers

 Writing: poets; playwrights; authors; storytellers

 Youth: under 29 years of age

Biographies

►ABUKAR, Hassan

YOUTH LEADERSHIP REPRESENTATIVE, Toronto Youth Cabinet, 55 John St., 11th Fl., Toronto, ON M5V 3C6. Born: Somalia, 1981/ in Canada since: 1990.

▶ Hassan Abukar arrived in Canada in 1990 from war-ravaged Somalia; within weeks he was in school and involved in school and community activities. He has since become an example of youth leadership in action, representing issues of concern to youth (e.g. AIDS, education, employment, the environment, diversity). **HIGHLIGHTS:** Ontario Delegate, Forum for Young Canadians Conference, Ottawa, 2001; Cdn Delegate, Youth Forum of the Americas, Quebec, 2001; Cdn/Somalian Delegate, Future World Leaders Summit, Washington, 2001; Vice-Chair, Toronto Youth Cabinet; VP, TDSB Super Council, 2000; Ontario Delegate, Interchange on Cdn Studies Conf., NS, 1998. And, in the larger community, he has been a youth mentor at the Eastview Community Centre; worked with SAPACCY; and, supports a number of Somalian and other youth organizations. **HONS.:** including: Harry Jerome Award, excellence in leadership, 2000; Herbert H. Carnegie Citizenship Award, 2001; Future Shop Future Leaders Scholarship, 2001; Outstanding Achievement Award, & Black Achievers Community Volunteer Awards, YMCA, 2001. **REVIEWED IN:** local & community publications. **EDUCATION:** pursuing BA, York U. **HEROES/ROLE MODELS:** Father; God. **MOTTO:** "Luck" is when hard work and preparation meet opportunity. **CONTACT:** hassan_abukar@hotmail.com; www.torontoyouth.com

►ACQUAAH-HARRISON, Kobèna

MUSICIAN/PRODUCER, Ice Hut Production, Toronto, ON. Born: Ghana.

▶ Kobèna (pron. *kaw-ben-na*) Acquaah-Harrison is a multi-talented musician and producer of musical events featuring African artists. Since 2000, he has been the Artistic Director of Toronto's AfroFest, a three-day outdoor festival featuring music from continental Africa; previously, he was the first elected president of the AfroFest Board, in 1994. He is also the producer of AfricaNight, a monthly music showcase at the Bamboo Club in Toronto, since 1994. He has been the radio host of the weekly *Sounds of Africa,* on CKLN 88.1 FM, since 1989. His music has been featured in film, TV commercials, and on a number of JUNO-nominated and - awarded CDs (Kaleefa, Jack Grunsky). As a musician, he has played with the Afro-Nubians, as guitarist; COBA, as drummer; Flash Bantou; Jama; Sikaya; has also been a featured guest artist with a number of other performers. He directed the first group of international performers to tour Guyana, during the 135th Anniversary of Emancipation, in 1999, performing in seven cities in ten days; is also a composer/conductor of Jungle Bouti Orchestra, a 12-piece African orchestra, which performs a blend of "African hip hop jazz" music from Africa, the Caribbean, and the Americas; was a contributing editor to *Word* magazine, 1989-93. He recently established the multi-media studio, Abandze Embassy Studios in Accra, Ghana, and is preparing to release his second CD. **COMMUNITY INVOLVEMENT:** well-known community activist, committed to groups like Each One Teach One, CAN:BAIA, Soul Discovery, and Black Habits; co-founder of several arts service organizations including Worlds of Music and the Music Alliance Projects (MAP). **HONS.:** including: Anansekrom, for contribution to traditional music in Canada (2001), and, Media Arts Excellence (1997), Ghanaian-Cdn Assn.; Toronto African Music Awards, Excellence in Media (1999), & Best Composer (1997); Coolest Musician in Toronto Award, *eye Weekly,* 1994. **WORKS:** in *Earthtone Music Guide; Word; Toronto Star.* **CONTACT:** Tel: 416-292-2544; icehutproduction@hotmail.com; www.junglebouti.com

▶**ADAMS, James L.**
ARTIST/PROFESSOR (Ret.), Douglas/Kwantlen University College,White Rock, BC. Born: USA/ in Canada since: 1969.
▶ Professor James Lowell Adams is an artist and a teacher. Originally from the US, he came to Canada in 1970 and taught at Douglas/Kwantlen University College until 2000; he was also a Canada Council Lecturer at University of Waterloo. In addition he has taught at The Laguna Beach School of Art and Design, the Philadelphia Museum of Fine Art, and the Fleisher Memorial Art School in Philadelphia. He has researched various media such as offset lithography, cinematography as a painter's art form, books as an art form, and the impact of flight on the visual arts. Current research examines the reinterpretation of the romantic landscapes and deity figures from the African continent. His work moves between painting and sculpture, although he is primarily a painter. He describes his work as dealing with shape, colour, and spatial relationships. From 1970-87, his work concerned flight-related images; since then his focus has been on: local landscape (South Surrey), figurative paintings (social commentaries), and sculpture (drawing on the Yoruba traditions). He has created and organized a number of exhibitions including *Creative Flight* and, for TV, *S.A.G.A.,* and *On View.* His works have been exhibited throughout Canada and the US and can be found in public and private collections. **COMMUNITY:** Chair, BC Festival of the Arts, 2002; Public Art Advisory, City of Surrey; Cultural Strategic Plan Task Force, Surrey. **HONS.:** several including: Fifty Best Books of the Year, 1976. **REVIEWED IN:** several art catalogues and local & provincial publications. **EDUCATION:** MFA, U. of Pennsylvania, 1968; BFA, Temple U., 1968. **HEROES/ ROLE MODELS:** Father; Eugene Feldman & Neil Welliver, professors at Graduate School. **MOTTO:** Life is clearly defined by how you face it when there are no witnesses. **CONTACT:** jima43@telus.net

▶**ADAMS, Leonard,** PhD.

PROFESSOR EMERITUS, Dept. of French Studies, University of Guelph, Guelph, ON. Born: Trinidad & Tobago/ in Canada since: 1966.

▶ Dr. Leonard Adams is, since 1996, University Professor Emeritus at Guelph University; he is internationally known for his contributions to the fields of 18th century French Literature and Religious History. He began his teaching career at U. of Guelph in 1967, first in the Dept. of Languages and Literatures, then in the Dept. of French Studies; he became a full professor in 1989 and the first Chair of the Dept. of French Studies (1992). He has written many articles, papers, abstracts and book reviews with a focus on 18th century French Literature and History. His *magnum opus* is a seven-volume edition of the Gallican correspondence of William Wake (Archbishop of Canterbury, early 18th century), which has been described by other specialists in the field as being "of real historical significance," since it is the first to document the main ecumenical effort of the period between French Catholic and Anglican theologians. Since retiring in 1995, LA continues his research on clerical and philosophical dissent in 18th century France, this time focusing on Pierre-François Le Courayer. LA could have also pursued a career in classical music; he has accreditation from the Paris Conservatory as a singer and has been the recipient of the top prize for his performances. He was a member of the Guelph Chamber Choir, from 1982-93. His musical career began in his native Trinidad, where, after completing his musical studies, he undertook a successful tour, in 1965, of the Eastern Caribbean, sponsored by the Extra-Mural Dept., University College of the West Indies, giving recitals in Grenada, Barbados, St. Lucia, and Antigua. **OTHER:** he and his wife have been foster parents to six children; he was a member of a committee on the environment, set up by Guelph City Hall. **WORKS:** several, including articles, abstracts, reviews, books: *William Wake's Galli-*

can Correspondence and Related Documents 1716-1731, seven volumes, 1988-93; *Coyer and the Enlightenment,* vol. 123 of *Studies on Voltaire and the Eighteenth Century,* 1974. **EDUCATION:** PhD, U. of London, UK, 1971; MA, Romance Philology & French Literature, McMaster U., 1967; Music Diplomas (FTCL, LTCL, LRSM): Trinity College of Music & Royal Schools of Music, London, England, 1963-66; Dip. Ed, London-UCWI, 1959; BA/Hons., London-UCWI, 1958. **MOTTO:** *Felix qui potuit rerum cognoscere causas/* Lucky is the one who can learn the roots of the universe. **CONTACT:** ladams@uoguelph.ca; Fax: 519-763-9572

▶**ADAMS, Pastor John**

MINISTERIAL DIRECTOR, Alberta Conference of Seventh-day Adventists, 37541 Highway 2, Red Deer, AB T4E 1B. Born: St. Vincent/ in Canada since: 1970.

▶ Pastor John Adams has been involved with the Seventh-day Adventist (SDA) Church as a pastor since 1982. Among his many accomplishments is the spearheading and building of the largest African-Canadian church in Western Canada. He is Ministerial Director of the Alberta Conference of the SDA Church (head office of the more than 8,300 Adventists in the province of Alberta and an integral part of the 12 million Adventists worldwide) and is involved in the leadership of three areas: Ministerial, Evangelism, and Ministry Director. He is "the pastor's pastor" to 42 church leaders, and 65 churches and companies. He is responsible for planning the evangelistic growth of the Adventist Church for the entire province, visiting and counseling with ministers and their families, speaking at their churches, conducting training workshops, and more. He is very active in the community and involved with the Afro-Canadian Leadership organization; has been a member of the Chief of Police Advisory body; volunteers with eight different community organizations. **HONS.:** Health & Well-Being

Award, BAASA, 1996. **REVIEWED IN:** local, regional, and church publications; *Alberta SDA Magazine; The Canadian Messenger.* **EDUCATION:** doctoral studies in progress; M.Div, Andrews U., US, 1986; B.Th, Cdn Union College, 1981. **MOTTO:** Not by might nor by power but by my Spirit, says the Lord. (Zech. 4:6) **CONTACT:** jr_adams@albertasda.org; Fax:403-343-1523

▶ADIBE, Michael

PRINCIPAL (Ret.), Office of the Auditor General of Canada, Ottawa, ON. Born: Nigeria/ in Canada since: 1968.

▶ Michael Adibe retired from the office of the Auditor General of Canada in 1997, after 29 yrs. of service in the Federal Public Service. **CAREER HIGHLIGHTS:** his Canadian career began in 1968 when he joined Statistics Canada, as Head of Deflation Section, National Accounts Div., responsible for the constant dollar estimates of Canada's GNP and derivation of the implicit price deflators and analysis of their trends; 1970, he transferred to the Treasury Board Secretariat, as Project Officer in Efficiency Evaluation Div.; 1972, became Senior Project Officer, leading teams that assisted federal Govt. departments in the development of operational performance measurement systems; 1976-80, he was Chief, Implementation Assistance Group, that provided consultative assistance to departments in the implementation and use of program performance measurement for planning, management control, and accountability purposes. In 1980, he transferred to the Office of the Auditor General, as Director, Control Evaluations Branch, where he directed audits of efficiency and effectiveness in Consumer and Corporate Affairs, and the National Library and Public Archives. In 1982, he moved to Audit Operations Branch and directed value for money audits in National Health and Welfare, IDRC, and government-wide effectiveness audits in selected departments. In 1983, he became Principal, responsible at different periods for a variety of functions and value for money audits including: 1983-85, managing revision of the Office's auditing manual and the publication of audit guidelines and bulletins; 1986-91, audits of Public Debt and Employee Pensions, Canada's participation in the World Bank and IMF, and Cooperative Assistance of the Int'l Atomic Energy Agency in Vienna; 1991-97, audits of Tax Assistance for Retirement Savings, and Excise Tax on alcohol, tobacco, gasoline and jewellery. **BACKGROUND:** Prior to coming to Canada, he worked in Nigeria in the Federal Office of Statistics, 1954-66, beginning as a Statistical Clerk. Then, through a series of promotions complementing his ongoing academic and professional training and development, progressed to Statistician, 1962-64, and Acting Senior Statistician, 1964-66. **COMMUNITY:** active in church as eucharistic minister, lay reader; member of Our Lady of Fatima Knights of Columbus Council. **HONS.:** academic scholarships & fellowship awards from the governments of Nigeria, Britain, and the European Common Market, 1960-62. **WORKS:** co-authored, "The Role of Performance Information in Improving the Management of Public Sector Programs," in *Annals of Public & Cooperative Economy,* 1979. **EDUCATION:** MA, Economics, Carleton U., 1974; Dipl., Statistics (with distinction), Inst. of Social Studies, The Hague, Netherlands, 1962; Dipl., Statistics (MIS), Inst. of Statisticians, London, UK, 1962. **HEROES/ROLE MODELS:** Alex Foti, advised him to study for MA in Economics; Ted McNamara, encouraged him to transfer to the Office of the Auditor General. **MOTTO:** Work as hard as if everything depends on you; and, pray as hard as if everything depends on God.

▶AGINAM, Obijiofor, PhD.

ASSISTANT PROFESSOR, Dept. of Law, Carleton University, 1125 Colonel By Dr., Ottawa, ON K1S 5B6. Born: Nigeria, 1969/ in Canada since: 1996.

▶ Dr. Obijiofor Aginam is an Assistant Professor of Law at Carleton University, with expertise in international law, global health and environmental issues. He teaches courses on: Public International Law; Global Governance, Human Rights, Environmental Justice, International Organizations, and Third World Development. **CAREER HIGHLIGHTS:** was a Global Health Leadership Officer, WHO, based in Geneva, 1998-2001. There, he worked on two projects involving international legal approaches to global governance of tobacco and infectious diseases; was also a member of the Legal Expert Group responsible for developing a Framework Convention on Tobacco Control (FCTC). While still in Nigeria, he was: an Attorney and Research Associate with a law firm focusing on human and environmental rights in oil and gas operations, 1994-96; Legal and Research Officer, Kainji Lake National Park, worked on legal issues concerning natural resources conservation, 1993-94; legal consultant for Nigerian National Park Board and part of the legal team that drafted the current National Parks legislation for Nigeria, 1994-96. He has also worked as legal consultant to WHO for negotiation of the FCTC by over 156 member states of WHO. **HONS.:** recipient of a number of academic awards & fellowships; Global Health Leadership Fellow, WHO, Geneva, 1999-2001. **WORKS:** articles in WHO publications; *J of Maritime Law & Commerce; Indiana J of Global Legal Studies; Chicago J of International Law;* book, *Humanizing Our Global Order* (co-editor), forthcoming. **EDUCATION:** PhD, UBC, 2002; LLM, Queen's U., 1998; LLB, U. of Nigeria, 1992. **HEROES/ROLE MODELS:** Martin & Caro Aginam, parents; Olisa Agbakoba. **MOTTO:** Work hard and defer the applause of the moment to the judgement of history. **CONTACT:** aginam@yahoo.com; Fax: 613-520-4467

▶AGNANT, Marie-Célie

ÉCRIVAINE, Montréal, QC. Née: Haïti/au Canada depuis: 1970.

▶ Marie-Célie Agnant est une écrivaine qui, depuis 1994, a publié huit ouvrages (poésie, romans, nouvelles). Conteuse, elle anime régulièrement des ateliers de contes. Elle participe également depuis 15 ans au festival annuel du « Bread & Puppet Theater » au Vermont. Ecrivain présente et attentive au monde qui l'entoure, elle souhaite que son œuvre reflète cet engagement. En dehors de ses occupations d'écrivain, comédienne, et conteuse, elle travaille à titre d'interprète et de traductrice (Espagnol, Français, Anglais et Créole); elle est accréditée comme interprète culturelle auprès des services sociaux et de santé de Montréal. **PRIX:** finaliste, Prix de Gouverneur Général, *Le Silence comme le Sang,* un recueil de nouvelles, 1998; finaliste Prix du Roman Desjardins, *La Dot de Sara,* un roman, 1996. **ŒUVRES:** *Vingt petits pas vers Maria,* 2001; *Le Livre d'Emma,* roman, 2001; *Alexis, fils de Raphaël,* 1999; *Le Noël de Maïté,* 1999; *Alexis d'Haïti,* roman, 1999; *Le Silence comme le Sang,* 1997; *La Dot de Sara,* 1995. **CONTACT:** annecelie@hotmail.com

▶AITCHESON, Adrian

FASHION DESIGNER, Roots, Toronto, ON. Born: Toronto, ON.

▶ Adrian Aitcheson is a Toronto-based clothing designer specializing in sportswear and urban fashion. He is the original founder of the clothing line, Too Black Guys, released in 1990, and which quickly became a pioneering urban fashion brand. In addition to designing the clothing, he was also responsible for marketing and sales. Too Black Guys retail stores opened in Toronto and New York, while sales extended to England, France, Germany, and Japan. The clothing was featured in popular videos by high-profile performers such as Mary J. Blige's *Real Love, Scenario,* by A Tribe Called Quest, and in movies such as *Dangerous Minds* and *Get on the Bus.* In 1999, AA joined Roots, one of Canada's most recognizable lifestyle brands, as a designer. He has since worked on the Roots menswear collection, and headed up the team that designed the Sydney 2000 Canadian Olympic collection and the Toronto Maple Leaf NHL collection. For the 2002 Winter Olympics, he led the team designing the US and Canadian team outfits, as well as the British parade outfits. Public response to the 2002 Winter Olympic collection was overwhelmingly positive, and the City of Toronto recognized his achievements with the award for Fashion Designer of the Year. **HONS.:** Award for excellence, Fashion Designer of the Year, City of Toronto, 2002; Men of Excellence Award, 1996. **REVIEWED IN:** nat'l & int'l publications; TV & radio coverage. **EDUCATION:** BA, Economics, U of T. **CONTACT:** aaitcheson@roots.com

►AKANDE, Zanana L.

EDUCATOR (Ret.), Toronto District School Board; **FORMER MPP,** Government of Ontario. Born: Toronto, ON.

▶ Zanana Akande has held positions as a teacher, administrator, and lecturer at all levels of education, and as an elected member of provincial parliament. As a consultant, she designed and coordinated programs for pupils with special needs, including gifted students and immigrant children adjusting to the Canadian system. As a principal, she was responsible for the redirection of large inner city schools with culturally diverse populations. In addition, she was an interviewer and panelist for MTV, and co-founder of *Tiger Lily,* a magazine giving voice to the perspectives of visible minority women. In 1990 she became the first Black woman in Ontario elected to provincial parliament, representing the riding of St. Andrew/St. Patrick, until 1994. During her term in government, she was appointed Minister of Community and Social Services, and later served as Parliamentary Assistant to the Premier. She was responsible for the design and implementation of the jobsOntario Youth Program, which created over 5,000 jobs for youth across the

province during the summers of 1991 to 1994. In addition, she was involved with many ministerial committees, including the Interministerial Committee on Youth Employment, focusing on effecting wider access to jobs for all youth. Now retired, she continues to work as a speaker and lecturer on topics of equity, effective communication, feminism, and social change. **COMMUNITY INVOLVEMENT:** has included: Brd., United Way of Greater Toronto, and served on several committees; Brd., Family Services Assn.; Brd., Elizabeth Fry Society; Doctors Hospital, and several others. Current involvements include: executive member, Toronto Child Abuse Centre; Brd., YWCA; executive member, Harbourfront Centre; Brd., Urban Alliance on Race Relations; executive member, Cdn Alliance of Black Educators; Brd., Community Unity Alliance. **HONS.:** has been the recipient of many awards including: ACAA, for education; Onyx Award, for "exemplary service to community"; Black History Makers Award; Arbor Award, U of T; Award of Distinction, Congress of Black Women; Plaque from visible minority civil servants in the Ontario Government, "In appreciation of your uncompromising struggle…for consistently representing the interests of racial minorities particularly in the Ontario Public Service." **REVIEWED IN:** *Millennium Minds,* 2000; *Some Black Women,* 1993. **EDUCATION:** continuing studies in Sociology; M.Ed, BA, U of T. **CONTACT:** Fax: 416-322-9637

►AKANO, Liz

BUSINESS TEACHER, Thames Valley District School Board, London, ON. Born: Nigeria/ in Canada since: 1979.

▶ Liz Akano is a business studies teacher in London who has been recognized by the Ont. Secondary School Teachers' Federation (OSSTF), the Congress of Black Women, and the YMCA, for her active involvement in human rights and community development organizations. These include: Foster Parents; President, Congress of

Black Women, London Chapter; Race Relations Advisory Committee; Cdn Org. for Human Rights; OXFAM; Amnesty International; Nigerian Org. for Human Rights and Democracy; African Assn. of London; Greenpeace, and many others. **HONS.:** Woman of Distinction Award, for arts, heritage, and culture, YWCA/YMCA, 2001; Special Recognition, OSSTF, 2001; Woman of Distinction Award, Congress of Black Women/ London, 2000. **REVIEWED IN:** articles in local media. **EDUCATION:** B.Ed, Technical/Industrial, U. of Manitoba, 1984; Dipl., Textile Tech., Mohawk College, 1982. **HEROES/ROLE MODELS:** Parents. **MOTTO:** It is not over until I win! **CONTACT:** lizakano@ideasnetworks.com; www.africastyles.com; Fax: 519-649-2960

▶ALCINDOR, Maryse

DIRECTRICE, Direction de l'éducation & de la coopération, Commission des droits de la personne et des droits de la jeunesse, 360, St-Jacques, 2ᵉ étage, Montréal, QC H2P 1P5. Née: Haïti/au Canada depuis: 1965.

▶ Maryse Alcindor travaille à la Commission des droits de la personne et des droits de la jeunesse du Québec, depuis 1985 et occupe actuellement le poste de Directrice à la direction de l'éducation et de la coopération. Auparavant, elle était enquêtrice-médiatrice à La Commission et a participé, entre autres, à deux grandes enquêtes: l'une sur le traitement des patients à l'hôpital Rivière-des-Prairies, et l'autre sur les relations entre la police et les groupes ethniques à Montréal. Dans ses différentes activités, elle travaille à améliorer les rapports entre les divers groupes et à promouvoir l'égalité dans les rapports entre les citoyens. Elle a commencé sa vie profesionnelle comme enseignante de français et d'histoire dans les écoles secondaires. Ensuite, elle s'est dirigée vers des études de droit; pendant ses études et après son Barreau, elle a fait un stage au cabinet de Juanita Westmoreland-Traoré et associés; 1981-85, elle a tenu son cabinet d'avocat avant de commencer son travail à la Commission. Sur le plan international, elle a organisé et coordonné des colloques et des conférences sur les droits de la personne et les droits des femmes. De 1994 à 2001, elle était responsable de l'organisation et de la supervision d'une session annuelle d'éducation aux droits à l'Université de Strasbourg, en France. **PRIX:** Enseignant de l'année, étudiants, l'Ecole secondaire, Henri-Bourassa, 1981. **ŒUVRES:** *Manuel de formation à l'intention des para-juristes,* 1995; plusieurs rapports et articles pour la Commission des droits de la personne et des droits de la jeunesse. **FORMATION:** Ecole nationale d'administration publique, 1988. Licence en droit, 1980; Bac, Pédagogie, 1966, U. de Montréal. Maîtrise en Arts, 1978; Bac, spécialisé en Histoire, 1974, UQAM. Bac, Enseignement secondaire, Haïti, 1965. **CONTACT:** Tél: 514-873-5146, poste 260

▶ALEXANDER, Norman E., MPM.

REGISTERED PROFESSIONAL BIOLOGIST (Ret.), BC Institute of Technology, Chilliwack, BC. Born: Vancouver, BC.

▶ Norman Alexander is a Registered Professional Biologist, otherwise described as a Forest Biologist. In this capacity, he was an Instructor at the BC Institute of Technology, 1967-93; during that time he acted as Chief Instructor and Dept. Head; developed and taught a number of courses including Forest Health course and Environmental Impact Assessment; assisted in Photo Interpretation, Silviculture, Forest Land Management, and Forest Ecology. He is described as "one to thank for a fundamental change in the way we view and manage our forests." He also completed consultancies for the Pacific Forestry Centre (field audit of forest insects and disease ranger function), BC Min. of Parks (forest pest management for parks managers), BC Min. of Forests (summary of pest management training needs). **OTHER:** he operated his own forestry consulting firm, 1969-87, during which time he achieved the following: for five yrs. was responsible for the in-service Forest Pest Management Training for the BC Min. of Forests; pioneered the direct delivery of forestry worker courses to Indian bands on their own lands; completed projects for Canadian Forest Products, BC Hydro, Alberta Parks, Okanagan Helicopters, Dept. of Indian Affairs and many private operations; conducted the 1994 National Validation Survey for Forest Technologists in BC; and, was an Instructor at the Nicola Valley Institute of Technology, teaching their Forest Health course, 1993-97. Before becoming a Forest Biologist, he also worked as a Forest Biology Ranger, at the Pacific Forest Research Centre, 1955-67; and as a logger and technician, 1950-52. **AFFIL/MBRSHP:** 28 yrs. in Scouting (from Cub, Scout, Rover Scout, Scoutmaster, District Scoutmaster and District Commissioner), which he credits as being a major influence in his life, 1939-67; BC AACP; National Black Coalition, Western Canada; skilled as a photographer, he has provided photos for Govt. of Canada reports, Min. of Forests; Big Brothers of Burnaby; founding member Professional Pest Management Assn. of BC; BC Forest Health Committee. **HONS.:** including: Distinguished Service Award, 2001, & Service Recognition Award, 1991, BC Institute of Technology; Award for contributions to the field of education, Congress of Black Women, 1993; Long Service Medal, Boy Scouts of Canada. **WORKS:** including: articles in *The Forest Chronicle;* wrote column, "Forest Facts," *Northwest Sportsman* magazine; photos used in Min. of Forests "Tree Doctor" diagnostic program; photo/illustrations in *Field Guide to Pests of Managed Forests in BC;* plus a number of reports completed for the Govt. of Canada, Govt. of BC Forestry & Forest Biology Divisions; Sr. author, *Brief to Pearse Royal Commission on Forestry,* 1975. **EDUCATION:** Master Pest Management (MPM), Simon Fraser U., 1976; Dipl. Photography, NJ Dept. of Education, 1973. **CONTACT:** normalex@telus.net

▶**ALEXANDER, Siobhan**

LEGAL COUNSEL, Bank of Montreal, First Canadian Place, 21st Fl., Toronto, ON M5X 1A1. Born: Toronto, ON, 1967.

▶ Siobhan Alexander is, since 2000, Legal Counsel, Personal and Commercial Client Banking Group, at the Bank of Montreal, and is responsible for providing legal advice to three major Bank Lines of Business (Everyday Banking, Insurance, and Term Investments). She articled at McCarthy Tetrault, 1996-97, then joined Aird & Berlis, 1998-99, as an Associate in Corporate and Securities Law. **AFFIL/MBRSHP:** African Canadian Legal Clinic; LSUC. **HONS.:** academic, including: J.S.D. Tory Fellowship, Legal Writing, 1996. **REVIEWED IN:** *Toronto Star,* 1999. **EDUCATION:** completing MBA, Wilfrid Laurier U.; LLB, U of T, 1996; BA, McMaster U., 1987. **MOTTO:** Do your best and let God do the rest! **CONTACT:** shevy@look.ca

▶**ALEXANDER, The Hon. Lincoln M., PC, CC, O.Ont., QC.**

LAWYER, LIEUTENANT-GOVERNOR (Ret.), Government of Ontario. Resides in Hamilton, ON. Born: Toronto, ON.

▶ The Hon. Lincoln Alexander has had a number of significant accomplishments during the course of his career, becoming the first Black elected to the House of Commons (1968-80), and the first Black in Canada to become Lieutenant-Governor (Ont., 1985-91). **BACKGROUND:** born in Toronto and raised in Hamilton, he served as a radio operator with the RCAF during WWII; after completing his studies at McMaster University and Osgoode Hall Law School in 1953, he began practising law. In 1965, he was appointed a Queen's Counsel and was partner with the Hamilton law firm, Miller, Alexander, Tokiwa, and Isaacs, 1963-79. In 1968, he was elected as an MP, and served in the House of Commons until 1980; in 1979, he was the Federal Minister of Labour. In 1980, he retired from politics and became Chair of the Ontario Workers' Compensation Board, until 1985. In 1985, he was appointed Lieutenant-Governor of Ontario and became the first member of a visible minority group to serve in this capacity in Canada, a post he held until 1991. An emphasis on youth and the promotion of improved race relations were hallmarks of his mandate. And, to commemorate his term as Lieutenant-Governor, the province of Ontario established The Lincoln M. Alexander Awards in 1993. **OTHER:** in 1991, he was appointed Chancellor of the University of Guelph, a position he still holds; he is, since 1996, Chair of the Cdn Race Relations Foundation; and, continues to be involved with a number of charities. He has been described by Dr. Daniel G. Hill as, "a proud chapter in Black Canadian history. A soldier, lawyer, and parliamentarian, he is a man of compassion and generosity who has given us pride and our children hope." **HONS.:** several including: Recipient of 7 Honorary Doctorate degrees; Lifetime Achievement Award, CABL, 1997; Canadian Forces Decoration, 1994; Companion, Order of Canada, 1992; GG 125th Anniv. Medal, 1992; Hamilton Gallery of Distinction, 1992; Award of Merit, City of Toronto, 1993; appointed to the Most Venerable Order of the Hospital of St. John of Jerusalem, Knight of Justice (K.St.J.), 1994; three schools and one highway have been named in his honour; Chancellor, U. of Guelph, since 1996. **REVIEWED IN:** *WWIC; Some Black Men,* 1999; *Millennium Minds,* 2000. **EDUCATION:** LLB, Osgoode Hall, U of T, 1953; BA, McMaster U., 1949. **CONTACT:** c/o CRRF, Tel: 416-952-3500

▶**ALEXANDER, Thérèse,** The Hon.

JUDGE, Provincial Courts British Columbia, 6263 Deer Lake Ave., Burnaby, BC V5G 3Z8. Born: Vancouver, BC.
▶ The Hon. Judge Thérèse Alexander is the great great-granddaughter of Charles and Nancy Alexander, Black settlers who came north from the US and settled in Saanich, BC, in 1858. TA trained as a classical ballet dancer and studied at Université de Québec à Trois Rivières and at La Sorbonne Nouvelle, in France, before completing her studies in law at the University of British Columbia. She was called to the bar of BC in 1984; was a founding partner in the law firm, Stone and Alexander, and conducted a general civil litigation practice until her appointment to the Provincial Court of BC in January, 1996. She currently presides in all divisions of the Provincial Court of BC and is one of three bilingual judges there. For five years she served as national chair of the Cdn Assn. of Provincial Court Judges Bilingualism Committee; 1997-2000, served as a director of the Cdn chapter of the Int'l Assn. of Women Judges. She has a long-standing interest in equality issues; 1997-2002 was a member of the Provincial Court of BC Chief Judge's Equality Committee; is currently a member of the Social Context Education Planning Advisory Committee of the National Judicial Institute; is the national chair of the Cdn Assn. of Provincial Court Judges Equality and Diversity Committee; is also actively involved in a number of community outreach activities. **OTHER:** 1993-95, was a part-time commissioner on the BC Motor Carrier Commission; was on the Advisory Council to the Law Society of BC Gender Bias Committee; was an elected member of provincial and national council of the Canadian Bar Assn. for six years and served for three years on the executive of the New Westminster Bar Assn. of which she was elected president in 1995. **HONS.:** CABL, 2000; Black Law Students Association, 1996. **EDUCATION:** LLB, 1983; BA, 1980, UBC. **CONTACT:** talexander@provincialcourt.bc.ca; Fax: 604-660-4527

▶**ALEXIS, Horace C.,** MD.

PHYSICIAN/PHILANTHROPIST, Horace C. Alexis, MD, Ste. 208-194 Main St., Ottawa, ON. Born: Trinidad & Tobago/ in Canada since: 1957.

▶ Dr. Horace Alexis came from humble beginnings in Trinidad. But, through hard work and determination, he became a physician who has maintained a strong commitment to community and to helping others. He came to Canada in 1957 to study medicine at the University of Ottawa. **HIGHLIGHTS:** after completing his internship at Toronto Western Hospital in 1967, he began his practice in Petrolia, Ontario. While there he engaged in a number of activities including the Petrolia Credit Union, the Sarnia VON, and was Chief of Staff at the Eleanor Englehart Hospital. In 1974, he moved from Petrolia to establish a private practice in downtown Ottawa; there he continued his community involvement by undertaking fundraising for initiatives like the James Robinson Johnston Chair in Black Cdn Studies at Dalhousie University. In 1996, he and a few other like-minded Black professionals, founded the Black Canadian Scholarship Fund, to assist young Blacks complete their university education; this fund is administered by the Ottawa Community Foundation. **OTHER COMMUNITY ACTIVITIES:** Brd., Ottawa Community Foundation; attends numerous functions to support community initiatives; and, during Black History Month, devotes much time to visiting schools to address students and teachers on accomplishments by Blacks, particularly to Canadian society. And, the love of racing horses that he developed in Petrolia has been nurtured over the years: currently he is the owner of a three-year-old standardbred which he plans to race. **HONS.:** including: first Pioneer Award, for his "outstanding efforts to make Ottawa-Carleton a more welcoming community for Newcomers," Catholic Immigration Centre, 1998; commendation from PM Chrétien for the establishment of the Scholarship Fund, 1998. **REVIEWED IN:** local & regional publications including: *Ottawa Sun; Ottawa Citizen; Doctor's Review; Millennium Minds,* 2000. **EDUCATION:** MD, U. of Ottawa, 1966. **CONTACT:** hcalexis@hotmail.com

▶**ALGOO-BAKSH, Stella,** PhD.
ASSOCIATE PROFESSOR, Dept. of English, Memorial University of Newfoundland, St. John's, NF. Born: Guyana/raised in Trinidad/ in Canada since: 1969.
▶ Dr. Stella Algoo-Baksh has been an English Professor at Memorial University since 1984. She was a lecturer, 1984-91; became an Assistant Professor, 1991-95; and became an Associate Professor in 1995. One of her areas of specialization is teaching Graduate Post-Colonial and Graduate Cdn Literature from Canadian and Post-Colonial perspectives. She wrote the first biography on Austin C. Clarke (see below); and served as editor of Memorial University's *The Teaching and Learning Newsletter.* **WORKS:** *Austin C. Clarke: A Biography; Austin C. Clarke and His Works;* reviews include: *Grammar of Dissent; Images of African & Caribbean Women; Island Wings: A Memoir; The Companion to African Literature* in the *Can J of African Studies.* **EDUCATION:** PhD, MA, BA, Memorial U. of Newfoundland. **MOTTO:** The pleasure and paradox of my own exile is that I belong wherever I am. (George Lamming) **CONTACT:** sbaksh@mun.ca; Fax: 709-737-4528

▶**ALLEN, Daniel H.**
DIRECTOR, Service Delivery Policy, Human Resources Development Canada (NHQ), Place du Portage, Phase IV, 140 Promenade du Portage, Hull, QC K1A 0J9. Born: Windsor, ON.
▶ Daniel Allen has worked with Human Resources Development Canada since 1972. From 1996 to March, 2002, he was Director, Human Resource Centres of Canada in the Essex, Kent, and part of Lambton counties. In his current position as Director, Service Delivery Policy, he is involved with developing national policy regarding delivery of various government-sponsored programs and services. Previously, he was Manager of the Windsor Canada Employment Centres, 1984-96. **OTHER:** his service to the City

of Windsor began in 1994, when he was city councillor, until 1997; since 1998 he has been Vice-Chair of the Police Services Board. **COMMUNITY:** Art Gallery of Windsor; Windsor UGRR Monument Committee; NA Black Historical Museum and Cultural Centre; United Way; Essex Golf and Country Club. **HONS.:** GG Award, for contribution to his fellow Canadians, his community, and to Canada, 1992. **EDUCATION:** BA, U. of Windsor, 1973. **HEROES/ROLE MODELS:** Mother; Trevor Wilson, colleague & friend. **MOTTO:** Remember that not getting what you want is sometimes a wonderful stroke of luck. (Dalai Lama) **CONTACT:** dan.allen@hrdc-drhc.gc.ca; Fax: 819-994-7580

▶ALLEN, Lillian
WRITER/POET/CULTURAL STRATEGIST/CREATIVE WRITING PROFESSOR, Ontario College of Art & Design, 100 McCaul St., Toronto, ON M5T 1W1. Born: Jamaica/ in Canada since: 1969.

▶ Lillian Allen is an award-winning and internationally renowned poet and writer of short stories and plays. As one of its main originators, she has specialized in the writing and performing of dub poetry, a highly politicized form of poetry which is often set to music. Her recordings *Revolutionary Tea Party* and *Conditions Critical,* won Juno awards, 1986 and 1988 respectively. Her works appear independently and in anthologies. She has spent close to two decades writing, publishing, and performing her work in Canada, the US, Europe and England. She has also worked in film, both as a featured artist (*Revolution from de Beat,* 1995; *Unnatural Causes,* 1989; *Rhythm and Hardtimes,* 1987) and as co-producer and co-director of *Blakk Wi Blakk* (1994), a film on dub poet Mutabaruka. **OTHER:** she is a leading expert on cultural diversity and culture in Canada and has been a consultant and advisor to all levels of government and to community groups. She has initiated or facilitated the establishment of a number of organizations in the Black community and in various culturally diverse communities. **AFFIL/MBRSHP:** several, including: member, Experts Advisory on the International Cultural Diversity Agenda; executive member, the Canadian Commission for UNESCO. **HONS.:** several including: Margo Bindhardt Award, City of Toronto & the Toronto Arts Council Fdn., 1998; nominee, Honorary Doctorate, U of T, 1992; Foremother of Canadian Poetry, League of Canadian Poets, 1992; Ontario Volunteer Service Award, 1989; Outstanding Contribution to the Arts Award, National Congress of Black Women, 1987; Juno Awards, for *Revolutionary Tea Party,* 1986, for *Conditions Critical,* 1988, and for Landmark Album of the Last 20 Years, 1988; from *Ms.* magazine, for *Revolutionary Tea Party,* 1987. **WORKS:** selected: *Psychic Unrest,* 2000; *Freedom & Dance* (CD), 1999; *Women Do This Every Day,* 1993; *Nothing But a Hero,* 1992; *Why Me,* 1991; *Conditions Critical* (album), 1988; *If You See Truth,* 1987; *Revolutionary Tea Party* (album), 1986; *Curfew Inna BC* (cassette), 1985; *De dub poets* (recording), 1984. In anthologies: *Wheel and Come Again,* 1998; *The Other Woman in Canadian Literature,* 1995; *Breaking Through: a Canadian Literary Mosaic,* 1990. Plays: *Market Place* (radio), 1995; *Love and Other Strange Things,* 1993, 1991; *Art and Motherhood,* 1985. Reports: *Cultural Diversity in Every Day Life,* 2002; *Creating Room for Inclusion – a Strategy for Cultural Diversity,* 2001; *First Steps on the Road to Racial and Cultural Equality: From Multiculturalism to Access.* **CONTACT:** Tel: 416-977-6000 ext. 691

▶ALLEYNE, Archie
MUSICIAN/DRUMMER, PO Box 65013, RPO Chester, Toronto, ON M4K 3Z2. Born: Toronto, ON.

▶ Drummer Archie Alleyne is a musical pioneer who has been on the music scene in Toronto since the mid-1950s. Known as "Mr. Swing Beat," he was the house drummer at Toronto's legendary Colonial Tavern and Town Tavern between 1955 and 1970, and played with such performers as Lester Young, Ben Webster, Billie Holiday, Milt Jackson, Stan Getz, Roy Eldridge, Carmen McRae, Zoot Sims and many others. He has toured the world with the trios of Teddy Wilson, Oliver Jones and Marian McPartland; and has appeared at Birdland, NY; The Blue Note, Chicago; Baker's Keyboard Lounge, Detroit; and at festivals in Europe and other parts of the globe. He is featured in the film *Oliver Jones in Africa* and appeared in the Toronto stage productions of *The Connection,* and *Lady Day at Emerson's Bar and Grill,* with Ranee Lee. In the '50s, at a time when few Black musicians were being employed by local clubs, he was not only a regular at one of Toronto's biggest jazz venues, he was also one of the early Black musicians to perform regularly on both CBC Radio and TV. He credits his success as a pioneer in these venues with his willingness and ability to do musical crossover, allowing whites as well as Blacks to recognize his musical genius. From 1970-82, he was co-owner of the popular soul food restaurant, the Underground Railroad. For AA though, it was a trip to Africa in 1989 with Oliver Jones that awakened his interest in his African heritage and exposed him to the roots of jazz. This trip changed his life and influenced his future musical activities. First, touched by the need for instruments by the only music school at the time in Nigeria, upon his return AA collected donations of instruments (guitars, saxophones, drums) and sent them back to the Peter King College of Music. Subsequently he was named the first "Grand Patron" of this institution. Two years after his return from Africa, he and Rudy Webb *(see: Webb, Rudy)* began work on *The Evolution of Jazz,* a show tracing the history of jazz from its African roots, through the experience of slavery in the US and the Caribbean, to its modern incarnation. This show has been performed in Toronto to positive critical response and is now being adapted for schools. AA was both a player and a consultant for a 1994 video documentary, *It Ain't All Jazz,* by JoJo Chintoh, profiling three of

Canada's most prolific musicians: Wray Downes, Sonny Greenwich, and Archie Alleyne. AA continues to play and perform. His current group, Kollage, co-led by saxophonist Doug Richardson *(see: Richardson, Doug),* is a popular fixture on the downtown jazz circuit; one of the group's mandates is to introduce younger Black jazz musicians to the larger jazz community, and to provide them with an easier entry into the world of professional music than that experienced by their predecessors. **HONS.:** several, including: playing for dignitaries such as Nelson Mandela, the Presidents of Iceland and the US, the Prime Minister of Israel, and the Duke of Edinburgh; "Canadian Black Music Pioneer" citation from the Cdn Black Music Awards, 1981. **REVIEWED IN:** nat'l newspapers & magazines; *Some Black Men,* 1999. **CONTACT:** archie.alleyne@sympatico. ca; www.kollage.com; Fax: 416-690-2694

▶**ALLEYNE, Brian C., MSc, DME.**
CLINICAL EPIDEMIOLOGIST, Associate Resources Management Consultants/**LECTURER,** University of Alberta, Edmonton, AB. Born: Curaçao/ in Canada since: 1969.
▶ Brian C. Alleyne is an epidemiologist who worked with the Alberta Occupational Health and Safety Dept., from 1979-97. In this position, he conducted epidemiological investigations to identify and document the effect of occupational health hazards and/or the effectiveness of protective measures. He has also been a lecturer in Epidemiology in the Dept. of Community Medicine at the U. of Alberta, and trained industrial workers in Occupational Health and Safety. **OTHER HIGHLIGHTS:** Research Associate, Dept. Epidemiology, McGill U., 1976-78, coordinated epidemiological investigations, such as the Northwest Quebec Health Study, commissioned in response to litigation against a pulp and paper company; Clinical Instructor, Dawson College, 1972-75; Bio-Chemist, F.W. Horner Pharmaceutical, assessed the bio-viability of new drugs, 1972. BA

originally trained as a Medical Technologist, and practised in this field in Trinidad (1959-63, 1967-68), in England (Chief Medical Technologist, Brampton Chest Hospital, 1965-67), and in Montreal (Sr. Medical Technologist, Royal Victoria Hospital, 1968-69). **AFFIL/MBRSHP:** Western Carnival Development Assn. Alberta (President, 1990-99), producers of CARIWEST, the annual festival of Caribbean Arts; Cdn Progress Club; Strathcona Family and Community Services Advisory Brd.; Federal-Provincial Working Group on Health and Safety for Laboratory Workers. **HONS.:** Community Service, BAASA, 2000; Progressian of the Year, 1991. **WORKS:** articles in: *J O M; Can J P H; Alberta Occupational Medicine Newsletter; Clinical & Investigative Medicine; Occupational Health & Safety Canada.* **EDUCATION:** courses: Industrial Hygiene, 1987; Epidemiology of Cancer, 1979; MSc, DME Clinical Epidemiology, McMaster U., 1976; BSc, Biochemistry, with distinction, SGWU (now Concordia U.), 1972; Advanced Registered Technologist CSLT, Canada, 1969; Fellow, Institute of Biomedical Sciences, London, UK, 1966. **CONTACT:** allthese@bigfoot.com

▶**ALLEYNE, John**
ARTISTIC DIRECTOR, Ballet British Columbia, Vancouver, BC. Born: Barbados.
▶ As Artistic Director of Ballet British Columbia (BBC) since 1992, John Alleyne has gained international recognition as a contemporary ballet choreographer whose work consistently challenges the boundaries of ballet. After graduating from his studies in 1978, he joined the Stuttgart Ballet; his dancing drew praise and he also began his choreographic career there, creating works for the company's workshops, such as *Phases* and *In Variation on a Theme.* In 1982, he joined the National Ballet of Canada (NBC) as a First Soloist, performing such roles as Solor in *La Bayadere* and Oedipus in *Sphinx.* He went on to become resident choreographer at the NBC, creating a variety of works including *Blue-Eyed Trek,* 1988; *Split House Geometric,* 1989-90; *Interrogating Slam,* 1991; and, for the students of the NBC, *Nightal,* 1987; and *Moving Vehicles,* 1989. From 1988-91, he choreographed several works for BBC, including *Flying to Paris,* 1989; *Go Slow Walter,* 1990; and *Talk About Wings,* 1991. Since 1992, he has created 10 new works for BBC, including *The Don Juan Variations,* 1995; *Remember Me from Then,* 1996, and *The Faerie Queen,* 2000. In addition to his work for BBC, he has also been commissioned to create works for other internationally renowned companies and festivals, including the NYC Ballet, the San Francisco Ballet, Les Ballets de Monte Carlo, Dance Theatre of Harlem, and the Stuttgart Ballet. His work has won him much critical acclaim and many awards acknowledging his significant contributions to the world of dance. **HONS.:** Harry Jerome Award, for Professional Excellence, BBPA, 1993; Dora Mavor Moore Award, for Outstanding New Choreography, for *Interrogating Slam;* Best Choreographer Award, at the 1990 Jackson, Mississippi Int'l Ballet Competition for his work *00:02:57.* **EDUCATION:** National Ballet School, Toronto, 1978. **CONTACT:** c/o rforzley@balletbc.com

▶**ALLEYNE-NIKOLIĆ, Eucline Claire,**
Ed.D.
REGISTRAR, Ontario Institute for Studies in Education (OISE), University of Toronto, 252 Bloor St. W., Toronto, ON M5S 1V6. Born: Guyana/ in Canada since: 1973.
▶ Dr. Alleyne-Nikolić has been the Registrar at the Ontario Institute for Studies in Education at U of T, since 1996. Prior to coming to Canada, she was an elementary school teacher in Guyana, 1960-66. At U of T she has held the following positions: Admissions Officer, Faculty of Nursing, 1973-76; Registrar, Faculty of Applied Science and Engineering, 1976-81; Associate Registrar, Woodsworth College, 1981-88; Registrar,

Faculty of Education, 1988-96. **AFFIL/MBRSHP:** has served on many committees within the university; Harry Gairey Scholarship Committee. **HONS.:** including: Chancellor's Award of Excellence, for outstanding contribution to the University, 1994. **REVIEWED IN:** *Canada Heirloom Series,* vol. 7; *WWIC.* **EDUCATION:** Ed.D, U of T, 1987; MA, Howard U., 1972; BA, Albion College, 1970. **CONTACT:** calleyne@oise.utoronto.ca; Fax: 416-923-7834

▶**ALLICOCK, Robert L.W.**

SALON OWNER/STYLIST, Salon Robert Allicock Montreal, 3541 Swail Ave., Montreal, QC H3T 1P5. Born: Guyana, 1961/ in Canada since: 1982.
▶ Robert Allicock is also known in Montreal as "stylist to the stars." He opened his salon in 1995 and was soon contracted to provide services to performers like Vanessa Williams, Angela Bassett, Queen Latifah, Vanessa Bell Calloway, and others. In 1998, he was the stylist on *The Cosby Show,* in New York. Described as a perfectionist, he attributes his rapid rise in the profession to well-developed client services, his ability to manage a highly skilled and motivated staff, and his award-winning styling skills. He has made many guest appearances on TV shows and is an international education platform artist for Brosis Agency Inc., a wholesale beauty supplier to the Canadian industry. Having earned the credentials as a master hairstylist by servicing many entertainers, business professionals and the community at large, he has hosted many radio programs dealing with the subject of hair care. In addition, he is a freelance beauty journalist and serves as an advisory member for *Panache* magazine; and, is a freelance beauty journalist for Montreal's *Community Contact.* **HONS.:** include, SIFA Hair Awards, 1998: Canadian Stylist of the Year, Int'l Stylist of the Year (male & female), Int'l Stylist of the Year (evening); Int'l Style of the Year, SIFA Hair Award, 1997. **WORKS:** monthly column, *Community Contact,* 1997-99; *The Real Scene.* **REVIEWED IN:** *Shop Talk* magazine; *Essence; Panache; Irie Times; Share.* **EDUCATION:** College Inter-Dec, Montreal, 1996; Dudley Cosmetology U. & Advanced Training Academy, 1995. **HEROES/ROLE MODELS:** Oprah Winfrey; Rosa Parks. **MOTTO:** An achievement is for today, but an education is for a lifetime. **CONTACT:** allicockr@aol.com; Tel: 514-344-0842; Fax: 514-344-8149

▶**ALLSOPP, W. Herbert L.,** Dr.

FISHERIES CONSULTANT, CEO, Smallworld Fishery Consultants Inc., 2919 Eddystone Cres., North Vancouver, BC V7H 1B8. Born: Guyana/ in Canada since: 1972.
▶ Dr. Herbert Allsopp has been the Hon. Consul General for Ghana in BC, since 1991. He is also CEO and principal fisheries development specialist of Smallworld Fishery Consultants Inc., the company he created in 1983. During the past 50 years, professional visits have taken him to over 110 countries, including every country in Africa. Since his company's start, he has completed over 87 assignments for agencies including the World Bank, Asian Development Bank, CIDA, UNIDO, UNDP, FAO, USAID, Sweden's IFS, Finland's FINNIDA, Iceland's ICECON, Canada's CESO. **CAREER HIGHLIGHTS:** Fisheries Associate Director, IDRC (Canada), 1972-83, where he organized and managed IDRC's initial worldwide fisheries program; first Senior Regional Fishery Officer for Africa, FAO/UN, 1966-72 (based in Ghana, he was responsible for the joint monitoring of FAO and UNDP fishery projects in Africa) and inaugural Secretary of two international fishery commissions (CECAF and CIFA); Marine Biologist and Development Advisor, Belize, FAO/UNDP, 1965-66; Fishery Development Advisor, Togo, FAO, 1961-65; Senior Fishery Officer in charge of fisheries, Guyana, 1949-61; UN Research Fellow, 1953-54, review of fishery development systems in 11 countries. **OTHER:** carried out original research on Manatees for control of aquatic weeds (Guyana,

Florida, and W. Africa); established the first shrimp culture production centre in S. America (Guyana, 1958); established a model resource management program for tropical spiny lobsters (Belize, 1964-66); introduced to S.E. Asian aquaculture, Brazilian fish breeding system by pituitary hormones and applied it through IDRC's initial program (1973-83) to over 20 countries; established prototype programs for the recovery of fish caught as by-catch in trawling for high-valued target species (to avoid waste discards of millions of tons of fish annually). **COMMUNITY ACTIVITIES:** Vancouver Institute; Aboriginal Rights Coalition; Caribbean Assn. of BC; Royal Commonwealth Society; CESO. **AFFIL/MBRSHP:** elected life member, Am. Fisheries Society (1954); Society of Limnologists and Oceanographers; Society of Ichthyologist and Herpetologists; Int'l Academy of Fishery Scientists; Aquaculture Assn. of Canada; Fellow, Institute of Animal Resource Ecology. **HONS.:** several including: Career Achievement Citation, U. of Wisconsin, 1989; Distinguished Service Award, IDRC, 1983; Commendation, outstanding service, FAO, 1971; Guyana Independence Medal, 1966; citations from Govts. of Togo (1964), Belize (1966), Djibouti (1979); UNESCO/FAO commendation letter for innovative research on *Control of tropical waterweeds by Manatees,* 1959/60. **WORKS:** selected: *Time,* 1960, Science section review on "Allsopp's Useful Manatees"; has written more than 60 technical studies & reports for publication by FAO, UNDP, IDRC, IFAD, CIDA, CESO on aquaculture in Asia & Africa, Caribbean fisheries, fisheries development and investment projects; contributed chapters to nine technical books. **EDUCATION:** Dipl. Fish Processing Technology, U. of Aberdeen, 1961; Pre-doctoral Assoc., U. of Washington, 1957; Dipl. Public Admin., UWI, 1955. MSc, Fisheries, 1949; BSc, Biology, 1948, U. of Wisconsin. **MOTTO:** Strive for excellence in everything you undertake; never be content with mediocrity; never stop learning. **CONTACT:** Fax: 604-929-1860

►**ANDERSON, Roy T.**
STUNT COORDINATOR/ACTOR, Action 4 Reel. Born: Dover, NJ.

▶ Roy Anderson is an actor, stunt man, and stunt coordinator who performed his first stunt in the film, *Class of 84,* in 1981. He completed his studies in 1988 and went on to appear in more than 200 movies and TV productions including: *Shaft; Bad Company; Ali; Baby Boy; Down to Earth; In Too Deep; Blues Brothers 2000; Kung Fu: The Legend Continues; Exit Wounds; Trial by Jury.* He has doubled for Mario Van Peebles, Robert Townsend, Jamie Fox, Billy Dee Williams, and Busta Thymes. He also holds several world records for stunts performed. Now in transition from stunt performer to stunt coordinator, he coordinated the films, *Against the Ropes,* starring Meg Ryan, and *Down to Earth,* starring Chris Rock. He has also supervised the action scenes on a variety of cable features for HBO and Showtime, including *Our America,* and *10,000 Black Men Named George.* **HONS.:** nominated for best driving (*Shaft*), World Stunt Awards, LA, 2001. **CONTACT:** action4reel@yahoo.com

►**ANDERSON, Wolseley W. (Percy),** PhD.
PROFESSOR EMERITUS AND SENIOR SCHOLAR, Social Sciences, York University, 4700 Keele St., Toronto, ON M3J 1P3. Born: Guyana/ in Canada since: 1966.

▶ Dr. Wolseley (Percy) Anderson has been Professor Emeritus of Social Science at York University since 1994. Over the past 40 yrs. he has lived, studied, and worked in Guyana, Jamaica, England, Kenya, and Canada. His academic and professional activities have been particularly concerned with: education and social change; race and ethnic relations; diversity in a global village context; and, strategies and techniques of planning for the development and effective utilization of human resources. A special area of interest and experience for him throughout his career has been "Canadian-Caribbean relations with particular attention to immigration trends"; through his work he has examined the patterns of adjustment and settlement challenges for Caribbean immigrants as they seek to integrate rather than assimilate. He has been very active in the promotion of leadership roles within a pattern of innovative community volunteer service. **COMMUNITY INVOLVEMENT:** within the Ontario Legal Aid System, he has served as chair of a legal aid clinic; founding member of a consultative committee between the Black community and the Toronto Police Services Brd.; member, Black Education Working Group; Urban Alliance on Race Relations. **WORKS:** has written a number of papers and monographs including: *Caribbean Immigrants,* 1993; *The Newcomers,* 1987. **EDUCATION:** PhD, OISE/U of T, 1971; MA, London Institute for Studies in Education, 1966; BA/Hons., UWI, 1961. **MOTTO:** If "to be" is "to become" then "service to others" is perfect freedom!

▶ANDRE, Irving

LAWYER/AUTHOR, Private Practice, 17 Chapel St., Brampton, ON L6W 2H2.

▶ Irving Andre is a criminal defence lawyer who has been in private practice since 1994. He has also held the following positions: VP, Licence Appeal Tribunal; Night Court Prosecutor, Ont. Min. Attorney General, 1996-99; Crown Prosecutor, Ont. Min. of Labour; Assistant Crown Attorney, Ont. Min. of Attorney General, 1991-93. **COMMUNITY INVOLVEMENT:** United Achievers Club; Sisserou Housing Development Corp.; John Howard Society; Kiwanis Club, Brampton; Peel Legal Aid Committee. He is also a published author. **HONS.:** including: United Achievers Recognition Award, 2001; Black History Makers Award, 1999; Cert. Appreciation, Peel Brd. of Education, 1998; Community Service Award, Dominica Assn., 1997. **WORKS**: fiction: *The Jumble Wedding,* 2001; *The Island Within,* 1999; *A Passage to Anywhere,* 1996; non-fiction: *Distant Voices,* 1999; *In Search of Eden,* 1992; along with articles in *Osgoode Hall Law J, Caribbean Quarterly.* **EDUCATION:** LLB, Osgoode Hall, York U., 1988; BA, UWI, Jamaica, 1981; partial PhD studies in History, Johns Hopkins U., MD, 1984. **CONTACT:** Fax: 905-459-5534

▶**ANGLADE, Georges,** Dr de 3ème cycle. **GÉOGRAPHE-ÉCRIVAIN, EX-PROFESSEUR TITULAIRE,** Dépt. de Géographie, Université de Québec à Montréal (UQAM). Né: Haïti/ au Canada depuis: 1969.

▶ Professeur Anglade est généralement décrit comme « homme en trois morceaux » pour ses activités nombreuses et variées. Académiques et scientifiques: chercheur et professeur titulaire d'université; politiques: mouvements démocratiques Haïtien, ancien ministre; littéraires: auteur de fiction et d'essais. Après avoir terminé ses études de doctorat en géographie, cartographie et démographie à Strasbourg, il entre à l'emploi de l'UQAM, en 1969, pour une carrière académique de 33 ans en géographie sociale. Il a aussi travaillé comme Consultant à la Direction générale Min. de l'Education/Québec. Sur le plan politique, il a été prisonnier politique (1974) sous la dictature duvaliériste et deux fois exilé politique par les forces militaires, en 1974 et 1991. De la chute des Duvaliers en 1986 jusqu'à 1996, il milite activement en politique et anime, à partir de Montréal, le MAS, d'où sortira un renouvellement de la question de la diaspora haïtienne. Il a été Conseiller aux Cabinet privé du Président Aristide, 1993-94; Président de la Conférence Internationale de Miami, Janvier 1994; Min. en charge des Infrastructures du pays Travaux publics, Transports et Communications, 1995; et, Conseiller au Cabinet du Président Préval, 1996. Comme écrivain, il a produit une douzaine d'ouvrages, une cinquantaine d'articles dans les revues internationales, des centaines de communications du politique et du scientifique. Il se signale depuis deux ans comme auteur de fiction . **PRIX:** Récipiendaire de nombreux prix et de distinctions surtout pour son travail lies aux Caraïbes; nombreuses subventions et bourses dont la Bourse du Conseil des Arts et des Lettres du Québec, 2001-2002; et sa distinction la plus récente et la plus globale pour l'ensemble de son oeuvre et de ses actions, la Mention d'Honneur du Prix Int'l José Marti de l'UNESCO, 2001. **ŒUVRES:** Sélectionnée: Roman: *Leurs Jupons Dépassent*, 2000; *Les Blancs de Mémoire*, 1999. Académiques: *Cartes Sur Table*, 1990; *Atlas Critique d'Haïti*, 1982; *Mon Pays d'Haïti*, 1977; *L'Espace Haïtien*, 1974. Politique: Manifeste *La Chance qui passe*, 1990. Ses articles se trouvent: *Haïti-Observateur; Cahiers de géographie du Québec; Collectif Paroles; Rev. canadienne des Sciences Régionales.* **ŒUVRES À SON PROPOS:** (dans) *Le Devoir; Le Nouveau Monde; Collectif Paroles; Le Nouvelliste; Environnement Africain; Haïti-Observateur.* **FORMATION:** Doctorat en géographie, 1969; Licence en lettres, 1967, Strasbourg. Licence en droit, Haïti, 1965; Diplôme en science sociales, Haïti, 1965. **MENTORS:** « le drame de ma génération a été justement cette absence de mentors; j'ai ressenti ce manque pendant 40 ans avant de pouvoir m'en passer. » **CONTACT:** anglade.georges@uqam.ca; Fax, phone répondeur: 514-488-4837

▶ANNOR-ADJEI, Ellen

CONCERT PIANIST, Toronto, ON. Born: Russia/ in Canada since: 1993.

▶ Ellen Annor-Adjei was born in Moscow into a family of mixed African and Russian ancestry; she began studying piano at age five and later attended the Musical College of Moscow State Tchaikovski Conservatory. Her repertoire of classical piano literature includes works by Bach, Beethoven, Chopin, Liszt, Moussorgsky, Balakirev, and Rachmaninoff. She has held a number of successful concerts in Russia, Europe and N. America. In Toronto, she has appeared in numerous group recitals at the Arts and Letters Club, Ford Centre and Glenn Gould Studio, and has performed a number of solo recitals. She has also performed at the Queen's Hall in Trinidad as part of the Steinway Concert Series, 1999; and, in a solo recital in Bermuda, sponsored by the Bermuda Musical and Dramatic Society, 2001; tour of the Czech Republic and Germany, 2002, featuring performances of Beethoven and Chopin piano concertos. **CONTACT:** elleannora@hotmail.com

▶APPELT, Pamela

CITIZENSHIP JUDGE (Ret.), Court of Canadian Citizenship. Resides in Oakville, ON. Born: Jamaica/ in Canada since: 1966.

▶ In 1987, Judge Pamela Appelt became the first Black woman to be appointed to the Court of Canadian Citizenship, a position she held until her retirement in 2000. She came to Canada in 1966 from the UK, after completing her studies in microbiology and biochemistry, and first worked as a biochemist at Queen Elizabeth Hospital in Montreal; she later worked as a researcher in medical biochemistry at McGill U. for several years. The main themes in her life are to help children and families have better lives; she speaks regularly to groups and organizations on issues of violence against women and children; she also speaks on issues concerning recent immigrants and visible minority women. Her knowledge of religious human rights has led to speaking engagements in Germany and France. In 1999, she was appointed by the Province of Ontario as a member of the Custody Review Brd. and the Child and Family Services Review Brd., which deal with young offenders. **COMMUNITY INVOLVEMENT:** Christian Women's Club; OBHS; BBPA; the Clarke Institute of Psychiatry; and York U. Currently she is involved with: Brd., United Way; Community Foundation of Oakville; advisor to the President of Northern Caribbean U.; International Center for Human Rights and Democratic

Development; founding member of Black-Jewish dialogue of B'nai Brith Canada; patron of PACE and John Brooks Foundation. **OTHER:** she is also an accomplished artist in the art of *découpage* and has displayed her work in exhibits in the US, Jamaica, and Canada; she is a former food editor for *Excellence* magazine. **HONS.:** several including, Hon. LLD, Northern University, Jamaica, 2002; honoured by the Friends of Ron Hubbard Society for her "outstanding community work and achievements." **EDUCATION:** M. Public Admin., Senior University, CA; graduate of West Indies College; studied Microbiology & Biochemistry, London, UK. **CONTACT:** pappelt@cogeco.com; Fax: 905-849-7924

▶APPIAH, Yvonne

EXECUTIVE DIRECTOR, CODE, 321 Chapel St., Ottawa, ON K1N 7Z2. Born: Ghana.

▶ Yvonne Appiah is the Executive Director of CODE (Cdn Organization for Development through Education), an NGO which has supported literacy and education projects in developing countries since 1959. Since becoming Executive Director in 2000, she has managed to increase the donor base by 25% and negotiate a significant five-year funding agreement with CIDA. **BACKGROUND:** she joined CODE in 1987 as the Coordinator of Volunteer Programs and later became National Coordinator for Project Love, moving the volunteer program from primarily a book-packing activity in ten cities into an award-winning global education program that increases awareness among Cdn youth in schools and community groups about international development issues and involves them in a "hands-on" partnership with their global neighbours. Project Love won the 1997 Govt. of Canada Literacy Innovation Award and the 1996 Jennie Mitchell Celebrate Literacy Award from the Int'l and Ontario Reading Assn. YA also managed to increase the number of schools involved from 27 in one city, in 1987, to 500 schools in over 150 communities across Canada, by 1998. In 1999, she became Program Manager, then Director of Development; in 2000, she assumed her present position. **OTHER CAREER HIGHLIGHTS:** CUSO Consultant, 1982-87; Host National Consultant, CIDA, 1982-87, conducted country briefing sessions for CIDA cooperants assigned to Ghana; 1976-81, Senior Public Relations Officer, the West African Examinations Council, a regional testing board developing and administering primary, secondary, and post-secondary level examinations in West Africa (Ghana, Nigeria, Sierra Leone, The Gambia, and Liberia); 1974-75, was host of a weekly TV program, *Mainly for Women,* Ghana Broadcasting Corp. **COMMUNITY ACTIVITIES:** Word on the Street, Ottawa; Ghana Assn. of Ottawa; Harambee Foundation (Black Orpheus Gala events); Multiculturalism Advisory Committee, Ottawa Brd. of Ed. **CONTACT:** yvonne@codecan.org; www.codecan.org

▶ARCELIN, André, MD.

MEDECIN, Clinique Medicale, 1155, boul. St-Joseph, Montreal, QC H2J 1L3. Né: Haïti/ au Canada depuis: 1964.

▶ Dr André Arcelin a étudié la médecine en Espagne et a commencé sa pratique médicale au Canada dans les hôpitaux universitaires de Montréal en 1964. Depuis, il a occupé les postes suivants: attaché à l'hôpital Jean-Talon de Montréal, depuis 1997, et à l'hôpital Sainte-Jeanne-d'Arc, depuis 1972; Directeur du Centre médical pour personnes âgées, Le Cardinal de Pointe-aux-Trembles, Mtl, 1972-80. Très actif dans les affaires communautaires et politiques il a été: Président du conseil élu par les Haïtiens de Montréal, 2000 à 2002; Conseiller à l'Académie des sciences de l'Homme du Canada, l'Institut des civilisations comparées de Mtl, 1993; membre de la délégation canadienne à l'assermentation du président J-B Aristide, Haïti, 1991; membre du comité chargé de préparer la participation du Canada à l'Exposition de Séville pour commémorer le 500e anniversaire de la rencontre des deux mondes, 1990; membre d'Imagine, le plus grand organisme philanthropique du Canada, 1990; membre du Comité pour l'équité en matière de l'emploi relevant du président du Conseil du Trésor du Canada, 1989; participant bénévole aux élections fédérales comme Coordonnateur d'évènements entre les communautés culturelles et les candidats PC, 1984, 1988; Vice-président du Conseil canadien du multiculturalisme, 1985-92; Président de l'école de danse (ballet) Eddy Toussaint, 1985-88. **AUTRES:** il écrit la poésie; il est conseiller spécial du Président d'Haïti. On Montreal's 2001, BHM Calendar, they wrote: He possesses an ability to cultivate awareness of the need for a more harmonious society, a skill that serves him well as a political activist and defender of the rights and interests of the Black community. Dr. André Arcelin has worked tirelessly to help the Black community gain its rightful place in a society where racism and discrimination still exist. He is also committed to Black youth, helping them to develop the self-esteem needed to build the kind of future envisaged by Dr. Martin Luther King Jr. to ensure that: "Our future belongs to us today." **PRIX:** plusieurs y compris: Prix Jackie Robinson, MABBP, 2001; Plaque, l'association des Médecins Haïtiens, 2000; Plaque, par la communauté Latino-américaine, 2000; Nommé *Role Model* par Harambee, organisme philanthropique de la communauté noire, 1992; Nommé *Role Model* de la communauté noire de Mtl et reçoit un trophée de la Vice-Prémiere Ministre du Québec (Mme Lise Bacon), 1990; certificat, Honneur au Mérite, Gouv. du Canada, 1988. **ŒUVRES:** sélectionnée: les préfaces des livres écrit par G. Préval; G. Dupervil; W. Cambrone. **FORMATION:** Dipl. Médecine, Faculté de Médecine, Séville, Espagne, 1964. **MENTORS:** Martin Luther King & Nelson Mandela, pour leur lutte pacifiste. **MOTTO:** Our future belongs to us today. **CONTACT:** Tel: 514-490-0648

►ARCHER, Hutton Gilbert

DIRECTOR, External Relations, Global Environment Facility, 1818H St. NW, Ste. G6-150, Washington, DC 20433, USA. Born: Guyana/ in Canada since: 1964.

► Hutton Archer is a senior communications executive who has been working with a number of international companies and organizations throughout the course of his professional life. Since 1996, he has been Director, External Relations, Global Environment Facility (GEF). The primary objective of the GEF is to serve as a mechanism for international co-operation by providing funding to meet the agreed global environmental benefits primarily in the areas of biological diversity, climate change, international waters, and ozone layer depletion. **CAREER HIGHLIGHTS:** Public Relations Officer, AlCan, Quebec and BC, 1971; Public Communications Advisor, Prime Minister and the Min. of Information, Guyana, 1972-78; concurrently, he was Head of the Guyana Film Center, 1972-78; Chief of Conference and Communications, Caribbean Community Secretariat, 1978-83; Associate Director, Public Affairs, IDRC, 1984-86; Chief of Communications, UNCHS, Kenya, 1986-90; Chief of Public Communication, International Civil Aviation Org., Montreal, 1990-96. **EDUCATION:** World Bank Executive Development Prog., Harvard Business School, 2001; MBA, US International U., 1988; Fullbright Fellowship, Communications, Boston U., 1981. MA, 1971; BA, 1968, McGill University. **HEROES/ROLE MODELS:** Mother. **MOTTO:** Groun' low, wata settle (water settles only in depressions, otherwise it flows freely). **CONTACT:** harcher@worldbank.org; www.gefweb.org

►ARMSTRONG, Bromley, CM, O.Ont.

LABOUR & CIVIL RIGHTS ACTIVIST (Ret.), Pickering, ON. Born: Jamaica/ in Canada since: 1947.

► Bromley Armstrong has led a life of activism in

the labour movement and in the community since his arrival in Canada in the late 1940s. **HIGHLIGHTS:** active in the United Auto Workers Union, local 439, 1948-56; member of Toronto and District Labour Council, 1949-56, served as auditor and member of the Fair Practices committee (for his local and Labour Council); was the youngest member of the 1954 Black delegation to Ottawa seeking change to Canada's immigration policy, which restricted the entry of non-white immigrants to Canada. He was involved in the fight to enforce the Employment and Accommodations Acts; conducted test cases in Toronto and London, and assisted in the desegregation of Dresden, Ont. Insurance broker, 1962-78; Adjudicator, Ont. Labour Relations Brd., 1980-96; Commissioner, Ont. Human Rights Commission, 1975-80; Advisory Council of Multiculturalism, 1972-75. Founding member of several community organizations including: First Caribbean Soccer Club; JCA (President, 1970-72) and Jamaican Canadian Credit Union; BIG Investments, 1972; National Council of Jamaicans, 1987; Urban Alliance on Race Relations, 1993-98; BBPA and the Harry Jerome Awards. Was also an active member of: UNIA; Toronto United Negro Assn. and the Toronto United Negro Credit Union (VP, 1950-54); Brd., Canadian Civil Liberties Assn., 1972-2002; Chair, Brd., Cdn Centre for Police Race Relations, 1993-98; Brd., Cdn Centre for Ethics and Corporate Affairs, 1997-2000. **HONS.:** several including: Baha'i National Race Unity & Harmony Award, 1998; Toronto Onyx Club Award, 1995; Stanley Knowles Humanitarian Award, OPSEU, 1995; Order of Canada, 1994; Human Rights Award, OFL, 1994; GG 125th Anniv. Award, 1993; Order of Ontario, 1992; Harry Jerome Award, for Community Service, 1990; Minister's National Award for Race Relations, 1990; Urban Alliance on Race Relations, 1988; Order of Distinction, Jamaica, 1983. **WORKS:** co-author: *Bromley: Tireless Champion for Just Causes,* 2000; published *The Islander,* community newspaper, 1973-77. **REVIEWED IN:** *WWIC;* in

community & nat'l newspapers; *Some Black Men,* 1999. **EDUCATION:** Waltham College, Jamaica.

▶**ARMSTRONG, Neil**
JOURNALIST/NEWS DIRECTOR, CHRY Radio, York University, 4700 Keele St., Toronto, ON M3J 1P3. Born: Jamaica/ in Canada since: 1995.
▶ Neil Armstrong is a journalist who began his broadcasting career with Radio Jamaica, as a broadcast journalist, 1991-94. Since 1995, he has been the News Director, spoken word coordinator and program coordinator at CHRY Radio, at York University in Toronto. Through his many community contacts he has brought a diverse array of individuals (authors, poets, youth leaders, rights activists, etc.) to public attention through his radio programs and provided mentoring to a number of high school co-op students. **OTHER:** has been a moderator of the Get Reel Film Festival seminars; chair, Caliban Arts Theatre. **COMMUNITY:** founding member, CABJ; JCA; OBHS; Jane-Finch Concerned Citizens Org.; Brampton Junior Chamber of Commerce; member, Obsidian Theatre. **EDUCATION:** Cert. Journalism, Ryerson U.; BA/Hons., Communication, UWI, Jamaica. **HEROES/ROLE MODELS:** Henry E. Armstrong, grandfather; Delores & Henry Armstrong, parents. **MOTTO:** Strive to do your best and help someone along the way. **CONTACT:** armstrongneil @hotmail.com

▶**ASAGWARA, K.C. Prince,** PhD.
RESEARCHER/POLICY & PLANNING ANALYST/ EDUCATOR, Winnipeg, MB. Born: Nigeria/ in Canada since: 1977.
▶ Dr. Prince Asagwara works in the Education and Training Department of the Government of Manitoba; he has worked for the Government of Manitoba since 1990, and has authored numerous research reports. **CAREER HIGHLIGHTS:** Employment and Training Services (ETS) 2000 Annual

Report; he is the author of *A Profile of the African Community of Manitoba,* Multiculturalism Secretariat, 1994. Taught in the Department of Educational Administration, Psychology and Foundations, Faculty of Education, U. of Manitoba, 1987-89 and 1996-99. Ed., *Can J of Educational Administration and Policy Studies* (CJEAP), 1997-1999; Member, Ed. Brd., *J of Educational Administration and Foundations,* 1986-1988, Department of Educational Administration, Psychology, and Foundations, Faculty of Ed., U. of Manitoba. Research Associate, 1996-97, Centre for Higher Education, U. of Manitoba. Taught sessional courses in the Dept. of Continuing Education, Red River College, 1991-94. **COMMUNITY INVOLVEMENT:** Manitoba Ethnocultural Advisory and Advocacy Council (MEAAC), has held a number of positions including Secretary-General, 2002; VP Finance & Administration, VP Community and Cultural Relations, VP Member Relations. Folk Arts Council of Winnipeg Inc. (FACWI), VP Festivals Development, 1996-2002. Social Planning Council of Winnipeg; Council of African Organizations in Manitoba Inc., founding member and Director of Social Activities, 1993-99; Founding member and President, Nigerian Assn. of Manitoba Inc. (NAMI), 1982-83. **AFFIL/MBRSHP:** Cdn Assn. for the Study of Educational Administration (CASEA); Cdn Society for the Study of Higher Education (CSSHE); Comparative and International Education Society of Canada (CIESC); Cdn Society for the Study of Ed. (CSSE). **HONS.:** Lt.-Gov.'s Dinner/ Reception, 2002; Graduate Fellowship Award, U. of Manitoba, 1988-89; Winnipeg Fdn. Fellowship Award, 1986-87; Earl of Dalhousie Scholarship Award, 1984-85; Graduate Fellowship Award, Dalhousie U., 1983-84. **WORKS:** several articles in refereed journals: *Education & Society; Canadian & International Education; The Urban Review;* etc. **EDUCATION:** PhD, 1989; MA, 1983, U. of Manitoba. MPA, Dalhousie U., 1986; BA, U. of Lethbridge, 1980. **HEROES/ROLE MODELS:** Dr. Okechukwu

Ikejiani, friend & advisor. **MOTTO:** I am the captain of my ship and the master of my domain. I am therefore at peace with myself. **CONTACT:** kasagwara@gov.mb.ca; asagwara@mts.ca

▶**ASANTE, Kabu**
EMPLOYMENT CONSULTANT/CEO, D&S Personnel Services, Ste. 5-425 Eddystone Ave., Toronto, ON M3N 1H8. Born: Ghana/ in Canada since: 1985.
▶ In 1981, Kabu Asante and his wife began their own employment agency, D&S Personnel. Today he is CEO of this company, which has 300 full-time employees on assignment across Toronto. Members of his agency are placed with companies and fill the positions of office, industrial and warehouse staff. Currently, D&S Personnel has two offices, one in North York and the other in Mississauga; a third office is planned for late 2002. D&S Personnel is the largest employer in the African community in Southern Ontario. **EDUCATION:** MA, International Development, U. of Guelph; BA/Hons., York U. **MOTTO:** With God, all things are possible. **CONTACT:** asante@on.aibn.com; Fax: 416-740-4652

▶**ATUANYA, Tony I.**
EXECUTIVE DIRECTOR, WADE Inc. 1144 Main St., Dartmouth, NS B2W 4R4. Born: Nigeria/ in Canada since: 1973.
▶ Tony Atuanya is the Executive Director of the Watershed Assn. Development Enterprise (WADE), whose focus is community economic development. During his tenure, WADE has planned, designed, developed and coordinated the implementation of the first Community Asset Map of a Black community in Canada. **COMMUNITY INVOLVEMENT:** Director of Economic Development for the Preston Area; volunteers as the Executive Director of the Preston Area Board of Trade; is the first Black elected to the NS Labour Development Board; inaugural chair,

North Preston Community Education Council. **WORKS:** ed./publ. *WADE News* (quarterly); *How to conduct a community asset map.* **REVIEWED IN:** *Chronicle Mail Star.* **EDUCATION:** BSc, Dalhousie U.; Electronic Engineering Technologist, Humber College. **HEROES/ROLE MODELS:** Father. **MOTTO:** Stay focused! **CONTACT:** Inno@accesswave.ca

▶ATWELL, Frances

PHARMACIST (Ret.), Winnipeg, MB. Born: USA/ in Canada since: 1923.

▶ Frances Atwell graduated from the University of Manitoba with her BSc in Pharmacy in 1948, thereby becoming possibly the first Black pharmacist in Manitoba. Over the course of her career, she worked in hospitals, in the community, in retail locations, and in replacement positions as she balanced her career with raising seven children. An accomplished singer, she was runner-up for the prestigious Rose Bowl at the Manitoba Music Festival in 1950 (to win the Rose Bowl, the contestant must vie with the winners of the "A" classes, e.g. soprano, opera, etc.). **AFFIL/MBRSHP:** continues her membership with the Manitoba Pharmacists' Assn. as a non-practising member; and, is active in the community, in her church, and in Caribbean seniors' activities. **HONS.:** 50-yr. Gold Pin, member in good standing of Manitoba Pharmacists' Assn., 1998; Award in recognition of achievements & community service, National Black Coalition of Canada/Winnipeg Chapter, 1983; Gold Cord recipient, Cdn Girl Guides, 1941. **EDUCATION:** BSc, Pharmacy, U. of Manitoba, 1948.

▶ATWELL, George

TEACHER (Ret.), Winnipeg School Board/ **COMMERCIAL BEEKEEPER,** Winnipeg, MB. Born: Trinidad & Tobago/ in Canada since: 1949.

▶ George Atwell taught in a one-room school in rural Manitoba; then, after earning his BA and B.Ed, taught high school for two years in Morris, Manitoba, then junior high in Winnipeg, 1959-74. After earning his Diploma in Agriculture in 1976, he became a commercial beekeeper for several years, selling his honey to the local honey producers' co-op. He was a member of the Royal Canadian Naval reserve, 1950-74, and retired with the rank of Lieutenant Commander. **COMMUNITY:** was active with the Boy Scouts, becoming chair of the local group committee. **EDUCATION:** Dipl., Agriculture, 1976; B.Ed, 1959; BA, 1956, U. of Manitoba. **MOTTO:** Trust in your own untried capacity. (Ralph Waldo Emerson)

▶ATWELL, Gerry

PERFORMER/VISUAL ARTS CURATOR, Winnipeg, MB. Born: Winnipeg, MB.

▶ Gerry Atwell is a multi-disciplinary artist who has worked in music, theatre, radio, film, and TV. He is currently expanding into the realm of visual arts as a curator; was awarded a Canada Council grant for Curator-in-Residence for Cultural Diversity, a one-year position being completed at the St. Norbert Arts Centre in Winnipeg; he curated a multi-artist installation exploring art by African-Canadian contemporary artists on the topic of "whether or not there exists an African Canadian Aesthetic" (May-June, 2002, Winnipeg). **CAREER HIGHLIGHTS:** stage play, *Life of the Party* included in Factory Theatre's Cross-Currents Festival, Toronto, 2002; as a screenwriter, his feature *Barbara James* was entered in the Taorima Film Festival in Italy, 2001, and closed the 2002 Get Reel Film Festival (April, 2002); his teleplay *The Hands of Ida* won a Blizzard award and was nominated for a Gemini; has also written a CBC radio drama, *Soul Games* and the stage play *Soul on Ice.* **BACKGROUND:** he studied piano and plays keyboards with musical acts in the genre of reggae/alternative, roots rock, and R&B; member of Eagle and Hawk (Aboriginal band), since 1999, which won a Juno Award, 2002. He has played with the CBC House Band, Ministers of Cool, and conceived of a concert series combining two local steel bands to perform with the Winnipeg Symphony, 2002. As an actor, he has appeared in *Wild Guys* at the Winnipeg Fringe Festival, 1999. **AFFIL/MBRSHP:** St. Norbert Arts Centre; Manitoba Assn. of Playwrights; CAN: BAIA; Winnipeg Folk Arts Council; Navy League of Canada; John Travers Cornwell Sea Cadet Corps. **HONS.:** Juno Award, to band, Eagle and Hawk, for Best Music of Aboriginal Canada, 2002; *The Hands of Ida:* Prairie Waves II, screenwriting competition, 1995, won Blizzard Award, and was nominated for a Gemini. **WORKS:** screen & radio plays; essays published in *Prairie Fire, Revue Noire.* **CONTACT:** gatwell@mb. sympatico.ca

▶AUGUSTINE, The Hon. Dr. Jean, PC, MP.

MEMBER OF PARLIAMENT, House of Commons, 433 West Block, Ottawa, ON K1A 0A6. Born: Grenada/ in Canada since: 1960.

▶ In 1993, The Hon. Dr. Jean Augustine became the first Black woman elected to the Parliament of Canada. Since then, she has been re-elected twice, representing the riding of Etobicoke-Lakeshore. On May 26th, 2002, she was appointed Secretary of State (Multiculturalism and Status of Women), making her the first Black woman to be appointed to Cabinet. **CAREER HIGHLIGHTS:** Parliamentary Secretary to Prime Minister Jean Chrétien, 1994-96; since 2002, is Chair of the Foreign Affairs and International Trade Parliamentary committee; and, has served on the Parliamentary Sub-committees on Human Rights and International Trade, as well as Citizenship and Immigration. She was the founding Chair of the Canadian Association of Parliamentarians on Population and Development, and also served three terms as Chair of the National Liberal Women's Caucus. During her time in office, she has presented a number of motions in the House of Commons; she is responsible for having February declared nationally as Black History Month; and for having the Famous Five Statue (of five activists for women's rights who succeeded in having women recognized as "persons" by the Constitution) installed on Parliament Hill. **BACKGROUND:** prior to her life in public office, JA was an elementary school principal with the Toronto District Catholic School Board, and served as Chair of the Metro Toronto Housing Authority. **COMMUNITY INVOLVEMENT:** Congress of Black Women; BBPA; Harbourfront Centre; Urban Alliance on Race Relations; Catholic Children's Aid Society; Toronto Mayor's Task Force on Drugs; York U.; Hospital for Sick Children. **HONS.:** several including: Hon. LLD, U of T; Kay Livingstone Award; ACAA; Women of Distinction Award, YWCA; Ontario Volunteer Award & Pin; Bob Marley Award. **REVIEWED IN:** *WWIC; WWCW; Millennium Minds,* 2000; *Some Black Women,* 1993. **EDUCATION:** BA, M.Ed, U of T. **CONTACT:** augustine.j@parl.gc.ca; Fax: 416-251-2845

▶AYLWARD, Carol A., LLM.

ASSISTANT PROFESSOR, Faculty of Law, Dalhousie University, 6061 University Ave., Halifax, NS B3H 4H9. Born: Halifax, NS.

▶ Prof. Carol Aylward is, since 1991, an Assistant Professor in the Faculty of Law at Dalhousie University where she teaches courses in Criminal Law, Critical Race Theory, and General Jurisprudence. She is also past Director of the Law Program for Indigenous Black and Aboriginal students. In this position, which she held for ten years, she designed, implemented and administered this Access Program, which was created in order to encourage indigenous minority students to consider law as a profession. Her liaison and outreach were both to attract students and to solicit the support of the NS bar, the Judiciary and the government to support this program by providing articling positions for these students. She has also produced, edited and co-directed for Dalhousie University, the mini-documentary,

Balancing the Scales, which looks at the role of affirmative action programs in Cdn law schools and examines the experiences of students in such programs. **OTHER:** she is the first Black Nova Scotian to obtain a master's degree in Law (LLM) from Dalhousie Law School; will be pursuing a doctorate in Law at Ottawa University. **AFFIL/MBRSHP:** Nova Scotia Barrister's Society Race Relations Committee; past Commissioner, NS Police Commission; past Commissioner, NS Human Rights Commission; Elizabeth Fry Society; NS Black Lawyers Assn. **HONS.:** several, including: CABL, 2001; Harry Jerome Award for Professional Excellence, 1998; Cert. of Appreciation, Congress of Black Women/Cherry Brook Chapter; Maritime Book Prize. **WORKS:** book: *Canadian Critical Race Theory,* 1999; brochure: *Myths & Facts;* articles in: *Can J of Women & the Law; UNB Law J.* **EDUCATION:** LLM, 1989; LLB, 1993, Dalhousie U. **CONTACT:** carol.aylward@dal.ca

► **AZAN, Kemeel**

HAIR STYLIST/SALON OWNER, Azan's Beauty Salon, 2nd Fl.-126 Davenport Rd., Toronto, ON M5R 1H9. Born: Jamaica/ in Canada since: 1958. ▶ Kemeel Azan has been in the hair business for over 40 yrs., as an educator, business owner, and stylist. He opened his first salon in 1962; by 1972, he owned and operated salons in four locations across Toronto, including Yorkville, and had a staff of 42 employees. Known for his high standards, skill in service delivery, and business development practices, a number of leading hair stylists currently operating their own establishments in Toronto, had trained or worked with him earlier in their careers. His is the salon of choice by Blacks in and from Toronto. With an active interest in training and development, KA has used his business experience to benefit others: wrote a manual on *How to Run a Small Business,* which was accepted into the school system; provides mentoring opportunities to secondary school students in his salon; speaks to and encourages youth on the importance of education and career choices; developed a training program and provided equipment to a school of cosmetology in Jamaica; has helped shape the careers of a number of young, aspiring individuals, including Tonya Lee Williams; and, launched a public relations campaign in support of Ben Johnson after his positive test for steroids at the Seoul Olympics. **OTHER COMMUNITY INITIATIVES:** was a member of Milestone Radio's lobbying team, which submitted briefs to the CRTC for the granting of a licence to what is now, FLOW 93.5FM (first Black-owned radio station); is a promoter of the annual Cotillion Ball; spearheaded the purchase and restoration of two Toronto churches on behalf of the Church of God of Prophecy (255 Blantyre Ave. and 2431 St. Clair Ave.) which together seat 1000 congregants. **HONS.:** including: ACAA, business, 1999; Beauty Industry Pioneer Award, Mascoll's, 2000; a number of awards from New York, Philadelphia, Detroit, & Washington as one of the most creative hairdressers; award from *Hair News* magazine, 1994. **REVIEWED IN:** *Globe and Mail; Toronto Star; Beauty Trade; Chatelaine,* etc. **EDUCATION:** Marvel Hairdressing School, Toronto; Perdue, New York; Pivot Point, Chicago. **HEROES/ROLE MODELS:** Parents; wife. **CONTACT:** Tel: 416-944-0262

▶BACCHUS, Natasha Cecily

ATHLETE/MEDALLIST, World Deaf Games. Toronto, ON. Born: Toronto, ON, 1977.

▶ Natasha Bacchus is a hearing-impaired athlete who has won a number of international competitions in running 100m and 200m events. She began running at the age of ten, in 1987 and, with encouragement from fellow athlete, Rohan Smith (*see: Smith, Rohan*) and coach Gary Lubin, began training for the World Summer Games for the Deaf (WSGD). In 1993, she participated in her first international competition, in Bulgaria at the WSGD, winning a gold for the 100m and a silver for the 200m; at WSGD in 1997, in Denmark, she won gold for the 100m and the 200m. In 1998, at the Indoor Track & Field Championships in Dortmund, Germany, she won four gold medals, for the 60m, 100m, 200m, and the 4x400m relay and was named "most outstanding athlete" of the Games. She has won 50 medals and 15 trophies in overseas competitions. In 1997, she received a scholarship from the Canada Deaf Sports Association to attend Gallaudet University, in the US (the only university in the world for the hearing impaired). In her first year, 1997-98, she broke the existing 55m and 100m records and was named "best female athlete of the year." In 2001, she also participated in the WSGD in Italy. She is currently enrolled in college and hopes to work with children; a role model and hero amongst other hearing impaired youth, NB is also seeking means of giving voice to their needs within the Deaf community. **HONS.:** including: Female Athlete of the Year, Gallaudet U., 1998; "most outstanding athlete," German Track & Field Assn., 1998; Jo-Anne Robinson Award, Female Athlete of the Year, 1997; Harry Jerome Award, Athlete of the Year, 1995; Award, outstanding achievement in athletics, Guyanese Heritage & Cultural Assn., 1994. **CONTACT:** chocolateg4@hotmail.com

▶BADOE, Adwoa, MD.

AUTHOR, Guelph, ON. Born: Ghana/ in Canada since: 1992.

▶ Dr. Adwoa Badoe trained as a physician in her native Ghana, but, unable to practise in Canada without re-doing her studies, she has turned to her second passion, writing, and has become a successful author of children's books. In less than ten years she has already published three books in Canada (see below), which have been well received by critics and by the general public. She writes contemporary children's books with ethnic content, as well as traditional African tales. Her books are illustrated with people of African descent. She also writes for the educational market in Africa with Macmillan UK, and Smartline Publishers (Ghana). She does storytelling and conducts African Dance workshops in local schools, libraries and in the community to increase awareness by children of the rich cultural heritage that surrounds them. She has also participated in Storytelling and Writers' Festivals in Southwestern Ontario since 1996. **WORKS:** books include: *A Pot of Wisdom: Ananse Stories,* 2001; *The Queen's New Shoes,* 1998; *Crabs for Dinner,* 1995; *Nana's Cold Days,* forthcoming. Reviewed in: local papers, *Globe and Mail, Toronto Star.* **EDUCATION:** MB Ch.B, 1988; BSc Human Biology, 1985, U. of Science & Technology, Kumasi, Ghana. **HEROES/ROLE MODELS:** Prof. K. Twum-Barima, father; Robert Munsch, author. **MOTTO:** I can do all things through Christ who strengthens me! **CONTACT:** adwoa_badoe@yahoo.ca

▶BAFFOE, Michael Kofi

EXECUTIVE DIRECTOR, Black Star Big Brothers, 5117, de Maisonneuve O., Montreal, QC H4A 1Z1. Born: Ghana/ in Canada since: 1987.

▶ Michael Baffoe is Executive Director of the Black Star Big Brothers, a mentoring program for young Black boys, aged 8-16, growing up in single-parent families. He designed and launched the program in 1994, to provide role models for boys at the critical age when a positive male figure is vital to development, to reduce the loss of interest in school and to pre-empt problems with the law. Black Star also runs an in-school mentoring program for boys and girls in inner-city schools, who are at risk of dropping out. Staffed by a coordinator, a counsellor and a secretary, the Black Star project has an advisory committee of 11 Black professionals including psychologists, doctors, pastors social workers and other professionals who formulate the standards and policies for the project. The response from families concerned and the community at large has been extremely positive. The program has been so successful that the National Strategy on Community Safety and Crime Prevention –a federal initiative to assist community groups across the country deal with the root causes of crime–has recently funded projects designed to help Ottawa's Somali community and Toronto's Tamils reach out to their youth with similar mentoring programs. **HONS.:** include, Award for Excellence in Clinical Practices, McGill U., School of Social Work, 1995. **WORKS:** "Demonizing African Culture in the Name of Christianity," in *Community Contact,* 1997. **REVIEWED IN:** community publications including: *Young People's Press; Montreal Gazette; Community Contact; The Monitor.* **EDUCATION:** MSW, 1993; BSW, 1992, McGill University. BA, U. of Ghana, 1979. **CONTACT:** mbaffoe @hotmail.com; www.blackstarbigbrothers.com

▶**BAILEY, Cameron**
FILM CRITIC/BROADCASTER, *NOW* Magazine/ Alliance Atlantis Broadcasting, Toronto, ON. Born: UK/raised in Barbados/ in Canada since: 1971.
▶ Cameron Bailey is the first Black film critic in Canada. He reviews for *NOW* magazine and CBC Radio's *The Arts Today.* He was for many years a regular reviewer on CTV's *Canada AM;* since

1998, he has co-hosted *The Showcase Revue* on Showcase TV. He has been a guest speaker at several Canadian universities, the Smithsonian Institute, Harvard University and the Banff Centre for the Arts. He is founder and former programmer of the Planet Africa section of the Toronto International Film Festival, and past chair of the Festival's Perspective Canada series; co-founder, Black Film and Video Network. His own film credits include co-writing the screenplay for *The Planet of Junior Brown.* The film was named Best Picture, 1998, Urbanworld Film Festival, NY and was nominated for a Gemini. His second feature, *oldschool* is currently in development. **WORKS:** in, *NOW; Take One; The Village Voice; Screen; CineAction!; Borderlines;* & the Banff Centre anthology, *Territories of Difference.* **REVIEWED IN:** selected: *Word; Toronto Star; Globe and Mail; The Australian; Xpress.* **EDUCATION:** BA/Hons., U. of W. Ontario, 1987. **CONTACT:** dubwise@sympatico.ca

▶**BAILEY, Daphne**
NURSING SPECIALIST (Ret.), D&B Footcare Business, Etobicoke, ON. Born: Jamaica/ in Canada since: 1960.
▶ Daphne Bailey is a nursing pioneer among Blacks in Canada. After completing her nursing studies in England, both as a State Registered Nurse and as a State Certified Midwife, she arrived in Canada in 1960 and worked at the Brantford General Hospital and at the Doctors Hospital throughout the 1960s. She then joined the Victorian Order of Nurses, from 1972-95, as a Community Health Nurse. While there she helped develop tools for the evaluation of nurses; was an early discharge nurse for mothers and babies; she later worked in the areas of footcare and as an Infusion Specialist; and, also taught "healthy aging" to Seniors. She is now the co-owner of D&B Footcare Business. **COMMUNITY INVOLVEMENT:** member of the JCA since 1963; involved with the North York Seniors HC; was on

Advisory Committee on Seniors' Issues for over six yrs., giving input to various levels of government; member, Richview United Church (in choir for 27 yrs.). **HONS.:** several, including Award for Volunteerism, Ont. Min. of Citizenship & Culture. **EDUCATION:** Cert. Gerontology, Ryerson Polytechnic, 1986; Cert., Footcare, Micheners Institute of Applied Arts & Science. BA, 1979; Public Health Cert., 1971, U of T. RN & State Midwife, England. **HEROES/ROLE MODELS:** Mother. **MOTTO:** Give back to the community and lay a foundation for those who will follow. **CONTACT:** ddelphi14@hotmail.com

▶ BAILEY, Donovan

OLYMPIC ATHLETE, c/o Rhonda Cohen, Lawyer, Toronto, ON. Born: Jamaica/ in Canada since: 1980.

▶ Donovan Bailey is a five-time World and Olympic Champion, and the first man in history to achieve, in a single year, the titles of Olympic Champion, World Champion and World Record Holder. *Track and Field News* named him "Sprinter of the Decade" (1990s) and one of the all-time most dominant sprinters. Winner of countless world-class sprint competitions, including eight-time Canadian Champion, Pan American Games Champion, Francophone Games Champion, Goodwill Games Champion, Commonwealth Games Champion, World Champion and Olympic Champion. He still holds the Olympic Record for the 100m and the World Record for the 50m. At the 1996 Atlanta Olympic Games, he set a World Record of 9.84 seconds in the 100m sprint and led Canada's men's 4x100m team to a Gold Medal victory. **BACKGROUND:** originally from Jamaica, he came to Canada at age 12, graduated from college with a diploma in Business Admin. and started his own telemarketing firm. He began to run seriously in 1994. He is the subject of a 1998 documentary, *Olympic Warrior: Donovan Bailey's War.* Recently retired from competitive athletics, he is involved

in several business initiatives and is a spokesperson who gives his time to a number of charities including the Canadian Cancer Society, Ontario Lung Association, Big Brothers, and Big Sisters. He is also the spokesperson for Skill Canada – Ontario. He created the Donovan Bailey Foundation, committed to the advancement and financial assistance of Canada's most talented amateur athletes. **HONS.:** many, including Athlete of the Year – Athletics Canada, Lou Marsh Trophy (1996; runner-up, 1995), Canadian Leadership Award (first athlete to receive this prestigious award); appointed by the Federal Minister of Canadian Heritage as President, Celebrate Canada! Committee (2002). **CONTACT:** rcohen@sherrardkuzz.com; www.donovanbailey.com

▶ bailey, maxine

MANAGER, Public Affairs, Toronto International Film Festival, Ste. 1600-2 Carlton St., Toronto, ON M5B 1J3. Born: England/ in Canada since: 1971.

▶ maxine bailey is a co-founder of Sugar 'n Spice Productions, which produced the plays, *Sistahs* (co-written with Sharon Lewis), *Stockholm(e),* nominated for Best Performance and Direction (Dora Mavor Moore Award), and *Afrocentric.* She also directed *Afrocentric* and *Stockholm(e).* Over the past ten years, she has worked with a number of theatre companies, including Company of Sirens, Factory Theatre, Theatre Passe Muraille and Nightwood Theatre, where she currently serves on the Artistic Advisory board. She is also a board member of Artscape, an organization creating spaces for Toronto artists to live and work, and the Obsidian Theatre Company. She has many years of experience at the Toronto International Film Festival Group, where her current role is Public Affairs Manager. **WORKS:** co-wrote, *Sistahs.* **REVIEWED IN:** entertainment columns & publications. **CONTACT:** sistahs@hotmail.com; Fax: 416-967-7669

▶**BAILEY, Nehemiah L.**
COMMUNITY ORGANIZER/EDUCATOR (Ret.), Toronto District School Board (TDSB), Toronto, ON. Born: Jamaica/ in Canada since: 1963.

▶ Nehemiah Bailey is known as a career educator and community leader. **CAREER HIGHLIGHTS:** began his professional life in Jamaica, first as a laboratory technician with UWI, then as an engineering technician with ALCAN/Jamaica Ltd.; taught technical and industrial arts education, in elementary and secondary schools 1958-63, in Jamaica. After completing his Industrial Arts and Technical Education program between Moose Jaw, SK and Toronto, ON, he returned to Jamaica; finding limited job opportunities there, he returned to Canada and worked for 17 yrs. in the field of aviation technology, with Litton Systems Canada Ltd. in Toronto. He then taught technical and vocational education with the TDSB, until his retirement in 1998. Since then he has been working as a realtor. **COMMUNITY INVOLVEMENT:** activities have been extensive over a 38 yr. period; JCA, since 1964; National Council of Jamaicans and Supportive Organizations; Toronto Police Community Liaison; participated in national consultations for WCAR/ 2001; Political Affairs and Govt. Relations Committee, Toronto Real Estate Board; Director, Canadian Ethnocultural Council. **HONS.:** including: 30-yrs. Voluntary Service Award, Ont. Min. of Culture; 25 yrs. Jamaican Canadian Assn. **WORKS:** member of committee that developed current Police Community Race Relations Policy of Ontario. **REVIEWED IN:** *Discovering Patterns in Human Geography.* **EDUCATION:** Cert., Industrial Arts & Technical Education, SK Technical Institute; Dipl., Ontario College of Education, U of T; Jamaica College of Arts, Science & Technology (now University of Technology). **MOTTO:** Mankind cannot improve itself without improving others; selfishness is a road to destruction. **CONTACT:** nbailey@trebnet.com; Fax: 416-751-7795

▶**BANCROFT, George W.,** PhD.
PROFESSOR EMERITUS, SCHOLARSHIP, University of Toronto. Born: Guyana/ in Canada since: 1948.

▶ Professor George Bancroft, educator and scholar, began his teaching career in Guyana and completed it at the University of Toronto. During that time, he made significant contributions to academia and to various government commissions on which he served. In 1987 he was awarded the title of Professor Emeritus from U of T. His teaching career in Canada began at Forest Hill Jr. High and at FH Collegiate, 1956-66; he next taught at the College of Education at Fairleigh Dickenson U. in NJ, 1967-69; he joined U of T in 1969 in the Faculty of Education; from 1971-77 he was Chair of the Dept. of History, Philosophy and Sociology of Education; served on the Hall Commission on Education, 1968. In 1980, he was seconded to the Ont. Min. of Citizenship and Culture where he served until 1983 as Executive Director then Sr. Policy Advisor to the Minister, Multiculturalism and Citizenship Div. **OTHER HIGHLIGHTS:** pioneered a study in Ontario on the effect of education on sons rising to higher positions than their fathers; Commissioner, Ontario Human Rights Commission, 1988-91; published a number of works on education and the experience of recent immigrants; participated in the making of a video for the Cdn Council of Christians and Jews, *Toward a Just Society,* 1999. During his career, GB was involved in many community organizations, professional groups, and advisory councils, including the Ont. Council of University Affairs; was founding chair of the Harry Gairey Scholarship, 1985-95. **HONS.:** named "Distinguished Educator," OISE/U of T, 1997; Sword of Honour, Sikh Social & Educational Society; Community Friend Award, Federation of Pakistani Canadians; Multicultural History Society of Ontario Award; ACAA; Award of Merit, OSSTF. **WORKS:** many including: *They Came From Abroad; The Novice and the Newcomer; A*

Place to Stand; and articles in: *Ont. J of Educational Research; Can Modern Language Review,* and other scholarly journals. **REVIEWED IN:** *Some Black Men,* 1999. **EDUCATION:** Sanskrit/Court Poetry in Translation; additional study, New School for Social Research, NY, 1966-69. PhD, Educational Theory, 1960; M.Ed, 1953, U of T. BA/Hons., McGill U., 1951; BA (intermediate), U. of London/Guyana, 1946.

▶**BANCROFT, Joseph (Dan),** BSM.

CITY AUDITOR (Ret.), City of Toronto, ON. Born: Barbados/ in Canada since: 1957.

▶ Joseph (Dan) Bancroft was a career public servant, first with the Federal Service then with the Municipal Government where he worked in the Audit Dept. for the City of Toronto, from 1958-1994. Over the years he progressed through the ranks until he became Head of the Audit Dept. and City Auditor, the first Black to hold this position. **COMMUNITY ACTIVITIES:** St. Anne's Anglican Church; Cdn Friends to West Indian Christians; founding member, Caribbean Cdn Assn. (became Barbadian Cdn Assn.); Order of Freemasons, a Master Mason for over 35 yrs. and, from 1987-91, was elected Most Worshipful, Grand Master of the Most Worshipful Prince Hall Grand Lodge, Free and Accepted Masons of the Province of Ontario and Jurisdiction; founder, Barbados Nurses' Assn. of Toronto, 1990. **AFFIL/MBRSHP:** EDP Auditors Assn.; Canadian Comprehensive Auditing Foundation of Canada; past member, Institute of Public Administration of Canada. **HONS.:** several awards from the community & the Fraternity; Bi-Centennial Award, for service to the community, Province of Ontario, 1984; Barbados Service Medal (BSM), for community service to Barbadian Nationals in Canada, Govt. Barbados, 1980. **EDUCATION:** courses in Accounting, Administration, Auditing & Management, Ryerson Polytechnic Institute & U of T. **MOTTO:** We pass this way but once; any good we can do, do it NOW. **CONTACT:** Fax: 416-536-4676

▶**BARCLAY, John V.**

DEPUTY GRAND MASTER, Independent United Order of Solomon/Canada, 2040 Weston Rd., Weston, ON M9N 1X4. Born: Jamaica/ in Canada since: 1968.

▶ John Barclay has been involved with the Independent United Order of Solomon since 1983; he is described as "having given dedicated service to the community in promoting charitable programmes for the improvement of human welfare through charitable events." His charitable activities on behalf of this Order include: organizing the first donation of a CT Scanner to the Mississauga Hospital; arranging shipment of medical supplies to Grenada and to Jamaica; organizing and delivering wheelchairs to First Nations in Hamilton; organizing humanitarian supplies for Jamaica following Hurricane Gilbert. In addition to his many community activities, he operated his own business, Barclay's Maintenance Services, from 1972-99. **EDUCATION:** Mechanics, Kingston Tech. High School, Jamaica, 1946. **HEROES/ROLE MODELS:** Lloyd Seivright, Grandmaster.

▶**BARNES, Kofi**

SENIOR COUNSEL & SPECIAL ADVISOR, Dept. of Justice, Federal Prosecution Service, PO Box 36, First Canadian Place, Toronto, ON M5X 1K6. Born: Ghana/ in Canada since: 1984.

▶ Kofi Barnes has been a member of the Department of Justice, since 1993; he is a Senior Counsel and Special Advisor. For several years he has prosecuted criminal cases on behalf of the Attorney General of Canada, with particular emphasis on Drug and Income Tax cases. He has a special interest in finding alternative ways of dealing with non-violent drug addicted offenders who commit minor offenses. He has always been interested in and committed to issues of social justice; in 1998, KB collaborated with others from the Ontario Court of Justice, members of the defence bar, law enforcement officers, and substance abuse treatment providers to design and implement Canada's first Drug Treatment Court, which was then introduced in the City of Toronto. This Court combines therapeutic principles with the court process, to provide judicially supervised drug addiction treatment for eligible, non-violent, drug-addicted offenders. Substance abuse treatment providers are an integral part of this process. KB is recognized as Canada's first Drug Treatment Court prosecutor and as one of the country's leading legal experts in this area; he has become a national spokesperson on this concept and has been featured on radio, TV, in magazines and newspapers to promote it. He is a frequent instructor at the Ontario Bar Admission Course. In addition, he has advised and trained national and international delegations of lawyers, judges, treatment providers and government officials on the design and application of such a system. **COMMUNITY:** volunteers with non-profit housing and drug addiction treatment providers to address issues of homelessness and drug addiction. **HONS.:** recipient of several professional merit awards, from the Dept. of Justice, Federal Prosecution Service. **EDUCATION:** LLB, Osgoode Hall, York U., 1991; BA, Trent U., 1988. **CONTACT:** kofi.barnes@justice.gc.ca

▶BARNES, Leesa

IT MANAGER/PRESIDENT, BITePRO, Ste. 133-429 Danforth Ave., Toronto, ON M4K 1P1. Born: Toronto, ON, 1974.

▶ Leesa Barnes began her career in IT after completing an undergraduate degree in History, 1997. Since then, she has held managerial positions at a variety of technology companies, most recently at Sun Microsystems; she has five yrs. of experience managing software, internet, e-business, and security projects. She is a founding member and President of BITePRO (Black IT eProfessionals), whose mandate is to provide professional development and networking opportunities for Blacks in the IT sector; in this capacity she is interviewed regularly on radio, TV and in print. She makes public presentations on online publishing, website development and, women in technology; she is also responsible for developing two websites, sportsfemmes.com and evesgarden.ca, both dealing with women's sports and health issues. **HONS.:** include, ACAA, youth category, 2000; academic awards. **REVIEWED IN:** local & nat'l publications including: *Toronto Star; Toronto Sun; Share;* profiled in, *Millennium Minds: Profiles of Black Youth,* 2000. **EDUCATION:** BA, York U., 1997. **HEROES/ROLE MODELS:** Angela Lawrence, *Style At Home* magazine. **MOTTO:** Nothing is more rewarding than owning what you create. **CONTACT:** leesa@makeda.ca

▶BARRETT, Danny

HEAD COACH, Saskatchewan Roughriders, Regina, SK. Born: USA/ in Canada since: 1985.

▶ Danny Barrett is the Head Coach of the Saskatchewan Roughriders and has been in this position since January, 2000. He is a former CFL quarterback with the Calgary Stampeders, the Toronto Argonauts, the BC Lions, and the Ottawa Rough Riders, where he played a total of 163 regular season games. He also played in two Grey Cup championships: 1987, with the Toronto Argonauts, and, 1991, with the Calgary Stampeders. In the 1991 Grey Cup, he set a CFL record with 34 completions. During the course of his playing career, 1983-96, he also played one season with the New Jersey Generals of the USFL. He began coaching in 1997 with the Calgary Stampeders, then spent two seasons, 1998 and 1999, as an Assistant Coach with the BC Lions; during his first season as the team's quarterback coach and assistant offensive coordinator, he was needed back on the field, so dressed as the team's backup quarterback for 15 games. During his three seasons as Assistant Coach, his teams reached the post-season play-offs each time. **EDUCATION:** Physical Studies, U. of Cincinnati,

1982. **CONTACT:** ryanw@saskriders.com; www. saskriders.com

▶BARTON, Brad, CM.

EDUCATOR/CEO, Bar Jun Consultants, Dartmouth, NS. Born: Acaciaville, Digby, NS.
▶ Brad Barton has had an extensive career in education, occupying teaching and senior administrative positions, before retiring to become an educational consultant. He also distinguished himself by becoming the first Black international volleyball referee in Canada. **CAREER HIGHLIGHTS:** (teaching): taught at elementary, junior, and senior high schools, 1963-72; was a vice-principal, 1972-77, Graham Creighton High School; served as a principal, 1977-92, in junior and senior high schools (Forest Hills High, Gordon Bell Junior and Senior High, Graham Creighton High, Bell Park Academic Centre, Charles P. Allen High); was the first principal of African descent in the province of Nova Scotia. From 1992-97, he occupied senior administrative positions including: Supervisor and Coordinator of Race Relations, Cross Cultural Understanding and Human Rights, Halifax County and Regional District School Board, 1992-94; Sub-system Supervisor and Supervisor of Schools, 1994-96. In these positions, he provided professional development in cross-cultural understanding and human rights for approximately 70 schools at the elementary, junior, and senior high school levels; he also developed Race Relations, Employment Equity, and Harassment Policies and Procedures for the Halifax Regional School Board, before his retirement in 1997. Since 1997, he is CEO of Bar Jun Consultants, which has provided services to federal, provincial and municipal government departments and educational entities on questions of equity, education, harassment, and diversity. In 2001, he prepared reports on achieving equitable educational opportunities for African Nova Scotia learners; and, from March 2001-April 2002, was Acting Executive Director of the Council on African Canadian Education (CACE). **VOLLEYBALL:** after qualifying as an international volleyball referee in 1975, he became the first Black Nova Scotian and Black Canadian to reach this level. He officiated at the Montreal Olympics in 1976, and at the Los Angeles Olympics in 1984; has also officiated at World Student Games in Romania, Japan, Cuba, Mexico, and Puerto Rico, and at Pan American Games. He continues to referee and has received a number of awards for his involvement with athletics. **COMMUNITY INVOLVEMENT:** has been extensive; currently, Brd., NS Home for Coloured Children; NS Police Review Brd.; Inner City Education Advisory, and many others. Previously: President & executive member, Black Educators Assn.; vice-chair and chair, CACE; Black Learners Advisory Cmtee (BLAC); President, National Council of Black Educators of Canada; Cdn Consultative Council on Multiculturalism; NS School Athletic Federation; President's Task Force for Blacks and Aboriginals, Dalhousie U. **HONS.:** several including, Member, Order of Canada, 2000; Recognition for "outstanding work in the Black community," Apex Invitational Golf Assn., 2000; Marjorie Turner-Bailey Athletic Achievement Award, Black Loyalist Heritage Society, 2000; Cert., Multi-Cultural Council of Nova Scotia, 2000; Volleyball Award, Dalhousie U., 1999; Appreciation Award, Black Educators Assn., 1999; inductee, Black Cultural Centre Wall of Honour, 1999; inductee, Digby Sports Wall of Fame, 1997; FK Stewart Fellowship, for Outstanding Leadership in Education in Canada, 1986; GG 125th Anniv. Medal, 1992; NS Official of the Year, 1984 & 1987; Hon. Member for Life, Cdn Volleyball Assn. **REVIEWED IN:** local and nat'l publications; *Journey: African Canadian History,* 2000; *Black to Business* magazine (BBI), 2000; *Black Focus* magazine, 1999. **EDUCATION:** completed courses at Dalhousie, Saint Mary's, & Mount Saint Vincent universities; School Administrators' Block Program, NS Dept. of Education, 1976; Associate Education

Degree, NS Teachers' College, 1966. **HEROES/ ROLE MODELS:** Mary Barton, mother; Dr. George McCuroy; Rev. Donald Skeir. **MOTTO:** Remember your roots. **CONTACT:** brad.barton@ns.sympatico.ca; Fax: 902-434-6110

▶BATCHELOR, Barrington deVere,
PhD, P.Eng.

PROFESSOR EMERITUS (Ret.), Civil Engineering, Queen's University, Kingston, ON. Born: Jamaica/ in Canada since: 1966.

▶ Dr. Barry Batchelor began his career in civil engineering in the United Kingdom and practised in Jamaica before moving to Canada where he taught in that discipline at Queen's University, from 1966-93. In addition, he has had extensive involvement in community activities on issues of Race Relations, Community Policing, and Human Rights. **CAREER HIGHLIGHTS:** Asst. Prof., Civil Engineering, 1966-68; Assoc. Prof., 1968-72; Assoc. Chairman (1971-74) and Chairman (1974-75), Div. III, School of Graduate Studies and Research; Professor, of Civil Engineering, 1972-93; during his Sabbatical leave, 1974-75, he was Visiting Professor at Cornell U., NY and at U. of Washington, Seattle. Upon his retirement in 1993, he was designated Professor Emeritus of Civil Engineering. Prior to teaching at Queen's, he worked with the Min. of Education in Jamaica, first as Executive Engineer, 1958-63, and then as Senior Executive Engineer, 1963-64. From 1964-66, he operated his own engineering firm and was the Principal in Franks and Batchelor, Consulting Engineers, Jamaica. **OTHER:** professional appointments included Consultant to Min. of Transportation and Communications, ON; Consultant to Florida Dept. of Transportation; Consultant to Transportation Research Board, US. Served as reviewer for *J of the American Concrete Institute, Can J for Civil Engineering, J of the Structural Division* (Am. Society of Civil Engineers). **AREAS OF RESEARCH:** include, Reinforced Concrete Structures; Model Analysis of Structures; Dynamics of Structures; Development of Highway Bridge Systems; Pre-stressed Laminated Wood Bridge Decks. **COMMUNITY INVOLVEMENT:** founding member and past-President, Kingston Cmtee for Racial Harmony; founding member, Mayor's Cmtee on Race, Ethnic, and Aboriginal Relations, 1991-94; Advisory Cmtee on Race and Ethnic Relations to the City of Kingston Police Board of Commissioners (founding member and Chair, 1989, 1990); Race Relations Advisor to the Principal, Queen's University, 1990-91; Principal's Advisory Cmtee on Race and Ethnic Relations, 1990-91. Has been a key community contact for several government ministries and departments at the Provincial and Federal levels on issues concerning human rights, race relations, and policing; organized a number of public workshops including: Policing in a Multicultural and Multi-Racial Community and Application of Bill 107 (1991); The Police and the People (1988); What are Your Rights? (1986); Multicultural Kingston: Past, Present, and Future (1984). **AFFIL/MBRSHP:** served on the Immigration and Refugee Brd., Convention Refugee Determination Div., 1988-91; Brd. of Governors, Kingston General Hospital; Fellow, Engineering Institute of Canada; Fellow, Cdn Society for Civil Engineering; American Society of Civil Engineers; American Concrete Institute; founding member, Institution of Engineers, Jamaica. **HONS.:** Distinguished Service Award, Queen's U., 1993. **REVIEWED IN:** *Who's Who in America; WWIC.* **EDUCATION:** National Defence College of Canada, 1982-83. PhD, Civil Engineering, Commonwealth Scholar, 1963; Dipl. in Concrete Structures, 1961, Imperial College of Science and Technology, U. of London. BSc/ Hons., Civil Engineering, U. of Edinburgh, 1956. **CONTACT:** DrDEVB@aol.com; Fax: 613-544-1095

▶BATCHELOR, Wayne B., MD, MHS,
FRCPC, FACC.

CARDIOLOGIST, Southern Medical Group, PA, Ste. 800-1401 Centerville Rd., Tallahassee, FLA

32308, USA. Born: Jamaica, 1965/ in Canada since: 1966.

▶ Dr. Wayne Batchelor is an Interventional Cardiologist and was Co-Director of Clinical Trials in Interventional Cardiology at the Terrence Donnelly Heart Centre, at St. Michael's Hospital in Toronto. He was also an Assistant Professor of Medicine at the University of Toronto. Until his move to Florida (Spring, 2002), where he now practises, he was the only Black Interventional Cardiologist in Canada. In addition, he is the author of over 50 published articles on cardiology, has written several book chapters in Interventional Cardiology textbooks and divides his time between research, teaching, and patient care. **AFFIL:** American College of Cardiology; Cdn Cardiovascular Society; Assn. of Black Cardiologists. **HONS.:** many academic honours and awards including: Dean's Award for Excellence in Clinical Research, U of T, 1999/2000; Junior Research Fellowship Award, Heart & Stroke Foundation/Canada, 1996-99. **WORKS:** over 50 publications (chapters in books & articles); *Circulation; J American College of Cardiology; American J of Cardiology; Cardiol Clin.; European Heart; Can J of Cardiology.* **EDUCATION:** MSc Clinical Research, 1999; Interventional Cardiology Fellowship, 1996-99, Duke U., NC. Cardiology Research Fellow, St. Michael's Hosp., 1995-96; Adult Cardiology Clinical Fellowship, U of T, 1994-95. MD, 1990; BA (with highest distinction), 1990, Queen's U. **HEROES/ROLE MODELS:** Dr. Barry Batchelor, father. **MOTTO:** Excellence is the best deterrent to racism or sexism. (Oprah, 1989) **CONTACT:** batch002@earthlink.net; Tel: 850-216-0120; Fax: 850-201-4834

▶**BAYLIS, Françoise, PhD.**
PROFESSOR, Bioethics & Philosophy, Faculty of Medicine, Dalhousie University, 5849 University Ave., Halifax, NS B3H 4H7. Born: Montreal, QC.

▶ Dr. Françoise Baylis is professor of medicine and philosophy in the Departments of Bioethics and Philosophy at Dalhousie University. She has considerable expertise in health care ethics, a notable research and publication track record, and national experience in policy-making. Her many research interests include novel genetic technologies, as well as research involving humans, women's health and feminist ethics. Her current research focuses on gene transfer technology, stem cell research and human cloning. This research is funded by the Canadian Institutes of Health Research (CIHR) and the Stem Cell Network (a member of the Networks of Centres of Excellence). In addition to her academic work, FB is involved in national policy-making primarily via her research contracts, public speaking and membership on a number of national committees. She has served on the Ethics Committees of the Royal College of Physicians and Surgeons of Canada and the Society of Obstetricians and Gynaecologists of Canada. For many years she was also a member of the National Council on Ethics in Human Research. Currently, she is a member of the Governing Council of CIHR, Co-Chair of the CIHR Standing Committee on Ethics and a member of the Science and Industry Advisory Committee (SIAC) of Genome Canada. **CAREER BACKGROUND:** Assoc. Prof., Depts. of Bioethics and Philosophy, Dalhousie U., 1996-2002; Asst. Prof., Dept. of Philosophy, U. of Tennessee, 1993-96; Clinical Associate, Medical Ethics, U. of Tennessee Medical Centre, 1993-96; Bioethicist, Hospital for Sick Children, Toronto, 1991-93; and, Research Associate, Westminster Institute for Ethics and Human Values, London, Ontario, 1989-90. **AFFIL:** Canadian Bioethics Society; American Society for Bioethics and Humanities; International Association of Bioethics; and Feminist Approaches to Bioethics. **HONS.:** several including: Award of Excellence in Medical Research, Bioethics, Dalhousie U., 2001. **WORKS:** several edited books, numerous peer-reviewed articles and monographs: *The Roles and Responsibilities of the Ethics Consultant: A Retrospective Analysis of Cases,* 2000; *Codes of*

Ethics: Ethics Codes, Standards and Guidelines for Professionals Working in a Health Care Setting in Canada, 1999; *The Politics of Women's Health: Exploring Agency and Autonomy,* 1998; *Health Care Ethics in Canada,* 1995; *In the Case of Children: Paediatric Ethics in a Canadian Context,* 1993; articles in *Bioethics; The Hastings Centre Report; CMAJ;* and *J Medical Ethics.* **EDUCATION:** PhD, Philosophy (specialization in Bioethics), 1989; MA, Philosophy, 1984, U. of Western Ontario. BA (First Class Honors), McGill U., 1983. **CONTACT:** francoise.baylis@dal.ca; www.bioethics.dal.ca

▶**BAYLIS, Gloria L.**

FOUNDER/CEO, Baylis Medical Company, Ste. 540-5253 Décarie Blvd., Montreal, QC H3W 3C3. Born: Barbados/ in Canada since: 1953.

▶ Gloria Baylis is a Registered Nurse by training, and founder of Baylis Medical Company (BMC), in 1983. The company began as a home office, importing and distributing a range of medical products with a focus on devices (including catheters) for neurosurgery. BMC has since grown into a leading developer and manufacturer of high-tech medical products in cardiology and pain management, with annual sales of $5-million, and offices in Montreal and Toronto. One of the most recent new devices is a home-based cardiac-monitoring system that electronically measures a patient's vital signs, allowing the physician at a hospital to monitor the patient's status. These and other innovative devices are developed for an international market. GB first attracted public attention in 1964, when she initiated a court challenge of discrimination in hiring against Montreal's Queen Elizabeth Hotel (then operated by the Hilton chain). After submitting her application for one of the advertised nursing positions, she was told that the vacancies had been filled: this was not the case as the position was subsequently offered to a white nurse. The case was tried in 1965 and the Queen Elizabeth Hotel and Hilton were found guilty of contravening the Discrimination Act of 1964; for the next 11 yrs. the hotels appealed, seeking to have the conviction overturned. In 1977, the original decision was upheld by the Quebec Superior Court. **HONS.:** Jackie Robinson Award, Business Person of the Year, MABBP. **REVIEWED IN:** local media, including *Montreal Gazette.* **CONTACT:** gbaylis@baylismedical. com; Fax: 514-488-7209

▶**BAYNE, Clarence S., PhD.**

PROFESSOR, Decision Sciences/Management Information Systems, John Molson School of Business, Concordia University, 1455 Maisonneuve Blvd., Montreal, QC H3G 1M8. Born: Trinidad & Tobago / in Canada since: 1954.

▶ Professor Clarence Bayne teaches in the Department of Decision Sciences/Management Information Systems. He is also Director of Graduate Diplomas in Administration and Sports Administration and Director, Entrepreneurship Institute for the Development of Minority Communities at the John Molson School of Business at Concordia U. He began teaching at Concordia U. in the Faculty of Commerce while completing his PhD in Economics at McGill U., in 1977. Prior to that and after completing his MA in 1960, he worked as a transportation economist at CN in Montreal. **COMMUNITY INVOLVEMENT:** Brd., founding Director and past-President, Black Theatre Workshop, 1970-80; Founder and VP, Quebec Brd. of Black Educators, 1970-2001; Founder and President, Black Studies Centre, Quebec, 1971-82, 1985-present; founding member, Nat'l Black Coalition of Canada, 1969, Nat'l President, 1970-71; Director, Black Community Council of Quebec, 1975-77; Founder and past-President, T&T Assn., Mtl, 1964-75; YMCA, 1978-80; President, Nat'l Council of Black Educators of Canada; Brd., Queen Elizabeth Health Complex, Mtl, since 2000. **HONS.:** several including: 30th Anniv. Award, Quebec Brd. of Black Educators, 2000; GG 125th Anniv. Award, 1992; Dr. Martin

Luther King Jr. Achievement Award, 1992. **WORKS:** co-authored: *Statistics Applied to Canadian Issues,* 1991, plus numerous research papers, articles, briefs & discussion papers. **REVIEWED IN:** many publications including: *WWCB; Concordia Magazine; Canada at the Millennium.* **EDUCATION:** PhD, Economics, McGill U., 1977. MA, Economics, 1960; BA, Poli. Sci. & Economics, 1958, UBC. **CONTACT:** bayne@jmsb.concordia.ca; www.johnmolson. concordia/diadsa

▶**BEAUREGARD, Kettly**

EX-CONSEILLÈRE MUNICIPALE, Ville de Montréal. Née: Haïti/ au Canada depuis: 1972.

▶ Kettly Beauregard a la distinction d'être la première femme noire élue à Montréal comme conseillère municipale, en 1994. Depuis, elle a été re-élue deux fois: en 1998, et en 2001; la dernière fois, elle a cédé sa place au Maire défait lui permettant de siéger comme chef de l'opposition. Pendant son séjour à la mairie, elle représentait le district de Marie-Victorin; faisait parti du comité exécutif de l'hôtel de ville; était responsable du dossier des affaires interculturelles; et, était Vice-présidente de la commission de la sécurité publique. Avant d'entrer le secteur public, elle occupait divers emplois autant à Ottawa qu'à Montréal au cours des années 1980 (municipalité d'Ottawa, Via Rail, Philipps, Commission de la fonction publique du Canada, etc.). En 1990, elle fonde un centre d'aide communautaire à Côte-des Neiges, un des quartiers les plus multi-ethniques au Canada. Cette volonté de changer des choses l'a amenée en politique. **AUTRE:** membre de la Chambre immobilière du grand Montréal. **ŒUVRES À SON PROPOS:** dans les médias locaux, y compris, *calendrier mois de l'histoire des noires,* Ville de Mtl, 2000. **FORMATION:** Bac, science politiques; formation en éducation; formation en informatique; agente immobilière. **CONTACT:** Tél: 514-259-6815; Fax: 514-899-1049

▶**BELL, David V.J.,** PhD.

PROFESSOR/DIRECTOR, Centre for Applied Sustainability (YCAS), York University, 4700 Keele St., Toronto, ON M3J 1P3. Born: Toronto, ON.

▶ Professor David Bell is a political scientist by training and has been teaching at York University since 1971. He is also Director, York Centre for Applied Sustainability, at York University, which he founded in 1996. Prior to that he was Dean of the Faculty of Environmental Studies, 1992-96, and Dean of the Faculty of Graduate Studies, 1981-87. **OTHER HIGHLIGHTS:** writer and host of a 12 -hour radio course for Open College, which aired on CJRT-FM, entitled *Sustainability: Canadian and Global Perspectives* (available on the YCAS website). He has written extensively, including several papers on sustainability. He is an editor of the *Int'l J of Sustainable Development;* editor of the "sustainable development theme" of the forthcoming UNESCO-sponsored *Encyclopedia of the Life Support Systems;* he has also served as consultant and advisor to governments at the local, provincial and national levels in Canada and Jamaica. **HONS.:** Morris Katz Memorial Lecture, 1997. **WORKS:** numerous articles, books including *The Roots of Disunity;* chapters in books, conference papers, including chapters in: *Canadian Politics 2000.* **REVIEWED IN:** *WWIC.* **EDUCATION:** PhD, Poli. Sci., 1969; AM (MA equiv.), Poli. Sci, 1967, Harvard University. BA, Poli. Sci, York U./U of T, 1965. **HEROES/ROLE MODELS:** Oscar Peterson; J. Douglas Salmon. **CONTACT:** dvjbell@yorku.ca; www.yorku.ca/ycas

▶**BENNETT, Karl,** PhD.

ASSOCIATE PROFESSOR, Dept. of Economics, University of Waterloo, Waterloo, ON N2L 3G1. Born: Jamaica/ in Canada since: 1959.

▶ Dr. Karl Bennett is an Associate Professor in the Faculty of Economics at the University of Waterloo, where he has taught since 1966. Areas of specialization: Economic Development (Trade Policy); Regional Economic Associations; Trade Policy in the Caribbean; The Informal Sector; Economic Development (Finance); Exchange Rate Systems; Capital Flight; Monetary Integration. **CAREER HIGHLIGHTS:** UN Consultant in the Caribbean, based in Trinidad, 1975; Chair, Dept. of Economics, 1981-87; taught at the Consortium Graduate School, UWI/Jamaica, summer of 1992; member of the Ontario Premier's Council on Economic Renewal, 1991-95. Since 1979, he has been a Research Associate with the Caribbean Centre for Monetary Studies, formerly the Regional Programme of Monetary Studies. **WORKS:** has written many monographs, chapters in books, and articles, which appear in: *Social & Economic Studies; J of Int'l Development.* **EDUCATION:** PhD, McGill U., 1973. MA, 1964; BA, 1962, Queen's U. **CONTACT:** kmbennet@watarts.uwaterloo.ca; Fax: 519-725-0530

🎭 🎨 🌐

▶**BENNETT-COVERLEY, The Hon. Dr. Louise Simone,** OM, MBE. **FOLKLORIST/PERFORMER/AUTHOR.** Resides in Toronto, ON. Born: Jamaica/ in Canada since: 1987.

▶ The Hon. Dr. Louise Simone Bennett-Coverley, otherwise affectionately known by her stage name "Miss Lou" is Jamaica's foremost and most renowned folklorist, writer, and storyteller. Known and admired the world over, she is credited with having created acceptance for the Jamaican dialect, and, through her artistry (seen in acting, broadcasting, theatre, literature and poetry), elevating it as a legitimate form of speech which is representative of a key component of Jamaican culture. **HIGHLIGHTS:** born in 1919 in then-colonial Jamaica, she began writing then performing verse in dialect from the age of 13, at a time when standard English was considered the norm and the ideal to which most people aspired. She began acting in 1936, while in high school, and was spotted by Eric Coverley, a pop-

ular musician (who would later become her husband); in 1945, she won a scholarship to the Royal Academy of Dramatic Arts in London; while there and still a student, she hosted the live radio show, *Caribbean Carnival* on the BBC; during a second stay in London, she hosted a second program for the BBC, *West Indian Guest Night,* which introduced emerging West Indian talent. In Jamaica, her verses, written in dialect were published in the country's newspaper, *The Daily Gleaner,* she also performed them on stage and on radio along with her prose monologues; she hosted radio shows, *Laugh with Louise* and *Miss Lou's Views* which were on the air for 15 yrs., as well as *Lou and Ranny;* on stage she appeared in a number of productions including the annual Jamaican pantomime (from 1943 until 1971, without interruption, and retiring from the stage in 1975); for 12 yrs., beginning in the 1970s, she hosted a popular TV program, *Ring Ding,* which allowed children from all parts of the country to participate and showcase their talent in the performing arts. Her film credits include *Calypso* and *Club Paradise;* her song, *Going Home,* used in the film *Milk and Honey,* was nominated for a Genie Award. In 1989, she was appointed Ambassador-at-Large for Culture by the Jamaican Government. Over the years LBC has performed and lectured throughout the world, promoting Jamaican history and culture and creating awareness and pride amongst Jamaicans for their folk stories and songs. Her works are said to, "have a sophisticated and subversive, political dimension and pillory both pretension and self-contempt. They ridicule class and colour prejudice, and criticize people ashamed of being Jamaican or ashamed of being black." (*Gazette,* York U., 1998). She is the author of a number of books and recordings (see below) and is the recipient of several awards. In March 2000, she was recognized by the Int'l Theatre Institute, Jamaica Chapter, as the "Most Important Theatre Personality of the 20th Century." Several established poet/performers, including Mutabaruka,

Linton Kwesi Johnson, and Yasus Afari have paid tribute to her in their works, for accentuating and promoting Jamaican culture through use of Jamaican dialect. **HONS.:** several including, Member of the Order of Merit (OM), for her distinguished contribution to the development of the Arts & Culture, Jamaica, 2001; Member of the Order of the British Empire (MBE), for work in Jamaican literature and theatre; Norman Manley Award for Excellence; Order of Jamaica, for work in the field of Native Culture; Hon. D.Litt, York U., 1988 and UWI, 1982; Gold Musgrave Medal, for contribution to the development of the arts in Jamaica & the Caribbean, 1978. **WORKS:** Recordings include, *Yes, M'Dear: Miss Lou Live,* 1983; *The Honourable Miss Lou,* 1981; *Carifesta Ring Ding,* 1976; *Listen to Louise,* 1968; *Miss Lou's Views,* 1967; *Jamaica Singing Games,* 1953; *Jamaica Folk Songs,* 1953. Poetry: *Jamaica Labrish,* 1966; *Anancy and Miss Lou,* 1979; *Selected Poems,* 1982; other publications: *Aunty Roachy Seh,* 1993; *Laugh with Louise;* and *Anancy and Miss Lou.* **EDUCATION:** Royal Academy of Dramatic Art, England; St. Simon's College, Excelsior College, & Friends College for Jamaica. **HEROES/ROLE MODELS:** Kerene Robinson, mother. **MOTTO:** *Tek kin teet kiba heart bun:* Use a smile to cover sorrow.

▶BENN-IRELAND, Tessa

AUTHOR/SENIOR LIBRARIAN, Markham Public Libraries, Markham, ON. Born: Guyana.

▶ Tessa Benn-Ireland has been a librarian for most of her professional life. Presently she is head of Children's Services and Programs with the Town of Markham Public Libraries. She is the first Black woman of Caribbean heritage elected to the Board of Trustees of York Region District School Board. She is the publisher of the *Black Business and Professional Women's Calendar,* since 1983 and co-author of *Some Black Women,* 1993. She has served on several Boards and Commissions in Ontario and is currently serving her second term as a member of the Board of Governors at Seneca College. **COMMUNITY:** has a lifelong record of service and civic accomplishment in her community; past-President, Markham African Caribbean Assn. **AFFIL/MBRSHP:** coordinator, Spelling Bee of Canada/York Region; Trustee, York Region Dist. School Board. **HONS.:** ABACUS Assn. of Canada, 1999; Race Relations Award, Town of Markham; Nubian Award of Excellence, 1995; GG 125th Anniv. Medal, 1992. **WORKS:** articles for children and on parenting; *Black Business and Professional Women's Calendar; Some Black Women,* 1993. **REVIEWED IN:** WWCW. **EDUCATION:** Dipl., Library Science, Ryerson, 1972; BA/Hons., U of T, 1982. **MOTTO:** Success is a four-letter word: "I Can." **CONTACT:** tbennirela @aol.com; Fax: 905-479-9479

▶BERGER, Marie-Josée, PhD.

DOYENNE, Faculté de l'Education, Université d'Ottawa. Née: Haïti/ au Canada depuis: 1969.

▶ Dr Marie-Josée Berger est entrée en fonction comme doyenne à la Faculté d'Éducation de l'Université d'Ottawa, le premier juillet 2002. Elle travaillait comme: Professeur agrégée d'Education à l'Institut d'Études pédagogiques de l'Ontario (OISE), de l'U. de Toronto depuis 1994, et depuis 1997, comme directrice du Centre d'Études Pédagogiques de la vallée d'Ottawa, de l'U. de Toronto. Elle a débuté cette carrière universitaire en prêt de service du Conseil des écoles publiques de langue française d'Ottawa-Carleton, où elle était conseillère pédagogique en mathématiques et sciences depuis 1991. Elle obtient le poste à OISE de façon permanente en 1997. Elle a débuté sa carrière dans l'enseignement (1971-1990) et a enseigné au Québec, au Nouveau-Brunswick et en Ontario. Le domaine de la lecture chez les enfants de l'école élémentaire était sa grande préoccupation. Ainsi, ses recherches ont porté sur l'intervention précoce en lecture, auprès des élèves à risques, en milieu minoritaire. Elle a aussi reçu plusieurs subventions qui lui ont permis de travailler avec ces élèves et leurs enseignants. **AFFIL/ASSN:** prés: Société canadienne pour l'étude de l'éducation; avant: Ontario Education Quality & Accountability Office; Comité aviseur du Recteur pour les affaires Francophones, U. d'Ottawa; Table des partenaires (Regroupement provincial des Réseaux et Centres de formation de l'Ontario), Ont. Min. de l'Education et de la Formation; Comité de programmation des cours en français; Centre de recherche en éducation Franco-ontarienne. **ŒUVRES:** livre: *Construire la réussite,* 1995. Articles dans: *Curriculum & Teaching Dialogue; Can J of Program Evaluation; Rev. du Nouvel Ontario; Vie pédagogique,* etc. **FORMATION:** Direction d'école, 1&2, 1991, 1992, U. Laurentienne. PhD, Education, 1988; M.Ed, Education/Psychopédagogie, 1976, U. d'Ottawa. B.Ed, UQAM, 1972. **MENTORS:** « ma mère, qui a toujours voulu que ces deux filles soient les futures reines du monde. » **MOTTO:** Impossible, n'est pas français. **CONTACT:** Tél: 613-562-5804; Fax: 613-562-5146

▶BERNARDINE, Marion

EDUCATOR/PRINCIPAL (Ret.), Toronto District School Board, ON. Born: Trinidad & Tobago/ in Canada since: 1971.

▶ Marion Bernardine is a noted educator, former principal and champion of equity issues. Before her retirement, she was the Principal of Regal Road PS, 1993-98, and worked with teachers, parents and students to ensure that all voices were heard and reflected in the curriculum. She actively sought to include parents as partners in their children's education; her dual-track school recruited and trained parents as volunteers; her units on anti-racism gained recognition from the Elementary Teachers Federation and were used by a number of school systems. In 1997, she was chosen as part of a team of educators to go to S. Africa and assist in developing educational out-

comes for the new system of education for that country. Since her retirement, she has undertaken consulting work for the Ont. Min. of Education. **WORKS:** curriculum documents; handbooks for parents; articles in the Newsletter for the Federation of Women Teachers' Assn. **EDUCATION:** M.Ed, U of T, 1974. MA, Ed. Psychology, 1971; BA, 1966, NY U. **MOTTO:** God counts the tears of women. (Kabalah) **CONTACT:** marion.bernardine @sympatico.ca

▶BERNHARDT, Kim

LAWYER, Grant & Bernhardt, Box 68507, 360A Bloor St. W., Toronto, ON M5S 1X1. Born: Toronto, ON.

▶ Kim Bernhardt is a lawyer who specializes in labour, employment, human rights, professional regulation, administrative, and constitutional law. From 1993-2001, she worked for the Ontario Nurses' Assn. (ONA), a union that represents 45,000 registered nurses and allied health professionals. She presented ONA's policy position and represented ONA members before arbitration boards and tribunals including the Worker's Compensation Appeals Tribunal, Employment Equity Commission, and the Ont. Human Rights Commission. She has also served on the Public Service Grievance Board and was a part-time appointee to the Human Rights Board of Inquiry. From 1989-92, she lived in the United Arab Emirates and taught business for the Higher Colleges of Technology. **AFFIL/MBRSHP:** has been involved in community and legal organizations concerned with equity, law, education, and social issues; Thistletown Community Services; OBHS; Amnesty International; Halton Board of Education, Equity Committee; Urban Alliance on Race Relations; CABL; Delos Davis Law Guild; National Assn. of Women and the Law (NAWL). **EDUCATION:** LLM, 1999; LLB, 1988, Osgoode Hall, York University. BA/Hons., U of T, 1977. **CONTACT:** kim.bernhardt@cogeco.ca

►BERRY, Ivan

PRESIDENT, Beat Factory/**HEAD,** International Division, BMG Music, Ste. 100-190 Liberty St., Toronto, ON M6K 3L5. Born: St. Kitts, 1963/ in Canada since: 1979.

► Ivan Berry is President of his own company, Beat Factory, and Head of the International Division of BMG Music/Canada. Since 1983, he has been working to develop urban music in Canada. In collaboration with Rupert Gayle, he started Beat Factory to manage Gayle's group; the company has grown into a corporation which now manages the careers of the top urban music artists in Canada. Their roster has included Glenn Lewis, Michee Mee, LA Luv, Index, Devon, Rupert Gayle, Organized Rhyme, and others. His most famous client is the hip hop group, Dream Warriors, which, since 1990, has scored many international top 10 hits and garnered numerous awards. Other clients currently include: Rupert Gayle (BMG Music), Mathematik, Diamond X, and Bliss. **OTHER HIGHLIGHTS:** signed the first Cdn rap artist to an international record deal; signed the most rap, hip hop and R&B artists to record deals and sold more of these records worldwide than any other manager. In 1996, he started a record label division of Beat Factory, which is distributed by EMI Music Canada. As a result this label is now the first urban music label in Canada to be nationally distributed by one of the five major record companies in the world. IB believes in giving back to the community and does so through his involvement with various community organizations; he also teaches a music management program at the Harris Institute of the Arts. **HEROES/ROLE MODELS:** Mother. **MOTTO:** To take advantage of an opportunity, you must first recognize it. **CONTACT:** ivan.berry@bmge.com; Fax: 416-586-6671

►BERTLEY, Frederic Marcus, PhD.

IMMUNOLOGIST/RESEARCH SCIENTIST. Harvard University Medical School/Boston Children's Hospital, Boston, MA, USA. Born: Montreal, QC, 1970.

► Dr. Fred Bertley is a Post-Doctoral Fellow at Harvard University's Medical School, and is the immunologist on an HIV vaccine laboratory team, working on the development and testing of a DNA vaccine for the prevention of HIV infection. **BACKGROUND:** during his doctoral studies and in collaboration with Johns Hopkins University, he conducted field studies and research in Haiti (1993), Sudan (1994), and at Iqaluit on Baffin Island in Nunavut Territory (1996 and 1998). Some of his research examined whether or not measles induced cell-suicide or immunity, and he studied Graft-versus-Host Disease (GVHD), a major complication of bone marrow transplantation. **COMMUNITY INVOLVEMENT:** Brd., Dudley Street Neighbourhood Initiative, and Chair, Education Cmtee., 2001-03; founder/ director, Mass Comprehensive Assessment System, 2001-02; Tutor, John D. O'Bryant Institute, Northeastern U., 2000-02; Tutor, the Garvey Institute, Montreal, 1990-99. **HONS.:** several, including, National Institute of Health (NIH) Research Fellowship, 2000-03; Merck Frosst Scholarship, 1999; President's Award, Quebec Black Medical Assn.; Jackie Robinson Scholarship, City of Montreal, 1998; Du Pont Pharma Scholarship, 1997; Bristol Meyer Squibb Scholarship, 1997. **WORKS:** articles and papers based on research have been presented at conferences and published in scientific journals. **REVIEWED IN:** *Millennium Minds,* 2000. **EDUCATION:** Post-Doctoral Fellow, Harvard University. PhD (Dean's Hon. List), Immunology, 1999; BSc, Math/Physiology, 1994, McGill U. **CONTACT:** Tel: 514-855-1425; Fax: 514-855-1426

►BERTLEY, John N., MD, FRCPC.

PHYSICIAN/INTERNIST/RESPIROLOGIST, Sir William Osler Health Centre, Toronto, ON. Born: Montreal, QC.

► Dr. John Bertley is a specialist in Internal Medicine, with a sub-specialty in Respirology. His areas of medical interest include: General Respirology; Bronchoscopy; Sleep Medicine; and the Intensive Care Unit (ICU). He works in association with the Sir William Osler Health Centre in Toronto, and served on the Executive Committee of the Ontario Lung Association. **HONS.:** several academic including, Dr. Charles H. Este Scholarship; City of Pierrefonds Scholarship; Medical Research Council of Canada Scholarship; *Bourse d'Excellence, Fonds de la Recherche en Santé du Québec.* **EDUCATION:** FRCPC, 1995. MD CM, 1989; BSc (with great distinction), 1983, McGill U.

▶**BERTLEY, June A.**
EDUCATOR/DIRECTOR-GENERAL, The Garvey Institute, 8409 Côte Vertu, Montréal, QC H4L 1Y4. Born: Barbados/ in Canada since: 1954.
▶ June Bertley is a career educator who began teaching in Barbados and is co-founder and Director-General of the Garvey Institute (GI) in Montreal, since 1981. The GI was established to provide education in a positive environment, with an emphasis on the contributions made by Blacks throughout history. It has three components: a primary school, which is registered with the Quebec Ministry of Education; the Institute, which offers tutorial, remedial and supplementary educational support to students enrolled in the public education system; and, the administration of the Deborah Bertley Scholarship Fund. From 1961-72, JB taught at various high schools in the Montreal area; she was also a lecturer in Trinidad at the Roman Catholic Women's Teachers Training College, 1966-67. **COMMUNITY INVOLVEMENT:** extensive, including various school committees; Black Liaison Committee; President, Quebec Task Force on Immigrant Women, 1984-2000; Brd., Union United Church; Cubs and Guides Leader; Secretary, Coloured Women's Club. **OTHER:** June Bertley, her spouse and four children [*see: Bertley* (one deceased)] are all graduates of

McGill University. **HONS.:** several including: Jackie Robinson Award, Business Person of the Year, MABBP, 2000; Mary Ann Shadd Award, AKAX, 2000; 25-yr. recognition for loyal service, Min. of Education, Quebec, 1993; Marcus Mosiah Garvey Centennial Award, UNIA, 1987. **EDUCATION:** M.Ed, McGill U., 1982; B.Paed, U. de Montréal, 1963; Class 'A' Teaching Dipl., Govt. of Quebec, 1961; BA, SGWU (now Concordia U.), 1959; Hons. Business Dipl., Sir George Williams Business College, 1955. **CONTACT:** Tel: 514-855-1425; Fax: 514-855-1426

▶**BERTLEY, Leo W., PhD.**
AUTHOR/JOURNALIST/EDUCATOR/PROFESSOR,
Dept. of History, Vanier College, St. Laurent, QC. Born: Trinidad & Tobago/ in Canada since: 1960.
▶ Dr. Leo Bertley is a career educator who is currently Professor of History at Vanier College, St. Laurent, QC. He has taught and lectured in schools and universities across Canada, in the Caribbean, the US, and the UK. **CAREER HIGHLIGHTS:** Adjunct Prof., History, St. Lawrence U., New York, 1986; Sessional Lecturer, Canadian History, McGill U., 1977; Sessional Lecturer in Black History, U. of Vermont; Researcher, Quebec Institute of French-Canadian Studies; first Principal and founding member, Da Costa-Hall Education Project; Principal, St. Michael's High School, 1960 (thus becoming the first person of African descent to head a public high school in Quebec); Master, Presentation College, Trinidad. In 1975, he wrote briefing documents on Canada's Black population for the Dept. of External Affairs; these were sent to 55 Canadian Consular Offices, High Commissions and embassies around the world. He also wrote, at the request of the Min. of Education of Quebec, *Anglophone Blacks in Quebec* for distribution to the province's teachers. **COMMUNITY INVOLVEMENT:** extensive, particularly in the area of education, Black history and culture; member of UNIA;

founding member, Garvey Institute; Cdn Historical Assn. He is the author of many articles and publications, and editor of community newspapers, *The Afro-Canadian* and *Afro-Can,* 1981-94. **OTHER:** Dr. Leo Bertley, his spouse and four children [*see: Bertley* (one deceased)] are all graduates of McGill University. **HONS.:** several including: Presentation College Golden Anniversary Award, 1998; Testimonial Dinner, at the Queen Elizabeth Hotel, Black Community Council of Quebec, 1995; Trinidad & Tobago Montreal Award, 1995; West Island Black Community Assn. Award, 1995; Pan African Movement of Barbados Award, 1995; Center for Int'l Development Programs, Southern U., Louisiana, 1995; Quebec Brd. of Black Educators, 1990; Community Service Award, MABBP, 1988; Marcus Garvey Centennial Award, 1987; National Award, Cdn Council for Multicultural & Intercultural Education, 1984; Multiculturalism Award, Govt. Canada; Explorations Award, Canada Council; Pan African Movement of Barbados Award. **WORKS:** selected: articles have appeared in Canadian & int'l newspapers & magazines: *Montreal Star; Montreal Gazette; Times of Zambia; Trinidad Express; Evening Standard; Contrast; Afro-Can; The Afro-Canadian.* Books: *This Noble and Apostolic Work: the Presentation Brothers in the Caribbean,* 1998; *Canada and Its People of African Descent,* 1977; *Montreal's Oldest Black Congregation,* 1976; *Black Tiles in the Mosaic,* 1974, 1975. Ed., *Look for Me in the Whirlwind,* 1981; *To My Someday Child,* 1977. **REVIEWED IN:** local, nat'l, & int'l publications, including, *A Legacy to Share,* 1996 (calendar by City of Montreal, BHM); *Millennium Minds,* 2000; *Some Black Men,* 1999; *Montreal Star; Barbados Advocate; The Gazette* (Mtl); *Trinidad Express; Evening Standard; Times of Zambia.* **EDUCATION:** seven academic degrees including: PhD, History, Concordia U., 1980. MA, History, 1970; BA/Hons., 1965; BSc, 1960, SGWU (now Concordia U.). M.Ed, Ottawa U., 1963; B.Paed, U. de Montréal, 1962; BA, McGill U., 1957; Class 'A' Teaching Dipl., QC, 1961. **CONTACT:** Fax: 514-744-7952

▶**BESS, Ardon**

ACTOR, Toronto, ON. Born: St. Vincent/ in Canada since: 1964.

▶ Ardon Bess is a pioneer in the performing arts in Canada; he began his professional acting career in 1968, after graduating from the National Theatre School as the first Black to attend and graduate from that institution. He is possibly best known for his role on the 1970s TV series, *King of Kensington,* in which he was cast as the Postman, 1975-80 (he was the first Black to be cast in an ongoing role in a Cdn TV series). His film and TV credits include: *Due South; Street Legal; The Littlest Hobo; Laughter on the 23rd Floor,* 2001; *10,000 Black Men Named George,* 2001; *On Hostile Ground,* 2000; *One Heart Broken into Song* (nominated for a Gemini), 1999; *Moving Target,* 1996; *Soul Survivor,* 1995; *Prince for a Day,* 1995; *Ordinary Magic,* 1993; *The Tai Babilonia Story,* 1990; *Hot Paint,* 1988; *Hostage,* 1988; *Head On,* 1981; *Fourth Floor; Highpoint,* 1980; *Prom Night,* 1980; *The Shape of Things to Come,* 1979; *High Ballin',* 1978; recently in *Soul Food* and *Drop the Beat.* His stage work includes: *Driving Miss Daisy,* which he has performed across most of Canada; *Coming Through Slaughter,* by Michael Ondaatje; *The Great White Computer,* by Peter Desbarats; *Prodigals in a Promised Land; Africa in the Caribbean,* a work he co-wrote with Jeff Henry, 1968, and performed for BTW. He has worked with Carol Burnett, Sydney Poitier, Morgan Freeman, and others. **AFFIL:** founding member, Obsidian Theatre Co. **HONS.:** including: ACAA, Arts, 2001; nominee, Gemini Awards, 2000 & 2001; Golden Sheaf Award, for *My Father's Hands;* Yorkton Film Festival, 2000; Outstanding Achievement Award, BFVN-Reel Black Awards, 1998. **REVIEWED IN:** local & nat'l publications. **EDUCATION:** National Theatre School. **MOTTO:**

What a beautiful day the Lord has made. **CONTACT:** ardon@sympatico.ca; Fax: 416-868-0101

▶BEST, J. Calbert, DCL.

CIVIL SERVANT/HIGH COMMISSIONER (Ret.), Federal Public Service, Ottawa, ON. Born: New Glasgow, NS.

▶ Dr. J. Calbert Best worked for over 39 yrs. in the Canadian Public Service, serving in a number of Assistant Deputy Minister positions before becoming an Ambassador. **CAREER HIGHLIGHTS:** National President, Civil Service Assn., the first Black to hold such a senior position in this association, 1957-66; Director, Personnel and Administration, Office of the Comptroller of the Treasury, 1969-70; Director-General Administration, Dept. of Supply and Services, 1970-73; Assistant Deputy Minister, Operations, 1973-75; Assistant Deputy Minister Administration, Dept. Manpower and Immigration, 1974-75; Director Applied Studies in Government, Commonwealth Secretariat, London, England, 1975-77; Special Policy Advisor to Deputy Min./Chair, Employment and Immigration, 1978; Assistant Deputy Minister, Immigration, 1978-85; Canadian High Commissioner to Trinidad & Tobago, 1985-88 (and the first Black Nova Scotian to hold such a position). **AFFIL/MBRSHP:** Chair, Min. Task Force on Sport, 1991-92; Commissioner, Core Sport Study, 1993-94; appointed member, President, Treasury Board's Task Force on the "participation of visible minorities in the Federal Public Service," 1999. **HONS.:** Hon. Doctor of Civil Law, U. of King's College, 1995; Centennial Medal, 1967. **WORKS:** co-author, *Sport: The Way Ahead,* 1992; and, various articles in periodicals. **REVIEWED IN:** *WWIC; Journey: African Canadian History,* 2000; *Some Black Men,* 1999. **EDUCATION:** BA, Dalhousie U., 1948; Dipl. Journalism, U. of King's College, 1948. **HEROES/ROLE MODELS:** Dr. Carrie Best, mother. **CONTACT:** best.cal26@sympatico.ca

▶BEY, Salome

SINGER/ACTOR, Toronto, ON. Born: USA/ in Canada since: 1964.

▶ Salome Bey is an award-winning jazz and blues singer who has enjoyed great success in Canada and internationally; she is known as "Canada's First Lady of the Blues" and has performed in a wide variety of productions, ranging from children's theatre, international jazz festivals, Broadway shows, to Royal command performances. **BACKGROUND:** originally from Newark, New Jersey, she first drew attention at age 14 when she won a talent contest at the Apollo Theater but, not having received her parents' permission beforehand, she was not allowed to collect the prize–a week of performance at the famous theatre. Later, she would leave her studies in law in order to pursue a career in entertainment; she formed a group with her brother and sister, called Andy and the Bey Sisters; they performed initially at local clubs and later across N. America and in Europe. She came to Toronto in 1964 and stayed, becoming very popular on the jazz circuit, performing at jazz festivals in Canada and around the world. **CAREER HIGHLIGHTS:** SB enjoyed great success in theatre and in the early 1970s won an OBIE (off-Broadway theatre) Award as Best Actress for her role in the New York version of the play, *Justine* (performed there as *Love Me, Love My Children*); appeared in the play, *Indigo,* which won a Dora Mavor Moore Award and was performed on stage and on CBC TV; also appeared in her own play, *Madame Gertrude.* She appeared in many TV specials with other leading performers including two CBC-TV specials, *Salome Bey's Christmas Soul,* 1995, and *Special Moments,* 1992, filmed live in Seville, Spain. Her recordings include: *Christmas Blue; I Like Your Company; Live* (with the Montreal Jubilation Choir); *Tears are Not Enough* (single and video); with Horace Silver (Bluenote Records), and, Andy and the Bey Sisters (RCA Records). Concert appearances included: Imperial Room, Massey Hall, Roy Thomson Hall in Toronto; at the Olympia in Paris, the Cotton Club in New York, Montreux Jazz Festival, Switzerland, Expo '86 (Vancouver) and Expo '92 (Seville, Spain). She performed twice for Queen Elizabeth II and at Nelson Mandela's first visit to Canada. SB continues to perform and host events in Toronto, sometimes with her daughters. **HONS.:** several including: OBIE Award, Best Actress, for *Love Me, Love My Children,* 1972; Dora Mavor Moore Awards, for *Indigo;* Grammy nomination, for cast album, *Your Arms are Too Short to Box with God;* Toronto Arts Award; three Black Music Awards; Martin Luther King Jr. Award. **REVIEWED IN:** *Some Black Women; WWCW; WWIC;* nat'l and int'l newspapers and magazines.

▶BIDDLE, Charlie

JAZZ MUSICIAN, c/o Justin Time Records, Ste. 101-5455, rue Paré, Montreal, QC H4P 1P7. Born: USA/ in Canada since: 1948.

▶ Charlie Biddle, bass player, is a musical institution in Quebec; he is responsible for the creation of the annual Montreal International Jazz Festival. In 1979, when he organized the first jazz festival the city had ever seen and called it *Jazz de Chez Nous,* he was told from many quarters that it would never work. He went ahead and the CBC broadcast the three-day event which turned out to be a phenomenal success. The following year, some of the original organizers planned the *Festival international de Jazz de Montreal,* but, due to financial constraints from the cost of staging the first event, CB was not one of the organizers of the new festival, but is still credited with being its founder. **BACKGROUND:** he came to Canada from the US in 1948, after completing his military duty, then studying music at Temple U. Upon his arrival in Quebec, he formed his own jazz band and travelled throughout the province, introducing jazz to towns which had never heard it before; he found a particularly warm welcome as a musician in the Eastern Townships. In 1967,

he was selling cars by day and playing nights at Montreal's Black Bottom club; with the preparations for Expo '67 underway, his wife, Constance, convinced the organizers to allow him to use the Youth Pavillion to produce jazz events. As a result, the international community was introduced not only to Charlie Biddle, but also to John Coltrane, Thad Jones and Pepper Adams. CB has played with all of the jazz greats and continues to do so. His four children are all active in Quebec's entertainment industry; together they are described as "the royal family of Montreal music." Towards the end of the '70s, CB and some friends opened Biddle's Jazz and Ribs in downtown Montreal, which has become a very popular restaurant and jazz venue for showcasing local and international talent. His last recording, *In Good Company,* 1996, includes Oliver Jones, Johnny O'Neal, Wray Downes, Ranee Lee, Richard Ring and Wali Muhammad. Over the course of his career, CB has played for kings, princes, prime ministers, and premiers. **OTHER:** throughout the '70s and '80s, he developed a career as a part-time actor, appearing in a number of films, most recently, *The Whole Nine Yards* (starring Bruce Willis), in which he performed two songs with daughter Stephanie Biddle, and, *The Buttercream Gang.* He is the subject of a documentary aired on Canal D's *Biographies,* 2001, entitled, *Charlie Biddle: une vie improvisée.* **HONS.:** including, Oscar Peterson Award, Montreal International Jazz Festival; honoured by Mayor Bourque, 2001, in recognition of his contribution to the cultural heritage of the City of Mtl; was invited to dine with Queen Elizabeth II. **CONTACT:** Tel: 514-738-9533; www.justin-time.com

▶BIDDLE, Sonya

ACTOR/FORMER CITY COUNCILLOR, Décarie/NDG, Montreal City Council. Born: Montreal, QC.

▶ Sonya Biddle is renowned as an actress, director and producer; she was also, until the 2001 municipal elections, a city councillor, the first Black Anglophone woman elected to Montreal's City Council. She was elected in 1998 to represent the Décarie District in the borough of Notre-Dame-de-Grace. During this term, she initiated a number of revitalization projects which benefited business, youth, and the community in general. She entered politics following a request by then-Mayor Pierre Bourque, and because she wanted to make a difference in her neighbourhood, which seemed to be on the decline. **ARTISTIC ACCOM-PLISHMENTS:** appearances in plays such as, *A Woman Alone, The Haunting,* and many major feature films including *The Bone Collector* with Morgan Freeman; co-producer for several musicians and musical festivals such as, The Montreal International Blues Festival, The Montreal Celtic Music Festival, and the Montreal Indigenous Music Festival; and, Associate Producer of a weekly TV series on Scotland. **COMMUNITY:** member, NDG Entrepreneur Centre; The Cinema V Action Committee; active supporter of *Chez mes Amis,* Boomerang Connections, and St. Raymond Community Centre; founding member of the NDG Community Inter-Racial and Inter-Cultural Committee. **CONTACT:** sonyabiddle@hotmail. com; Fax: 514-872-2937

▶**BISHOP, Henry V., Dr.**
CHIEF CURATOR, DIRECTOR, Black Cultural Centre for Nova Scotia (BCC NS), 1149 Main St., Dartmouth, NS B2Z 1A8. Born: Weymouth Falls, NS.
▶ At the start of his career, Dr. Henry Bishop was employed as a Communications Officer with the Black United Front (BUF) of NS, then worked independently in graphic design and photography. This led to his association with the BCC NS, which he joined as a curator trainee in 1982. At the same time, he worked with the NS Museum complex and co-curated the nationally travelled exhibit, *Africville, a Spirit that Lives On,* 1985. His goal is to "create understanding and respect

for all people with the use of positive cultural experience." He is also active in developing educational programs for schools and social agencies; he has been featured on many radio and TV programs, including Japan Radio. **HONS.:** Hon. Doctorate, Fine Arts, NS College of Arts & Design, 2000. **WORKS:** co-authored two books: *Out of the Past and Into the Future,* 1994; and, *In Our Time,* 1996. **REVIEWED IN:** *Black to Business; CACE; Blacks in the Maritimes.* **EDUCATION:** B.Visual Arts, NS College of Art & Design, 1975; add'l studies in African Music, History & Culture, Dalhousie U.; studies in Museumology, Mount Saint Vincent U. **HEROES/ROLE MODELS:** Mother; Dr. W.P. Oliver, friend. **MOTTO:** Keep the faith…faith will keep you. **CONTACT:** mail@bccns.com; www. bccns.com

▶**BLACKETT, Adelle, LLM.**
ASSISTANT PROFESSOR, Faculty of Law, McGill University, 3644 Peel St., Montreal, QC H3A 1W9. Born: Montreal, QC, 1967.
▶ Adelle Blackett is an Assistant Professor in the Faculty of Law, McGill University, since 2000. Her areas of expertise are labour law, international trade, development and human rights. **CAREER HIGHLIGHTS:** Labour Law and Labour Relations Specialist, ILO (UN), Geneva, 1994-95, 1998-2000; Associate in Law (Teaching Fellow), Columbia University, NY, 1996-98. **HONS.:** Boulton Research Fellowship, McGill U., 1999; Cheryl Rosa Teresa Doran Award, McGill U., 1994. **WORKS:** articles in: *Columbia Human Rights Law Review; Indiana J Global Legal Studies; Columbia J Transnational Law.* **EDUCATION:** JSD Candidate; LLM, 1998, Columbia University. BCL & LLB, McGill U., 1994; BA, Queen's U., 1989. **CONTACT:** adelle.blackett@mcgill.ca

BLACKMAN, Craig
▶**GENERAL MANAGER,** Rehabilitation and Training Services, COSTI Immigrant Services, 700

Caledonia Rd., Toronto, ON M6B 4H9. Born: Toronto, ON.

▶ Craig Blackman is the General Manager, Rehabilitation and Training Services at COSTI (Canada's largest education and social service agency with a specific mandate to provide services to newcomers and their families). His responsibilities are to assist individuals with physical, emotional, social or medical barriers to employment in their efforts to enter or re-enter the workforce; and, with the Youth portfolio also added to his mandate, he is also responsible for providing social recreational programs to at-risk youth. **OTHER HIGHLIGHTS:** Instructor at Seneca College, teaching courses on rehabilitation to the general public, courses are also required for adjusters throughout Canada, by the Institute of Insurance; coach and founder of the I Be Fast Track Club, specializing in sporting activities for youth, ages 5-13; coach of North Toronto Boys' Basketball; 3T Director of Programs, specializing in the development of programs for at-risk youth; Coordinator and Coach of Athletics in the Ontario Summer Games. A former international class athlete himself, he was a member of Canada's Pan Am Games Team for athletics, 1971, and a member of Canada's Olympic Team in athletics, 1972; in 1966, the International Track & Field Assn. ranked him number three in triple jump in the World, Junior category. **HONS.:** including: All-American Award, National Collegiate Athletic Assn., 1971 & '72; Man of the Year, National Black Coalition, 1966. **REVIEWED IN:** *Who's Who in Canadian Sports, Toronto Life.* **EDUCATION:** NCCP, Level 3 Coaching Certification, 1999; Registered Rehabilitation Professional, 1994; BSc, Special Ed. & Broadcast Communication, U. of Oregon, 1974. **HEROES/ROLE MODELS:** Mary Allen, grandmother; Lloyd Percival & Noel Creft, life coaches. **MOTTO:** You can make it happen! **CONTACT:** sajia@idirect.com

▶**BLACKMAN, Gordon**

HIGH SCHOOL TEACHER (Ret.), Lakeshore School Board, Montreal, QC. Born: Trinidad & Tobago/ in Canada since: 1962.

▶ Gordon Blackman taught History and English at John Rennie High School in Montreal for nearly 33 yrs., beginning in 1965. His most significant contribution to the field of education was the development and teaching of a Black History course. **HIGHLIGHTS:** in 1993, he began work on curriculum to meet the needs of Black students; by 1994, his students were involved in an integrated approach to the study of Black history; under his supervision, they wrote and published the *Black History Magazine;* wrote, acted and produced two videos entitled *Our Legacy* and *Let Us Tell You About Our People.* **OTHER:** 1996, sat on the committee that produced and revised, based on their original research, *Some Missing Pages: The Black Community in the History of Quebec and Canada;* this teaching resource is now available on-line; he was motivated in this endeavour by the belief that, "Black youth, by being exposed to, and knowing their history, will be in a better position to understand and appreciate their heritage and culture." He has also been active in the community promoting Black History Month and other initiatives aimed at increasing awareness and appreciation of Black history and Black culture. Prior to coming to Canada, GB taught for 12 yrs. in Trinidad. **HONS.:** several including: one of the finalists for the GG Award for Excellence in Teaching Canadian History, 1997; *Encyclopaedia Britannica* Award, for outstanding contribution to education, 1993. **WORKS:** articles on Black history; Black history curriculum: participant in producing *Some Missing Pages: The Black Community in The History of Quebec and Canada.* **REVIEWED IN:** *Montreal Gazette; The Society; CCT News; Traces.* **EDUCATION:** graduate studies (History), Concordia U.; BA, McGill U.

▶BLACKMAN, Margot
COMMUNITY ADVOCATE/NURSING TEACHER
(Ret.), Vanier College, Montreal, QC. Born: Barbados/ in Canada since: 1961.

▸ As a child in Barbados, Margot Blackman always wanted to be a missionary. Many say that through her activities as a nurse, teacher, social organizer, church worker, philanthropist, advocate and counsellor she has fulfilled this ambition, with Montreal being the mission field. **BACKGROUND:** she is described by many as a "community stalwart" for her involvement in community building over a 38-yr. period. After completing her schooling in Barbados, she taught from 1951-56 at both the elementary and the secondary school levels; with the assistance of her cousin, Rev. H.E. Blackman, she was awarded a scholarship to study nursing at the St. John's Episcopal Hospital School of Nursing in NYC. **CAREER HIGHLIGHTS:** 1961-66, she was a staff nurse, team leader, and charge nurse in the Paediatrics Dept., Montreal's Jewish General Hospital. After completing a Bachelor degree in Nursing, she taught for three years at the School for Nursing Assistants, at the Jewish General Hospital. In 1971, she received a position as a nursing teacher at Vanier College, where she remained until her retirement in 1994. In 1974, she obtained a Certificate in Teaching at the College level. Over the years she mentored and advised many nurses, particularly those who were Black. **COMMUNITY INVOLVEMENT:** has been extensive and was spent at: St. Paul's Anglican Church; Union United Church; the Negro Community Centre; the *Afro-Can* (then *Afro-Canadian*) newspaper and *Community Contact;* member editorial committee, reporter and photographer for 13 yrs. with *Afro-Can.* Current volunteer activities: *Community Contact;* active in the Barbados Assn., Mtl, (re-named, Barbados House) 1970-81, and was one of the founders and editors of the association's magazine, *BAM News;* included Barbados House in two international exhibitions sponsored by the YWCA, in the '70s; organized the 10-yr. anniversary celebration of Barbados House which was attended by over 400 people. As an avid lover of folklore, she compiled and published a collection of Barbadian sayings, 1982. And, in addition to "giving to her community in Montreal," she has also sent nursing, science and math books to St. Vincent, Montserrat, Guyana, and to the Community College and Queen Elizabeth Hospital in Barbados. **OTHER:** has made presentations on radio (CBC, CJAD, CFMB) on Black culture, and on feminism in the Black community. **HONS.:** several including: Tribute organized by Barbados House, 1999. **WORKS:** including, *Compilation of Bajan Proverbs,* 1982; articles in *Nation* (Barbados); *Barbados Advocate; Jamaica Gleaner; Contrast; BAM News; Afro-Can; Bim* magazine, and others. **REVIEWED IN:** *Community Contact.* **EDUCATION:** Cert. Teaching at the College Level, 1974; BN, 1968, McGill University. Dipl., St. John's Episcopal Hospital School of Nursing, NY, 1959. **CONTACT:** Tel: 514-489-4540

▶BLACKWOOD, Yvonne
BANKER, Royal Bank of Canada/**AUTHOR,** Toronto, ON. Born: Jamaica/ in Canada since: 1976.

▸ Yvonne Blackwood has held several management positions within the Royal Bank, from Loans Officer, Branch Manager, to Sr. Account Manager Business Banking; in 1999, she was appointed Community Banking Advisor. **AFFIL/MBRSHP:** Tropicana Community Services Organization; Ontario Development Corp.; Trillium Foundation; Metro Toronto Children's Aid Society; YMCA Black Achievers Program; chairs the Black Cultural Committee, Royal Bank. Fellow, Institute Cdn Bankers; Associate, Institute of Bankers, UK. **OTHER:** wrote a weekly column in *Pride News* magazine; wrote a bi-weekly column, *Toronto Star* and a monthly column in *African Connection.* **HONS.:** Cert. for volunteering, Ont. Min. of Citizenship & Culture; Community Volunteer Recognition, Heritage Skills Development Centre, and City of Markham. **WORKS:** has published several short stories; first book: *Into Africa, a Personal Journey,* 2000. **REVIEWED IN:** community newspapers and in the Royal Bank's 1990 Annual Report, for her community work. **EDUCATION:** studies at U of T & Ryerson U.; University of Technology (formerly CAST), Jamaica. **CONTACT:** yebblack@ hotmail.com

▶BLAIR, Ned

COMMUNITY ACTIVIST. PRESIDENT, Organization of Black Tradesmen & Tradeswomen of Ontario, Toronto, ON. Born: Guyana/ in Canada since: 1970.

▶ Ned Blair has been involved in various community development initiatives for more than 30 yrs. One of his greatest achievements is presiding over the Organization of Black Tradesmen and Tradeswomen of Ontario (OBTTO) since 1992. Prior to the organization's formation, Blacks were denied access to jobs on construction sites. The OBTTO was established to counter this imbalance and received funding and support from government agencies, the private sector and unions. It has managed apprenticeship programs that trained over 1,000 youth (male and female), and forced a change in the hiring practices on construction sites. Occupational fields include carpentry, electrical, steelwork, automotive, tool and die, and masonry. Partners for this program include the federal and provincial governments, Honda Canada, Ontario Hydro, Carpenters' Union, Iron Workers' Union, George Brown and Centennial Colleges. Another achievement was collaborating with the Adventist Development Relief Agency (ADRA), to bring critically ill children from Guyana for surgery at Sick Children's Hospital in Toronto. **COMMUNITY INVOLVEMENT:** as chair for Special Projects with Toronto Kaiteur Lions Club, he sought funding to establish a retirement home for Caribbean seniors through the JobsOntario Homes Program; initiated a partnership with Queen's U. Teaching Hospital (Kingston, ON), to undertake research among Guyana's indigenous peoples, since 1989; co-founded the Alliance of Guyanese-Canadian Oganizations, 1990, the umbrella body for all Guyanese organizations; cmtee member, Harry Jerome Awards, BBPA; life member, Guyana Berbice Assn., since 1982; founded the Hopetown Assn. and the Guyana Essequibo Assn., and many others. Has been active in several other community organizations including: JCA; Caribbean Cultural Committee; OBHS; St. Thomas Health Care Group. To help those outside of Canada, he has shipped medical, educational, and recreational equipment and supplies to hospitals, schools, and community centres in Guyana, and established two libraries in rural areas. **OTHER:** NB works at Steelcase, one of the largest manufacturers of office furniture in NA. **HONS.:** several including: Prostate Cancer Sensitization Award, for promoting awareness, Anthurium Foundation, 2001; Harry Jerome Award, for community service, BBPA, 1999. **REVIEWED IN:** Guyana media, local and community publications; *Quartermark* (Steelcase corporate magazine). **HEROES/ROLE MODELS:** Dr. Rudy Grant, friend; Archdeacon Oscar Agard, friend. **MOTTO:** Education is the key! **CONTACT:** nblair@steelcase.com; Fax: 416-245-0222

▶BLAKE, Ronald E. A.

DIRECTOR OF STUDIES, Higher Marks Educational Institute Inc., Ste. 109-1440 Bathurst St., Toronto, ON M5R 3J3. Born: Jamaica/ in Canada since: 1966.

▶ Ronald Blake is the founder and Director of Studies of the Higher Marks Educational Institute Inc., in Toronto. Specializing in remedial and intervention education, the private institute addresses the needs of students who face academic, self-esteem, and self-confidence problems in the regular school system. Over its 23-year history, more than 6,000 students have been assisted. Higher Marks, whose impact on education has been the subject of TV documentaries on: CBC, CTV, WTN, Sask.-TV and Rogers Cable, is also the creator of the Prophonics self-help reading system. REB is also a leading lecturer on Black history. **HONS.:** People of Excellence Award; Harry Jerome Award for professional excellence, BBPA; Certificate, for contributions in the field of education, Ontario Government; Award, for service to the community, Onyx Lions Club; Award, for service to the community, *Contrast* newspaper. **WORKS:** *How to Motivate the Student* (booklet); books: *Jamaica: Great Nation, Great Problems, Great Future,* 1999; *Ruler in the Kingdom of Men,* 1991. **EDUCATION:** MSc, Education and Resource Development; BA/Hons., U. of Guelph. **MOTTO:** Try to SERVE, not to SURVIVE. **CONTACT:** Tel: 416-532-5563; Fax: 905-887-4108

▶**BLANCHETTE, Howard,** MD, FRCSC, FACOG.
CHAIR, Dept. of Obstetrics & Gynecology, Danbury Hospital, 24 Danbury Ave., Danbury, CT 06810, USA. Born: Winnipeg, MB.
▶ Dr. Howard Blanchette has been the Chair of the Dept. of Obstetrics and Gynecology (OB/GYN) at the Danbury Hospital in Connecticut, since 2000. His previous professional and academic positions include: Chair, Dept. of OB/GYN, Metro West Medical Center, MA, 1996-2000; private practice, 1976-96; Associate Clinical Professor, Yale School of Medicine, since 2000; Clinical Professor, Tufts U., School of Medicine, since 1998; was Adjunct Clinical Professor at the Boston U. School of Medicine, 1996-2000; and, a Lecturer at the Harvard Medical School, 1996-2000. At U. of Southern California's School of Medicine, he was made an Emeritus Clinical Professor, 1998, after the following appointments: Asst. Clinical Prof., 1979-

84; Assoc. Clinical Prof., 1984-88; Full Clinical Prof., 1988-98. **AFFIL/MBRSHP:** Examiner, American Brd. of OB/GYN, since 1998; President, California Academy of Medicine, 1994; President, San Francisco Gynecological Society, 1990-91; National Perinatal Assn., 1998-2001; President, Medical Staff, Alta Bates Hospital, 1988. **His father, A.R. Blanchette (1910-1977), left St. Kitts in 1928 to study medicine at Howard University. The Depression brought an end to his studies and he joined the railway. He became a key organizer in Mtl for railway porters and advocated on their behalf for better working conditions and better wages; once the Brotherhood of Sleeping Car Porters (BSCP) was recognized in Canada, he became the country representative.** **HONS.:** several including: Outstanding Service Award, MA House of Representatives, 2000; OB/GYN Resident Teaching Award, Tufts Medical Center, 1999; President's Award, Medical Staff, Alta Bates Hospital, 1995; Community Award, City of Berkeley & Berkeley Primary Care Access Clinic, 1994; Distinguished Service Award, Alta Bates Medical Center, 1993; Earl Henriksen Award, U. of S. CA School of Medicine, 1983-84. **WORKS:** *American J of Obstetrics & Gynecology; J of Reproductive Medicine.* **EDUCATION:** Residency OB/GYN, LA County, U. of S. CA Medical Center, 1975. MD, 1971; BSc, 1965, McGill U. **HEROES/ROLE MODELS:** Don Gadbold, PhD, Fraternity brother. **MOTTO:** Arete–Greek for "competitive excellence." **CONTACT:** howard.blanchette@danhosp.org; Fax: 203-796-7982

▶**BLIZZARD, Stephen V.,** MD, D.Av.Med.
AVIATION MEDICINE CONSULTANT, Nepean, ON. Born: Trinidad & Tobago/ in Canada since: 1958.
▶ Dr. Stephen Blizzard is an MD specializing in Aviation Medicine. He is also a military jet pilot and is licensed as a commercial pilot and flying instructor. Most of his career was spent in the Royal Canadian Air Force (RCAF); he is one of only four Black Air Force jet pilots Canada has

ever had, and the only one who is also a flight surgeon. **CAREER HIGHLIGHTS:** after completing his studies in Edinburgh, Scotland, he taught at the Ontario Veterinary College (now U. of Guelph). He joined the RCAF from 1960-69, and was a member of the Canadian Forces (CF), 1976-83, where he was a Squadron Leader, then a Major. In 1982, he was Deputy Commanding Officer with the National Defence Medical Detachment. He was Sr. Consultant for Safety and Human Factors as well as Chief of Civil Aviation Medical Unit with the Dept. of Civil Aviation Medicine, 1983-95. Since 2000, he has been a Senior Consultant of Marine Medicine with Transport Canada. **OTHER:** he has written and presented a number of papers; in 1975 he presented the first paper on Aviation Medicine in the Commonwealth Caribbean on "The Aerial Transportation of Patients." **AFFIL/MBRSHP:** Fellow, Int'l Aerospace Medical Assn.; past-President Int'l Civil Aviation Medical Assn.; past-President Cdn Society of Aerospace Medicine; Member and Selector, Int'l Academy of Aviation and Space Medicine (membership limited to 250 worldwide); past-President Cdn Aerospace Medicine Aeromedical Transport Assn. (CAMATA). **HONS.:** many including, Cdn Peacekeeping Medal, 2001; MABBP, 1992; Serving Brother, Order of St. John, 1982; UN Peacekeeping Force Medal (Egypt), 1979; Cdn Forces Decoration, 1977. **WORKS:** including: *The Role of the Doctor in Civil Defence; Clinical Aspects of Brucellosis in Man; Patient Care in Flight; Photochromic Lenses in the Aviation Environment.* **REVIEWED IN:** many, including: *Millennium Minds,* 2000; *Flight Lines.* **EDUCATION:** Dipl., Aviation Medicine, UK, 1980; MD, U. of Western Ontario, 1963; BSc, MRCVS (member, Royal College of Veterinary Surgeons, UK), U. of Edinburgh & Royal School of Veterinarian Studies, 1953. **HEROES/ROLE MODELS:** Carmen King, friend, advisor; Dr. Ian Anderson, mentor in Aviation Medicine. **MOTTO:** Never give up! **CONTACT:** sblizz@magma.ca; Fax: 613-226-5768

▶**BLYDEN-TAYLOR, Brainerd**
FOUNDER/ARTISTIC DIRECTOR, The Nathaniel Dett Chorale, 100 Old Orchard Grove, Toronto, ON M5M 2E2. Born: Trinidad & Tobago/ in Canada since: 1973.

▶ Brainerd Blyden-Taylor is the Founder/Artistic Director and Conductor of The Nathaniel Dett Chorale, a new Canadian professional chamber choir, which began in 1998 and is dedicated to the creation and performance of Afrocentric music of all styles (incl: classical, spiritual, gospel, jazz and blues). He was inspired by African-Canadian composer R. Nathaniel Dett (1882-1943), a prominent figure among early 20th century Black musicians, who promoted an awareness of their heritage through composing new works, exploring new musical forms, and fostering an appreciation of existing spirituals and folk songs. **OTHER HIGHLIGHTS:** Conductor of The Ontario Youth Choir, 2002; Music Director, St. Timothy's Anglican Church; is a Master Teacher/ Consultant, coaching teachers and students in choral technique and is often solicited as a clinician/ adjudicator; was the Artistic Director of the Orpheus Choir of Toronto, and the Orpheus Chamber Choir, 1987 to 2002; past-Music Director, Oakwood Wesleyan Church, Humbercrest United Church, and St. Paul's Anglican Church; has also directed a number of university, youth and concert choirs. In addition, he has been the Music Director for a number of events across Canada, such as the Martin Luther King Jr. Tribute, NS; Canada 125 "O Canada Project"; NB, Choral Federation Youth Sing; International Gospel Festival, NS. **MOTTO:** Fill the cup that clears today of past regrets and future fears. (Omar Khayyam) **CONTACT:** unicorn7@rogers.com; www.nathanieldettchorale.org

▶**BOATENG, Kwaku-Barima**
ATHLETE/HIGH JUMPER, Canadian Track & Field Team, Montreal, QC. Born: Ghana, 1974/ in Canada since: 1994.

▶ Kwaku-Barima Boateng is a high jumper and is considered one of the brightest young stars in Canadian Track & Field. He is a former member of the Ghana national team, highlighted by an appearance at the 1994 Commonwealth Games in Victoria; following the Games, he applied for refugee status and remained in Canada with five other Ghanaian athletes. **HIGHLIGHTS:** Silver Medal, Commonwealth Games, 2002; placed 2nd at the Francophonie Games, 2001; Gold Medal (jointly with Mark Boswell), Pan American Games, 1999; four-time Canadian national high jump champion (1995, '96, '98, and '99); placed in top three in many international high jump competitions; is ranked between 3rd and 5th in the world; personal best is 2.34m. **EDUCATION:** completed a degree in computer graphics and multimedia. **CONTACT:** kwakub1@hotmail.com

▶**BON, Trevor,** MD, FRCPS.
PHYSICIAN, GERIATRICS AND INTERNAL MEDICINE, St. Joseph's Care Group, 35 Algoma St. N., Thunder Bay, ON P7B 5G7. Born: Winnipeg, MB, 1969.
▶ Dr. Trevor Bon completed his medical studies at the University of Toronto, then specialized in Geriatric Medicine, a sub-specialty of Internal Medicine. Since 1999, he has been on staff at St. Joseph's Care Group in Thunder Bay, where he is the Physician Advisor for Complex Chronic Care, and on active staff at Thunder Bay Regional Hospital. He is a founding member of AABHS and Camp Jumoke (a summer camp for children with Sickle Cell Anemia). **EDUCATION:** Geriatric Medicine, 1999; Internal Medicine, 1998, RCPSC. MD, U of T, 1994; Biochemistry, U. of Western Ontario. **HEROES/ROLE MODELS:** Father. **CONTACT:** bont@tbh.net; Fax: 807-346-9015

▶**BONNY, Yvette,** MD, FRCPC.
PROFESSEUR EMÉRITE/HÉMATOLOGUE, Hôpital Maisonneuve-Rosemont, 5415, boul. de l'Assomp-

tion, Montréal, QC H1T 2M4. Née: Haïti/ au Canada depuis: 1962.
▶ Dr Yvette Bonny est pédiatre et hématologue; directrice de la section pédiatrie de l'unité de transplantation médullaire à l'hôpital Maisonneuve-Rosemont (HMR), jusqu'à l'an 2000. En avril, 1980, elle a réussi la première greffe de la moelle osseuse (GMO) au Québec (*first doctor in Quebec to carry out a bone marrow transplant*). Elle est professeure agrégée de clinique à l'Université de Montréal; 1980-97, elle a été responsable de la section pédiatrique de GMO de l'Est du Canada. À cause de ses réussites médicales, elle a été l'objet de deux émissions: *En toute liberté,* SRC TV, 1994; *À moitié sage,* Canal Communautaire, 1994. Active dans la communauté, elle est membre du CA, Kouzin-Kouzin, entraide bénévole, auprès des jeunes. **PRIX:** Médecin de Mérite des 20 dernières années, *Actualité Médicale,* 2000; Femme de Mérite, santé, YWCA, 1996; Hématologue de l'Année, 1996; Médecin de Cœur et d'Action, l'Association des MD de la langue Française, 1993; Professeur Émérite, HMR, 1989. **ŒUVRES:** *Vie médicale au Canada Français; Am J Hematology; New England J Medicine; Psychotherapy & Psychomatics; Transplantation; Blood.* **ŒUVRES À SON PROPOS:** « 100 Québécoises au sommet de l'action », *Entreprendre,* 1999; *Reader's Digest,* 2000; *l'Actualité Médicale; Amina; Gazette de Femmes; Chatelaine.* **FORMATION:** Fellow, RCPSC, 1970; Spécialiste, hématologie, CSPQ, 1969; Spécialiste, pédiatre, CSPQ, 1969; Docteur en Médecine, faculté de Médecine d'Haïti. **MENTORS:** Martin Luther King: avoir un rêve, le réaliser et le communiquer aux autres. **MOTTO:** Vouloir c'est Pouvoir! **CONTACT:** pelogad@sympatico.ca; Fax: 514-731-2386

▶**BORDEN, George**
CAPTAIN (Ret.), Royal Canadian Air Force (RCAF)/ Canadian Forces (CF)/ **POET-SONG-WRITER/HISTORIAN,** Dartmouth, NS. Born: New Glasgow, NS.

▶ Captain George Borden served in the Royal Canadian Air Force (renamed Canadian Forces, 1968) from 1953-1985, retiring with the rank of Captain. He then served for five years as executive assistant to the provincial Minister of Social Services, becoming the first Black in NS to hold such a position. From 1988-91, he was the first provincial Literacy Coordinator for Blacks in NS. He is also well known as a poet-songwriter having written the complete lyrics for *The Easter Suite,* 1999, a cantata of ten original gospel songs, performed in 1999. **COMMUNITY:** Executive Director, BUF NS, 1984; Executive Director, Black Cultural Society of Nova Scotia, 1993-94. **HONS.:** CF Peacekeeping medal, 2000; GG 125th Anniv. Medal, 1992; CF Decoration (32 yrs. service), 1985; Centennial Medal, 1967. **WORKS:** Selected: a trilogy on the Black experience: *Canaan Odyssey,* 1988; *Footprints, Images and Reflections,* 1993; *A Mighty Long Way,* 2000. Articles in: *Ebony Black Express; Contrast; Provincial Monitor.* Works in: *Fire on the Water,* 1991; *KOLA; Canada's Black Battalion,* 1986. **REVIEWED IN:** *Journey: African Canadian History,* 2000; *Fire on the Water,* 1991; *KOLA.* **HEROES/ROLE MODELS:** Dr. Carrie Best, community elder; great poets & playwrights. **MOTTO:** For all that you get out of life, you owe it to put something back in. **CONTACT:** mightylongway@access-wave.ca; Tel: 902-435-5698

▶BOVELL, Keith T., MB BS, FRCPC.
MD, GASTROENTEROLOGIST & INTERNIST, Private Practice, Ste. 201-49 Emma St., Guelph, ON N1E 6Z1. Born: Guyana/ in Canada since: 1980.
▶ Dr. Keith Bovell is a gastroenterologist, consultant and internist. In addition to his private practice, he is also a member of staff at Guelph General and St. Joseph's hospitals. After completing his studies in the UK, he came to Canada in 1980 and worked as a family physician in Saskatchewan, until 1983. He re-certified in internal medicine, 1986, then completed a clinical fellowship in gastroenterology at McMaster U., 1986-87. From 1990-91, he was Chief of Dept., Internal Medicine, Guelph General Hospital. **RESEARCH INTERESTS:** gastroduodenal motility with special reference to gastrointestinal dysmotility in diabetes mellitus; upper gastrointestinal motility disorders; and, biliary tract endoscopy. His area of special interest is the treatment of infectious hepatitis B & C. **OTHER:** he is the founder and director of Guelph Annual Day in Internal Medicine, since 1991; founder and coordinator, SW Ontario Gastroenterology/GI Surgery Gut Club, 1996; Medical Advisor, Waterloo-Wellington chapters of the Cdn Liver Fdn., and, the Cdn Ileitis and Colis Fdn. **COMMUNITY:** Soccer Coach; past-President, Saultos Gymnastics Club. **WORKS:** several seminar & presentation papers; "The control of fat-mediated pyloric motility," *Gastroenterology,* 1990; "Total Parenteral nutrition in inflammatory Bowel Disease," *Medifacts,* 1987. **EDUCATION:** ABIM, 1987; FACG, 1989; FRCPC, Gastroenterology, 1987; FRCPC, Internal Medicine, 1986; MRCP, London, UK, 1979; MB BS, King's College, U. of London, UK, 1975; Queen's College, Guyana, 1970. **HEROES/ROLE MODELS:** Mother; Headmaster, Queen's College, Guyana. **CONTACT:** Fax: 519-763-2144

▶BOYD, George
PLAYWRIGHT/JOURNALIST, Montreal, QC. Born: Halifax, NS.
▶ George Boyd spent several years as a journalist with the CBC before devoting himself to being a full-time playwright. Born and raised in Nova Scotia, he became the province's first Black national TV news anchor, on CBC's *Newsworld,* in 1992. As a playwright, he has written two works for screen: *Consecrated Ground,* 1990; *Dead Reckoning: The Lanier Phillips Story,* 1999. His stage credits include: *Shine Boy,* 1988; *Gideon's Blues,* 1992; *Consecrated Ground,* 1999, for which he received a GG award nomination for drama. With several works in progress for

both screen and stage, he has also written extensively for radio. These credits include: *Gideon's Blues; House of Flowers;* and, *God is My Warden,* for which he wrote the title song. His work has been received with positive reviews, particularly as they tell stories reflecting the experiences of indigenous Blacks in Canada. In 1995, he was appointed Writer-in-Association at the Neptune Theatre in Halifax. **HONS.:** including: GG Award nomination, for Drama, 2000; Hon. Diploma, NS Community College, 1998; Cert. of Artistic Merit, BCC/NS, 1988; Cert. of Appreciation, BUF, 1988; Atlantic Journalism Award, 1988. **WORKS:** including: *Two by George; Consecrated Ground.* **REVIEWED IN:** *Journey: African Canadian History,* 2000. **EDUCATION:** NS Institute of Technology, Saint Mary's University. **CONTACT:** ge_boyd@yahoo.com

▶**BOYD, Suzanne**
EDITOR-IN-CHIEF, *FLARE* Magazine, Rogers Media, 777 Bay Street, 7th Fl., Toronto, ON M5W 1A7.
▶ Suzanne Boyd is the Editor-In-Chief of *FLARE* magazine, since 1996, Canada's best-selling fashion and beauty magazine, foreign or domestic. **CAREER HIGHLIGHTS:** began her journalism career as a news reporter and features writer of *The Nation* (Barbados newspaper). She first joined *FLARE* in 1990, as an Associate Beauty Editor; after freelancing in 1992 for the *Toronto Star* (fashion section) and *Chatelaine* magazine, she re-joined *FLARE* and was appointed Beauty, Health, and Fitness Editor in 1993; was promoted to Associate Editor in 1994. Since her appointment to Editor-In-Chief, SB has not only maintained the magazine's fashion and beauty positioning, but has also enhanced it with a commitment to editorial and artistic excellence as well as more relevant and topical content in the areas of arts and entertainment, health, social, and current affairs. **OTHER:** in 1998, SB spearheaded *FLARE*'s 20th Anniversary celebration by producing, the

"FLARE presents: Made in Canada, photographs by Bryan Adams," a book, from which all proceeds go to the Canadian Breast Cancer Foundation. She is also the editorial director of *FLARE Pregnancy* and *FLARE & Co.: This Is Your Life;* serves as a judge for the *FLARE* Volunteer Awards, and for high profile fashion awards such as the Smirnoff International Fashion Awards; appears regularly in print and electronic media as a commentator on women's issues and popular culture. **AFFIL/ MBRSHP:** CABJ; Fashion Design Council of Canada. **HEROES/ROLE MODELS:** Manuel Rodenkirchen; Bonnie Brooks; Michael Griffith. **MOTTO:** *Ad Astra Per Aspera:* To the stars through difficulties. **CONTACT:** www.flare.com; Fax: 416-596-5184

▶**BRAITHWAITE, Daniel**
COMMUNITY ORGANIZER/TRADE UNIONIST, Toronto, ON. Born: Sydney, NS (deceased 20 July 02).
▶ Daniel Braithwaite had a long history of community involvement, advocating for change in discriminatory practices, organizing community support groups and, as a union representative, educating employees on their rights. Originally from Nova Scotia, he moved to Toronto in 1927 with his parents; in his teens he was already active in the Young Men's Negro Assn. and with the Negro Youth Club, the youth division of UNIA; he met Marcus Garvey during his visit to Toronto in 1937, and became even more determined to work for the "upliftment" of his race. When he volunteered to join the Air Force in 1942, he was denied because of his colour; when he was later drafted into the Army, he initially refused but later served until his discharge in 1944. In 1947, he helped found the Toronto Negro Veterans' Assn., which is now the Toronto Negro Colour Guards; this Assn. later petitioned and succeeded in persuading the Ontario Govt. to allow Black nurses to train and be employed in Ontario Hospitals. He was a founding member,

1944, of the Joint Council of Negro Youth and increased awareness in the Black Community of their human and civil rights. He was a founding member of the Toronto Negro Study Group, 1948, which sought ways of increasing unity among Blacks in the community; founding member of the *Canadian Negro Newspaper,* 1950, which advocated for better treatment of Blacks in Toronto; also a member of the Toronto Negro Citizenship Committee, 1950, which helped to ease immigration laws, thereby allowing Blacks from the Caribbean to enter the country. In 1954, he led a community effort to have the Toronto Brd. of Education remove the book *Little Black Sambo* from the curriculum, as it portrayed Blacks in a stereotypical and negative manner; the fight was finally won in 1956. **OTHER:** his trade unionist days grew out of his employment with the Dunlop Plant; he was on the executive of Local 132 of the United Rubber Workers Union and served as the first chair of the Fair Employment Practices and Human Rights Committee; there he was responsible for conducting educational programs, both within the Union and the company's hiring department. He continued to be very active in the community over the years, supporting a number of groups including the OBHS. **HONS.:** including: Hall of Fame Award, ACAA, 2001; Cert. Appreciation, JCA, 1993; Award of Appreciation, Sydney Toronto Assn., 1995; Award of Appreciation, UNIA, 1991. **REVIEWED IN:** community and local publications; profiled in *Some Black Men,* 1999. **EDUCATION:** Motor Mechanic, Central Tech High School, 1939. **HEROES/ROLE MODELS:** Parents; BJ Spencer Pitt, lawyer, former UNIA President; Marcus Garvey; Paul Robeson. **MOTTO:** Up you mighty race, you can accomplish what you will! (Marcus Garvey)

▶**BRAITHWAITE, F. Carlton,** PhD.
ECONOMIST/ENTREPRENEUR/COMMUNITY LEADER, Ottawa, ON. Born: Jamaica/ in Canada since: 1962.

▶ Dr. Carlton Braithwaite, a former sprinter and mathematics teacher, has extensive experience in the Canadian public and private sectors. From 1966-82 he worked for the federal government, serving as Chief, Econometric Research Div., Statistics Canada, then as Sr. Economist, Economic Council of Canada. During this time he authored and co-authored over 30 papers and several studies and books, a number of which led to changes in methodologies at Statistics Canada, the Economic Council and elsewhere as well as influenced government practices and policies. He also established himself as one of the leading economists on investment in Canada. In 1983, he moved to the private sector where he formed and presided over the Uniprop Group of Companies, which invested mainly in the real estate and high-tech industries. In a few years the group amassed holdings in excess of $100-million. In 1987, he co-founded the Commonwealth Club of Ottawa, later renamed Commonwealth Club International, an international business and social club. During 1995-1997, he also served as a member, Brd. of Directors, Ontario Realty Corp. and as an Associate of the Glen Ardith-Frazer Corp., an independent investment management company. Since 1997, he has been an independent distributor for Morinda Inc., a leading natural health and wellness network marketing company. He is also actively involved in a number of community organizations. **AFFIL/MBRSHP:** several including, City of Ottawa Advisory Group on Visible Minorities; Consultative Group for Black Canadian Studies Chair at Dalhousie U.; Alumni President, Ottawa Coronary Health Improvement Program; Director, Exec. Brd., Queen's U. Alumni Assn.; Queen's U. Council. **HONS.:** several athletic & academic awards, Skelton Clarke Fellowship, Queen's U. Inaugural Harry Jerome Business Award, BBPA, 1990. From Morinda: Founders' Club Member, 1997, Black Pearl Distributor, 1998, Millennium Founders' Club, 2000. **WORKS:** several papers, studies and books; *The Impact of Investment Incentives on Canada's*

Economic Growth, 1983; *An Econometric Analysis of the Determinants of Investment in Cdn Manufacturing,* 1971. **EDUCATION:** PhD, Economics, Queen's U.; MA, Economics, McMaster U.; BA, Economics, Mathematics (Pure & Applied), London/ UCWI. **CONTACT:** fcbraithwaite@rogers.com; Fax: 613-748-0135

▶BRAITHWAITE, Jack

LAWYER/PARTNER, Gatien♦Braithwaite Law Firm, 1970 Paris St., Sudbury, ON P3E 3C8. Born: Montreal, QC.

▶ Jack Braithwaite is a partner in the law firm of Gatien♦Braithwaite. He has significant experience in wrongful dismissal and other employment-related litigation. He specializes in employer representation in Human Rights, Workplace Safety and Insurance Board matters, Occupational Health and Safety prosecutions, Ont. Labour Relations Board proceedings, as well as public and private sector arbitrations. He collaborated in writing a leading textbook entitled *Canadian Employment Law,* published by Canada Law Book and was Associate Editor of the *Dismissal and Employment Law Digest,* a national publication for lawyers. **OTHER:** has taught both a sports law course and a criminal law course at Laurentian University and occasionally lectures at U. of Western Ontario on Occupational Health and Safety matters; has delivered several papers and presentations to various professional and business organizations; attended the International Criminal Tribunal for Rwanda in Arusha, Tanzania as an Observer and served in an advisory capacity on procedural matters. **AFFIL/MBRSHP:** several, including: Advocates Society; CABL; HRPAO; NBA, in the USA; Chair, Greater Sudbury Chamber of Commerce; Brd., Ontario Chamber of Commerce; Governing Council, Ontario Chamber of Commerce; National Advocacy Council, Cdn Diabetes Assn. **WORKS:** contributed to *Canadian Employment Law; Dismissal and Employment*

Law Digest. **EDUCATION:** LLB, U. of Alberta. MA, Admin. & Policy Studies; Dipl. Teaching, McGill University. BA; BSc, Concordia U. **CONTACT:** jbraithwaite@gatienlaw.com; www.gatienlaw.com

▶BRAITHWAITE, John B.

CITY COUNCILLOR, City of North Vancouver, 141 West 14th St., North Vancouver, BC V7M 1H9. Born: Toronto, ON.

▶ John Braithwaite is a veteran of the social work profession, with over 39 yrs. experience; he is also a veteran city councillor with over 20 yrs. in elected office. He was first elected as a councillor, North Vancouver in 1972, serving until 1976. He returned to municipal politics in 1983, and has been re-elected consecutively since then. Currently he sits on a number of committees including: Waterfront Industrial Noise Control; Social Planning Advisory; Community Energy System; National Action Committee on Race Relations, Federation of Canadian Municipalities; Judicial Council of BC; Parks and Recreation. **CAREER HIGHLIGHTS:** Executive Director, North Shore Neighbourhood House, 1956-80; BC Min. of Social Services, 1980-87; medical Social Worker, Burnaby Hospital, 1987-1995. He has also been a consultant to a number of organizations, including: Squamish Band Council, to develop social and recreational services on the Mission Reserve; former Vancouver Indian Centre, board and staff training coordinator; instrumental in reorganizing Kiwassa Neighbourhood House, into a broad-based community service agency. **COMMUNITY INVOLVEMENT:** founding member, Black Action Coalition Cmtee; Special Needs Cmtee, North Vancouver School District; North Shore United Way; Victorian Order of Nurses; volunteered in Sport and Youth Services and coached the first Black basketball team (Harlem Nocturnes), which became provincial champions, 1964; involved in North Shore Cmtee, special needs of the physically and mentally challenged. **HONS.:** several at local, provincial, & nat'l levels including: National Black Coalition; Black Historical Society of BC; North Shore Neighbourhood House; True Resolution Lodge; GG 125th Anniv. Medal. **EDUCATION:** MSW, 1956; BSW, 1955; BA, 1951, U of T. **CONTACT:** jbraithwaite@cnv.org; Fax: 604-987-5552

▶**BRAITHWAITE, Leonard A.,** CM, QC.
BARRISTER, SOLICITOR, & NOTARY PUBLIC, 250 Wincott Dr., Richview Sq., Toronto, ON M9R 2R5. Born: Toronto, ON.

▶ Leonard Braithwaite has practised law since 1958 and was appointed a Queen's Counsel in 1971. In 1963, he became the first Black elected to any Parliament in Canada, and served as MPP/Etobicoke, 1963-75; during that time he was the Opposition Party Critic for Labour, as well as the Critic for Community and Social Services. He was elected to Etobicoke City Board of Control and the Metro Toronto Council, Controller, 1982-88. **OTHER HIGHLIGHTS:** he was elected as Alderman/Etobicoke Ward 4, 1962-64; Brd. of Education Trustee, Ward 4, Etobicoke; lecturer, U of T, Institute of Business Administration; Management Systems Analyst, Phillips Canada, 1955. Enlisted in RCAF, 1943; served in Canada and with the No. 6 Bomber Group in Yorkshire, England; transferred to RCAF/ Reserve, 1946. **AFFIL/MBRSHP:** selected: Kiwanis; Thistletown Lions Club; Toronto Brd. of Trade; Phi Delta Phi, legal fraternity; former Brd. of Governors, CNE, Etobicoke General Hospital and West Park Hospital; former member, Etobicoke Brd. of Health and Etobicoke Planning Brd.; past-President Delos Davis Law Guild; LSUC; BBPA; Harvard Club. **COMMUNITY:** from 1962-88, he sponsored many Etobicoke boys' and girls' teams in soccer, baseball, hockey, and lacrosse; teams were known as "Braithwaite Legal Eagles." **HONS.:** Harry Jerome Award, for Professional Excellence, BBPA, 2002; Achievement Award, CABL, 2001; elected Bencher, Governing Council,

LSUC, 1999; ACAA, Politics, 1998; Order of Canada, 1997; Community Service Award, Toronto Onyx Lions Club, 1996. **REVIEWED IN:** many newspapers, magazines; *Some Black Men,* 1999. **EDUCATION:** LLB, Osgoode Hall, 1958; MA, Business Admin., Harvard U., 1952; B.Comm., U of T, 1950. **CONTACT:** Tel: 416-249-2288; Fax: 416-249-2280

▶**BRAITHWAITE, Rella Aylestock**
WRITER/HISTORIAN, Toronto, ON. Born: Listowel, ON.

▶ Rella Aylestock Braithwaite has been researching and recording the history of Blacks in Canada since the 1960s and has, through her publications, made significant contributions to the existing body of work. She began writing to ensure that her children knew their heritage; she wrote for *Contrast* newspaper for ten years, producing well-researched columns on Black history; in 1973, she co-authored a booklet, *Women of our Times,* for the first Black Women's Congress. In 1975, she published a book on outstanding Black women, *The Black Woman in Canada;* and, in 1978, she worked with teachers at the Ont. Min. of Education, on a Black Studies Guide for students. Her main publications appeared in 1993 (*Some Black Women*) and 1999 (*Some Black Men*). Over the years, she has addressed groups of students and adults on Black history and shared her extensive collection of Black memorabilia. **COMMUNITY:** involvement has been extensive including local church, school and charities; Int'l Soroptimist Professional Women's Club; in 1973, she was appointed to the Ont. Advisory Council on Multiculturalism for three yrs., by then-premier, William Davis; covered Scarborough Brd. of Education meetings for the *West Hill* newspaper; joined the Ont. Black History Society, 1978 and served as co-chair for three terms. **HONS.:** several including: Hall of Fame Award, ACAA, 1998; Scarborough Bicentennial Civic Award, 1996; Kay Livingstone Award, Congress of

Black Women, 1989; Plaque for accomplishments, Assn. of Black Women, 1983; Black Woman of the Year, Negro Colour Guard, 1973. **WORKS:** books: *Some Black Men: Profiles of over 100 Black Men in Canada,* 1999; *Some Black Women,* 1993; *The Black Woman in Canada,* 1975; *Women of our Times,* 1973. Articles in: *Contrast; Africa Speaks; West Hill Newspaper.* **HEROES/ROLE MODELS:** Parents; older sisters. **MOTTO:** My husband and I believe it is very important to have faith in God and to have a good relationship with our family. **CONTACT:** aylestock@ hotmail.com

▶**BRATHWAITE, Keren Sophia**
ASSOCIATE DIRECTOR, Transitional Year Programme, University of Toronto, 49 St. George St., Toronto, ON M5S 1A1. Born: Antigua/ in Canada since: 1967.
▶ Keren Brathwaite is an educator who has spent most of her life as an advocate of equity and anti-racism in education. She is a founding faculty member of the Transitional Year Programme (TYP) at U of T, which began in 1969 as a means of increasing access to university by groups that are usually under-represented, namely Blacks, Aboriginal, the working class, and single parents. She is Associate Director of the TYP and also lectures on Literature and Writing. One of her recent successes includes seeing two Black students complete the TYP (2000-01) then be awarded National Scholarships (awarded on merit) to continue their studies at U of T. Other educational initiatives: encouraging greater parent involvement in education, including education in the home; advocating for more inclusive and anti-racist curriculum and pedagogy; founding contributor to the Organization of Parents of Black Children (OPBC); Cdn Alliance of Black Educators/CABE; the Black Heritage Program in the former Toronto Board of Education; and, the Black Educators' Working Group. She has participated on many task forces and in organiza-

tions for human rights and equity, and was a member of the Secondary Education Reform Advisory Committee, Ont. Min. of Education, which monitored the reform of Ontario's secondary schools from a five-year to a four-year system. **HONS.:** several including: Jus Human Rights Prize, an award of excellence, U of T, 1999; Distinguished Educator Award, OISE/U of T, 1998; Leadership Award, Toronto Brd. of Education, 1996; Award, Congress Black Women, 1996; Outstanding Achievement Award, Ont. Min. of Citizenship & Culture, 1994; Award of Merit, City of Toronto, 1993; Special Award, Black Students' Conference, 1991. **WORKS:** forthcoming: *Access and Equity in the University;* co-editor, *Educating African Canadians,* 1996; "The Black Student & the School: A Canadian Dilemma," in *African Continuities,* 1989; co-authored *Black Students in Toronto Schools,* 1988; ed., *Stories from Life,* 1987. **EDUCATION:** completed course work for PhD; M.Ed, OISE/U of T, 1968; Dipl. in Education, 1965; BA, 1964, U. London/UWI. **MOTTO:** Education is something not to play carelessly with. **CONTACT:** keren.brathwaite@utoronto.ca

▶**BRATHWAITE, Shirley N., MD,**
FRCPC.
PSYCHIATRIST/PROFESSOR, Royal Ottawa Hospital, 1145 Carling Ave., Ottawa, ON K1Z 7K4. Born: Barbados/ in Canada since: 1974.
▶ Dr. Shirley Brathwaite is a forensic psychiatrist who has been on staff at the Royal Ottawa Hospital (ROH) since 1978, and a member of staff at the University of Ottawa, since 1979. **CURRENT POSITIONS:** since 1982, she is Unit Director, Forensic Outpatient Service, ROH; Assistant Professor, U. of Ottawa, since 1986; Consultant Psychiatrist, Min. of Correctional Services, since 1989, providing assessment and treatment of inmates, as well as probationers, parolees, and screening of the newly arrested for fitness to stand trial. **PREVIOUS POSITIONS:** completed latter part of her residency at the National Defence

Medical Centre, 1977-78; Clinical Fellow, Forensic Unit, ROH, 1978-79; became Staff Psychiatrist at ROH, 1978-82; Lecturer, Dept. of Psychiatry, U. of Ottawa, 1979-86. **AFFIL/MBRSHP:** American Academy of Psychiatry and Law; Cdn Academy of Psychiatry and Law; Medicolegal Society of Ottawa; Cdn Psychiatric Assn; Black Psychiatrists of America; previously, member, Ontario Criminal Code Review Board; Scientific Program Committee, 2nd World Congress on Prison Health Care, 1981-89; Hard to Serve Children Cmtee, Ottawa, 1978-81; Multicultural Health Services Task Force; National Council of Barbadian Assns.; Youth Services Bureau, 1988-94. **HONS.:** Award, Professional Excellence, BBPA (Ottawa), 1994; GG 125th Anniv. Medal, 1993; Volunteer Service Pin, Prov. of Ontario, 1993. **WORKS:** papers include: "Mental Health Legislation in Canada," 1999; "The Mentally Disordered Offender," 1993; "Aggression as a Presenting Symptom in an Outpatient Forensic Psychiatry Population," 1991. **EDUCATION:** FRCPC, Psychiatry, U. of Ottawa, 1978; MB BS, UWI, 1971. **CONTACT:** Tel: 613-722-6521

▶BRAXTON, Evelyn
COMMUNITY ORGANIZER, Coloured Women's Club, Longueuil, QC. Born: St. Kitts/ in Canada since: 1929.

▶ Evelyn Braxton arrived in Montreal from St. Kitts in 1929. Soon afterwards, she joined the Union United Church and taught Sunday School, a practice which continued for many years. She has since served on practically all the church boards; was VP of the United Church Women, and was Chair of Missions and Service. She successfully reinstated the church bazaar, which had been inactive for many years, introduced the soup lunch to the church and is a member of the Black Aging group. In 1960, she joined the Coloured Women's Club and continued to serve her community; for 14 yrs. was President of the Ladies Auxiliary to the Brotherhood of Sleeping Car

Porters; became Worthy Matron of the Eve Chapter of the Grand Lodge and "revitalized the group to one of size and substance." At the end of her term she continued to promote activities that would benefit seniors (including Christmas dinners, Christmas hampers, bus outings); she also regularly visited the sick in community and area hospitals. During her earlier years, EB travelled extensively and, upon her return, would give lectures and share pictures of her adventures. She welcomed into her home foreign students who were studying in Montreal. As a pioneer Black on Montreal's South Shore, where she has lived for close to 50 yrs., she has contributed to the shaping of the community; was interviewed on CBC TV and local newspapers in celebration of the 95th anniversary of the Coloured Women's Club, 1997. **HONS.:** include, Cert. of Appreciation, Black Aging; 25-yr. pin for devoted service, Grand Lodge, Eve Chapter.

▶BRIN, Derek
MUSIC PRODUCER/COMPOSER, Fierce Music Group, Ste. 1715-705 King St. W., Toronto, ON M5V 2W8. Born: Toronto, ON, 1968.

▶ Derek Brin is a music producer who has produced, remixed and engineered over 80 recordings for international release. As a composer, he has scored music for over 1,800 episodes of TV series and a few one-hour documentary specials. He produced the Billboard No. 1 hit, *Stronger,* by Kristine W; and, has programmed for songwriter, Diane Warren, producer for Guy Roche, Jud Friedman, and Allen Reich. As a composer, he has worked with Yorgen Ellison (wrote for N Sync, Celine Dion), Anselm Douglas, Sammy McKenna (wrote for Aretha Franklin & Patti Labelle), Carlos Morgan, Rupert Gayle, and others. **HONS.:** several including: Producer of the Year, Caribbean Achievement Awards; Urban Music Award; Album of the Year (Ivana Santili), Best R&B single, Female (Belinda); Certified Double Platinum (US), *Pokemon* soundtrack;

twice Certified Gold (US) Robyn & Blue Streak Soundtrack; three Juno awards & five nominations; CAN-PRO Award for Best Children's Programming for the TV series, *Adventures in Evergreen Forest.* **WORKS:** in "Producer's Corner" in *Mic Check* magazine; "Mastering techniques," *Cubase Int'l Update* magazine. **REVIEWED IN:** *Billboard; DMC;* plus several websites and international magazines. **EDUCATION:** De La Salle College, 1986. **HEROES/ROLE MODELS:** Mother; Martin Luther King Jr. **MOTTO:** Do what you need to do, to do the things you want to do. **CONTACT:** derek_brin@hotmail.com; www.geocities.com/Hollywood/Location/254; Fax: 416-955-9197

▶**BROOKS, C. John,** Dr., CM, O.Ont., OD(JM).
HUMANITARIAN & COMMUNITY ADVOCATE, The John Brooks Community Foundation, Toronto, ON. Born: Jamaica/ in Canada since: 1963.
▶ Dr. John Brooks' career of community involvement began in Jamaica and continued when he came to Canada with his family in 1963. He co-owned and operated one of the first Caribbean-oriented nightclubs in Toronto, the Latin Quarter. However, this establishment only operated as a nightclub in the evenings; during the day it was a drop-in centre for recently arrived immigrants. Over the years, he organized sports activities between students and the police; helped to establish the Regal Rd. Public School Daycare Project; raised funds for famine relief in Africa; supported the Jamaican Bobsled Team; founded the National Domino League; and helped to organize many other activities for youth in the community. In 1981, the Caribbean Excelsior Fraternal Assn. set up the John Brooks Scholarship Fund to provide bursaries to deserving students, in Canada and Jamaica, achieving academic excellence. He continues to be active in the community, addressing youth and community organizations, and supporting worthwhile initiatives. **HONS.:** many including: plaque "for outstanding contributions

to the African-Canadian Community," JCA, 2001; Order of Ontario, 1997; ACAA 1995; Order of Canada, 1993; Civic Award of Merit, City of Toronto, 1993; Hon. LLD, Queen's U., 1992; Harry Jerome Award, BBPA, 1992; Mac-Donald-Cartier Achievement Award, 1991; Order of Distinction, Govt. of Jamaica, 1986; Ontario Medal of Good Citizenship, 1984. **REVIEWED IN:** community and nat'l publications; profiled in *Millennium Minds,* 2000; *Some Black Men,* 1999. **HEROES/ROLE MODELS:** Inspired & assisted by his wife, Patricia. **MOTTO:** I cannot impress upon you enough the importance of working with those who are less fortunate than yourselves. Our responsibilities to them must include actions that will help with their upliftment. (convocation address, Queen's U., 1992) **CONTACT:** Fax: 416-656-4317

▶**BROWN, Jeri**
JAZZ PERFORMER, Justin Time Records/ **PROFESSOR OF MUSIC,** Concordia University, Montreal, QC. Born: USA.
▶ Jeri Brown is a classically trained jazz performer who, during her training under Frank Summerside, performed in the US and throughout Europe (Sweden, Germany, Norway, and Holland). In addition to performances with the Cleveland Chamber Orchestra and the St. Louis Symphony Orchestra, she began performing more stylistic renditions of standards from theatre, film and pop culture. She was heard by Bob McKee, the drummer and bandleader on the Mike Douglas show at the time, who invited her join his group in Ohio. This exposure and training led to performances with many renowned artists, including Ellis Marsalis, Billy Taylor and Dizzy Gillespie. From there she moved into the front rank of jazz vocalists in the Cleveland area. In addition to classic jazz standards, she developed as a lyricist, recitalist, concert soloist and recording artist, and has become one of the world's most respected jazz vocalists. She has

written and recorded lyrics in collaboration with such composers as Henry Butler, Kenny Wheeler, Cyrus Chestnut, Avery Sharpe and Greg Carter. Her recorded vocal improvisations of contemporary jazz with Kenny Wheeler, Fred Hersch and D.D. Jackson, as well as her choral and vocalese arrangements with Abdullah Ibrahim and Jimmy Rowles, have won her special recognition as an arranger. A popular figure on the European performing circuit, she performs a large repertoire of selections from Ellington, Gershwin, Legrand and Porter. Recent performances include the Montreal International Jazz Festival and the Orleans Jazz Festival, where she opened for Chick Corea. To date she has released eight recordings with Justin Time Records, with the most recent, *Image in the Mirror: the Triptych* being nominated for a Juno (others include, *April in Paris,* 1996; *Fresh Start,* 1995; *A Timeless Place,* 1993; *Unfolding: The Peacocks,* 1992; and, *Mirage,* 1991). She has also participated in recordings for the CBC and film projects for BRAVO! and Vision TV. Outside of performing, JB is an Associate Professor of Music at Concordia and McGill universities. She has also taught at the Oberlin Conservatory of Music, at the U. of Akron in Ohio, and at the U. of Massachusetts; she is also an Oral Culturalist with Columbia U. in Ohio; and, is the founder and artistic director of Jongleur, an artists' training group in NS, which she began in order to encourage and support local talent. **HONS.:** CHOC de l'Année, *Jazzman,* 1995. **EDUCATION:** holds degrees in Counselling, Education, Music, and English. **CONTACT:** www.justin-time.com

▶**BROWN, Rosemary,** PC, OC, OBC, CD(JM).

MLA (Ret.)/**RIGHTS ACTIVIST,** Vancouver, BC. Born: Jamaica/ in Canada since: 1951.

▶ Dr. Rosemary Brown has the distinction of being the first Black woman in Canada to be elected to public office, in 1972 in BC, serving as a Member of the Legislative Assembly (MLA) in the provincial legislature until 1986. She is also the first Black woman in Canada to run for the leadership of a federal political party, 1975, finishing, after four ballots, a close second in the NDP leadership race. **HIGHLIGHTS:** she came to Canada in 1951, to complete her studies and later worked in social work in the 1960s; worked with the Children's Aid Society of Vancouver, the Riverview Mental Hospital, the Montreal Children's Hospital, and as a counsellor at Simon Fraser University (SFU). In 1987, she was the Ruth Wynn Woodford Professor of the Endowed Chair in Women's Studies at SFU; is a former CEO of MATCH International and continues in the role of President of this NGO, which works with women in developing countries. She has participated in many national and international conferences on peace, women's issues and human rights. In 1993, she was appointed Chief Commissioner of the Ontario Human Rights Commission, and served until 1996. **AFFIL/MBRSHP:** founding member, Vancouver Status of Women Council; founding member, Institute of Public Affairs, Dalhousie U.; Judicial Council, BC. **HONS.:** several including: 15 honorary degrees from universities across Canada, including UBC, U of T, McGill, Mount Saint Vincent, Dalhousie; Order of Canada; Order of BC; Order of Distinction, Commander, Govt. of Jamaica; Member, Privy Council; Award, National Coalition of Canada; Black Historical & Cultural Society, BC. **WORKS:** include, autobiography, *Being Brown,* 1989. **REVIEWED IN:** *WWIC; WWCW; Millennium Minds,* 2000; *Some Black Women,* 1993; *Journey: African Canadian History,* 2000. **EDUCATION:** MSW, 1965; BSW, 1962, UBC. BA, McGill U., 1955. **CONTACT:** rmbrown@telus.net

▶**BROWNE, Christene**

FILMMAKER, Syncopated Productions Inc., 441 Delaware Ave., Toronto, ON M6H 2V1. Born: St. Kitts, 1965/ in Canada since: 1970.

▶ Christene Browne is an award-winning film-maker who has been working as a producer and director for over ten years. Her first feature film, *Another Planet,* released in 1999, made her the first Black woman in Canada to write and direct a dramatic feature film. Other films produced include: *A Way Out; Them That's Not,* the fourth film in the NFB series on the feminization of poverty; *Jodie Drake: Blues in my Bread,* for the CBC's, *Adrienne Clarkson Presents; No Choice;* and, *Brothers in Music,* which was nominated Best Documentary under 30 minutes, Yorkton Short Film Festival, 1991. Her films have been screened, broadcast, and distributed internationally. CB's experience in the film and television industry is broad-based; in addition to producing, directing, writing, and researching, she has also acted as film programmer, curator and media arts instructor. **HONS.:** several including: Best Film, for *Another Planet,* Black Int'l Cinema 2000, Germany; Bronze Apple Award, for *Them That's Not,* Nat'l Educational Film & Video Festival, USA, 1995; Special Jury Prize, for *Them That's Not,* Yorkton Short Film Festival, Canada, 1994. **EDUCATION:** Film Studies Program, Ryerson U. **MOTTO:** In life there are no mistakes, just lessons. **CONTACT:** syncopated@sympatico.ca; Fax: 416-531-4870

▶BROWNIE, Edward

BIOCHEMISTRY RESEARCH TECHNOLOGIST, University of Alberta, Edmonton, AB T6G 2E2. Born: Jamaica/ in Canada since: 1968.

▶ Edward Brownie is a Biochemistry Research Technologist in the Dept. of Biochemistry at the University of Alberta. Previous positions in Jamaica included: Senior Technologist, Alumina Partners; Veterinary Laboratory Technician, Dept. of Agriculture; Teacher, Min. of Education; Chemist, Sugar Laboratory, West Indian Sugar Co. **COMMUNITY ACTIVITIES:** Cdn Rainbow Educational and Community Services; McClure United Church; Vice-President, Jamaica Assn.,

N. Alberta; National Black Coalition Canada, Edmonton Chapter; President, Parents Assn. of the Edmonton Public School All City Choirs. **HONS.:** several academic & others including: Telus Award, Science & Technology, BAASA, 1997; Award for Academics & Leadership, Chemical Technology Advisory Committee, 1968; Chemcell Scholarship Award, 1967. **WORKS:** in: *Can J Biochemistry; J Biological Chemistry; Biochemistry;* also cited in, *J Biochemistry & Cell Biology; J Molecular Biology; Protein Science.* **REVIEWED IN:** *Edmonton Sun,* 1997; *Edmonton J,* 1997; U. of Alberta, *Dept. of Biochem. AnnualReport,* 1997; *Chemical Assn.* magazine, 1967. **EDUCATION:** BSc, Microbiology, U. of Alberta, 1987; Dipl., Chemical Research Technology, N. Alberta Institute Technology, 1968. **HEROES/ROLE MODELS:** Mother; Ms. Gunnings, elementary school teacher. **MOTTO:** Do today what others won't do, so you can do tomorrow what others can't do. **CONTACT:** ebrowniee@ netscape.net; Fax: 780-492-0886

▶BRUCCOLERI, Claudette

TEACHER, Calgary Board of Education, 512-18th St. NW, Calgary, AB T5N 2G5. Born: Jamaica/ in Canada since: 1980.

▶ Claudette Bruccoleri is a teacher with the Calgary Board of Education (CBE). She is the creator and facilitator of a Social Justice Education course, which is being taught at Queen Elizabeth Jr./Sr. School in Calgary, with the aim of increasing awareness and acceptance of people from diverse ethno-cultural and religious backgrounds. This course is possibly the only one of its kinds being taught within the Calgary school system. Previously, she worked in establishing a private school for racialized students, and worked with a team of educators in Montreal in establishing the Greaves Academy. She is a member of the committee on Equity with the CBE; member, ARUSHA Board of Calgary; regular presenter on women's health issues, in Montreal and Calgary.

WORKS: in progress: paper on African Cdn female leaders in education. **EDUCATION:** B.Ed, Union Nebraska College, 1989; BSc, Nursing Education, Northern U., Jamaica, 1979. **HEROES/ROLE MODELS:** Sylvia Greaves, principal; Harriet Tubman, crusader. **MOTTO:** It's not over until I win. **CONTACT:** cmaddan@shaw.ca

▶BRUCE, Lawrence S.

VICE-PRESIDENT, Black Loyalist Heritage Society, PO Box 1194, Shelburne, NS B0T 1W0.

▶ Lawrence Bruce is past Vice-President of the Black Loyalist Heritage Society (BLHS), a not-for-profit group incorporated in 1990, whose mandate is, "to discover, interpret, safeguard, and promote the heritage and history of the Black Loyalists who first arrived in NS from 1783." The group's activities to date include: archaeological digs in Birchtown, 1993-94, with Saint Mary's U.; archaeological survey at Birchtown and Fort Point, 1995; installation of plaque honouring Black Loyalist Settlers at site of the Black Burial Grounds, 1996; Monument erected commemorating the site of the first African Methodist Episcopal Church (1873/4-1948/9), 1997; renovated historical site and opened BLHS museum, 2000. As per the BLHS literature, "these projects helped to inform the public of the African-American origins of Birchtown, archaeology, and the impact of the Black Settlers on, not only NS, but Canada." **HONS.:** BLHS awarded Race Relations Award, NS Human Rights Commission, 2000; received the first NS Multicultural Volunteer Award, 1999. **MOTTO:** Hard work will pay off in the end. **CONTACT:** Tel: 902-875-3124

▶BRUCE, Ronald A., CGA, CIS, CIA.

CORPORATE INTERNAL AUDITOR, SaskPower, 2025 Victoria Ave., Regina, SK S4P 0S1. Born: Barbados/ in Canada since: 1972.

▶ Ronald Bruce is a career internal auditor with over 25 yrs. experience. He joined SaskPower in 1983, where he has been the Corporate Internal Auditor. Prior to becoming Head of Internal Audit, he held similar positions at Saskatchewan Oil and Gas Corp. (now Nexen Canada Ltd.) and with the Govt. of the NWT in Yellowknife. **CAREER HIGHLIGHTS:** seconded to TANESCO (Tanzania Electric Supply Co.) as a member of the Deloitte and Touche project team, 2000; acting VP, Finance, SaskPower; Fort Smith Region of the Govt. of the NWT as regional finance director; internal auditor, consultant and special advisor on Nanisivik, a Canadian Arctic mega project involving construction of a town, lead-zinc mine, harbour, airport, and highway, 1977-81. **BACKGROUND:** Prior to his career in internal auditing, he worked in administration and sales in the insurance industry; was a manufacturing supervisor for the electronics industry; in medical sales for the pharmaceutical industry, and in public accounting. He was also a high school teacher and an instructor with the universities of Alberta and Athabasca extension programs. **COMMUNITY INVOLVEMENT:** within his church is auditor for a parish in the Qu'Appelle diocese; past President of SK's Caribbean Cdn Assn.; 20-yr. involvement in Regina's annual Mosaic Festival (festival of cultures); founder and coordinator, Caribe Folk and Gospel Singers; coordinator of the Caribe Steel Orchestra, since 1994; mentor and counsellor to youth and adults, particularly in the Regina Caribbean community; involved with the YMCA for past 20 yrs.; certified level three soccer coach (National Coaching Certification Program), and has been coaching a youth team for 12 seasons, which won the city championship during six consecutive seasons; active member of Toastmaster, 1984-90, and in 1988, achieved the DTM, the highest level in toastmastering; past Toastmasters Area Governor; past member, Optimist Club of Regina, with responsibility for the inter-school oratorical contest. Most recently, RB has been practising the art of storytelling with an interest in West Indian authors. **EDUCATION:** CISA, 1990; CIA, 1989; CGA, 1976; MBA, Marketing &

Management, U. of Windsor, 1974; B.Comm, U. of Windsor, 1973; BA, Economics & History, UWI, 1970. **CONTACT:** rbruce@saskpower.com

▶BRUEGGERGOSMAN, Measha

SOPRANO/OPERA SINGER, Germany. Born: Fredericton, NB, 1977.

▶ Measha Brueggergosman, is an international, prize-winning opera singer, who has performed in England, New York, Switzerland, and Germany. In June 2002, at the inaugural International Jeunesses Musicales Voice Competition, held in Montreal, QC, she won first place overall in a field of 251 international vocalists; in addition, she won awards for Best Canadian Performance, Audience Choice Award, and Best Interpretation of a new work. After completing her BA/Music degree at U of T, she was awarded a Canada Council grant to pursue graduate and pre-doctoral studies in Germany, with Canadian soprano, Edith Wiens. In 1998, she premiered the title role of the new Canadian opera, *Beatrice Chancy,* by George Elliott Clarke, which toured Halifax, Toronto, and Edmonton, and starred in the CBC TV version; her performance was nominated for a 2001 Gemini Award. **OTHER:** has performed at the National Arts Centre, for the Royal Family, and for Nelson Mandela. Combined with her studies, future performances are scheduled for radio and TV, and with the Cincinnati Opera, as well as throughout the US, Germany, Switzerland, and Canada. Being featured in a CBC TV documentary, *Opening Night.* **HONS.:** include: Jeunesses Musicales Int'l Voice Competition, Mtl; Wigmore Hall Int'l Song Competition, England; Kirsten Flagstad Award, New York; Robert Schumann, Germany; George London Foundation, NY. **REVIEWED IN:** several including: *Maclean's; ELLE; Time* (Canada); *U of T Alumni Magazine.* **EDUCATION:** pre-doctoral studies; Master of Voice Performance, 2001, Germany. BA/Music, U of T, 1999. **CONTACT:** swgbag@ nbnet.nb.ca; Fax: 506-457-1594

▶BRUNEAU, Ethel

MASTER TAP DANCE PROFESSOR, Ethel Bruneau Dance School, 2132 Herron Rd., Dorval, QC. Born: USA/ in Canada since: 1953.

▶ Ethel Bruneau, formerly known on the show business circuit as "Miss Swing" or "Queen of Afro Cuban," arrived in Montreal in 1953, with Cab Calloway and his band. She grew up in Harlem and, as a child, attended the Mary Bruce Starbud Dance School and the School of the Performing Arts; she settled in Montreal in the '50s (and remembers when all the roads were only dirt) and worked the Montreal "Las Vegas" circuit; was the MC at Rockheads Paradise, a Montreal landmark. From 1959-60 she travelled the US with Pearl Bailey's Big Review; she popularized Black Rhythm Tap or "Hoofin'" in Montreal. She is one of only two people in Canada teaching this style and has preserved this "hand me down dance art-form." After the decline of the nightclub era in Montreal, she dedicated herself to teaching people of all ages, in this style. She opened her first dance school in 1960 with ten children; attendance soon grew to 200 and she has not stopped teaching since. One of her highlights in recent times was being praised by Gregory Hines as the "Tap Queen of Montreal" after one of her star pupils, Travis Knight (*see: Knight, Travis*), danced for Hines at the 1996 Montreal Jazz Festival, perfectly imitating his own complicated tap dance choreography. In 1998, she choreographed a segment for her top tap students to perform at the GG Awards. She is a Montreal legend who continues to teach dance classes seven days/week and, at the age of 66, shows no sign of slowing down. She is an example of focused determination who says, "lack of money from a student has never deterred her from teaching those who were interested in learning to dance"; in return she only demands their desire, their undivided attention, and their dancing feet. **HONS.:** several including: Rosetti Lifetime Achievement Award for her contributions to the performing arts, 2000; Martin Luther King Award, Sounds of Blackness, 1999. **REVIEWED IN:** *Community Contact; Montreal Gazette;* featured in NFB film; performed on CBC TV's *On the Road Again,* 2000; many radio and TV interviews with CBC, CTV, Global TV, CJAD. **HEROES/ROLE MODELS:** Mary Bruce, first dance teacher. **MOTTO:** Give me strength to carry on. **CONTACT:** Tel: 450-678-6107

▶BUREY, Rev. Owen Leslie

MINISTER, Sandwich First Baptist Church, 3652 Peter St., Windsor, ON N9C 1J8. Born: Jamaica/ in Canada since: 1966.

▶ Rev. Owen Burey is the pastor of the Sandwich First Baptist Church in Windsor, Ontario, a church built by former slaves following their arrival in Canada via the Underground Railroad (built in the 1840s then re-built in 1851). The church is one of the oldest in the Windsor area and is now part of the African-Canadian Heritage Tour. He has been the pastor since 1986, is also a teacher by training and has worked in correctional services. In 1992, he became a Chaplain, coordinating pastoral services for the Min. of Community and Social Services, Southwestern Regional Centre. **COMMUNITY:** VP, National Council of Jamaicans in Canada; Moderator, Amherstburg Baptist Church; Brd., St. Joseph's Hospital; Int'l Services Canadian Red Cross Society; Kiwanis Club; Kent County Task Force Committee on Family Violence; Children's Aid Society; Volunteer Probation Officer, Kent County. **HONS.:** including: Volunteer Award, Govt. of Ont., 1995 & 2000; Volunteer Award, Govt. of Canada. **WORKS:** Social Service Commissions Report, 1986. **EDUCATION:** M.Div., McMaster Divinity College, 1981. B.Ed, 1977; BA, 1975, U. of Windsor. **MOTTO:** A winner never quits and quitters never win! **CONTACT:** Tel: 519-252-4917; Fax: 519-254-3427

▶BUSH, Rochelle

LOCAL HISTORIAN & COMMUNITY ACTIVIST, Harriet Tubman Centre for Cultural Services, 92 Geneva St., St. Catharines, ON L2R 4N2. Born: St. Catharines, ON.

▶ Rochelle Bush is involved in a number of activities to preserve the historical contributions of Blacks in the Niagara region. She is the Historical Director of the Salem Chapel of the British Methodist Episcopal (BME) Church and was instrumental, in 1999, in having this church designated as a National Historic Site due to its association with Harriet Tubman, who according to local and oral history, worshipped there. The official designation was granted in July, 2000; that same year, she spearheaded the Millennium Fund project to raise funds for the historic preservation of the exterior of the church. She is also the Director of the Harriet Tubman Centre for Cultural Services, created in 1997 to provide presentations and heritage tours of the UGRR in St. Catharines and Niagara. RB is also the junior historian of the Zion Baptist Church, which was led by Pastor Anthony Burns, an escaped slave, whose recapture in 1854 incited the Boston Riots. **HONS.:** Harriet Tubman Achievement Award, Albany, NY, 2001; Community Volunteer Award, St. Catharines, 1999. **CONTACT:** htccs@netcom.ca; www.netcom.ca/~htubman; Fax: 905-688-9422

▶BUTTERFIELD, Joan

ARTIST, Brampton, ON. Born: Bermuda/ in Canada since: 1964.

▶ Joan Butterfield is an artist, born and raised on the island of Bermuda; she immigrated to Canada in 1964. She studied in New York, Boston and Toronto, where she now resides and continues to practise her craft. Her works are created using the 17th-century art form of "Three Dimensional Decoupage." Drawing from her heritage as a Black Bermudian woman now living in Canada, her images exalt the virtues of the African Diaspora. She has several solo and group exhibits a year both in Canada and the US, her works can be found on display in museums, universities, libraries, city councils and hospitals throughout the world. In addition to creating works of art, she is curator of the Human Rights Through Art travelling exhibit for the city of Toronto, The Bank of Montreal, the LSUC, and the Canadian Human Rights Commission. In 1988, Essence Art (a division of *Essence* magazine) discovered her work and introduced her to the American public at Art Expo. In 2000, her gallery launched the Pathway to Success poster to school project; with the assistance of corporate sponsors, the posters, which portray images of Black children, are distributed to schools in selected areas. In 2001, she was chosen to participate in The Paper Trail exhibit at Toronto's Harbourfront Centre, which included artists from around the world displaying their paper creations. **CONTACT:** www.joanbutterfieldartist.com

▶**CADER, Eric**
AGENT D'EDUCATION, Interlink Consulting Services/ **DIRECTEUR DE LA PROGRAMMATION FRANÇAISE,** CIUT 89,5FM, University of Toronto Radio, ON. Au Canada depuis: 1980.
▶ Eric Cader est, depuis 1981, animateur/facilitateur de projets culturels, colloques et d'ateliers dans les milieux francophones et anglophones du Québec et de l'Ontario. **ACTIVITÉS PRINCIPALES**: initiateur de projets; agent d'éducation et formateur à la Commission d'équité en matière d'emploi; co-fondateur et Président du festival African Film Now/Le cinéma africain; correspondent-représentant de RFI à Toronto; Animateur-facilitateur de forums, soirées culturelles, au ministère du Procureur général depuis 1994. Animateur d'un magazine francophone, (*Pot-pourri–la voie des sans voix*) depuis 1986, à la radio CIUT 89, 5FM, chaque dimanche de 11h à 13h. Il a aussi travaillé avec la chaîne française de TVO/TFO comme animateur. A travers toutes ses activités il cherche d'encourager la compréhension et la tolérance raciale; il anime des conférences et des ateliers sur le bénévolat, les conseils d'administration, les politiques anti-racistes, l'équité dans l'emploi, la violence et la tolérance à l'école et dans la société. Il participe à de nombreux ateliers et rencontres au Canada et à l'étranger dans le domaine de l'audiovisuel, du journalisme radio, de la production, et de la présentation des programmes culturels. Il est aussi producteur-adjoint du magazine culturel *Les Arts et les autres* à TV5. **PRIX:** Plaque de reconnaissance et certificats, Min. du Solliciteur général, de l'Ontario, 1994; reconnaissances des organismes communautaires, des entreprises privées et publics au Canada et à l'étranger, 1994; Bourse d'études, RFI, Paris, 1990. **OEUVRES À SON PROPOS:** *L'Express* de Toronto; *Où sont nos modèles?* une série d'ateliers pour les écoles à Toronto et au Québec, recherche et production pour RFI et CIUT. **FORMATION:** Train the Trainers, OISE/U de T, 1993; Animation/réalisateur, RFI, Paris, 1990; Cert. Journalisme et Radio,

U. de Montréal, 1983. **MOTTO:** Il y a toujours quelque chose à faire… **CONTACT:** ecader@sympatico.ca; Fax: 416-759-0914; www.ciut.fm

▶**CALLENDER, Chloe E.**
EDUCATOR/RACE RELATIONS CONSULTANT (Ret), Waterloo District Catholic School Board, Waterloo, ON. Born: Trinidad & Tobago/ in Canada since: 1958.

▶ Chloe Callender has spent a lifetime as an educator, community development worker, and leadership trainer. She has focused her talents on promoting positive ethnocultural relations in diverse areas that include English as a second language, fine arts, special education, conflict resolution, and youth. **CAREER HIGHLIGHTS:** teacher, Waterloo District Roman Catholic School Board, 1968-89; Race Relations Consultant, 1989-95; former coordinator of programs for homeless and other at-risk youth in the Kitchener-Waterloo (K-W) area, 1995-97. **AFFIL/MBRSHP:** Affiliate Director of Ontario Teachers of ESL; Anti-Racism Ethnocultural Educators Network, 1990-96; K-W Police Community Advisory Committee; Holocaust Education Committee, 1993-96; Congress of Black Women of Canada, first president of the K-W chapter (1988-93), past-President of Ontario Region (1993-96) and past-President of Ontario Provincial chapter (1988-92); co-founder K-W Caribbean-Canadian Cultural Assn.; Ontario Arts Council, 1976-86; served two terms on Brd. of Governors and Senate, Wilfrid Laurier U.; serves on Brd., K-W YWCA; Cdn Network for Peace and Conflict Resolution; Brd., St. Mary's Hospital, Kitchener. **OTHER:** in 1995, she co-facilitated a ten-day Symposium for Commonwealth students, with focus on styles and programs for conflict resolution. Since her retirement, she and a partner have formed a consulting team, Skylark, which provides workshops on community building and encourages people to "accept, respect and celebrate" cultural diversity in schools, the workplace, and community in general. **HONS.:** including: guest of honour at Mayor of Kitchener's Annual fundraising dinner, 2001; Outstanding Achievement Award, Ont. Min. of Citizenship, Culture, Tourism, & Recreation, 1993; Award of Merit, in promoting leadership & ethnocultural relations among Canadian youth, Society for Educational Visits & Exchanges in Canada (SEVEC), 1993; K-W Woman of the Year Award, for her work in the area of Multiculturalism, 1991; Volunteer of the Year Award, for community contribution, 1991. **REVIEWED IN:** local & community publications; profiled in, *Women Worth Knowing*, 1995; *Vista*, 1993. **EDUCATION:** Dramatic Arts Sr. Qualifications, U of T, 1986; Special Ed. Specialist, U. of Western Ont., 1983; Dipl. Special Ed., Birmingham Poly. Inst., UK, 1980; BA, U. of Waterloo, 1974; Toronto Teachers' College, 1964. **HEROES/ROLE MODELS:** Mother; Joseph McKay, former colleague. **MOTTO:** You can do just about anything if you prepare, give it your best shot, and go for it. **CONTACT:** mgecalle@sciborg.uwaterloo.ca

▶**CALLENDER, Murchison G.**, Dr., FAAO.
PROFESSOR EMERITUS, School of Optometry, University of Waterloo, Waterloo, ON. Born: Trinidad & Tobago/ in Canada since: 1958.

▶ Dr. Murchison Callender joined the School of Optometry in the Faculty of Science, at the University of Waterloo, in 1968, and remained until his retirement in 1996. During this time, he was promoted to full professor and held several administrative positions, including Admissions Officer and the Director of the Contact Lens Clinic. Amongst his many contributions to the School and the University, his most enduring is considered to be the development of a clinical and didactic teaching program dealing with contact lenses, as well as the initiation of research in this field. His particular interest has been and continues to be the transition of scientific knowledge from fundamental theory to clinical practice. **HIGHLIGHTS:** he has been recognized for his research on the physiology of the eye in contact lens wear, as well as the microbiological evaluation of contact lenses and care products. He has been a consultant to the major contact lens and contact lens disinfecting systems manufacturers and has been involved in several FDA clinical investigations of their products; has served on various committees for the Cdn Assn. of Optometrists and continues to be a consultant to that Assn. on matters pertaining to contact lens wear. He is also a member of the Cdn National Bureau of Medical Devices Standards Committee for contact lenses and care products. In recent years, his research has been in experimental myopia and he has been collaborating in the investigation of the anatomical and biochemical mechanisms associated with the refractive changes in the developing chicken's eye. **OTHER:** he has published numerous papers and has lectured on these topics internationally; though now retired, MC is still actively involved in research, clinical teaching and vision care programs in the Caribbean. Since 1974, he has led the U. of Waterloo, School of Optometry Caribbean Vision Care Programme; here, optometry interns, under his supervision, provide eye care biannually to local residents who have limited financial means. His personal goal is to facilitate the development of eye and vision care internationally. **AFFIL:** Councillor, Int'l Society for Contact Lens Research; Int'l Assn. of Contact Lens Educators; Assn. for Research in Vision and Ophthalmology; British Contact Lens Assn.; Cdn Assn. of Optometrists; Trinidad and Tobago Assn. of Optometrists. **HONS.:** several including, Fellow, American Academy of Optometry. **WORKS:** articles in: *Optom Vis Sci*; *Opt Soc Am*, *Tech digest*; *Ophthal Physiol Opt.; Pract Optom*; *J Comp Physiol.* **REVIEWED IN**: Perspectives section, *Kitchener-Waterloo Record*, 2002. **EDUCATION:** M.Phil, Vision Science, U. Aston, Birmingham, UK. Doctor of Optometry (OD); MSc, Physiology, U. of Waterloo. BSc, Biology,

SGWU (now Concordia U.). **CONTACT:** mgecalle@sciborg.uwaterloo.ca; Fax: 519-725-0784

▶**CALLISTE, Agnes,** PhD.
ASSOCIATE PROFESSOR & BLACK STUDENT ADVISOR, St. Francis Xavier University, PO Box 5000, Antigonish, NS B2G 2W5. Born: Grenada/ in Canada since: 1973.
▶ Dr. Agnes Calliste is an Associate Professor in the Dept. of Sociology/Anthropology at St. Xavier University. From 1993-96, she was Dept. Chair. In addition to teaching, she was Liaison Officer for Black and Native students, 1987-90, and Special Advisor to them, 1991-92. In 2000, she was appointed Black Students' Advisor; she is also the faculty advisor to Brothers and Sisters of the African Diaspora Society, a student organization which she helped students to initiate.- **PREVIOUS CAREER HIGHLIGHTS:** Assistant Professor of Sociology, U. of Manitoba, 1981-84; taught at York U. and was the Lead Instructor of the Black Cultural Heritage Program, Toronto Brd. of Education, 1980-81; Instructor, OISE, 1977-80; substitute teacher with Toronto Separate School Board, 1973-80; prior to coming to Canada, she taught elementary to secondary school, 1965-73, in Grenada. As a sociologist, she has devoted much time and effort to addressing issues of inequity and injustice in Cdn society. She has collaborated with Dr. George Dei on a number of works concerning systemic racism, including publications; has been involved with many community organizations; is the co-chair of the African Liaison Committee, which advises the administration on issues of access and equity for students of African descent. **HONS.:** including: Award, for outstanding contributions to education, Black Educators Assn., 2001; Award, for dedicated services to the Black communities, Congress of Black Women, Antigonish-Guysborough, 2001; Special Services Award, Cdn Sociology & Anthropology Assn., 1999. **WORKS:** including, *Anti-Racist Feminism: Critical Race & Gen-*

der Studies, ed., 2000; *Power, Knowledge & Anti-Racism Education*, ed., 2000. Articles/essays in: *Can Review of Sociology & Anthropology*; *Educating African Canadians*; *Race, Gender, & Class*; *J Black Studies*; *J Can Studies*. **REVIEWED IN:** *Millennium Minds*, 2000; *Society Société*; *WWCW*. **EDUCATION:** PhD, Sociology of Education, 1980; MA, Sociology of Education, 1975, OISE/U of T. BA, UWI, 1971. **CONTACT:** acallist@stfx.ca; Fax: 902-867-2448

▶**CAMPAYNE, Hazel, D.Min.**
DIOCESAN MULTICULTURAL CONSULTANT, The Anglican Diocese of Toronto, 135 Adelaide St. E., Toronto, ON M5C 1L8. Born: Guyana/ in Canada since: 1980.

▶ Dr. Hazel Campayne is a Multicultural Consultant with the Community Ministries of the Anglican Diocese of Toronto; in this capacity she has been providing consultation, training, and support to parishes and diocesan groups on issues of multiculturalism, particularly the No Longer Strangers project, since 1994. **BACKGROUND:** an educator by profession, from 1965-80, she was the Headmistress of St. Rose's High School, one of Guyana's leading secondary institutions, where a number of creative programs were initiated, and whose graduates have gone on to excel across the professional sectors, whether in Guyana, the Caribbean, or other parts of the world. In Guyana, HC was involved in ecumenical, human rights, and social justice issues, which increased as the political situation in Guyana intensified leading to her departure for Canada. She continued to be concerned with her country's needs and for ten yrs. organized teams of educators to conduct Summer Institutes for students and teachers in disadvantaged areas of Guyana; she was also part of a team which monitored the country's elections in 1992. **CAREER HIGHLIGHTS:** in Canada, has done work in her parish, Our Lady of Lourdes, on the inclusion of newer Canadians and initiated greater involvement of Black Roman Catholics, which includes a music ministry and BHM celebrations; worked with the Ont. Anti-Racism Secretariat, examining faith communities and how they were addressing concerns of racism; in 1994, was a member of the Ecumenical Monitoring Program for S. Africa and a monitor during the country's historic elections that year. In the No Longer Strangers project, she assists with the integration of the many people from diverse cultures now living in Toronto. This initiative was the result of a study completed by the late Rev. Dr. R. Moseley, whose report, *No Longer Strangers: Ministry in a Multicultural Society*, underscored the need for the Anglican Church to be more inclusive of congregants from its worldwide community, now living in Toronto. Out of this has emerged the annual BHM Eucharistic Celebration, attended by over 2,000. **OTHER:** participated in the closing Assembly and festival for the World Council of Churches Ecumenical Decade of Churches in Solidarity with Women, in Harare, Zimbabwe, 1998; attended General Assembly, World Council of Churches, 1998 and 2001; delegate, Canadian Council of Churches, to the NGO Forum and WCAR in S. Africa, 2001. **AFFIL/MBRSHP:** includes: Chair, Canada-Caribbean Working Group, Canadian Council of Churches; founding member, ENOWAH, which held its first international conference in 2001; in 1981, she initiated a Guyana Human Rights support group in Canada, (now the Canada-Guyana Forum); Brd., GATE (chaplaincy ministry for women ex-prisoners); Program Cmtee, Doctor of Ministry Programs, Toronto School of Theology; Women's Inter Church Council; Cdn Catholic Org. for Development and Peace; OBHS. **HONS.:** Woman of the Year, for work with youth, Rotary Club, Guyana, 1975. **EDUCATION:** D.Min, Toronto School of Theology & U of T, 1990; M. Religious Studies, St. Michael's College; Post-Grad., Cert. Education, London U.; M.Ed, OISE/U of T; BA, UWI. **HEROES/ROLE MODELS:** Ora & James Campayne, parents; Berenice Campayne, sister. **MOTTO:** Do not let others define who you are. Be faithful to who and what God has called you to be and to do. **CONTACT:** hcampayne@toronto.anglican.ca; www. toronto.anglican.ca; hacampayne@canada.com

▶CAMPBELL, Constantine A., PhD, CM.

SOIL RESEARCH SCIENTIST EMERITUS, CONSULTANT, Eastern Cereal & Oilseed Research Centre (ECORC), Ottawa, ON. Born: Jamaica/ in Canada since: 1959.

▶ Dr. Constantine Campbell is recognized worldwide as one of the foremost specialists in research pertaining to soil organic matter and all aspects of nitrogen in soils and crops. He is a leading authority on degradation of nitrogen (N) in American prairie soils, especially regarding losses of amounts and quality of organic matter. Throughout his career, he worked almost exclusively with Agriculture Canada, retiring in 1998. Since then he has been working as a consultant in soil and environmental sciences, and continues to conduct research at ECORC as an Honorary Research Associate. **CAREER HIGHLIGHTS:** lecturer in Soil Chemistry and Soil Physics, U. of Sask., 1964-65; Research Scientist, Agriculture Canada, 1965-75. In 1978, he was promoted to Sr. Research Scientist; 1975-90, he was the Leader of the Soil Management and Conservation Program, as well as Head, Soils and Environment Section for Agriculture Canada, Swift Current, SK. From 1978-79, he was Visiting Scientist with CSIRO, in Queensland, Australia. He attained the post of Principal Research Scientist with Agriculture and Agri-Food Canada, at Swift Current, SK, in 1985. He was Adjunct Professor, Dept. of Soil Science, U. of Sask., 1978-95; he transferred to ECORC in Ottawa in 1997, where he retired, 1998. Through his research he demonstrated that soil organic matter is a key environmental indicator on the health status of prairie soils; his research has received attention nationally and internationally and is used in the development

and testing of plant growth models. **RESEARCH HIGHLIGHTS:** carbon dating–demonstrated how the C-dating technique could be used to measure the dynamics of soil organic matter turnover; refined concept of potentially mineralizable N; conducted studies on the influence of different crop rotations on soil quality indices and soil productivity; and, provided research basis to enable fertilizer N use efficiency to be optimized for production of spring and winter wheat, and forage grasses on the Cdn prairies. Was active in extension and technology transfer through presentations, written articles, radio and TV interviews; spoke to universities and professional societies in W. Canada and the US on topics including: tillage management, crop response to fertilizers, snowtrapping, water use efficiency, organic farming, soil degradation, and others. **AFFIL/MBRSHP:** Agricultural Institute of Canada; Cdn Society of Soil Sciences; Cdn Society of Agronomy; American Society of Agronomy. **HONS.:** several including, inducted to Sask. Agricultural Hall of Fame, 1999; Sask. Order of Merit, 1998; appointed Scientist Emeritus, Agriculture & Agri-Food Canada, 1998; Order of Canada, 1998; foundation founded in his honour, 1997, for U. of Sask. student to train in Soil Sciences at Swift Current; Distinguished Service Award, Sask. Institute of Agrologists, 1997; Fellow, American Society of Agronomy, 1993; Fellow, Soil Science Society of America, 1993; Outstanding Research Award, Cdn Society of Agronomy, 1991; Distinguished Agrologist Award, SK Institute of Agrologists, 1990; Fellow, Agricultural Institute of Canada, 1988; Fellow, Cdn Society of Soil Science, 1988; Agronomy Merit Award, Wheat Pools of the Prairie Provinces & Western Co-op Fertilizers, 1986. **WORKS:** has authored and co-authored approx. 190 scientific publications, 12 chapters in books, 3 books. **REVIEWED IN:** scientific publications; also profiled in *WWIC*; *Millennium Minds*, 2000. **EDUCATION:** PhD, Soil Science, U. of Sask., 1965. MSA, Soil Science, 1961; BSA,

Agricultural Chemistry, 1960, U of T. **CONTACT:** campbellca@em.agr.ca; Fax: 613-759-1924

▶**CAMPBELL, Denise Andrea**
YOUTH ACTIVIST/FORMER PRESIDENT, National Action Committee Status of Women (NAC), Toronto, ON. Born: Jamaica, 1975/ in Canada since: 1980.

▶ Denise Campbell, at age 26, became the youngest president of NAC, Canada's largest feminist organization; she had been active in the community for many years as a youth activist and community organizer. In 1999, she became the first Young Feminist VP of NAC and created the Young Women Network when she took office; she has travelled extensively as a motivational speaker, addressing issues of racism, women, and youth empowerment; she has appeared on local and national media, and was featured in educational videos on volunteerism, child poverty, etc. She often represents a youth perspective for various media, including CBC TV and radio, YTV, Much Music. In 1996, she co-hosted *GirlTalk* on WTN for ten episodes, and co-produced an educational video on gender issues with young women; also hosted a six-part series on international development, *Global Villagers*, and is now working on the eight-part follow-up on globalization. She has also participated in a number of global conferences including: the G-7 and People's Summits, 1995; Social Summit in Copenhagen, 1995; the World Conservation Congress in Montreal, 1996; the Rio+5 Earth Summit in New York, 1997; the UNESCO Conference on the Environment and Education in Greece, 1997; the 2000 Commission on the Status of Women meeting at UN Headquarters; UN 4th World Conference on Women, Beijing, China, 1995; co-created Challenge the Assumptions!, a multimedia educational package on systemic gender issues with 150 young women from 10 countries; participated in the UNWCAR in S. Africa with a two yr. project working with young women to explore the barriers they face at the intersection of race and gender; consultant, McConnell Fdn., for launch of a national student engagement program. **COMMUNITY INVOLVEMENT:** Trillium Fdn.; New Vision Optimist Club; Students' Commission/ *TG Magazine*; Cdn Feminist Alliance for Int'l Action; Royal Commission on Learning; National Youth Week. Due to NAC's financial constraints, DC resigned as President in the Fall of 2001. **HONS.:** several including: Young Woman of Distinction, YWCA; Harry Jerome Award, Youth; Youth Achievement Award, YTV; GG 125th Anniv. Medal; Lincoln Alexander Anti-Racism Award. **WORKS:** paper, *Challenge the Assumptions*. **EDUCATION:** completing MA, McGill U.; BA/Hons., U. of Ottawa. **HEROES/ROLE MODELS:** Joan Grant-Cummings; Stoney McCart. **MOTTO:** Courage is not the absence of fear....rather the realization that there is something far more significant than fear. **CONTACT:** denise@tgmag.ca; Fax: 416-597-0661

▶**CARNEGIE, Herbert, O.Ont.**
HOCKEY PIONEER/COMMUNITY LEADER, Toronto, ON. Born: Toronto, ON.

▶ Herbert Carnegie was born in Toronto in 1919. In his youth, he wanted only to play hockey, and in the 1940s and '50s supported his family through his career as an amateur hockey player. However, despite his obvious talent and abilities, he was not given the opportunity to play for the NHL. Unsuccessful in his desire to become a professional hockey player, he channelled his energy into other areas that would benefit the next generation: he started the first hockey school for boys in 1955. There he wrote the *Future Aces Creed,* which encouraged children to respect themselves and others, to play and work cooperatively, and to develop self-confidence and self-esteem. Since then he has been a leader in the community, sharing his vision of how people can live together in harmony. The Future Aces Philosophy, supported by several boards of education, has been introduced to more than 100 schools to encourage, guide and inspire young people. And HC, while in his eighties, continues to make numerous presentations in schools each year in order to spread this message. In addition, he had a successful career in business, becoming a Senior Accounts Executive with Investors Group; in 1987, he established the Herbert H. Carnegie Future Aces Foundation, which provides 25 bursaries of $1,000 each per year, to civic-minded students in financial need. To date, $250,000 in bursaries has been awarded. In recognition of his significant contributions to the larger community over the course of his life, HC has received many honours (see below). In addition, the Herbert H. Carnegie Centennial Centre was named in his honour by the City of Toronto, 2001. He is the subject of a radio documentary, *Black Ice*, 1998, on CBC Radio; and is the subject of two documentary films: *Too Colourful for the League*, 2000, and *Stories of Our Becoming*, 1995; and, is the real-life comic book character in two special issues of *Spiderman*, 1990. **HONS.:** several including: Harry Jerome President's Award, BBPA, 2002; inducted into six Halls of Fame, including Canada's Sports Hall of Fame, 2001; five medals, including Order of Ontario, 1998; Cert. of Recognition, B'nai Brith, 2001; Black History Month Award, City of Toronto, 2000; GG 125th Anniv. Medal, 1992; winner of 16 golf championships including Canadian Seniors Golf Championship, 1977 & '78. **WORKS:** autobiography, *A Fly in a Pail of Milk*, 1999. **REVIEWED IN:** most local, community, & nat'l publications; *Some Black Men*, 1999. **CONTACT:** future_aces@email.com; www.future-aces.org; Fax: 905-947-9131

▶CARRENARD, Patrice
DIRIGEANT D'ENTREPRISE/PDG, VISICOM MEDIA, #401–6200 boul. Taschereau, Brossard, QC J4W 3J8. Né: Drummondville, QC, 1970.
▶ Patrice Carrenard est un jeune entrepreneur qui, avec deux collègues d'enfance, a créé Visicom

Média, en 1996, une entreprise spécialisée dans le développement de logiciels et d'outils pour les gestionnaires de sites Internet. Avec leur premier produit, *WebExpert*, ils avaient du succès; ce produit était le premier éditeur de pages Web conçu en français. Immédiatement après, la compagnie a fait sortir par la suite, d'autres produits innovateurs: le logiciel *FTP Expert*, qui permet le transfert de fichiers Internet; le *Gif Movie Gear*, version française, un logiciel conçu pour l'animation de sites Web; *GoGraph*, un site de graphiques, ainsi que d'autres produits sortaient de l'entreprise Visicom. En 1998, l'équipe a décidé de se lancer dans le marché anglophone; au présent, la compagnie prépare de lancer la 5e version de son produit-vedette, *WebExpert*. En 2000, elle a réalisé un chiffre d'affaires de $1,1 millions, pour l'année 2001 elle prévoit atteindre $1,6 millions. Elle emploie 14 personnes, et travaille sur le plan national et international; elle compte parmi ses clients France Télécom et bien d'autres. Pour leur prochain défi, les responsables de l'entreprise Visicom cherchent à faire les produits multilingues afin d'avoir accès au marché en Amérique du sud. **PRIX:** plusieurs, y compris: Prix Canada Innovation, Chambre de Commerce de la Rive-Sud, 2001; Jeune Entreprise Rive-Sud, BDC, 1999; Elan et productivité, Semaine de la PME, BDC, 1999; Prix Cator, prix d'excellence, Communauté haïtienne, 1998. **ŒUVRES À SON PROPOS:** plusieurs, y compris les journaux: *Entreprendre*; *Montréal Gazette*; *Haïti-Observateur*; *J de Montréal*. **FORMATION:** Cert. Informatique; Bac, en Urbanisme, UQAM. **MOTTO:** Rome ne s'est pas construit en un jour. **CONTACT:** patricec@visic.com; www.visic.com

▶CARRINGTON-MCCRACKEN, Iris
JOURNALIST/SOCIAL ACTIVIST (Ret.), Pointe-Claire, QC. Born: Toronto, ON.
▶ Iris Carrington-McCracken studied Journalism and Public Administration before embarking on the career which ultimately led her to the Cana-

dian North. Her activities there included: Operations Manager, CBC Northern Radio, Rankin Inlet/ Frobisher Bay, 1980-81; Local Education Authority Development Coordinator, Baffin Region, Government of the Northwest Territories (GNWT), 1981-84; member, Task Force on Spousal Assault for the GNWT, secondment, 1984; Policy Advisor, Dept. of Education, GNWT; Coordinator, Family Violence Prevention Program, responsible for the implementation of three-year Action Plan in response to the Task Force on Spousal Assault Report, 1985-1990. **OTHER CAREER HIGHLIGHTS:** writer, producer, CBC, 1969; Executive Director, YWCA, 1969-71; Administrative Services, Ville Marie Social Service Centre, 1971-78. **COMMUNITY:** founding member, Black Studies Centre; Negro Theatre Arts Club; Brd., Negro Community Centre; founding member, Montreal Negro Alumni Group, formed in 1955 to ensure that Black youth had role models from professionals within the community, provided scholarships and tutorial services; founding member, National Congress of Black Women. **OTHER:** she is writing a book on the role of Blacks in the history and development of Canada's Northwest Territories. **EDUCATION:** B. Journalism, Lincoln U., Missouri; Cert., Public Admin., Ryerson Polytechnic; social work courses, McGill School of Social Work. **MOTTO:** Do it Now!

►CARTER, George E., Mr. Justice

JUDGE (Ret.), Ontario Court of Justice, Toronto, ON. Born: Toronto, ON.

▶ Mr. Justice George Carter was born in Toronto of West Indian parents who came to Canada in 1920 from Barbados. He graduated from the School of Law at the University of Toronto in 1945; he served his Articles and completed Osgoode Hall in 1948 and was called to the Bar in 1949. He served two years of Articles in the Chambers of B.J. Spencer Pitt, Esq. His own private practice was of a general nature with emphasis on civil litigation. In 1969,

he was appointed a Queen's Counsel. And, in 1979, he was sworn in as a Provincial Court Judge. In July, 1996, he retired from the Bench.

►CARTER, Jean

JOURNALIST, CBC Radio, 250 Front St. W., Toronto, ON. Born: UK/ in Canada since: 1984.

▶ Jean Carter is an on-air journalist with CBC Radio. **CAREER HIGHLIGHTS:** co-produced, *Understanding Umaah* on Toronto's Muslim community, after Sept. 11, 2001; reported on Walkerton Water Disaster, 2000; was acting National Reporter for Maritimes (1994 and 2000), and Parliamentary Bureau (1994); broke national story on Nova Scotia girls who were abducted and forced into prostitution, 1992; reported on Westray Mine Disaster, NS, 1992; wrote and produced 20-min. documentary on racism in Halifax bars, 1990. **HONS.:** including: Awards & Honourable Mentions from Radio-TV News Directors Assn. of Canada, 2000, 1991-94; CBC Radio Award, for programming excellence, 1996; Gabriel Award, Station of the year, CBC Radio Halifax, 1993; Cdn Assn. of Journalists, 1992. **EDUCATION:** BAA, Journalism, Ryerson U., 1988. **MOTTO:** What you fear, you create. **CONTACT:** jean_carter@cbc.ca; www.cbc.ca

►CARTER, Rubin "Hurricane"

FORMER BOXER/ACTIVIST, Association in Defence of the Wrongfully Convicted (AIDWYC), Toronto, ON. Born: USA/ in Canada since: 1985.

▶ Rubin "Hurricane" Carter was the number one contender for the Middleweight Boxing title in the US when he was accused of murder in 1966, in New Jersey. He was tried and convicted twice, but maintained his innocence throughout and wrote his life story, *The Sixteenth Round: From Number 1 Contender to #45472,* in 1974. This mobilized a great deal of support from celebrities like Bob Dylan (who later penned the song, *Hur-*

ricane), Muhammad Ali, Ellen Burstyn and others. But, their efforts and many public rallies, were unsuccessful. During a second trial, though the original principal witnesses recanted their perjured statements, RHC's conviction was upheld; it is believed that Carter was deliberately framed because of his militant views during the civil rights movement, advocating Black empowerment "by any means necessary." After being befriended by Lesra Martin, a teen from an inner-city area in the US, then living with an adopted family in Canada, a new attempt was made by Martin's housemates to have the case re-examined in 1983. They were successful and in 1985, RHC's previous convictions were overturned by Judge Lee Sarokin. Lawyer F. Lee Bailey described the Carter case as, "one of this century's most important legal sagas." **CURRENTLY:** RHC lives in Toronto; he lectures frequently at bar associations, universities, law schools, high schools, and libraries throughout N. America and other countries; he speaks on issues of literacy, education, wrongful convictions, *habeas corpus*, and the death penalty. He has testified before the US Congress on the need for preserving federal review of State Court Convictions; and, has testified before the General Assembly of the United Nations. He is on the Board, Southern Center for Human Rights (Atlanta, GA); Death Penalty Focus (CA); the Alliance for Prison Justice (Boston). He is the Executive Director of the international organization, AIDWYC (Toronto), which works for the release of those wrongfully imprisoned; one such case was Guy Paul Morin's, whose two convictions were ultimately overturned. **OTHER:** RHC is the subject of books and a 1999 film starring Denzel Washington, *The Hurricane*; featured in *Sports Illustrated*, and in programs on NBC, CBC, CNN, and the BBC. **HONS.:** Hon. Middleweight Boxing Championship, 1993. **WORKS:** *The Sixteenth Round: From Number 1 Contender to #45472*, 1974. **REVIEWED IN:** *Hurricane*, 2000; *Lazarus & the Hurricane*, 1992. **CONTACT:** Fax: 416-203-9088

▶**CARTER-HENRY LYON, Grace**
FOUNDER/MUSICAL DIRECTOR, The Heritage Singers, Pickering, ON. Born: Jamaica/ in Canada since: 1973.

▶ Grace Carter-Henry Lyon is best known as the founder and Musical Director of the Heritage Singers, a group founded in 1977. Its aims are: to promote the development of Caribbean folk music and theatre; use folk singing and dance as tools to bridge cultural gaps internationally; enhance, ethnic, historic and social traditions; and, to share that heritage with the larger community. Since its inception, the group has performed in a number of international locations, including Jamaica, the US, the Netherlands, Taiwan, Germany, and Mexico; produced recordings and videos; and, been the subject of a CBC documentary. Partial proceeds from their performances have been given to charitable organizations including: Ronald McDonald House; The Daily Bread Food Bank; the JCA; Save the Children Canada, and others. **OTHER:** GCHL has worked in the Real Estate industry for over 20 yrs. and has received many awards marking her success; since 1997 she has achieved sales in the top three per cent in Ontario. **COMMUNITY:** Jamaican Cultural Committee; the Arts and Culture Committee, Metropolitan Toronto Community Folk Arts Council; Maple Downs Investment. **HONS.:** Harry Jerome Award, for Excellence in Business, BBPA, 2002; Woman of Excellence Award, Congress of Black Women, 2000. Several in Real Estate: Emerald Award, 1999, 1997; Award for professionalism, Homelife Canada, 1995; Gold Award Member, since 1988. **EDUCATION:** Institute of Cdn Bankers, U of T; Trinity School of Music; Royal School of Music; Ontario Real Estate Assn. **MOTTO:** Life is a journey to be enjoyed, not a sentence to be served. **CONTACT:** glyons@treb-net.com; Fax: 905-839-7528

►CARTY, Donald

WWII VETERAN, Royal Canadian Armed Forces, Toronto, ON. Born: Saint John, NB.

► Donald Carty is a veteran of WWII and has been involved in the military or military training most of his life. This interest in serving his country was likely influenced by his father and two of his uncles who served in WWI. He appears in the 2001 documentary, *Honour Before Glory*, by Anthony Sherwood, which tells the story of the No. 2 Construction Battalion (the all-Black unit in which Canadian Blacks served in WWI). His community involvement, particularly with youth, has been extensive and includes: Cubs and Boy Scouts; community camp counsellor; RCAF; Brd., OBHS; YMCA; Bathurst Lions International. **HONS.:** has received several including: Boys Scouts Canada, (Appreciation Award, 1997 & Woodbadge Award, 1973); RCAF, CVSM & Clasp; ACAA, 1999; Hall of Fame. **REVIEWED IN:** community newspapers; *Maclean's*; and books including: *Blacks in Canada, A History*, 1971. **EDUCATION:** Ryerson Institute, 1952. **HEROES/ROLE MODELS:** Father. **MOTTO:** People tend to accept you on the level that you present yourself.

►CHAMBERS, Juanita, PhD.

PSYCHOLOGIST/PROFESSOR EMERITUS, University of Alberta, Edmonton, AB. Born: Montreal, QC.

► Dr. Juanita Chambers was born in Montreal in 1913 and, though her elementary schoolteacher told her she would grow up to be a domestic, she went on to graduate at the top of her class at all levels and become a psychologist, radio announcer, and university professor. **BACKGROUND**: in 1947, she taught nursery school at the YMCA, which led to a great interest in the psychological development of the child. In 1950, she returned to university for graduate studies; at the time she was also a radio consultant for African Affairs for the CBC and was one of the first public "personalities" to discuss apartheid in S. Africa. **CAREER HIGHLIGHTS**: from 1954-58, she was Psychologist-in-Chief at the Montreal Mental Hygiene Institute and recognized as one of the best interpreters of the WISC IQ Test; 1958-60, she was Senior Psychologist at the Montreal Children's Hospital, and was responsible for the coordination of diagnostic services of the Psychology Dept. with other units; she also worked with the Director of Psychiatry in setting up Ward 7D, one of the first in-patient wards in child psychiatry in Montreal. In 1960, she became Director of Psychological Services at Harterre School (a remedial boarding school for emotionally disturbed children) and managed to raise the professional standards of the teachers, re-organize the school program, and introduce psychological services for each child; during this time she also lectured part-time at SGWU (now Concordia U.), and participated in the planning of a provincial training program for careworkers. In 1964, she became Asst. Director of the Psychiatry Annex (annexed to the Montreal Children's Hospital); in 1965, she was a Research Consultant for the Quebec Assn. for Retarded Children, and became a part-time lecturer at the U. de Montréal where she gave 15 lectures on Developmental Psychology on the French TV Network. In 1967, she was invited to join the University of Alberta as Associate Professor of Educational Psychology; soon thereafter, she became a full Professor, Chair of the Dept. of Educational Psychology, and an Advisor on the Council for the Faculty of Extension. **OTHER:** she was the first Faculty member appointed to look into the schooling of Aboriginal children throughout the province of Alberta; she also carried out a study on the incidents and treatment of brain-damaged children in Alberta. In addition, she taught summer courses in Child Psychology at Lethbridge U. and at the U. of New Brunswick. Amongst all these accomplishments there are a number of firsts: first female to participate in the McGill mock parliaments, 1934; first female Chair, Dept. of Educational Psychology, U. of Alberta; first President, Assn. of Early Childhood Educators; first academic instructor to teach Aboriginal post-secondary courses in education at St. Paul, AB. In her own words, JC considers one of her greatest achievements to be "raising the status of the Faculté St-Jean" when she conducted an inquiry into the schooling of Francophones, by travelling to French schools in Saskatchewan and BC. **HONS.:** several including, creation of the Juanita Chambers Excellence in Community Service Award, Psychologists' Assn. of Alberta, 2000; John Ware Lifetime Achievement Award, BAASA, 1998; 50th Anniv. Plaque, for being 1st President (1946-48), Assn. Early Childhood Educators, 1996; Professor Emeritus, U. of AB; Award for outstanding contribution & service to Black women of AB, Black Women's Assn., 1989; Cert. Merit, for the film *Troubled Children*, Fed. Cdn Amateur Cinematographers, 1967. **WORKS:** include: *Troubled Children*, documentary (wrote, directed, & produced), 1966; "Maternal Deprivation & the Concept of Time in Children," *Am J Orthopsychiatry*, 1961; "The Adopted Child," *Can Mental Health*, 1959. **REVIEWED IN:** *Lethbridge Herald; The Edmonton J; Epilogue, U of AB Newsletter; Edmonton Sun.* **EDUCATION:** PhD (cum laude); MA (cum laude), U. de Montréal. BA/Hons., French, McGill U.

▶**CHAMBERS, Mary Anne**
SENIOR VICE-PRESIDENT, Scotiabank, 888 Birchmount Rd., Toronto, ON M1K 5L1. Born: Jamaica/ in Canada since: 1976.
▶ Mary Anne Chambers is a Senior Vice-President at Scotiabank. She joined the bank in 1976, as a Computer Programmer/Analyst; after completing her degree in 1988, with a major in Commerce, she moved quickly up the corporate ladder. Since 1990, she has held the position of Vice-President in a number of divisions: International and Executive Office Systems Development; Projects and Program Management; Retail Services, Corporate and Commercial Services;

and, currently holds the position of Senior Vice-President of Electronic Banking Services. **COMMUNITY INVOLVEMENT:** Chair, Brd. of Directors, United Way of Canada-*Centraide Canada* (member since 1994); U of T, Governor since 1993, and three yrs. as Vice-Chair, Governing Council; Rouge Valley Health System; Cdn Merit Scholarship Foundation, Brd. of Trustees; United Way, Greater Toronto, seven yrs., Brd. of Trustees; Air Cadet League Canada, Governor, three yrs.; Canadian Club, Director, 1995-2001, President, 1998-99. Through her various community outreach initiatives, she has advanced the interests of youth through corporate sponsorship; launched a benefactor relationship with the Cdn Merit Scholarship Foundation through which the Canadian Club of Toronto grants five annual scholarships to university-bound students; she also sponsors a Basic School in Jamaica. **HONS.:** including: named "Great Mind," U of T's 175th anniversary celebrations, 2002; Diamond Award, for community service, Variety Children's Charities, 2002; Black History Makers Award, United Achievers' Club Brampton, 2000; Arbor Award, for outstanding voluntary service, U of T, 1999; Cert. Excellence, Human Rights & Race Relations Centre, 1998; ACAA, for achievement in business, 1997; Woman on the Move Award, *Toronto Sun*, 1996. **REVIEWED IN:** *U of T Alumni Magazine; Toronto Star; Millennium Minds*, 2000. **EDUCATION:** Executive Management Program, Queen's U.; BA, Commerce, U of T, 1988. **MOTTO:** Make a difference! **CONTACT:** maryanne. chambers@scotiabank.com; Fax: 416-750-6472

▶**CHAMBERS, Michael**
PHOTOGRAPHIC ARTIST/PUBLISHER, Nok Photo Publishing, Ste. 206-300 Campbell Ave., Toronto, ON M6P 3V6. Born: Jamaica/ in Canada since: 1972.
▶ Michael Chambers is a photographer who has been described as "the quintessential Canadian artist," for his challenging photographic work,

which has captured and captivated a generation. Working primarily in black and white, his work is described as "breathtakingly beautiful and deeply disturbing." In the early '90s, he was a contributing photographer to *NOW* and *Word* magazines. In 1995, his image, *The Watermelon* became one of the most controversial in contemporary art. In 1998, he presented a ten yr. retrospective at the Thames Art Gallery (Chatham, ON), ...*And Spectators are no More*, which was well received. He has exhibited internationally in the US, Japan, S. Africa, the UK, and the Caribbean. In addition to his works for galleries and museums, he has collaborated on films including: *Journey to Justice*; *Esther, Baby and Me*; *Raisin' Cain*; and the forthcoming, *The Gospel According to Mary*. He was the subject of the NFB documentary, *The Photographer: An Artist's Journey*; he is the subject of the jazz recording, *Michael the Photographer,* by Neil Braithwaite and David Williams. He has been interviewed and profiled in the media, including TV and print, and his work appears in national and international publications. **OTHER:** creative director, *Dragon* magazine; produced three AIDS Awareness posters for the AIDS Committee of Toronto (ACT); raises awareness of sweatshop abuse for OXFAM Int'l; has been mentoring university students since 1993; lectures across Ontario, including AGO, Science Centre, Chatham Cultural Museum. **HONS.:** including, Mosaic Image Award, 2000. **REVIEWED IN:** nat'l & int'l publications including: *Revue Noire; British J Photography; Elle* (Canada)*; Mix* magazine; *Soul; Venus; QX* int'l magazine; *Gleaner; Toronto Life; Photo Digest*; *Globe and Mail; Toronto Star.* **EDUCATION:** BFA, York U., 1983. **CONTACT:** nokphoto@rogers.com; Tel/Fax: 416-536-2689

►CHARLES, Bernadette

POET/STORYTELLER, Kulanga Production, Montreal, QC. Born: Grenada/ in Canada since: 1980.
▶ Bernadette Charles, a.k.a. Kulanga, is a writer, performance poet, and storyteller who uses music and poetry to "re-capture her social and religious heritage." Born and educated in Grenada, she taught elementary school until 1980, when she immigrated to Canada to study cosmetology, after which she owned and managed a number of beauty salons in the Montreal area, and is still the owner of Salon de Coiffure Bebak. In the early 1990s, she attended Concordia University, became involved in community organizations (i.e. Congress of Black Women, Montreal West Island Black Community Assn.) and began writing poetry. By 1992, she had published her first book of poetry and by 1997, had recorded *The Call*, which combines spoken word with African drumming; her most recent work, *Kabakajah* is a CD with her poems accompanied by music. She is the owner of her own publishing company, Kulanga Productions, and is an active promoter of Afrocentric cultural activities, such as Kwanzaa and Black History Month. **WORKS:** *Kabakajah*, CD with recorded poems; *The Call*, 1997*; Slave Spirit Speaks*, (poetry) 1992. **EDUCATION:** Political Science, Concordia U. **CONTACT:** kulanga@canada.com

►CHARLES, Maurice A., Mr. Justice

JUDGE (Ret.), Provincial Court of Ontario, Toronto, ON. Born: Guyana/ in Canada since: 1963.
▶ Mr. Justice Charles has the distinction of having been a judge in Guyana, Ghana and Canada during the course of his career. **CAREER HIGHLIGHTS:** after qualifying as a solicitor in 1944, he began practising civil and criminal law in Guyana, 1945-49; was then appointed a District Magistrate as a member of Britain's Overseas Judicial Service, and exercised Civil and Criminal jurisdiction until July, 1956; was transferred to Ghana, 1956, serving as a District Magistrate; promoted to Senior Magistrate, 1957; was then appointed a member of the Commission of Inquiry in Ghana for an alleged conspiracy to

overthrow the government of the day and to kill then-president Nkrumah; in 1959, was appointed by the Governor-General of Ghana as a Judge of the High Court of Ghana; exercised unlimited jurisdiction in civil and criminal cases, as well as Appellate Jurisdiction over decisions of District Magistrates and County Court Judges; in 1967, he retired as the most senior High Court Judge. After coming to Canada and qualifying as a barrister and solicitor of the Law Society of Upper Canada, 1969, he was appointed to the Ontario provincial judiciary, thereby becoming the first Black criminal court judge in Ontario, a position he held until his retirement in 1995. He continues to practise criminal law and to act in an advisory capacity on cases, as requested. **OTHER:** he has given a number of lectures and presentations, including an address to the law graduates of both U of T and Dalhousie U., on the Charter of Rights and Freedoms. **EDUCATION:** Law Society of Upper Canada, 1969; LLB, U. of London, England, 1952; Solicitor, Law Society of England, 1944. **CONTACT:** Fax: 416-449-8654

►CHEESMAN, Sean

DANCER/CHOREOGRAPHER, Edmonton, AB. Born: Edmonton, AB.

▶ Sean Cheesman has choreographed for, and danced with, the world's top entertainers, including Michael Jackson, Janet Jackson, Prince, Vanessa Williams, Tina Turner, Whitney Houston, Britney Spears, and Cher. He began his career as a figure skater and dancer, then studied dance at the Alvin Ailey American Dance Center in New York. Afterwards, he toured with Janet Jackson as a choreographer and dancer. He choreographed the Diamonds and Pearls tour for Prince, as well as tours for *La Bouche* and Faith Hill. He also acts and appeared in *The Bodyguard*, in 1992, with Whitney Houston; in that film he also choreographed the dance sequences. His other TV work includes Prince's ABC special, *The Ride Divine* (choreographer); the NBC

TV series, *Guys Next Door* (choreographer); MTV awards and *Soul Train Awards*. In addition, he conducts dance workshops and seminars in N. America, Europe, and Asia. And, he has written, directed, and choreographed large-scale musicals in Japan. **HONS.:** many, including: two MTV awards for choreography; nominee, Bob Fosse Choreography Award. **REVIEWED IN:** nat'l and int'l entertainment publications. **CONTACT:** sean-mcheesman@yahoo.ca

►CHRISTENSEN, Carole Pigler, D.Ed.

PROFESSOR, School of Social Work & Family Studies, University of British Columbia (UBC), Vancouver, BC V6T 1Z2. Born: USA/ in Canada since: 1969.

▶ Dr. Carole Pigler Christensen is a professor and a former Director of UBC's School of Social Work. **CAREER HIGHLIGHTS:** prior to her UBC appointment, she was a Professor at McGill University, 1970-91, where, as a pioneer in the area of cross-cultural and anti-racist studies, she initiated undergraduate courses and a graduate-level concentration in cross-cultural and anti-racist practice; she also developed and taught courses in Human Sexuality at McGill, 1976-91, and appears to be the first Black woman in Canada to be a certified Sex Therapist and Sex Educator. She is also a registered clinical member of the American Assn. for Marriage and Family Therapy. She chaired the Cdn Assn. of Schools of Social Work's Task Force on Multicultural and Multiracial Issues in Social Work Education, 1988-1991, which produced a report ("Social Work Education at the Crossroads: The Challenge of Diversity"), leading to accreditation standards cognizant of these issues. In 1990, she became the first Black woman to be appointed Director of a school of social work in Canada. She was the second female Director of UBC's School of Social Work in the school's 75-yr. history. During her mandate, she negotiated funds for the Jack Bell Building, and outlined the design for the building, which now houses the UBC School of Social Work. She is also the initiator and Program Director of the Multicultural Family Centre in East Vancouver, designed to assist immigrants and refugees to access health and social services. The Centre resulted from a grant awarded to CPC by Multiculturalism and Citizenship Canada, 1990-94. **OTHER:** she was a Lecturer at the Danish School of Social Work (Copenhagen) where she developed and taught courses in family therapy; has also been involved in training professionals for effective practice with a multicultural and multiracial clientele at home and abroad. She is a co-founder of the Assn. of Black Human Service Workers, (Montreal, QC). Her publications and current professional activities are in the areas of multicultural and anti-racist practice, model building, and research; her current research examines access to health care for visible minority immigrant women. **HONS.:** several including: End Racism Award, BC Min. of Multiculturalism & Immigration, 2000; Distinguished Service to Families Award, BC Council for the Family, 1997; Community Service Award, Congress of Black Women/BC, 1994; Fulbright Scholar, Copenhagen, Denmark, 1960-61. **WORKS:** including: articles in *J Multicultural Social Work; Can Ethnic Studies; Women and Therapy; Counselor Education and Supervision; J Social Work & Human Sexuality*, and several others. Book: *Linking Schools of Social Work to Aboriginal Students & Communities: Exploring the Issues*, 1994; also chapters in books. **REVIEWED IN:** *The Province; Education Leader; News & Views on Education*; newsletter, Adoptive Parents Assn. BC; UBC reports; major Danish newspapers. **EDUCATION:** D.Ed, Counselling Psychology, McGill U., 1980; MSW, U. of Michigan, 1963; BA, Howard U., 1960. **HEROES/ROLE MODELS:** Mother. **MOTTO:** The more we care for the happiness of others, the greater is our own sense of well-being. (Dalai Lama) **CONTACT:** cchriste@ interchange.ubc.ca; Fax: 604-822-8656

▶**CHUMPUKA, Florence**
LEGAL COUNSEL, Federal Department of Justice, 284 Wellington St., Ottawa, ON K1A 0H8. Born: Zambia/ in Canada since: 1989.
▶ Florence Chumpuka is Legal Counsel in the Public Law Policy Sector, Human Rights Unit of Justice Canada, a position she has held since 1997. She is responsible for the legal and policy development of the Canadian Human Rights Act; provides legal and policy advice to other Govt. depts. and territorial governments on the application of the Canadian Human Rights Act in relation to immigration, employment and Aboriginal issues. Additionally, she is involved in the interpretation of Canada's international obligations vis-à-vis their domestic implications. In August, 2001 she was part of the team advising the Canadian government delegation in negotiations at the UNWCAR in Durban, S. Africa. **OTHER CAREER HIGHLIGHTS:** she was a Policy Advisor with Health Canada before joining the Departmental Legal Services Unit as Legal Counsel for First Nations and Inuit health, and advised on Constitutional, Charter, health information, self-government and transfer issues; served as a Special Advisor to an Ont. provincial government Cabinet Minister and AG with responsibilities for judicial appointments and OIC appointments of members to agencies, boards and commissions, 1990-97; had served in the Min. of Labour and Min. of Citizenship as a Policy Advisor involved with the policy formulation of labour and human rights policy relating to the Pay Equity Act, Employment Standards Act and Employment Equity. She considers one of her greatest achievements to be the increase in diversity (e.g. women, Aboriginal persons, visible minorities, and people with disabilities) in judicial appointments, from three per cent in 1990 to 48% in 1994. She is also a former provincial prosecutor, and represented the Min. of Labour before the Ontario Board of adjudication tribunal in administrative hearings of Employment Standards Act viola-

tions. **OTHER:** in the Dept. of Justice, she is one of the co-founders of a peer support group to foster greater diversity in the workplace; in the community she is involved with a non-profit organization, Women's Place/*Place aux femmes*, which promotes inclusiveness and women's economic independence. Before moving to Canada, FC practised law as Parliamentary Counsel to the Zambian Parliament, 1980-1989. **WORKS:** "World Conference Against Racism and the Human Rights Issues," *inter pares* (Justice Canada). **REVIEWED IN:** *inter pares* (Justice Canada: www.justice.gc.ca/interpares_e/). **EDUCATION:** National Accreditation, 1994; Cert. Legislative Drafting, 1986, U. of Ottawa. Cert. Parliamentary Practice & Procedure, London, England, 1983; LLB, U. Zambia, 1980. **CONTACT:** fchumpuk@ justice.gc.ca; Fax: 613-745-0816

▶CIRIAQUE, Marie-Claudette

ORGANISATRICE COMMUNAUTAIRE, « Pour une action bénévole engagée au sein de la communauté ici et ailleurs », bur. 2-401, rue des Carrières, Montréal, QC H2S 3P9. Née: Haïti.

▶ Marie-Claudette Ciriaque s'est engagée dans l'action bénévole depuis plus de 30 ans; elle participe à divers titres à de nombreux projets d'aide aux plus démunis, notamment au Canada et ailleurs, par le biais de projets d'alphabétisation, d'éducation populaire, de construction d'écoles et de dispensaires. Une de ses priorités est l'association dont elle est fondatrice, L'association d'aide aux femmes et aux enfants analphabètes et démunies de Docajou (Haïti)–Ed Pou Malerèz Lan DOKAJOU (EPMANDOK). Déjà, elle a aidé à construire un centre d'alphabétisation, et une clinique de premiers soins. Après le cyclone Georges, elle a été désignée par le regroupement des 26 associations régionales haïtiennes à Montréal, pour les représenter en Haïti auprès des sinistrés du cyclone. En dehors de ses activités communautaires, elle est très actives dans les médias (radio, télévision, théâtre, etc.). **VIE ASSOCIATIVE:**

Assn. des Retraités d'Origine Haïtienne du Québec et du Canada; Conseil national des citoyens et citoyennes d'origine haïtienne; Fédération de l'âge d'or du Québec; Société pour le reboisement d'Haïti, etc. **PRIX:** y compris, Hommage du groupement des femmes d'affaires noires et de professions; Reconnaissance et mérite de l'Entraide bénévole Kouzin Kouzin; Cert., Radio Centre-Ville. **ŒUVRES À SON PROPOS:** publications communautaires, *Amina*, 2002; *Bulletin-Info-SORHICA*; magazine *Soleil des Iles*; *J PAMH*; *Bulletin Collaboration Santé Internationale*; *calendrier du MHN*, 2001; *J Horizon*; *J de Montréal*; *La Presse*, etc. **CONTACT:** Tél: 514-270-2299

▶CLARK, Eugene
PERFORMER/SINGER/SONGWRITER/PRODUCER,
Toronto, ON. Born: US.

▶ Eugene Clark is an actor, singer, songwriter and producer. He starred for two years in Disney's *The Lion King*, as Mufasa (original Toronto cast at the Princess of Wales Theatre, Toronto). Other stage performances include: *Jacob Two-Two Meets the Hooded Fang; Night and Day*; and, *The Threepenny Opera*. He has starred in a number of American and Canadian TV series including: *Night Heat* (received Gemini Award); *ENG; Sweating Bullets;* and *TEKWARS*. As a composer, songwriter and producer, he has recorded three CD's: *Eugene Clark's Love Letters; As Long As I Give; Y-jam;* and, *How Great thou Art*. In 1984, his song, *Letter from a Concerned Citizen (Starvation in Africa)*, was selected by the Canadian Red Cross to promote their National Public Awareness and Fundraising Campaign; and in the mid-1980s, his song, *Call Me*, was used in the Sick Kids and Variety Village telethons, to help raise funds for children's charities. **OTHER:** since childhood, he has combined both the performing arts and athletics; he was a professional football player (was captain of the UCLA Bruins Football Team and played in the

Hula Bowl; played for the Toronto Argonauts); and, is a personal trainer. He was also a stand-up comedian at the Yuk-Yuks Comedy Clubs. **HONS.:** Gemini Award, Best Supporting Actor in a Dramatic Series, for *Night Heat*. **EDUCATION:** BA, Psychology/ Sociology, UCLA. **CONTACT:** eugeneaclark7@hotmail.com; www.eugene-clark.homestead.com

▶**CLARKE, George Elliott,** PhD.
PROFESSOR/POET/AUTHOR/PLAYWRIGHT,
Dept. of English, University of Toronto, 7 King's College Circle, Toronto, ON M5S 3K1. Born: Windsor, NS.
▶ Dr. George Elliott Clarke is a Professor of English, a published poet, author, playwright, and a cultural activist. Born and raised in Nova Scotia, he has, through his writings, brought attention to the rich historical and cultural traditions of Blacks in the Maritimes. **CAREER HIGHLIGHTS:** currently he is a Professor of English at U of T; previously, he taught English and Canadian Studies at Duke University, NC, 1994-99; and, 1998-99 he was appointed the Visiting Seagram's Chair in Canadian Studies at McGill U. Before completing his studies and becoming an academic, he worked at a variety of jobs: parliamentary aide, House of Commons, Ottawa, 1987-91; newspaper editor in Waterloo and then Halifax; social worker in Halifax, 1985-86; and, legislative researcher, provincial parliament, Toronto, 1982-83. His writings consist of poetry, a verse novel, two verse plays, and literary criticism: *Whylah Falls* was adapted for radio and aired on the CBC; in 1997, the stage version premiered in Halifax; the play, *Beatrice Chancy* was made into an opera and has been performed on stage and broadcast on CBC TV; he wrote the screenplay for the film, *One Heart Broken into Song*, which was directed by Clement Virgo (*see: Virgo, Clement*). **HONS.:** several including: GG Award for English Poetry, for *Execution Poems*, 2001; two Hon. Doctorate degrees (Dalhousie U., 1999,

& UNB, 2000); Outstanding Writer in Film & Television, 2000; Bellagio Fellowship, 1998; Portia White Prize for Artistic Achievement, 1998; Archibald Lampman Award, 1991. **WORKS:** poetry: *Blue*, 2001; *Execution Poems*, 2001; *Provençal Songs*, 1993 & 1997; *Gold Indigoes*, 2000; *Saltwater Spirituals and Deeper Blues*, 1983; *Lush Dreams, Blue Exile*, 1994; a verse-novel, *Whylah Falls,* 1990 & 2000; two verse plays, *Whylah Falls: The Play*, 1999 & 2000, and *Beatrice Chancy*, 1999; editor, *Eyeing the North Star: Directions in African-Canadian Literature,* 1997; *Fire on the Water: An Anthology of Black Nova Scotian Writing*, 2 vols. 1991-92. Articles in: *Dalhousie Review; J Can Studies; European Romantic Review; Essays on Can Writing; Transition;* etc. **REVIEWED IN:** *WWIC*; *Millennium Minds*, 2000; *Some Black Men*, 1999; *Studies in Can Literature*; *J Can Studies*; *Can Poetry.* **EDUCATION:** PhD, English, Queen's U., 1993; MA, English, Dalhousie U., 1989; BA/Hons., U. of Waterloo, 1984. **HEROES/ROLE MODELS:** Walter Borden, actor; John Fraser, professor. **MOTTO:** *Ingenium ad imperio* (Talent equal to power). **CONTACT:** Tel: 416-946-3143; Fax: 416-406-5898

▶**CLARKE, LaFerne**
EXECUTIVE DIRECTOR, Family Services Hamilton-Wentworth, Ste. 101-105 Main St. E., LL, Hamilton, ON L8N 1G6. Born: Jamaica/ in Canada since: 1987.
▶ LaFerne Clarke is known locally as "a community leader, social worker, and former member of the Police Services Board." In 2001, she was appointed Executive Director of Family Services of Hamilton-Wentworth; she assumed this position after serving as Executive Director of Big Sisters, Kitchener-Waterloo, 1996-2001. She has a record of innovative program development, which sustains long-term individual and systemic change; is successful in supporting and facilitating community development. **OTHER HIGHLIGHTS:** Practicum Instructor, Faculty of Social Work,

Wilfrid Laurier U., since 1998; Social Worker who has been providing counselling to teens, adults, seniors and immigrant families; she completed her placement for her MSW with the YWCA in Zimbabwe, 1994-95, and with the YWCA, Kitchener-Waterloo, 1993. She has also worked in the business sector: in marketing, with The Centre in The Square, Kitchener; with the City of Kitchener in Employment Equity, and Training and Development. Before coming to Canada, she pursued a career in Business Administration, and Marketing, 1970-87. **COMMUNITY:** World Wide Opportunities for Women, since 1996; Congress of Black Women, since 1988. Past Brd. member: Waterloo Regional Police Board; Big Sisters of Canada; Focus for Ethnic Women; New Generation Housing Co-operative; YWCA. **HONS.:** including: Award for outstanding community service, Black History Assn., Waterloo-Wellington, 1997; Award for Community Service, United Way, Kitchener-Waterloo, 1996. **WORKS:** "Building Positive Relationships: An Evaluation of Process & Outcomes in a Big Sister Program," *J of Primary Intervention*, 2001. **REVIEWED IN:** local publications; *The Daily Gleaner; Int'l Who's Who of Professionals*, 1997. **EDUCATION:** MSW, Wilfrid Laurier U., 1995; Cert. & Dipl., Graduate Institute of Marketing, London, UK, 1983; Cert. Marketing & Cert. Supervisory Management, U. of Technology, Jamaica. **MOTTO:** To whom much is given, much is asked. **CONTACT:** lclarke@fshw. on.ca; Fax: 905-523-8699

▶**CLARKE, Neville**

ARTIST, Ajax, ON. Born: Jamaica/ in Canada since: 1974.

▶ Neville Clarke is an artist known primarily for his portraits and his works in watercolour. His paintings are said to "reflect the current social and economic situation"; for him the figure is the medium through which he communicates and expresses sympathy, hope and human dignity. Through his paintings, NC explores the issues of Black identity, hopes to re-educate Canadian society, and aims to influence and encourage Black creativity. His wife, Janice, is often the subject of his paintings. He lectures and presents on Canadian Art at a number of locations including the Varley Gallery in Unionville. **CURRENT ACTIVITIES:** preparing a new body of work based on the various stages of pregnancy, which will be exhibited at the Robert McLaughlin Gallery, in Oshawa, in 2003. **AFFIL/MBRSHP:** member of the Society of Cdn Artists; the Ontario Society of Artists; the Canadian Institute of Portrait Artists; founder, Society of African-Canadian Artists. Since 2001, he is the President of the Cdn Society of Painters in Watercolour, the first person of African descent to hold this position. **HONS.:** Recipient of many awards; one of his paintings has been included in the Prince of Wales Collection, UK, 2001; outstanding established Artist Award, Our Image, 2001; Charles Comfort medal, 2000; twice winner of the A.J. Casson Medal, 1995 & 1999. **REVIEWED IN:** *A Dictionary of Canadian Artists*; exhibition catalogues, including *Towards a Meaningful Expression*; profiled in local and community newspapers. **EDUCATION:** OCA, Hon. Graduate, Florence, Italy, 1984; OCA, 1983; Sheridan College, 1980; and study tours in Holland and the UK. **MOTTO:** Whatever the mind of man can conceive and believe, it can achieve. (Napoleon Hill) **CONTACT:** clarke@primus.ca

▶**CLARKE WALKER, Marie**

TRADE UNIONIST/ PAST VP NATIONAL DIVERSITY, Canadian Union of Public Employees. Born: UK/ in Canada since: 1972.

▶ Marie Clarke Walker was the first person ever elected to the position of National Diversity Vice-President at the Cdn Union of Public Employees (CUPE), 1999-2001. In this position she was responsible for representing the issues and concerns of all workers from diverse ethno-cultural and religious orientations within the

Union; represented CUPE at the UNWCAR, 2001, in S. Africa. Her current position is Equity VP, for CUPE Local 4400, at the Toronto District School Board. CUPE is Canada's largest union whose 485,000 members work for school boards, hospitals, municipalities, universities, public utilities, homes for the aged, day care centres, children's aid societies, libraries, transit systems, emergency services and other publicly funded employers. In June, 2002, she was elected Executive Vice-President of the Canadian Labour Congress. **COMMUNITY:** active in the Peace Games, Scarborough Basketball Assn., and issues concerning reparations to Blacks as a result of slavery. **EDUCATION:** completing BA, York U.; ECE, Seneca College, 1998; Cert., Human Services Worker, Durham College, 1992. **HEROES/ROLE MODELS:** Parents. **CONTACT:** marie8@canoemail.com; Fax: 416-284-7551

►**CLAYTON, Cyril A., CWO, MMM, CD.**
CHIEF WARRANT OFFICER (Ret.), Department of National Defence, Royal Canadian Regiment, Williamswood, NS. Born: Halifax, NS.

▶ Chief Warrant Officer Cyril Clayton joined the Canadian Army as a regular in 1958, at the age of 17, after serving two years in the army militia. When he retired, 40 yrs. later, he was one of only three Blacks to have reached the rank of Chief Warrant Officer (CWO) in the Infantry Corps, and the first to become Regimental Sergeant Major (RSM) of a major Cdn Base. **CAREER HIGH-LIGHTS:** after his basic training, he was assigned to the 1st Battalion Cdn Guards at Camp Petawawa; he was transferred to the Black Watch Royal Highland Regiment of Canada at Camp Gagetown, NB, in 1959; in 1961, he was promoted to Lance Corporal and served as a Machine Gun Detachment Commander and Section Second-in-Command; in 1964, he was promoted to Full Corporal and employed as a Rifle Section Commander. He began his overseas experience in 1966: went to Norway as a member of the newly creat-

ed Ace Mobile Force; UN Tour of Duty in Cyprus, 1967, as an Observation Post Commander; 1969, promoted to the rank of Sergeant and employed as Platoon Sergeant of a Rifle Platoon. At the time, he was the youngest Sergeant in the Unit. In 1971, he was posted to the Cdn Forces Officer Candidate School at CF Base Chilliwack, as an Instructor. Again, he was one of the first Blacks in the Cdn Military to be employed there; was promoted to Warrant Officer in 1975; in 1980, he was promoted to Master Warrant Officer; he was promoted again in 1981 ("while so employed"), to CWO and was made RSM of the Cdn Contingent UN Middle East on the Golan Heights in Israel; from 1982-86, he carried out the duties of Company Sergeant-Major and Drill Sergeant-Major; in 1986, he was promoted to CWO and became RSM of the RCR Battle School at CFB Petawawa; in 1989 he was appointed RSM of the School of Infantry at CFB Gagetown; and, in 1993, he was appointed RSM of the Combat Training Centre, CFB Gagetown, thereby becoming the first Black to be RSM of a major (more than 1,000 personnel) Cdn base. After 40 yrs. of service, CWO Clayton retired from the military, in 1996. **OTHER:** he is still very active in the community with a number of youth and community organizations; is in the process of collecting information and documenting the role of Blacks in the Military throughout Canada; participated in the preparation of the exhibit, Blacks in the Military, curated by the Halifax Naval Museum, which toured throughout Atlantic Canada. **HONS.:** several including: Medal of Military Merit (MMM); UN Peacekeeping Medal, UN, Cyprus; UN Disengagement Observer Force Medal; GG 125th Anniv. Medal; CF decoration with two bars. **WORKS:** article, *The Company Sergeant Major*, Gagetown, NB. **REVIEWED IN:** military publications; *Toronto Sun;* local & regional newspapers.

►**COLLINS, David**
ACTOR, Toronto, ON. Born: Winnipeg, MB.

▶ David Collins is a teacher, actor and director with a long list of stage, film, radio, and TV credits. As a teacher he has led acting classes at York University and George Brown College. He has developed and facilitated drama programs for grass roots arts organizations such as Fresh Arts, Dixon Hall, Regent Park Community Centre, and St. Christopher House. He has also led workshops in primary, secondary and post-secondary schools throughout Southern Ontario with Shakespeare in Action. As a performer, he has appeared in leading roles from the classics to the most contemporary theatre, including: *Twelfth Night,* Vancouver Playhouse; *A Taste of Honey*, Theatre New Brunswick; the Shaw Festival; *Romeo and Juliet*, Ford Centre; *The Adventures of a Black Girl in Search of God*, du Maurier Theatre. Canadian TV appearances have included: *Nikita*; *Psi Factor*; and *Due South*. He has also appeared in films such as, *To Die For* and Showtime's *Love Songs*. **OTHER:** he has been actively involved in the development of new plays with Nightwood Theatre, Cahoots, and Canadian Stage, in Toronto. He is an active founding member of Obsidian Theatre Co., which is dedicated to the exploration, development, and production of the Black voice on the world stage. **HONS.:** nominee, Dora Mavor Moore Award, for Best Actor, in *The America Play,* 1995. **EDUCATION:** MFA, York U. **CONTACT:** davidrcollins@rogers.com; Fax: 416-538-3890

▶COLLINS, Enid M.

PROFESSOR EMERITUS, NURSING, Ryerson University, Toronto, ON. Born: Jamaica/ in Canada since: 1961.

▶ Professor Enid Collins is a pioneer in the field of nursing. She began her career in Jamaica before immigrating to Canada in the early 1960s. By the time of her retirement in 2001, she had been teaching nursing for over 30 yrs. **CAREER HIGHLIGHTS:** her first position in Canada was as an obstetrical nurse at the Royal Victoria Hospital in Montreal, where she worked with immigrant women. Their limited knowledge of the language and the system in which they found themselves increased her awareness of the impact of culture shock and led her to become an advocate for this group. After two years, she enrolled at McGill U. and completed studies in Public Health and Nursing Education. She later completed graduate degrees in Nursing, as well as Sociology, and Equity in Education. In 1969, she began teaching at the Hospital for Sick Children School of Nursing, where there were no Black nursing students and no other Black instructors. In 1973, she went on to teach at the Ryerson School of Nursing, and remained there until her retirement in 2001. During this time, she served as a mentor and role model, particularly to students and colleagues from racialized groups. **OTHER:** her research interests have included investigation of nurses' complaints related to workplace discrimination. She continues to conduct research on career mobility among immigrant women in Nursing, recognizing that, despite the gains and the increase in numbers of nurses from diverse ethnic backgrounds, many still face a glass ceiling in career advancement. **AFFIL/MBRSHP:** JCA; Sickle Cell Assn.; Women for PACE; U. Hospital of the WI Nurses' Assn. **HONS.:** including, Professor Emeritus, Ryerson U., 2001; Race & Ethnic Relations Leadership Award, North York City Council, 1997. **WORKS:** "Cultural Perspectives in Chronic Illness," in *Health and Cultures: Exploring the Relationships*, 1993; ed., *Holistic Education Newsletter*, OISE, 1994. **EDUCATION:** Doctoral candidate; M.Ed, U of T, 1992; MSN, State U., NY, 1980; BN, McGill U., 1969; RN, Kingston Public Hospital. **MOTTO:** Courage, perseverance, and self-esteem are the ingredients of success. **CONTACT:** ecollins@acs.ryerson.ca

▶COLLINS, Erma B.

PROFESSOR (Ret.), George Brown College, Toronto, ON/ **COMMUNITY VOLUNTEER.** Born: Jamaica/ in Canada since: 1960.

▶ Professor Erma Collins, educator and community volunteer, began her teaching career in Jamaica in 1956, at the elementary school level, and retired in 1998 from George Brown College as Professor of Business English. **HIGHLIGHTS:** her career at George Brown ran from 1966-98; during that time she also served as Chairperson, English and Liberal Studies Dept., St. James Campus, 1987-91. As chairperson, she monitored the development and delivery of 60 post-secondary courses in English, French and Social Sciences. **COMMUNITY INVOLVEMENT:** while engaged professionally, she also found time to serve the community over a 40-yr. period. While teaching primary school in Jamaica, she also ran a community library, tutored students, and served on the executive of the Agricultural Society; during her years as a high school English teacher, she also taught basic English to adults and ran a girls' recreation program five nights per week. Since arriving in Canada in 1960, community activities include: the JCA; BBPA; the Black Educators' Group; Executive, Nat'l Council of Jamaicans and Supportive Org. in Canada; active supporter of the Provincial Liberal Assn.; the CNIB; member, Community Advisory Committee, B'nai Brith Canada. **HONS.:** several including: Harry Jerome Award, BBPA, 2000; Award of Merit, John Brooks Community Foundation, 1998; Urban Alliance Race Relations Award, 1998; Award of Merit, Scarborough, 1996; Volunteer Appreciation Award for 25 yrs. of service, JCA, 1994; GG 125th Anniv. Medal, 1992; Volunteer Service Award, Ont. Min. of Citizenship & Culture, 1986. **WORKS:** several articles and a book, *Brush Up Your English*, 1979. **REVIEWED IN:** community & local newspapers; *Some Black Women*, 1993. **EDUCATION:** M.Ed, OISE/U of T, 1975; BA, U. of Manitoba, 1963; Dipl. Teaching, St. Joseph's Teachers' College, Jamaica, 1955. **MOTTO:** All of us have a reason for giving back to our community. **CONTACT:** ecollins@idirect.com; Fax: 905-472-2617

▶ **COMESEE, Auntie**
PERFORMER/STORYTELLER, Toronto, ON. Born: Guyana/ in Canada since: 1980.
▶ "Auntie Comesee" is the character name by which Pauline Thomas is known. This character, which she developed while in Guyana, represents a country woman who uses local dialect, colourful anecdotes, folk humour and wisdom to illustrate her points; the character is similar to Louise Bennett's "Miss Lou" (*see: Bennett-Coverley, Louise*). PT is a classical singer by training, and has become a dramatist and storyteller whose work in theatre has entertained many members of the Caribbean and Guyanese community, both on stage and on the air. While her work through the character of Auntie Comesee initially met with some opposition by members of the Guyanese population, most have now come to accept the importance of embracing all aspects of a culture's identity, including the Creole spoken by rural inhabitants. She was a member of the Guyana Delegation to Canada's Expo '67, and performed classical pieces as well as patriotic and folk songs. Her success with the character of Auntie Comesee has led to many opportunities. Since settling in Canada, she has become a regular feature and entertainer at Caribbean and Guyanese events and is seen as one who preserves the Guyanese culture by telling popular folk stories and anecdotes in Creole. **OTHER:** she is director of both the adult and the children's choirs at Fellowship Baptist Church in Markham, Ontario, and continues to do solo work as a classical singer. Currently, at over 80 yrs. of age, she is completing a BA at U of T. **HONS.:** several including, ACAA, Arts & Entertainment, 2000; Plaque, on Guyana's 31st Anniv. of Independence, in recognition of her role in keeping Guyanese culture alive in Canada, 1997. **CONTACT:** mckenziewilliams@rogers.com

►COMPTON, Wayde

WRITER/EDITOR, Vancouver, BC. Born: Vancouver, BC, 1972.

► Wayde Compton is a writer, poet and editor, whose writings have appeared in several journals and anthologies. His first book, *49th Parallel Psalm*, is described as, "a history-in-verse of the Black presence in British Columbia," a presence which began in the 1840s and which "puzzlingly" has been omitted from many written records. The book was praised by *january magazine* as "dizzying, exhilarating and seductive…[an] unbearably lucid book that crackles with anger and subversive energy." He is also the editor of *Bluesprint: an Anthology of Black British Columbian Literature and Orature*, 2002, a collection of writings, speeches, stories and poems by Blacks in BC, dealing with issues of race, community, gender, and genre, a first of its kind for BC. After completing his MA in English at SFU, he was the Writer-in-Residence at Green College, UBC. **HONS.:** shortlisted for the Dorothy Livesay Prize, 2000. **WORKS:** ed., *Bluesprint: an Anthology of Black British Columbian Literature & Orature*, 2002; *49th Parallel Psalm*, 1999; articles and poems in several anthologies and literary journals. **REVIEWED IN:** *Globe and Mail; Toronto Star; Vancouver Sun; National Post; FFWD Weekly; Can Literature: a Quarterly of Criticism & Review; Can Content.* **EDUCATION:** MA, English, Simon Fraser U., 2001. **CONTACT:** wcompton@sfu.ca; www.sfu.ca/~wcompton

►COOK, Verda

COMMUNITY VOLUNTEER, Toronto, ON. Born: Toronto, ON.

► Verda Cook was born in Toronto in 1917 and has been involved in serving the community for most of her life. In 1979, she retired from the National Council of the YMCA where she had worked for 31 yrs. and had become the head of her department. Through her involvement with the YMCA, she became the President of the Association of Office Personnel and the National Council Liaison. **COMMUNITY INVOLVEMENT**: Scarborough Women's Community Project; served on the planning committee of A Day with Black Women, which was a component of the Festival of Women and the Arts, 1975; founding member of the Cdn Negro Women's Assn. and served two years as president; member, steering committee for the first Cdn Congress of Black Women; founding member, National Black Coalition; was the Ont. Regional Director of the Sickle Cell Society of Canada, 1982-84; continues to volunteer with the OBHS, the Scarborough Village Seniors' Assn., and, the Ecumenical Network of Women of African Heritage (ENOWAH). **HONS.:** including, Recognition of Contributions, ENOWAH, 2001; Cert. Appreciation, for service to the Black community, Assn. of Black Women, 1993; GG 125th Anniv. Medal, 1992; Kay Livingstone Award, Congress of Black Women/Ontario, 1991; Queen's Silver Jubilee Medal, for contributions to the community, 1977. **REVIEWED IN:** *Some Black Women*, 1993.

►COOLS, The Hon. Anne Clare

SENATOR, Senate of Canada, Ottawa, ON. Born: Barbados/ in Canada since: 1956.

► Senator Anne Cools was appointed to the Senate under the advice of former prime minister Pierre Trudeau, in recognition of her long career in community organization and ensuring social services in the field of family violence and family conflict. Throughout her career, she has been an innovator and leader in the creation of social services to help battered women, families in crisis, and those affected by domestic violence. **CAREER HIGHLIGHTS:** in 1974, she founded Women in Transition (WIT), one of the first shelters for battered women in Canada, and served as its Executive Director. She succeeded in having WIT registered as a United Way member agency and assisted other battered women's shelters in Ontario to get started. In 1987, under her guidance, WIT opened a second women's shelter. She served as a Field Instructor to students at Seneca College (1977-89), with the Faculty of Social Work, U of T (1977-78), and with Ryerson Polytechnic (1978-80); since 1999, she is a Field Supervisor in the PhD Program, Dept. of Educational and Counselling Psychology, at McGill U. As a long-standing Liberal Party supporter, she ran twice for Federal office, 1979 and 1980 (she is the subject of an NFB film, *The Right Candidate for Rosedale*); she was also Vice-Chair of the GTA Liberal Caucus, 1993-95. As a Senator, she has worked on a number of Bills including: Bill C-20, the Clarity Bill regarding Quebec Secession; Bill C-41, amending the Divorce Act; Bill C-37 and Bill C-42, amending the Judges Act; Bill C-21, amending the Unemployment Insurance Act. She is currently the Deputy Chair of the Standing Senate Committee on National Finance and is also a member of the Senate Standing Committee on Legal and Constitutional Affairs. She was also a leading member of the Special Joint Senate-Commons Committee on Child Custody & Access. She has also served on several other Senate Committees, including Standing Committee on Social Affairs, Science and Technology, the Standing Committee on Banking, Trade and Commerce, and the Task Force on the Meech Lake Accord. **COMMUNITY INVOLVEMENT:** LaMarch Centre for Research on Violence and Conflict Resolution; Prayer Book Society of Canada; Black Education Project; Black Theatre Canada; Metro Toronto Social Planning Council. **HONS.:** several including: Cert. of Recognition as Canada's first Black Senator, from Howard University; Bob Marley Day Award, for promoting equality, peace, and harmony, 2001; Person of the Year, Real Women of Canada, 1999; Spiritual Mother of the Year, NA'AMAT, 1997; ACAA, for outstanding achievement in politics, 1997. **REVIEWED IN:** nat'l publications; *WWIC*; *WWCW*; *Millennium Minds*, 2000; *Some Black Women*, 1993. **EDUCATION:** BA, McGill U. **CONTACT:** Fax: 613-992-8513

▶**COOPER, Afua,** PhD.
PROFESSOR OF SOCIOLOGY/POET, Ryerson University, 350 Victoria St., Toronto, ON M5B 2K3. Born: Jamaica/ in Canada since: 1980.
▸ Afua Cooper is a well-known poet and historian. She is the author of four books of poetry, and is credited with co-authoring the first book on Black women's history in Canada, *We're Rooted Here and They Can't Pull Us Up: Essays in African Canadian Women's History*, 1999. She is also the first woman in Canada to graduate with a PhD in African-Canadian History. She currently teaches at Ryerson University; in 2002, curated two exhibits in Toronto, on Black history and life in nineteenth century Toronto, displayed at the Royal Ontario Museum, and at MacKenzie House. **HONS.:** including, Honourable Colonel, for contributions to the study of Kentucky's history and life of Blacks, (Kentucky's highest award), Louisville, KY, 2002; Fellowship, Brown U., 2001; Joseph Brant Award, Best Book on Ontario History, 1997; *Casa de las Americas* prize for poetry, 1992. **WORKS:** including, *Utterances & Incantations: Women, Poetry, & Dub*, 1999; *Memories Have Tongue*, 1992; articles in: *Atlantis, a Women's Studies J; Can Rev of American Studies; Ontario History*. **EDUCATION:** PhD, History, U of T, 2000. **MOTTO:** God is good, I thank Her for Her goodness.

▶**COOPER-WILSON, Jane**
HISTORIAN/ARTIST/WRITER, TigerLily Enterprises, P.O. Box 2, Duntroon, ON L0M 1H0. Born: Collingwood, ON.
▸ Jane Cooper-Wilson, local historian and artist, has undertaken the task of protecting the cultural heritage of her ancestors through research, writing and local restoration initiatives. In 1997-98 she was the driving force behind the restoration and re-dedication of the inter-racial Bethel-Union Pioneer Cemetery, in Sunnidale Township, where many of her relatives, descended from those who

had escaped to Canada via the UGRR, are buried. As an artist, she has also produced a number of paintings, most notably the Millennium Mural, commissioned by the Town of Collingwood and the Blue Mountain Foundation for the Arts, unveiled Fall, 2001. Her artwork can be found in private and public collections (e.g. Cdn Wildlife Federation, JS Redpath Collection). Having researched her family history and tracing them to Madagascar, then the US, before their arrival in Canada, she is currently writing a historical novel entitled *Morgan's Seed*, based on the life of her ancestor, John Morgan Sr., born in Madagascar in 1763, and who died in Old Sunnidale Township at the age of 110. **HONS.:** Robert G. Kemp Award, for literary & artistic excellence, 2000. **HEROES/ROLE MODELS:** James J. Cooper, father. **CONTACT:** janiew100@yahoo.ca

►COOPSAMMY, Madeline F.

WRITER/POET, Winnipeg, MB. Born: Trinidad & Tobago/ in Canada since: 1968.

▶ Madeline Coopsammy is a teacher who writes poetry and short stories. Through her works and her community involvement, she has been active in issues relating to immigrant women and equality in education. Her poetry and short stories have been published in anthologies and journals in Canada and the US. The 1995 conference held in Toronto and celebrating 150 years of East Indians in Trinidad was entitled, *The Second Migration,* from the title of one of her poems. **WORKS:** poems include: *Immigrant; For My Daughter; In the Dungeon of My Skin; The Second Migration;* and have been published in magazines & anthologies. Short stories: *The Tick-tick Bicycle; The Boy from Petitville; The Sedge is Withered;* have been published in: *Caribe & Excite* magazines, and in *The Whistling Bird: Women Writers of the Caribbean; The Insiders in Jahaji: An Anthology of Indo-Caribbean Fiction.* **EDUCATION:** M.Ed, B.Ed, U. of Manitoba. BA/Hons., Delhi U., India. **CONTACT:** mcoopssa@shaw.ca

►CRAWFORD, Rachael

ACTOR, c/o Fusion Artists Inc., Ste. 401-401 Richmond St. W., Toronto, ON M5V 3A8. Born: London, ON, 1969.

▶ Rachael Crawford is an actor who has appeared in TV and film. She is one of Canada's most recognizable film actors with credits including lead roles in *Pale Saints, When Night is Falling, Curtis' Charm,* and Clement Virgo's award-winning, *Rude,* which earned her a Genie Award nomination for Best Performance by a Supporting Actress, and which premiered at Cannes, 1995. TV credits include*: Traders;* she was a regular on several series, *Between Brothers, Here and Now, Brewster Place* and *ENG*; she also appeared in episodes of *The Outer Limits* and *Side Effects.* Her performance in the TV movie, *The James Mink Story,* co-starring Lou Gossett, Jr., was nominated for a Gemini Award for Best Performance by a Lead Actress; she has also starred in the TV movies, *In His Father's Shoes,* and, *We The Jury.* **HONS.:** Gemini Award nominations: *Inside Stories*; *The James Mink Story*; *Traders*; Genie Award nominations: *Rude*; *Pale Saints.* **CONTACT:** Fax: 416-408-4867

►CRAWLEY, Iona

NURSE/RECRUITMENT-RETENTION CONSULTANT, School of Nursing, Dalhousie University, 5869 University Ave., Halifax, NS B3H 3J5. Born: Halifax, NS.

▶ Iona Crawley, a nurse by training, is currently a consultant with the School of Nursing at Dalhousie University and is responsible for the recruitment and retention of African-Nova Scotian students to this program. She is the first to occupy such a position. **CAREER HIGHLIGHTS:** first Black to serve on Halifax School Brd., 1971-79; owned and operated the first Black Business School in Atlantic Canada, 1984; founder and director of Wee Care Developmental Centre for Disabled Children, 1973-80; founder of Sister to

Sister, the first Black Women's Breast Cancer Support Group, 1999; first Black to serve on the Brd. of Directors, Saint Mary's U., and chaired their Affirmative Action Council, 1989-92. She has also carried out a significant amount of work on domestic violence within the Black population in NS. In 2001, she spearheaded the making of an educational video, entitled *No More Secrets* (produced by Sylvia Hamilton, *see: Hamilton, Sylvia*), to encourage women to break the silence about this condition to which many are subjected. **HONS.:** several including: inductee, Dr. W.P. Oliver Wall of Honour, 2002; Dr. W.P. Oliver Award, for work with African Nova Scotians in Literacy & Adult Education, 2000; YWCA Women's Recognition Award, for Community Service, 1986 & 2001 (the only woman to have received this twice); several other awards & certificates for work with disabled children, volunteerism, and adult education. **WORKS:** several articles on Early Childhood Education; papers on breast cancer and the Black community. **REVIEWED IN:** *Chatelaine*, 1977 & '76, "Top 50 women in Canada"; local and community papers. **EDUCATION:** Developmental Disabilities, New York U., 1973. Mount St. Vincent U. & Institute of Early Childhood Education, 1978, '73, '66. **HEROES/ROLE MODELS:** Wilphemina Williams, former teacher. **CONTACT:** icrawley@hfx.eastlink.ca; Fax: 902-876-8249

▶CRICHLOW, Wesley, PhD.
ACTIVIST/ASSISTANT PROFESSOR, Dept. of Law, Carleton University, 1125 Colonel By Dr., Ottawa, ON K1S 5B6.

▶ Dr. Wesley Crichlow is an Assistant Professor in the Dept. of Law at Carleton University, since 2000. He is best known as a community and gay rights activist and advocate who seeks to raise awareness about social and legal obstacles faced by Blacks who engage in non-heterosexual practices. **ACTIVITIES:** has been a visiting professor at the Akwesasne First Nations Reserve Adult Education program and a visiting instructor at the First Nations Technical Institute, Tyendinaga Mohawk Territory, through Carleton U.'s School of Social Work. He has lectured on race and ethnic relations at Carleton U. with the Centre for Research-Action on Race Relations. He has also been involved in research on the treatment of Young Offenders by the legal system and developed, with members of a research team, a form of restorative justice to deal with those in the system. He is a former owner of the bookstore, A Different Booklist, in Toronto. **HONS.:** Professor of the Year Teaching Award, B.Ed. Pre-Service Program, OISE/U of T, 2002; article, "Buller Men and Batty Bwoys" nominated for Lambada Non-Fiction Literary Award, 2001. **WORKS:** including: "Buller Men & Batty Bwoys," in *A Queer Country*, 2001; *Facing Race Before the Courts*, on Nat'l Judicial Institute website for judges, 2000; *Black Male Rastafariansism: Racism & Stereotyping*, for the Quebec HRC, 2000; "Migration, Identity, and a Black Same-Sex Consciousness," in *Ma'ka Diasporic Juks: Contemporary Writings by Queers of African Descent*, 1997; "Understanding the World of the Black Child" in *Orbit*, 1994. **EDUCATION:** PhD, 1998; M.Ed, 1990, OISE/U of T. BA/Hons., York U., 1988. **MOTTO:** Learn to unlearn and make life experience teachable moments. **CONTACT:** Tel: 613-520-2600 ext. 3823; wcrichlow@oise.utoronto.ca

▶CROOKS, Charmaine
OLYMPIAN/IOC MEMBER, International Olympic Committee/NGU Consulting, Vancouver, BC. Born: Jamaica/ in Canada since: 1973.

▶ Charmaine Crooks is a five-time Olympian, representing Canada from 1980-97 in athletics and competing in track events (400m, 800m, and 4x400m relay). **CAREER HIGHLIGHTS**: was the Opening Ceremonies Flag Bearer at the 1996 Olympics; an Olympic Silver Medallist (1984); Pan Am World Cup and Commonwealth Games Gold Medallist; she was 11 times national champion in the 400m and 800m (from 1980-97); is the first Canadian woman to run the 800m in under two minutes. She was elected, 1996 and 2000 as a member of the IOC; was a member of the Toronto 2008 Olympic Bid Committee and is a member of the 2010 BC Olympic Bid Committee; founding member of the independent IOC Ethics Commission, 1999-2001, and current member of the IOC Press Commission. **CURRENT ACTIVITIES:** is President of NGU Consulting, which provides strategic counsel for sports organizations and corporations at an international level; is a freelance TV host, producer and motivational speaker; co-hosted CBC TV's *In the Company of Women*, 1999/2000; has worked on air as host or analyst on programs such as the Canada Winter and Summer Games (CBC, TSN); hosted the first nationwide TV program on cycling and fitness, *Cycle*, which aired on CBC and OTN; since 1997, has hosted the internationally televised World Athletics Gala from Monaco; is the creator and producer of the *Comic Relief*-style show, *No Laughing Matter*, which raises funds for breast cancer research. CC volunteers her time in support of various national and international charities, which focus on children and women. She recently created Sports-Cares, helping disadvantaged youth get involved in sports and healthy lifestyles. **AFFIL/MBRSHP:** sits on several corporate and non-profit boards; member, AIM Mutual Funds, serves on Corporate Advisory Brd. and Governance Cmtee; continues to volunteer with athletic bodies: Chair, Pan American Athletes Commission; Brd., Cdn Centre for Ethics in Sport; Executive Brd., Cdn Olympic Cmtee, Director of Int'l Relations; co-Chair, 2003 World Weightlifting Championships; Past co-Chair of Federal Govt. Task Force on financing for amateur sports in Canada, 2002. **HONS.:** including, inducted into Athletics Hall of Fame, U. Texas, 2001; BC Business "Top 40 under 40," 1997; Bruce Kidd Award, for athletic leadership, 1996; GG Award, for community service, 1993; John F. Bassett Award, for out-

standing community work and sporting excellence, 1991; BC Track & Field Athlete of the Year, 1990, '91; Olympic Silver Medal, 4x400m, 1984. **REVIEWED IN:** nat'l and int'l publications; *WWIC*; *WWCW*. **EDUCATION:** BA, U. of Texas/El Paso, 1985. **HEROES/ROLE MODELS:** Parents. **MOTTO:** Never give up! **CONTACT:** www.ccrooks.com

▶CROOKS, Kipling

PRESIDENT/OWNER, K.K. Machine Products Inc., 64, boul, Huot, ND de l'isle Perrot, QC J7V 5V6. Born: Jamaica/ in Canada since: 1973.

▶ Kipling Crooks is the president and owner of KK Machine Products, a high-tech machine shop he started in 1984. Since its inception, the company has been manufacturing state-of-the-art machined components for technologically advanced companies in the telecommunication, aerospace, and electronic industries. Clients include: Nortel (worldwide), CMC, Mitec, EMS, LSI Technologies, and many others. **OTHER:** he was a non-commissioned officer in the Royal Engineers and Air Corps for 12 yrs.; was a member of Concordia University's Board for the Faculty of Commerce and Administration for four yrs.; and, established the KK Charity Foundation, in 1999. **HONS.:** Jackie Robinson Award for Outstanding Achievement in Business, MABBP, 1990. **WORKS:** *Montreal Gazette*, 1999. **REVIEWED IN:** *Industrial Machinery; L'Etoile; La Presse*. **EDUCATION:** Royal Engineering College, 1962. **HEROES/ROLE MODELS:** Mother. **MOTTO:** No impossibilities, just degrees of difficulties. **CONTACT:** kip@kkmp.com; www.kkmp.com

▶CURLING, Alvin, CD(JM).

MEMBER PROVINCIAL PARLIAMENT (MPP), Legislative Assembly of Ontario, Toronto. Born: Jamaica/ in Canada since: 1965.

▶ Alvin Curling is the MPP for the riding of Scarborough-Rouge River in the Ontario Legislature. In 1985, he became the first Liberal MPP elected to the riding of Scarborough North (now Scarborough-Rouge River). In his first win in 1985, he amassed the highest total vote in Canadian history, and has since been re-elected four times, making him one of the longest-serving Members in the Ontario Legislature. **HIGHLIGHTS:** under the David Peterson government, AC served as Minister of Housing, 1985-87; served as Ontario's Minister of Skills Development with special responsibility for Literacy, 1987-89; 1990, was the Parliamentary Assistant to the Premier and the Minister of Intergovernmental Affairs; served on the Premier's Council on Science and Technology. As a member of the Official Opposition, he has served as Ontario Liberal Critic for Housing, Urban Affairs, Solicitor General, Youth Employment, Colleges and Universities, Human Rights and the Disabled. And, he has held caucus positions as Deputy Opposition House Leader and Deputy Whip; currently, he is the Critic for Training, Skills and Development. **OTHER:** was an Educational Administrator at Seneca College; worked in management of housing and land settlement in Jamaica before immigrating to Canada. **COMMUNITY:** has served on a number of Boards and committees, including: Chair, Advisory Brd., Caribana Cultural Committee; World Hunger Project; President, World Literacy of Canada; Advisory Brd., Chinese Cultural Centre; Brd. of Directors, Tri-Vision. **HONS.:** several, including, Order of Distinction, Commander, Govt. of Jamaica, 2001. **EDUCATION:** Seneca College; York U.; U. of Technology, Kingston, Jamaica. **HEROES/ROLE MODELS:** Father. **MOTTO:** Action feels better than words. **CONTACT:** alvin_curling-mpp@ontla.ola.org; www.alvincurling.com

▶**DADSON SR., Joseph E.,** P.Eng.
BIO-MEDICAL ENGINEER/PRESIDENT/CEO, Newsol Technologies, Ste. 10-5250 Finch Ave. E., Toronto, ON M1S 5A5. Born: Ghana/ in Canada since: 1962.

▶ Joseph Dadson Sr. is a bio-medical engineer who has specialized in the creation and development of portable dialysis machines. He is the President of Newsol Technologies, a company he founded in 1997, which specializes in an Automated Peritoneal Dialysis System including machines, disposable products and solutions. **CAREER HIGHLIGHTS:** 1976-97, co-founder and CEO of Medionics International, where he invented the first portable Volumetric Peritoneal Dialysis machine, significant for its reduction of handling-induced peritonitis (peritoneum infection) and for increasing patient mobility; he invented a Quick Connect-Disconnect Cap, which reduced the incidence of peritonitis while resulting in greater convenience and cost-saving for dialysis treatment; also invented the disposable Y-Set that has become the industry standard and which has reduced peritoneal dialysis infection rate from once per year to once per three years or even less frequently. His most recent invention is the smallest dialysis machine ever and incorporates a number of distinctive operating and diagnostic features. JED began his professional career as a Technical Administrator in the Nephrology Dept., Toronto General Hospital, 1972-83. **AFFIL/MBRSHP:** member of the Cdn Standards Assn. and co-founder of the Assn. of Ontario Medical Manufacturers. **HONS.:** including: Cdn Black Achievement Award, Science, *Pride*, 1994; GG 125th Anniv. Medal, 1993; Achievement & Civic Recognition Award, Business, Town of Markham, 1992; Harry Jerome Award, Business, BBPA, 1991; Award for Excellence in Product Innovation, Markham Brd. of Trade, to Medionics International, 1990; Gold Medal for Small Business, Canada Awards for Business Excellence, Govt. of Canada to

Medionics International, 1987. **WORKS:** holds a number of patents in Canada, US, & Japan, related to dialysis inventions. **EDUCATION:** Graduate Studies, Bio-Medical Engineering, U. of NB, 1970; B. Applied Sc., UBC, 1968. **MOTTO:** Only the best is good enough! **CONTACT:** jdadson@newsoltech.com; www.newsoltech.com

▶**DALEY, Sandy**

ACTOR/ENTREPRENEUR, Chocolate Dolls Productions, Toronto, ON. Born: Jamaica/ in Canada since: 1987.

▶ Sandy Daley is an actor who has appeared in film, TV, music videos and theatre; she starred in *Another Planet* by Christene Browne, the first Canadian feature film to be written, directed, and produced by a Black woman (*see: Browne, Christene*). *Another Planet* appeared at a number of international film festivals and won the Best Foreign Film Award in Germany. SD is also an entrepreneur and owns Chocolate Dolls Productions, which consists of a clothing line and the Chocolate Doll Calendar, which highlights achievements of Canadian women in the entertainment industry. **REVIEWED IN:** *Sophisticate's Black Hair*; *Hollywood Film Festival Report*; community & nat'l publications. **EDUCATION:** Corporate Communications, Centennial College, 1994. **MOTTO:** I will not live and wonder, "what if?" **CONTACT:** sandydaley88@hotmail.com; www.chocolatedolls.com

▶**DANIEL, Juliet,** PhD.

ASSISTANT PROFESSOR, Dept. of Biology, McMaster University, LSB-331, 1280 Main St. W., Hamilton, ON L8S 4K1. Born: Barbados, 1964/ in Canada since: 1989.

▶ Dr. Juliet Daniel is an Assistant Professor in the Dept. of Biology at McMaster U., a position she has held since 1999. She teaches a second-year undergraduate course in cell biology and a third-year course on molecular biology of the nucleus. Her areas of research are related to cancer and include Cadherin-mediated cell adhesion, signal transduction and tumor metastasis. After completing her doctorate at UBC in microbiology in 1994, she was awarded a post-doctoral research fellowship at St. Jude Children's Research Hospital in Memphis, Tennessee. JD's work has already been published in a number of leading scientific journals; her most significant discovery to date has been the cloning and identification of a new transcription factor, which she has named "Kaiso," in honour of calypso music. Her research objective is to determine Kaiso's role in cell adhesion, signal transduction and/or tumor progression. In the long term, her findings may lead to the development of therapeutic strategies and animal models for the treatment of malignant tumors. **HONS.:** several academic and research awards including, Ontario Premier Research Excellence Award, McMaster, 2001-2006; Poster Award, Vanderbilt Ingram Cancer Center Retreat, 1999; NSERC pre- (1989-91) & post- (1994-96) doctoral scholarships. **WORKS:** in *Hybridoma*; *J Cell Biology*; *J Biological Chemistry*; *Molecular and Cellular Biology*; *Genomics*; *Oncogene*. **REVIEWED IN:** *Millennium Minds*, 2000. **EDUCATION:** PhD, Microbiology, UBC, 1994; BSc, Life Sciences, Queen's U., 1987. **HEROES/ROLE MODELS:** Dr. Leda Raptis, colleague; Dr. Colin Nurse, colleague. **MOTTO:** We are what we repeatedly do. Excellence, then, is not an act, but a habit. (Aristotle) **CONTACT:** danielj@mcmaster.ca; www.science.mcmaster.ca/biology

▶**DANIEL-LEWIS, Emily Louise**

ADMINISTRATIVE ASSISTANT/SOCIAL WORKER (Ret.), Negro Community Centre, Verdun, QC. Born: Montreal, QC.

▶ Emily Louise Daniel-Lewis has the distinction of being one of the first women of African descent to receive a Bachelor of Arts degree from Sir George Williams College (now Concordia U.), in 1944. But, due to employment practices at the time, it was still difficult for educated Blacks to secure employment in their professional fields. Working in a number of administrative positions in the business sector, she made significant contributions to community organizations including: the Negro Community Centre, 1944-80; YWCA; Girl Guides of Canada; founding member, The Pioneer Girls, which assisted domestics who came to Canada under the government program; Co-op Club, Union United Church; Congress of Black Women; Altrusa International of Montreal, professional women's service club; founding member, Council of Black Aging Community; United Red Feather, now Centraide; Montreal Council of Women; St. George's Anglican Church and Sunday School. **HONS.:** including, Community Afro-Quebec of Little Burgundy, 1993; Council of Black Aging Community, 1992; Caribbean Pioneer Women, 1989; Negro Community Centre, 1964. **EDUCATION:** Associate of Social Work, McGill School of Social Work; BA, Sir George Williams College (now Concordia U.); Licentiate in Music (Piano), McGill U. **HEROES/ROLE MODELS:** Father: "I still remember his kindness to others & his love of life." **MOTTO:** Look for the good at all times!

▶**DAVIDSON, Patricia, MD, FACP.**
INTERNIST & CARDIOLOGIST, Private Practice, Ste. 118-106 Irving St. NW, Washington, DC 20010, USA. Born: Montreal, QC.

▶ Dr. Patricia Davidson is a medical internist and cardiologist, originally from Montreal, who now practises in the Washington area. She is one of fewer than 30 Black women cardiologists in the US. She has been praised for her pioneering work in medicine, particularly in the area of women's health in cardiovascular diseases, and is recognized throughout the US as an expert in this area. **HIGHLIGHTS:** served as Assistant Professor in the Division of Hypertension and Cardiology at the U. of Maryland Medical School, 1985-88; was an Instructor of Medicine at the Howard U. Medical School, 1982-83; and serves as a Master Faculty member for Women and Heart Disease for the American Medical Women's Assn. (AMWA). **OTHER:** because of her expertise and particular interest in heart disease in women, particularly African Americans and other ethnic populations, PD is regularly interviewed on radio, TV and in print on health and heart disease; also speaks regularly to local and national organizations on this topic. She worked with congresswoman Maxine Waters in the preparation of the amendment to the Women's Health Research and Prevention Act, and was cited in the Congressional Record upon passage of the bill. **AFFIL/MBRSHP:** Diplomat, American Brd. of Internal Medicine; Fellow of the American College of Physicians; Assn. of Black Cardiologists, 1988-90; American Heart Assn., 1992-98, and chaired Task Force on Women and Heart Disease, 1993-94; appointed Governor, region 3, by the American Medical Women's Assn.; currently chair of the Task Force on Ethnic Women's Health. **HONS.:** several including, First Inductee into the Washington, DC Hall of Fame, Medicine, Class of 2000; Silver Heart Award, American Heart Assn., 1999. **WORKS:** research has been published in: *Minority Health Today, Practical Cardiology*; wrote a chapter in *Ethnic Factors in Health Disease.* **EDUCATION:** Residency (Surgical, Medical) & Fellowship (Cardiology): Howard U., Washington, DC, 1979-85; MD, U. Louisville Medical School, KY, 1978; MSc, Atlanta U., GA, 1974; BSc, U. of Michigan, 1972. **CONTACT:** padavidsonmd@aol.com; Tel: 202-726-4600

▶**DAVIS, Rev. Erica**
MINISTER, British Methodist Episcopal Church, 83 Essex St., Guelph, ON N1H 6K5. Born: St. Vincent/ in Canada since: 1973.

▶ Rev. Erica Davis was ordained in 1994 and was appointed Minister of the Guelph British Methodist Episcopal (BME), a church that had been closed since 1979. She is one of three female ministers in the BME church across Canada. The Guelph BME is significant as it was built in 1880 by fugitive slaves who arrived in the area via the UGRR. Since re-opening the church, ED also works at researching and sharing the history of Blacks in the Guelph area and telling of their contributions to the community of the day. She has also, in recent years, organized a series of lectures and presentations (BME Black History Lecture Series) at the church to increase awareness of Black history. **OTHER:** by training, she is a Quality Control Chemist; is president of the Methodist Student Group, U. of Guelph, a group she started in 1989; is also a chaplain at the Homewood Health Centre and the Guelph General Hospital. **REVIEWED IN:** *Guelph Mercury; Guelph Tribune.* **EDUCATION:** M.Div., McMaster U., 1996; BA, Religious Studies, U. of Waterloo, 1994; BSc, U of T. **MOTTO:** Hard work never kills anyone, but it will help one to achieve his/her goals if s/he persists. **CONTACT:** Tel: 519-763-7137

▶DAVIS, Rodney, CA.
PROPRIETOR/CHARTERED ACCOUNTANT, Nappy's Inc./Chartered Accounting Practice, Pickering, ON. Born: Jamaica/ in Canada since: 1968.

▶ Rodney Davis is the president and one of the founders of Nappy's Inc., a chain of hair salons. Nappy's was founded in 1990 with a mission to improve the service and quality of men's and women's haircare services in Toronto; the company now has five locations throughout southwestern Ontario. **CAREER HIGHLIGHTS:** he began his career at KPMG-Peat Marwick Thorne, 1989-95, as a Senior Audit Consultant and Manager in Corporate Finance, and Mergers and Acquisitions. In 1995, he left KPMG to join Southam Inc., Canada's largest newspaper publisher, with

revenues of $1.3-billion annually; soon he was appointed to the position of VP, Finance, and Corporate Controller responsible for all aspects of the company's accounting, finance and treasury, including public financial reporting, business plan approval, capital budgets and newspaper acquisitions. While at Southam, he was instrumental in the negotiation and purchase of the *Financial Post* and the launch of the *National Post* newspaper. He then joined Maxxcom Inc., where he served as VP, Corporate Development, planning and executing the company's corporate development program and leading the acquisition program for Cybersight, while taking the company public on the Toronto Stock Exchange. In June 2000, he joined MGI, a provider of visual media software products and infrastructure, as their CFO. **COMMUNITY INVOLVEMENT:** interim CEO, Caribana; Ontario Science Centre; Canadian Stage Theatre; CAN: BAIA; Innoversity. **HONS.:** recognized as one of "distinguished Peel Region graduates," Positively Peel Campaign, 1993. **EDUCATION:** CA, Institute Chartered Accountants, 1992; B.Bus.Mngmt, Ryerson U., 1989. **CONTACT:** rodneyd-ca@rogers.com; www.nappyshairshoppe.com

▶DAVIS, Wells
OWNER & MANAGING PARTNER, Clarity – Independent Strategic Consultancy, and Urban Engine Communications, 510 Front St. W., Toronto, ON M5H 3H3. Born: Jamaica, 1965/ in Canada since: 1967.

▶ Prior to starting the firms, Clarity and Urban Engine, Wells Davis was head of the Strategy Dept. of Canada's largest advertising and communications agency, MacLaren McCann. He and his team were responsible for developing communications strategies for some of Canada's largest companies, including GM, Royal Bank, Microsoft, Rogers Cable, Nissan, Apple, Ford, Xerox, H&R Block, the Toronto Zoo, and others. These strategies were then used in the development of TV, print, magazine, internet, promotions, and direct mail communications. In addition to his expertise in advertising, he is also a professional researcher; prior to joining MacLaren McCann, he spent three years with DesRosiers Automotive Research as a Sr. Consultant and Managing Editor. There, he conducted industry forecasts and wrote a newsletter on the automotive industry; he regularly conducts primary research for his advertising clients; and has appeared on CBC *Newsworld* and CBC Radio as an expert on advertising. **HONS.:** has contributed to award-winning campaigns for clients (e.g. Toronto Zoo, Rogers Cable, GM, Ford, Nissan, Shoppers Drug Mart). **WORKS:** contributes to trade press and the media on effective use of strategic planning. **EDUCATION:** Public Policy & Administration, York U.; Canadian Securities Institute. **HEROES/ROLE MODELS:** Beverly Davis: "she taught me how to persevere & how to love." **MOTTO:** Ain't nothing to it but do it! **CONTACT:** Tel: 416-848-9789; wdavis@skyadmedia.com

▶DAWKINS, Ettie E.

DIRECTOR OF MARKETING, Ettie Dawkins Fashion Sales Agency, Ste. 106-111 Peter St. Toronto, ON. Born: Jamaica/ in Canada since: 1968.
▶ Ettie Dawkins is a former model who is now Director of Marketing of her own company. Since 1996, she has been holding the Cotillion Ball, an annual event designed to provide Black youth with an opportunity to learn and practise good social conduct and proper etiquette. She initiated this activity in order to empower youth through education and social awareness, and to facilitate their ability to interact with others in a wide variety of social and professional situations. **HONS.:** Harry Jerome Award, BBPA, 2001; Cert., for Year of Volunteers, City of Toronto, 2001; PACE Maker Award, 1993; GG 125th Anniv. Medal, 1992; Hadassah Book of Life, 1977. **REVIEWED IN:** *Toronto Star*; *Canadian Living* magazine; *Jamaica Gleaner; The Black Canadians*, 1998. **CONTACT**: Fax: 416-593-5979

▶de B'BERI, Boulou E.

FILMMAKER/ACTIVIST, Montreal, QC. Born: Cameroon/ in Canada since: 1992.
▶ Boulou de B'beri is recognized as a critically engaged filmmaker and activist; currently he is concluding a PhD dissertation in Communication Studies (Concordia U.), with the focus on discourse analysis and cultural studies. His research addresses questions of the materiality of image in cinema and knowledge transmission of African heritage in the Americas, narrative questions of African oral tradition, and discourse analysis of media in traditional and intercultural milieu. He is the author of many articles dealing with questions of Scriptural Economy of Black African Cinemas. His last documentary film, *Looking for My Pygmalion–Mémoires*, 2001, dealt with the issues of being Black in Quebec; it was acclaimed in Toronto's Get Reel Black Film Festival 2001, and is in the program of many film festivals around the world. In 2001-02, he was a Doctoral Fellow at the Center for Black Studies, University of California at Santa Barbara; he is also a trained modern and traditional dancer. **HONS.:** nominee, *Looking for My Pygmalion–Mémoires,* Reel Black Film Festival, 2001. **WORKS:** in progress, *Beyond Discourse, Experience of Verb in Black African Cinemas* (book); ed., a volume of the *J of Film Studies, CINEMAS*, 2000. **EDUCATION:** PhD in progress, Concordia University. MA, Film Studies, 1998; MA, 1997; Cert., Creative Writing, 1995, UQAM. **CONTACT:** be2beri@canada.com; http://boulou.fr.st

▶deGRAFT-JOHNSON, Ama, MD, FRCPC.

ANAESTHESIOLOGIST/CLINICAL PROFESSOR, Hamilton Health Sciences Centre, 237 Barton St., Hamilton, ON L8L 2X2. Born: Ghana/ in Canada since: 1973.
▶ Dr. Ama deGraft-Johnson is an anaesthesiolo-

gist at the Hamilton Health Sciences Centre; she is also an Assistant Clinical Professor of Anaesthesia at McMaster University. She is a member of the Agape Samaritan International HQ in the US. **HONS.:** Outstanding Female Professional, Ghanaian-Canadian Business & Professional Assn., 1997. **EDUCATION:** specialized in Anaesthesia, McMaster U., 1981; MB, ChB, U. of Ghana, 1971. **MOTTO:** You only get out of life what you put in. **CONTACT:** adegjohn@attcanada.ca

▶**DEI, George J.S.,** PhD.
PROFESSOR & CHAIR, Dept. of Sociology, Ontario Institute for Studies in Education (OISE), University of Toronto, 252 Bloor St. W., Toronto, ON M5S 1V6. Born: Ghana/ in Canada since: 1979.

▶ Dr. George Dei is Professor and Chair of the Dept. of Sociology and Equity Studies in Education, and is cross-appointed to the Dept. of Anthropology, U of T. He served as the first Director of the Centre for Integrative Anti-Racism Studies (CIARS) at OISE/U of T from 1996-2000. Research and teaching areas include: anti-racism and domination studies; sociology of race and ethnicity; international development; indigenous knowledge and anti-colonial thought; political ecology; and ethnography. **HONS.:** several, including: Community Partnership Award, TCDSB, 2001; Ghanaian News Award, for education & community development, 2000; Research Associate, Joint Centre of Excellence for Research on Immigration & Settlement, 1998-present; Volunteer Services Award, Min. of Citizenship, 1996; Fellow, Society for Applied Anthropology, Washington, DC, 1996-present. **WORKS:** selected, 8 books including: *Inclusive Schooling,* 2001; *Power, Knowledge and Anti-Racism Education,* 2000; *Removing the Margins: The Challenges and Possibilities of Inclusive Schooling,* 2000. Also, 27 chapters in books, 46 papers in refereed journals. **EDUCATION:** PhD, U of T, 1986; MA, McMaster

U., 1980; BA, U. of Ghana, 1978. **HEROES/ROLE MODELS:** Mother. **CONTACT:** gdei@oise.utoronto.ca; Fax: 416-926-4751

▶**DEVERELL, Rita Shelton,** Dr.
VICE-PRESIDENT, New Concept Development, Vision TV, 80 Bond St., Toronto, ON M5B 1X2. Born: USA/ in Canada since: 1967.

▶ Dr. Rita Shelton Deverell is Vision TV's Vice-President, New Concept Development, and Executive Producer of the network's award-winning human affairs programming. She is by training and experience, an actor, broadcaster, writer, arts consultant, and university professor. Since joining Vision TV in 1988, she has been the founding producer of the Gemini Award-winning human affairs programs *Skylight,* and *It's About Time*, and the creator of *Arts Express*, a series on spirituality and the arts. **PREVIOUS ACTIVITIES:** Host and producer of CBC's *Take 30* and *Access*; Acting Director of the School of Journalism, U. of Regina. **HONS.:** include, Urban Alliance on Race Relations 25th Anniv. Award, 2000; Cdn Black Achievement Award, media, 1995; Award, for outstanding contribution, WIFT/Toronto, 1995; *Maclean's* Honour Roll of Outstanding Cdns, 1993; Dodi Robb Award, Media Watch, 1993; Canada Award, Gemini Awards, 1993; Writers Club Award, for excellence in presenting diversity; Professional Woman of the Year, YWCA/Regina, 1987; among "Women to Watch," *Chatelaine*, 1986. **WORKS:** chapter in, *Deadlines and Diversity.* **REVIEWED IN:** *Millennium Minds*, 2000. **EDUCATION:** Ed.D, Educational Theory, U of T; MA, History of Religions, Columbia U.; BA, Adelphi U. **HEROES/ROLE MODELS:** Parents and numerous industry role models. **CONTACT:** c/o: alang@visiontv.ca; www.visiontv.ca

▶**DEVONISH, Terrie-Lynne**
VICE-PRESIDENT, LEGAL COUNSEL AND COR-

PORATE SECRETARY, HSBC Securities (Canada) Inc., 66 Wellington St. W., Toronto, ON M5K 1B7. Born: Toronto, ON, 1971.

▶ Terrie-Lynne Devonish is currently Vice-President, Legal Counsel and Corporate Secretary at HSBC Securities (Canada) Inc., where she has worked since 2000. She heads the legal department and is responsible for providing legal advice to all areas of the business on issues including regulatory compliance, research, contracts, litigation, employment, and corporate governance. Positions held since being called to the bar, 1997: Associate, Fraser Milner Casgrain LLP, 1997-2000; and, Legal Counsel, BMO Nesbitt Burns, 1999-2000 (on secondment). **AFFIL/MBRSHP:** CABL; Cdn Bar Assn; Women in Capital Markets; Ministerial Advisory Committee, Min. of Citizenship and Immigration. **COMMUNITY:** co-chair, Harry Jerome Awards; youth mentor, Each One Teach One; Pianist, Christie Street Baptist Church. **HONS.:** include: Ont. Volunteer Award, 2000; John Brooks Community Fdn. Volunteer Award, 1995; Harry Jerome Scholarship, 1991; and, several academic awards & bursaries. **WORKS:** co-authored presentation to Federated Press Securities Conference, 2000, 2001. **EDUCATION:** LLB, Osgoode Hall, York U., 1995; BA, Collège Glendon, York U., 1992. ARCT (Piano), Royal Conservatory of Music, 1990. **HEROES/ROLE MODELS:** Mother. **MOTTO:** *Je me souviens*: I remember who I am and where I've come from. **CONTACT:** terrie_devonish@hsbc.ca; Fax: 416-868-5484

▶**DICK, J. Emmanuel**

EDUCATOR (Ret.)/**COMMUNITY ORGANIZER,** National Council of Trinidad & Tobago Organization in Canada, Toronto, ON. Born: Trinidad & Tobago/ in Canada since: 1964.

▶ Emmanuel Dick is a pioneer who became the first Black principal in a Toronto Board of Education public high school. **CAREER HIGHLIGHTS:** trained in Trinidad in the field of welding, machine shop and steamfitting; he began teaching welding, machine shop and mathematics shortly after his arrival in Canada, at the college level in Oshawa, and at the secondary school level with the Toronto Board of Education, 1967-80; during this time, he pursued his own education, preparing himself for promotion and greater administrative responsibilities within the education system. In 1979, he became Technical Director/Head of Dept.; in 1980, he was promoted to Vice-Principal, a position he held until 1983, when he was promoted to the position of Principal and remained in that post until his retirement in 1999. **COMMUNITY INVOLVEMENT:** founder and President of the National Council of Trinidad and Tobago Org. in Canada, since 1987; Brd., United Way, 1988-93; Cdn Ethnocultural Council (CEC), since 1992, President, 1995-99; Brd. of Inquiry, Toronto Police Force; Cdn Alliance of Black Educators; Advisory Committee, Secretary of State, Multiculturalism, 2000-01. During his community service and, particularly during his mandate with the CEC he emphasized access to jobs, training and upward mobility of skilled immigrants. **HONS.:** including, ACAA, 2000; Award for Volunteerism, Ont. Min. of Citizenship, 1995; Arbor Award, for volunteer service in the field of Race Relations, U of T, 1993; Dumas Award, achievement through volunteering, 1988. **EDUCATION:** M.Ed, OISE/U of T, 1979; B.Ed, 1974, U of T; BA, York U., 1973; Certified Technical Instructor, Purdue U., IN, 1970; Technical Teacher's Certification, Manchester U., UK, 1962. **MOTTO:** Grow and blossom where you are planted. **CONTACT:** manniedick@hotmail.com

▶**DIDY**

ARTISTE/PEINTRE, Les Entreprises Didy, Montréal, QC. Né: Togo/ au Canada depuis: 1969.

▶ Didy, (Didier-Dorothe Deokor), s'intéresse très jeune au dessin, à la peinture et à la musique. Entre 6 et 10 ans, il vendait déjà ses œuvres. Dans les années 60 il étudie la musique au Conservatoire municipal Malherbes de Paris, prend des cours privés en peinture et de danse, et fréquente l'école de Louvre à Paris. Arrivée au Canada, il étudie l'art graphique, l'illustration et l'anatomie au CEGEP Ahuntsic, l'histoire de l'art à l'UQAM, la publicité et l'intégration des arts dans l'environnement (art public) à l'U. de Montréal. **ACTIVITÉS PRINCIPALES:** pendant six ans, il dirige sa propre compagnie de graphisme et de publicité. Depuis 1981, il se consacre à la peinture. Sa démarche artistique reflète une thématique de la culture africaine dont il s'inspire. Dans ses productions, on perçoit une combinaison harmonieuse qui repose sur les vieux fonds de mythes et légendes. Selon lui, « la peinture n'est pas un art de loisir, mais un moyen pour lutter. » Il a participé et participe toujours à de nombreuses expositions, en solo et en groupe, au Canada, aux EU, Europe, Afrique, et aux Caraïbes. **AUTRES:** il fit partie d'un orchestre local où il eut l'opportunité de jouer en compagnie de Cozy Cole et Louis Armstrong; en 1971, il fit une brève apparition à la Place des Arts en 1971 en titre de membre de la troupe de Maurice Béjart. **PRIX:** y compris, Lauréat du concours d'affiches Mois de l'Histoire des Noirs, 2000; Trophée, « Artiste peintre par excellence », 1989; Diplôme honorifique de l'U. de Cuba, Faculté de Médecine, Holguin, Cuba, 1987; Lauréat concours d'Affiches Vues d'Afrique, Montréal, 1987; nommé « Personnalité » dans le répertoire des personnalités ethniques du Québec, Institut des civilisations comparées de Mtl, 1987. **CONTACT:** didy63@hotmail.com; www3.sympatico.ca/d.deokor-didy

▶**DILLON-MOORE, Patricia (Pat)**
PUBLICIST/SPOKEN WORD PERFORMER, National Film Board of Canada (NFB), Montreal, QC. Born: Montreal, QC, 1966.
▶ Pat Dillon-Moore is a publicist with the NFB, responsible for promoting the NFB films produced in Montreal and Atlantic Canada to media

outlets across Canada, as well as those in the US, supporting theatrical, community and film festival screenings. She is also a writer and performer; in 1986, she was the lead actress in the NFB film, *Sitting in Limbo*, which won a number of awards and favourable reviews around the world. Her stage credits include a number of productions for Black Theatre Workshop, including Trevor Rhone's *Smile Orange*; as a spoken word artist, she has written and performed monologues for her series *Clemmie is Mi Frien'*, drawing on North American/ Jamaican culture and dialect. **HONS.:** including, Woman of the Year, AKAX, Montreal, 1994; Special Merit Prize, for *Sitting in Limbo*, National Black Programming Consortium, Ohio, 1987. **EDUCATION:** Financial Analysis & Management, McGill U.; Creative Arts, Dawson College, Mtl. **HEROES/ROLE MODELS:** Ms Louise Bennett, Grand Dame of Jamaican theatre & culture. **MOTTO:** One one coco fulls basket. **CONTACT:** p.a.dillon@nfb.ca

▶**DOGBE, Julius,** His Worship.
JUSTICE OF THE PEACE, Ministry of the Attorney General. Richmond Hill, ON. Born: Ghana/ in Canada since: 1969.
▶ His Worship, Julius Dogbe is a Justice of the Peace with the Ontario Ministry of the Attorney General, a position he has held since 1997. **CAREER HIGHLIGHTS:** 1980-97, he was with the Employment Standards Branch in the Ministry of Labour, as Regional Manager (1986-91), and Area Manager (1991-97); 1980-86, he was a consultant with DARS Consulting, and provided strategic planning and management for projects concerning renewable natural resource management and policy, biodiversity conservation, trade and environment. At the beginning of his professional career, he worked as a Mechanical Foreman then Mechanical Technologist in Mauritania, Ghana, and W. Germany; he then worked in the Operations Dept. of the Clarkson Refinery with Gulf Oil Ltd., 1972-79. **COMMUNITY:**

COSTI, 1990-97; CANACT, 1984-97; Assn. of Ghanaians in Toronto, 1969-88. **WORKS:** reports & papers including: *Production Management in Developing Countries*; *Rural Development as a Strategy for Integrated Resource Management.* **EDUCATION:** MES, York U., 1977; BA/Hons., U of T, 1974. **CONTACT:** dogbe@sympatico.ca; Fax: 905-737-8754

▶DONKOR, Rev. Dr. Samuel

SENIOR PASTOR, All Nations Full Gospel Church, 4401 Steeles Ave. W., Toronto, ON M3N 2S4. Born: Ghana.

▶ Rev. Dr. Samuel Donkor is the Senior Pastor of All Nations Full Gospel Church, which he founded in 1986. His ministry began in 1982 and he was ordained in 1986 after completing his studies. Since its inception, All Nations has established 11 branches in Ontario and two in the US. Outreach activities in Canada include a food bank, Bible college (founded in 1993), Cell Ministry, and Summer School. A Christian university is being planned for Ghana. **OTHER:** founding member and first President, African Canadian Ministers' Assn., 1994; Founder/President, International Ministers' Fellowship, 1999. **HONS.:** Ghanaian Cdn Achievement Award, religion, *Ghana News*, 2000; Award, Pastor of the Year, *Vox* newspaper, 1999; ACAA, religion, 1997. **WORKS:** chapter in prayer book, *Heal Our Land.* **REVIEWED IN:** community publications; listed in *WW in Executive Business*, 2000. **EDUCATION:** D.Div, Institute Church Management, Madras, India, 1995. D.Min., 1993; M.Th.S., 1991; B.Th.,1989, Canada Christian College. Dipl. Pastoral Theology, Evangelical Church Alliance Bible Institute, 1986; Dipl., Electronic Engineering, Humber College, 1984. **CONTACT:** Tel: 416-665-9964; Fax: 416-665-7303; drsdonkor@anfgc.org

▶DORSEY, Robert Edward

PRESIDENT/MANAGEMENT CONSULTANT, 3rd Dimensions & Associates Ltd., 2880 Carling Ave., Ottawa, ON K2B 7Z1. Born: USA/ in Canada since: 1937.

▶ Robert Dorsey is a Management Consultant who is working in a group with CN, Via Rail, and Ottawa Central Railways developing a rapid transit rail system in the Ottawa-Carleton area. Since 1979, he has also been promoting CANTRAK Auto train, which could provide seasonal rail service (for passengers and their autos) to three high-traffic areas in Canada and the US. From 1985-2001, he was involved in a waste-to-energy recycling program, with KEYCEPT in the US. Earlier in his career, he worked as an Industrial Management Consultant in Toronto and Montreal; was Director of Finance and Administration with the exploration arm of the Kenting Group of companies in Alberta; was a Sr. Business Administrator with the Calgary YWCA; and, served as Executive Director of Goodwill Industries, in Windsor, 1977-79. In 1999, he initiated a project that resulted in the making of a video (entitled, *Lest We Forget, Blacks Served Too*) honouring Blacks who served for Canada in WWII, including Senator Calvin Ruck, Dr. Stephen Blizzard, and others. **REVIEWED IN:** *Ottawa Citizen*, 1981; *Windsor Star*, 1979. **EDUCATION:** B.Comm, McGill U. **HEROES/ROLE MODELS:** John H. Flandreau, former business partner. **CONTACT:** Fax: 613-725-1028

▶DORSINVILLE, Max, PhD.

PROFESSOR/WRITER, Dept. of English, McGill University, 853 Sherbrooke O., Montreal, QC H3A 2T6. Born: Haiti/ in Canada since: 1954.

▶ Professor Max Dorsinville has been teaching at McGill University since 1970. His teaching and research areas of specialization are Postcolonial and Modernist literature, with a special interest in Haitian and Caribbean literature. From 1970-1987, in the Dept. of English, he has held the positions of Lecturer, Assistant, then Associate Professor, becoming a full Professor in 1987. From 1975-80, he was the Director of the French Canada Studies Program at McGill. As a writer, he has produced many works (see below). He has a particular interest in publishing the works of his uncle, Roger Dorsinville (1911-1992), *«écrivain, chercheur qui a vécu 25 ans en Afrique et qui a laissé un héritage considérable que je m'occupe de diffuser et de traduire en anglais; deux livres déjà édités.»* **WORKS:** *Roger Dorsinville Memoirs of Africa*, ed., 2002; *Postcolonial Stories by Roger Dorsinville,* ed., 2001; *The Rule of François Duvalier in Two Novels by Roger Dorsinville*, ed. 2000; *Erzulie Loves Shango*, 1998; *James Wait et les lunettes noires*, 1995; *Caliban Without Prospero*, 1974. **REVIEWED IN:** *The Empire Writes Back*, 1989; *Théorie caraïbes*, 1996. **EDUCATION:** PhD, City U., NY, 1972. MA, 1968; BA, 1966, U. of Sherbrooke. **HEROES/ROLE MODELS:** Roger Dorsinville, uncle. **MOTTO:** *Les affinités par élection.* **CONTACT:** max.dorsinville@mcgill.ca

▶**DORTELUS, Daniel, L'honorable**
JUGE, Cour du Québec, Palais de justice, 1, rue Notre-Dame Est, Montréal, QC H2Y 1B6. Né: Haïti/ au Canada depuis: 1972.
▶ Monsieur le juge Daniel Dortélus a accédé à la magistrature du Québec le 15 mai, 2002, et devient la deuxième personne noire d'être nommée à la Cour du Québec. Après avoir terminé ses études de droit à l'U. du Québec à Montréal en 1985, et il a été admis au barreau du Québec in 1986. Il débute sa pratique du droit aux Services Juridiques Communautaires de Pointe St-Charles et Petite Bourgogne, à Montréal. Par la suite, il a ouvert son propre cabinet. De 1988 jusqu'à sa nomination à la Cour du Québec, il a exercé le droit en pratique privée. Il a été membre de deux tribunaux, soient: le Tribunal des droits de la personne du Québec, 1990-96; et, la Commission Nationale des Libérations Conditionnelles, 1995-98. Il a agi comme conseiller juridique et a siégé au conseil d'administration

de divers organismes publics et communautaires. De 1995-97, il était membre du Comité Droit à l'Egalité du Programme de Contestation Judiciaire du Canada, dont le mandat était, entre autre, de sélectionner et d'accorder du financement à des causes types promouvant le droit à l'égalité à travers le Canada; en 1990, il a été nommé membre du Conseil Consultatif de l'Emploi et de l'Immigration par le gouv. fédéral. **PRIX:** plusieurs, incluant: prix des Bâtisseurs, Table ronde MHN, 2000; prix pour «son implication communautaire et son engagement vers l'excellence professionnel, » CABL, 1998; Cert. d'honneur, Ville de Mtl, 1997; prix Mathieu da Costa, Ligue des Noirs du Québec, 1992; Trophée Jackie Robinson, MABBP, 1990. **ŒUVRES À SON PROPOS:** plusieurs articles dans des journaux locaux et communautaires; était une des personnalités honorées et incluses dans le premier calendrier produit pour le Mois d'Histoire des Noirs, ville de Mtl, 1994. **FORMATION:** Bac, Droit, UQAM, 1985. **CONTACT:** dortelusconstant@qc.aira.com; Fax: 514-931-9362

▶**DOUYON, Emerson, PhD.**
PSYCHOLOGUE/PROFESSEUR, Centre de Psychologie René Laennec, 1100, av Beaumont, Montréal, QC. Né: Haïti/ au Canada depuis: 1963.
▶ Le Dr Emerson Douyon est Psychologue et Professeur pendant plus de 30 ans, auteur de nombreuses études et recherches. Il s'est notamment distingué pour son expertise dans les relations ethniques et la délinquance juvénile. Il a commencé sa vie professionnelle en Haïti avant de s'installer au Québec. **ACTIVITÉS PROFESSIONNELLES:** Chargé de cours (psychologie), École Normale supérieure et Faculté de Médecine, U. d'Haïti, 1956-62; également Psychologue-consultant, Min. de la Santé, de la justice et des affaires sociales, Gouv. d'Haïti; Professeur de psychologie criminelle, École de criminologie,

U. de Mtl, 1967-94; Chargé de cours, Faculté de l'Éducation permanente, U. de Montréal, Les minorités ethniques et la question criminelle, 1993-98; Professeur invité, DEA, Droit social, Faculté de Droit, U. de Montpellier, France, 1988-89; Psychologue-Consultant, Centre de psychologie Laennec, depuis 1994; expertise psycholégale, Chambre de la jeunesse/ Cour supérieure à Mtl/Tribunal des droits de la personne, 1980-2001; Évaluateur-conseil, projet de recherche-action sur la négligence parentale, Vivons famille-Combattons la négligence, Kouzin-Kouzin, 1999-2002. **VIE ASSOCIATIVE:** Inspecteur-enquêteur et expert agrée, Ordre des psychologues du Québec, 1998-2002; Conseil consultatif, Commission du droit, Canada, 1998-2003; comité national, services institutionnels à l'égard des enfants placés au Canada, 1998-99; comité aviseur, Mtl Black Demographic Project, 1999-2001; conseil d'administration de l'Institut interculturel de Mtl, 1999-2001; conseil d'administration du Centre d'ethnothérapie communautaire, 1999-2001; Comité ethnoculturel consultatif national, Service Correctionnel du Canada, 2001-04; Commissaire, Commission des droits de la personne et des droits de la jeunesse/Québec, 1999-2004. **PRIX:** plusieurs y compris: Citoyen d'honneur, Ville de Montréal, 1998; Cert., Honneur au mérite, Min. de la Citoyenneté et de l'Immigration, et Secrétariat d'État, 1999. **ŒUVRES:** plusieurs rapports et études; articles dans: *Psychologie Québec; Santé Mentale au Québec; l'Interculturel; Revue Internationale d'études transculturelles et d'ethnopsychanalyse clinique; Etudes de démographie: les noirs au Québec, mutations et défis.* **ŒUVRES À SON PROPOS:** *calendrier, Mois de l'Histoire des noirs*, Ville de Mtl, 1999. **FORMATION:** Cert., cours Int'l de Criminologie, École de Criminologie, 1967; PhD, Psychologie, 1965; Lic. Psychologie, Institut de Psychologie, 1955; BA, Psychologie, 1953, U. de Montréal. Dipl. d'études supérieures, U. d'Haïti, 1952. **MENTORS:** Prof. Noël Mailloux: « il m'a permis

de réaliser un rêve de jeunesse. » **MOTTO:** Échouer même est enviable pour avoir tenté. **CONTACT:** emersondouyon@sympatico.ca; Fax: 514-738-2587

▶**DOWNES, Marguerite A. (Peggy),** Major, OMM, CD.
AIDE-DE-CAMP/ADMINISTRATIVE OFFICER, Canadian Forces Army Reserve, Toronto, ON. Born: Dartmouth, NS.

▶ Major Marguerite (Peggy) Downes joined the Royal Canadian Army Service Corps Militia in Halifax, in 1955, then transferred to the Toronto Reserves in 1956. Over the course of her career, she has become the highest ranking Black female officer in the Canadian Forces Army Reserves in Ontario. She retired as Officer-in-Command, Charlie Squadron and is currently with the Queen's York Rangers Army Cadets. She is also a Commissaire with the Superior Crt. of Justice and has been serving as Aide-de-Camp since 1980 to Lieutenant-Governors: John Black Aird, Lincoln Alexander, Hal Jackman, Hilary Weston, and currently to Lt.-Gov. James K. Bartleman. **AFFIL/MBRSHP:** member, Royal Cdn Military Institute; Toronto Signals Officers Club; Hon. Life member, Cdn Women's Army Corps, and Argyll and Sutherland Highlanders; was an active member of the Toronto Negro Colour Guard (previously a men's-only veterans' group); member of the Empire Club and the Royal Commonwealth Society. **COMMUNITY INVOLVEMENT:** has been extensive: since 1977, Musical Director, Toronto First Baptist Church and founder, Voices of Joy gospel choir; Beverly Mascoll Charitable Fdn.; Kay Livingstone Visible Minority Assn./NS; has also been involved in fundraising for the James Robinson Johnston Chair in Black Cdn Studies, Dalhousie U.; fundraises for the Sickle Cell Foundation's Camp Jumoke; volunteers with the Out of the Cold Program. **HONS.:** several, including, Lifetime Achievement Award, ACAA, 2002; Vice-

127

Regal commendation & Lt.-Gov's Volunteer Award, 2001; Hon. Doctor of Humanities, 2001, N. Carolina Theological Institute; Order of Military Merit, 1988; CF Medal, three bars; GG 125th Anniv. Medal, 1992. In 2000 was named one of the "100 Most Influential East Enders." **REVIEWED IN:** *WWIC*; *Some Black Women*, 1993; & in community newspapers.

▶**DOWNES, Wray,** FTCL.
CLASSICAL/JAZZ PIANIST, c/o Justin Time Records, Ste. 101-5455, rue Paré, Montreal, QC H4P 1P7. Born: Toronto, ON.
▶ Wray Downes has been given the title, "Grand Man of the Piano" for his accomplishments and innovations, including becoming the first Canadian to win a scholarship, in 1942, to study at Trinity College of Music (founded in 1875), in London, England. **BACKGROUND:** during the 1950s and '60s, he played live with jazz greats Sonny Stitt, Clark Terry, Dizzy Gillespie, Oscar Peterson, Billie Holiday, George Benson, Mel Tormé, and Lester Young. At the same time, he worked for the CBC, as a composer, arranger, performer, on radio and TV (*Music Hop*, *Show on Shows*). During the '70s and '80s, he performed, recorded, and toured throughout Canada and the US. He also collaborated with the Archie Alleyne-Frank Wright Quartet, with vocalist Joe Williams, and was Assistant Musical Director with the Peter Appleyard Quartet. He has performed for dignitaries like Nelson Mandela, the President of Finland, the Hon. Lincoln Alexander, and others. **OTHER:** has been on the Faculty of the Music Dept. of Concordia (1990-94, 1995-98) and McGill (1994-98) universities, and has conducted jazz seminars and clinics across Canada. WD was one of the subjects in the film, *It Ain't All Jazz*, 1997, along with Archie Alleyne (*see: Alleyne, Archie*) and Sonny Greenwich. He has released recordings with Sackville Records and Justin Time, the latest being, *For you....E*, 1996, with Archie Alleyne and Dave Young.

HONS.: over 75 awards, medals, and scholarships, particularly from his classical training, including: Beethoven Open, Stratford; Crescendo Piano, Stratford; Niagara Falls Piano; Trinity College of Music Award (first Canadian recipient since the founding of the College), 1949. **REVIEWED IN:** *Jazz in Canada: 14 Lives*, 1982. **EDUCATION:** completed in England, Europe, and Canada; Conservatoire National de Musique de Paris. Fellowship, 1950; Licentiate, 1946; Associate, 1943, Trinity College London, England. **CONTACT:** Tel: 514-738-9533

▶**DUNCAN, Alvin**
WWII VETERAN, Royal Canadian Air Force. Oakville, ON. Born: Oakville, ON.
▶ Alvin Duncan is a veteran of WWII and a veteran of the Battle of Britain. He served in the RCAF and was a radar operator; he was one of only two Blacks who were allowed, at the time, to service the highly confidential radar equipment being used in the Allied cause, 1942-46. He has received many awards and decorations for his contributions and, in 1996, the Cdn government allowed Britain to issue to AD and his comrades, the Certificates of Appreciation, which had been prepared since 1946, for the radar technicians who had been involved in the Battle of Britain. Following the war, AD worked with the Avro Aircraft Plant in Toronto, which was building the CF-100 at the time; when the plant closed in 1959, he opened his own business, Al Duncan TV. **COMMUNITY:** has been involved in a number of activities; has been a Scoutmaster; has a keen interest in the history of the Oakville area, particularly its African American history, and belongs to the Oakville Historical Society; is well known for his presentations to school classes on the subject of the Underground Railroad and has shared the results of his research with the Oakville Museum. He is credited with having one of the most extensive privately owned libraries in the Oakville area.

HONS.: including, Defence Medal; Victory Medal; Volunteer Medal and Clasp; Royal Cdn Legion Medals, for members of Air Force Telecommunications Assn.; Citation to Radar Technicians, Battle of Britain, Secretary of State for War, UK, 1946 (rec'd 1996); Plaque from General D. Eisenhower, 1944; Plaque, House of Commons, honouring Canada's WWII Radar Veterans, 1997; and, the week of Oct. 7-13, 1997, was proclaimed Radar Veterans' Week in Ottawa. **WORKS:** in *Hamilton Spectator*; information to Oakville Museum & Oakville Black History, 2000. **REVIEWED IN:** newsletters, *Toronto Star.* **EDUCATION:** Ryerson Technical (now Ryerson U.), 1947; Oakville High, 1932. **MOTTO:** *Non palmo sine pulvere*: no rewards without effort. (High School motto)

▶**DUNCAN, Carol B., PhD.**
ASSISTANT PROFESSOR, Dept. Religion & Culture, Wilfrid Laurier University, 75 University Ave., Waterloo, ON N2L 3C5. Born: UK/ in Canada since: 1973.
▶ Dr. Carol B. Duncan teaches in the Dept. of Religion and Culture at Wilfrid Laurier University. Her areas of specialization include the religion and culture of the African Diaspora with an emphasis on Caribbean religion in Canada. She also conducts research on religion and popular culture; has published and presented academic papers within Canada and internationally; participates in many academic and community initiatives. **AFFIL/MBRSHP:** American Academy of Religion; Cdn Society for the Study of Religion; Cdn Women's Studies Assn. **HONS.:** several including: Merit Award, WLU, 2001; Access Awareness Award, for support & encouragement provided to students with disabilities, York U., 1997; university-wide Teaching Award, York U., 1996; John O'Neill Award for Teaching Excellence, Dept. of Sociology, York U., 1995. **WORKS:** in *J of the Assn. for Research on Mothering*; *Small Axe: A Caribbean J of Cultural Criticism; Canadian Woman Studies J; Vox Feminarum.* **EDUCATION:** PhD, Sociology, 2000; MA, Sociology, 1991, York University. BA, U of T, 1988. **CONTACT:** cduncan@wlu.ca; Tel: 519-884-0710 ext. 3692; Fax: 519-884-9387

▶**DUNCAN, George**
CITY MANAGER, City of London, 300 Dufferin Ave., London, ON N6A 4L9. Born: Hamilton, ON.
▶ George Duncan assumed his current position as City Manager of the City of London, Ontario, on August 1st, 2002. Previously, he was Chief Administrative Officer (CAO) of the City of Richmond, BC for five years (1997-2002), where his responsibilities included: overseeing the administration of the corporate body (business units/operation) of the City, its officers and employees; keeping Council up to date on corporate matters; ensuring that Council policy was implemented and by-laws enforced; leading the Council's senior executive team; and setting the overall strategic direction for short and long term corporate goals. **HIGHLIGHTS:** under his leadership as CAO, Richmond restructured its service delivery model to adopt a high performance, customer service-based approach. Examples of strategies and initiatives implemented during his mandate include: the Blowout Bureaucracy Program, which reduced the turnaround time for development and building approvals; the Customer Service Strategy, which improved delivery of service to the community; a Corporate Efficiency Strategy that saved $6-million in operating costs with no reduction in programs; a Neighbourhood Services Program, which brought custom designed programs directly to neighbourhoods; and, a Community Safety Program that integrated emergency services to provide better service to the population. As a result of these innovations and the accompanying improvement in operations and morale, the city has been recognized with over 40 major

awards at both at the national and international levels. Included in these are two consecutive Willis Awards for Excellence in Administration and Exceptional Innovation – the highest award presented to local government administration in Canada. Other awards include: in November 2001, the City of Richmond was named by *Maclean's* magazine and Media Corp. as one of the Top 100 Employers in Canada; in May 2002, the city was the recipient of the 2002 BC Medical Association (BCMA) Excellence in Health Promotion – Business Sector Award, for its corporate wellness program. GD himself has received a number of prestigious awards for his management and leadership practices including the 2002 Award of Excellence, from the BC Human Resources Management Assn. (BCHRMA). This award honours outstanding individuals, teams and organizations whose people-practices reflect the leadership and innovation that enhance the results of the organizations. **BACKGROUND:** prior to joining the public sector, GD worked for 14 yrs. in the private sector, first with the Engineering Dept. of Proctor & Gamble, then as an entrepreneur employing up to 70 people in his operations in both Ontario and BC. He joined the City of Richmond in 1987, serving as General Manager of the Engineering and Public Works Dept. before becoming CAO in 1997. **HONS.:** several including, Award of Excellence, BCHRMA, 2002; recipient of two awards from the International City/County Management Assn. (ICMA), an organization of his counterparts around the world, Philadelphia, 2002. **CONTACT:** Tel: 519-661-5493

▶**DUPERVAL, Raymond,** MD, FRCPC.
PROFESSEUR/CHEF DU SERVICE D'INFECTIO-LOGIE, Faculté de médecine, Université de Sherbrooke, Sherbrooke, QC J1H 5N4. Né: Haïti/ au Canada depuis: 1976.

▶ Dr Raymond Duperval est spécialisé en maladies infectieuses; il est Professeur titulaire à l'Université de Sherbrooke, où il travaille depuis, 1976. Il est aussi chef du Département de microbiologie et d'infectiologie au Centre Hospitalier universitaire de Sherbrooke (CHUS), depuis mai 2000. **D'AUTRES ACTIVITÉS:** Directeur régional pour le Réseau national des essais cliniques anti-VIH au Canada; président du Comité de pharmacologie et toxicologie, CHUS; président du Comité des essais cliniques, CHUS; Directeur programme d'accueil pour médecins non diplômés du Canada. **INTÉRÊTS EN RECHERCHE CLINIQUE:** l'Antibiothérapie; l'Infection VIH et ses complications; la Maladie des légionnaires; le Paludisme; et les Infections chez les patients immuno-compromis. **AUTRES:** En dehors de son travail, sa recherche et ses cours, il est Consultant avec GAP-VIES, un groupe communautaire aidant les gens d'Haïti qui habitent à Montréal; comme loisir, il joue la musique haïtienne dans un groupe avec ses fils et quelques amis; ils ont même enregistré deux CDs qui ont été bien reçus. **ŒUVRES:** *Can J Infect. Dis.; Pediatric Radiology; Sida et Infections à VIH: Aspects in Zone Tropicale.* **ŒUVRES À SON PROPOS:** *Heirlooms,* vol.7, gouv. du Canada. **FORMATION:** étude post-doctorale, maladies infectieuses, U. Minnesota, Mayo Graduate School of Medicine, 1976; FRCPC, médecine interne, U. de Sherbrooke, 1975; MD, U. Louis Pasteur, Strasbourg, 1970. **CONTACT:** Raymond.Duperval@USherbrooke.ca; www.usherb.ca/rech/microbio

▶**DURITY, Felix,** MD, FRCSC.
PROFESSOR/HEAD, DIVISION OF NEURO-SURGERY, Dept. of Surgery, University of British Columbia (UBC), 910 West 10th Ave., Vancouver, BC V5Z 4E3. Born: Trinidad & Tobago/ in Canada since: 1956.

▶ Dr. Felix Durity is a Professor and Head of the Division of Neurosurgery, Dept. of Surgery in the Faculty of Medicine at UBC, a position he has held since 1992. He is also a member of staff, Division of Neurosurgery, at Vancouver

General Hospital (VGH); previously, he had been Head of the Division of Neurosurgery at VGH, from 1992-97, and 2000-01. **OTHER CAREER HIGHLIGHTS:** as Head of Neurosurgery at UBC, he has been instrumental in its development from a purely clinical division to a first class, state-of-the-art clinical division, as well as a highly productive academic division; since 1996, he has been successful in recruiting five highly sought-after neuroscientists to UBC. He has successfully led the drive for research funding, which increased from $50,000 in 1991 to over $800,000 by 1997; he was successful, with others, in obtaining funding for the first program for stereotactic radiosurgery in Western Canada, established as a joint effort between the Div. of Neurosurgery and the BC Cancer Agency, and was available to patients in 1997. The research funding has also allowed the Div. of Neurosurgery, under his leadership, to participate with the Rick Hansen Institute in establishing a National Neurotrauma Initiative, which has received committed grants for the next five yrs. from various provincial governments. At the Vancouver Hospital and Health Sciences Centre, he has succeeded in fundraising initiatives which support research scientists and the purchase of specialized operating room equipment. His clinical work focuses on trauma and problems related to increased intracranial pressure, cerebrovascular disease and skull base surgery; he is a founding member of the N. American Skull Base Surgery Society. **AFFIL/MBRSHP:** involved in many hospital and university committees; Canadian Stroke Society; Congress of Neurological Surgeons; Trauma Assn. of Canada; Western Neurosurgical Society; reviewer, *CMAJ*. **HONS.:** several including, A.D. McKenzie Award, for Undergraduate & Postgraduate teaching, 2001; H. Rocke Robertson Award in Surgery, best surgical teaching, 3rd Year Medicine, 2000 & 1986; Award for Clinical Excellence, Vancouver Hospital & Health Sciences Centre, 1995. **WORKS:** articles in: *Neurosurgery;*

J Otolaryngology; New England J Medicine; Recovery. Chapters in books: *Atlas of Neurosurgical Techniques*, 2000; *Surgery of Cranial Base Tumours*, 1993; *Blood Flow & Metabolism in the Brain*, 1975. **REVIEWED IN:** *Vancouver Sun*, 2001; *Globe and Mail*, 2000; *The Best Doctors in Canada*, 1998. **EDUCATION:** FRCSC, Neurosurgery, 1970; MD, 1963; BA, 1958, UBC. **MOTTO:** Be strong, insightful, brave, and loving. **CONTACT:** neuros@interchange.ubc.ca; fmdurity @interchange.ubc.ca; Fax: 604-875-4036

▶**DWYER, Mike**
TRACK AND FIELD COACH, Toronto, ON. Born: Jamaica/ in Canada since: 1976.

▶ Mike Dwyer is a former Olympian who is now coaching other young athletes to develop their skills in track & field events. Shortly after coming to Canada in 1976, and with the encouragement of gym teacher, James Dodd, he pursued his interest in track, competing in 100m, 200m, and 4x100m events. He participated in the following: 1981 Canada Games; '86 and '90 Commonwealth Games; '87 and '91 World Championships (4x100m); '85 and '87 World Student Games (100m, 200m, 4x100m); '91 Pan Am Games (100m, 200m, 4x100m); '89 Goodwill Games (4x100m); '87 Pan Pacific Conference Games (100m, 200m, 4x100m); '88 Olympics, but did not compete due to injuries; '99 CIAU, 60m title. He has been coaching since 1991; is currently a level III coach and a member of the Cdn Professional Coaching Assn. During the *Jeux de la Francophonie*, 2001, he was the men's and women's sprint coach. **HONS.:** several for track & field. **EDUCATION:** BA, York U., 2000. **HEROES/ROLE MODELS:** James P. Dodd, gym teacher; George Neeland, Val Grose, & Peter Cross, coaches. **CONTACT:** michael_sub20@ hotmail.com

►EARLE, Gordon

SENIOR PUBLIC ADMINISTRATOR (Ret.)/**FORMER MP**, Government of Nova Scotia & Canada. Upper Tantalon, NS. Born: Halifax, NS.

▶ Gordon Earle spent his professional life in senior government administrative positions and, as an elected official, became the first Black from NS to be elected to the Canadian Parliament. **CAREER HIGHLIGHTS:** in 1968, he was hired as the first staff person for the NS Human Rights Commission, and was instrumental in the establishment of the office and the drafting of the province's first Human Rights Act. By 1971, he was promoted to Chief Human Rights Officer/NS; during that time he completed a study on the feasibility of establishing a provincial Ombudsman's office. In 1972, NS' first Ombudsman invited GE to be his assistant, a position he held until 1982. From 1982-94, GE was appointed provincial Ombudsman by the Govt. of Manitoba. After completion of the maximum two terms, he returned to NS and accepted a post as Deputy Minister/Dept. of Housing and Consumer Affairs. In 1996, GE retired from the civil service and in 1997, was elected to the House of Commons, the first Black from NS to do so, and served until Nov. 2000. During that time, he was the NDP spokesperson for Citizenship and Immigration, Multiculturalism, Aboriginal Affairs, National Defence, and Veteran Affairs. **COMMUNITY INVOLVEMENT:** founded the Hammonds Plains Karate Club, which brought youth from different backgrounds together for recreational activities; BCC/NS; honorary Brd. member, NS Home for Coloured Children; past-President of NS/AACP; Brd., CNIB; Brd., YMCA/Halifax; Director, Bayside Baptist Youth Camp. **OTHER:** as evidence of his and his wife's commitment to youth, they provided care for six long-term foster care children; they were also foster parents for nearly 13 yrs.; in addition, they provided Open Custody supervision for Young Offenders who served their sentences in the Earle home. **HONS.:** Judge J. Elliott Hudson Award, University of King's College; Silver Medal, in recognition of contribution and assistance in Ombudsman's field, Govt. of West Germany; Induction into Dr. W.P. Oliver Wall of Fame, BCC/NS. **REVIEWED IN:** *Journey: African Canadian History, 2000.* **EDUCATION:** post-graduate studies in Sociology; BA, U. of King's College, 1963. **CONTACT:** gordon.earle@ns.sympatico.ca

►ECHOLS, Edith McGruder, MSW.

SOCIAL WORKER (Ret.), Women's Christian Alliance, Philadelphia, PA, USA. Born: Toronto, ON.

▶ Edith McGruder Echols graduated from the University of Toronto's Social Work program in 1939, after completing her BA in 1937. After receiving her MSW from the School of Social Work at Atlanta University, she remained in the US in order to work in her field. Her professional experiences took place in Philadelphia and included: Bureau of Childcare, 1943-64; Dept. of Public Welfare, 1965-1967; Women's Christian Alliance, 1968, until her retirement in 1977. Since then, she has been active in the local Senior Citizens' Centre and the Lutheran Church's Women committee activities. **EDUCATION:** MSW, School of Social Work, Atlanta U., GA, 1942. Cert. Social Work, 1939; BA, 1937, U of T.

►EDEH, Rosey

OLYMPIC ATHLETE (Ret.)/**TV BROADCASTER**, Cable News Network (CNN), CNN Center, Alta, GA. Born: UK/ in Canada since: 1972.

▶ Rosey Edeh is a former world athlete and Canadian Olympian. **CAREER HIGHLIGHTS:** was a member of the 1988, '92, and '96 Canadian Olympic Teams; member of the 4x400m relay team that placed fourth at the 1992 Barcelona Olympics; placed sixth in the 400m hurdles at the 1996 Atlanta Olympics (setting a new Cdn record); placed first at the 1992 World Cup in Cuba; is a six-time Canadian champion and won a silver medal at the World Student Games, 1989 in Germany. **CURRENTLY:** she is a broadcaster with CNN. Previously, she was a sports columnist for CBC radio, profiling lesser-known amateur athletes. She is also a highly skilled photographer and has completed a number of modelling contracts in recent years; was featured on the cover *of ELLE* Quebec in 1997. She gives back to the community by speaking to youth about achieving their goals. **HONS.:** including, Student of the Year, Concordia U., 1998/99; nominated, Quebec Female Athlete of the Year, 1996; Quebec Female Track & Field Athlete of the Year, 1992, '93, '95, '96. **WORKS:** wrote articles for *Panache* magazine, 1997-2001. **REVIEWED IN:** several, local, nat'l, int'l; "15 Cdn women to watch in the New Millennium," *Chatelaine*, 2001; *Elle*, 1997. **EDUCATION:** BA, Rice U., TX. **HEROES/ROLE MODELS:** Maya Angelou; Oprah Winfrey. **MOTTO:** Know thyself! **CONTACT:** rosey.edeh@turner.com

▶**EDEY, David**
VICE-PRESIDENT, ADVISOR, Tandem Financial Services, Westmount, QC. Born: Montreal, QC.
▶ David Edey is an Advisor and Vice-President with the Tandem Wealth Management Group, in Montreal; he has been in the Cdn Financial Services industry since 1985. **CAREER HIGHLIGHTS:** author of two books on personal investments; has conducted public and corporate workshops on finance; has written articles on personal finance and investing issues for national publications; has been a columnist in *Investment Executive* newspaper since 1991; is a regular contributor to a personal finance show on Montreal's CJAD radio, as well as *Money Talks* and *Canada's Money Show,* he has also appeared on CBC business programs such as *Canada's Money Show.* **WORKS:** in business columns & publications; *Smart Money Strategies for the Canadian Mutual Fund Investor*, 1998; co-authored, *Beyond Mutual Funds,* 2000. **EDUCATION:** BA, Economics, Concordia U., 1984. **CONTACT:** davide@twmg.net

▶**EDMONDS, Pamela**
ARTIST/WRITER/CURATOR, Montreal, QC. Born: Montreal, QC.
▶ Pamela Edmonds is an artist, writer, and curator who resides in Montreal and Halifax; she is interested in developing and curating projects that focus on the creative production of Black Canadian artists, and in work that deals with issues surrounding the ideologies of race, gender, cultural identity and representation. She also works in film and video, and has directed experimental documentaries (*X-isle*, 1999, and *Deliberate Body*, 2000), and curated screening events such as: Africadian Visions: Contemporary Film From Black Nova Scotia, at the Winnipeg Cinematheque, 2001; No Place Like Home: The Search for Place and Space in Cinemas of the Black Diaspora, Centre for Art Tapes, Halifax, 2000; and, REEL Black Film Night, Oxford Theatre, Halifax, 1999. Her curatorial projects include: *Generations and Feminisms* at SAW Gallery in Ottawa, 1999; *SisterVisions III: Through Our Eyes*, Art Gallery of NS, 2000; *Cultural Memory: The House that Mom Built*, 2000, University College of Cape Breton Art Gallery; her most recent project was curating *Black Body: Race, Resistance, Response*, at the Dalhousie Art Gallery, 2001. **OTHER ACTIVITIES**: former co-editor, Black cultural journal, *Kola*; was VP, Black Artist's Network of NS; and, with Anthony Joyette, is one of the founding members of the Cdn League of Black Artists. **REVIEWED IN:** programs from curated events; *Black Body: Race, Resistance, Response*, 2001. **EDUCATION:** MA, Art History (in progress); BFA, Art & Art History, 1997, Concordia U. **CONTACT:** pamella@netcom.ca

▶**EDOGHAMEN, Robin**
EXECUTIVE DIRECTOR, Metro Street Focus Organization; **PROGRAM COORDINATOR,** Africanadian Mediation and Community Services, 2nd Fl., 590 Jarvis St., Toronto, ON M4Y 2J4. Born:

Nigeria/ in Canada since: 1990.

▶ Robin Edoghamen is the Executive Director of Metro Street Focus, an organization he founded in 1995, which offers practical assistance to the needy on the streets of Toronto, "...who may be grappling with issues of hunger and deprivation, poverty, addiction, mental illness, unemployment, and homelessness." As a certified mediator, he is the founder of the Africanadian Mediation and Community Services (AMCS), 2001, whose objectives are to facilitate resolution of interpsonal conflicts in the African/Black communities in Ontario, where he is the present coordinator of the program. And, as a former employee of the Canada Immigration and Refugee Board, he also counsels on immigration issues and conflict resolution. **AFFIL/MBRSHP:** is involved with a number of professional and community organizations. **HONS.:** 2001: Int'l Year of Volunteers Award; Ont. Min. of Citizenship; Appreciation Award, City of Toronto; Award for hard work & dedication, Nigerian Cdn Assn.; Award, for his "excellence & hard work," Edo Assn., 2000. **REVIEWED IN:** *AfriCanadian J.* **EDUCATION:** currently pursuing MA, Int'l Studies & Diplomacy, York U.; Dipl. Law, Toronto; Admin. Studies & Post Cert., Public Admin., Nigeria. **HEROES/ROLE MODELS:** Father; Nelson Mandela. **CONTACT:** metro@lefca.com; www.lefca.com/metro

▶EDWARDS, Brother Leeroy

PHOTOGRAPHER/POET, Montreal, QC. Born: Trinidad & Tobago/ in Canada since: 1954.

▶ Brother Leeroy Edwards, a.k.a. "The Happy Wanderer," is an icon in the Montreal Black community. He is known as a poet and a photographer, and has one of the largest collections of photographs by a non-professional photographer in Canada: over 11,000 pictures of key moments in contemporary Black history, his personal life, and his travels around the world. He has been featured on TV and in local magazines and newspapers. In his professional life, he worked for Air Canada until his retirement at age 65, having worked there for "32 years, four months and 14 days"; until age 62, he had a 100% record for attendance and punctuality. Allowed travel privileges through his employer, he has been around the world seven times, visited 52 countries and 134 major cities. **HONS.:** including, Ambassador, Air Canada 50th Anniv., for loyalty & dedication to the company; Editor's Choice Award, National Library of Poetry, 1997. **WORKS:** poems in: *The Best Poems & Poets of 2001.* **REVIEWED IN:** several community & local publications, including, *Montreal Gazette, Community Contact.* **MOTTO:** Live the life you love; love the life you live.

▶EDWARDS, Haskell G., D.Min.

PASTOR, Seventh-day Adventist Church, HQ, 1110 King St. E., Oshawa, ON L1H 1H8. Born: Trinidad & Tobago/ in Canada since: 1973.

▶ Dr. Haskell Edwards has pastored Seventh-day Adventist (SDA) congregations in the Toronto area since 1974, including the 1,000-member Toronto West Church, the first Black SDA church in Canada. He developed and conducts Family Achievement workshops in Canada and the US, to help individuals deal with the impact of migration on family relationships, family function, development of children and youth, and provides motivation on achieving goals. He also founded the Adventist Counselling Centre, primarily to meet the therapeutic needs of families adjusting to the Cdn cultural context. He directed several departments of the Ontario Church, and in this capacity he established the Touch of Love ministry, which assists the homeless in Toronto by providing meals on a daily basis. In addition, he is a founding member of the Metro Black Clergy Community Assn. of Toronto. **HONS.:** including, Award for Service, 1999 & 1994, Seventh-day Adventist Church; Award for 14 yrs. service, West Indian Ministerium, 1989. **WORKS:** *The Immigrant Family: Framework for Adaptation &*

Excellence. **EDUCATION:** D.Min, 1990; M.Div, 1969; MA, 1967, Andrews U., MI. BA, Religion, Atlantic Union College, MA, 1965. **MOTTO:** Those who find stumbling blocks along the way must turn them over and reshape them into stepping stones. **CONTACT:** family1999@hotmail.com

▶**EDWARDS, Jacqueline**
RECRUITMENT OFFICER, Federal Correctional Service of Canada, 440 King St. W., Kingston, ON. Born: Jamaica/ in Canada since: 1975.

▶ Jacqueline Edwards was hired as a Correctional Officer with the Correctional Service of Canada, in 1995; currently she is a Recruitment Officer in Kingston, Ontario. **RESPONSIBILITIES:** promoting the Correctional Service of Canada as a viable career option, and increasing the awareness of career opportunities within the federal government. She is a member of the hiring board which assesses applicant's skills and abilities in the correctional officer recruiting process. Since 1999, she has led a Recruitment Outreach Project in the Greater Toronto Area, to better inform the diverse ethnocultural groups, aboriginal communities, and educational institutions on career opportunities within the Correctional Service of Canada in particular, and in the Public Service in general, and to assist those from diverse cultural backgrounds to learn about positions available within the various federal departments. **OTHER:** JE is a strong advocate for increased cross-cultural understanding and the improvement of race relations within the Correctional Service of Canada and throughout the Public Service sector. She fulfils numerous speaking engagements, multicultural community town hall sessions, attends job fairs and regularly facilitates diversity-awareness workshops. **AFFIL/MBRSHP:** chaired the regional Racial Harmony Cmtee of Corrections Canada (Ontario); VP of ABLE; President, National Council of Visible Minorities in the Public Service, formerly first VP and Ontario Director; mentor through Women in Motion.

HONS.: including, Recipient of Multicultural Award, Corrections Canada, 2002; Officer of the Year, and Community Award, ABLE. **REVIEWED IN:** featured in Corrections Canada recruitment campaign. **EDUCATION:** Dipl., Law & Security Program, Humber College, 1994. **MOTTO:** Make it happen! **CONTACT:** edwardsjj@csc-scc.gc.ca; Fax: 613-545-8504

▶**EDWARDS, Madeline**
COMMUNITY ORGANIZER/MANAGER (Ret.), Geriatric Psychiatric Outreach, Centre for Addiction & Mental Health, Toronto, ON. Born: Jamaica/ in Canada since: 1962.

▶ Madeline Edwards was, until her retirement in 2002, the Manager of Geriatric Psychiatric Outreach at the Centre for Addiction and Mental Health, (CAMH). This is a specialty area which provides assessment, treatment, on-going community follow-up and, when necessary, in-patient hospitalization of older persons with severe mental health problems. Since the 1980s the primary focus in her nursing career was gerontology, with a commitment to helping seniors live to their fullest potential in safety. She has also been active in a number of community initiatives designed to benefit disadvantaged groups. **CAREER HIGHLIGHTS:** Staff Development Coordinator/ Nursing Supervisor, St. Joseph's Health Centre, 1982-87; Staff Development Coordinator, Runnymede Hospital; Staff Nurse, the Clarke Institute of Psychiatry; College Instructor for seven years with the Registered Nurses Association Program; and, coordinated nursing practicum at Riverdale and Toronto Western hospitals and Lambert Lodge; also provided mentoring support to nursing students, particularly those from diverse ethno-racial groups. **COMMUNITY INVOLVEMENT:** founding member, Congress of Black Women, Mississauga and Area Chapter; spearheaded the conception and development of the Congress' non-profit housing facility, Camille's Place, and is currently Chair; founding member, Peel Community Care Access Centre. **HONS.:** several including: Kay Livingstone Award, 1998; Harry Jerome Award, BBPA; Certificates for volunteering from Halton Peel District Health Council, Toronto Public Health, George Brown School of Nursing, & Ryerson U. **REVIEWED IN:** *Toronto Star*; *Share*. **EDUCATION:** Management Cert., 2001; BA, 1979, York University. Teaching Techniques, George Brown College, 1971; State Registered Midwife, Scotland, 1962; State Registered Nurse, England, 1961. **HEROES/ROLE MODELS:** Mother; Jean Augustine, friend; Janette Balfour, niece. **MOTTO:** I will rise again! **CONTACT:** madelinedwards@hotmail.com

▶**EGUAKUN, George**
MANAGER, Market Research & Analysis, Saskatchewan Power Corp., 8SE 2021 Victoria Ave., Regina, SK S4P 2A4. Born: Ghana, 1965/ in Canada since: 1991.

▶ George Eguakun worked as a Civil Engineer in Ghana before coming to Canada. Following his course of study in Transportation Planning and Management at the University of NB, he worked with Manitoba Public Insurance: with the Road Safety Dept., responsible for establishing and maintaining an evaluation strategy to support policy and program initiatives in road safety, 1996-98; as a Sr. Business Analyst in the Public Affairs Div., responsible for establishing continuous improvement processes and developing service quality standards, 1998-2000. Since 2000, he has been the Manager of Market Research and Analysis, SaskPower, responsible for conducting and analysing results of the company's market research studies. **COMMUNITY:** Ghanaian Community Assn.; founder, Black Chamber of Commerce, MB; owner, Patience Custom Catering and Restaurant; organized Winnipeg's first Black Business Expo, in 1998. **HONS.:** Award, for excellence in community service, *Ghanaian News*, 2001. **WORKS:** in, *Proceedings of the Can Multidisciplinary Road Safety*

Conference, 1995-99; articles in, *J Accident Analysis & Prevention.* **EDUCATION:** PhD, in progress; EMBA, in progress; MSc, Transportation Engineering & Business Mngmt., 1993, U. of NB. BSc, Civil Engineering, U. of Science & Technology, Ghana, 1987. **HEROES/ROLE MODELS:** William Eguakun, uncle. **MOTTO:** Begin with the end in mind. **CONTACT:** geguakun@yahoo.ca

▶**EKONG, Chris,** MB BS, FRCSC, FACS, FICS.
CLINICAL PROFESSOR, SURGERY/NEUROSURGERY, University of Saskatchewan, 122 Medical Office Wing; 1440 14th Ave, Regina, SK. Born: Nigeria/ in Canada since: 1974.

▶ Dr. Chris Ekong has been a neurosurgeon with the Regina Health District since 1982; he is also Clinical Professor of Surgery (Neurosurgery) at the University of Saskatchewan. Since 2000, he has been Director of the Canadian Clinical Neuro-Technology Research Unit, a unit he started in order to investigate electronic technologies and apply them in clinical practice, and to aid in the instruction of neurosciences. This Unit is housed in the Regina General Hospital. **AFFIL:** member, Examination Board for Neurosurgery, Royal College of Surgeons of Canada; Fellow, American College of Surgeons; Fellow, International College of Surgeons. **WORKS:** over 50 papers, abstracts, & presentations in the field of neurosurgery. **REVIEWED IN:** *The Physician,* 2001. **EDUCATION:** FRCSC, U of T, 1981; MB BS, Ibadan, Nigeria, 1972. **HEROES/ROLE MODELS:** Dr. Odeku, Neurosurgeon, Nigeria; Dr. Charles Tator, Neurosurgeon, Toronto. **CONTACT:** ekongc @medi-fax.com; www.medi-fax.com/dr_ ekong

▶**ELABOR-IDEMUDIA, Patience,** PhD.
ASSOCIATE PROFESSOR, Dept. of Sociology, University of Saskatchewan, 9 Campus Dr., Saskatoon, SK S7N 5A5. Born: Nigeria/ in Canada since: 1982.

▶ Dr. Patience Elabor-Idemudia is an Associate Professor in the Dept. of Sociology at the University of Saskatchewan where she has been teaching since 1995. **CAREER:** began teaching at Brock University, Dept. of Sociology as a Sessional Lecturer, 1993; Sessional Lecturer, Women's Studies, U of T, 1989-94; Assistant Prof., Dept. of Sociology and Anthropology, Wilfrid Laurier U., 1994-95. Areas of specialization include: sociology of the family; women's studies; race and ethnic relations; women/gender and development. She has also conducted workshops on prejudice, discrimination, anti-racism education, conflict resolution and diversity, as well as race relations, employment equity and multiculturalism. Previously, she worked as an Agricultural Research Officer, Rubber Research Institute of Nigeria, 1980-82. **AFFIL/MBRSHP:** Cdn Sociological and Anthropology Assn; West Africa Research Assn.; Cdn Assn. of African Studies; Inter-Church Coalition on Africa; Cdn Research Institute for the Advancement of Women. **HONS.:** several academic awards; PEO International Peace Scholarship, 1989-92. **WORKS:** include a monograph, 9 chapters in books, many conference papers, articles in academic journals: *Can Woman's Studies; The Negro J of Education;* and periodicals: *Economic Justice Update.* **EDUCATION:** PhD, Sociology of Education, OISE/U of T, 1993; MSc, Agricultural Extension Education, U. of Guelph, 1985; BSc, State University College, Oneonta, NY, 1977. **HEROES/ROLE MODELS:** Mother; Prof. Dorothy Smith. **MOTTO:** It's not how much but how well. **CONTACT:** idemudia@sask.usask.ca; www.usask.ca/sociology

▶**ELLIS, Keith A.A., PhD, FRSC.**
PROFESSOR EMERITUS, Dept. Spanish & Portuguese, University of Toronto. Born: Jamaica/ in Canada since: 1956.
▶ Dr. Keith Ellis taught Latin American Literature and Culture at U of T, from 1963 to 2000.

His area of specialization is Latin American poetry and the short story; he is widely considered to be one of the world's leading authorities on the poetry of Caribbean writer Nicolás Guillén. In 1998, he made history by becoming the first Canadian to be awarded an honorary doctoral degree by the 270-year-old University of Havana. In 1994, he was a Visiting Professor, Stanford University, and he has given invited lectures at several universities including Yale, Cambridge, the University of the West Indies, Bordeaux, and others. **AFFIL/MBRSHP:** Fellow, Royal Society of Canada, national academy, 1988; was Juror for the *Casa de las Americas* Literary Prize, 1988; Cdn Assn. Latin American Studies; JCA; Cdn-Cuban Friendship Assn.; Hon. Member, Union of Artists and Writers of Cuba; served on Executive Committee, Brd. of Trustees, Royal Ontario Museum. **HONS.:** include, Hon. D. Fil., University of Havana, 1998; Medal of Distinction for National Culture, Cuba, 1998; Cdn Hispanists' Prize, Best Book; Medal, City of Poitiers, France, 1978. **WORKS:** including, *A Cuban Poet at Niagara Falls*, 1997; *The Role of Science in Cuban Culture*, 1995; *Nicolás Guillén: New Love Poetry*, 1994; *Nicolás Guillén (1902-1989): A Life of Poetic Service*, 1991; *Cuba's Nicolás Guillén: Poetry and Ideology*, 1985. **EDUCATION:** PhD, 1962; MA, 1961, U. of Washington. BA, U of T, 1958. **CONTACT:** zellis @yorku.ca

▶**ELLISTON, Inez, PhD.**
EDUCATOR & COMMUNITY VOLUNTEER LEADER, Toronto, ON. Born: Jamaica/ in Canada since: 1967.
▶ Dr. Inez Elliston is an educator, writer, consultant and leader in community volunteerism, whose expertise has been developed through her professional activities and her community involvement. The focus of her work and volunteer experiences has been "the identification and elaboration of issues, the search for solutions,

and the encouragement of collaboration in devising strategies for the accommodation of diversity, combatting racism, discrimination, and other inequities." **CAREER HIGHLIGHTS:** first Coordinator of the Multiculturalism and Race Relations Committee, 1988-94, of the Scarborough Brd. of Education; was responsible for the implementation of 14 major policy recommendations, including multicultural training for staff and improved assessment of immigrant children in the school system; Education Officer, Min. of Education and Training, 1994-96; Vice-principal, Continuing Education, 1986-90; Coordinator, Adult Day School and Multicultural Centre, 1978-82. In her honour, the Scarb. Brd. of Ed. (Toronto School Dist. 16) established the annual Dr. Inez Elliston Award for achievement in Anti-racist and Ethnocultural Equity, for two schools demonstrating excellence in education and equity in accommodating diversity (1995-98). She is Patron of Women for PACE and has established a bursary in her name for Early Childhood Education. **AFFIL:** Cdn Council for Multicultural and Intercultural Education; Delta Kappa Gamma Int'l Society for Key Women Educators; Governing Council, U of T; Cdn Federation of University Women. **HONS.:** include: Appreciation for significant contribution to community, City of Markham, 2002, and City of Scarborough, 1994; John Hubbard Humanitarian Award, lifetime achievement, 2001; Malvern Youth Club Award, lifetime achievement, 2000; ACAA, 1996; Outstanding Contribution, JCA, 1996; Outstanding Achievement Award, Cdn Council for Multicultural and Intercultural Education, 1990; Citation for Citizenship, Govt. of Canada, 1989; 15-yr. Volunteer Service Award, Min. of Citizenship, 1987. **WORKS:** many articles & reports including: *Multiculturalism in Canada: Issues & Perspectives*; *Education in a Changing Society; Effective Schooling for an Increasingly Diverse Student Population.* **REVIEWED IN:** WWCW; WW in Toronto; *Some Black Women; Jamaican Canadians: A Commitment to Excellence.* Also reviewed in several community publications. **EDUCATION:** PhD, 1976; M.Ed, 1972, U of T. M.Ed, Boston U., 1965. Dipl. Ed., London U., UK, 1962; BA, London U./UWI, 1961. **MOTTO:** Sometimes God's purpose in shattering the peace in our lives is to remind us that He has a purpose for everything...make friends with your trials, and you will learn from them. (*Our Daily Bread*) **CONTACT:** ieliston@idirect.com

▶**EMERENCIA, Emerita**
MULTIDISCIPLINARY ARTIST & EDUCATOR. Prologue to the Performing Arts (Artist Representative). Toronto, ON. Born: Aruba/ in Canada since: 1975.

▶ Emerita Emerencia is a multilingual, multidisciplinary artist and educator who works in the media of dance, theatre, song, and storytelling to convey her message. Originally trained as a teacher in Aruba, and not able to practise in Canada without re-training, she pursued an interest in theatre. She is one of the first recipients of the Chalmers Award, 1979, allowing her to study theatre (New Federal Theatre), then dance (Alvin Ailey) in New York. In 1984, she had a leading role in Black Theatre Canada's, *A Caribbean Midsummer Night's Dream*, which won a Dora Mavor Moore Award for Innovation and Artistic Excellence. She was hired by U of T as a dance instructor, and has been teaching both at Hart House and in the Dept. of Athletics and Health Sciences since 1984. In 1991, she was among the choreographers chosen by the National Ballet of Canada for their Creating Dance in the Schools project; in 1996 and '97, was one of five librettists selected by the Cdn Opera Co. for their Creating Opera in the Schools project. In 1998, she travelled to Kenya to present a workshop and to tour with her show, *Food for Thought*, during the IDEA '98 World Congress of Drama/Theatre and Education. As a storyteller, she has performed across Ontario, in Montreal, the Yukon Territories, and the Caribbean. Her story-based presentations have been performed in Dance Immersion's Showcase at Harbourfront; and, she is currently a Course Director of Movement for fourth-year Theatre students at York U. **WORKS:** "Nikiboko," *Pippin*, 2000; "In the Spirit," *Drama Contact*, 1998; "The Artist as an Entrepreneur," *The Arts Paper*, 1997. **REVIEWED IN:** *Dance Current; Yukon News; Pippin* (Toronto storytelling magazine); local and regional media. **EDUCATION:** Theatre, York University. Studied at the Stella Adler Conservatory for Acting; Alvin Ailey Dance Center; apprenticeship, New Federal Theatre, NY, 1979-84. B.Ed, Aruba, 1975. **HEROES/ROLE MODELS:** Amah Harris, theatre director; Lavinia Williams, dance teacher. **MOTTO:** To learn is better than to know. **CONTACT:** contactme@eemerencia.com; www.eemerencia.com

▶**ENYOLU, Evans Rick A.,** PhD.
PUBLISHER/PRINCIPAL CONSULTANT, Multitech Consulting International Inc., 1801 Fernam St., Pickering, ON L1V 4S9. Born: Nigeria/ in Canada since: 1975.

▶ Dr. Evans Enyolu is an economist by training who is now an author and consultant on human rights, economic issues, environmental health problems, non-profit management, sustainable development, and strategic planning. Earlier in his career he served as a senior staff economist for a number of federal government depts. In 1992, he was Program Evaluation Manager at the Dept. of Justice in Ottawa; he has also taught e-conomics, statistics, environmental management and international development at U. of Ottawa and U of T. He is the principal partner in Multitech Consulting Int'l, a firm specializing in E-Commerce, research, policy advice, project planning, management and evaluation. **COMMUNITY ACTIVITIES:** PACT; Red Cross; Nigerian Cdn Assn.; Community Resource Centre, Scarborough; Ontario Hydro Liaison; Domestic Violence Prevention Group; Cdn Adult and Youth Action; Unity Council; Black/ African Cdn

Toronto Community Planning Cmtee; Order-In-Council Appt. (Govt. of Ontario), to Early Years Challenge Fund Program (a matching program that challenges businesses, volunteer and charitable groups to help communities develop new early years programs for all parents and children). **HONS.:** Equity/Human Rights Award, City of Toronto, 2000; Environment Award, Ontario Hydro, 1999. **WORKS:** ed. *Third World Debt Trap*, 2001*; National Investment Options with Venture Capital*, 2000; *Urban Housing Markets*, 1989; ed., *Int'l J of Waste Management; Nigerian Industrial Organization and Policy* (forthcoming). **EDUCATION:** Dipl. E-Commerce, Prime Tech Institute. PhD, Resource Management; MA, Economics; Grad. Dipl., Int'l Development, U. of Ottawa. BA/Hons., Economics, Carleton U. **MOTTO:** Gear your goals to heavenly gains. **CONTACT:** mulconmail@yahoo.ca; www.multitechworldnet.net

▶**ESHO, David**
REALTOR, Prudential Elite Realty, Ste. 100-5090 Explorer Dr., Mississauga, ON. Born: Nigeria/ in Canada since: 1972.

▶ David Esho has been a realtor since 1989 and works with Prudential Elite Realty in Mississauga. He specializes in residential, commercial, and investment properties. From 1980-82, he taught courses in micro-economics and the Canadian economy at Seneca College of Applied Arts and Technology. He has also made two bids at municipal office, running as a candidate in the 1994 and 2000 municipal elections. He is a member of the Brampton Race Relation Action in Council, and was elected as a member to the Institute of Marketing, UK, 1982. **HONS.:** inducted into Honour Society (2000) and Leading Edge Society (2001), Prudential Real Estate World Wide; Granite Award (real estate), 1999. **REVIEWED IN:** local publications, including *Brampton Guardian*; *Share*; *Toronto Star*; *AfriCanadian J.* **EDUCATION:** BAS, Admin. Studies, 1981; BA, Economics, 1980, York University.

Dipl. Marketing, Seneca College, 1977. **HEROES/ ROLE MODELS:** Uncle. **MOTTO:** With God, all things are possible. **CONTACT:** davesho@sprint.ca; Fax: 905-629-0496

▶ ESTRIDGE, Christopher

ARTIST, c/o The Publicity Group, Ste. 300-438 Parliament St., Toronto, ON M5A 3A2. Born: USA/ in Canada since: 1992.

▶ Christopher Estridge is an artist who began his career in New York before moving to Canada in 1992. Encouraged to pursue his interest in drawing, he initially thought to make his career in fashion; after studying at the Fashion Institute of Technology in New York, he worked in the fur salon of Bergdorf Goodman. But, realizing that his dream to create "art" outside of the confines of "fashion" was not being met, he established his own business allowing him to have more time to devote to his art made up of found objects or paintings in the *gouache* style (painting with opaque pigments, ground in water and thickened with a gum-like substance). In 1970, through his affiliation with This and That Gallery in Manhattan, his art began to attract public attention. His large assemblages, composed of objects rescued from the trash became popular and were featured in New York magazines. Since then, his work has been exhibited widely across the US, and his paintings have also been featured in movies such as *Getting Away with Murder*. In Toronto, his work is displayed at the Trias Gallery. **EDUCATION:** Parson's School of Design; School of Visual Arts; Fashion Institute of Technology, New York. **CONTACT:** kpennant@thepublicitygroup.com

▶ ESTRIDGE, Winston

PRESIDENT, Enterprise Solutions North America, Nortel Networks, 2221 Lakeside Blvd., M/Stop 991/16B/20, Richardson, TX, USA. Born: St. Kitts/ in Canada since: 1971.

▶ Winston Estridge has been the President of Nortel Networks' Caribbean, Mexico, and Latin America business since 2001, with complete responsibility for Nortel's business in this region. **CAREER HIGHLIGHTS:** has held numerous executive-level positions with Nortel including: President of Nortel Networks' Enterprise business in N. America, 1999-2001, where he led the company's sales and marketing thrust to Enterprise customers. From 1996-99, he was Senior Vice-President for Nortel's Enterprise Data Networking business in N. America, which included Bay Networks, following his company's acquisition of Bay in 1998. In this position he led Nortel's N. American data thrust to Enterprise customers; his organization leveraged Nortel's core strengths in the wide area network (WAN) products along with Bay's strong data networking portfolio in the campus and local area network (LAN) environments, to offer complete, differentiated, end-to-end solutions to businesses in N. America. He has been with the Nortel family of companies for over 25 yrs. running organizations in the Middle East, Latin America, the Caribbean, the US and Canada. **OTHER:** member, Brd. of Directors, Inroads. **EDUCATION:** MBA, U. of Miami, 1986; B.Ed, U of T, 1977; BSc, Saint Mary's U., NS, 1975. **MOTTO:** If you are willing to work for it then you can accomplish it. **CONTACT:** estridge@ nortelnetworks.com; Fax: 972-684-3772

▶ EVANS, Doris

VOLUNTEER & SENIOR CITIZENS ADVOCATE, Dartmouth, NS. Born: Kentville, NS.

▶ Doris Evans is a retired teacher, with 35 yrs. experience and many years devoted to community service. Some of her activities include: several years' involvement with the BCC/NS; founding member, Black Educators Assn., 1969; founding member, Black Professional Women's Group; initiated and implemented the Seniors Group in East Preston; participated in the educational TV series, *Seniors Need to Know*; member of the Seniors Writers' Guild and assisted with the production of two publications (*Yarns Worth the Telling* and *Poor Houses of Nova Scotia*); VP, Halifax Regional Seniors Council; Brd., Preston Area Boys and Girls Club. **HONS.:** several including: Multicultural Assn., 2000; Plaque from BCC/NS for involvement in Black Battalion Memorial, 1999; Community Leader Award, Cdn Red Cross, 1992; award from Black Educators Assn. for 35 yrs. of service, 1985; YMCA, Recognition of Women, 1982. **WORKS:** co-authored: *Telling the Truth: Segregated Schools of NS.* **EDUCATION:** earned BA equivalent through summer courses from various universities; Teacher's Cert., NS Teachers' College, 1946. **CONTACT:** Fax: 902-434-2306

▶**EWING, Brendon**

MANAGER, Personal Financial Services, RBC Financial Group, 1597 Bedford Hwy, Bedford, NS B4A 1E7. Born: Halifax, NS, 1969.

▶ Brendon Ewing is a senior manager at one of the largest branches of RBC Financial Group in the Atlantic District; he is also the only Black branch manager in this area. RBC Financial Group has approx. 150 branches and business units, employing nearly 3,260 financial services professionals in the Atlantic District. Recently, BE was selected as one of two employees to represent RBC Financial Group, Atlantic Region, in a national TV advertising campaign. **HONS.:** including, six-time nominee & five-time winner of the Top Performer Award for sales, customer service, & leadership, RBC Fin. Group, 1993-98; two-time Royal Performance Conventional Finalist & runner-up, for Top Performer in the County, 1994-96, RBC Fin. Group; recipient of Lt.-Gov. medal for academic achievement, NS Community College, 1989. **EDUCATION:** completing Personal Financial Planning designation; Dipl. Business Admin., NS Community College, 1990. **HEROES/ ROLE MODELS:** Rodger Smith, Mervyn Broome, & Sharon Oliver, friends. **MOTTO:** God, grant me the serenity to accept the things I cannot change; the courage to change the things I can; and, the wisdom to know the difference. **CONTACT:** brendon.ewing@rbc.com

▶FALCONER, Julian N.

BARRISTER, SENIOR PARTNER, Falconer Charney Macklin, 8 Prince Arthur Ave., Toronto, ON M5R 1A9. Born: Canada.

▶ Julian Falconer is a barrister whose practice takes him to civil, administrative, and criminal courts. He has appeared as a senior counsel on matters before each level of court, including the Supreme Court of Canada. In addition to cases of commercial litigation, he has also been involved in human rights and public interest litigations. Having specialized in inquests into the deaths of people in custody, all of whom were marginalized individuals, he was named "Voice for the Powerless" by the *National Post*. His institutional clients have included: the United Church of Canada; Urban Alliance on Race Relations; Chinese Canadian National Council, Toronto; Brampton Caledon Community Living; Organization of Ethnic Employees, Metropolitan Housing Authority. In 1995/96, he successfully represented lawyers in Ontario in class action proceedings over compensation from the Ontario Legal Aid Plan. In June 2000, he co-chaired a conference on Alternatives to the Use of Lethal Force by Police, which brought police and community together to find solutions to fatal police shooting of suspects. **HONS.:** include, Vision of Justice Award, Black Law Students' Assn., 2000; honoured by U of T, as "one of 20th century's 100 most notable graduates for his work on social change in the context of Coroners' Inquests." **WORKS:** has written on constitutional law, issues of race, and the justice system; co-authored book on *Ontario Coroner's Act*, 2001. **REVIEWED IN:** local & nat'l media; profiled in *U of T Alumni Magazine*, 2000. **EDUCATION:** LLB; BA, from: U of T, U. of Alberta, McGill U. **CONTACT:** giselle@ fcmbarristers.com; Fax: 416-929-8179

▶FARRELL, Lennox

TEACHER/COMMUNITY ORGANIZER. Toronto District Catholic School Board, 4640 Finch Av. E., Toronto, ON M1S 4G2. Born: Trinidad & Tobago/ in Canada since: 1969.

▶ Lennox Farrell is a teacher and community organizer who has been at the forefront advocating for social change in Toronto since the 1980s. **HIGHLIGHTS:** successfully negotiated with former City of North York for the transfer of a building to be used by the community as the Marcus Garvey Centre for Leadership and Enterprise; negotiated with the City of Toronto for use of a building as HQ for Caribana; was part of a team that, over a three-year period, met numerous times with the North York Brd. of Education on issues in education concerning Black youth (e.g. streaming, representation in materials and staff, etc.); campaigned for greater police accountability and fairness in the media concerning the portrayal of Black youth; and is involved with many community organizations. He is also a writer of short stories, poetry, pamphlets and essays; his works have been included in print and on electronic media, in community, professional and educational publications. **HONS.:** Canada Annual Centennial Medal, 1995; Jane-Finch Community Award, 1995, '89, '80; Award for "merit in teaching," Ont. English Catholic Teachers Assn., 1993. **REVIEWED IN:** *NOW; Globe and Mail; Toronto Star.* **EDUCATION:** M.Ed, B.Ed, BA, 1973-80, U of T. **HEROES/ROLE MODELS:** Parents. **MOTTO:** The future might hopefully come to the virtuous; but it is definitely taken by the organized. **CONTACT:** lenfar@yahoo.com; Fax: 416-665-4373

▶FARRELL, Vernon W.

PRINCIPAL (Ret.)/ **EDUCATIONAL CONSULTANT,** InclusivEd Associates, 4 Ashglen Way, Unionville, ON L3R 3A7. Born: Trinidad & Tobago/ in Canada since: 1965.

▶ Vernon Farrell was a Principal with the Toronto District School Board (TDSB), from 1971, until his retirement in 1998. Since then, he is an Educational Consultant with InclusivEd Associates, has taken short-term contracts with the TDSB, and has worked on the Board's Cross-Cultural Communications Project. His work was motivated by the belief that: "All students can learn; validation of students' life experiences and culture enables them to see themselves in inclusive curricula as subjects rather than objects." **HIGHLIGHTS:** Community Zion Intervention Program, assisting underachieving Black students; developed a motivational program for Black honours students; founded and edited *Focus* newsletter, a publication of the African Heritage Educators' Network (AHEN), 1991; founded Project 90, a Saturday morning tutorial program for Black students. During his tenure at Brookview Middle School, 1995-98, he restructured the school's focus to include high academic expectations. As a result, the school's benchmarks rose above the system's grade averages in mathematics and literacy. He was a Host Principal, Faculty of Education, York University; was affiliated with the Faculties of Education at U of T, York and Waterloo universities, 1971-97, as a Supervising Principal to teacher candidates. **COMMUNITY INVOLVEMENT:** AHEN, 1990-96; Skills for Change; BBPA; researched for the Brd. of Education, Developing an Anti-Discriminatory School Environment, 1990-91; presented and facilitated a number of workshops on curriculum development and anti-racism. **HONS.:** including, Community Service Award, Town of Markham, 1998; New Pioneers Leadership Award, Skills for Change, 1996; Harry Jerome Award for Leadership, BBPA, 1996. **WORKS:** *Share* newspaper; *Focus* newsletter; *Akili J.* **REVIEWED IN:** community publications, *Toronto Star; Ghanaian News; Share.* **EDUCATION:** M.Ed, OISE/U of T, 1976. Principal's Cert., Ont. Min. of Education, 1971. **CONTACT:** vwfarrell@rogers.com

▶**FARROW-LAWRENCE, Jacquie**
MUNICIPAL CLERK, Municipality of Annapolis County, PO Box 100, Annapolis Royal, NS B0S 1A0. Born: Digby, NS.

▶ Jacquie Farrow-Lawrence was appointed Municipal Clerk, Municipality of Annapolis County, in 1995, and thereby became the first person of African-Aboriginal ancestry to hold such a position in Canada. She joined the Municipality in 1981 as Administrative Secretary. Following a number of promotions, she was appointed Acting Municipal Clerk in 1994; her responsibilities included administration, HR, lockup facilities, animal control/by-law enforcement, administration of unsightly/dangerous premises. In 1995, she assumed her present position. **AFFIL/MBRSHP:** Education Chair, Assn. Municipal Administrators/ NS; Municipality Employment Equity Committee; founding member Council on African Cdn Education; active on several Provincial committees (municipal elections review, etc.). **WORKS:** *Reflections to the Third Power*, ed./publ., 1990. **EDUCATION:** Dipl., Public Management, 1997; Municipal Admin. Program, 1994, Henson College, NS. Business Admin. Program, George Brown College, Toronto, 1979. **HEROES/ROLE MODELS:** Mother & grandmother; Ron Grant, former Clerk. **MOTTO:** Everything I need to know about life, I learned from watching *Star Trek.* **CONTACT:** clerk@annapoliscounty.ns.ca; Tel: 902-532-3131; Fax: 902-532-2096

▶**FEARON, Gervan, PhD.**
ASSISTANT PROFESSOR/ECONOMICS, Atkinson College, York University, 4700 Keele St., Toronto, ON M3J 1P3. Born: Toronto, ON.

▶ Dr. Gervan Fearon is an Assistant Professor of Economics, teaching at York University since 2001. In addition to teaching, he has worked in the public & private sectors. **CAREER HIGHLIGHTS**: taught at U of T in the Division of Management, 1998-2001; continues to teach at the Centre for Industrial Relations at U of T; also taught on a part-time basis at U. of Western Ontario (1997-98), Ryerson Polytechnic (1992-99), U of T, 1992-99, and U. of Guelph, (1984). Public sector: Executive Assistant to the Deputy Minister, Ont.

Min. of Agriculture, Food and Rural Affairs, 1994-96; Senior Analyst, Fiscal Planning, Ont. Min. of Finance, 1993-94; Policy Advisor, Ont. Min. of Agriculture and Food, 1987-91; Research Associate, Cdn Agricultural Services, Chase Econometrics, Div. of Chase Manhattan Bank, Pennsylvania (1984-85). Private sector: is the CEO of Launch Fusion Communications Inc., an award-winning website (www.launchfusion.com), which provides on-line access to over 200 international newspapers and radio stations; is the President of Nucore Business and Economic Services, an economic and business consulting firm; testified before the Copyright Board of Canada on the establishment of a levy on blank cassette tapes and CDs in support of Canadian musicians. **HONS.:** including, WebMaster Award, 2002 & Golden Web Award, 2001, Int'l Assn. of Web Masters & Designers; Volunteer Contribution Award, Tropicana Community Services Org., 2001; Volunteer Award, Higher Marks Educational Institute, 1999 & 2000; Professor of the Year, Management & Economics Students' Assn., U of T, 2000. **WORKS:** a number of research reports & papers; articles, "Endogenous Public Sector Budgeting," in *Can J Economics*; "Labour Union Political Contributions & Campaign Spending," in *Int'l Advances in Economic Research.* **EDUCATION:** PhD, Economics, U. of Western Ontario, 1999; Queen's Strategic Leadership Program, School of Business, Queen's U., 1995. MSc, Agricultural Economics, 1984; BSc, Agricultural Economics, 1981, U. of Guelph. **HEROES/ROLE MODELS:** W. Arthur Lewis; Nelson Mandela; Albert Einstein. **MOTTO:** Yesterday happened, tomorrow will happen, and today is about what we do. **CONTACT:** gfearon@yorku.ca; gervan@launchfusion.com

▶**FÉQUIÈRE, Madeleine, FCI.**
WORLDWIDE DEPARTMENT DIRECTOR, TREASURY/ CREDIT RISK, Abitibi Consolidated Inc., Ste. 800-1155 Metcalfe St., Montreal, QC H3B 5H2. Born: Haïti.

▶ Madeleine Féquière is a Certified Credit Professional with 17 yrs. extensive national and international experience in Credit Risk Management within the Paper for Communications, Telecommunications, Software, Pharmaceutical, Process Control and Food Industries. **CAREER HIGHLIGHTS:** she has held Credit Risk Management positions with companies such as Teleglobe Inc., Microsoft/SI, Foxboro Inc., and ADM/ Ogilvie. In December 2000, she was appointed Worldwide Department Director, Treasury/ Credit Risk Management at Abitibi-Consolidated Inc., headquartered in Montreal. Abitibi-Consolidated is the world's leading newsprint and uncoated groundwood manufacturer, the fifth leading producer of lumber in NA, and has approx. 17,000 employees, 27 paper mills, 22 sawmills and two manufacturing facilities. **OTHER:** MF is an accredited Fellow with the Canadian Credit Institute (www.creditedu.org); an active member of the National Assn. of Credit Managers (www.nacm-canada.org); and, member, Finance Credit Int'l Business (www.fcibglobal.com). She is a regular contributing writer to publications for credit professionals, and is an experienced lecturer in the field of Credit Risk Management. **COMMUNITY INVOLVEMENT:** President, *Résidence Projet Chance* (www.projectchance.org), low-cost housing for single mothers pursuing full-time academic studies; President, *l'Alliance des Femmes d'Affaires et Professionnelles Haïtiennes de Montréal* (www .lapham.com), whose mission is to contribute to the advancement and promotion of Quebecois women of Haitian origin, within the business, political and social sectors; past-President, Mathieu Da Costa BDC. MF has a particular interest in the advancement of women to positions of power. **HONS.:** recipient of several honorary awards for her implication in social and community causes and for her contribution to the promotion of her profession. **WORKS:** articles in *National Credit News; E-Credit News* (on-line newsletter for members of the American Credit Assn.).

EDUCATION: enrolled in Exec. MBA; FCI, Cdn Credit Institute & *Haute Etudes Commerciales*; BA, Concordia U. **HEROES/ROLE MODELS:** Monette Malewski, "power with class and simplicity." **MOTTO:** To go F A R, one has to be Flexible, Adaptable, and Resilient. **CONTACT:** madeleine. fequiere@abicon.com; www.abicon.com

▶**FERNANDES, Lester**
GEOLOGIST (Ret.), COMINCO Ltd. Resides in: Mississauga, ON. Born: Guyana/ in Canada since: 1998.

▶ Lester Fernandes is a retired geologist who was involved with some important mineral discoveries in Mexico and in S. America. During the course of his career, he worked as an Exploration Manager in the Caribbean and Central America, as General Manager of Mineracao Cominco in Brazil, and most recently, as a General Manager with Cominco Peru, from 1994-98. Previously, he worked as mine geologist at Noranda's *Mina Julia* in Chile, as Associate Professor of geology at the U. of Guyana, and in the Guyana Geological Survey Dept., where he led the team that discovered the Upper Mazaruni diamond and gold fields in Guyana, 1958. He was also a participant in the discovery of Cominco's Maria copper mine in Sonora, Mexico in the 1970s. **WORKS:** presented papers on findings at the Fourth Caribbean Geological Conference, 1968; article in *Geological Survey Guyana Records 4*, 1968; *Records 2*, 1965; at the Fifth inter-Guiana Geological Conference, 1961. **EDUCATION:** MSc, Applied Mineral Exploration, McGill U., 1962; BSc, Mining Geology, Royal College of Mines, Imperial College, London U., 1957. **MOTTO:** I do not sleep to dream, but dream to change the world. (from Martin Carter's poem, *Looking at your hands*) **CONTACT:** fernandesll@aol.com

▶**FERRIER, Ross**
INVESTMENT ADVISOR, CIBC Wood Gundy, 123 Commerce Valley Dr. E., Thornhill, ON L3T 7W8. Born: Sudbury, ON, 1971.

▶ Ross Ferrier is an Investment Advisor with CIBC Wood Gundy. He was a member of the RBC Dominion Securities President's Club in 1997 and 1998. RF was a competitive recruit to Merrill Lynch Canada Inc., in 1999, then achieved Executive Club status with CIBC Wood Gundy (formerly Merrill Lynch Canada Inc.), in 2001. Previously, from 1990-96, he played professional baseball with the NY Mets. **REVIEWED IN:** baseball career: *Florida News; Miami Herald; Toronto Star; USA Today; Baseball America; Mississauga News*; *NY Mets* news, etc. Investment career: *Investment Executive; Toronto Star; National Post.* **EDUCATION:** Level II Life Insured, 2000; Professional Financial Planner, 1999; Cdn Securities, 1997; BA/Hons., Econ/Math, U. of Waterloo, 1994. **HEROES/ROLE MODELS:** Michael Lee-Chin; Vernon G. Michael. **MOTTO:** You're either in…or in the way! **CONTACT:** ross. ferrier@cibc.ca

▶**FIELDS, The Reverend Stephen**
INCUMBENT, The Anglican Church of St. Stephen, 2259 Jane St., Downsview, ON M3M 1A6. Born: Barbados/ in Canada since: 1993.

▶ The Reverend Stephen Fields has been the Incumbent (minister) at The Church of St. Stephen since 1996. **CAREER HIGHLIGHTS:** after completing his Master of Sacred Theology degree (STM) in New York, he returned to Barbados in 1982 and spent the next 11 yrs. serving the church at the parochial and diocesan levels. In 1993, he was invited to be the Associate Priest at the Church of St. Michael and All Angels, Toronto. He was appointed to his present Incumbency on July 1, 1996. Active in his own parish, he also coordinates ministry events within the Black Anglican community in Toronto, such as the first and subsequent Black History Eucharistic services, 1996-99, in the Diocese of Toronto, and coordinated the planning of the fifth Caribbean

Anglican Consultation (CAC), which was held in Toronto, 1999, and assisted with the planning of CAC-6 in Nassau, Bahamas, 2001. The CAC is a biennial conference, which began in 1991, for the Clergy and Laity in the Anglican Church in N. America and the Caribbean. Its purpose is to examine the ministry and ministry needs of the clergy and those of the congregants from the Caribbean and the Caribbean Diaspora, to determine how the congregants are contributing to the life of their church communities and how the Church is responding to their needs. Participation is no longer limited to clergy but is open to all who minister with and among people of Caribbean heritage. Since 1996, he has served as the Chaplain to the Caribbean Chorale of Toronto, an ecumenical choir of Caribbean heritage, established in 1993. **HONS.:** Award of Recognition for leadership in the Caribbean Anglican Community in NA, 1999. **WORKS:** "Alienated for Years, Black Anglicans Still Faithful to their Church," *The Anglican*, 1997; co-author, "Black Anglicans Travel Long Road Towards Acceptance in Diocese," *The Anglican*, 1995. **REVIEWED IN:** "Black Priest gives Church Lessons in Cultural Diversity," *Toronto Star*, 1996; "Overwhelming Community Response to Church Outreach Programme," *Jamaican Weekly Gleaner*, 1996. **EDUCATION:** Master of Sacred Theology, The General Theological Seminary, NY, 1982; BA/Hons., Theology, UWI, 1980; Dipl. Theology, Codrington College, Barbados, 1980. **MOTTO:** I can do all things through Him who strengthens me. **CONTACT:** stelumar@sympatico.ca; www.saintstephenstoronto.com

▶**FITZ-RITSON, Don,** DC, FCCRS, DACRB. **DIRECTOR,** Advanced Therapeutic Centre, Ste. 800-8 King St. E., Toronto, ON M5C 1B5. Born: Jamaica/ in Canada since: 1969.

▶ Dr. Don Fitz-Ritson is a chiropractor by training and specializes in the treatment of chronic pain with a combination of laser, chiropractic and nutrition. Since 1999, he has incorporated NeuroLink into his practice for treating all health conditions; he has been teaching and practising since 1979. **CAREER HIGHLIGHTS:** he is the Director of the Advanced Therapeutic Centre, which he opened in 1996. He has lectured in Europe, the US, throughout Canada, in Hawaii, and in Barbados; he teaches at the Cdn Memorial College of Chiropractic (CMCC) where he has held the following positions: Lecturer in Neuroscience, 1979-83; Asst. Prof., 1983-2002; Adjunct Prof., Post Graduate Div., 1983-90. During this time, he also held the position of Chair, Chiropractic Science Dept., 1987-88. **OTHER PROFESSIONAL POSITIONS:** Consultant, FDA Low Back Study, and VP, R&D, Accelerate Health Care Centres, 1999 to present; VP, Posture Research Institute, since 1995; VP, Physical Rehabilitation, Int'l Managed Healthcare Centres, 1993-95; Director, Chiropractic Health Centre, 1980-94. **CURRENT PROJECTS:** developing a low-back disc exerciser; developing specific Laser Protocols for Bone Spurs; writing a book, *Worker Health–Sitting*; developed a Cervical Traction Unit, presently being clinically tested. He has spoken on radio, TV and in the press on lower back pain, whiplash injury, the spine and other related topics. **WORKS:** 18 research papers and three book chapters. **REVIEWED IN:** *Jamaican Canadians: A Commitment to Excellence*, 1987; *Globe and Mail*. **EDUCATION:** Diplomate, Am. Chiropractic Rehab. Brd., 2000; Fellow, College of Chiropractic Rehabilitation Specialists/Canada, 1996; Graduate courses in Neurophysiology, U of T, 1979-83; Doctor of Chiropractic, CMCC, 1979; BA/Hons., U. of Waterloo, 1974. **MOTTO:** Always do your best. **CONTACT:** info@backmagic.com; www.backmagic.com

▶**FLEGEL, Peter**
YOUTH ADVOCATE/COMMUNITY ORGANIZER, Black Youth in Action, 29 Burton Ave., Westmount, QC H3Z 1J6. Born: Haiti, 1978/ in Canada since: 1979.

▸ Peter Flegel is co-founder and former co-chair of Black Youth in Action (BYIA), an association that advocates for Black youth and provides services designed to facilitate their integration into the social, economic, and political life of Quebec and Canada. **HIGHLIGHTS:** completely bilingual, PF has been a spokesperson on a number of issues of particular interest and concern to Quebec's Black population, and to gays and lesbians of diverse ethnic backgrounds; was one of the organizers of Quebec's first round table on "racism, sexism, and homophobia," and the province's first Black media forum; helped to organize and co-moderated the Black Community Political Rally, the first bilingual political rally in Quebec bringing together representatives of the four main federal political parties (2000 federal elections) to debate issues of concern to Montreal's Black population. Sits on the Board, NCC/Charles H. Este Cultural Centre; attended UNWCAR in S. Africa, 2001; has spoken at academic conferences including the ACS' Minorities of African Descent in the Americas. He has been the subject of short documentaries on Global TV and Canal Vie. **OTHER:** composes, sings and arranges music; has sung backup for Michael Bolton, Paul Anka, Chris de Burgh, and others. **HONS.:** include, GG Academic Medal, Dawson College; Arts Sector Awards, Social Science & Humanities, Dawson College; Powell Entrance Scholarship, for academic excellence & community involvement, McGill U. **WORKS:** "Homophobia in the Black Community," *Community Contact*; "The Challenges of Human Rights Praxis," *Human Rights Tribune*; "Challenges to Cdn Multiculturalism: the case of Black Montreal," *Can Issues*. **REVIEWED IN:** several publications including, *BHM Calendar, 2002; Montreal Gazette; La Presse; Le Devoir; J du Barreau.* **EDUCATION:** MA, in progress; BA, 2001, McGill University. DEC, Dawson College, 1998. **MOTTO:** Our basic challenge is to discover how to organize our strength in terms of economic and political power. (Martin Luther King Jr.) **CONTACT:** philodoc@hotmail.com

▶**FOGGO, Cheryl**
WRITER/JOURNALIST/FILM DIRECTOR. c/o The Jennifer Hollyer Agency, Toronto, ON. Born: Calgary, AB.
▸ Cheryl Foggo is an award-winning writer of fiction, non-fiction, poetry, and plays; she also writes for TV and film. She is a descendant of the migration of Black Oklahomans who settled in Amber Valley, AB and Maidstone, SK, in 1910. **FILM CREDITS:** wrote and directed, *The Journey of Lesra Martin,* 2002, about the young man who was the catalyst for the freeing of Rubin "Hurricane" Carter (*see: Carter, Rubin*), a National Film Board (NFB) production; *Love Hurts,* 1998, finalist for the Alberta Motion Picture Industry Awards; *The Higher Law,* co-written for *North of Sixty*; for two and a half seasons, she was a member of the TV series, *North of Sixty's,* story-writing team; *Carol's Mirror,* 1992, winner of numerous national and international educational film awards. **BOOKS:** include *Pourin' Down Rain,* her first book and a chronicle of her ancestors' journey from Africa to America to northwestern Canada. This book was a finalist for the Alberta Culture Non-fiction Award, 1990. Her first young adult novel, *One Thing that's True,* was nominated for the GG, the Blue Heron, the Mr. Christie and the R. Ross Annett Book Awards, 1997; and, a screen adaptation of this book has been completed. **THEATRE:** her play, *Heaven,* about a Black school teacher who arrives from the East to teach in Amber Valley, in 1927, was a finalist for Theatre BC's National Playwriting Competition (2000) and was produced by Lunchbox Theatre (2001); *Heaven* is also being developed as a full-length play for the Obsidian Theatre Co. in Toronto, for their 2003/04 season; *Heaven* has also been commissioned by CBC Radio for national broadcast. The play, *Turnaround,* was co-written with her husband (also a playwright, with whom she has collaborated on films and plays) and was produced by Lunchbox and Quest Theatres, 1999/2000, and was a finalist for the

Betty New Play Award. **HONS.:** several including: *I Have Been in Danger*, finalist, R. Ross Annett Book Award, 2001. Best Educational Program, Gold Apple Award & Short Drama Award, for *Carol's Mirror*, 1992; one of three winners of the Great North Television Writing Competition, 1995; Mr. Christie Book Award & GG Award nomination for *One Thing That's True*, 1997; Overall Achievement Award, BAASA, 1998. **WORKS:** articles in, *Canadian; Calgary Magazine; Western Living; The Herald*. Books: *I Have Been in Danger*, 2001; *One Thing That's True*, 1997; *Pourin' Down Rain*, 1990. **REVIEWED IN:** *Avenue Magazine*, as "One of Ten Calgarians to Watch." **EDUCATION:** Journalism Program, Mount Royal College, Calgary. **CONTACT:** martini@ucalgary.ca; Fax: 403-288-1138

▶**FORDE, Keith**

SUPERINTENDENT OF POLICE, Toronto Police Service, 40 College St., Toronto, ON M5G 2J3. Born: Barbados/ in Canada since: 1969.

▶ Keith Forde has been policing in the City of Toronto for over 30 years. In January 2001, he was promoted to the rank of Superintendent, making him the highest-ranking minority officer in the history of the Toronto Police Service. With this promotion, he was assigned to head the Service's Community Policing Support. **CAREER HIGHLIGHTS:** was the Officer in Charge of the Police Service's Professional Standards Complaints Review Unit; was the Unit Commander of 11 Division in the west end of Toronto for five yrs., 1992-97. With over 29 yrs. in leadership roles, he is described as having exhibited strength and objectivity in conflict resolution and problem solving. He has served in various policing units including Motorcycle Patrol, Uniform Patrol, Undercover Drug Enforcement, Detective Branch; as a Liaison Officer; and on the Police Services Board. He has held senior management positions at Duty Operations, 52 Div., 11 Div., Toronto Police Services Board Internal Prosecut-

ing Services Unit, and the Professional Standards Complaints Review Unit; 1995-97, he was Aide-de-Camp to the Hon. Henry N.R. Jackman, then Lt.-Gov. of Ontario. **HONS.:** numerous awards and recognitions, ACAA; Chief of Police Excellence Award; City of York Award; Parkdale Gold Star Appreciation Award; Province of Ontario Award; Barbadian-Cdn Assn. Award and the Bob Marley Award; Human Rights and Race Relations Gold Medal, Town of Ajax; Black History Achievers Award. **REVIEWED IN:** *Pride; Share; Caribbean Camera; Toronto Star; Toronto Sun.* **EDUCATION:** Management Development Program, U of T, 1991; Public Admin., Ryerson U.; Investigative Science & Police Studies, Seneca College, 1984. **CONTACT:** keithforde@sympatico.ca

▶**FOX, Lovena**

ACTOR/SINGER/SONGWRITER, Vancouver, BC. Born: Vancouver, BC.

▶ Lovena Fox is an actor, singer and songwriter who has many credits to her name in each field. **THEATRE:** she completed a US tour with the Tony-Award winning musical, *Ragtime*, for which she was nominated Best Actress, 2001 National Broadway Theater Awards; she was involved with *Ragtime* from 1996, having been cast by the Chicago, Broadway, Los Angeles, and Vancouver production companies. Other theatre credits include: *Jekyll and Hyde; Sophisticated Ladies; Ain't Misbehavin'* (nominated for a Jessie Award); *The Colored Museum; Black and Gold Revue; It's Time to Sing; Razz M'Jazz*; and, *Little Shop of Horrors.* **SONG:** she was the lead singer of the duo, Love and Sas, which recorded for BMG/RCA; she was lead vocals on four top-10 singles in Canada, for which the group won two Juno Awards (Best R&B single, 1992 and 1993); one of these singles, *Don't Stop Now*, reached No. 42 on *Billboard Magazine's* charts in the US. She has also sung background vocals for Bon Jovi, the band, Little Caesar, Colin James, and the Payolas. LF began her singing career with the R&B band, HB Concept, which won the CBC Fame Game and the West Coast Music Award, for "most promising act"; she also performed on the National Talent show, *Star Search*, and a number of variety shows; her performances have taken her to England, Germany, Israel, Egypt, and Cypress. Her latest CD, *Holdin' Out* was released in 2001. **FILM AND TV CREDITS:** *Cousins; Boy Meets Girl; Secrets of a Married Man; Airwolf II; Stir Crazy; Secret Lives*, and others. **HONS.:** MuchMusic Award, Best R&B Video, 1993; Juno Award, Best R&B single, 1992, 1993. **CONTACT:** www.lovenafox.com

▶**FRANCIS, Flora H. Blizzard**

AUTHOR/LIBRARIAN (Ret.), University of Guelph, ON. Born: Trinidad & Tobago/ in Canada since: 1959.

▶ Flora Blizzard Francis began working as a librarian in Trinidad, in 1952, and continued in this profession until her retirement in 1994, from the University of Guelph. **CAREER:** Librarian, Trinidad, 1952-58; Librarian, U. of Guelph, 1959-94; from early 2000 to mid-2001, Librarian, Brantford Symphony Orchestra. Over the course of her career, she compiled two bibliographies and wrote articles for library journals. **AFFIL/ MBRSHP:** 1960-95: American Library Assn., Cdn Library Assn.; Institute of Professional Librarians of Ontario (IPLO); Assn. Cdn Map Libraries and Archives (ACMLA); Soroptimist Int'l, since 1971; Guelph Spring Festival Volunteer, 1965-2001; St. George's Anglican Church. **HONS.:** including, Ont. Volunteer Service Award, for 35-yrs. volunteering with the Guelph Spring Festival, 2001; Hall of Fame Award, Soroptimist Int'l, 1996; Teaching & Learning Committee Award, for compilation of slide & phono disc, West Indian Collection, U. of Guelph, 1984. **WORKS:** books: *A Black Canadian Bibliography*, 2000; *West Indians in Canada*, 1970. Articles in: *Cartographica; Ontario Newsletter; Ontario Library Review; Can Library J.* **EDUCATION:** MLS, 1978;

BLS, 1969, U of T. BA, Waterloo Lutheran U. (now Wilfrid Laurier U.), 1965; Associate, Library Assn. (British), 1958; Eastern Caribbean Regional Library School, T&T, 1958. **MOTTO:** Slow and steady wins the race! **CONTACT:** ffrancis @uoguelph.ca

▶**FRANCIS, Ken K.,** CFP.

CEO & PRESIDENT, Ken K. Francis Financial Services, Ste. 207-550 St. Clair Ave. W., Toronto, ON M6C 1A5. Born: Trinidad & Tobago/ in Canada since: 1967.

▶ Ken Francis has been a broker and has operated his financial services office since 1978. He has also been an agent of the Crown Life (now Canada Life) Insurance Co. since 1969, and is one of the leading brokers in Canada. **CAREER HIGHLIGHTS:** life membership, Million Dollar Round Table (MDRT), an international organization whose members are in the top five per cent in sales of all financial and insurance brokers in the world; Top of the Table, three times (top three per cent of the MDRT); member, Court of the Table, 16 times (annual sales over $2-million Cdn, in premium); 25 times Crown Life President's Circle. In 1997, he became a Certified Financial Planner. **COMMUNITY:** Waverley Lodge, no. 361, since 1975; Bathurst Lions Club, 1980s; Caribana Cultural Committee; St. George's Anglican Church. **HONS.:** won a number of awards related to insurance and financial services: 29 National Quality; at Crown Life, 25 Crown Quality; 25 President's Circle; three Century Club; five Royal Crown Life Club, Leader of Excellence. **REVIEWED IN:** *Toronto Life*; Crown Life *Sales Pulse*; Crown Life *Contact.* **EDUCATION:** CFP, 1997; MBA, Syracuse U., 1995; Life Underwriters Training Courses, 1971-90; Dipl., Business Management Program, Ryerson Polytechnic, 1971. **MOTTO:** Reach for the top! **CONTACT:** ffrancis@uoguelph.ca

▶FRANCIS, Mayann

EXECUTIVE DIRECTOR, Nova Scotia Human Rights Commission, PO Box 2221, 1690 Hollis St., Halifax, NS B3J 3C4. Born: Sydney, NS.

▶ Mayann Francis has been the Executive Director of the Nova Scotia Human Rights Commission since 1999. In 2000, she was also appointed Ombudsman for the province of Nova Scotia, and thereby the first woman to hold the position of Ombudsman in Nova Scotia. **CAREER HIGHLIGHTS:** Assistant Deputy Minister, Ontario Provincial-Municipal Education and Training Secretariat, 1997-99; Assistant Deputy Minister, Ontario Women's Directorate, 1994-97; was the first Black woman appointed to this position; was the first Black woman appointed by the provincial government in NS, with Deputy Head status. She was also Employment Equity Officer, Dalhousie U., 1990-93; and, Administrative Manager, Equal Employment Opportunity Coordinator, Office of the District Attorney, NY, 1986-1990. Of her various experiences and being a pioneer in public administration, she notes: "Being the first and most often the only Black, has not been easy. The expectations of people are far greater than anyone can imagine. It is because of my belief in God and my spirit that I have been able to survive. I believe that my spirit can climb as high as I want it to." **COMMUNITY INVOLVEMENT:** Brd.,Voluntary Planning; co-chair, International Project Advisory Committee (Brazil), and past Brd. member; United Way of Canada; Beverly Mascoll Community Foundation. **AFFIL/MBRSHP:** previously: member, Brd. of Governors, University College of Cape Breton; Black Educators Assn.; Black Social Workers. **HONS.:** Award, for exemplary contribution and commitment to improving race relations, Multicultural Education Society of NS, 2001; Harry Jerome Award, for Professional Excellence, 2000; recognized by Congress of Black Women/Preston, NS "for outstanding work in human rights," 2000; Special Recognition Award, Rubena Willis Counselling Centre for Assaulted Women and Children, Ontario, 1996. **WORKS:** in, *Multicultural Health Assn. Bulletin; St. Paul's J; Dalhousie News; Southender.* **REVIEWED IN:** selected: *Globe and Mail; Halifax Chronicle Herald; The Halifax Daily News; Cape Breton Post; Millennium Minds,* 2000. **EDUCATION:** M. Public Admin., New York U., 1984; BA, Saint Mary's U., NS, 1972. **HEROES/ROLE MODELS:** Archpriest G.A. Francis & Thelma Francis, parents; Beverly Mascoll . **MOTTO:** Stay positive and focused. Always remember your spirit and give thanks to our Creator. **CONTACT:** francime@gov.ns.ca; Fax: 902-424-2407

▶FRANCIS, Pat, D.Div.

SENIOR PASTOR, FOUNDER, Deeper Life Christian Ministries, 1224 Dundas St. E., Unit 20, Mississauga, ON L4Y 4A2. Born: Jamaica/ in Canada since: 1976.

▶ Dr. Pat Francis is the Senior Pastor and Founder of Deeper Life Christian Ministries Int'l, Deeper Life Family Church, Deeper Life Community Services, and Pat Francis Ministries. Leaving her profession as a radiographer, in 1990, she began her ministry while volunteering in the foreign missions field. She travelled to countries in Africa, Asia, S. America and the Caribbean, "preaching the gospel and equipping local converts for effective Christian service." The church's weekly attendance is reported at over 3,000; major focus of the Ministry is reaching children and youth at risk; programs have been developed to provide academic, social, and spiritual enhancement to young people. Her TV program, *Washed by the Word* airs weekly and is seen across Canada, the US, in Uganda, and the Caribbean. In addition, she is President and CEO of Admarie Int'l, a multi-media company. **AFFIL/MBRSHP:** Brd., Evangelical Fellowship of Canada; member, Women Presidents' Organization of N. America. **HONS.:** include: Black History Makers Award, 2002; Black Woman of Distinction Award, 2000; Black Women Appreciation Award, 1995. **REVIEWED IN:** community & local newspapers, *Who's Who of Professionals.* **EDUCATION:** D.Div, 1996; M.Div, 1994, School of Theology. Dipl. Radiography, UWI; Certified Psychotherapist & Counselor, CICC. **MOTTO:** God will give you the ability to achieve if you have the faith to believe. **CONTACT:** info@deeperlife.net; www.deeperlife.net; www.patfrancis.org

▶**FRANCIS, Verlyn F.**

LAWYER, Law Office of Verlyn F. Francis, Ste. 2000-393 University Ave., Toronto, ON M5G 1E6.

▶ Verlyn Francis completed her studies in law in 1996 and opened her office in 1997, specializing in corporate/commercial, family, estates, civil litigation and mediation. In 2001, she was a law instructor in the School of Legal and Public Administration at Seneca College. **COMMUNITY ACTIVITIES:** Brd., Toronto Board of Trade; Toronto Community Foundation; past Chair, Harry Jerome Scholarship Fund. In 2001, she developed and implemented strategic plans that garnered $100,000 for 30 bursary awards, and persuaded volunteers and senior executives of corporations to donate time and resources towards post-secondary bursaries and grants. **HONS.:** including, Volunteer of the Year Award, BBPA, 2001; several academic prizes. **EDUCATION:** Advanced Family Mediation, LSUC, 1999; LLB, Osgoode Hall Law School, York U., 1995; BA (partial), U of T. **CONTACT:** verlyn.francis@sympatico.ca

▶**FRANÇOIS, Pierre**

MECHANICAL ENGINEER/TEACHER (Ret.), Pierre Mechanical Engineering Consultant, Toronto, ON. Born: Trinidad & Tobago/ in Canada since: 1972.

▶ Pierre François trained in mechanical engineering in Trinidad; there he was Assistant Mechanical Engineer, Trinidad Government Railway, then Mechanical Supervisor, Public Transport Corp.

In Canada, was a part-time teacher of technology with the Toronto District School Board (TDSB), 1980-98; worked with CN Railways, 1973-85, as an Automotive Technician; was an Automotive Mentor/Coach at Centennial College, 2000. He continues to act as a Society of Auto Engineers Consultant to the TDSB. **MBRSHP:** Institute of Road Transport Engineers; Society of Automobile Engineers; Cdn Alliance of Black Educators; U of T Alumni Assn. **HONS.:** Arbor Award, for volunteerism, U of T, 2000. **WORKS:** article, "Tractor-trailer Air Brake System Improvement," Institute of Road Transport Engineers publication. **EDUCATION:** B.Ed, 1997; Technical Education Dipl., 1979, U of T. BA, Athabasca U., 1996; BSc, Eng., Jackson State U., FLA, 1972.

▶**FRASER, Felix (Fil), CM.**

WRITER/JOURNALIST/FILMMAKER, Edmonton, AB. Born: Montreal, QC.

▶ Fil Fraser has been a life-long journalist, radio, television and film producer. Now based in Edmonton, he has taken on a role as Adjunct Professor of Communication Studies at Athabasca University, where he will help to develop a new website dedicated to media study and a number of master's level courses in media and communications. From 1995 until his retirement in 2000, he served as the President and CEO of Vision TV, in Toronto. **CAREER HIGHLIGHTS:** born and raised in Montreal, he began his broadcasting career at CKFH in Toronto, later working as an announcer, a hockey broadcaster, disc jockey and newsman at radio stations in Timmins, Barrie, and Montreal. In 1958, he moved to Regina and worked in public relations before founding the *Regina Weekly Mirror*, in 1960, which chronicled the introduction of Medicare by Tommy Douglas. In 1969, having moved to Edmonton, he joined the Metropolitan Edmonton Educational TV Assn. and was program manager of Canada's first educational TV station, which went on the air in March, 1970. He was the co-host of CBC

Edmonton's evening news and public affairs program, 1971-73, and served as the summer replacement host of *Take 30,* the national public affairs program. During the 1970s he wrote, produced and directed several documentary films for TV, and in 1976 he produced, *Why Shoot the Teacher,* one of the country's most successful feature films. He followed with *Marie Anne,* in 1977, and *The Hounds of Notre Dame,* in 1980. All received theatrical distribution and won awards. In 1974, he organized and chaired the first Alberta Film Festival, later founding the now renowned Banff International Television Festival. In 1977, he was a member of the Alberta Task Force on Film, whose report led to the establishment of the Alberta Motion Picture Development Corp. In 1985, he was appointed by the Communications Minister to the Federal Task Force on Broadcasting Policy. Their 1986 report formed the basis for a new Cdn Broadcasting Act. After being appointed to the Cdn Multiculturalism Council in 1987, he organized and chaired a National Forum on Broadcasting and Multiculturalism, Reflections in the Electronic Mirror, held in Toronto, 1988. From 1989-92, he was Chief Commissioner of the Alberta Human Rights Commission; later developing and teaching a course on The Evolution of Human Rights to third year students in the Faculty of Law at U. of Alberta. **AFFIL/MBRSHP:** founding member and Chair of Specialty and Premium TV Assn.; former director, Alberta Performing Arts Foundation; member, U. of Alberta Senate, 1970-76; founding member, Academy of Cdn Cinema; former Chair, Media Awareness Network; Governor, Cdn Journalism Foundation; CABJ; former director, Ontario Heritage Foundation; director, Cdn Broadcast Museum Foundation; he also sits on a number of corporate boards. **HONS.:** Fil Fraser Lecture Series, launched in his honour by CABJ, 2001; Order of Canada, 1991; Lifetime Hon. Director of the Banff Int'l Television Festival; Dave Billington Award, 1990; Alberta Achievement Award, 1978; Gov. Emeritus, Banff

Centre School of Fine Arts. **WORKS:** forthcoming, *A Memoir of Camelot* (working title) on Alberta's support of the arts during the 1970s; numerous articles & stories in newspapers, magazines & journals; his memoir on Cdn multiculturalism appeared in the 100th Anniv. issue of *Saturday Night Magazine.* **REVIEWED IN:** *WWIC; Some Black Men,* 1999. **EDUCATION:** McGill U. **HEROES/ ROLE MODELS:** Felix Blache Fraser, father, Canada's first Black real estate developer; Rheo Thompson, broadcaster, CFCF Montreal. **MOTTO:** Stand tall, but never forget whose shoulders you are standing on. **CONTACT:** fbfraser@telusplanet.net

▶**FRASER, Frank M., P.Eng.**
VP MARKET DEVELOPMENT (Ret.), MDS Nordion. Kanata, ON. Born: Montreal, QC.
▶ Frank Fraser is a Professional Engineer, who has played a significant role in developing food irradiation techniques and thereby representing Canadian industry and innovation internationally. **CAREER HIGHLIGHTS:** when he joined Atomic Energy of Canada Ltd. (AECL) in 1964, it was as a Project Engineer designing irradiation facilities to sterilize disposable medical products. He later headed up the Industrial Irradiation Division, and became VP Market Development, the position he held until his retirement in 1999. As VP, Market Development for MDS Nordion (formerly the Commercial Products Div. of AECL), he developed and implemented programs, which saw the spread of Canadian technology to many countries. He is a pioneer and champion of cobalt 60-based technologies, and has brought food irradiation to the attention of the world. Canadian-developed food irradiation procedures are rapidly gaining acceptance throughout the world as a safe, cost-effective means of extending the shelf life of food in countries where spoilage rates can approach 50%. He participated in the design, supply, and installation of more than 75% of MDS Nordion's industrial irradiation plants currently operating in more than 40 countries. He

was instrumental in establishing the Food Technology Services facility in Florida (the world's first dedicated commercial-scale food irradiation facility), as well as the Canadian Irradiation Centre at Laval, Quebec. He has also played a leading role in developing procedures to safely irradiate cosmetic raw materials, pharmaceutical products, and for the stabilization of sewage. **AFFIL/MBRSHP:** past Chair, Int'l Atomic Energy Agency (IAEA) Task Force of Int'l Experts on Irradiation Technology; past Chair, Assn. of Int'l Industrial Irradiation (AIII); represented Canada at a number of int'l meetings and consultations on food irradiation; chaired the Int'l Meeting on Radiation Processing (IMRP); chaired a Gamma Processing Seminar; has given several radio and TV interviews on food irradiation. **OTHER:** prior to his career at the AECL, he was an athlete playing both hockey and football; was likely the first Black Canadian halfback to play in the CFL; from 1956-64 he played with the Montreal Alouettes, Ottawa Rough Riders, Winnipeg Blue Bombers, Regina Roughriders, and the Edmonton Eskimos; he was recognized as one of the fastest halfbacks in the CFL; was a member of the 1962 Grey Cup-winning team, the Winnipeg Blue Bombers. He continued his involvement with sports by coaching junior football and minor hockey. **HONS.:** including, Ontario Marketer of the Year; Hon. Life Member, for service to the Assn. of Int'l Industrial Irradiation, 1999; City of Kanata Recognition Award, for leadership & commitment to youth; honoured at Int'l Meeting on Radiation Processing, Holland; member of Who's Who in American Colleges. **WORKS:** has delivered papers in US and internationally on food irradiation. **REVIEWED IN:** trade magazines and *Ascent Magazine* (Atomic Energy of Canada), 1985; *AEC Source*, 1985; *Ottawa Citizen*, 1992. **EDUCATION:** BSc, Mechanical Engineering, Tennessee State U. (TSU), 1964. **HEROES/ROLE MODELS:** Roy Errington, former president & founder, AECL; Dr. J. Parsons, TSU. **MOTTO:** You can achieve anything if you believe in yourself. A

man's inhibitions are self-inflicted. **CONTACT:** ffraser@compmore.net

▶**FRASER, James H.,** CWO, MMM.
CHIEF WARRANT OFFICER (Ret.), Canadian Forces, Department of National Defence. Resides in Porters Lake, NS. Born: Dartmouth, NS.
▶ CWO James Fraser joined the Canadian Forces in 1964 and retired in 1998. During that time he had many accomplishments: one of very few members of a minority group to obtain the rank and appointment of Master Warrant Officer (MWO) in an Infantry Company; only the second Black soldier in Canada to be appointed Regimental Sergeant Major (RSM) of an Infantry Battalion; first Black Serviceman to be appointed as an Area RSM. **CAREER HIGHLIGHTS:** after completion of his basic training in 1965, served six yrs. as a rifleman and section second in command and as a company signaler for tour of UN peacekeeping duty in Cyprus; served seven yrs. in the 2nd Battalion as a section-in-command, section commander, recruit instructor, and for a second tour of duty in Cyprus; 1977, posted to Germany as a section commander in the Anti-Armour Platoon; with promotion to Warrant Officer, served as a platoon second-in-command, 1979-81; following the Europe Tour, he returned to the School of Infantry in Gagetown, was promoted to MWO, 1982, and served as Sergeant Major of G Company; completed his third tour of duty in Cyprus, 1983-84. On promotion to the rank of CWO, 1988, he was posted to the Air Defence Artillery School Tactical Cell until 1990; July, 1990, he was appointed RSM of the 1st Battalion. Upon completion of his three-year tour, he was appointed Area RSM of Land Force Central Area, 1993-97; this included being RSM of the UN Disengagement Force Golan Heights Israel-occupied Syria. **HONS.:** several including, Member, Order of Military Merit, 1998.

▶FRITZBERG, Daléus

ORGANISATEUR COMMUNAUTAIRE, Centre d'Union Multiculturelle & Artistique des Jeunes (CUMAJ), bur. 201-10125, rue Parthenais, Montréal, QC H2B 2L6. Né: Haïti/ au Canada depuis: 1972.

▶ Daléus Fritzberg, est membre-fondateur et directeur général du CUMAJ depuis 1989. Il est aussi intervenant et organisateur communautaire auprès des jeunes de diverses communautés culturelles et auprès du Service de Police de la Communauté Urbaine de Montréal (SPCUM). **ACTIVITÉS PRINCIPALES:** 1998-1999, il était directeur de la table-ronde du Mois de l'Histoire des Noirs; en 1995, il était observateur des élections législatives en Haïti pour le gouvernement canadien auprès de l'Organisation des États américains, ainsi qu'attaché culturel au consulat général d'Haïti à Montréal. Outre ses engagements politiques et communautaires, il est animateur de plusieurs émissions radiophoniques en français et en créole, dont Krik-Krak, Radio Centre-Ville et VWA PA NOU, Radio CFMB 1410 AM. Il travaille pour les médias depuis plusieurs années, notamment comme chroniqueur et recherchiste au canal 9 (Vidéotron) pour l'émission *De ville en ville* de 1993-95, et pour l'émission *Publi-Cité* de radio CKUT entre 1991 et 1993. Il a aussi été producteur de spectacles et créateur artistique à titre d'auteur, compositeur et interprète de chansons. En 1990 et en 2001, il s'est présenté comme candidat aux élections municipales à Montréal. **PRIX:** y compris: Prix Claire Heureuse, Personnalité de l'Année, 1996; Médaille d'or, 1985 et Mention d'excellence, 1984, Concours des artistes peintres du Québec. **FORMATION:** Études, Cinématographie et Scénarisation, 1993; Cert. en Arts-plastiques, 1991, UQAM. Dipl., Journalisme communautaire, Radio Centre-Ville, 1989; Dipl., Sciences humaines, Collège Marie Victorin. **MENTORS:** Toussaint L'Ouverture, 1er génie et l'instigateur de la lutte des esclaves à St. Domingue. **MOTTO:** Instaurer la paix à l'intérieur de sa propre personne pour faire échec à toutes les guerres. **CONTACT:** Tél: 514-389-6644; Fax: 514-389-2136; cumaj@vif.com

▶FUHR, Grant

FORMER GOALTENDER, NHL/**GOALTENDING CONSULTANT,** Calgary Flames, AB. Born: Spruce Grove, AB.

▶ Grant Fuhr played 19 seasons in the NHL and was a leading goaltender, becoming only the sixth in NHL history to record over 400 career wins before his retirement in 2000. **CAREER HIGHLIGHTS:** was drafted by the Edmonton Oilers in 1981 where he played until 1991, during which time they won five Stanley Cups (1984, 1985, 1987, 1988, and 1990); he played six times in NHL All-Star Games (1982, 1984-86, 1988, and 1989); he set an NHL record for most assists/points by a goaltender, by recording 14 assists, in the 1983-84 season; he posted a career high of 40 wins and four shut-outs, in the 1987-88 season; then in 1991, after setting a number of records and awards, he played his final season with the Edmonton Oilers, where he still holds the franchise record for most wins (226). He then played for the Toronto Maple Leafs, from 1991-93, when he was traded to the Buffalo Sabres; there, in the 1993-94 season he and Dominik Hasek won the Jennings Trophy for the lowest GAA. In 1994-95, he was traded to the Los Angeles Kings; 1995-96, he was signed as a free agent by the St. Louis Blues and that season he played in a career high of 79 games with 76 consecutive starts (setting a new NHL record by a goaltender). In the 1996-97 season, he posted 33 wins with the Blues, his second highest number of wins in a single season; in the 1998-99 season with the Blues, he played in 39 games, and posted a 2.44 GAA, which was a career best. He played his final season, 1999-2000 with the Calgary Flames. Since officially retiring from playing in 2000, he is a goaltending consultant to the Calgary Flames. **HONS.:** several including, William M. Jennings Trophy (shared with Dominik Hasek), 1994; Vezina Trophy, league's top goaltender, 1988; Stanley Cup, with the Edmonton Oilers, 1984, 1985, 1987, 1988, and 1990. **REVIEWED IN:** nat'l and int'l publications. **CONTACT:** Tel: 403-777-3684; phanlon@calgaryflames.com

▶**GALABUZI, Grace-Edward**
RESEARCH ASSOCIATE/COMMUNITY ACTIVIST,
Centre for Social Justice, Toronto, ON. Born: Uganda/ in Canada since: 1982.

▶ Grace-Edward Galabuzi has been operating his own consulting firm for project management and research since 1996. During that time he has conducted studies and written reports on immigration and settlement; human rights; employment equity; community economic development, and many other topics. **CAREER HIGHLIGHTS:** he is the author of a 2001 report on the economic condition of racialized groups in Canada, "Canada's Creeping Economic Apartheid"; is a research associate at the Centre for Social Justice and a doctoral candidate at York U.; worked in the Ontario NDP government as a special assistant to the premier and in the Ontario public sector as a senior policy analyst on justice issues; is a former provincial coordinator of the Alliance for Employment Equity, and has been involved in many community campaigns around social justice issues including anti-racism, education, anti-poverty and police reform; he has also been a course director at George Brown College and York U. In the Summer of 2001, he acted as convener for the Building Hope Coalition Against Violence, discussing the problems of youth violence with youth living in the most affected areas. **COMMUNITY ACTIVITIES:** CUPE; founding member, White Ribbon Campaign; African-Canadian Heritage Assn.; founding member, AfroFest; Urban Alliance on Race Relations. **HONS.:** Canadian Windows on Int'l Development Award, IDRC, 2001. **WORKS:** several including: "Canada's Creeping Economic Apartheid," Centre for Social Justice, 2001. Position papers: "Implementing Employment Equity in Ontario," 1990; "Fair Access to Professions & Trades in Ontario," for NDP, 2000; forthcoming, "Racializing the Division of Labour." **EDUCATION:** PhD candidate; MA, Poli. Sci., 1997, York University. BA, Economics, U. of Winnipeg, 1987. **MOTTO:** Above all else, civilization is about the struggle for social justice. **CONTACT:** ggalabuz@yorku.ca

►GALE, Lorena

ACTOR/PLAYWRIGHT/DIRECTOR, Curious Tongue, 941 Salsbury Dr., Vancouver, BC V5L 4A5. Born: Montreal, QC.

▶ Lorena Gale is an international actor, playwright, and director. She has appeared in over 50 stage productions across Canada and has played over 80 roles in film and on TV. **HIGHLIGHTS:** she starred in her bilingual one-woman show, *Je me souviens*, which has been produced in Halifax, Calgary, Victoria and Vancouver, and was nominated for three Jessie Richardson Awards, including Best Actress and Best Production. She was the first Black woman to be accepted at the National Theatre School of Canada; was the Artistic Director of Black Theatre Workshop, 1984-85; was the creator and director of the Program for the Artistic Development of Artists of Colour in Theatre, Vancouver, 1992-94; is currently Artistic Director of Curious Tongue Productions. Her most memorable stage performances include Normal Jean in *The Coloured Museum*, and Hecuba in *Age of Iron,* for which she received both a Jesse Richardson Nomination (*Iron*) and Award (*Museum*). Other plays authored: *Angelique*, her first full-length play, was produced in Calgary, Detroit and New York, Off-Broadway at Manhattan Class Company, and was also presented in Dublin, Ireland. *Angelique* was nominated for three Betty Mitchell Awards (Calgary) and eight Audelco Awards (Harlem, NY); *What Colour is Black? Art, Politics and Racial Identity* premiered in the Halfbred Performance Series at The Grunt Gallery, Vancouver, 1995. **HONS.:** including, 10 Best Plays of 2000, *Vancouver Sun,* for *Je me souviens*; nominee, Jessie Richardson Award, for *Je me souviens,* 2000; 8 Audelco nominations including Best Production, for *Angelique,* NY, 1999; Winner, du Maurier National Playwriting Competition, for *Angelique,* 1995; Jessie Richardson Award, Best Supporting Actress, for *The Colored Museum,* 1991; Best Director, for *Irene & Lillian Forever,* Quebec Drama Festival, 1986. **WORKS:** *Je me souviens: memories of an expatriate anglophone Montrealaise, Québecoise, exiled in Canada,* 2001; *Angelique,* 2000. Excerpts in: *Bluesprint,* 2002; *Going it Alone,* 1998; *Beyond the Pale: Dramatic Writings by First Nations and Writers of Color,* 1996; *Another Perfect Piece,* 1995; Essays in: *CanPlay; Canadian Theatre Review; "…but where are you really from?": Stories of Identity and Assimilation in Canada,* 1997. **EDUCATION:** enrolled in graduate Liberal Studies, SFU, 2002; National Theatre School, 1979; Social Sciences, Marianapolis College, 1975. **HEROES/ROLE MODELS:** Victor Garraway, teacher; Judith Koltai, movement specialist. **MOTTO:** Just do it! **CONTACT:** lgale@intergate.bc.ca; Fax: 604-254-3949

►GANNON, Louis

EXECUTIVE DIRECTOR, Better Business Bureau of the Maritime Provinces Inc., 1888 Brunswick St., Ste. 601, Halifax, NS B3J 3J8. Born: Halifax.

▶ In 1996, Louis Gannon became the first African Nova Scotian to be appointed as Executive Director of the Better Business Bureau in the Maritimes (BBB/Maritimes), which serves 1,500 members. Since then he developed the first Annual Awareness Campaign with a focus on education and preventative initiatives. In 1988, he became the first Black to be appointed CEO of a Canadian YMCA in Charlottetown (PEI), a position he held until 1996. During his tenure he introduced a number of innovative programs including: Each One Teach One, and Carry the Books as well as the Ball; he also introduced an anti-racism program to Junior High students in the schools of PEI entitled, Appreciating our Differences and Similarities. Previously, he had been with the YMCA/Halifax since 1972, occupying positions ranging from Youth Director, Int'l Development Officer, to General Manager/Support and Community Services. **COMMUNITY INVOLVEMENT:** member, Human Rights Commission Cmtee; member, Black Educators Assn.; the African NS Music Awards; Racism and the World Black Response Society; past member, NS Barristers' Society, the Halifax Rotary Club, Dalhousie Legal Aid Cmtee. **OTHER:** an avid sportsman, he is Asst. Coach, Men's varsity basketball and Asst. Coach, St. Pat's Men's varsity basketball team, and, since 1972, has been participating in the annual Provincial Black Basketball Tournament. **HONS.:** several, including, Music Heritage Award, 1999; GG 125th Anniv. Medal, 1993; merits of appreciation, City of Halifax, Mayor's Office, 1988, Halifax Minor Basketball; Halifax School Brd.; & St. Patrick's Alexander School. **REVIEWED IN:** *Journey: African Canadian History*, 2000. **EDUCATION:** BA, Phys. Ed., Dalhousie U., 1974; Executive Leadership programs, United Way; Administration & Management Studies, Acadia U. **HEROES/ROLE MODELS:** Rocky Jones, friend. **MOTTO:** Each one, teach one. **CONTACT:** lagannon@sprint.ca; Fax: 902-429-6457

►GARNER, Linton

REGIONAL SERVICES DIRECTOR, Quebec Division, Canadian MedicAlert Foundation, Montreal, QC. Born: USA/ in Canada since: 1964.
▶ Linton Garner has a lengthy history of working on behalf of the Black community in Quebec, both through his employment and his community involvement. **CAREER:** former Director of Marketing at Athena Educational Partners, responsible for planning the strategic and tactical deployment of resources; Director, Health and Social Services, Alliance Quebec; Senior Advisor on Intercultural and Interracial Relations, Montreal Urban Community; Regional Coordinator for Access to English Language Services, Regional Council on Health and Social Services; former Director, Unity Boys and Girls Club; Community Organizer with Project Genesis; Youth Diversion Worker, West Island YMCA. He joined the Canadian MedicAlert Foundation as Regional Services Director (Quebec Div.) in mid-2002. **COMMUNITY:** editorial committee, McGill U. Black Demographic Project; past-President, Negro Community Centre; co-founder, Federation of Cosmopolitan Chambers of Commerce, Montreal; Brd., *Maison des Jeunes Côte-des-Neiges*; Corbo Commission of Quebec on Racism in the Montreal Police Force; Regional Advisory Committee on Drugs and Alcohol; Black Community Council of Quebec; co-founder, West Island Black Community Assn.; Chair, Task Force on Racism in Quebec; Cdn Council on Multicultural Health; past-President, *Alliance des communautés culturelles sur la santé et les services sociaux*. **EDUCATION:** DEC, Social Sciences, Dawson College, 1973. **MOTTO:** If not you, WHO? If not now, WHEN? **CONTACT:** Tel: 514-875-7466; treetop@videotron.ca

►GAYLE-ANYIWE, Brenda C. Hope, PhD.

PROFESSOR, Faculty of Business, Seneca College of Applied Arts and Technology, 1750 Finch Ave. E., Toronto, ON M2J 2X5. Born: Jamaica/ in Canada since: 1972.
▶ Dr. Gayle-Anyiwe has been a Professor of Economics at Seneca College in the Faculty of Business since 1980, teaching courses in micro- and macro-economics, Canadian economic issues, and international trade. **CAREER:** Consultant, 1992-99, Cdn Assn. of Insurance and Financial Advisors (CAIFA), preparing instructors' manual and students' study guide; Acting Chair, Liberal Studies Division, Seneca College, 1991-92. Prior to coming to Canada, she held the following positions in Jamaica: Economist and Executive Assistant to the Managing Director, Jamaica Development Bank, 1969-72; Economic and Commercial Assistant, US Embassy, 1969; Senior Research Officer, Bank of Jamaica, 1967-69. **HONS.:** including, Ford Foundation Research Fellowship, 1976-78; Commonwealth Scholar-

ship, 1972-77. **WORKS:** including, co-author, Study Guide for use with *Understanding Economics: a Contemporary Perspective*, 2002; *Instructors' Manual Study Guide, Economics LUAC/CAIFA*, 1996. **EDUCATION:** PhD, Economics, U. of Ottawa, 1979; MA, Economics, U of T, 1974. MSc, Economics & Business Admin., 1969; BSc/Hons., Economics, 1966, UWI. **CONTACT:** brenda.gayle-anyiwe@senecac.on.ca

▶**GAYLE-BENEDEK, Theresa**
FINANCIAL CONSULTANT/PRESIDENT, Benetheque Managerial Services, 1070 Laird Blvd., Montreal, QC H3R 1Z1. Born: Jamaica/ in Canada since: 1956.

▶ Theresa Gayle-Benedek was a financial consultant with diversified experience in treasury management, asset/liability management, portfolio management and corporate finances. Now a semi-retired business consultant, she operates, since 1989, her own firm, Benetheque Managerial Services. Previously, she worked with Steinberg Inc., 1964-91; her last position was Director of Treasury Services. **COMMUNITY:** is best known for her involvement with the Montreal Assn. of Black Business and Professional Persons (MABBP) for 14 yrs., and served as an executive member for several organizations including: Jamaican Assn. of Montreal; Matthew Da Costa Business Development Corp.; *Le Centre de Recherche-Action sur les Relations Raciales*; Black Theatre Workshop; Women's Centre of Montreal; participated in projects and workshops concerning youth and the Montreal Black community. **AFFIL/MBRSHP:** founding member, Cash Management Assn. of Canada; Treasury Management Assn. of Montreal; Treasury Management Assn. of Canada. **HONS.:** GG 125th Anniv. Medal, 1992. **REVIEWED IN:** *Jamaican Canadians: A Commitment to Excellence*; *WWCB*; *Une Femme, Un Vote*; *Cash Management Review.* **EDUCATION:** Certificates from Canadian Securities Institute & American Management Assn.;

B.Comm, Concordia U., 1960. **MOTTO:** Discipline is the gateway to success and good fortune. **CONTACT:** btheque@aol.com; Fax: 514-486-1361

▶**GEORGE, Gbadebo Oladeinde**
NIGERIAN AMBASSADOR (Ret.), Nigerian Ministry of Foreign Affairs. Resides in Gloucester, ON. Born: Nigeria/ in Canada since: 1987.

▶ Ambassador George served as a career diplomat for Nigeria in several countries over a 30-year period, including 15 years as Head of Mission or Department. He began his professional career in journalism as a broadcaster with what is now the FRCN (Federal Radio Corp. of Nigeria). He was the first Nigerian correspondent in Ghana, during their pre-Independence elections, 1956, and their Independence Celebrations, 1957. He was also in New York when Nigeria became the 99th Member of the United Nations in 1960. That same year, he joined the Ministry of External Affairs, where he remained until 1990, occupying the following posts: External Affairs Officer in Ghana, Cameroon, Gambia, Senegal, and Zaire, up to 1974; Consul General of Nigeria in New York, 1976; Deputy Permanent Representative to the UN, 1976-78, and to the UN Security Council; Nigerian Ambassador to Angola, 1978-84; Dean of the Luanda Diplomatic Corps, 1983-84; Director, European Affairs Dept., Lagos, 1984-87; Nigerian High Commissioner to Canada, 1987-90. Upon his retirement in 1990, he chose to stay in Canada. **EDUCATION:** Balliol College & Institute of Commonwealth Studies, Oxford U., 1965; School of Journalism, U. of Missouri, 1955. **CONTACT:** Fax: 613-746-2227

▶**GEORGE, Kenrick**
PRESIDENT/CEO, Aaron Multi-Tec Systems, Unit 60-3011 Markham Rd., Toronto, ON M1X 1L7. Born: Trinidad & Tobago/ in Canada since: 1971.

▶ Kenrick George is the President and CEO of Aaron Multi-Tec Systems (AMS), a company he founded in 1989, which specializes in telecommunications products, services and solutions to organizations (including government, small/large companies, and educational institutions) throughout N. America and the Caribbean. His experience and that of his executive management team was acquired through their previous technical and managerial positions with Bell Canada and Nortel; clients and operating partners include Digitronics, Nortel, and others. He is also the Chair of Xn-Net. **COMMUNITY:** has founded, chaired, and/or supported a number of community business development initiatives, including *Pride News* Magazine and Youth Clinical Services. **EDUCATION:** BA, Economics, York U., 1982; Dipl., Gen'l Business & Dipl., Gen'l Accounting, Seneca College, 1977. **MOTTO:** Success is how you deal with adversity. **CONTACT:** ken.george @aaronmultitec.com; www.aaronmultitec.com

▶**GIBSON, Leonard (Len)**
DANCER/CHOREOGRAPHER/TEACHER, Vancouver, BC. Born: Athabasca, AB.

▶ In the world of dance, Len Gibson is a legend. He was born in Alberta in 1926; his grandparents had first settled there in 1911; his parents later moved to BC. He began his career in dance at age five; as a self-taught tap dancer he performed in local shows when they toured through Vancouver. After studying ballet in BC, he moved to New York at age 19 when offered a scholarship to study at the Katherine Dunham School. There, he was introduced to the Afro-Cuban style and completed courses in ballet, tap, jazz, Spanish, oriental percussion, costume and visual design. He toured Europe in the 1960s performing as an actor, singer, dancer and choreographer; he was also a principal dancer with Vancouver's Theatre Under the Stars; he was billed mostly as a "song and dance man" when he toured throughout Canada and Europe. He was one of the dancers in the '60s film classic, *Cleopatra* (starring Elizabeth Taylor and Richard Burton). LG eventually settled in Toronto where, for 30 yrs., he operated his own Studio of Dance and Theatre Arts. He also taught at Sheridan College and at the Yorkville Performing Arts Studio. He performed, directed, and choreographed for stage, film, TV, radio and in productions such as: *Fiddler on the Roof; West Side Story; Guys and Dolls; Hello Dolly; Finian's Rainbow*; Salome Bey's, *Indigo*, and many more. Now residing in Vancouver, he continues to teach and choreograph, and often works with his sister (Thelma Gibson-Towns) and her group, The Afro Jazz Drum and Dance Ensemble. He is described as having been instrumental in launching the careers of many of his former students, and touching them personally with his sincerity, his professionalism, and his humanity. **HONS.:** include, Lifetime Achievement Award, Harry Jerome, 2000; Award of Distinction, Black Dancers in Canada. **HEROES/ROLE MODELS:** Leona Risby, mother. **MOTTO:** You can't keep a good person down.

▶**GIBSON-TOWNS, Thelma**
PERFORMER/DIRECTOR, Afro Jazz Drum & Dance Ensemble, Vancouver, BC. Born: Athabasca, AB.

▶ Thelma Gibson-Towns has been an actor, singer, and dancer who has toured throughout Canada, Europe, Central America, and the Caribbean. **HIGHLIGHTS:** radio and TV experience on CBC (performed with brothers Len and Austin Gibson on *Bambula*, a live TV show), Radio Trinidad, CKVU; stage and floor shows including feature vocalist with Oasis; has had principal roles in *Poltergeist; Mean to be Free; A Raisin in the Sun; Show Boat;* she acted with Sylvester Stallone, in *First Blood*, and appeared in a number of commercials, the more recent ones concerning senior citizens. She was a member of the Cdn contingent at the Second World Black and African Festival of Arts and Culture in Lagos, Nigeria, 1977, and was appointed Theatre Officer; she also wrote and performed the song, *I*

Hear the Drum. In addition, she has been the Executive Director and choreographer for the Afro Jazz Drum and Dance Ensemble; taught Afro-Cuban dance at Lanbara City College, the YWCA, and Hastings Community Centre; developed a Black History show, performed on TV with brother, Len Gibson, 2000; annually coordinates a show to entertain seniors in the Vancouver area. **HONS.:** including: Black History Month Award of Appreciation, for outstanding & dedicated service, True Resolution Lodge, 1990; Award, Black Historical & Cultural Society of BC, 1983; Multicultural Arts Award, Folkfest, 1980. **REVIEWED IN:** *Vancouver Courier; Vancouver Sun; Vancouver Herald; The Afro News.* **EDUCATION:** studied percussion with Babatune Olatunje; Drama, King Edward Drama School, 1956; Goodman School of Fashion, 1954; studied dance with Len Gibson, Toronto. **HEROES/ROLE MODELS:** Brothers Len, Austin, & Sylvester; Leona Risby, mother, who also provided foster care for 17 children during her life. **MOTTO:** There's no such word as "can't." **CONTACT:** Fax: 604-255-7011

▶**GITTENS, Rudolph O.** MD, FRCSC, FACS.
ORTHOPEDIC SURGEON/SPORT MEDICINE CONSULTANT, Private Practice, Ottawa, ON. Born: Trinidad & Tobago/ in Canada since: 1953.
▶ Dr. Rudolph Gittens is an Orthopedic Surgeon and Sport Medicine Consultant. He was the Team Physician for the Ottawa Rough Riders Football Club, 1966-1989, and the Ottawa 67's Major Junior A Ice Hockey Team, 1968-96. He is also a Clinical Assistant Professor, Orthopedics, Dept. of Surgery, U. Ottawa; and, Lecturer in Orthopaedics, Dept. of Surgery, UWI, Barbados. In addition, he has been part of the Canadian Soccer Assn. for 19 yrs. and associated with the Men's and Women's National Team Program since 1984, travelling throughout the world with the Under 17, Under 20, Pan American, Olympic and World Cup Teams. **AFFIL/MBRSHP:** Canadian Soccer Assn., Chair since 1992; Chair, Medical Commission, CONCACAF; American Academy of Sports Physicians, President since 1993; Sports Medical Committee, FIFA; Medical Advisor, Help the Aged Canada. **HONS.:** including, Sport Medicine Physician of the Year, 1999, Sport Medicine & Science Council of Canada, 1999; Aubrey Sanford Meritorious Award, Cdn Soccer Assn. **WORKS:** *FIFA Magazine*, 1996, 1997. **EDUCATION:** FRCSC; FACS; Fellow, American Academy of Sports Physicians; MD, U. of Ottawa, 1966; BSP, U. of Sask., 1957. **MOTTO:** Go the last mile! **CONTACT:** rudy.gittens@sympatico.ca; Fax: 613-731-6873

▶**GLANVILLE, Carlton R.W.**
CHARTERED ACCOUNTANT, Carlton R.W. Glanville, MBA, CA, 108 George St., Hamilton, ON L2P 1E2. Born: Jamaica/ in Canada since: 1965.
▶ Carlton Glanville is a Chartered Accountant who, after completing his studies at McMaster University, in 1969, articled with the chartered accounting firm of Clarkson Gordon & Company (now Ernst & Young). He obtained his CA designation in 1972 and was appointed Manager in the firm, in 1975. He has operated his own accounting practice in Hamilton ON, since 1980. **COMMUNITY ACTIVITIES:** Society for Hamilton Area International Response; member, Mayor's Race Relations Committee; Caribbean Cultural Assn.; Hamilton Wentworth Council on Police, Race and Community Relations; National Council of Jamaicans and Supportive Organizations in Canada. An avid table tennis player, he was a member of the Jamaica Table Tennis Team, which competed in the West Indies Championships, in 1961. **WORKS:** "Hamilton: more than steel and the Tigercats Football Team," *Jamaica Weekly Gleaner*, 2001. **EDUCATION:** MBA, 1972; B.Comm, 1969, McMaster U. **HEROES/ROLE MODELS:** Hugh Buchanan, friend. **MOTTO:** If you

can keep your head when all about you men are losing theirs and blaming it on you, if you can trust yourself when all men doubt you… yours is the Earth and everything that's in it…(Rudyard Kipling) **CONTACT:** carltong@glanville.ca; Fax: 905-522-5298

▶**GLASGOW, Valerie, RN, MScN.**
CLINICAL NURSE EDUCATOR, Mount Sinai Hospital/ **FACULTY INSTRUCTOR,** Ryerson University, Toronto, ON. Born: Jamaica/ in Canada since: 1970.
▶ Valerie Glasgow is both a Clinical Nurse Educator in the Mothers' and Infants' Health Program at Mount Sinai Hospital, and a Faculty Instructor and Advisor in the Basic Nursing Degree Program at Ryerson University. She has an extensive background in maternal-child health nursing, with expertise in antepartum, intrapartum, and postpartum nursing for women in high-risk, at-risk, and low-risk categories. **CAREER HIGHLIGHTS:** has been in the nursing profession since 1979, serving until 1994 as a Staff Nurse in Perinatology at Mt. Sinai; was a Casual Staff Nurse in High-Risk Antepartum/Postpartum Perinatology at Women's College Hospital, 1989-96; 1994-2001, was a Clinical Case Coordinator, Maternal Infant Program at Mt. Sinai; she was also, 1999-2000, Nursing Unit Administrator, Antepartum and Postpartum. She is a Preceptor for third- and fourth-year nursing students from U of T, Ryerson, Queen's, and McMaster universities. **AFFIL/MBRSHP:** Assn. Women's Health, Obstetrics and Neonatal Nurse; Sigma Theta Tau International; VP, Cdn Black Nurses Assn. **OTHER:** developed the Young Mothers Prenatal Group, a program developed for young pregnant women; she has also made presentations at conferences on breastfeeding challenges and sickle cell anemia. **HONS.:** include, Nursing Excellence Award, Mt. Sinai Hospital, 2002 & 1995; Morris Gross Bursary Award, Mt. Sinai Hospital, 1997. **EDUCATION:** MSc Nursing, D'Y-

ouville College, NY, 1997; BSc Nursing, Ryerson U., 1994; Dipl., Nursing, George Brown College. **CONTACT:** vglasgow@mtsinai.on.ca

▶**GODDARD, Horace, PhD.**
DIRECTOR, COMMUNITY SERVICES, English Montreal School Board, 6000 Fielding Ave., Montreal, QC H3X 1T4. Born: Barbados/ in Canada since: 1970.
▶ Dr. Horace Goddard is an educator and a writer. Since 1995, he has been the Director of Community Services with the English Montreal School Board. Trained in education, he taught elementary and high school in Montreal, 1977-87; was Vice-Principal of LaSalle High School, 1987-90; then Principal of Parkdale School, 1990-93. From 1993-95, he was the Coordinator of Personnel Services. He is also active in the community and involved in a number of organizations including: Black Community Resource Centre; Quebec Board of Black Educators; National Council of Black Educators; Cdn Assn. of Commonwealth Language and Literary Studies. As a writer, his works include poetry, fiction and children's stories. **HONS.:** including, Award for contribution to the field of education, Quebec Board of Black Educators, 1996; Medal of Appreciation, Boys & Girls Club, 1987. **WORKS:** selected: books: *Paradise Revisited,* 1997; *A Common Tongue: Interviews with Cecil Abrahams; Rastaman, Poems for Leonta,* 1982; works also included in anthologies & magazines (*KOLA, Caribe*). **REVIEWED IN:** *BHM Calendar,* 2000. **EDUCATION:** PhD, 1985; MA, U. de Montréal. M.Ed, 1988; Dipl. Ed, 1977, McGill U. BA/Hons., Concordia U., 1975. **HEROES/ROLE MODELS:** Ricardo Gill, former professor & colleague. **CONTACT:** hgoddard@emsb.qc.ca; Fax: 514-483-7213

▶**GOMEZ, Henry**
MUSICIAN/ACTOR, King Cosmos Entertainment/ **EDUCATOR,** Toronto District School Board, ON.

Born: Trinidad & Tobago/ in Canada since: 1969.
▶ Henry Gomez, a.k.a. King Cosmos, is a veteran calypsonian and soca performer who has been performing on the Toronto music scene for several years. He is one of Canada's best-known performers of Caribbean music. Musical releases include: *Culture Shock*, 1990; *Half Breed*, 1993; *Dis One Hot*, 1998; *Fire*, 2000. He is also an accomplished stage, film, TV and radio actor, having performed in productions for CBC Radio, Black Theatre Canada, Black Theatre Workshop, Centaur Theatre, The Globe Theatre, Theatre London, and others. He is also a high school teacher with the Toronto District School Board. **AFFIL/MBRSHP:** founding member and first Secretary/ Chair, Org. of Calypso Performing Artists; former Chair, Caribbean Cultural Committee, organizers of Caribana. **HONS.:** include, Chalmers Award, 1981; Cdn Reggae Music Award, 1999; Sunshine Award nominee, 1999; Cdn Calypso Monarch, 1995. **WORKS:** "Politicization of the Artist: The Artist as Citizen," *Can Theatre Review*, 1995; "The Invisible Visibles: Minorities in the Media," *Currents*, 1983. Composer of *Reparations* and *Sketches of Trudeau*. **REVIEWED IN:** *Share*; *Caribbean Camera; Pride*; *Toronto Star*; *Globe and Mail*; *NOW*; Trinidad & Tobago publications; *Revue Noir.* **EDUCATION:** BA, 1987; MFA, 1982, York University. B.Ed, 1985, U of T; Dipl., Ryerson, 1976. **HEROES/ROLE MODELS:** Samuel Blyden Forde, former headmaster. **MOTTO:** You can't help others unless you can help yourself. **CONTACT:** kingcosmos@hotmail.com; mp3.com/kingcosmos

▶**GOODING, Victor E., PhD, P.Eng.**
FUTURE TECHNOLOGY DEVELOPMENT SPECIALIST, Telesat Canada, 1601 Telesat Court, Ottawa, ON K1B 5P4. Born: Barbados/ in Canada since: 1969.
▶ Dr. Victor Gooding is a specialist in satellite communications who first joined Telesat Canada, a satellite operator and communications service

provider, in 1980. Previously, he had been an Assistant Professor of Electrical Engineering at Queen's University. Since 1997, he has been a Future Technology Development Specialist, responsible for developing Anik satellites and satellite applications. The current emphasis of his team is on broadband multimedia satellites utilizing advanced technologies such as spot beams, on-board processing and higher frequencies. His primary responsibility is management of a $60-million Canadian Space Agency contract relating to the development and implementation of the Anik F2 Ka-band Multimedia System; Anik F2, planned for launch in 2003, will be one of the largest satellites ever built and possibly the first in N. America with a commercial Ka-band payload. **HIGHLIGHTS:** other positions at Telesat: 1980, Sr. Engineer, Communications Systems Engineering Group, responsible for system analysis and network design for voice, data, and video services carried on Canada's first communications satellites, the Anik A- and B-series; from 1981, he worked on projects for direct-to-home satellite TV distribution, radio programming distribution, satellite video-conferencing and VSAT services. In 1983, as a member of the team planning the implementation of the Anik E-series of satellites, they were responsible for identifying the optimum system design to satisfy the company's various target markets; he was also involved in the development of mobile satellite facilities and services, in support of MSAT, Canada's mobile services satellite. In 1985, he became Communications Services Manager, and was, until 1989, responsible for corporate strategic planning relating to potential opportunities and threats to Telesat's satellite business. One key result of this work was the company's deployment of a system of teleports in major cities across Canada. In 1989, he returned to the Communication Systems Engineering Div., as a Traffic Planning Engineering Specialist responsible for traffic planning on the Anik satellites. In 1994, VG became an independent consultant and took leading roles in projects requiring a wide range of engineering expertise and functions, including work for Stentor, CANARIE, Industry Canada and ARABSAT; in 1996, he joined TMI Communications, the operator of MSAT, and was made engineering team leader for a number of mobile satellite service development projects. In 1997, he re-joined Telesat and occupies his present position. **OTHER:** during his youth, VG excelled in athletics: at SGWU (now Concordia U.), he played varsity soccer for four years and was named soccer MVP in 1973; he competed at the national level in track, 1973-80; representing Queen's U. in 1975, he set three Ontario university records in Track & Field and won all sprint titles between 1973 and 1976; he was selected to the Barbados Olympic team in 1976, where the 4x400m relay team set a Barbados national record. He is currently VP, Queen's Track & Field Booster Club; he also coaches youth soccer. **HONS.:** several including, Track & Field Hall of Fame, Queen's U., 1994; Telesat Award of Excellence, for Anik E satellite planning, 1985; NSERC Graduate Scholarship, 1974. **WORKS:** several conference papers including: "Planning the Next Generation of Satellites," 1984; "Jointly Optimal Filters for Data Transmission over Multi-route systems," 1978; "M-ary PSK Transmission via a Coherent Two-Link Channel," 1977. **EDUCATION:** PhD, 1977; M. App. Sc, 1974, Queen's University. B.Eng, SGWU (now Concordia U.), 1973. **HEROES/ ROLE MODELS:** Rolf Lund, Track & Field coach, Queen's U.; Edwin Moses, Olympic athlete & physicist. **MOTTO:** Just do it! **CONTACT:** vgooding@rogers.com; Fax: 613-748-8712

▶GORDON, Donald Keith, PhD, OD(JM).

PROFESSOR (Ret.), University of Manitoba, Winnipeg, MB. Born: Jamaica/ in Canada since: 1956.

▶ Dr. Donald K. Gordon taught at the University of Manitoba, 1970-2001, and was coordinator of Latin American Studies, 1993-96. **CAREER HIGHLIGHTS:** in 1984, he attained the rank of full Professor; was guest lecturer at UWI/Trinidad, 1977; and, a Courtesy Professor at the U. of South Florida, 1984-85, 1991-92, and 1998-99. He initiated the *Black Historical Calendar,* published by the Afro-Caribbean Assn. of Manitoba (ACAM); he was its coordinator, 1973-87, and a consultant to the project, 1988-94. He retired from U. of Manitoba in July 2001. **OTHER:** from 1981-1999, DKG served as Jamaican Honorary Consul at Winnipeg. **COMMUNITY INVOLVEMENT:** Richmond Kings soccer coach, 1971-80; President, ACAM, 1972; producer of folk music album, *Sun, Spirit and Soul*, by the Afro-Caribbean Singers, 1975 (CD, 2002); producer of video *An Audio-Pictoral History of the ACAM*, 1988, updated for 25th anniversary, 1993, and for ACAM's 30th anniversary, 1998. **HONS.:** several including, Order of Distinction (Officer Class), "in recognition of...service to the Jamaican community in Canada," Govt. of Jamaica, 2000; Plaque awarded, "for service as Jamaican Honorary Consul, Winnipeg," Jamaican Assn. of Manitoba 1999; Plaque awarded by ACAM for "past President & Valuable Contribution ...in appreciation of 23 yrs. of service," 1993; Plaque from students in graduating class, 1979 & 1992. **WORKS:** books: *Lo jamaicano y lo universal en la obra del costarricense Quince Duncan*, 1989; *Los cuentos de Juan Rulfo*, 1976. Articles in: *Afro-Hispanic Review; Can J of Latin American Studies; Can Modern Language Review; Cuadernos Americanos*; *Hispania*. Included in: *The Directory of Caribbean Personalities in Britain & N. America*, 1985. Articles in many other publications including: *Contrast; Jamaica Gleaner; Our Voice; The Spectrum*; *Toronto Star*; *Winnipeg Free Press*. **EDUCATION:** PhD, Spanish American Literature, U of T, 1969. **MENTOR:** Prof. Kurt L. Levy, thesis advisor & friend. **MOTTO:** Keep on keeping on. **CONTACT:** dkgordon2@yahoo.com; Fax: 204-269-5319

►GORDON, Kevin

WRITER, Oakland, CA, USA. Born: Guelph, ON, 1968.

▶ Kevin Gordon is an author and doctoral law student; he is also a former semi-professional tennis player and backpacker. He was nationally ranked as a Junior tennis player, both in Canada and the US; had been No.1 in Manitoba in each Junior age group; played briefly on the semi-pro circuit in Portugal; and, after receiving his level one certification from the US Professional Tennis Assn., he began teaching, running his own tennis camps in the summers of 1988-89; he also held a number of positions as Director of Junior Tennis (until 2001) in camps and racquet clubs in Massachusetts and Illinois. He has traveled to over 50 countries throughout the Caribbean, N. and S. America, Africa, and Europe. His coming of age book, *Not Yet African*, was published in 1998. **WORKS:** *Not Yet African*, 1998; *American Dreamers*, forthcoming. **REVIEWED IN:** *Jamaican Canadians: A Commitment to Excellence,* 1987. **EDUCATION:** completing doctoral studies in law, U. of California, Berkeley; BA, Harvard U., 1991. **HEROES/ROLE MODELS:** Prof. Donald K. Gordon, father. **CONTACT:** kupugani@aol.com

►GRANGE, Hamlin

JOURNALIST/PRESIDENT, ProMedia International Inc., 202B-260 Carlaw Ave., Toronto, ON M4M 3L1. Born: Jamaica/ in Canada since: 1964.
▶ Hamlin Grange is President of ProMedia International Inc., a company specializing in media production and consulting. He began his career as a reporter for the *Rocky Mountain News*, in Denver; was later managing editor for *Contrast,* then Canada's leading Black community newspaper. He next worked for three years with the *Toronto Star*, then was a reporter for Global TV and CBC TV, progressing from Assignment Editor, Municipal Affairs Reporter, to host, interviewer and news anchor. He hosted *Newsworld*,

TVO's *Workweek*, and the CBC's *More to the Story*. Interested as well in international public television, he has been an organizer and presenter at the Best of INPUT conferences at the CBC for several years; November 2000, he helped launch the first Caribbean INPUT in Jamaica. A strong advocate of diversity in the media, he has mentored Blacks and members of other ethnocultural groups in the media. He is co-founder of Innoversity™, a not-for-profit initiative of ProMedia International that presents the international Innoversity™ Creative Summit; the first was held in 2002 and brings together those with creative ideas and media executives from Canada and around the world. **AFFIL/MBRSHP:** co-founder of the Harry Jerome Awards and Scholarship Fund; currently President of CABJ; Brd., BFVN; Brd., YMCA/ Toronto. **HONS.:** several including, B'nai Brith Human Rights Award for Journalism; a BFVN Achievement Award; ACAA; awards from the NY & Houston Int'l Film & Video Festivals. **EDUCATION:** BSc, Journalism, U. of Colorado. **CONTACT:** hamlin@promedia.ca

►GRANT, Gerald, PhD.

ASSISTANT PROFESSOR, Eric Sprott School of Business, Carleton University, 1125 Colonel By Dr., Ottawa, ON K1S 5B6. Born: Jamaica/ in Canada since: 1974.
▶ Dr. Gerald Grant is an Assistant Professor at the Eric Sprott School of Business at Carleton University; he is Coordinator of the Information Systems teaching area and Chair, Enterprise Systems/E-business Committee. This committee is responsible for leading the E-business focus of the school and for establishing and managing the school's high technology e-Lab. **RESEARCH AREAS:** enterprise information systems and enterprise process institutionalization; E-business architecture; E-government; information systems in global organizations; information and communication technology for social and economic development; IT in developing countries; evolu-

tionary and resource-based views of information systems. **CAREER HIGHLIGHTS:** Faculty of Management, McGill U., 1997-98; Dept. Information Systems and Computing, Brunel U., UK, 1997; Vice-Principal, Financial Administration, 1990-92, and Assistant Professor in Management and Information Systems, 1986-90, at Solusi U., in Zimbabwe. **INTERNATIONAL CONSULTANCIES:** Commonwealth Secretariat, UK, responsible for establishing the Commonwealth Business Network (COMBINET), an electronic networking program aimed at linking Chambers of Commerce and Industry associations in commonwealth countries; Commonwealth Network of IT for Development (COMNET-IT), Coordinator, 1994-95; assisted in establishing COMNET-IT as an international foundation based in Malta, 1995. Now serves as Business Development Consultant to the foundation, coordinating international workshops such as: From the Digital Divide to the e-Economy, Malta, 2002; Enhancing Public Service Delivery through IT, Malta, 1997; Regional Initiative for Information and Communications Technology Strategies, Malaysia, 2001; Regional Initiative on Informatics Strategies, Jamaica and S. Africa, 2001. **OTHER:** member, Advisory Brd., Ottawa Manufacturers Network. **HONS.:** including, Organizational Leadership Award, Information Resources Management Assn., 1999. **WORKS:** several including, ed., *Managing Telecommunications and Networking Technologies in the 21st Century: Issues and Trends*, 2001; ed., *Guidelines for Sectoral ICT Policy & Planning*, Malta, COMNET-IT paper, 2001; "The Growth Gap," *Financial Post*, 1999. **REVIEWED IN:** "Changing the way business thinks," in *This is Carleton*, 2001. **EDUCATION:** PhD, London School of Economics & Political Science, U. of London, 1996. MBA, 1985; BS, Business Admin., 1978, Andrews U., Michigan. **CONTACT:** gerald_grant@carleton.ca; Fax: 613-520-4427

▶**GRANT, Otis "Magic"**

PROFESSIONAL BOXER/ENTREPRENEUR, Stele Promotions; Otis Grant & Friends, 5038-A Labrosse, Pierrefonds, QC H8Y 2Y6. Born: Jamaica, 1967/ in Canada since: 1978.

▶ Otis "Magic" Grant is the former WBO Middleweight Champion of the world, 1997. He is also a two-time NA Boxing Federation Middleweight Champion, 1992 and 1995; the Continental America Super Middleweight Champion, 1990; and the former Canadian Middleweight Champion, 1991. In addition, he is a former member of the Cdn National Boxing Team and was a Silver Medallist at the 1987 Pan-Am Games. With these accomplishments, he was one of the very few boxers to hold three belts simultaneously in two different weight classes. His professional record is: 31 wins; two losses; one draw. His amateur record is: 100 wins; 18 losses; 0 draws. **OTHER:** following a serious car accident in 1999, his boxing career is on hold; however, he is still very active in the community; has founded a charitable organization, Otis Grant and Friends Foundation, whose main focus is an annual food drive, which has donated over 30 tons of food, clothing and toys to organizations working with the needy in the Greater Montreal Area. As a result of his success in the ring and his humanitarian work in the community, OG is well regarded by the local population; he has given back through his foundation, through speaking engagements and his work with special-needs children in the Resource Dept. at Lindsay Place High School. **HONS.:** several including: creation of the Otis Grant Award, at Lindsay Place High School, 1998; Martin Luther King Jr. Award of Excellence, 1998; Jackie Robinson, Professional of the Year, MABBP, 1998; Achievement of Excellence, MABBP, 1991. **REVIEWED IN:** *Montreal Gazette*; *National Post; La Presse; J de Montréal.* **EDUCATION:** BA, Recreation & Leisure, Concordia U., 1993. **MOTTO:** Take advantage of every opportunity that will make you a better person and a credit to our society. **CONTACT:** Tel: 514-683-9791; Fax: 514-683-7240; www.otisgrant.com

▶**GRANT, Rudolph W.,** PhD.
PROFESSOR EMERITUS, York University, Toronto, ON. Born: Guyana/ in Canada since: 1965.
▶ Dr. Rudy Grant taught at York University from 1967 until his retirement in 2000. **CAREER HIGHLIGHTS:** Lecturer, Government Training College for Teachers, Guyana, 1962-65; following his studies at U of T, 1965-70, he was a researcher at the London University Institute for Commonwealth Studies, UK, 1975-76; was then a consultant with UNESCO, 1976-79 (completed assignments in France, Guyana, Barbados, Libya, Colombia, and Surinam, while on leave from York University); researched at the Harvard Graduate School of Education, from 1986-90; was a moderator with the Caribbean Examinations Council; and, lectured at the University of Guyana in 1993. His research has centred on Caribbean regional integration and on Third World educational issues. His work has been published in the Caribbean, North America, and Europe. **EDUCATION:** PhD, Poli. Sci., 1970; MA, Poli. Sci., 1967; MA, Education, 1966, U of T. Dipl. Ed. (Academic), London U., 1963. Dipl. Ed. (Teaching), 1961; BA/Hons., 1960, UWI. **MOTTO:** If you do not know, do not be afraid to ask; if you know, do not wait to be asked; help. It's never too late to start either process. **CONTACT:** rwgrant@yorku.ca

▶**GRANT, Sheryl**
ASSISTANT MANAGING EDITOR, The Halifax Herald Ltd., PO Box 610, 1650 Argyle St., Halifax, NS B3J 2J2. Born: Halifax, NS.
▶ In 1999, Sheryl Grant was promoted to the position of Assistant Managing Editor with The Halifax Herald Ltd. As such, she is likely the only Black Assistant Managing Editor in Canada, at a mid-sized daily newspaper. The papers under her responsibility are: *The Chronicle Herald, The Mail Star,* and *The Sunday Herald.* She joined the *Halifax Herald* in 1980 as a journalist, covering general, municipal, then legislative affairs; then became an editor on *The Chronicle Herald* and *The Mail Star;* in 1998, with the launch of *The Sunday Herald,* she became editor of *Your Time* and then the books section. **HONS.:** New Media Fellowship, Newspaper Assn. of America, 2001-02. **REVIEWED IN:** several including, *Journey: African Canadian History,* 2000. **EDUCATION:** BA, Journalism, U. King's College, Halifax, 1980; BA, Dalhousie U., 1978. **MOTTO:** How can we make it work? **CONTACT:** sgrant@herald.ns.ca; www.halifaxherald.com; Fax: 902-426-1158

▶**GRANT, Yola**
LAWYER/ACTIVIST, Grant & Bernhardt, Barristers in Association, 360A Bloor St. W., Box 68507, Toronto, ON M5S 1X1. Born: Jamaica/ in Canada since: 1973.
▶ Yola Grant has been practising labour and employment law, as well as human rights and constitutional law since her call to the Ontario bar in 1989. In her practice she has had a number of notable successes: 1994-98, serving as Tribunal Counsel to the Pay Equity Hearings Tribunal, Employment Equity Tribunal, and the Board of Enquiry (Human Rights), she worked primarily with legislation aimed at eliminating discrimination in pay and employment systems; developed the first procedural rules to ensure fairness in the human rights hearing process; from 1990-94, she prosecuted numerous occupational health and safety violations in the construction, industrial, and mining sectors. She has also worked as counsel to unions and as a policy analyst with Ontario's Min. of Labour. As a volunteer member of LEAF, she acted as co-chair of the National Legal Cmtee and participated in a number of significant cases involving women's equality rights. As counsel, she argued successfully before the Supreme Court of Canada against

an allegation of judicial bias concerning Nova Scotia's first Black female judge; argued before the Ontario Court of Appeal for children's constitutional right to have their "non-status" single mother obtain "landed status" and remain in Canada to provide for their care. **OTHER:** extensive involvement in the anti-apartheid and anti-racism movement during 1980s and 1990s; was an elections observer to the first national "one person, one vote" elections in S. Africa, 1994; served as tribunal counsel to the first int'l inquiry (Toronto, 1999) into the May 1998 massacre in Barrancabermeja, Colombia. **AFFIL/MBRSHP:** CABL; LEAF; Sickle Cell Assn. of Ontario. Previously: Metropolitan Toronto Housing Co. Ltd.; Toronto Org. for Domestic Workers' Rights (INTERCEDE); North York Women's Shelter. **HONS.:** Tory Research & Writing Award, 1987; Torkin, Manes & Cohen Award, academic standing and work in legal clinics, 1987. **WORKS:** *Can J of Women & the Law.* **EDUCATION:** LLB, York U., 1987. MSc Physical Chemistry, 1980; BSc/Hons. (*cum laude*), 1978, U of T. **MOTTO:** *Carpe Diem!* **CONTACT:** yolagrant@equality-rights.com; www.equality-rights.com

▶GRANT STATES, Violet

SYMPHONY/MUSIC TEACHER (Ret.), Montreal Women's Symphony. Verdun, QC. Born: Montreal, QC.

▶ Violet Grant States was accepted into the Montreal Women's Symphony under Canada's first woman conductor, Ethel Stark, in 1943, and thereby became the first Black to be a member of a major Canadian symphony. Her original dream had been to train as a school teacher at Macdonald College but, while accepted into the program, she was told by the Dean that there would be little likelihood of [white] parents allowing her to teach their children. Denied permission to continue her studies there, she soon won a scholarship to the *Conservatoire de Musique et d'Art Dramatique de la Province de Québec*, and

began building a clientele of young piano students, most of whom were white. While attending the first concert of the Montreal Women's Symphony in 1940, she vowed to become a member; in order to do this she needed to play a wind instrument so switched her major from piano to clarinet at the *Conservatoire*. When her teacher thought she was ready, she auditioned and won a position in the 80-member all-women orchestra. In 1947, they became the first Canadian Symphony to play at Carnegie Hall, NY. She remained with the Montreal Women's Symphony until 1965, when she finally went to McGill U. to complete her studies in music. In addition to the symphony, VGS also taught piano privately for 28 yrs., always with a waiting list of new students; taught school for 22 yrs. as a Music Specialist and class teacher, from kindergarten to the end of high school; and, taught high school bands during which time (over seven years), she was assigned 1,000 music students per week. Outside of her teaching, VGS served as Organist and Choir Director at Union United Church for 15 yrs., and taught at the Baha'i summer schools in Maine, Alaska, and Jamaica. **CURRENT ACTIVITIES:** she is involved in research on Canadian Black History; assisted in having a plaque erected to honour the early Black railway porters' contributions to the development of Canada (Windsor Station, Montreal); member of a team which fought to have an unmarked slave cemetery (slaves were buried under a huge rock) in St. Armand, QC, consecrated and national recognition accorded for the site's historical importance. **HONS.:** Scholarship for piano & clarinet at the *Conservatoire de Musique et d'Art Dramatique de la Province du Québec*. **REVIEWED IN:** *Negro Digest* magazine; interview CBC Radio, 2001; interview posted on www.artscanada.cbc.ca, 2002. **EDUCATION:** B.Ped, U. de Montréal, 1971; B.Mus., McGill U., 1969; *Conservatoire de Musique et d'Art Dramatique de la Province de Québec*, 1952. **HEROES/ROLE MODELS:** Parents. **MOTTO:** You can do it. I know you can!

▶GRAY, Rev. Darryl

MINISTER, Union United Church, 3007 Delisle St., Montreal, QC H4C 1M8. Born: USA/ in Canada since: 1990.

▶ Rev. Darryl Gray is the Pastor of the historic, Union United Church, Montreal's oldest Black church, established in 1907. Previously, he was the Pastor of the Guysborough Road United Baptist Church in NS. In addition to being a minister, he has also worked as a human and civil rights activist, newspaper columnist, lecturer on Black community economic development, race relations and cross-cultural understanding, conflict mediator and youth counsellor. Originally from the US, he served the church in Georgia, S. Carolina, and Kansas; he was elected as a State Senator in Kansas, the only Black at the time from that state. **HIGHLIGHTS:** while in NS, he was the publisher/editor of the *Provincial Monitor*, then NS's only Black news publication; was president of the NS Black Business Consortium, which was instrumental in facilitating minority set-aside programs in municipal and provincial government, allowing Blacks and other minority contractors to gain experience and have access to lucrative government contracts; as Development Coordinator for two NS communities, he introduced sustainable economic development community programs, and a training program for Black community organizations. Since arriving in Montreal, he has been involved in a number of community initiatives: Brd., NCC/Charles H. Este Cultural Centre, which will restore the Centre and see Montreal's first Black museum created; has begun a Prison Ministry Program that serves five correctional institutions; was the host and producer of the only weekly Black TV program in Quebec, now named *Soul Call*; does a weekly commentary on CJAD radio; co-chaired the 2000 Montreal Conference on Black Business and Economic Development, with the Black Coalition of Quebec; co-chaired first bilingual Black Community Election Rally, which mobi-

lized a large Black voter turnout for the 2000 federal elections. **COMMUNITY:** Montreal Black Council on Aging; Cdn Bible Society; Minority Apprenticeship Program; Black Legal Education and Support Foundation; Jamaican Assn. Montreal. Has also been involved in civil and human rights organizations: Southern Christian Leadership Conference (US); NAACP; Operation PUSH; National Rainbow Coalition; Cdn Centre on Racism and Prejudices; Harambee Centres; founder, Martin Luther King Jr. Legacy Cmtee (Montreal). **HONS.:** several including, Rosa Parks Award, Canadian Human Rights Commission, 2002; Black Star Award, for outstanding community commitment, 1999; Minister's Award, for Excellence in Race Relations, NS Min. of Multiculturalism & Citizenship, 1992. **REVIEWED IN:** *BHM Calendar*, 2001. **EDUCATION:** pursuing M.Div., Religious Studies, McGill U.; Conflict Mediation, Henson College & Dalhousie Law School; Dipl., Community Economic Development, NS Community College; BA, Benedict College, S. Carolina. **HEROES/ROLE MODELS:** Mary Jane Gray, grandmother. **MOTTO:** I can do all things through Christ who gives me strength. **CONTACT:** unionchurch@qc.aibn.com; Fax: 514-932-8846

▶GRIFFITH, Clyde

RECREATION & LEISURE CONSULTANT (Ret.), BC Provincial Government. Victoria, BC. Born: Trinidad & Tobago/ in Canada since: 1955.

▶ Clyde Griffith is a pioneer in the field of recreation for the public sector in BC. He was the first Recreation Director for the cities of Delta, 1961; Surrey, 1965 (prepared design plan and site location for the Surrey Fine Arts Theatre Complex, 1964); Port Coquitlam, 1968 (prepared design and site location plans for PC Recreation Centre, the first multi-purpose ice arena and recreation centre in the province; also prepared first five-year plan for Parks and Recreation). From 1973-95 he was a Recreation Consultant for the BC

Provincial Government, in the Recreation branch of the Ministry of Housing, Recreation and Consumer Services. In this capacity, he was also involved with many special projects including: Mission Staff Member of the BC Summer Games, the Canada Summer and Winter Games, three terms each; BC Rep. on National Cmtee for Skills Management Development; BC Rep on National Olympic Cmtee, Youth Div.; Govt. Liaison with Commonwealth Heads of Govt. Conference, 1987; Team Attaché for Trinidad & Tobago, Commonwealth Games, 1994. **COMMUNITY:** President, BC Black History Awareness Society, 1997-99; 25-yr. Executive member of BC/Yukon Red Cross Water Safety Branch; Chair, Education Cmtee responsible for authoring *The Black History Resource Guide*, portraying the contributions of Black Pioneers to BC; the guide has been distributed to schools throughout the province. **HONS.:** including, 25-yr. Volunteer Services Award, Cdn Red Cross, 1999; nominee, Order of BC, 1994; Service Recognition, Govt. Recreation Branch, 1993; Int'l Student of the Year, 1962. **WORKS:** chaired cmtee which produced *The Black History Resource Guide*, 1996. **REVIEWED IN:** *Millennium Minds*, 2000; "Recognition Profile," *UBC Alumni*, 2000; *Provincial Ministry Profile*, 1993; also in many local and provincial publications. **EDUCATION:** Dipl., U. of Oregon, 1974; MA, Community Development, U. of Nebraska, 1967; BPE & Recreation Management, UBC, 1964. **HEROES/ROLE MODELS:** Hon. Justice Leggatt, friend; Emery Barnes, friend. **MOTTO:** Nothing is impossible with God. **CONTACT:** candggriff@ shaw.ca; Fax: 250-472-2296

►GRIMMOND, Claude N.

MEDIATOR/TRAINER/FACILITATOR, Conflict Management Services (CMS), Ste. 101 9251-8 Yonge St., Richmond Hill, ON L4C 7L9. Born: Guyana/ in Canada since: 1963.

▶ Claude Grimmond began his professional career as a teacher over 29 yrs. ago. He taught at Westview Centennial Secondary School in North York, for a number of years and was a Program Team Leader in the Creative Arts Department; there, he was noted for his work in the area of conflict mediation. **ACHIEVEMENTS:** implemented the Positive Peer Culture program at Westview in 1981, where students were taught to resolve conflicts through mediation rather than through adversarial means; co-produced the video, *You've Got the Key*, which instructs students and teachers in dealing with racial conflict in school; chaired and served on the Brd. of Directors of the Jane-Finch Legal Clinic, which also helps needy students gain access to legal advice; he has been operating CMS since 1990. **AFFIL/MBRSHP:** accredited Family Mediator, Ontario Assn. for Family Mediation; roster Mediator, Ont. Mandatory Mediation Programs; roster Mediator, College of Teachers; Brd. of Directors, Blue Hills Child and Family Services. **HONS.:** including, Inaugural Alumni Award for Excellence in Teaching (initiated at the Faculty of Education's 25th Anniv.), York U., 1998; North York Mayor's Award, 1996. **WORKS:** articles in *Interaction J*; co-author, *You've Got the Key, An Anti-racist Approach to Conflict Mediation Guide.* **REVIEWED IN:** *Toronto Star.* **EDUCATION:** MES, Dispute Resolution, Faculty of Environmental Studies, 1998; B.Ed, 1990, York U. **MOTTO:** Keep your eyes on the prize. **CONTACT:** cgrimmond@echo-on.net; Fax: 905-884-0299

►GRIZZLE, Stanley G. CM, O.Ont., OD(JM).

CITIZENSHIP COURT JUDGE (Ret.), Court of Canadian Citizenship, Toronto, ON. Born: Toronto, ON.

▶ Judge Stanley Grizzle was the first African-Cdn appointed as a citizenship court judge, 1978-83, and re-appointed, 1999-2000; sleeping car porter, Canadian Pacific Railway (CPR), 1940-60; letter carrier, Canada Post, 1960-61; Clerk Examiner & Labour Relations Officer, Ont. Labour Relations

Brd., 1961-78. Military service: Corporal, Cdn Army, 1942-46, served in Canada, Scotland, England, France, Belgium, Holland and Germany. **COMMUNITY INVOLVEMENT:** extensive, selected: founding member & secretary, Young Men's Negro Assn., 1938; VP, Toronto CPR Div., Brotherhood of Sleeping Car Porters, 1950-53; Pres. & Chair, Grievance Cmtee, 1953-59; Secr. Treasurer, 1959-62; founder, Railway Porters' Trade Union Council, 1958; Toronto Labour Council, 1955-61; Toronto Labour Cmtee for Human Rights, 1956-61; organizer & spokesperson for delegations of Blacks to provincial and federal governments urging changes to immigration laws & adoption of a human rights code, 1954-56; VP, Cdn Assn. for the Advancement of Coloured People, 1959-60; candidate for the Ontario Legislature, 1959; founding member, JCA, 1962; Toronto Negro Bus. and Prof. Men's Assn., which sponsored Toronto's first Black history display, 1963; chair, founding cmtee, National Black Coalition of Canada, 1969; Brd., Urban Alliance on Race Relations, 1977-78; Cdn Civil Liberties Assn., 1974-2000; founding member, OBHS, 1978-2000; and many others. **OTHER:** is one of the subjects in the NFB documentary, *Journey to Justice*, which won the TIFF's award for Best Documentary, 2001. **HONS.:** several including, Race Relations Award, Urban Alliance on Race Relations, 1998; Order of Canada, 1995; inductee, Cdn Labour Hall of Fame (first visible minority), 1994; Order of Ontario, 1990; Harry Jerome Award, 1987; Community Services Award, Nat'l Black Coalition, 1978; Order of Distinction, Jamaica, 1978. **WORKS:** including, *My Name's Not George: the Story of the Sleeping Car Porters in Canada* (autobiography), 1998; *Discrimination: Our Achilles Heel?* booklet and broadcast across Canada, 1959. **REVIEWED IN:** selected, *WWIC*; *Some Black Men*, 1999; *Toronto Life*, 1990; *The Lawyers Weekly*, 1998. **MOTTO:** If you don't know where you've been you don't know where you're going.

▶**GUDGE, Leyland,** MSW.

CONSULTANT, Family Services & Anti-racism/ Multicultural Organizational Change, 60 Bradley Rd., Markham, ON L3S 1A8. Born: Guyana/ in Canada since: 1974.

▶ Leyland Gudge has been active in the field of social services and community work for over 30 yrs. **CAREER HIGHLIGHTS:** in Guyana, 1967-72, he was General Secretary of the YMCA in Georgetown and Albouystown; following his arrival in Canada, he continued working with the YMCA and 1978-79, was appointed Executive Director of the YMCA Multicultural Centre in Toronto's St. Clair-Oakwood area, responsible for the design, development and delivery of recreational, educational and social programs, as well as for piloting multiracial and multilingual programs to the growing Caribbean community in this area, which had been predominantly Italian. From 1979-83, he joined the Children's Aid Society (CAS) of Toronto and was a Family Services/ Community Worker with Caribbean families in Toronto's west end; 1983-88, was appointed to the CAS senior management position of Executive Assistant, Multicultural Program and was responsible for pioneering and managing the first multicultural program in a mainstream social service institution, aimed at improving CAS service delivery to Toronto's growing, culturally diverse communities. During this time, he also became Manager of Public Relations with the CAS. From 1988-89, he was on secondment to Harambee Child & Family Services, to set up this agency intended to assist Black and Caribbean families; he played a key role in the design and development of its inaugural service-delivery system. From 1990-94, he was the Director of St. Clair Community Youth Services, which served predominantly Black youth in west-end Toronto; also designed and implemented various school-based programs aimed at supporting Black and Caribbean students across Toronto and in York and Halton Regions. Since 1994, he works as an independent consultant, providing organizational direction and strategic program development expertise to both community-based and mainstream organizations across Ontario. **AFFIL/ MBRSHP:** 1986-92, member, Child and Family Services Review Brd.; Vice-Chair, Caribana, 1986-88; founding member, Black Consultative Cmtee on Police Relations, Toronto Police Services Brd.; Ontario Assn. Social Workers. **HONS.:** including numerous citations for work in education, youth, and community work; Volunteer Recognition Award, Markham Multicultural Assn., 1990; nominee, Cdn Black Achievement Award, *Pride*, 1986. **REVIEWED IN:** *Toronto Star; Share; Pride.* **EDUCATION:** MSW, U of T, 1996; BA/Hons., York U., 1994; Cert., Life Skills Counselling, George Brown College, 1980; Cert., Public Relations/ Journalism, Humber College, 1978. **CONTACT:** leylandgudge@sympatico.ca

▶**GUY, Sol**

GLOBAL HIP HOP ENTREPRENEUR, Toronto, ON. Born: Grand Forks, BC, 1974.

▶ Sol Guy is one of Canada's leading music executives in the Urban Music sector, and has already worked with major labels including BMG and Arista Records. Beginning his career as a performer, he and friends formed the hip hop group, Ragamuffin Rascalz, in 1991; their first full-length album, *Really Livin'*, sold 20,000 copies. In 1994, he and Dugai Barrington formed their own management label, Figure IV Records, to handle the group's business interests. He was recruited by BMG Music Canada, in 1995, as an Urban Product Manager; this move was also beneficial for his group, now known as The Rascalz who, in 1997, became the second Canadian rap group to sign with a major record label. Their album, *Cash Crop* reached Gold status, selling 60,000 copies. Offered a position with Arista Records in New York as an international marketing manager, he began working from the US in 1998; this position allowed him to travel and see the influence of hip hop internationally. By implementing street-based awareness and targeted marketing strategies, he helped to further establish the global network of urban music on an international platform. This improved the marketing and promotion of Urban Music. After eight months with Arista, he and a partner established Time Zone International, an international consulting firm, which works at maximizing exposure for artists such as Puff Daddy, Outkast, KRS-One, and Jill Scott. The roster of artists managed by Figure IV has grown to include Kardinal Offishall and K-OS. In 2001, SG left Figure IV to pursue other interests inside and outside of the music industry, stating: "The overall goal at this point is to help people; if I cannot do that with what I learned then it is all for naught." One of his personal interests is to introduce a greater sense of consciousness and responsibility among artists he manages, to recognize that the images they portray in their music and their videos can greatly influence those who listen to, and purchase their material. **HONS.:** include: Special Achievement Award, UMAC, 2001. **HEROES/ROLE MODELS:** Father. **MOTTO:** Positive Energy Activates Constant Elevation (PEACE). **CONTACT:** www.newgro@hotmail.com

▶**GYLES, Carlton L., DVM, PhD.**

PROFESSOR OF BACTERIOLOGY, Dept. of Pathobiology, University of Guelph, ON. Born: Jamaica/ in Canada since: 1959.

▶ Dr. Carlton Gyles is a microbiologist who teaches bacteriology at the University of Guelph; from 1981-86, he was Dean of the Faculty of Graduate Studies. He is also the Associate Network Director and Group Leader of the *Escherichia* Research team, with the Canadian Network on Bacterial Pathogens of Swine. He is described as one of the world's leading experts on E. coli, and is responsible for discovering the E. coli heat-labile enterotoxin and E. coli plasmids with genes for enterotoxin and drug resistance; he is also the first to clone and sequence the gene for E. coli verotoxin 2e, to purify the edema disease toxin, and to develop a toxoid vaccine against edema diseases of pigs. **RESEARCH AREAS:** pathogenesis of E. coli infections; role of verotoxins in disease; and, rapid methods for detection of bacterial food-borne pathogens. **HONS.:** several including, Hon. Diplomate, American College of Veterinary Microbiologists, 1998; Beecham Award, for excellence in research, Ontario Veterinary College, 1990; Canada-France Exchange Scientist, 1984 & 1990; Postdoctoral Fellow, Medical Research Council, 1968-69; five convocation awards including the gold medal, for highest academic performance, Ontario Veterinary College, 1964. **WORKS:** over 100 research publications in refereed journals, 17 book chapters, and three books edited; articles in, *Can J Vet Res; J Clin Microbiol; Vet Microbiol; Appl Environ Microbiol; Can J Microbiol*; Editor, *Animal Health Research Reviews,* 2001. **EDUCATION:** PhD, 1968; MSc, 1966, U. of Guelph. DVM, Ontario Veterinary College, U of T, 1964. **MOTTO:** We have a responsibility to ourselves and to society to be the best that we can be. **CONTACT:** cgyles@ovc.uoguelph.ca; www.medvet.umontreal.ca/reseau/ang/scientists/gyles

▶**GYLES, Shirley**
PRESIDENT, The Coloured Women's Club of Montreal. Born: Montreal, QC.
▸ Shirley Gyles is the president of The Coloured Women's Club (CWC) of Montreal, the first and oldest Black women's organization in Canada. The group was founded in 1902, by seven American women whose husbands worked for the railway; the women originally came together socially to counter the loneliness they experienced when their husbands were away. At that time, there were few social agencies to alleviate hardship or to aid the poor and the less fortunate. What began as a social club grew to be an organization aimed at assisting Blacks in Montreal in

any way possible. One of the many activities of the CWC included providing warm clothing and assistance in settling into the community to students who arrived from the West Indies to attend McGill U., as they were often unprepared for Canadian winters and Canadian discrimination. Over the years, the CWC has played a key role in the community, providing support where needed and bursaries to students. In 1907, the Club's members helped with the creation of the Union United Church, the oldest Black congregation in Montreal; members have also been involved in the operations of the Negro Community Centre (NCC). And, in the interest of uniting Black women across Canada, the CWC co-founded the Congress of Black Women and hosted two of their meetings, in 1973 and 1974. In 1999, the members published a cookbook, edited by SG; proceeds from the sale of this publication enabled the Club to establish a permanent scholarship fund to help Black students. And, in order to inform the public about the Black experience in Canada, for the past four years, SG has organized and conducted Black Heritage tours to the Underground Railroad. **OTHER:** SG worked for 36 yrs. as a Traffic Controller for AT&T Canada, before retiring; also serves on the Board of the NCC and the South Shore Black Community Assn. She has been the president of the CWC since 1997. **HONS.:** Club's benevolent work recognized by the *Min. des Relations avec les Citoyens et de l'Immigration du Québec*, 1997; Solidarity Prize created by the Quebec Government and awarded annually, named Anne Greenup Solidarity Prize, in honour of the Club's first President. **WORKS:** *The Coloured Women's Club Millennium Cookbook,* 1999. **REVIEWED IN:** local & community papers, *Montreal Gazette,* 2000; featured on Global TV, 2002. **HEROES/ROLE MODELS:** Evelyn Braxton, friend & fellow club member. **CONTACT:** sagyles@sympatico.ca; Fax: 450-465-0853

►HALSTEAD, Joseph A.G.

COMMISSIONER, Economic Development, Culture, and Tourism, City of Toronto, 100 Queen St. W., Toronto, ON M5H 2N2. Born: Jamaica/ in Canada since: 1966.

▶ Joe Halstead, in his capacity as Commissioner of Economic Development, Culture, and Tourism, is also responsible for Parks and Recreation, as well as Special Events. He has occupied this position since the amalgamation of metropolitan Toronto with its surrounding boroughs, in 1997. Previously, he spent 24 yrs. with the Ontario Public Service, serving in five different provincial ministries in a broad range of management positions, rising to the position of Assistant Deputy Minister of the Provincial Ministry of Culture, Tourism, and Recreation. **AFFIL/MBRSHP:** involved in sports and recreation both as a volunteer and in his professional life, he has been active with various organizations: Canada Games Council; Coaching Assn. of Canada; Inter-provincial Sport and Recreation Council; Cdn Olympic Assn.; Toronto Raptors Foundation; Premier's Roundtable on Volunteerism; Toronto Community Foundation. He was the City's lead person on Toronto's bid for the 2008 Summer Olympic Games; Executive Lead for the World Youth Day Conference and the Papal visit in 2002. **REVIEWED IN:** local, nat'l publications, radio & TV coverage; *Who's Who of Executives & Professionals.* **EDUCATION:** BA, Poli. Sci. & Economics, York U., 1973; Cert., Technology, Bristol College of Science & Technology, UK, 1967. **HEROES/ROLE MODELS:** Hon. Lincoln Alexander, fraternal brother. **MOTTO:** Commitment! **CONTACT:** jhalste@city. toronto.on.ca; Fax: 416-395-0388

➤HAMALENGWA, Munyonzwe

LAWYER, Munyonzwe Hamalengwa, Barrister & Solicitor, Ste. 900-45 Sheppard Ave. E., Toronto, ON M2N 5W9. Born: Zambia/ in Canada since: 1977.

▶ Munyonzwe Hamalengwa is a lawyer who specializes in criminal, constitutional, immigration, international, and family law. He has been in private practice since 1991. **HIGHLIGHTS:** founder and Principal, Nelson Mandela Academy of Applied Legal Studies, teaches law courses to paralegal students, since 1996; writes weekly column on legal issues, *Pride* newspaper, since 1998. Director, African Studies Program, York U., 1986-87; taught political science and social science, York U., 1980-89. Active in the realm of international human rights, he has completed diploma and certificate courses with the International Institute of Human Rights (France), the Cdn Human Rights Foundation (PEI), the UN (Switzerland), the Hague Academy of International Law (The Netherlands), and the Antioch School of Law (Washington, DC). **AFFIL/MBRSHP:** African Human Rights Research Assn.; Forum for African Students in Toronto; CAN: BAIA; Refugee Lawyers Assn. Int'l Society for the Reform of Criminal Law; Int'l Third World Legal Studies Assn.; Brd., Board of Inquiry, Human Rights Code of Ontario, 1995-98; Brd., Liquor Licence Board of Ontario (LLBO), 1991-94. **WORKS:** selected in: *Social Justice; Human Rights and the Administration of Criminal Justice; The Law & Economic Development in the Third World; J Human Rights Quarterly; Africa: A Continent in Crisis;* books: *Class Struggles in Zambia,* 1992; forthcoming, *The Practice of Law in Canada.* **EDUCATION:** PhD candidate; LLM, 2001; LLB, 1989, Osgoode Hall, York University. Diplomas & Certificates, Int'l Human Rights Law (incl., Strasbourg, 1983 & '85; Geneva, 1983; The Hague, 1985, etc.); Cdn Human Rights Law, 1989; Grad. Dipl., Int'l Trade Law, Antioch School of Law, Washington, DC; MA, Int'l Affairs, Norman Patterson School of Int'l Affairs, Carleton U., 1980; BA, York U., 1979. **MOTTO:** It counts for something when education, knowledge, experience, fearlessness and advocacy skills sit comfortably together. **CONTACT:** mhamalengwa@sympatico.ca; Tel: 416-222-8111; Fax: 416-222-7518

173

►**HAMILTON, Sylvia,** Dr.

FILMMAKER, Maroon Films Inc., Box 10, RR #3, Grand Pre, NS B0P 1M0. Born: Beechville, NS.

▶ Sylvia Hamilton is a respected Canadian filmmaker and writer. She began her professional life in social and community development, working with high school dropouts in Halifax in the 1970s, then, with community-based organizations across Canada for the Company of Young Canadians. She trained as a reporter and announcer, worked for private radio stations and freelanced for the CBC. **CAREER HIGHLIGHTS:** During the 1980s she was a Program Officer for the federal Dept. of Secretary of State, then Asst. Regional Director, then Acting Regional Director. Her interest in communications led her to writing and filmmaking. She worked with the NFB in Halifax and with Studio D, the NFB women's studio in Montreal. Through her films and in her writing, she has brought the life experiences of Black Nova Scotians into the mainstream of Canadian arts. Her films include: *Black Mother, Black Daughter,* 1989; *Speak It: From the Heart of Black Nova Scotia,* 1993; *Against the Tides (Hymn to Freedom Series),* 1994; *No More Secrets* (about violence against Black Women), 1999; *Portia White: Think on Me* (only major work on this Canadian contralto, called "Canada's Marian Anderson"), 2000. Her films have been screened widely and internationally, and have won numerous awards. **OTHER:** continues to develop film projects through her company, Maroon Films; in 2001, she was appointed Nancy's Chair in Women's Studies at Mount Saint Vincent U. **COMMUNITY:** throughout her career, she has volunteered with a number of artistic, social, and cultural organizations, locally, provincially, and nationally. **AFFIL/MBRSHP:** National Chair, WTN Foundation; has been active in the Writers' Federation of NS and the Cdn Independent Film Caucus. **HONS.:** several including, Hon. LLD, Dalhousie U., 2001; Pioneer Award, CBC Television, 2000; Commemo-ration Award, City of Halifax, 2000; Women of Excellence, 1996; Race Unity Award, Baha'i Canada, 1996; Hon. D.Litt, Saint Mary's U., 1995; Gemini Award & NHK Japan Broadcasting Maeda Prize (for *Speak It*), 1994; Golden Sheaf Award (for *Black Mother, Black Daughter*), 1990. **WORKS:** poetry in: *Dalhousie Review; Fiery Spirits, Canadian Writers of African Descent,* 1995; *Fireweed,* 1986 & 1983; *Other Voices: Writings by Blacks in Canada,* 1985. Articles/essays in: *Atlantis; A Women's Studies J,* 1995; *And Still We Rise,* 1993; *Canadian Women Studies-Les cahiers de la femme,* 1982*; Workshop Guide: No More Secrets,* 1999; co-editor/contributor, *We're Rooted Here and They Can't Pull Us Up: Essays in African Canadian Women's History.* **REVIEWED IN:** *Millennium Minds,* 2000. **EDUCATION:** MA, Dalhousie U., 2000; Dipl., Atlantic School of Broadcasting, 1979; BA, Acadia U., 1972. **CONTACT:** Tel: 902-542-1609

►**HAMIS, Ahmed R.**

ENVIRONMENTAL COORDINATOR, Regional Municipality of Halton, 1151 Bronte Rd., Oakville, ON L6J 6E1. Born: Nigeria/ in Canada since: 1979.

▶ Ahmed Hamis is an Environmental Coordinator/ Industrial Waste Abatement Inspector with the Regional Municipality of Halton, since 1989. His responsibilities include: performing industrial waste inspections and assessing the adequacy of pollution control systems in existing industries; evaluating industrial waste discharge applications and issuing appropriate discharge approvals to new industries. Previously, he was an Industrial Waste Monitoring Technician, 1988-89, and a Plant Operator, 1987-88 with the Region of Halton. Active in the community, he is serving his second term as President of the Nigerian Cdn Assn., since 1999; he is also co-founder and Chair of the Assn. of Northern Nigerians in Canada. **HONS.:** Award for contribution to the Nigerian community, Miss Nigeria/Canada

Pageant, 2001; Outstanding Leadership Award, Assn. N. Nigerians, 2001; Leadership Award, Nssarawa State, Nigeria, 2000. **EDUCATION:** Cert., Internal Auditor, Cdn Standards Assn., 1998; work-related courses, Ont. Min. of the Environment, & Municipality of Halton; BSc, Environmental Science, Lake Superior State U., Michigan, 1986; Dipl., Engineering Technology, Sault Ste. Marie College, 1984. **CONTACT:** ncapresident @netscape.net; Fax: 905-825-8771

▶**HANSRAJ, Luther**

ACTOR/PRODUCER/DIRECTOR, Toronto, ON. Born: Guyana/ in Canada since: 1974.

▶ Luther Hansraj is an actor, producer, director, and educator with over 27 years experience in the performing arts. He began his career with Black Theatre Canada in 1976 and went on to perform on stage, in film, TV, and radio. **CAREER HIGH-LIGHTS:** stage: *A Caribbean Midsummer Night's Dream* and *Playboy of the West Indies;* film and TV: *Fields of Endless Day; Ghost of a Chance* (with Redd Foxx); *Cocktails* (with Tom Cruise); *Equus* (with Richard Burton); *Street Legal; Scales of Justice*; and, several readings for CBC Radio. He has represented Canada at a number of international festivals including the Netherlands Stage Door Festival, and the Taiwan Nan Ying Folklore International Festival. He has also worked in the UK and the US. Locally, he has toured schools and universities as an actor, workshop leader, trainer and mentor, promoting accessibility for artists from diverse ethno-cultural backgrounds in theatre, film and TV. He has served as juror and advisor for the Ontario Arts Council, Dora Mavor Moore Awards, Chalmers Awards, Harry Jerome Awards, and Canada Council for the Arts. He is a founding member of the Harold Awards for Alternative Theatre. **HONS.:** including: Award of Recognition, Ont. Society for Services to Indo-Caribbean Canadians, 2000; ACAA, 1997; Harry Jerome Award, 1996; Dora Mavor Moore Award, for innovative artistic excellence, *A Caribbean Midsummer Night's Dream*, 1983. **EDUCATION:** U of T; George Brown College; Royal Conservatory of Music; Dipl., Radio & TV Broadcasting, National Institute of Broadcasting.

▶**HAREWOOD, John L.**

ACADEMIC ADVISOR/PROFESSOR (Ret.), Faculty of Arts, University of Ottawa, ON. Born: Barbados/ in Canada since: 1958.

▶ John Harewood has worked in both academic and government settings: he spent 35 yrs. with the University of Ottawa, 25 yrs. as an Academic Advisor and nine yrs. as an Assistant Professor in the Dept. of Classical Studies. He also taught at Carleton U. and gave private ESL lessons to diplomats from S. America, Africa, Europe and Asia. In government, he served as a Consultant for CIDA, Employment and Immigration, the Multiculturalism Directorate, and the Ont. Min. of Education. He was also, for several years, Chief Oral Examiner of English as a Foreign Language Examinations for Cambridge U. at U. of Ottawa. **OTHER:** he has written poems, essays, and skits, which have been performed on radio, stage, and during Black History Month celebrations. He is a member of the theatre group, Third World Players. **COMMUNITY:** Arts and Cultural Cmtee, Ottawa; National Black Awards; Intercultural Immigrant Services; Black Canadian Scholarship Fund; United Way. **HONS.:** including, University recognition, 25 yrs. of service, U. of Ottawa, 2001; Cert. Recognition for service, Assn. for Higher Education, Ottawa, 2000; Award for Community Service, Barbados-Ottawa Assn., 1999. **WORKS:** articles/essays in: *Multiculturalism & the Black Presence in the Canadian Mosaic*, (ed. V. D'Oyley), 1979; *Echos du Monde Classique/Classical News and Views; Contrast.* **EDUCATION:** M.Ed, U. of Ottawa, 1989. MA, Classics, 1964; BA/Hons., 1961, U of T. Cert. Education, NF, 1962. **HEROES/ROLE MODELS:** Father, brother, uncle. **MOTTO:** Nothing is too difficult with time and effort. **CONTACT:** harewood@uottawa.ca; Fax: 613-562-5973

▶**HARRIS, Claire**
AUTHOR, Calgary, AB. Born: Trinidad & Tobago/ in Canada since: 1966.
▶ Claire Harris is an award-winning poet living in Calgary; she has been described by the *Ottawa Citizen* as "One of the best poets in Canada today." Her works include: *Fables from the Women's Quarters,* 1984; *Translation into Fiction,* 1984; *Travelling to Find a Remedy,* 1986; *The Conception of Winter,* 1989; *Drawing Down a Daughter,* 1992; *Dipped in Shadow,* 1996; *She,* 2000. **BACKGROUND:** in addition to teaching high school English and drama from 1966 to 1994, she travelled widely, living and working abroad. From 1981-89, she was the poetry editor at *Dandelion Magazine*; she has also worked on the Calgary project, Poetry Goes Public, which publishes poster poems of major poets. Now, in addition to devoting herself to writing on a full-time basis, she also lectures and conducts workshops for young writers. **AFFIL/MBRSHP:** Writers' Guild of AB; Amnesty Int'l; Inter Pares; League of Cdn Poets. **HONS.:** short-listed for AB Writers' Guild Prize, for *She,* 2001 & for *Dipped in Shadow,* 1996; nominated for GG Award in poetry, for *Drawing Down a Daughter,* 1993; AB Culture Special Award for poetry, for *Conception,* 1990; Writers' Guild of AB & AB Culture Poetry Prize, for *Travelling,* 1987; AB Achievement Award, 1987; Commonwealth Prize for poetry, *Fables,* 1985. **WORKS:** has also co-authored/co-edited texts such as: *Kitchen Talk,* 1992; *Grammar of Dissent,* 1995. **EDUCATION:** Dipl., Mass Communication, U. of Lagos, Nigeria, 1975; Dipl. Ed., UWI, Jamaica, 1963; BA, U. College, Dublin, 1961. **CONTACT:** Fax: 403-230-8653

▶**HARRIS, Jeffrey F.**
LAWYER/PARTNER, Myers, Weinberg, 240 Graham Ave., Winnipeg, MB R3C 0J7. Born: Winnipeg, MB.
▶ Jeffrey F. Harris has been practising law since 1983; he has been a partner with Myers, Weinberg since 1996. Prior to that he was a founding member and partner with Keyser Harris, 1987-96. In addition to trial work in civil, criminal and child protection cases, he has represented First Nations and First Nations organizations in negotiating resolutions in matters concerning land claims, education, labour matters, self-government and justice issues. **HIGHLIGHTS:** his practice is focused almost exclusively on matters related to Aboriginal peoples and governments; he is counsel to two First Nations Child and Family Service Agencies and has been retained by a third to represent it in an inquiry; he is counsel to two Manitoba First Nations bands negotiating a comprehensive land claim, two others negotiating a flood claim, and an Ontario First Nation band involved in litigation over land rights under a Treaty. He was appointed to the Organizing Committee of the N. American Indigenous Games held in Winnipeg in August, 2002; he has also acted for the Minister of Indian Affairs in investigating and reporting on a challenged election on a First Nation; in 1998, he prepared a paper for the Assembly of Manitoba Chiefs on issues surrounding the assumption of jurisdiction in education by First Nations in Manitoba. **AFFIL/MBRSHP:** radio and TV commentator on criminal, civil, and aboriginal issues; United Way; Manitoba and Cdn Bar Assn.; Royal Lifesaving Society; Lester Beach Assn.; Heritage St. Norbert; Laurier Club. **EDUCATION:** LLB, 1982; B.Ed, 1976; BA, 1974, U. of Manitoba. **CONTACT:** jharris@myersfirm.com

▶**HARRIS, Paul F.**
OWNER/MANAGER (Ret.), Supreme Electric Manufacturing Ltd., Belair, MB. Born: USA/ in Canada since: 1928.
▶ Paul Harris was a pioneer as the owner and manager of his own electrical manufacturing

company, Supreme Electric Manufacturing, for close to 30 years. In his own words, "without any formal training or schooling in the electrical field, I, with my wife's encouragement was able to learn 'on the job' and successfully manage this company." His company manufactured water heater elements which were then supplied to Winnipeg Hydro and Manitoba Hydro; he also manufactured heating coils which were supplied to wholesalers and repair stores across Western Canada to BC. **EDUCATION:** Wilberforce U., Ohio; United College (now, U. of Winnipeg). **HEROES/ ROLE MODELS:** Parents.

►**HARRISON, Herman (Herm)**
FORMER FOOTBALL PLAYER/PHILANTHROPIST, Calgary, AB. Born: USA/ in Canada since: 1964.
▶ Herm Harrison is well known in Calgary for his community involvement and his support of many charities, particularly those concerning children. He first came to the attention of Albertans when he played in the CFL for the Calgary Stampeders, 1964-73, as a linebacker and tight end. **FOOTBALL HIGHLIGHTS:** the Stampeders played in three Grey Cups (1968, '70, '71) and won in 1971; voted Most Popular Player, 1968; voted Canadian All Star for five yrs.; awarded Western All Star in Canada for six yrs. In one of many career records, he scored four touchdown passes in one game (Sept. 1970, against the Winnipeg Blue Bombers); still holds a number of unbeaten all-time football records. **OTHER:** during the last five yrs. of his football career and afterwards, he worked with Moffat Communications, selling radio advertising; he was General Manager of CKXL and CHFM radio stations, 1979-86, but left the management position to continue selling advertising; he won many awards for consistently being a top performer. **COMMUNITY:** extensive involvement; volunteers for speaking engagements, supports many charities and raises millions of dollars for various causes, including Special Olympics; Children's Wish Fdn.; United

Way; Kids Help Phone; Discovery House; CNIB. **HONS.:** football: John Ware Memorial Trophy, BAASA; inducted into Football Hall of Fame, 1993; Stampeder Wall of Fame, 1987; received Football's President Award & Outstanding Player, 1968. Radio & advertising: Employee of the Year, 1987; Master Sales Award, seven times and was a member of the Million Dollar Club. **WORKS:** has written for local publications, including the sports section of *Guide: Play & Fashion Magazine.* **REVIEWED IN:** local & nat'l newspapers & magazines; profiled in *Stampeder Fact Book.* **EDUCATION:** MA, Elementary Psychology; BA, Education Psychology, Arizona State U. **HEROES/ROLE MODELS:** Lela Harrison, mother; Calvin George; Frank Kush, Head Coach, Arizona State U. **MOTTO:** Every day above ground is a good day. **CONTACT:** hharrison76@shaw.ca; Fax: 403-288-4276

►**HARTLEY, Max,** Sgt.
POLICE SERGEANT (Ret.), Halifax Regional Police, Halifax, NS. Born: Shelburne, NS.
▶ Sgt. Max Hartley joined the Halifax Police Dept. in 1969, and rose to the rank of Sergeant by 1993, before retiring from the Halifax Regional Police in 1999. During his career, he worked in patrol, criminal investigation, and special enforcement. **HIGHLIGHTS:** co-recipient (along with Sgt. Darrell Downey) of Police Accommodation for efforts in saving two children from a house fire. In 1998, he was recognized by the Halifax Regional Police as the first African-Nova Scotian to be promoted in rank in the province's Regional Police Services. Since 1993, he has been a Racial Sensitivity Instructor, providing the first ever racial sensitivity training to the Executive Management of the Halifax Police Dept. and has lectured several times as an invited speaker on issues concerning the police, Black communities and Black history to the Halifax Regional Police's second recruit class (1998), to officers throughout Canada and at the Cdn Police College

in Ottawa. **OTHER:** credits retired Chief of Police Vincent MacDonald, with improving police relations in the Black community and on Black community issues. **AFFIL/MBRSHP:** member, Visible Minority Recruiting Cmtee, responsible for the hiring of the first visible minority police recruit class (1993); founder/President, Racial Minority Police Officers Assn. (RMPOA); facilitated appointment of the first Black honorary Police Inspector, Chaplain Lionel Moriah, to the Halifax Regional Police. **CONTACT:** joanne.hartley@ns. sympatico.ca; Fax: 902-457-1989

► **HARTY, Corita**
REGIONAL DIRECTOR, Human Resources, Ontario and Nunavut Region, Health Canada, Ste. 1131-200 Town Centre Crt., Toronto, ON. Born: Jamaica/ in Canada since: 1975.
► Corita Harty is, since 1999, the Regional Director of Human Resources, Ontario and Nunavut Region, for Health Canada. She has over 16 yrs. experience in areas of multiculturalism, official languages, and international relations; also has expertise in training and development, particularly in partnerships and project development. **CAREER:** was an Executive Advisor, Public Service Commission, 1997-98; occupied a number of positions (Sr. Program Manager, Training Specialist, Sr. Policy/Program Manager) with Canadian Heritage, 1989-97. **OTHER:** she is the founding President of the National Council of Visible Minorities in the Federal Public Service (NCVM), which was created in 1999 to assist government employees from diverse ethno-cultural groups achieve employment equity and equal opportunity for promotions and senior positions. **HONS.:** Deputy Minister's Award for Team Excellence, since 1999. **EDUCATION:** M.Ed Admin., 1993; B.Ed, 1985; BA, French & German, 1983, Ottawa U. **CONTACT:** ingridharty@ hotmail.com; Fax: 416-973-4219

► **HERRERA JACKSON, Denise**
CONSULTANT/TECHNICAL WRITER, Farrell Haynes Associates, Toronto, ON. Born: Trinidad & Tobago/ in Canada since: 1976.
► Denise Herrera Jackson is a journalist, technical writer, trainer and business analyst in information technology. She has been engaged as a consultant in IT since 1992, working with organizations such as IBM, Kasten Chase Applied Research, Media Synergy, Media Lynx; telecommunications entities such as Bell Canada, Unitel; banks such as TD Canada Trust and N. American Trust; entertainment management such as SOCAN; government bodies such as the Ministry of Finance. Previously, she worked as a full-time employee at Imperial Oil Ltd. for 13 yrs. in marketing, statistical analysis, and technical communication. She also managed and marketed the Corporate Manuals Group. **COMMUNITY INVOLVEMENT:** Harbourfront, since 1995; YWCA Women of Distinction Awards; worked on inaugural Martin Luther King celebrations in Toronto; co-producer Caribbean theatre and other events; Caribbean Cultural Committee, secured corporate sponsorship; Harriet Tubman Games; member, marketing and campaign team for MPP Alvin Curling; Black Secretariat, marketing research and conference planning; Toronto chapter, Society for Technical Communication; Project Management Institute, Toronto chapter. **HONS.:** Hon. Brd. Member, Harbourfront; Award of Achievement, Int'l Technical Communication Competition, 1988. **WORKS:** several business manuals, guides, on-line documentation; wrote the on-line help for Canada 411 web-enabled telephone white pages on www.sympatico.ca; wrote on-line user document for @loha, an animated e-mail system for home offices. **EDUCATION:** pursuing IT Management, Ryerson; MES, York U., 1984; BA, Journalism, U. of Western Ontario, 1975. **HEROES/ ROLE MODELS:** Dr. Rita Cox; Jean Sheen; Ita Ferdinand-Grant. **MOTTO:** Never start something that you cannot complete! **CONTACT:** sanscoche@ yahoo. com

►HEZEKIAH, Jocelyn, PhD.
NURSING EDUCATION CONSULTANT, Burlington, ON. Born: Trinidad & Tobago/ in Canada since: 1959.

▶ As a Nursing Education Consultant, Dr. Jocelyn Hezekiah has completed contracts in Canada, Dominica, Jamaica, Nepal, Pakistan, Thailand, and Trinidad. **CAREER HIGHLIGHTS:** Associate Professor of Nursing, McMaster U., 1987-97; Field Faculty Advisor in Pakistan for three years on an Aga Khan/CIDA project, to develop the leadership skills of local nurses and health-care workers; headed a community college nursing program and was Chair of Basic Nursing programs at Humber College; participated in the successful transfer of two hospital schools of nursing to the community college; initiated a common semester for the Nursing diploma and the Nursing Assistant programs, which was done for the first time in Canada. **AFFIL/MBRSHP:** President, Registered Nurses Assn. of Ontario, 1977-81 (first Black to be elected to this position); previously, member of the Min. of Colleges and Universities Committee on Clinical Experience for Diploma Nursing Programs; served on a number of professional and government committees dealing with nursing education; served on the Board of the Canadian Nurses Assn. and participated in the development of the first Code of Ethics for nurses in Canada; Sigma Theta Tau Int'l (the Honour Society of Nursing). **OTHER:** received funding to complete studies on: Caribbean nursing leaders; health promotion strategies for victims of genital mutilation; the history of nursing education in Trinidad & Tobago; rural women and power in Pakistan; also, wrote the first historical book on nursing leaders in the Caribbean (see below). **HONS.:** Plaque for Community Contribution, National Black Coalition/Edmonton Chapter, 1987. Awards: Ont. Min. of Health, 1968; Nurses Assn., Quebec, 1964; Mtl General Hospital Auxiliary, 1963. **WORKS:** incl.: *Breaking the Glass Ceiling: The Stories of Three Caribbean Nurses,* 2001. Articles in: *Can J Nursing Research; Health Care for Women Int'l; Int'l J Nursing Studies; Advances in Nursing Science; Int'l J Health Services.* **REVIEWED IN:** many publications, including: *Toronto Star; Globe and Mail; RNAO News; Trinidad Guardian; The Express; Newsday; Share.* **EDUCATION:** PhD, U. of Alberta, 1987; M.Ed, OISE/U of T, 1969; BN, McGill U., 1965. RN, 1954; Midwife, 1956, UK. **HEROES/ ROLE MODELS:** An Irish head nurse. **MOTTO:** If at first you don't succeed, try, try again. **CONTACT:** jhez@primus.ca; Fax: 905-639-9326

►HIBBERT JR., Leroy
MULTICULTURAL OUTREACH COORDINATOR, LUSO Community Services, 608 Hamilton Rd. E., London, ON N5Z 1S9. Born: Toronto, ON, 1971.

▶ Leroy Hibbert Jr. is the Multicultural Outreach Coordinator with the London Urban Services Organization (LUSO), a community agency created in 1979, which now provides social services to the community, in all of its diversity. As the coordinator of this program, LH provides workshops on self-esteem, conflict resolution, assertiveness training, race relations and multicultural education for secondary and elementary schools as well as community groups and associations; he has also introduced an essay/poetry writing contest to mark March 21 (Int'l Day for the Elimination of Racial Discrimination). Initially, 700 students participated and with this success the event has now become an annual poster drawing contest. He coordinated a Cross-Cultural Anti-Racism Education Conference at the U. of Western Ontario for youth, administrators, and educators, which attracted 300 participants. He is also a member of the London Race Relations Advisory Committee and, in this capacity, speaks regularly to groups of youth, administrators and various associations in the London area; has also appeared on TV discussing aspects of racism and hate groups following certain local incidents;

and, has been a panelist/facilitator at conferences on conflict resolution. **HONS.:** Frank Brennan Award, centre for children and families of the Family Court Clinic, 2001; Community Award, Congress of Black Women/London Chapter, 1998; Race Relations Award, Baha'i Community, 1998. **EDUCATION:** Dipl., Recreation Leadership, Fanshawe College, 1992. **HEROES/ROLE MODELS:** Parents; Dr. Fred Price; Kenneth Hagin. **CONTACT:** leroy@lusocentre.org; www.lusocentre.org

►**HILL, Dan**
SINGER/SONGWRITER/PRODUCER, c/o Jason Campbell, Big Picture Entertainment, 2820 Erica Place, Nashville, TN 37204. Born: Oakville, ON.
▶ Dan Hill has been writing and performing hit songs to critical acclaim since the 1970s. Over the course of his career, he has had four number one songs, twelve top ten records, a Grammy Award, five Juno Awards, four platinum albums, two gold albums, and written a novel. His songs have been performed by Celine Dion, George Benson, Barry Manilow, the Backstreet Boys, Tammy Wynette, Michael Bolton, Rod Stewart, Tina Turner, Cleo Laine, and many others. **CAREER HIGHLIGHTS:** in 1978, he had his first hit, *Sometimes When We Touch,* which rose to number three on the pop charts and earned him his first Grammy nomination. In 1987, his duet with Vonda Sheppard on *Can't We Try*, was number six on the pop charts and was *Billboard*'s Song of the Year; 1988, *Never Thought (That I Could Love)*, rose to number one on the charts. He has also been extremely successful writing and producing for others including Celine Dion, winning a Grammy Award, 1996, for his production and songwriting on the CD, *Falling Into You.* A single from that CD, written by DH, *Seduces Me,* was re-released on Dion's *Collector's Series*. DH has collaborated with other songwriters like Keith Stegall; their song, *Love of My Life*, performed by Sammy Kershaw, 1997, rose to number one on the US country charts; other songs by

the duo include *I Do (Cherish You),* 1997; *She's In Love*, 1999; and *Maybe Not Tonight*, 1999, also did well on the music charts. *I Do (Cherish You)*, originally performed by Mark Wills, was recorded by the pop group 98 Degrees and was featured in the movie, *Notting Hill,* which starred Julia Roberts and Hugh Grant. He sang the title song, *It's a Long Road* for the Sylvester Stallone film, *First Blood*. Between writing and performing his own works and writing for others, DH has become one of the industry's most respected and sought-after songwriters. **HONS.:** several including: ASCAP Award, for one of the year's most played songs (*Love of My Life*); Harold Moon Award (to a Canadian songwriter for international contributions to songwriting); two Gold albums in Canada (*Dan Hill* and *Hold On*); three Platinum albums in Canada (*Longer Fuse, Frozen in the Night, Dan Hill Collection*); five Juno Awards, Grammy Award, Producer, for *Falling Into You*, sung by Celine Dion, 1996; nominee, Grammy Award for Male Vocalist for *Sometimes When We Touch.* **WORKS:** novel, *Comeback.* **CONTACT:** Fax: (Agent) 615-292-0749

►**HILL, Lawrence**
WRITER, c/o Harper Collins, Toronto, ON. Born: Oakville, ON.
▶ Lawrence Hill is a writer of novels, short stories, books on the history of Blacks in Canada, and other non-fiction. He has also been a journalist and a teacher of creative writing. In addition to publishing two novels, two works of non-fiction, a children's history book and a number of short stories (see below), he has also pursued other forms of writing. He was a writer and media relations officer with the Ont. Min. of Economic Development, Trade and Tourism, 1995-98; a sessional instructor of creative writing at Ryerson University, 1993-98; a Senior Writer for various Ontario Govt. communications branches; and was a reporter, *Winnipeg Free Press*, 1982-85 (Ottawa Correspondent, in final year). Currently he is

researching his next novel, *Migration*; and, on occasion, serves as a Writing Mentor with the Writers-in-Electronic Residence program. **HONS.:** including, Gold Awards, Best Speech & Best Feature Article, Communicators' Forum, 1996. **WORKS:** books incl.: *Black Berry, Sweet Juice: On Being Black & White in Canada*, 2001; *Any Known Blood*, 1997; *Women of Vision: A History of the Canadian Negro Women's Association*, 1996; *Trials & Triumphs: The Story of African-Canadians* (children's history book), 1993. **EDUCATION:** MA, Writing, Johns Hopkins U., Baltimore, 1992; BA/Hons., U. Laval, 1980. **CONTACT:** lawrencehill@sprint.ca; www.lawrencehill.com

▶**HILL III, Dan G.,** PhD, OC, O.Ont.
FOUNDER/PRESIDENT EMERITUS (Ret.), Ontario Black History Society, Toronto, ON. Born: USA/ in Canada since: 1951.

▶ Dr. Daniel Hill III, sociologist, historian, lecturer and civil rights activist, contributed significantly to improving the rights of ethnic minorities in Ontario during the course of his career, particularly with the Ontario Human Rights Commission and as Ombudsperson for Ontario. **HIGHLIGHTS:** originally from the US, he and his wife, Donna, also a human rights activist, came to Canada in the 1950s; 1955-59, he was employed as a Research Director with the Social Planning Council of Metropolitan Toronto; 1962, he became the first Director of the newly formed Ontario Human Rights Commission, established in 1961 to administer and enforce the Ontario Human Rights Code. During his mandate, eight regional offices were opened; 4,000 formal complaints were investigated and about 30,000 informal cases, not covered by the law, were processed; 1971, he became Chair of this Commission; during his tenure he contributed to advances in public awareness about human rights issues; later, he established his own consulting firm and was a lecturer in the Dept. of Sociology and Social Work at U of T; he was also Special Advisor to U of T's President, to the Ontario AG, and to the Toronto Mayor's Committee on Community Race Relations; amongst his many accomplishments was the production of a Training Manual on Race Relations for the Metro Toronto Police Dept. In 1978, DGH, his wife, and some other community builders, joined to form the Ontario Black History Society (OBHS); serving as the group's president until 1983, he established the foundation upon which the organization continues to operate, encouraging research and promoting awareness of contributions by Blacks to Canadian history. From 1984-89, he served as Ombudsman for the province of Ontario, the first Black to hold this position (the office was opened in 1975 for the purpose of addressing complaints against provincial government ministries and agencies). **COMMUNITY:** over the years he has been involved with many groups and community organizations and acknowledged their contributions as pioneers in the community, including: the Cdn Negro Women's Assn., which sponsored a Negro History Week in 1958; the Negro Business and Professional Men's Assn., which sponsored a Black History Exhibit with the Toronto Public Library, in 1963; and, Gwen and Leonard Johnson's Third World Bookstore, which opened in 1968, and was the first major business providing Black-focussed books and art in Toronto. He is President Emeritus of the OBHS and an Honorary Fellow of the Multicultural History Society of Ontario. **OTHER:** DGH is the author of numerous books and articles on human rights and Canadian Black history. **HONS.:** several including: Hon. LLD, U of T, 2001; Officer, Order of Canada, 1998; Dr. Daniel G. Hill Scholarship & Student Support fund established by the Faculty of Social Work, U of T, 1994; Order of Ontario, 1993; Daniel G. Hill Community Service Award, established by OBHS, 1993; Hon. LLD, St. Thomas U., 1986; Dr. Hill & his wife, Donna, received Cdn Labour Congress Award, for outstanding service to humanity, 1984. **WORKS:** several including: *The Freedom*

Seekers: Blacks in Early Canada, 1981; *Negroes in Toronto: A Sociological Study of a Minority Group*, 1960. **REVIEWED IN:** several including: *WWIC*; *Millennium Minds*, 2000; *Some Black Men*, 1999. **EDUCATION:** PhD, Sociology, 1960; MA, 1950, U of T. Studies at Oslo U., Norway, 1948; BA, Howard U., Washington, DC, 1948.

▶HINKSON, Steven

LAWYER/PARTNER, Hinkson, Sachak, McLeod, Ste. 1201-67 Yonge St., Toronto, ON M5B 1J8. Born: England, 1963/ in Canada since: 1966.

▶ Steven Hinkson is a lawyer and a partner in the firm Hinkson, Sachak, McLeod. He appeared before the Supreme Court of Canada in a groundbreaking case, Regina vs. Williams; this case entrenched challenges for cause based upon race in jury trials. **REVIEWED IN:** *Hamilton Spectator*; *Globe and Mail*. **EDUCATION:** LLB, Osgoode Hall, York U., 1990; BA/Hons., U. of Western Ontario, 1987. **MOTTO:** Pursue your dreams! **CONTACT:** shinkson@idirect.ca; Fax: 416-363-9917

▶HOLAS, Patricia W.

CREATIVE DIRECTOR/AUTHOR, Pan-African Publications, PO Box 83023, Ottawa, ON K1V 1A3. Born: Trinidad/grew up in Grenada/ in Canada since: 1969.

▶ Patricia Holas is the founder and Creative Director of Pan-African Publications, a company she created in 1993, dedicated to promoting the accomplishments of Blacks in Canada. **BACKGROUND:** Senior Coordinator for National Campaigns, Canada Safety Council, 1989-96; various positions with banks and as an Assistant Editor with the Federal Government, 1976-89; also taught high school in Grenada and in Ottawa, 1966-70 and 1973-76. In 1993, she began publishing calendars through her company. In 1994, she created *Home Alone*, Safety Cards for Kids, on behalf of the Canada Safety Council. She has also produced a series of publications

with profiles of Black achievers, youth and adults. Her most recent publication, *Millennium Minds*, 2000, profiling 100 Black Canadians, has been received with much enthusiasm. **HONS.:** Solicitor General's Award, for *Home Alone*, 1994. **WORKS:** in 1993: *Black Profiles: A Calendar; Black Sisters; Black Inventors; Blacks in the Arts; Black Pioneers of Canada; Black Youth: A Millennium Calendar*. **EDUCATION:** BA, U. of Ottawa, 1973. **HEROES/ROLE MODELS:** Chief Justice Julius Isaac, mentor, friend. **MOTTO:** Life is not a rehearsal –live it fully. **CONTACT:** wpholas@cyberus.ca; Fax: 613-737-3334

▶HOLDER, Peter Anthony

RADIO HOST/BROADCASTER, Standard Broadcasting –CJAD 800 AM, Montreal, QC. Born: Montreal, QC.

▶ Peter Anthony Holder is a broadcasting veteran with over 20 yrs. experience. Since 1990, he has been the host of CJAD 800 AM's, *Holder Overnight*, a talk and interview program heard in the Montreal area, Monday-Friday (11pm-2am). He is particularly appreciated for his promotion of community initiatives which target youth. He is also a part-time Producer-Announcer on Radio-Canada Int'l and on the Canadian Forces Network, which is broadcast to various parts of the world and is accessible by shortwave and satellite. His broadcast experience extends to TV where he has been involved with *Just for Laughs*, and produced several shows such as *Roots Canadian Tribute Series*. He was the co-host for three years on Global TV's annual coverage of Montreal's Carifesta Parade. **OTHER:** freelance TV reporting for Hockey World on CFCF; scorer for major league baseball, and provided statistics to clients such as *USA Today* and Associated Press; on-camera reporter for CFCF 12's *Today's Magazine*; entertainment editor and reporter for CFCF Radio and CFQR; began his on-air career as an afternoon drive announcer on CFJR, in Brockville, Ontario. **HONS.:** Jackie Robinson

Award for Professional Person of the Year, MABBP, 1994. **WORKS:** in, *Today's Magazine; The Chronicle; Senior Times; Downtowner; Afro-Can.* **MOTTO:** What's wrong with trying to be the best?! **CONTACT:** peter@peteranthonyholder.com; www.peteranthonyholder.com

▶**HOLNESS, Renn O., MB BS, FRCSC, DABNS**

PROFESSOR, NEUROSURGERY/DIRECTOR OF SURGICAL EDUCATION, Dept. of Surgery; Dalhousie University, Rm. 3814, 1796 Summer St., Halifax, NS B3M 3A7. Born: Jamaica/ in Canada since: 1972.

▶ Dr. Renn Holness is Professor of Neurosurgery and Director of Surgical Education in the Dept. of Surgery at Dalhousie University. He is also, since 1977, Staff Neurosurgeon at the now-Queen Elizabeth II Health Sciences Centre (QE2 HSC). In 1992, he became the first neurosurgeon in Canada to perform fetal tissue transplants for Parkinson's disease. **HIGHLIGHTS:** Dept. of Neurosurgery, Dalhousie U.: Lecturer, 1977-81; Assistant Professor, 1981-83; Associate Professor, 1983-87; Program Director, Neurosurgical Residency, 1983-90; Professor and Head, Dept. Neurosurgery and Victoria General Hospital, 1987-94; Professor and Head, Div. Neurosurgery, Dept. of Surgery, Dalhousie U. and QE2 HSC, 1994-2000. Chair of Examining Board in Neurosurgery, RCPS Canada, 1996-2000. He was a guest lecturer at Morehouse Medical School, GA, 1999, and was the Peter Moyes Lecturer, at UBC, 1993. **OTHER:** and, staying true to his roots and his interest in medical education in developing countries, ROH returns regularly to the Caribbean to carry out surgery and to assist in the training and the examination of medical students and neurosurgical trainees. **AFFIL/MBRSHP:** Cdn Neurosurgical Society (secretary, 1992-94; president, 1995); Editorial Board, *Can J Neurological Sciences*; Director/Dean, UWI Clinical Training Programme, Bahamas (Jan-Nov. 2000). **HONS.:**

several including: QE2 HSC Distinguished Service Award, 2000; UWI 50th Anniv. Alumni Achievement Award, 1998; Distinguished Graduate Award, UWI, 1996. **WORKS:** in, *J Neurosurgery; Can J Surgery; Transplantation & Implantation Today; Can J Neurosurgical Sciences; The New England J of Medicine.* **REVIEWED IN:** *Canada at the Millennium; The Medical Post; Black Focus.* **EDUCATION:** Sr. Fellow, Neurosurgery, St. Michael's Hospital, 1977; Sr. Resident, Paediatric Neurosurgery, 1976; Resident, Neurosurgery, 1975; MB BS/II, UWI, 1968; BSc/ Hons., Anatomy, UK, 1965; MB BS/I, UWI, 1964. **CONTACT:** renn.holness@dal.ca; Fax: 902-473-2097

▶**HOOKS, Gwendolyn**

AUTHOR/TEACHER (Ret.), County of Leduc, AB. Born: Keystone, AB.

▶ Gwen Hooks is a retired teacher who taught for 35 yrs. with the County of Leduc. Since retiring, she has pursued her interest in writing and researching local Black history; her book, *The Keystone Legacy: Recollections of a Black Settler*, tells of the daily struggles and experiences of the Black pioneers who moved to what became Keystone, Alberta from Mississippi, Oklahoma, Kansas, and other parts of the US; they formed Keystone, one of five Black communities in Alberta. GH has also published two volumes of poetry. **HONS.:** Achievement Award, BAASA, 1997; Golden Poets Award, World of Poetry, 1988, 1991, 1992; Friend of Heritage Award, 1985. **WORKS:** *The Keystone Legacy: Recollections of a Black Settler*, 1997; *As Time Goes By*, Vol. 1, 1992;Vol. 2, 1997. **REVIEWED IN:** *Globe and Mail*; *Leduc Representative*; *Legacy* (Alberta's Heritage magazine). **EDUCATION:** Teaching Cert., 1942; B.Ed, 1975, U. of Alberta. **HEROES/ROLE MODELS:** Velma Cartier, teacher/ friend. **MOTTO:** It's never too late to learn!

►HOOPER, Charmaine

SOCCER PLAYER, Women's United Soccer Association, Atlanta, GA. Born: Guyana/ in Canada since: 1979.

▶ Charmaine Hooper is a professional soccer player who has had a wealth of international experience. Born in Guyana, she began playing soccer as a child in Zambia, where her father was posted with the Guyana High Commission. In addition to playing professionally for Canada, she has also played for the US, Italy, Japan, and Norway. **CAREER HIGHLIGHTS:** all-time leading goal scorer for the Canadian National team; was a member of the CONCACAF All-Tournament Team, 1999; member of FIFA World All-Star Team, 1999; voted MVP, FIFA World All-Star Exhibition Game, scoring two goals against the US in a 2-1 win (previously, Canada had lost 18 games to the US); most capped player in the history of Canada's national soccer teams, men or women; was team MVP and League leading scorer in Norway, 1993; played four yrs. in Japan and won Golden Boot Award as top scorer twice, and League MVP, 1994-98; at North Carolina State U., where she was awarded a full scholarship, she was all-time leading scorer and three-time team MVP; played for the All-American team, 1987-89. In 2001 she signed with the Atlanta Beat and is now a member of the Women's United Soccer Assn. **HONS.:** including: named honorary ambassador of the 2002 U-19 Women's World Cup; HC Kennet Award, most outstanding female athlete of the year, 1989-90; MVP, FIFA All-Star Exhibition; MVP & lead scorer, Norway, 1993; Golden Boot Award twice, for top scorer, Japan. **REVIEWED IN:** nat'l & int'l publications; *Millennium Minds*, 2000. **EDUCATION:** BSc, Food Science, North Carolina State U., 1991. **CONTACT:** chooper11@aol.com

►HOPE, Jay

CHIEF SUPERINTENDENT, Ontario Provincial Police, 777 Memorial Ave., Orillia, ON L3V 7V3. Born: Toronto, ON.

▶ Chief Superintendent Jay Hope, a 23-year veteran of the Ontario Provincial Police (OPP), is the highest-ranking Black police officer in Canada. He is also the first Black officer to be promoted to the rank of Superintendent (2000) in the OPP, then to Chief Superintendent (2001). And, he is the first Black to command a region with over 700 detectives and uniformed personnel. A significant career highlight was being acknowledged as having created the Greater Toronto Area's most innovative traffic programs, which succeeded in reducing personal injury collision and death rates. The programs were: Operation Move Over, Operation Corridor, and The Cottage Patrols. In addition, he was appointed Deputy Chief Aide-de-Camp to Lt.-Gov. Hilary Weston in 2001, the first Black officer to achieve this distinction. **HONS.:** ACAA, 2001; Finalist in the IACP (Int'l Assn. of Chiefs of Police) Traffic Safety Awards, 2001; finalist as Police Officer of the Year, 1996. **REVIEWED IN:** community newspapers; *Globe and Mail*; *Toronto Star*; *Toronto Sun*; *U of T Alumni Magazine*. **EDUCATION:** Human Resources Management, Ryerson U., 1997; BA/Hons., U of T, 1979. **MOTTO:** Never say die! **CONTACT:** jay.hope @jus.gov.on.ca; Fax: 705-329-6188

►HOPKINSON, Nalo

AUTHOR, Box 92527, Toronto, ON M5A 2K0. Born: Jamaica/ in Canada since: 1977.

▶ Nalo Hopkinson is a science fiction and fantasy writer, who has a number of novels and short stories to her credit. She also teaches courses in science fiction; was an instructor at the Clarion West Science Fiction and Fantasy Writers' Workshop 2001, Seattle Community College; taught creative writing at U of T, 2001; and has taught creative writing in high schools across Canada through Writers-in-Electronic-Residence. **HONS.:** John W. Campbell, for Best New Writer, 1999; *Brown Girl in the Ring* and *Midnight Robber* listed among Best Books for the Teen Age, 1998 & 2000, by the NY Public Libraries; *Brown Girl* also won Locus Award, first novel category; and Warner Aspect First Novel Award, 1998. **WORKS:** selected: *Skin Folk*, 2001; *Midnight Robber*, 2000; ed., *Whispers from the Cotton Tree Root: Caribbean Fabulist Fiction*, 2000; short story *Riding the Red*, CBC Radio, 2000; *Brown Girl in the Ring*, 1998. Short stories have appeared in *Fireweed, Exile*, and *Possibilities* magazines. **EDUCATION:** MA, writing popular fiction, Seton Hall College, 2002; Clarion Science Fiction & Fantasy, Michigan State U., 1995; BA/Hons., York U., 1982. **CONTACT:** nalo@web.ca; www.sff.net/people/nalo

►HUDSON, Maurice

SECONDARY SCHOOL PRINCIPAL, Peel District School Board (PDSB), 3545 Morning Star Dr., Mississauga, ON L4T 1Y3. Born: Jamaica/ in Canada since: 1970.

► Maurice Hudson is the Principal of Lincoln M. Alexander Secondary School in Peel District. He was appointed to this position in 1999, and was responsible for closing two schools and managing the amalgamation and transition to the present school, of which he is Principal. Previously, he was the Principal of Westwood Secondary School. In 1997, he served on the Synthesis Team, Ont. Min. of Education and Training, which developed new curriculum direction for secondary schools in Ontario. And, in 1995, he led the design and writing of an Anti-racism and Ethnocultural Equity Policy for PDSB. In 1989, he was appointed Justice of the Peace, Province of Ontario. **COMMUNITY INVOLVEMENT:** Anti-racist Multicultural Educator's Network; since 1984, established a mentoring and scholarship program for youth from Black and Caribbean backgrounds; president, non-profit organization that secured funding, planned construction and manages a 156-unit non-profit housing corporation. Since 1985, he sits on Boards for Peel Memorial Hospital, United Way of Peel, United Achievers Club of Brampton, and the Peel Multicultural Council. **HCNS.:** including, Community Partnership Award, PDSB, 2000; GG 125th Anniv. Medal, 1993; Citizen of the Year, City of Brampton, 1992. **EDUCATION:** completing D.Ed, California Coast U.; MSc, Education, Niagara U., 1986; B.Ed, U of T, 1981; BA, Wilfrid Laurier U., 1981. **MOTTO:** One man with courage makes a majority. **CONTACT:** mauricehudson@peelsb.com; Fax: 905-677-9232

►HUGGINS, Arleen

BARRISTER & SOLICITOR; PARTNER, Koskie Minsky, Ste. 900-20 Queen St. W., Box 52, Toronto, ON M5H 3R3. Born: Toronto, ON, 1963.

► Arleen Huggins is a partner in the firm of Koskie Minsky, which has 32 lawyers. The firm specializes in civil litigation, pension and employee benefits, and union-side labour law. Her areas of personal expertise are employment and human rights law, commercial litigation, and real estate litigation. She has argued cases in the Ontario Superior Court of Justice, the Court of Appeal for Ontario, and has appeared as co-counsel in the Supreme Court of Canada on behalf of the Women's Legal Education and Action Fund (LEAF). She is often a speaker with the Continuing Legal Education program of the Ont. Bar Assn. **AFFIL/MBRSHP:** member, CABL; ACLC (past Brd. and Legal Cmtee member); and LEAF. **WORKS:** in, *Can Insurance Law Review*; various articles on the *Employment Standards Act* and *Employment Standards Act, 2000.* **EDUCATION:** LLB, 1989; BA/ Hons., 1986, U of T. **CONTACT:** ahuggins@koskieminsky.com; www.koskieminsky.com

►HUGGINS, Dorette

DIRECTOR OF COMMUNICATIONS, Dept. of Justice Canada, Ontario Regional Office, Ste. 3400-

130 King St. W., Box 36, Toronto, ON M5X 1K6. Born: Nevis/ in Canada since: 1974.

▶ Dorette Huggins is the Director of Communications with the Federal Dept. of Justice, Ontario Regional Office. Her responsibilities include creating and directing the new Communications Section to provide strategic internal and external communications advice to the Sr. Regional Director, the regional management team, and the national Director of Public Affairs. **CAREER HIGH-LIGHTS:** Communications Advisor, HRDC, 2000-01, where she wrote speeches for the Associate Deputy Minister; Bilingual Human Rights Officer, 1996-2000, Cdn Human Rights Commission, Ont. Regional Office, responsibilities included providing information to the public on the Canadian Human Rights Act. While studying in France, she completed journalism internships with *Le Monde* and Agence France-Presse, 1990; was a freelance journalist with *The Financial Post*; and, from 1984-86, was a writer with the PMO and Office of the Leader of the Opposition, for then-PM John Turner. **AFFIL/MBRSHP:** president, BFVN, 1996-98; founder of *Human Rights Through Art* exhibit, 1997; founder *EDSIS*, a quarterly international journal on issues of concern to the environment and development of small island states, 1996. **WORKS:** articles in, *The Financial Post; Paris Passion; Le Monde; EDSIS.* «John Adams et ses réflexions sur Condorcet,» in *Condorcet homme des lumières et de la révolution: Les actes du colloque international de recherches sur Condorcet,* 1994. **EDUCATION:** Dipl., *l'Institut d'Etudes Politiques de Paris,* France, 1995; BA/Hons., Glendon College, York U, 1980. **MOTTO:** If it's to be, it's up to me! **CONTACT:** dorette@interlog.com

▶**HUNTE, Wesley,** O.St.J., CD.
WARRANT OFFICER (Ret.), Canadian Forces. Montreal, QC. Born: Barbados/ in Canada since: 1957.

▶ Warrant Officer Wesley Hunte served in the Canadian Forces Infantry and Medical Corps, 1961-1982. During this time he was promoted to the rank of Warrant Officer, 1969; received the Order of St. John (O.St.J.), 1976; and, was promoted to the rank of Corps Staff Officer in 1986; since retiring, he is with the Supplementary Strength Unit. While with the Medical Corps, he was responsible for updating members of the regiments in First Aid and First Aid Training; and for ensuring that members of the unit were healthy and cared for, whether in the garrison or in the field, during recruiting campaigns or functions. **COMMUNITY INVOLVEMENT:** serves on committees to improve housing for the disadvantaged and provide adequate public transportation for the disabled; founding member of the NDG Black Community Assn.; instrumental in ensuring that First Aid instruction was available to community organizations; initiated the W.O. Wesley Hunte Challenge Cup to be awarded in recognition of community services, 1975; chaired the Royal Canadian Legion March of Dimes Campaign, branch level; involved with Royal Cdn Legion for over 30 yrs.; member of the St. John Ambulance Brigade and the Quebec Council of Mtl for over 30 yrs.; Barbados ex-Police Assn.; Barbados House and many other Black community organizations. **HONS.:** Honour Roll Life Membership, Cdn Grenadier Guards, W.O., & Sergeants Mess, 1982; Order of St. John; Cdn Forces Decoration, 1976; Commendation for excellence in performance of duty, 1975; Cdn Centennial Medal, 1967. **MOTTO:** In service of humanity.

▶**HUSBAND, Gwen**
CHURCH VOLUNTEER & COMMUNITY ORGANIZER, Union United Church (UUC), 3007 Delisle St., Montreal, QC H4C 1M8. Born: Montreal, QC.

▶ Gwen Husband has been actively involved with the Union United Church (the oldest Black congregation in Montreal, started in 1907 by railway porters and their wives) all of her life. She is referred to as the "in-house historian." Her parents (father arrived 1913 from the Caribbean, her mother, 1916, from Nova Scotia) were early members and active in the Church's development. Her father was involved in the creation of the Brotherhood of Sleeping Car Porters (BSCP) of the CPR and her mother was a founding member of the Ladies Auxiliary to the BSCP, 1944. **HIGHLIGHTS:** While GH has been involved in most aspects of UUC's activities, she has been most involved with the Hostesses, of which she is a founding member (1958); she coordinates three fundraisers which they host each year. One such event is the annual Mother's Day Tea, the oldest such event in the Black community and which honours three women from the Church and/or the wider community. In 1972, GH was an active member of the Church's 65th Anniversary Committee; and, under her direction, in 1982, the *Hostesses' Memory Book* was compiled and published, to commemorate the 75th anniversary of the Church. This reference book provides biographical sketches of about 800 families, while identifying and profiling institutions, agencies, and societies which have provided important rallying points for the Black community. And, in 1991, 1996, and 2001, she was the driving force behind the publication of three photo directories of over 500 families from the current congregation of the UUC. **COMMUNITY INVOLVEMENT:** UNIA; the Negro Community Centre; and the Negro Theatre Guild. In addition to her extensive church and community involvement, she also worked with Bell Canada over a 31-yr. period, starting as a stenographer, then holding supervisory and managerial positions. **HONS.:** several including, Plaque, in recognition of her many years of service on the Finance & Stewardship Committee, UUC, 1997; Plaque, for dedicated service, Women's Support Group, UUC, 1999; honoree, *BHM Calendar*, 2002. **HEROES/ROLE MODELS:** Parents (father died at 98 yrs., mother at 101 yrs.). **MOTTO:** If you look upon your service as

something for private gain, your real value to any organization is questionable. Give of yourself; be prepared to meet and survive all challenges. **CONTACT:** Fax: 514-932-8846

▶**HYPPOLITE, Marc-Arthur**
WARDEN, Regional Reception Centre/Special Handling Unit, Ste-Anne-des-Plaines, QC. Born: Haiti/ in Canada since: 1970s.
▶ Marc-Arthur Hyppolite is Warden of the Regional Reception Centre (RRC) in Ste-Anne-des-Plaines, Quebec, which also contains Canada's only super maximum-security institution, the Special Handling Unit (SHU), for the country's most dangerous and violent offenders; it also has a special unit for women offenders requiring maximum security, and a structured environment for offenders with special mental health needs. He is the first and only Black to become a warden within Canada's Correctional Service. **CAREER HIGHLIGHTS:** MAH began his professional career as a probation officer with the Ont. Min. of Corrections, in 1984, after briefly working with Statistics Canada and with the Montreal Police. Since then he has advanced through the administrative structure with the following positions: Case Management Officer, Millhaven, where he completed correctional treatment plans for inmates and parolees and assisted with the re-integration of offenders into the community, 1984-87; Case Management Officer/Parole Officer, Ottawa, 1987-89; Section Supervisor/Area Manager, Peterborough, 1989-90; Parole, Area Director, St. Catharines, where he managed all aspects of Community Corrections for the Niagara Peninsula, 1990-94. After being on secondment with the Min. of Immigration and Citizenship, as a Control Analyst in both the International Service and the Organized Crime Divisions, 1994-95, he was appointed Deputy Warden and served in a number of facilities as Deputy (Frontenac Institution, 1995; Collins Bay Institution, 1996) then Acting or

Interim Warden (Collins Bay and Frontenac), before being appointed Warden of Cowansville Institution, in 1997, a medium-security facility containing one of the most diverse ethno-racial and linguistic populations in Quebec, including the Rock Machine or Banditos (rivals to the Hell's Angels). He remained in this position until September 2000 when he was appointed to his current position of Warden at the RRC, including the SHU, where his responsibilities include the overall management of the facility, international, inter-regional, and regional issues relative to the transfer of offenders, as well as the assessment and placement of all federally convicted offenders. **OTHER:** while working within the correctional system with some of the most difficult offenders, MAH promotes rehabilitation through training for those who are interested and has introduced initiatives (e.g. use of a mediator and inmate representatives) to decrease incidents of violence and resolve disputes between staff and inmates. **COMMUNITY INVOLVEMENT:** speaks to youth groups on crime prevention and seeks to increase public awareness of the correctional system. **AFFIL/MBRSHP:** founding member, Aboriginal & Ethnocultural Advisory Cmtee, 1991. **REVIEWED IN:** several professional publications; "The SHU: The very worst of the worst," *Sun Media*, 2001; "A One-of-a-kind Training Program," *Let's Talk*, Correctional Service of Canada newsletter, 2000. **EDUCATION:** Executive Training Program, CCMD (sponsored by PSC and the Treasury Brd.), 1995. M. Applied Criminology, 1983; BA, Sociology, 1981; BA, Psychology, 1980, U. of Ottawa. **HEROES/ROLE MODELS:** Martin Luther King Jr.; John F. Kennedy; Nelson Mandela; Ole Insgstrup, former Commissioner. **MOTTO:** Whatever you do in life, do it well and with conviction. **CONTACT:** Fax: 450-478-7661

▶IBHAWOH, Bonny

KILLAM SCHOLAR/LECTURER, Dept. of History, Dalhousie University, 6135 University Ave., Halifax, NS. Born: Nigeria, 1967/ in Canada since: 1998.

▶ Bonny Ibhawoh is the Izzak Walton Killam Scholar and Teaching Instructor at Dalhousie University, in the Dept. of History, since 1999; he is also an Instructor in human rights, University of N. Carolina, since 2002. He is considered an expert on human rights issues in Africa; is the Carnegie Fellow in Human Rights at the Carnegie Council, since 2000. Previously, he was a Visiting Research Fellow, Danish Center for Human Rights, Copenhagen, 1997-98; and, Lecturer/Researcher in African History at the Edo State U., Nigeria, 1995-99. **HONS.:** many academic awards including: Killam Scholarship for doctoral studies, Dalhousie U., 1999. **WORKS:** in, *Human Rights Quarterly; Netherlands Quarterly of Human Rights; African World Review.* **EDUCATION:** PhD candidate, Dalhousie U.; MA, History, U. of Ibadan, Nigeria, 1994; BA/Hons., Bendel State U., Nigeria, 1989. **MOTTO:** There is no such thing as darkness, only a failure to see. **CONTACT:** bibhawoh@is2.dal.ca; Fax: 902-494-3349

▶IEN, Marci

TV NEWS ANCHOR, CTV NewsNet, PO Box 9, Stn. O, Toronto, ON M4A 2M9. Born: Toronto, ON, 1969.

▶ Marci Ien is a TV News Anchor with CTV Newsnet, and a member of the *Canada AM* team, anchoring CTV's flagship morning program during the week. **BACKGROUND:** her TV career began at age ten when she was cast along with 11 other children on the show, *Circle Square*. The program dealt in a creative way with issues children often face: lying, peer pressure, cheating, making friends and other topics of interest and concern to teens and pre-teens. Her six yrs. on *Circle Square* allowed her extensive travel opportunities as the program gained in popularity internationally; viewers in the Caribbean, in particular, enjoyed the program and, as a result, several segments of the show were filmed there. **CAREER:** in 1991, MI graduated from Ryerson Polytechnic U. and was hired by Ontario Network TV (ONTV) where she worked as a weekend newswriter; was soon promoted to general assignment reporter with occasional anchoring duties; her news serial *Journey to Freedom*, a look at Canada's role in the slave trade and the Underground Railroad (UGRR), earned her a News Directors' Award for Excellence in 1995. That same year, she began reporting at Queen's Park, covering political news for ONTV's regional newscast as well as its national program, *Canada Tonight*. In 1997, MI debuted as a member of CTV's news team in Atlantic Canada, covering stories throughout the Maritimes and Newfoundland, including the Swiss Air disaster off Peggy's Cove, Nova Scotia, in 1998. That same year, she returned to Toronto to anchor CTV Newsnet, the network's 24-hour cable news service. **COMMUNITY:** has co-hosted the Harry Jerome Awards, and speaks regularly to groups of young people about pursuing their dreams. **HONS.:** Special Award, for series on *Journey to Freedom*, Radio & TV News Directors' Assn., 1995. **EDUCATION:** BAA, Radio & Television, Ryerson U., 1991. **MOTTO:** Reach for the moon, and if you happen to miss, you'll be among the stars, and that's not a bad place to be! **CONTACT:** mien@ctv.ca; Fax: 416-291-5337

▶**IGALI, Daniel**
FREESTYLE WRESTLING CHAMPION, c/o Landmark Sport Group. Surrey, BC. Born: Nigeria, 1974/ in Canada since: 1994.

▶ Daniel Igali is Canada's first Olympic and World Wrestling Champion, having won the gold medal at the 2000 Summer Olympic Games in Sydney, Australia. He also won the gold medal, Commonwealth Games, 2002. Originally from Nigeria, he began wrestling early as it was part of Ijaw culture (as hockey is to Canada); he competed in his first amateur freestyle wrestling event at age 16, in 1990, and won the gold medal; in 1993, he became the African champion in wrestling; in 1994, he competed in the Commonwealth Games in Canada and stayed, due to the political situation in Nigeria at the time. **HIGHLIGHTS:** Enrolled at Simon Fraser University (SFU), he continued to wrestle and was undefeated in 116 matches; for his success in developing his wrestling skills, he credits his coaches (Mike Jones and Dave McKay) and his personal trainer, Wayne Wilson. In 1998, he won the silver medal at the 1998 World Championships; in 1999, he won the gold medal and the World Championship in Turkey, despite recovering from a serious knee injury; in recognition of this win and becoming Canada's first World Champion in Wrestling, he was awarded the Canadian Amateur Male Athlete of the Year which he dedicated to his host mother in Canada, Maureen Matheny, who had died of cancer five days after his win in Turkey. Since completing his bid to win gold at the Olympics, DI has graduated from SFU and is raising funds to build a school in his home village in Nigeria; it will be named after Matheny, who herself had been a teacher and principal for 25 yrs. DI was a member of the Toronto 2008 Olympic Bid team and is a member of the Vancouver 2010 Olympic Bid team. He is a regular speaker at schools and community events; his sponsors to date are Cheerios and General Mills. **HONS.:** including, Athlete of the Year, Cdn Sports Award, 2001; Lou Marsh Trophy, Canada's Top Athlete, 2000; *Maclean's* magazine Honour Roll, 2000; Athlete of the Year, Cdn Sports Award, 2000. **HEROES/ROLE MODELS:** Grandmother; Maureen Matheny, host mother. **CONTACT:** landmark@netcom.ca; Fax: 416-593-4984

▶**IGINLA, Jarome**
HOCKEY PLAYER, Calgary Flames/National Hockey League, c/o 1251 Avenue of the Americ-

as, NY, NY 10020-1189, USA. Born: Edmonton, AB, 1977.

▶ Jarome Iginla became the second Black athlete ever to win a gold medal at the Olympic Winter Games. This occurred in Salt Lake City, Utah, 2002 (the first was Venetta Flowers, one week earlier, in the two-woman bobsled team, for the US). As a member of the Team Canada hockey team, JI played a pivotal role in securing the team's first gold medal in 50 yrs. by scoring a total of three goals in the Games, two of which were scored in the final game between Canada and the US. **CAREER HIGHLIGHTS:** he was first drafted in 1995, 11th overall in the Entry Draft, by the Dallas Stars; a few months later, he was traded to the Calgary Flames, where he plays Right Wing. Known for his scoring abilities, JI led all NHL rookies in the 1996-97 season with 50 points (21 goals, 29 assists); in the 1999-2000 season he reached a career high of 29 goals and 34 assists; in the 2001-2002 season, he was the only player to surpass the 50-goal mark. In 1996, at the World Junior Hockey Championships in Boston, MA, he led Canada to the gold medal, with 12 points (five goals, seven assists) in six games, earned his first All-Star Team honours, was named the Tournament's Most Outstanding Forward, and was the scoring champion. **COMMUNITY INVOLVEMENT:** outside of hockey, JI supports a number of charities and works with disadvantaged youth, encouraging them to become more involved in sports; as a proactive representative of NHL Diversity, he often accompanies Willie O'Ree (the first Black to play in the NHL, 1958; *see: O'Ree, Willie*) in conducting hockey clinics. **OTHER:** born of a Nigerian father and an American mother, JI began playing hockey at an early age and credits his parents and grandparents with being supportive of his interest in the sport. **HONS.:** several including, Maurice "Rocket" Richard Award, for most goals scored (52), 2002; Art Ross Trophy, for most points scored (96), 2002; Lester B. Pearson Award, voted by peers as "the League's most outstanding player," 2002; 2nd place as MVP for Hart Trophy, 2002; NHL Player of the Week, Oct. 29, 2001; runner-up, Calder Trophy, 1997. **HEROES/ROLE MODELS:** Elvis Iginla & Susan Schuchard, parents; Rick & Frances Schuchard, grandparents. **CONTACT:** www.calgaryflames.com; info@nhl.com; Fax: 212-789-2080

▶**IGWEMEZIE, Jude O.,** PhD, P.Eng. **PROFESSIONAL ENGINEER, CEO,** Applied Rail Research Technologies (ARRT), 9446 McLaughlin Rd. N., Brampton, ON L6X 4H9. Born: Nigeria/ in Canada since: 1978.

▶ Dr. Jude Igwemezie has been involved with rail-related research since 1981. He is an expert in structural mechanics, stress and failure analysis, design, testing and assessment of railway engineering structures, and derailment investigations. He has significant experience in the impact of rail grinding and lubrication on rail life, track force, rail stresses, tie stresses, and track alignment. Since 1988, he has authored or co-authored over 60 articles, reports and publications on railway track, bridge structures, and vehicle components. He has made significant contributions to the rail industry and was the first to develop a methodology for setting railhead wear limits; several NA railroads have successfully implemented his recommendations. **HIGHLIGHTS:** designed derailment containment barriers for residential areas; designed the high relief joint-bar that allows more rail wear for several N. American railroads; developed an expression for estimating the design load of concrete ties used on open deck railway bridges; developed a relationship between dynamic load that will cause rail to fracture and rail temperature, residual stresses, railhead defect size and rail fracture toughness; developed a standard for residual stress in rails (subsequently adopted by the American Railway Engineering Assn.); developed new rail wear limits for rails used by Canadian Pacific (CP), British Columbia (BCR), Calgary Transit, Illinois Central, Montana Rail Link (MRL), and Kansas City Southern Railroads; designed special tie plates that eliminate rail roll over derailments and minimize wood tie splitting stresses; designed special tie plates that fasten rail joints to wood ties, to reduce insulated and non-insulated joint damage. He is the founder and President of a number of companies: ARRT, 1992, a railway consulting, engineering, and research co.; UniP Tie Co., 1994, to market the UniP steel tie and fastener he invented for use in heavy haul and light rail track; NorFast Inc., 1998, created to market his premium elastic rail fasteners. **OTHER:** He is the holder of several patents and has many others pending; also acts as an industry expert on derailment and track component failures, and has appeared as an expert witness in litigations in both the US and Canada. He is very active in the American Engineering and Maintenance of Way Assn. and chairs one of the sub-committees. In 1997, he was invited by the American Railway Engineering Assn. to address the membership on rail management, during their annual conference in Chicago. **PREVIOUS ACTIVITIES:** Principal Researcher, CIGGT, Queen's U., 1991-94; Adjunct Assistant Professor, Queen's U., 1988-94; Manager and Sr. Structural Engineer, DS-Lea Assoc., 1991-92. **AFFIL/MBRSHP:** Iron and Steel Making Society; Cdn Society for Civil Engineers; Engineering Institute of Canada; Reg. Prof. Engineers of Ontario. **HONS.:** including, Harry Jerome Award for Professional Excellence, BBPA, 2001; Outstanding Contribution to the Nigerian Community, 2000; Gold Medal, Industrial Systems category, for the UniP steel tie & fastener, Cdn Design Engineering Awards, 1997. **WORKS:** articles in, *Can J of Civil Engineering; ASCE J of Structural Engineers*; as well as technical reports for CP, CN, BCR, MRL, CSX, Illinois Central, Kansas City Southern, and others. **EDUCATION:** PhD, Engineering, 1988; M.Eng, 1984; B.Eng, Civil Engineering, 1982, McGill U. **HEROES/ROLE MODELS:** Prof. Saeed Mirza, McGill U.; Warren G. Wood, Chair CPCS Transcom Ltd.

MOTTO: The harder you work, the luckier you get. **CONTACT:** jude@arrt-inc.com; www.arrt-inc.com

▶**IKEJIANI, Alexander O.**
BARRISTER & SOLICITOR, Dept. of Justice Canada, Ottawa, ON. Born: Germany, 1971/ in Canada since: 1971.

▶ Alex Ikejiani is a lawyer currently working with the Dept. of Justice in Ottawa and is a member of the environmental group within the legal services division of the Dept. of Fisheries and Oceans. He advises government officials on ocean and constitutional law. Since graduating from Dalhousie Law School in 1997, his other professional experiences include: articled with the Office of the Attorney General (AG) in Nova Scotia, 1997-98; was hired by the Office of the AG in 1998, as a member of the litigation team providing litigation and advisory support in the areas of constitutional, tax and general civil litigation to departments of Finance, Labour, Education, and Human Resources. In 2001, he was seconded to the Federal Prosecution Unit in Halifax, servicing the Dept. of Fisheries and Oceans, and was involved in conducting criminal prosecutions in the Gulf Region (NB, PEI), and examining Aboriginal fisheries cases, based on the treaty and aboriginal right to fish for food and ceremonial purposes. A highlight of his legal career to date, was an appeal presented before the NS Court of Appeal, on behalf of the Office of the AG, concerning the retroactive payment of taxes on *ultra vires* legislation. **WORKS:** in, *Constitutional Curriculum Review*, 1995. **EDUCATION:** LLB, Dalhousie U., 1997; BA, U. of Manitoba, 1994. **HEROES/ROLE MODELS:** Parents. **MOTTO:** Everything comes to those who wait. **CONTACT:** aikejiani@hotmail. com

▶**IKEJIANI, Charles,** MD, FRCSC.
ORTHOPAEDIC SURGEON, Private Practice, Georgian Professional Centre, Ste. 303-125 Bell Farm Rd., Barrie, ON L4M 6L2. Born: Nigeria,

1967/ in Canada since: 1971.

▶ Dr. Charles Ikejiani is an Orthopaedic Surgeon, currently practising in Barrie, Ontario. He maintains a private practice and is affiliated with the Royal Victoria Hospital. He completed his medical training at Dalhousie University; Fellowship, Trauma and Reconstruction, U of T and St. Michael's Hospital; Hip and Knee Arthroplasty, University of Manitoba and St. Boniface Hospital. **HONS.:** include, Research Award (CSCI/MRC), best resident research paper, Dalhousie U., 1999. **WORKS:** conference & research papers; article in, *J Clinical Orthopedics.* **EDUCATION:** FRCSC Orthopaedics, 2000; MD, 1995, Dalhousie University. BSc, Acadia U., 1989. **HEROES/ROLE MODELS:** Parents; Dr. D.P. Petrie, Orthopaedic Surgeon. **MOTTO:** Do your best. **CONTACT:** cikejiani @hotmail.com cikejiani@hotmail.com

▶**IKEJIANI, Okechukwu,** MD, FRCPath., CON.

PATHOLOGIST (Ret.), Duncan Professional Consultants, Orleans, ON. Born: Nigeria/ in Canada since: 1971.

▶ Dr. Okechukwu Ikejiani has had many careers between his native Nigeria and Canada, including that of professor, pathologist, advisor, and diplomat. He began his post-secondary education in Canada, completing his BSc at U. of New Brunswick, 1942. He completed his MSc (Microbiology), at U. of Chicago, 1943, but left there when he was refused entry into medical school. At U. of Michigan he was admitted to the joint PhD and ScD programs. There, he worked in the Serological Laboratory of Prof. Reuben Kahn, discoverer of the Kahn Test. During OI's stay there, the laboratory developed the Kahn Verification Test (which established the optimum temperature for detecting antibodies to syphilis and tropical diseases). OI then won a position as demonstrator in the Faculty of Pathology and Microbiology at the Banting Institute in Toronto, 1945-47; in 1946 he entered medical school at U

of T, completing the program in 1948. **CAREER HIGHLIGHTS:** Lecturer, Pathology, U. College, Ibadan, 1948-50; Medical Director, National Clinic and National Clinic Laboratories, Lagos, 1950-56; Medical Director, Pfizer Laboratories, Lagos, 1954-66; Commissioner, Rehabilitation Commission, Biafra, 1967-69; Coordinator, Refugee Medical Service, Biafra, 1967-70. At that time, he was also appointed Ambassador Plenipotentiary for Sierra Leone, Haiti, Jamaica, Guyana, Barbados, Trinidad & Tobago, and Greece, 1966-69. In 1971, he returned to Canada and held the following positions: Pathologist, General Hospital, Ottawa, 1972; Pathologist-in-Chief and Director of Laboratories, for Glace Bay and New Waterford Hospitals, 1972-97; Consultant Pathologist at Sydney's Regional Hospital, 1972-97; Program Director, Accredited Medical Laboratory Technology Training, Glace Bay, 1972-90; Medical Director, Glace Bay Community Hospital, 1973-92. **AFFIL/MBRSHP:** between Nigeria and Canada included: Brd., Glace Bay Community Hospital, 1973-92; NS Medical Society; President, Nigerian Medical Assn., 1962-66; Chair and Pro-Chancellor, U. of Ibadan, 1960-65; Brd., Nigeria Ports Authority, 1960-65; Chair, Nigeria Railway Corp., 1960-65; Chair, Eastern Regional Pharmaceutical Corp., 1960-65. **HONS.:** several including, Hon. D.Litt, U. College, Sydney, NS, 1994; Hon. DSc, U. of Nigeria, 1988; Hon. DSc, Lincoln U., PA, 1955; Recipient, Commander of the Order of the Niger (CON). **WORKS:** three books, including: *Nigeria: Political Imperative*; several scientific articles in: *Amer J Hygiene; West Africa Med J.* **EDUCATION:** FMCP, Nigeria, 1978; FWACP, 1978; FRC(Path), 1962; MD, U of T, 1948; LMMC, 1948; MSc, Microbiology, U. of Chicago, 1943; BSc, U. of NB, 1942. **CONTACT:** oikejiani@sprint. ca; Fax: 613-841-9824

▶**IMRIE, Kathy**

ACTOR/ENTREPRENEUR, Imre Background Talent Agency, 291 Withrow Ave., Toronto, ON M4J

1B6. Born: Trinidad & Tobago/ in Canada since: 1963.

▶ Kathy Imrie moved to Canada in 1963, but in order to pursue her desire to act, she moved to NYC in 1969, where she studied acting techniques at the Negro Ensemble Company, Warren Robinson Workshop Studio, and Alvin Ailey Dance Studio. She has worked in film, TV, and on stage; she is best known for her role opposite Richard Roundtree in *Shaft's Big Score*. Other film and TV credits include: *Common Ground; Welcome to Africville; All My Children*; and episodes of *Night Heat* and *Street Legal*. In NYC, she performed on stage at La Mama, Henry Street Playhouse and Lafeyette. Theatre credits: *Lament for Rastafari; Moon on a Rainbow Shawl; Coups and Calypso; And the Girls in Their Sunday Dresses*. She returned to Canada in 1987, where she has continued acting in theatre and film, as well as commercials and voiceovers. In 1998, she opened her own company, Imre Background Talent Agency. **CONTACT:** imre_bg@hotmail.com; Fax: 416-405-9548

▶ INCE, Thelma Coward
PERSONNEL ADMINISTRATOR (Ret.), Dept. of National Defence, Dartmouth, NS. Born: Halifax, NS.

▶ Thelma Coward Ince was the first Black Senior Secretary in the Dept. of National Defence (was secretary to the Chief of Staff to the Admiral), at a time when Canada had 75 ships in the Navy. Later, she was promoted to the position of Manager, Administrative Services, becoming the first Black manager in the Ship Repair Unit Atlantic, one of the few industrial organizations within the Dept., which was responsible for repairing all ships in the Cdn Navy found on the Atlantic Coast. This Unit had approx. 2,000 employees; at the time (1979-1992), fewer than 100 were women and there was only one female Manager, who happened to be Black. She was among the managers posted in the foyer of the $193-million

edifice when Prince Charles and Princess Diana dedicated the building. At the time, it was the most modern industrial repair facility east of Montreal and the only government building of its kind. **OTHER:** in 1954, TCI joined the Navy becoming the first Black female Naval Reservist in Canada. **COMMUNITY:** is deeply involved in the health care system as it affects minorities; sits on the Board of the Health Assn. of African Canadians; appointed Commissioner to the Advisory Commission on AIDS, by the Lt.-Gov. of NS; member of a committee responding to the Canadian Ethnocultural Council; Brd., Black Community Work Group of Halifax; and, sits on committees involved in the Capital District Health Authority and the Atlantic Health and Wellness Institute; Brd., Halifax Inner City Initiative, which is involved in duplicating the model used in Michigan (now a multi-million dollar business) to revitalize the downtown area. This project is called, Focus Hope. **REVIEWED IN:** *Journey: African Canadian History*, 2000. **EDUCATION:** completing BA, Sociology, 2002. **MOTTO:** The cycle of learning will never be done for me. **CONTACT:** te_eince@hotmail.com; Fax: 902-426-8699

▶ ISAAC, Julius Alexander, The Hon.
Mr. Justice
FEDERAL COURT JUDGE, Federal Court of Appeal, 12th Fl.-90 Sparks St., Ottawa, ON K1P 5B4. Born: Grenada/ in Canada since: 1951.

▶ The Hon. Mr. Justice Julius Isaac was appointed Justice of the Supreme Court of Ontario in 1989. In 1991, he was appointed Chief Justice of the Federal Court of Canada and remained in that position until August, 1999, when he was appointed a supernumerary judge with the Federal Court of Appeal. **CAREER HIGHLIGHTS:** member of the bars of Ontario, Saskatchewan, Grenada, and Alberta; practised criminal, general civil litigation, and corporate-commercial law in Ontario and Saskatchewan, 1960-69; partner, Acker & Isaac, Guelph, Ont., a general practice covering civil, criminal, family, corporate and commercial litigation, 1965-69; Legal Advisor and Corporate Secretary to Government Finance Office and various Crown Corporations, 1962-65; Senior Magistrate, Grenada, 1969-70; Legal Advisor, Ontario Securities Commission, 1970-71. From 1971-89, he was with the Federal Dept. of Justice with the following responsibilities: Chief, Federal Prosecutions, Toronto; Regional Director, Alberta; Asst. Deputy Attorney General (Criminal Law); counsel for the Govt. of Canada in appeals before the Supreme Court of Canada. **OTHER:** over the years, he has delivered a number of lectures and presented papers on various aspects of the law, including: Narcotic Control and Food and Drug Acts; Cdn Charter of Rights and Freedoms; Combines Investigation Act; the authority of the Federal Govt. to police Indian Reserves; nature and scope of Prosecutorial Discretion in Canada; problems in tax litigation in the Federal Court of Canada; int'l criminal law; the future for visible minorities in the Public Service of Canada. **COMMUNITY INVOLVEMENT:** 1952-94: Negro Citizenship Cmtee; Grand United Order of Oddfellows; Caribbean Cultural Cmtee; Cdn Brotherhood of Railway Transport and Other Workers; Johnston Chair in Black Studies; Black Artists in Action. **HONS.:** including, Jackie Robinson Distinguished Achievement Award, MABBP, 2001; Hon. LLD, UWI, 2000; Silver Jubilee Award of Grenada, 1999; Award for "outstanding contribution to legal profession," CABL, 1997; Black Achievement Award (Law), 1994; Hon. Doctor of Civil Law, U. of Windsor, 1994; GG 125th Anniv. Medal, 1992; Queen's Counsel, 1975. **REVIEWED IN:** *WWIC*; *Millennium Minds*, 2000; *Some Black Men*, 1999. **EDUCATION:** Specialist in Criminal Litigation, LSUC, 1988. LLB, 1958; BA, 1955, U of T. **CONTACT:** indrani.laroche@fct-cf.gc.ca; Fax: 613-947-4679

▶**ISAACS, Camille Nicola**
MANAGER, Market Strategy & Services, Standard Life Investments Inc., Montreal, QC. Born: Jamaica/ in Canada since: 1993.

▶ Camille Isaacs was a Foreign Service Officer in the Min. of Foreign Affairs and Foreign Trade in Jamaica, for over eight years prior to coming to Canada in 1993, where she made a career change and is now a marketing professional in the financial services sector. Since 1995, she has worked with The Standard Life Group, first as Marketing Coordinator, Group Pension Sales, 1995-97; then, Manager, Investment Marketing-Mutual Funds, 1998-99; and, since 2000, as Manager, Market Strategy and Services, playing a significant role in defining the company's overall market strategy in NA. In addition she is responsible for the development and delivery of marketing services for Standard Life Investments Inc. Her professional experiences before moving to Canada included: Economist, National Export-Import Bank of Jamaica, responsible for advising senior management on the impact of foreign and domestic economic trends on the quality of the Bank's credit risk, 1993; Min. of Foreign Affairs and Foreign Trade, in the divisions of Protocol, Foreign Trade, and Trade Policy, 1984-92. **AFFIL/MBRSHP:** *Centraide*/United Way; Montreal Assn. for the Blind; *Assn. Marketing de Montréal*; American Marketing Assn.; Cdn Pension & Benefits Institute; Investment Funds Institute of Canada; Pastel Society of Eastern Canada. **EDUCATION:** MBA, Marketing & Int'l Business, U. of Miami, 1991; BA, Language & Linguistic Studies, UWI, 1983; industry certifications: certif., Financial Planning, Cdn Institute of Financial Planning. **CONTACT:** cisaacs@sympatico.ca

▶**ISAACS, Joy Enid**
HUMAN RESOURCE CONSULTANT (Ret.), City of Toronto, ON. Born: Guyana/ in Canada since: 1968.

▶ Joy Enid Isaacs worked for several years as a Human Resource Consultant with the City of Toronto, and was responsible for advancing the

City's mandate of encouraging greater diversity in its employee base. In this context she designed and implemented outreach strategies to create awareness amongst the designated groups (visible minorities, native peoples, women, and people with disabilities) about employment opportunities with the City. She was also responsible for managing the Job Opportunity for Youth (JOY) program. In 1994, she was appointed a commissioner with the Ontario Advocacy Commission; her role was to assist a province-wide network of advocates empower vulnerable adults in making decisions about their lives. **COMMUNITY ACTIVITIES:** Women's Health in Women's Hands; Ethno-Racial People with Disabilities Coalition of Ontario; New Directions; Ontario March of Dimes; St. Stephen's Community Centre. **OTHER:** since retiring in 2001, she manages Goldyn Enterprises, providing specialized travel and entertainment packages to tour groups from the US. **HONS.:** include, Volunteer Award, Goodwill Toronto, 1999; Recognition Award, Coalition of Visible Minorities, 1994; Volunteer Award, New Directions, 1993. **REVIEWED IN:** *Share;* City of Toronto newsletter. **EDUCATION:** BA, U of T, 1981. **HEROES/ROLE MODELS:** Judge Juanita Westmoreland-Traoré, friend; Nelson Mandela; Maya Angelou. **MOTTO:** If you do not possess the knowledge, surround yourself with those who do.

►ISAACS, Orin

MUSICIAN, Moca Music, PO Box 1216, Stn. B., Mississauga, ON L4Y 3W5. Born: Toronto, ON, 1969.
► Orin Isaacs is, since 1997, the Musical Director of *Open Mike with Mike Bullard*, Canada's only late night talk/variety show. A skilled bass guitarist committed to the development of Urban Music in Canada, he has also been musical director for the country's biggest award shows: The Juno, Gemini, Genie, and NHL Awards. Early in his career, which began at the age of 17, he played and toured for five years with artists such as

Salome Bey, Arrow, Devon, Dream Warriors. In 1992, he decided to try music production so opened his own company, Bassmint Productions, which, during its five-year run, produced or recorded five Juno Award-winning albums. During this time he also signed a publishing deal with EMI music publishing and began composing for TV, with Fox's game show *Studs* being his first major undertaking. With a growing clientele, he built his own 24-track recording studio, North 49th St. Sound. His client list then included EMI Records, BMG, Virgin, Sony, Toronto Raptors, and shows such as *Ooh La La, Stars on Ice, Rap City*, and many others. After writing and producing for others for many years, OI has recently released his own debut CD, *Where I'm From*. **HONS.:** Craft EVA Award, for best music in a corporate video, 1997; Urban Music Industry Special Achievement Award; Reel Black Award, composition; Men of Excellence; featured in *Men on the Move* calendar; along with many awards for his community service. **EDUCATION:** Bathurst Heights; George Harvey. **HEROES/ROLE MODELS:** Mother; Mr. Love, high school teacher. **MOTTO:** Don't blame others for your failures. **CONTACT:** orin@mocamusic.com

▶JACKSON, D.D.

JAZZ PIANIST/COMPOSER, c/o Justin Time Records, Ste. 101-5455, rue Paré, Montreal, QC H4P 1P7. Born: Ottawa, ON, 1967.

▶ D.D. Jackson is a jazz pianist and composer from Canada, now residing in New York. He was born to an African-American father and a Chinese mother, and named Robert Cleath Kai-Nien Jackson. Trained as a classical pianist, he switched to playing primarily jazz in the early 1990s (incorporating gospel, blues, bebop, traditional African, depending on his collaborators at the time). He has released eight recordings as leader, with Canada's Justin Time Records and two with RCA Victor (BMG). DDJ has performed extensively on the international stage with solo piano concerts in Berlin, Tel Aviv, Italy, the JVC Jazzfest, with his trio in Portugal, Macedonia, and Hong Kong, and with the DD Jackson group at the Newport Jazz Festival, Bell Atlantic Jazz Festival, and others. He has appeared on BET and one of his concerts from the Montreux Detroit Jazz Fest was broadcast on National Public Radio's *JazzSet with Brandford Marsalis* and many others. DDJ is also a commissioned composer having worked on *Mytholojazz*, his *New York Suite*, and is working with George Elliott Clarke (*see: Clarke, George E.*) on a new opera, tentatively entitled *Quebecité*. **OTHER HIGHLIGHTS:** plays with the David Murray Big Band and has collaborated on recordings; participated in a concert in France at Paris' *Cité de la Musique*, performing the music of Billy Strayhorn and Duke Ellington. He has also been working with Taj Mahal, Bob Weir (the Grateful Dead), and Avery Brooks on a stage musical on Negro Baseball League pitcher, Satchel Paige. He has toured West Africa and performed and recorded with Senegalese musicians, namely, Mor Thiam on his debut CD for Justin Time, *Back to Africa*. DDJ is currently re-exploring his classical roots and recorded Gershwin's *Rhapsody in Blue* with the ProMusica Chamber Ensemble in Ohio, 2001.

His most recent jazz recording is *Sigame*. **HONS.:** several, including: Juno Award (and three additional Juno nominations), for *.....so far*, as Best Contemporary Jazz album, 2000; rated No. 1 Talent Deserving Wider Recognition, *Down Beat Critics Poll*, 2000; Jazz Composer of the Year, SOCAN, 2002; Composer of the Year, *Jazz Report* magazine, 2000 & 1996. **WORKS:** writes a bi-monthly column, "Living Jazz," in *Down Beat* magazine; "Ridin' the Wave," *Down Beat* magazine, 2001. **EDUCATION:** M.Music, Jazz, Manhattan School of Music, 1991; B.Mus., Classical Piano, Indiana U., 1989. **HEROES/ ROLE MODELS:** Don Pullen; Jaki Byard. **CONTACT:** dd@ddjackson.com; www.ddjackson.com

▶JACKSON, Ovid

MEMBER OF PARLIAMENT, Bruce-Grey-Owen Sound, House of Commons, Government of Canada, Ottawa, ON. Born: Guyana/ in Canada since: 1965.

▶ Ovid Jackson, Member of Parliament (Liberal) for Bruce-Grey-Owen Sound has been serving his constituency at the federal level since 1993. He was first elected to public office in 1974, serving until 1983, as Alderman, City of Owen Sound; he was then elected Mayor in 1983, and served until 1993. As MP, he has served on the following Standing Committees: Citizenship and Immigration, Health, Transport and Policy Development; he also served as Parliamentary Secretary to the President of the Treasury Board and the Min. responsible for Infrastructure. Presently, he is Chair of the Standing Committee on Transport and Government Operations. **BACKGROUND:** Field Mechanic, Min. of Works and Hydraulics, Guyana; Technical Teacher and Automotive Specialist, Owen Sound, 1968-93. **COMMUNITY:** Regional Community Talks; Police Services Board; Kiwanis. **HONS.:** including: GG 125th Anniv. Medal, 1992; St. John Ambulance. **REVIEWED IN:** *Some Black Men*, 1999. **EDUCATION:** BA, U. of Western Ontario; City & Guilds General Engineering Cert., Ont. College of Education. **CONTACT:** Jackson.O@parl.gc.ca; Fax: 613-957-0979

▶**JACKSON, Richard Lawson,** PhD, FRSC.
PROFESSOR EMERITUS, Spanish, Carleton University. Kanata, ON. Born: USA/in Canada since: 1963.
▶ Dr. Richard Jackson has been Professor Emeritus in Afro-Hispanic Studies at Carleton University since 1995, following a 30-yr. teaching career. After completing his studies in Romance Languages in 1963, he taught Spanish at Carleton U. throughout most of his career. **HIGHLIGHTS:** Lecturer, 1963-64; Assistant Professor, 1964-67; Associate Professor, 1967-75; from 1976-95, he was a full Professor. He also taught for one year, 1980-81, at U. of Tennessee, where he was Professor and Head of Romance Languages. The author of several books and articles, he also undertook a number of editorial responsibilities: co-founder and associate editor, *Afro-Hispanic Review*; advisory and contributing editor, *Callaloo;* advisory editor, *J of Caribbean Studies*. In addition to his involvement within the university, he also served as: External Examiner to institutions such as UWI, UBC, UCLA/San Diego, U. Illinois; Laval U. **HONS.:** Fellow, Royal Society of Canada, 1994; Afro-Hispanic Award from Hispanic Literature & Culture Conference, 1991; Research Achievement Award, 1991; Merit Award, 1977. **WORKS:** several books including: *Black Writers and Latin America: Cross-Cultural Affinities*, 1998; *Black Writers and the Hispanic Canon in Latin America*, 1997; *Black Writers in Latin America*, 1979; *The Black Image in Latin American Literature*, 1976. Also has many chapters in books; articles in: *Afro-Hispanic Review; Hispania; Chasqui; Latin American Research.* **EDUCATION:** PhD, Romance Languages, 1963; MA, Spanish, 1960, Ohio State University. BA, Knoxville College, TN, 1959. **HEROES/ROLE**

MODELS: James Hamlett. **MOTTO:** Nothing to it but to do it and once you do it, then it's done. **CONTACT:** richardjack@rogers.com

▶**JACOB, Selwyn**
FILMMAKER/PRODUCER, National Film Board of Canada/NFB, Ste. 200-1385 W. 8th Ave., Vancouver, BC V6H 3V9. Born: Trinidad & Tobago/in Canada since: 1968.
▶ Selwyn Jacob is an award-winning filmmaker, based in Vancouver, who has produced or directed more than a dozen films since joining the NFB in 1997, as one of three Cultural Diversity Producers. Current projects include: *The Journey of Lesra Martin*, about a former street youth who helped to free Rubin "Hurricane" Carter from prison; and *A Chinese Cemetery at Harling Point*, about the first Chinese cemetery in Canada. **FILMOGRAPHY:** includes documentaries such as *Jeni LeGon: Living in a Great Big Way*, a portrait of one of the first Black women entertainers in Hollywood to sign a long-term contract with a major Hollywood studio (*see: LeGon, Jeni*); *John McCrae's War: In Flanders Fields*, a look at the WWI Cdn army doctor who wrote the poem, *In Flanders Fields*. Prior to joining the NFB as producer, SJ was an independent filmmaker who directed two award-winning NFB releases: *Carol's Mirror* (1991), a film for schools about racism and equality; and, *The Road Taken* (1996), portraying the Black sleeping car porters working the Canadian railroad. Some of his other films include: *Obaachan's Garden,* 2001; *When a Child Goes Missing*, 2000; *Java Jive*, 1999; *Yuxweluptun: Man of Masks*, 1998; *Nuclear Dynamite*, 2000; *Britannia*, 2000; *Beaverbrook: The Various Lives of Max Aitken*, 2000; *T'Lina: The Rendering of Wealth*, 1999; *Al Tasmim*, 1995, on the struggle to save Edmonton's Al Rashid mosque. And, early in his career he produced, *We Remember Amber Valley*, 1984, a chronicle of Alberta's first Black community; and, *The Saint from North Battleford*, 1989, the story of Rueben

Mayes, the first Canadian (who also happened to be Black) to be named Rookie of the Year in the NFL (*see: Mayes, Rueben*). **HONS.:** several including, Premier's Award of Excellence, for work with Alberta Curriculum Standards Branch, 1998; Canada Award, for *The Road Taken*, Gemini Awards, 1998; John Ware, Lifetime Achievement Award, BAASA, 1997; Kathleen Shannon Award, & Best Documentary, for *The Road Taken*, Yorkton Short Film & Video Festival, 1997; Best Educational Award, Birmingham, and Golden Apple Award, Oakland for *Carol's Mirror*, 1993; Michael Blaustein Biography Award, for *Jeni LeGon*, Pittsburgh. **REVIEWED IN:** "Choosing the Road Taken," *New Trail*, (U. of Alberta Alumni publication), 1997. **EDUCATION:** MSc, Film, U. of S. California, 1975; B.Ed, U. of Alberta, 1970. **HEROES/ROLE MODELS:** Fil Fraser, friend. **CONTACT:** s.jacob@nfb.ca; www.nfb.ca

▶**JAILALL, Peter**
TEACHER/POET/STORYTELLER, Mississauga, ON. Born: Guyana/ in Canada since: 1970.
▶ Peter Jailall taught with the Peel Board of Education from 1975-98. Since his retirement, he devotes himself, on a full-time basis, to writing poetry and short stories; he is also a storyteller. In this capacity, he regularly visits schools in the GTA, to read poetry and to tell stories; he is the author of two books of poetry. And, as he had been doing throughout his teaching career, he returns regularly to Guyana and offers his services as a volunteer teacher. He is a full member of the League of Canadian Poets. **HONS.:** Nominated for Mississauga Arts Award, 2000. **WORKS:** books of poetry: *This Healing Place & Other Poems*, 1999, 2nd ed.; *Yet Another Home*, 1997. **EDUCATION:** completing MA, OISE/U of T; B.Ed, U of T; BA, York U.

▶**JAMES, Carl E., PhD.**
ASSOCIATE PROFESSOR, Faculty of Education,

York University, 4700 Keele St., Toronto, ON M1J 3P3. Born: Antigua/ in Canada since: 1971.
▶ Dr. Carl James is an Associate Professor at York University, in the Faculty of Education. Previous positions: Course Director, School of Physical and Health Education, U of T, 1992-95 and 1997; Visiting Course Director, Dept. of Teacher Training, U. of Uppsala, Sweden, 1997, '98 and '99; Coordinator, Tanzania Project, Sheridan College, 1989-92; Assistant Professor, Faculty of Education, York U., 1993-97; Associate Professor, Faculty of Education and Graduate Prog. in Sociology and Social Work, York U. since 1997. He is the author, co-author, and editor of many works on multicultural education (see below). **HONS.:** Award, Pickering Caribbean Cdn Cultural Assn., for dedication to youth & support to the Assn., 1992; President's Award of Excellence, Sheridan College, 1991; Fraser Award, for contribution to social development and social services, 1988. **WORKS:** selected: *Opportunity & Uncertainty: Life Course Experiences of the Class of '73*, 2000; *Seeing Ourselves: Exploring Race, Ethnicity & Culture*, 1995; ed.: *Talking about Identity: Encounters in Race, Ethnicity & Language*, 2000; *Experiencing Differences*, 2000. Articles in: *Pedagogy, Culture & Society; Int'l J Qualitative Studies in Education; Can Women's Studies J; Can J of Education; Urban Education.* **EDUCATION:** PhD, Sociology, 1986; MA, Sociology, 1980; BA/Hons., 1978, York U. **CONTACT:** cjames@edu.yorku.ca; Fax: 416-736-5913

▶**JAMES, June Marion, MD, FRCPC, FAAAI.**
CONSULTANT, ALLERGY AND ASTHMA, Winnipeg Clinic, 425 St. Mary Ave., Winnipeg, MB R3C 0N2. Born: Trinidad & Tobago/ in Canada since: 1960.
▶ Dr. June Marion James is one of the most renowned allergy specialists in Canada. She is a partner at the Winnipeg Clinic and Assistant Professor of Medicine at the University of Manitoba;

she is also responsible for having developed the first Family Asthma Program in Manitoba. She was the first Black woman admitted to U. of Manitoba's medical program, and graduated in 1967. She first specialized in Pediatrics, then switched to clinical immunology and allergy; she joined the Winnipeg Clinic in 1976 as an Allergy and Asthma Specialist. She has been teaching at U. of Manitoba in the Faculty of Medicine since 1974: Demonstrator, 1974-76; Clinical Lecturer, 1976-80; then as Assistant Professor, since 1980. **HIGH-LIGHTS:** she considers one of her most significant achievements to have been effected through the Harambee Housing Co-op: while president of this group, it succeeded in obtaining funding to build a 54-unit housing cooperative, providing quality but affordable units. This is now a much sought-after residence and houses a population which is culturally diverse. The recreation centre was named after her late husband, Dr. Ralph James. **AFFIL/MBRSHP:** elected to College of Physicians and Surgeons/Manitoba, 1990, and serves as President, since June 2002; past-Chair, Allergy and Immunology Section, Manitoba Medical Assn., 1993-98; past-President, Manitoba Allergy Society; Provincial Drug Standards and Therapeutic Committee, 1986-94. **COMMUNITY INVOLVEMENT:** currently: Winnipeg Foundation; Canadian Scholarship Trust Foundation; CAA Manitoba; Manitoba Museum Foundation; formerly: United Way; Citizenship Council of Manitoba; National Congress of Black Women (and Manitoba Chapter); Congress of Black Women Foundation; Manitoba Museum of Man and Nature; Manitoba Advisory Committee for Federal Judicial Appointments. **HONS.:** many including: Physician of the Year, Manitoba Medical Assn., 2000; Citation for Citizenship, Govt. of Canada, 1993; GG 125th Anniv. Medal, 1992; Cross of Lorraine, for the establishment of the Asthma Program in Manitoba, Cdn Lung Assn., 1980; Woman of the Year Award, YWCA, 1981. **WORKS:** articles and co-authored two books. **REVIEWED IN:** *WWIC*; *WW in Int'l Women*; *Canada at its Millennium.* **EDUCATION:**

Fellow, American Academy Allergy, Asthma and Immunology, 2002; FRCPC, Allergy & Clinical Immunology, 1976; FRCPC, Paediatrics, 1973; MD, 1967; BSc (Med.), 1967; BSc, 1963, U. of Manitoba. **HEROES/ROLE MODELS:** Grandmother; parents. **MOTTO:** Strive towards excellence. **CONTACT:** jmjames@shaw.ca; Fax: 204-254-6426

▶**JARRETT, Carolyn Joyce,** Dr.
OPTOMETRIST, Private Practice, Ste. 505-155 University Ave., Toronto, ON M5H 3B7. Born: Jamaica/ in Canada since: 1974.

▶ In 1981, Dr. Carolyn Joyce Jarrett became the first Black female optometrist practising in Ontario. Over the years she has also been involved in a number of community initiatives. In 1980, she was part of a team to provide eye care to patients in Jamaica, as part of a joint Canadian-Jamaican Lions Club Sight Project; was on the Board of the Glaucoma Research Society, 1992-97; was a clinical examiner for the Canadian Examiners in Optometry (licensing body), 1998-99. In 2001, she volunteered with the St. Thomas Health Care Organization conducting eye examinations at the Eye Care Clinic in Jamaica. In addition, she conducts motivational seminars with youth, encouraging them to believe in themselves and to achieve their goals. She also participates in Outreach Programs to senior citizen homes in Toronto and speaks on "the importance of Eye Health in the Aging Population." **HONS.:** Contact Lens & Overall Proficiency Awards, U. of Waterloo, 1981. **REVIEWED IN:** *Share,* 2000-01 & *Contrast,* 1981. **EDUCATION:** Doctor of Optometry (OD), 1981; BSc, Chemistry, 1977, U. of Waterloo. **HEROES/ROLE MODELS:** Father. **CONTACT:** sbraithw@interlog.com

▶**JARVIS, Michael**
FILMMAKER, Recfilm, c/o Characters, 150 Carleton St., Toronto, ON M5A 2K1. Born: Montreal, QC, 1970.

▶ Michael Jarvis is an independent filmmaker (director, writer, producer) whose career in the film and video industry began at an early age with an acting role in the opera, *Aida*. He attended Dawson College and Concordia U. where he worked on, wrote, and directed numerous short films and documentaries. **HIGHLIGHTS:** he began working at *L'Office Vidéo and Film Productions* where he made his professional debut directing industrial, commercial, and music videos, notably Sarah Simon's *Fait Moi Danser*. He did freelance work with Artisan Films on *The Ring* as a unit manager, and *The Long Awaited Journey*; worked as Asst. Director, actor and researcher for the documentary, *A Season of Change: The Jackie Robinson Story*. In 1997, he formed his own production house, *Les Productions Reconnaissance* Film Productions (Recfilm). The first project was a short film, *Mathieu Da Costa: The Untold Story*, a story about one of the first free Black men to land in N. America during the early 1600s. The film premiered at the Montreal *Vue d'Afrique* Festival and won the Reel Black Award at the ten-year anniversary of the BFVN during the Toronto Int'l Film Festival (TIFF). He then directed and co-produced a short feature film that he had researched for over three years, *Angelique*, set in New France in 1734, based upon the true story of Marie-Josèphe Angelique, a Black slave who was accused, tried, and convicted, of setting fire to Montreal. *Angelique* made its debut at the Montreal World Film Festival, 1999; it was then featured at the African Film Now – Kumba Festival in Toronto, Montreal's *Vue d'Afrique* Festival, the African Diaspora Festival in New York, Los Angeles Pan African Film Festival, and at the Reel World Film Festival, 2001. In Spring 2001, *Angelique* made its TV debut on CBC and is now being developed into a full-length film script. Other projects have included: six PSA for the CRRF; co-directing, *On Thin Ice: Blacks in Hockey*; and music videos for *Forgiveness, Struggle Report,* and *Dans Mon Coeur*; the docudrama, *Acrobats and Maniacs*, released at the

2002, TIFF. He is currently working on two films, *Inside Out* and *24hrs of haze*. **HONS.:** include, Reel Black Award, for *Mathieu Da Costa*, BFVN. **EDUCATION:** BAC, Cinema/Film Production, Concordia U. **MOTTO:** A picture can tell a thousand words; dreams are infinite… **CONTACT:** Tel: 416-731-0037; recfilm@sympatico.ca

▶**JEAN, Michaëlle**
JOURNALISTE-PRÉSENTATRICE, Société Radio Canada (SRC), Montréal, QC. Née: Haïti/ au Canada depuis: 1968.
▶ Michaëlle Jean a commencé sa carrière à l'université comme professeur, mais après avoir accepté des invitations de collaboration dans les projets de reportage, elle s'est orientée vers le journalisme. Elle a fait ses études en Italie (Pérouse, Florence, et Milan) dans le cadre d'une maîtrise en littérature comparée et un Bac en langues et littératures hispaniques et italiennes. Pendant qu'elle faisait ses études, elle a oeuvré pendant 8 ans (1979-1987) auprès de Regroupement provincial des maisons d'hébergement et de transition pour femmes victimes de violence conjugale au Québec. **RÉALISATIONS:** Elle a coordonné un travail de recherche qui a donné la première enquête en Amérique du Nord portant sur l'incidence des agressions à caractère sexuel rapportées par des femmes violentées par leur conjoint; l'étude a été citée lors d'un débat à l'Assemblée nationale, juin 1987. Pendant qu'elle enseignait, elle a reçu une invitation du magazine québécois, *Parole Métèque* de rédiger une série de portraits des femmes haïtiennes, suivant la chute du régime Duvalier, 1986; en 1987, elle a été invitée de collaborer dans le tournage d'une documentaire en Haïti, *Haïti, nous sommes la; Ayiti nou la*, avec l'Office National du Film du Canada. Le film a été tourné pendant une période de turbulence: des premières élections libres au pays. **ACTIVITÉS PRINCIPALES**: en 1988, elle a débuté comme reporter à l'émission, *Actuel*, à la

télé de SRC; en 1989, elle faisait partie de l'équipe du *Journal* et faisait *Montréal ce soir*; 1991-92, elle a co-présenté l'émission *Virages* sur l'évolution des valeurs et le choc des générations dans la société québécoise; du 1992-95, elle travaillait avec l'équipe du magazine télévise, *Le Point*, qui couvre l'actualité nationale et internationale; en 1995, elle devient journaliste-présentatrice à RDI, la 1ère chaîne francophone d'information continue en Amérique du Nord; pendant cette période, elle anime *Le monde ce soir, l'Edition québécoise, Horizons francophones, Grands reportages, Le Journal RDI* et, *RDI à l'écoute*. Elle traitait aussi des grands dossiers: *La moitie du monde*, 15 émissions autour des grands thèmes débattus à la Conférence de l'ONU sur les femmes à Pékin (Prix média d'Amnesty International, 1995); *L'enfance volée*, sur la pédophilie; *Le Sommet de la Francophonie à Hanoi; La rétrocession de Hong Kong à la Chine; Le Pape à Cuba; Une révolution à finir*, à l'occasion des 40ans de la révolution cubaine. En 1999, elle participe au film documentaire, *L'heure de Cuba* dont la présentation fut suivie d'un débat en studio; avant, elle avait participé à deux autres films avec le cinéaste Jean-Daniel Lafond, *Tropique Nord*, 1994 (en étant noir et québécois), et *Haïti dans tous nos rêves*, 1995 (sur le thème de l'exil et l'engagement), qui a gagné grand prix du film politique au festival Hot Docs à Toronto, 1996. Now, she is also the host of CBC Newsworld's *Passionate Eye: Sunday Showcase, Passionate Eye on Monday, and Rough Cuts*. **PRIX:** y compris: Prix Raymond Charette (première femme et première télé journaliste), 2000; l'une des Femmes de l'année, 1998, *Elle* Québec; Femme de Mérite en communication, YWCA, 1998; Premier Prix de journalisme, conférence des femmes à Pékin, 1995; Prix Anik, meilleur reportage pour *Les grandes familles et le pouvoir de l'argent en Haïti*, 1994; Prix Mireille Lanctôt, pour le reportage *Partir à zéro,* sur la violence conjugale, 1989; Prix d'excellence en études françaises. **FORMATION:** U. de Milan, 1985; U. de Florence, 1984; U. de Pérouse, 1982. Maîtrise, littérature comparée; Bac, langues et littératures hispaniques et italiennes, U. de Montréal. Parle couramment 5 langues (l'anglais, le français, l'italien, l'espagnol, le créole Haïtien; et elle lit le portugais). **CONTACT:** Tél: 416-205-8777; Fax: 416-205-6080

▶**JEANTY, Bernard, CA.**
CHARTERED ACCOUNTANT/PARTNER, Schwartz Levitsky Feldman, 10th Fl.-1980 Sherbrooke W., Montreal, QC H3H 1E8. Born: USA, 1965/ in Canada since: 1970.
▶ Bernard Jeanty returned to school in 1984 to study accounting after losing his job as a full-time professional DJ in Montreal nightclubs. He enrolled in the accounting program, in his own words, "not even knowing what accounting was, except to know it sounded secure": he liked it right away. After graduating in 1988, he joined the firm of Schwartz Levitsky Feldman in 1989, which specializes in audits, taxation, turnaround financing, business consulting and valuation, trusteeship, etc., and is recognized as the 10th largest firm in Canada, under its international affiliation, HLB. In 1990, BJ passed his Chartered Accounts exam and obtained his CA title; since then, he advanced very quickly in the firm to become, at the age of 35, a partner in 2001. Until 1994, he had continued working as a DJ in nightclubs while working full-time and pursuing his studies. In his words, not only has he "succeeded IN life, he has succeeded HIS life." **HONS.:** including, Jackie Robinson Award, Professional of the Year, MABBP, 2001. **REVIEWED IN:** *La Presse*; *Montreal Gazette*. **EDUCATION:** CA, *Ordre des Comptables Agrées du Québec*, 1990; Bac, Administration des Affaires, UQAM, 1988. **HEROES/ROLE MODELS:** Parents. **MOTTO:** *Toute mauvaise chose a une fin*–all bad things have an end. **CONTACT:** bernard.jeanty@slf.ca; Fax: 514-933-9710

▶**JEFFERS, Garvin**
HIGH SCHOOL PRINCIPAL (Ret.), Protestant School Board of Greater Montreal, Dollard des Ormeaux, QC. Born: Trinidad & Tobago/ in Canada since: 1956.
▶ Garvin Jeffers was a career educator who taught from 1961 until his retirement in 1997. **CAREER HIGHLIGHTS:** Mathematics and Black Studies teacher at several high schools; in 1973 he became Head of the Mathematics Dept. at the High School of Montreal; he continued in this position at Westmount High from 1976-91 when he was promoted to Vice-Principal; in 1994, he became the Principal of Westmount High, until his retirement in 1997. **COMMUNITY INVOLVEMENT:** he initiated a number of remedial programs including the Saturday Morning Tutorial Program; Negro Community Centre; Black Community Resource Centre; Quebec Board of Black Educators; Black Studies Centre; first Principal of Bana summer program and Principal of Da Costa Hall Summer School. **HONS.:** including, Award for community service, West Island Black Community Assn., 2001; Awards for leadership, commitment & dedication to education, Quebec Brd. of Black Educators, 1989, 1995, 2000; Award for outstanding work in education, Muhammad's Mosque, 1996; Award for fostering respect & unity between the races, Baha'i of Westmount, 1996. **EDUCATION:** MSc, New York State U., 1973; Dipl. Ed., McGill U., 1962; BA, SGWU (now Concordia U.), 1961. **CONTACT:** garvin@total.net

▶**JEMMOTT, Rev. Father Anthony**
INCUMBENT, All Saints Anglican Church, 12935 Keele St., King City, ON. Born: Barbados/ in Canada since: 1982.
▶ Rev. Father Anthony Jemmott was ordained in 1973, in the Anglican Church in Barbados, then spent nearly 20 yrs. serving in Montreal. Since 2001, he has been the Incumbent of All Saints Church in King City, Ontario; previously he was

Rector of Trinity Memorial Church, and the Honorary Canon of Christ Church Cathedral in Montreal, 1991-2001. In 1990, he was nominated to be of Bishop of Montreal; he ended as first runner-up out of a field of 19 candidates. He was the Regional Dean of Western Montreal, 1993-96; and, from 1985-1991, was the first Rector of St. Lawrence Church. While in Montreal he was a founding member of Montreal's Black Star Project (like Big Brothers; *see: Baffoe, Michael*), and served on the Board of the Queen Elizabeth Health Complex. **HONS.:** including, Caribbean-Anglican Consultation Award, for service to Caribbean people in Canada, 2001. **WORKS:** report, *Women in the Church*, Barbados, 1978. **EDUCATION:** MA, Religion, Concordia U., 1988; Dipl. Min., UTCWI, Jamaica, 1973; BA/Hons., Theology, UWI, 1973. **HEROES/ROLE MODELS:** Senator Clarence Jemmott, father; Canon Andrew Hatch. **CONTACT:** agejem @sympatico.ca; Fax: 905-833-6268

▶**JENKINS, Ferguson Arthur**
BASEBALL COMMISSIONER, Canadian Baseball League, Ste. 440-1140 W. Pender St., Vancouver, BC V6E 4G1. Born: Chatham, ON.
▶ Ferguson (Fergie) Jenkins is the newly appointed Commissioner of Baseball of the new Canadian Baseball League (CBL) whose first season will begin in 2003. During a very successful 19-season major league baseball career, FJ achieved a number of milestones: he is the only Canadian to be inducted into the National Baseball Hall of Fame in the US and is the Black pitcher with the most wins ever in the major leagues; he is the only pitcher in 40 yrs. to have pitched six straight, 20-win years; he is among the all-time leaders in wins (284), games started (598), innings pitched (4,499), shutouts (49) and strikeouts (3,192); he is the only pitcher in Major League history to strike out more than 3,000 batters while giving up fewer than 1,000 walks (997); he became only the fourth pitcher (of six) to win 100 games in both the American and National Leagues.

HIGHLIGHTS: his career began in 1963 in the minors with the Philadelphia Phillies until he was traded to the Chicago Cubs, where he started as a Pitcher in 1967; he considers 1971 his best year, leading his team with 24 wins, pitching 30 complete games and 325 innings; in 1973, he was traded to the Texas Rangers where he became their first 20-game winner, in 1974, when he posted 25 wins; he then played with the Boston Red Sox; after two yrs. was traded back to the Rangers; four yrs. later he became a Cub again, for two yrs., until he retired in 1983. In 1988, he became the pitching coach for the then-Oklahoma City 89ers, the Texas Rangers' farm club; during that time, he bought a ranch and began raising Appaloosa horses, an activity that he has continued over the years. In 1995-96, he was the pitching coach for the Chicago Cubs; and, in 1995, was the honorary coach for the '95 All-Star Game. For several years, he worked with the Major League Baseball Players Alumni Assn., raising money for charities through public appearances and speeches. In his new position as Commissioner, FJ will direct league policy and make appearances promoting the CBL and encouraging community involvement; the post-season championship will be played for The Jenkins Cup. **HONS.:** several including: voted "one of the top 100 baseball players of the 20th Century," Society for American Baseball Research, 1999; National Baseball Hall of Fame in 1991; Canadian Baseball Hall of Fame, 1987; National League Cy Young Award, 1971; Pitcher of the Year, NL, *The Sporting News*, 1971. **WORKS:** his autobiography, as told to George Vass, *Like Nobody Else: The Fergie Jenkins Story,* 1973; *Inside Pitching*, with David Fisher, 1972. **REVIEWED IN:** *Journey: African Canadian History*, 2000; *Some Black Men*, 1999. **CONTACT:** www.canadianbaseballleague.com

JENNINGS, Marlene

MEMBER OF PARLIAMENT, NDG-Lachine, House of Commons, Government of Canada. Constituency Office, Stc. 204-6332 Sherbrooke St. W., Montreal, QC H4B 1M7. Born: Montreal, QC.

▸ Marlene Jennings was first elected to the House of Commons in 1997, thereby becoming the first Black woman from Quebec to be elected to the Parliament of Canada. She was re-elected in November 2000, to represent the riding of Notre-Dame-de-Grace-Lachine. In September, 2001, the prime minister appointed her as Parliamentary Secretary to the Min. for International Cooperation. She is a member of the Standing Committee on Foreign Affairs and International Trade, and a member of its sub-committee on Human Rights and International Development. She is also a member of the sub-committee on National Security of the Standing Committee on Justice. During her first mandate, she served on Standing Committees for Natural Resources and Government Operations, Public Accounts, and Industry, Science and Technology. She was also Secretary of the National Liberal Caucus, 1997-2001; and has served as Secretary-Treasurer, and Chair of the Quebec Liberal Caucus. **BACKGROUND:** MJ is a lawyer by training and was called to the Quebec bar in 1988; she served on the Quebec Police Commission, 1988-90; then as Deputy Commissioner for Police Ethics, province of Quebec, 1990-97; has been involved in a number of national and international conferences on policing, police ethics, race relations and minority women's issues. She has also served with many not-for-profit community organizations. **HONS.:** Jackie Robinson Award for Professionals, MABBP. **EDUCATION:** partially completed Executive MBA, Concordia, 1990; LLB, UQAM, 1986; studies in English & Psychology, McGill U. **HEROES/ROLE MODELS:** Judge Westmoreland-Traoré, friend; Luciano Del Negro, husband & friend. **MOTTO:** Every time you get a "no," you're that much closer to getting a "yes." "No" doesn't mean "no," it just means "no for now." **CONTACT:** jennim@parl.gc.ca; www.marlenejennings.com

▶JOHN, Dexter

LAWYER, Donahue Ernst & Young LLP, Ste. 1800-222 Bay St., Toronto, ON. Born: Montreal, QC, 1969.

▶ Dexter John has been an Associate in Corporate Securities with Donahue Ernst and Young, since 2000. During that time he has worked on corporate transactions dealing with financing for high-tech companies, the statutory plan for the amalgamation of two Canadian mining companies, and initial public offerings of shares in Canada for a high-tech company. **BACKGROUND:** Legal and Policy Counsel, Investment Dealers' Association of Canada, 2000; Student-at-law, Stikeman, Elliott, 1999; Junior Counsel, Market Operations Branch, Ontario Securities Commission, 1996; Junior Counsel, Toronto Stock Exchange, 1996. **OTHER:** during the course of his undergraduate studies at York U., he was an All-Canadian sprinter and a participant at the 1992 Olympic Trials. **HONS.:** Sparks Award for Law, Queen's U., 1998. **EDUCATION:** LLB, Queen's U., 1998; Canadian Securities Course, 1998; BA, mathematics for commerce, 1993. **CONTACT:** dexter.john@ca.eyi.com; Fax: 416-943-2735

▶JOHNSON, Allister

PROGRAM COORDINATOR/COMMUNITY VOLUNTEER, North Preston Holistic, Cultural and Academic Enrichment Program, 60 Johnson Rd., North Preston, NS B2Z 1A1. Born: North Preston, NS.

▶ Allister Johnson has been active in his community as an educator and as a volunteer for many years. He is program coordinator at the North Preston Holistic, Cultural and Academic Enrichment Program, which is provided under the African Canadian Education Act (for which he and others insisted, in order to ensure that the needs and interests of the Black population were included in decisions related to education). He is a former board member of the Watershed Assn. Development Enterprise (WADE), and from 1997-2001 was chair. He led the group in developing a successful community economic development (CED) approach; they completed an asset-mapping project cataloguing the labour market and infrastructure assets of the Preston area. (WADE has also published a book on CED, *We Can't Walk Alone.*) He is a founding member of the North Preston Community Education Council, which succeeded in transforming a local elementary school into an Afrocentric one (only all-Black public school in NS); was president of the North Preston Community Development Assn. (formerly North Preston Ratepayers Assn.), from 1989-98, and initiated socio-economic development planning strategies for the area. During his mandate, he also addressed issues of race relations, municipal landfill siting, and community/police relations. In 1996, he developed and implemented the Census Communications Strategy, targetted to the Black population in NS; this strategy was expanded in 2001 to include the ethnically diverse population in the entire Atlantic Region. **WORKS:** co-authored chapter in, *We Can't Walk Alone*, 2000; co-authored *The Genealogy of William & Charlotte Cain*, 1999. **EDUCATION:** Cert., Community Economic Development, 2000; Cert., Leadership & Communication, 1977. **MOTTO:** Adequate hindsight and good insight beget good foresight. **CONTACT:** aljohnson@accesswave.ca

▶JOHNSON, Ben

ATHLETE/COACH, c/o IAPG, Box 94, Richmond Hill, ON L4C 4X9. Born: Jamaica/ in Canada since: 1976.

▶ Ben Johnson won a number of international competitions in the 100m, setting a number of world records and receiving the Olympic Champion Award in 1985. He had also been awarded: Sports Excellence Award, 1986; World Champion Award, 1987; named Outstanding Male Athlete of the Year, 1986 and '87; Ontario Athlete of the Year, 1985; and, inducted into the Canadian Amateur Sports Hall of Fame, 1988. However, in 1988, after winning gold in the 100m at the Seoul Olympics, he tested positive for the use of performance-enhancing drugs and was stripped of his medal and world record (9.79 sec.). Vilified by the media, he went from "Canadian hero" to "Jamaican immigrant" in a matter of hours. This positive test led to the Dubin Enquiry into the use of drugs in amateur sports in Canada and revealed the widespread use of steroids. BJ was initially banned from competition for two yrs., but was subsequently banned from competition for life in 1993. After petitioning from a number of MPs, led by MP Jean Augustine, the ban was lifted by Athletics Canada in 1999. He now provides coaching services to professional and semi-professional athletes. **CONTACT:** www.benjohnson-979.com

►**JOHNSON, Beverley C.H.**

HUMAN RIGHTS OFFICER, Ontario Public Service Employees' Union (OPSEU), 100 Lesmill Rd., Toronto, ON M3B 3P8. Born: Jamaica/ in Canada since: 1973.

▸ Beverley Johnson is the first and only Human Rights Officer with the Ontario Public Service Employees' Union, a position she has held since 1991. With nearly 100,000 members in the union (including ambulance services, child care, hospital workers, etc.), her responsibilities include: responding to questions on human rights and equity, whether from members, staff or union executive; being available for consultation on issues related to bargaining of collective agreements; consultation on issues of harassment; sitting on caucuses and HR committees regionally, nationally, and as part of coalitions with other unions, like the OFL. **BACKGROUND:** prior to joining OPSEU, she was the first Human Rights Intake Officer at the Ontario Human Rights Commission, 1973-91, and was responsible for dealing with complaints and providing public education on issues of human rights. **OTHER:** she is possibly the first Black woman to be appointed to the Ontario Judicial Appointments Advisory Committee. This group is responsible for identifying, recruiting and screening all candidates to determine their eligibility for the position of judge within the Ontario provincial courts. Based upon their recommendations, the AG will then make appointments. **COMMUNITY:** she is a founding member of the following: Toronto Chapter, Congress of Black Women; Ontario Coalition of Visible Minority Women; Coalition of Black Trade Unionists. She is the first and only woman to chair the Caribbean Cultural Committee and is a lifetime member of the Metro Children's Aid Society. **HONS.:** including: nominee for JS Woodsworth Award, NDP, 2000; Carolyn J. Holmes Humanitarian Award, CBTU, 1997. **REVIEWED IN:** *Share; Jamaica Gleaner; Excellence* magazine. **EDUCATION:** Dipl. Public Admin., Ryerson Polytechnic, 1981; Dipl. Personnel Admin., UWI, 1969; Dipl. Social Admin., London School of Economics, 1963; BA, SGWU (now Concordia U.), 1962. **CONTACT:** bjohnson @cbtu.ca; Fax: 416-292-3972

►**JOHNSON, E. Bruce**

PHARMACIST/CO-OWNER, City Drug Store Ltd., 369 Main St., Yarmouth, NS B5A 1E7. Born: Yarmouth, NS.

▸ Bruce Johnson is the first Black Nova Scotian to become a pharmacist and has been working in this sector since 1974. Very involved in his local community, he chairs the following: Yarmouth-Shelburne Black Employment Partnership Committee; Yarmouth Boys and Girls Club; Yarmouth Regional Business Corp.; Tri-County Housing Authority. He is also a member of the Board of the BBI. **EDUCATION:** BSc Pharmacy, Dalhousie School of Pharmacy, 1974. **HEROES/ ROLE MODELS:** Parents. **MOTTO:** Life is what you make it. **CONTACT:** citydrugstore@ns.sympatico.ca; Fax: 902-742-6407

►JOHNSON, Errol W. Clive
INSURANCE & FINANCIAL SERVICES EXECUTIVE,
Clarica, Ste. 1201-625 René Lévesque W., Montreal, QC H3B 1R5. Born: Jamaica/in Canada since: 1966.

▶ Errol Johnson, in 1994, became the first Black in the city of Dollard-des-Ormeaux, a Montreal suburb, to be elected to City Council; he was re-elected for a second term in 1998, but was unsuccessful in his 2001 bid under the new amalgamated municipal structure. **CAREER HIGHLIGHTS:** has been successful in his professional life as an insurance and financial services representative for Clarica (formerly Mutual Life), since 1973. During that time he has received a number of professional awards including being a member of the Million Dollar Round Table, 1975, and receiving the Award of Excellence Diamond Ring. He also ventured into the world of business when, in 1973, he began Natam Inc. to import Black dolls from the US so that his daughter and other children would have access to dolls which looked like them. **COMMUNITY INVOLVEMENT:** founding member MABBP and Mathieu da Costa Business Development Corp.; Quebec Chair, fundraising, James Robinson Johnston Chair in Cdn Black Studies; Jamaican Assn. of Montreal; plays guitar with his band, The CEOs. **AFFIL/ MBRSHP:** Commissioner of Oaths, province of Quebec, since 1989; Board of Directors, Via Rail, 1993-96; Advisory Committee to the President, Treasury Board of Canada, 1986-91. **HONS.:** including: Harry Jerome Award, Business, 2001; Jackie Robinson Special Award, MABBP; Plaque, for contribution to economic development in Quebec, QC Min. of Industry & Commerce, 1998; Plaque, Jamaica Assn./Mtl, 1989; Plaque, for community involvement, Jamaican Cdn Community Women's League/ Mtl. **REVIEWED IN:** community & nat'l publications including: *Millennium Minds*, 2000; *Toronto Star; Montreal Star; Montreal Gazette; Community Contact*. **EDUCATION:** BA, SGWU (now Concordia U.),

1973. **HEROES/ROLE MODELS:** Parents. **MOTTO:** No mountain is too high to climb; you can if you believe in yourself. **CONTACT:** errol.johnson@ clarica.com; Fax: 514-393-3775

►JOHNSON, Kaye
COORDINATOR, RACE RELATIONS, Annapolis Valley Regional School Board, PO Box 340, Berwick, NS B0P 1E0. Born: Montreal, QC, 1962.

▶ Kaye Johnson became involved in organizing and presenting workshops on anti-racism and social justice in the 1980s. Since 1998, she is the Coordinator of Race Relations, Cross Cultural Understanding and Human Rights (RCH), for the Annapolis Valley Regional Board; in this capacity, she organizes workshops and conferences on these topics for students, grades 1-12, for staff, parents, and the general public. Previously, 1995-98, she was the Regional Educator for Southwest NS, for the Black Learners Advisory Committee of the Black Educators' Assn. (BEA). **COMMUNITY INVOLVEMENT:** spent 17 yrs. in the Air Force Reserves, as a musician (tuba), radio operator, and teacher of basic training courses; 1994, served in Honour Guard of the Canada Remembers Unit (Belgium, France, Netherlands, UK); Multicultural Education Council/NS; founding member, Camp Kujichagulia; Valley African Heritage Society; Family Literacy Assn., NS; Hants Disabilities Partnership; federal NDP candidate in 2000 by-election and general election. **HONS.:** Cdn Decoration Medal, 12 yrs. service; GG 125th Anniv. Medal. **WORKS:** in, *The New Democrat*, 2002; papers & reports concerning RCH. **EDUCATION:** M.Ed in progress, Acadia U.; MSW, Social Admin. & Policy, 1994; BA, 1985, Carleton University. DEC, Vanier College, 1982. **HEROES/ROLE MODELS:** Changiah Ragaven, social activist; Dawn Brown, sister, author. **MOTTO:** Life is an act of faith; struggle is optional. (Ayanla Vanzant) **CONTACT:** kaye.johnson@avrsb.ednet. ns.ca; Fax: 902-538-4630

▶**JOHNSON, Lillie**
DIRECTOR OF NURSING (Ret.), Leeds, Grenville, and Lanark District Health Unit, ON. Born: Jamaica/ in Canada since: 1960.

▶ Lillie Johnson began her career in nursing in Scotland in the 1950s, came to Canada in 1960 where she continued her studies in Public Health Nursing, and obtained her BScN degree while occupying a number of nursing and senior administrative positions. Before retiring in 1989, she had become possibly the first Black Public Health Director of Nursing in Ontario. She also used her training and experience to foster greater community awareness on health-related matters, and founded the Sickle Cell Association of Ontario. **CAREER HIGHLIGHTS:** began her professional life as an elementary school teacher in Jamaica; after studying nursing in Scotland and midwifery in England, she worked in Oxfordshire as a domiciliary nurse and midwife, 1942-1950; returned to Jamaica and worked at the University College of the West Indies as a staff nurse, 1955-57; staff nurse at Beth Israel Hospital, New Jersey (US), 1958-60. In Canada, she held the following positions: staff nurse with the Victorian Order of Nurses (VON) and York County Regional Health Unit; became a Master Teacher (1973), Health Services Div., at Humber College, teaching basic and postgraduate nursing programs in maternal and child health; Nursing Consultant at the Ontario Min. of Health, 1974-81. From 1982-88, she was the Director of Nursing for Leeds, Grenville and Lanark District Health Unit (Kingston/Ottawa area), responsible for a staff of over 50 health care professionals, in the promotion and development of public health nursing programs to meet identified needs of the community. During this time, she also advocated for better living conditions for farm workers from the Caribbean working in the area. Over the years, she was also a resource person for the Early Childhood Education Program at Queen's University. **OTHER:** after retiring in 1989, she returned to Jamaica as a CUSO cooperant (1989-95) and was responsible for starting a clinic in Kingston, sponsored by Kiwanis/Seventh-day Adventists Church and working with underprivileged and high-risk families; over 10,000 patients receive medical, nursing, and preventative health care. **COMMUNITY INVOLVEMENT:** has been extensive: initiated peer counselling support for women from visible minority groups working in administrative positions; provided counseling and support to adolescents for coping with dating, peer pressure, communicating with parents, etc; and, as a Board member of YWCA in Toronto and Richmond Hill, organized support groups for women who had immigrated to Canada on the domestic plan. Participated in the first conference organized by the National Congress of Black Women and the Council of Jamaicans; Founder (1981) and a lifetime member of the Sickle Cell Assn. of Ontario, and currently chair of the Education Committee; lifetime member of PACE; Jamaican-Canadian Assn.; Area Council for CUSO. **HONS.:** several including, Certificates of Recognition: Women's Cmtee of the JCA, 2002; University Hospital of the West Indies, Graduate Nurses Assn./Canada Chapter, 2000. People's Plus Community Award, Nigerian Sickle Cell Awareness Group, 2001; Citation, for work done at Penwood Medical/Dental Clinic, CUSO, 1995. **REVIEWED IN:** *Int'l Who's Who of Professional & Business Women.* **EDUCATION:** BScN, 1969; Dipl., Public Health Nursing, 1964, U of T. Cert. Family Planning Training, London, England, 1957; Midwifery, Queen Charlotte & Churchill Hospitals, England, 1955; RN, Western General Hospital, Edinburgh, Scotland, 1954. **MOTTO:** SHARE! **CONTACT:** c/o JCA Tel: 416-746-5772

▶**JOHNSON, Molly**
SINGER/SONGWRITER/PHILANTHROPIST, c/o EMI Music, Toronto, ON. Born: Toronto, ON.

▶ Molly Johnson is well known on the Canadian music scene, now as a jazz singer, and previously as a rock performer. In the 1980s she formed the art/rock band, Alta Moda and released an album on Sony Music. In the early 1990s, she was lead singer for the Juno Award-winning band, the Infidels and was signed to the record label IRS Records. During this time, she was also performing jazz at local venues in Toronto, with her trio, Blue Monday. From performing at Toronto's bohemian Cameron Public House, she has moved to more prestigious venues, including Massey and Roy Thomson Halls, as well as the Imperial Room at the Royal York Hotel. She has also performed for dignitaries such as Nelson Mandela, Princess Diana, and Prince Philip. MJ released her self-titled jazz album, *Molly Johnson*, to critical and popular acclaim in 2000, on the label, Song Corp. This album was re-released by EMI Music Canada in March 2002. Her newest jazz recording, *Another Day*, was released by EMI Music in June 2002. Both albums have been well received by critics and consumers. **COMMUNITY INVOLVEMENT:** well known for her philanthropy and her commitment to charitable causes; is the founder and driving force behind the Kumbaya Foundation, established in 1992 to raise funds for the care of people living with AIDS and HIV; to date, close to one million dollars has been raised through the annual Kumbaya Festival, which is broadcast live across Canada by MuchMusic and features much of Canada's leading musical talent. **REVIEWED IN:** all major newspapers and magazines, including *Rolling Stone, NOW.* **EDUCATION:** National Ballet School of Canada; Banff School of Fine Arts. **HEROES/ROLE MODELS:** Parents; June Callwood; Margaret Atwood; Peter Gzowski. **MOTTO:** Go big or go home! **CONTACT:** mary.mill@emimusic.ca; www.mollyjohnson.com

▶**JOHNSON, Veronica**
EDUCATOR, Lester B. Pearson School Board, Dollard-des-Ormeaux, QC. Born: Jamaica/ in Canada since: 1968.
▶ Veronica Johnson completed her undergraduate

degree at SGWU (now Concordia U.) in four yrs. while working full-time; in addition, she wrote her final exam, on which she earned an "A," five days before her first child was born, in 1973. This drive and determination over the years have contributed to her success as an educator (over 25 yrs.), mother (three children), and three-time campaign manager for husband Errol Johnson's city councillor bids, 1994, 1998, 2001 (*see: Johnson, Errol*). **CAREER:** after working in banking for a number of years, she taught with the Protestant School Board, 1976-89; she currently teaches Adult Education with the Lester B. Pearson School Board and was instrumental in getting Black History added to the Adult Education curriculum. With this success, she was allowed to conceptualize and teach the first course in Black History to adult learners for that board. She also served for three years on the Cdn Advisory Council on the Status of Women and for five years in the Refugee Div., Immigration and Refugee Board. **COMMUNITY INVOLVEMENT:** West Island Community Shares; West Island Black Community Assn.; *Table de concertation jeunesse de l'ouest de l'ile*; Greendale School Committee; she has lectured on Black History, multiculturalism, and self-esteem in Black children and is a frequent speaker at community functions; has been encouraging greater financial independence for women, and that citizens become more involved in their community. **HONS.:** including: Plaque for outstanding & dedicated service, West Island Black Community Assn.; Award of Merit, Greendale Home & School Assn.; Plaque, in appreciation for unfailing support, Caribbean Pioneer Women of Canada; & several letters of appreciation. **WORKS:** in, *The Oracle; WIBCA Insight* (and served as editor); *The Guardian* (church newspaper). **REVIEWED IN:** local & nat'l publications including: *Montreal Star; Community Contact; Montreal Gazette; The Chronicle.* **EDUCATION:** M.Ed, partially completed; BA, 1973, SGWU (now Concordia U.). Cert., ESL, 1988; Dipl., Education, 1976, McGill U. **HEROES/ROLE**

MODELS: Martin Luther King Jr.; Sojourner Truth; Harriet Tubman. **MOTTO:** If your mind can conceive it, and if your heart can believe it, you can achieve it! **CONTACT:** errol.johnson@sympatico.ca

►JOHNSTON, Roy
WWII VETERAN, Royal Canadian Air Force/ Tool Room Foreman (Ret.), Gray Tool Co., Toronto, ON. Born: Toronto, ON.

▶ Roy Johnston is a WWII veteran. He joined the Royal Canadian Air Force in 1942 and was sent overseas, serving in England, Holland, Belgium, and Germany in the Air Observation Post, attached to the Artillery. Following his return to Canada, he resumed his position as a toolmaker with the Gray Tool Co., where he had begun working in 1940. In 1970, he was promoted to Tool Room Foreman, a position he held until his retirement in 1988. Since retiring he engages in a number of activities including volunteering at the AGO. **OTHER:** he also has the distinction of possibly being the first Black School Trustee with the Toronto Board of Education, a position he held from 1970-76 for Ward 3. And, during his youth, he protested, along with other community activists, certain discriminatory practices to which Blacks were subjected, including a protest of the Palais Royal dance hall, which would not admit Black youth on its premises. **REVIEWED IN:** *The Toronto Telegram* (now *The Toronto Star),* 1941-42; *Toronto Star,* 1992. **EDUCATION:** Western Tech Commercial High School, 1940. **HEROES/ ROLE MODELS:** Mr. Slade, Machine Shop Teacher; Wilson Brooks, friend.

►JOLLY, Brandeis Denham
BUSINESS OWNER, Flow 93.5FM, Ste. 400-211 Yonge St., Toronto, ON M5B 1M4. Born: Jamaica/ in Canada since: 1955.

▶ Denham Jolly has been the owner of a number of successful business initiatives in Canada and the US. **HIGHLIGHTS:** his career began in Jamaica

when he worked in nutrition; in Toronto, he taught chemistry and physics at Forest Hill Collegiate for seven yrs.; 1978-79, he owned Woodhaven Manor, a nursing home in Texas; from 1978-83, he owned and operated two medical laboratory companies (Edbec Paramedicals and Standard Medical Diagnostics); 1982-84, he was the publisher of *Contrast* the then-leading Black community newspaper in Toronto; he is the president of Tyndall Nursing Home, and operated the Toronto West Days Inn. In 2000, after several years of lobbying for a Black-owned urban music radio station, the CRTC granted him a licence and in early 2001, Flow 93.5FM went on the air in Toronto. **AFFIL/MBRSHP:** founder and first President, BBPA; JCA; Caribana; BADC; Black Inmates Organization; Harriet Tubman Games; Brd., Toronto Central YMCA; Brd., Surrey Place. **HONS.:** including, Daniel G. Hill Community Service Award, OBHS; Black History Makers Award, United Achievers of Brampton; Community Service Award, Onyx Lions Club; President's Special Award of Merit, BBPA; GG 125th Anniv. Medal. **REVIEWED IN:** *Millennium Minds,* 2000; *WW in Ontario; Some Black Men,* 1999; *Who's Who of Professionals.* **EDUCATION:** BSc, McGill U. **CONTACT:** Tel: 416-214-5000; Fax: 416-214-0660

►JONES, Ann
CLINICAL NURSE SPECIALIST, NEPHROLOGY, Toronto, ON. Born: Jamaica/ in Canada since: 1974.

▶ Ann Jones is a Clinical Nurse Specialist, who facilitates the care of patients requiring dialysis. In this role, she assists dialysis patients to maintain an optimal level of health by assessing their needs, providing education, and making referrals to members of the multidisciplinary team. Since1994, this work with dialysis patients has led to a desire to raise awareness within the Black population about the impact of hypertension and diabetes (the two leading causes of kidney failure) on kidney function. She joined the AABHS as a means of achieving this goal; with her colleagues in AABHS, she has made presentations on relevant topics and conducted blood pressure screenings at community events, such as the Camp Jumoke Walkathons. In 1999, she and two physician colleagues from AABHS, presented their study on trends in kidney failure among ethnic groups in Toronto, at a conference sponsored by the International Society on Hypertension in Blacks. The findings showed that Blacks, Orientals and East Indians were at a higher risk than Caucasians, of developing kidney failure thus requiring dialysis or kidney transplants. This was the first Canadian study of its kind. The results of this research have since been published in relevant medical journals. **HONS.:** for, development of a foot care and screening program for people with diabetes, 2000. **WORKS:** articles in, *CANNT J*, 2000; *Blood Purification*, 2000; *Ethnicity and Disease*, 1999. **EDUCATION:** MSc, Community Health Nursing, D'Youville College, NY, 2002; BSc, Nursing, Ryerson U., 1992; BSc, Biology & German, U of T, 1987. **MOTTO:** This above all, to thine own self be true! **CONTACT:** ajones6805@ aol.com

▶**JONES, Beryle Mae,** PhD.
ASSISTANT PROFESSOR, University of Winnipeg & University of Manitoba. Born: Jamaica/ in Canada since: 1963.

▶ Dr. Beryle Mae Jones is a career educator who retired in April 2002, as an Asst. Prof. from the Education Dept. at U. of Winnipeg. **CAREER HIGHLIGHTS:** taught English, French and Drama within the Transcona/Springfield School Div., 1967-85; Head, Dept. of English, John W. Gunn Jr. High School, 1974-84. From 1989, she lectured as Asst. Prof., U. of Winnipeg, in the Bachelor of Ed. program, teaching courses in applied linguistics (Language and Literacy in Education), and Multicultural Ed.; taught in the Centre for Academic Writing, in the English Dept.; sessional instructor, Faculty of Ed., U. of Manitoba

since 1992, and taught Aboriginal students in N. Manitoba through the Inter-University Northern Program, 1995-96. **OTHER:** served on National Steering Cmtee, Cdn Black Communities Demographics Project, McGill School of Social Work; consultant, Black Youth Helpline, 1994; consultant, Council Caribbean Org., MB, 1993-94; consultant, course developer and tutor, summer workshop for teachers in the Eastern Caribbean, 1978-83 and 1991-94; consultant, placement of recently arrived West Indian students in Manitoba schools, MB, Dept. of Ed., 1975-81; curriculum development and tutor, Summer Institute for teachers, U. of Haile Selassie, Addis Ababa, Ethiopia, with Cdn Project Overseas, 1972. **AFFIL/MBRSHP:** past-President, MB Multi-Resource Centre; Black Educators Assn. of MB; President, MB Assn. for Multicultural Ed.; Social Studies Cultural Advisory Team; Cdn Citizenship Fdn.; Citizenship Council of MB; founding President, Immigrant Women's Assn. of MB; founding President & co-chair National Council, Congress of Black Women, MB chapter; United Way; UN Assn. Canada/MB. **HONS.:** Black Community Award, BHM Cmtee, 1999; Citation for Citizenship Award, Citizenship & Immigration Canada, 1998; Role Model Award, Black Youth Helpline, 1997; Service Award, Citizenship Council, MB, 1996; Award of Distinction, Immigrant Women's Assn., 1993; Award of Distinction, Congress of Black Women, MB, 1991; Doctoral Fellowship, SSHRC, 1987-88, 1988-89; Post-Grad. Scholarship, MB Teacher's Society, 1986-87, 1987-88. **WORKS:** selected in, *Educating Citizens for a Pluralistic Society*, 2001; *Can Ethnic Studies J*; *re/Visioning: Canadian Perspectives on the Education of Africans in the Late 20th Century, 1998.* Co-author: *Focus on Bias: A Resource for Teachers*, MB Dept. Ed. **EDUCATION:** PhD, Sociolinguistics, U. of London, UK, 1989. M.Ed, Secondary English & Drama, 1974; B.Ed, English & French, 1969, U. of Manitoba. BA, U. of Winnipeg, 1967; Dipl., Ed., Shortwood Teachers'

College, Jamaica, 1960. **HEROES/ROLE MODELS:** Stanford A. Jones, father; Ina Reid, teacher. **MOTTO:** Set personal goals and believe you can! **CONTACT:** bjones@uwinnipeg.ca

▶JONES, Byron

EDUCATOR/PRINCIPAL, Munroe Junior High School, 589 Roch St., Winnipeg, MB R2K 2P7. Born: St. Vincent/ in Canada since: 1966.

▶ Byron Jones has been the principal of Munroe Jr. High School since 1992; it is a dual-track school offering French Immersion, Special Education and English programs. A teacher by training, he taught with the River East School Div. at the junior and senior levels and served as an administrator at three different schools for 19 yrs. In addition to teaching, he sits on two Provincial Social Studies committees for Manitoba and all of Western Canada and the NW Territories; he has presented workshops on various topics to principals, teachers and parents in Alberta, Saskatchewan, and rural Manitoba. In addition, he has been active in the federally funded, CIDA-operated program, Organization for Cooperation in Overseas Development, workshops which have been held throughout the Caribbean. **COMMUNITY:** Social Planning Council of Winnipeg; provincial rep. Parkinson's Society Canada; founding member, Black Educators' Assn., MB; Council of Caribbean Org., MB; co-founder and director of SICES, which deals with live-in caregivers from the Caribbean; has an extensive background in sports, excelling in cricket and has represented Manitoba in national competitions in Edmonton and Vancouver; has coached third division-level soccer and has been an organizer of cricket and soccer for over two decades. **HONS.:** including: Award, for outstanding professional contribution to the Caribbean community, 2000. **WORKS:** in, *re/Visioning: Canadian Perspectives on the Education of Africans in the Late 20th Century*, 1998. **EDUCATION:** M.Ed, 1988; B.Ed, 1973; BA, 1972, U. of Manitoba. **MOTTO:** With a little effort we

can all make a big difference! **CONTACT:** byjones@pop.merlin.mb.ca; Fax: 204-667-6211

▶JONES, Denise

PRESIDENT/EVENTS ORGANIZER, Jones & Jones Productions, Ste. 239-67 Mowat Ave., Toronto, ON M6K 3E3. Born: Jamaica/ in Canada since: 1981.

▶ Denise Jones is President of Jones & Jones Productions and Rhythm Canada Talent Agency. In business since 1987, Jones & Jones is a boutique-style agency offering a variety of services to a diverse clientele. The company provides event management and entertainment services to the corporate, academic, and religious sectors, and is a leading concert promotions, music management, and marketing company, producing over 30 concerts per year and booking over 150 artists. In 1997, DJ was included in Music Women to Watch, by the Georgia-based, Music Women Int'l; and was named by the *Toronto Star*, one of 1997's "People with clout in the entertainment industry." In addition to speaking at conferences and seminars, Jones also performs comedy routines with her husband. **AFFIL/MBRSHP:** founding and current chair, Reggae Cmtee, Cdn Academy of Recording Arts and Sciences (producers of the JUNO Awards); Brd., Cdn Independent Record Producers Assn.; Independent Meeting Planners Assn. of Canada. **HONS.:** including, Platinum record sales over 100,000 units (2002), and Gold record sales over 50,000 units (2000), for marketing of records in Canada; ACAA, for her work in the entertainment industry, 1998; Pioneer Award, for her "groundbreaking work developing & promoting Cdn Music," Urban Music Assn., 1998; Juno Award, for promoting Cdn artists & music, 1997. **WORKS:** *Tribute to Bob,* musical "rocumentary" on the life of Bob Marley, 2000; ed., an Afro-Caribbean cookbook, 1984; musical docu-drama, *Mr. Garvey,* 1989. **EDUCATION:** BA, Communications, U. of Windsor, 1977. **HEROES/ROLE MODELS:** Mother; Marcus Garvey. **MOTTO:** Don't bury your thoughts, put your dreams into reality. (Bob Marley). **CONTACT:** jones.jones@sympatico.ca; Fax: 905-452-8385

▶JONES, Lionel L., Mr. Justice

JUDGE (Ret.), The Court of Queen's Bench of Alberta, Edmonton, AB. Born: Edmonton, AB.
▶ Mr. Justice Lionel Jones began his law career in 1964 as a Crown Counsel for the Attorney General (AG) of Alberta, and retired in 2001 as a Justice of the Court of Queen's Bench of Alberta and a member, *ex officio*, of the Court of Appeal of Alberta. From 1966-69 he was a Legislative Draftsman, to the Dept. of the AG in Alberta. He then served as a Crown Counsel from 1969-72; from 1972-77 he served as a Sr. Crown Counsel in the Dept. of Justice, Govt. of Canada, until his appointment to the Provincial Court. LLJ was appointed as a Judge of the Provincial Court of Alberta in 1977; in 1995, he was appointed as a Justice of the Court of Queen's Bench of Alberta, a position he held until his retirement in June, 2001. **OTHER:** he has also been *ad hoc* lecturer to the RCMP, Province of AB Justices of the Peace, and to college and university students on law-related topics. **HONS.:** include, John Ware Memorial Lifetime Achievement Award, BAASA, 1996; first recipient of the James Bell Award for "outstanding courage & achievement against challenging odds," National Black Coalition of Canada, 1990. **EDUCATION:** LLB, 1963; BA, History, 1960, U. of Alberta. **CONTACT:** lion1@telusplanet.net

▶JONES, Oliver, Dr., OC, CQ.

JAZZ PIANIST/COMPOSER, c/o Justin Time Records, Ste. 101-5455, rue Paré, Montreal, QC H4P 1P7. Born: Montreal, QC.
▶ Oliver Jones is one of Canada's best-known jazz pianists. Born in Montreal in 1934, he performed in his first public concert at age five and had his club debut four yrs. later. He studied for 12 yrs. with Daisy Peterson Sweeney (sister of Oscar

Peterson) and decided to pursue a career in music. He spent two decades in Puerto Rico, outside of jazz, working as musical director for shows in local clubs; it was not until the late 1970s that he began his career in jazz and, until his retirement in 1999, was highly sought after. **CAREER HIGHLIGHTS:** with the launch of Justin Time Records in 1983, he was the first-time leader of their first recording, *Live at Biddles Jazz and Ribs*. From 1983-98, he released 15 albums with this label including, *The Many Moods of Oliver Jones*, 1984; *Speak Low, Swing Hard*, 1987; *Just Friends*, 1989; *A Class Act*, 1991; *Just 88*, 1993; *Yuletide Swing*, 1994; *From Lush to Lively*, 1995; *Have Fingers, Will Travel*, 1997; and, *Just In Time*, 1998. During the course of his career OJ played with many jazz greats including, Charlie Biddle, Dave Young, Ray Brown, Ed Thigpen, Clark Terry, and others. Having toured internationally, he has performed in S. America, Europe, Africa, Australia and New Zealand; he has also appeared at most international jazz festivals and was the subject of an NFB documentary, *Oliver Jones Live in Africa*. Since retiring, he devotes his time to being an advocate for jazz and jazz performers in Canada. He is also a member of the du Maurier Arts Council. **HONS.:** include, Composer of the Year Award, *Jazz Report* magazine, 1996; Order of Quebec & Order of Canada (Officer), 1994; Felix Awards, Best Jazz Album of the Year for *Just 88* (1994), *Just Friends* (1989) & *Yuletide Swing* (1995); Hon. Doctorate in Music (St. Francis Xavier U., 1996; McGill U., 1995; Laurentian U., 1992); Martin Luther King Jr. Award, for contributions to the Black community in Canada, 1993; Juno Award, for *Lights of Burgundy*, 1986. **CONTACT:** oliver.jones@sympatico.ca; www.justin-time.com

▶JONES, Robert William (Bud), CD.

BIBLIOPHILE/HISTORIAN/LECTURER, Anne Packwood Quebec Afro-Canadian Research Institute (AP/QACRI). Brockville, ON. Born: Montreal, QC.

▶ Robert William Jones, a.k.a. Bud Jones, was born in the St-Henri District of Montreal, a seventh-generation Canadian of African descent whose ancestors came to Canada from Maryland in 1849, via the UGRR. Professionally, BJ is a decorated career soldier of 30 yrs., and a veteran of WWII and Korea. After the war, his involvement in sports garnered him acclaim as a Canadian boxing champion and led to his induction into Canada's Boxing Hall of Fame. In 1975, following his retirement from the military, he entered and completed the Boston Marathon. He also accepted a position as a security investigator at Concordia U., which accorded him time to research his family tree and to organize the memorabilia, artifacts, books, photos and historical material that he inherited from family and relatives. Aware that his family had been involved in the history and development of a number of Black communities and institutions, he expanded his research to all of Canada. As a board member of the Negro Community Centre, he lectured and held exhibits on Canadian Black History; served on the editorial staff of the *Afro-Can*, Montreal's Black newspaper and published historical articles on Canada's Black community. Seeing the need for a Black Cultural Centre in Quebec, which could house a Black museum, archive, and library, he founded and organized the Anne Packwood Quebec Afro-Canadian Research Institute. He then lectured across Canada at churches, schools, universities, and historical institutions, upon request. In June 1992, he was invited by the PM, Brian Mulroney, to exhibit his collection of Black Canadian memorabilia and historical photos to Queen Elizabeth II at the opening of the Canadian Museum of Civilization, in Hull, Quebec. In 1995, '96, and '97, he exhibited his collection at Queen's University, in Kingston, Ontario. He was invited back as a guest lecturer; at the same time he participated in the founding of the university's Black Student Collective. Recently, he completed his studies on slavery in Kingston and the Bay of Quinte areas. To support this new endeavour, BJ relocated to

Brockville, Ontario. Though in semi-retirement, his research, library, and photo collection on the history of Blacks in Canada, are made available to students, authors, and organizations, and have been used by the NFB, CBC TV, and others. **HONS.:** CF Decoration (CD); inducted into Canada's Boxing Hall of Fame. **MOTTO:** Together we discover. **CONTACT:** budjones@recorder.ca; Fax: 613-345-3239

▶**JONES, Roger B.**
THE ABILITY MARKET CONSULTANT, Vancouver, BC. Born: Truro, NS.
▶ Roger B. Jones, "The Ability Guy," is a recognized expert on disability issues and a sought-after speaker nationally and internationally. He was a main presenter at the first International Conference on Individualized Funding and Self-determination in Seattle WA; was chosen to be part of a global delegation that wrote a declaration at the conference, which has been published and is being distributed to governments and organizations around the world. He was invited to be the keynote speaker at a similar conference in San Diego, Fall, 2002. **HIGHLIGHTS:** he was only the second person after Rick Hansen to give the keynote address at the Aging with a Spinal Cord Injury Conference. He established the Susan Marshall Fighting Spirit Award, which is presented annually by the Canadian Paraplegic Association in Halifax and Vancouver; facilitated diversity seminars and helped to establish a committee for persons with disabilities at the Canada Customs and Revenue Agency; actively involved in anti-racism and cultural awareness initiatives; has been a keynote speaker at the BHM Opening Ceremonies in British Columbia and a panelist at the BC Federation of Labor Diversity Conference, among others. He has toured Atlantic Canada as a spokesperson for the Texaco Drive to Survive Program and currently speaks to thousands of youth in BC schools with the program, Above and Beyond. In 1998 he was appointed by the

Govt. of BC to sit on the Board of Governors for Douglas College; is currently an advisor to U. of Calgary and Douglas College for their Disability Studies Degree Program; contracted by the province of BC to assess their Strategy for the Coordination of Disability Issues and co-wrote a report for the Minister of Advanced Education, Training and Technology. **OTHER:** co-founder of *The Afro News* newspaper; has been the subject of many local and national newspaper articles, and has been a guest on several radio and TV programs in Vancouver, such as *The Rafe Mair Show* and *Cross-Cultural*. He is featured in a documentary entitled *Access Challenge*, along with two other persons with disabilities who participated in a wilderness adventure. **AFFIL/MBRSHP:** Competent ToastMaster (CTM); Cdn Professional Speakers Assn.; Int'l Federation of Professional Speakers; Chair, Black Cultural Assn. of BC. **HONS.:** several including: Cert., "for extraordinary antiracism dialogue with youth," Vancouver City-wide Youth Initiative; Community Service Award, True Resolution Lodge; recipient of two awards, for facilitating a series of diversity seminars at Canada Customs and Revenue Agency. **WORKS:** in print and online publications; book, *The Ability Market*, forthcoming. **CONTACT:** roger @walkandroll. com

▶**JOSEPH, Richard (Rick)**
EXECUTIVE DIRECTOR, NS Environmental Industry Association, Ste. 206-2, 1 Research Dr., Dartmouth, NS B2Y 4M9. Born: Saint John, NB.
▶ Rick Joseph is the Executive Director of the Nova Scotia Environmental Industry Association, a province-wide business organization whose purpose is to promote environmental products and services, and contribute to sustainable development in the province. Since beginning his mandate in 2000, the Association has hosted a number of international conferences and workshops; these have raised the profile of the industry, locally, nationally and internationally. Earlier in his career, RJ was Executive Assistant to the Min. of Environment for NS, 1993-98; was the Executive Director of the Black United Front, 1985-87; was the first Personnel Manager in the Provincial Government of NS with the Dept. of Mines and Energy, 1978-81, and, from 1963-74, was a member of the RCAF/CF as a member of the Royal Canadian Navy. **EDUCATION:** Dipl., Marketing & Int'l Business, 2000; BA, 1977, Saint Mary's University. Dipl. Adult Ed, St. Francis Xavier U., NS, 1995. **HEROES/ROLE MODELS:** Dr. Bridglal Pachai, professor/friend; Les Brown, author/motivational speaker. **MOTTO:** If it is to be, it is up to me. **CONTACT:** linric.joseph@ns.sympatico.ca; Fax: 902-466-6889

▶**JOYETTE, Anthony**
PAINTER/WRITER, Montreal, QC. Born: St. Vincent/ in Canada since: 1976.
▶ Anthony Joyette is a visual artist and writer, originally from St. Vincent, who has lived and worked in Montreal since 1976. He maintains a multidisciplinary practice in painting, drawing, writing and publishing; the common thread throughout his work is that of a shared Black Canadian vision. He is the founder of the Canadian League of Black Artists Inc. and current editor of *Cacique*, a Black Canadian art and culture magazine; member of the Quebec Writers' Federation; and, one of the founders and a former editor of *KOLA*, a Black literary and cultural journal. He expanded his artistic expression to include writing when he realized that the general public in Canada was largely unaware of the presence of Black artists and the value of their work. His paintings have appeared on the covers of several Cdn books; he has exhibited his paintings in cities throughout N. and S. America, and his work can be found in private collections in N. America and the Caribbean. **HONS.:** several including, Cert. of recognition, Organization of American States, 1997; World of Poetry Award, 1990; Cert. of achievement, McDonald's & the

Int'l Freelance Photography Org., 1990; Quebec Black Community Award, for painting & visual arts, 1977 & '78. **WORKS:** in, *KOLA; Cacique; Black Body: Race, Resistance, Response,* 2001; ed., *Vincentian Poets 1950-1980,* 1990; collection of poems, *The Germination of Feeling,* 1980. **REVIEWED IN:** local and community publications; *A Black Canadian Bibliography,* 2001. **EDUCATION:** Collège Marie-Victorin; Concordia U. **MOTTO:** Aim for the stars but if you don't make it, at least you'll land on the moon. **CONTACT:** ajoyette@aol.com

▶**JULIEN, Stanley J.**

VICE-PRESIDENT, BMO Nesbitt Burns, First Canadian Place, 24th Fl, Toronto, ON M5X 1A1. Born: Trinidad & Tobago/ in Canada since: 1972.
▶ Stanley Julien joined the Bank of Montreal (BMO) in 1994 and is currently VP of Asset Portfolio Management at BMO Nesbitt Burns, the investment banking arm of the BMO. His career in Finance began in 1988 with the CNR as a junior tax analyst; he then worked with the Ontario Financing Authority, under the Ont. Min. of Finance, in a variety of positions, the last being as a Policy Analyst, Corporate Finance, 1990-94. After joining the bank in 1994, as a Commercial Banking Officer, he was promoted to Director, Special Accounts Management Unit. In this capacity he was successful in restructuring several accounts and returning them to performing status. **AFFIL/MBRSHP:** is active in the community and provides mentoring support to junior colleagues in the banking sector, he is also co-founder of the Nat'l Assn. of Urban Bankers (NAUB), Toronto Chapter, 1997, and past-President, 1999. This group, which has its HQ in the US, was formed to provide support and mentoring to those interested in a career in the financial services sector, particularly those of ethnoculturally diverse origins. NAUB has since been renamed the Urban Financial Services Coalition (UFSC), to include all who work in the Financial Services sector. SJ is also the past-Chair of the International Strategy Committee, NAUB/UFSC, 2000-01. **EDUCATION:** MBA, Dalhousie U., 2002; B.Comm, Concordia U., 1988. **MOTTO:** Anything is possible! **CONTACT:** stanley.julien@bmo.com; Tel: 416-867-6378

▶**JUMELLE, Yolène**

SOCIOLOGUE ET JURISTE, Tribunal Administratif du Québec, 500, boul. René Lévesque O., Montréal, QC H2Z 1W7. Née: Haïti/ au Canada depuis: 1971.
▶ Mme Yolène Jumelle est Membre, Tribunal administratif du Québec; Professeur invitée à la Faculté de droit, Cours de droit international, 1999; Faculté de droit, de l'U. du Rwanda, (1998) suivi des finissants en droit; cours de droit international privé. **D'AUTRES ACTIVITÉS:** 1989-96, Commissaire, Commission de l'Immigration et du Statut de Réfugie; 1976-89, Agent de relations humaines, Travailleuse sociale, Centre des Services Sociaux du Montréal; 1975-76, Professeur, CEGEP du Vieux Montréal; 1971-73, Co-fondatrice, Maison d'Haïti et Responsable des services aux immigrants et futurs immigrants; 1968-70, Journaliste, réalisatrice, et animatrice, Radio Port-au-Prince. **VIE ASSOCIATIVE:** Centre de recherche action sur les relations raciales; YMCA & YWCA; Comité Femmes de Centraide; participante à une série télévisée sur les femmes et les études féministes; Congrès des Femmes Noires (présidente, 1988-89; vice-présidente, 1984-88); co-fondatrice de la Maison des Jeunes de l'Ouverture, 1981-93 (la seule maison à caractère ethnique au Québec); co-fondatrice du journal *Haïti-Presse* à Montréal où elle a aidé à amener des journalistes de race noires sur les écrans; invitée à plusieurs reprises à Radio-Canada sur des sujets concernant Droits humains et l'inter culturalisme. **PRIX:** y compris: Citoyenne d'honneur de la Ville de Mtl, 1997; Prix Jackie Robinson, *Professional Person of the Year,* MABBP, 1991; 1989-1998, honorée par La Mai-

son d'Haïti, Maison des Jeunes de l'Ouverture, Congrès des Femmes Noires du Canada, Femmes d'Affaires de la Chambre de Commerce de Montréal. **ŒUVRES:** présentations: « Femmes noires et féministes »; « L'héritage noir au Canada »; « Femmes de couleur et média »; « Place des femmes de couleur dans le mouvement féministe. » **FORMATION:** LLB, 1983; Maîtrise, Sociologie, 1976, UQAM. Scolarité de doctorat, 1979; Bac, Service Social, 1973, U. de Montréal. **CONTACT:** jumyol@hotmail.com; Fax: 514-486-5210

▶**JUNOR, Kevin R.,** CWO.
REGIMENTAL SERGEANT-MAJOR (RSM), Canadian Forces, Toronto Scottish Regiment, Toronto, ON. Born: England, 1963/ in Canada since: 1973.
▶ CWO Kevin Junor joined the Canadian Forces (CF) in 1980, as an infantry soldier in the Toronto Scottish Regiment (formerly, The Queen Mother's own); since 1998, he has been promoted to the rank of CWO and appointed to the position of Regimental Sergeant-Major. He is possibly one of the youngest to achieve the rank of CWO and RSM, by age 35. He participated in the Queen Mother's 90th and 100th birthday celebrations in England, Scotland, and Canada, as well as her funeral (April 9, 2002). He was the first Black to be appointed RSM for the Land Force Central Area infantry training exercise conducted in Kentucky, 1999. In civilian life he works with the Ont. Min. of Transportation (MTO), and was, until early 2001, a strategic policy advisor, responsible for completing environmental scans of various transportation initiatives and advising the Minister and senior officials on policy decisions. He has since moved to the position of Learning and Development Consultant, where he designs training programs for Ministry staff to enhance their service-delivery capabilities. **COMMUNITY:** he is an ordained minister and Associate Pastor, New Way Community Church; is National co-chair, Defense Visible Minority Advisory Group; and, is involved with communi-

ty groups including the United Way. **HONS.:** including, CF Decoration, 1992; Best Junior Non-Commissioned Officer, 1982. **WORKS:** including, *The road to eternal life*, 1987; *QEW Commercial Vehicle Road Survey*, 1992; *Windsor-Sarnia Commercial Vehicle Road Survey*, 1992. **REVIEWED IN:** articles in military publications & newsletters; *Can Monarchist News*; *Toronto Star*; *Jamaica Gleaner*; *Scottish Regimental J.* **EDUCATION:** B.Theology, International U. of Biblical Study, 1991; Civil Engineering Technician, Seneca College, 1984. **HEROES/ROLE MODELS:** CWO Jim Fraser, 1st Black Area CWO for Land Force Central Area; MWO Wade McNaughton; Rev. R.W. Davy, Bishop, Pentecostal Church. **MOTTO:** Challenges and obstacles are only opportunities for growth. **CONTACT:** kevin.junor@mto.gov.on.ca; Junor.KR@Forces.ca; Fax: 416-235-4255

▶**KABUNDI, Marcel, LLM.**

**GESTIONNAIRE, PROGRAMMES ETHNOCULTU-
RELS,** Programmes de Réinsertion sociale, Service correctionnel du Canada, Ministère du Solliciteur Général du Canada, 8ᵉ étage, Section F, 340, av Laurier ouest, Ottawa, ON K1A 0P9. Né: République Dém. du Congo (ex-Zaïre)/ au Canada depuis: 1984.

▶ Marcel Kabundi est Gestionnaire national des programmes pour les minorités ethnoculturelles délinquantes au Service correctionnel du Canada. Il enseigne également le droit correctionnel à la section de Droit Civil de la Faculté de Droit, U. d'Ottawa. Avant de venir au Canada, il était magistrat en Rép. Démocratique du Congo ainsi que professeur de droit. Il est aussi auteur et, pendant plus de trois ans, il a conçu et produit une émission de télévision communautaire sur la chaîne 3 à Ottawa-Hull, *Focus sur l'Afrique*. **AFFIL/MBRSHP:** membre, National Association of Blacks in Criminal Justice (USA); membre de l'association internationale des criminologues francophones (Genève); fut membre du Conseil des communautés culturelles et de l'immigration du Québec; Conseil des relations interculturelles du Québec, premier noir d'être élu Gouverneur au Conseil des Gouverneurs de la Société canadienne de la Croix Rouge; président de la Fondation internationale des amis de l'Afrique. Il est aussi formateur national de l'Alliance de la Fonction Publique du Canada et président de la section local du syndicat des employés du Solliciteur général du Canada. **ŒUVRES:** plusieurs articles scientifiques et livres dont: *L'Afrique sans masque; Se protéger contre le vol; Réussir sa réinsertion sociale; Successful Community Reintegration (*Collectif*); Communautés culturelles et justice.* Il collabore actuellement à la rédaction d'un dictionnaire critique de sciences criminelles. **FORMATION:** en cours, LLD; LLM, U. d'Ottawa. MSc en Criminologie, U. de Montréal; LLL, U. de Kinshasa. **MENTORS:** André Normandeau, Ph.D, criminologue et professeur émeritus, U. de Montréal. **MOTTO:** La vie est un combat de tous les instants. **CONTACT:** kabundim@istar.ca; Fax: 613-996-0428

▶**KACELENGA, Ray, PhD.**

PRINCIPAL ENGINEER, General Dynamics Canada, 102-68ᵗʰ Ave. NE, Calgary, AB T2E 8P2. Born: Zimbabwe/ in Canada since: 1988.

▶ Dr. Ray Kacelenga has been a member of the Landmine Detection Systems Group at General Dynamics Canada (GD Canada) since 1997, where he is the principal engineer responsible for the design of multiple-sensor data fusion and target-tracking algorithms for the detection of buried landmines. The landmine detection sensors, which include a Minimum Metal Detector array, a Ground Penetrating Radar array, a Forward Looking Infrared camera, and a Thermal Neutron Activation sensor, are mounted on a low ground pressure and remotely controlled vehicle. RK is responsible for directing the design and integration of inertial navigation algorithms for the mine detection vehicle. The remotely controlled mine detection system is the world's first in production and four systems were delivered to the Cdn Dept. of National Defence in early 2002. While at GD Canada, RK has conducted data fusion R&D for the US Army Communications Electronics Command and for the UK Min. of Defence, and currently leads the company's R&D effort into alternative statistical data fusion and automatic target detection algorithms. **BACKGROUND:** prior to coming to Canada and after completing his studies in the UK, RK was a lecturer at the University of Malawi, 1985-88, where he taught analog and digital electronics and microprocessor technology courses; in graduate school, at the University of Calgary, he conducted research into Simulated Annealing and Genetic optimization algorithms for the design of finite-precision digital filter structures for use in the communications and bio-medical industries. From 1994-97, he taught Digital Signal Processing, Control Systems theory, and mathematics courses at the Calgary Devry Institute of Technology. **WORKS:** selected non-classified publications include: *Voting Fusion Adaptation for Landmine Detection,* 5th Int'l Conference on Information Fusion, July 2002; from SPIE's 16th Annual Int'l Symposium on Aerospace/Defense Sensing, Simulation, and Controls, 2002: "Bayesian Approach to Sensor Fusion in a Multisensor Landmine Detection System"; "Detection and Classification of Landmine Targets in Ground Penetrating Radar Images"; "Target Tracking for Landmine Detection." "Improved Landmine Detection System for the Cdn Army," 31st European Microwave Conf., 2001; "Data Fusion in a Multi-Sensor Mine Detection System," 2nd Int'l Conf. Information Fusion, 1999; Digital Filter Architecture Design, PhD thesis, U. of Calgary, 1995. **EDUCATION:** PhD, Electrical & Computer Engineering, 1995; MSc, Electrical Engineering, 1990, U. of Calgary. MSc, Electronics, U. of London, UK, 1984; BSc/Hons., Electrical & Electronic Engineering, Huddersfield U., UK, 1983. **MOTTO:** One step at a time. **CONTACT:** ray.kacelenga@gdcanada.com

▶**KADIRI, Yahaya Z., MD, FRCPC.**
ANAESTHESIOLOGIST/INTERNIST, Southlake Regional Health Centre, 596 Davis Dr., Newmarket, ON L3Y 2P9. Born: Nigeria/ in Canada since: 1974.
▶ Dr. Yahaya Kadiri has been an anaesthesiologist since 1977, and since 1979, has been on staff at the Southlake Regional Health Centre (former York County Hospital) in Newmarket. **CAREER:** he began his medical training in Nigeria; completed his Anaesthesia Residency at University of Toronto hospitals, 1977; completed his Research/Intensive Care Training at St. Michael's Hospital, 1978; was on staff at Toronto General Hospital, 1978-79; from 1986-91, he was Chief, Dept. of Anaesthesia, and also Co-Director, Intensive Care Unit, 1986-88, then

Director, Intensive Care Unit, 1988-91. **HONS.:** including several academic awards, 1971-78. **EDUCATION:** Fellow, RCPC, 1977; Fellow, American College of Anaesthesiology, 1978; Diplomate, American Board of Anaesthesiology, 1978; Intensive Care Training, St. Michael's Hospital, Toronto, 1978; Anaesthesia Residency, U of T Hospitals, 1977; Anaesthesia Training, University College Hospital, Ibadan, Nigeria, 1973; MB BS/Hons., U. of Ibadan, 1971. **MOTTO:** Always put yourself where God has put you; if you don't, you devalue yourself. **CONTACT:** yzkadiri@rogers.com; Fax: 905-508-4631

▶**KAFELE, Paul Kwasi**
DIRECTOR, Corporate Diversity, Centre for Addiction & Mental Health (CAMH), 33 Russell St., Toronto, ON M5S 2S2. Born: Jamaica/ in Canada since: 1978.
▶ Paul Kwasi Kafele has worked, taught, and volunteered for over 20 yrs. in Toronto in the areas of equity, diversity, human rights, strategic planning, organizational development, and community development. Currently, he is the Director of Corporate Diversity at CAMH, the largest mental health and addiction facility in Canada. Prior to joining CAMH, he was executive director of the JCA and the Black Secretariat; he also worked with the Anti-Racism Secretariat at the Ont. Min. of Citizenship and Culture. **COMMUNITY:** United Way; Community Social Planning Council of Toronto; Scarborough Conflict Resolution Services; African FoodBasket; African Canadian Cultural Collective. He has focused much of his community work on youth and social justice issues; is a founding member of the Black Action Defense Committee, and Ujamaa Young Peoples' Assn. **OTHER:** has written on cross-cultural counselling, community development and youth leadership; he is currently writing a book on eldership in the African Canadian community; is a published poet who performs regularly. **HONS.:** many community awards for his work in the field

of equity and human rights. **WORKS:** including, three training manuals in the *Progressive Paradigms* series. **EDUCATION:** completing MES in African Healing Therapies, York U.; studied Poli. Sci. & Economics, U of T. **HEROES/ROLE MODELS:** Malcom X; Winnie Mandela; Mutabaruka, poet/activist. **CONTACT:** paul_kafele@camh.net; Fax: 416-595-9997

▶**KAKEMBO, Patrick N., PhD.**
DIRECTOR, African Canadian Services, NS Dept. of Education, 2021 Brunswick St., PO Box 578, Halifax, NS. Born: Uganda/ in Canada since: 1985.
▶ Dr. Patrick Kakembo has been the Director of African Canadian Services, since 1999. Previously he was Assistant Director, 1996-99, and directed research for the Black Learners Advisory Committee's (BLAC) landmark *BLAC Report on Education*, 1992-94. This report delineated the obstacles to equality for African-Canadian students and resulted in significant changes in the way the NS school system deals with African-Canadian students and their needs, from pre-school through to adult education. **WORKS:** "The Emergence of the Black Learners Advisory Committee in NS." **REVIEWED IN:** *African-Canadians in Nova Scotia: 300 Years of Mistrust.* **EDUCATION:** MPA(M), 2002; PhD, 1989, Dalhousie University. BA/Hons., Makerere U., Uganda, 1982. **HEROES/ROLE MODELS:** Vincent D'Oyley; Brad Barton; Robert Upshaw. **MOTTO:** Always aim for the moon; even if you miss you'll land among the stars. **CONTACT:** kakembpn@ gov.ns.ca; Fax: 902-424-7210

➤**KASSIM, Ola A., MD, FRCPC, FCAP.**
PATHOLOGIST-IN-CHIEF & DIRECTOR OF LABORATORY SERVICES, West Parry Sound Health Care Services, 10 James St., Parry Sound, ON P2A 1T3. Born: Nigeria/ in Canada since: 1977.

▶ Dr. Ola Kassim has been the Regional Forensic Pathologist for the Districts of Parry Sound-Muskoka and N. Simcoe, since 1985. He is also the Chief of Pathology and Director of Laboratory Services and the Duty Physician at the Whitby Psychiatric Hospital. From 1983-85, he was a Lecturer in the Dept. of Pathology, Faculty of Medicine, U of T; was also Associate Staff Pathologist at Sunnybrook Medical Centre, 1983-84. **AFFIL/MBRSHP:** Society of N. Ontario Pathologists. **COMMUNITY:** BBPA; Yoruba Cultural and Heritage Assn.; Rotary Club/Richmond Hill; Assn. of Nigerians. **HONS.:** Metro Toronto Civic Award, 2000; Academic Excellence, Nigerian Cdn Assn., 1999; Leadership Award, Cultural Assn., 1996, '97; Community Leadership, Yoruba Cultural Assn., 1996, '98. **WORKS:** selected co-authored articles include: "Myocardial Infarction in Utero"; "Harmatoma of the Larynx"; "Ovarian carcinoid tumour with massive retroperitoneal fibrosis." **EDUCATION:** Fellow, American College of Pathologists, 1983; M.Public Admin., Queen's U., 1999; MD, Faculty of Medicine, U of T, 1981; BSc, MB, U. of Ibadan, 1975. **CONTACT:** okquincy @aol.com; Fax: 905-746-9584

▶**KAVANAGH, Anthony**
ARTISTE/SHOWMAN, s/c L. Gosselin, Agent/ Soulman Productions, 1570, Croisssant Seville, Brossard, QC J4X 1J4. Né: Montréal, QC, 1969.
▶ Comédien québécois, d'origine haïtienne, Anthony Kavanagh a connu un succès immense en France. À l'âge de 20 ans, en 1989, un prix des *Auditions Nationales Juste pour Rire* démarre sa carrière. Il participe durant un an aux *Midis Fous de CKOI* et devient collaborateur régulier à l'émission *Cent Limites*. Il devient tour à tour: comédien dans la série télévisée, « *Super sans plomb* » et dans une série américaine *Voodootaxi* de CBC, animateur de son propre talk-show « *...et Anthony* », membre régulier du circuit des *Lundis Juste pour rire*. Il était la révélation du Festival Juste pour rire en 1992. Il devient porte-

parole du programme *Jeunes pour rire*, et de nombreuses prestations tant sur les scènes extérieures qu'aux Galas du Festival Juste pour rire à Montréal et en Floride, porte-parole dans le cadre du même festival pour les sites extérieurs en 1994. À l'occasion des célébrations du 350ème anniversaire de Montréal, il était maître de cérémonie du *MusicHall*. Il accompagne Céline Dion dans deux tournées pan canadiennes. Une prestation sur la scène de *l'Apollo Theatre*, des présences dans les *comedy clubs* New-Yorkais le voit briller. Il fut choisi parmi 600 comédiens anglophones pour une série sur le réseau ABC, où il assura la première partie de Julio Iglesias et Natalie Cole; Festival d'humour de Montreux, 1995, et prestations en 1996 et 1997, la première partie de Céline Dion à Bercy et au Zénith de Paris; participation au Festival d'humour de Cologne en Allemagne, prestation à une émission spéciale suisse-allemande; invité à l'émission française « *Ça se discute* » TV5, gagnant du *Grand Jeu dictionnaire* à Bruxelles, participation à l'émission française, « *La fureur* » en compagnie de Johnny Hallyday; doublage de la voix d'Eddy Murphy pour le film d'animation *Mulan* de Walt Disney. En 1995, il initie son *one man show*, « *Kavanagh!* » qui l'a amené en France, d'abord à Lyon en 1998 et, fort de ce succès, le spectacle traverse ensuite le pays. Pendant sept mois il était à l'affiche du Théâtre Trévise à Paris et en 1999, il a joué à l'Olympia de Paris. Depuis, il est apparu à la télévision à maintes reprises; il a animé en direct sur TF1 les *NRJ Music Awards* en 2001 et en 2002. **AUTRES:** en plus de ses activités artistiques, il appuie des causes sociales telles que, La Marche du Club 2/3, fondation destinée à récolter des fonds en faveur des pays du tiers-monde; l'International Juste pour jeunes; la Fondation Diane Hébert pour le don d'organes, en 1997; et la Fondation Québécoise de la Migraine et des Céphalées en 1996. **ŒUVRES:** participe aux Editions Michel Lafon en qualité de Directeur de Collection; a écrit la préface du livre, *Si la vie est un jeu, en voici les règles* (de Cherie Carter Wright). **CONTACT:** cat@dconseils.com; www.anthony-kavanagh.com

▶ **KAWUKI-MUKASA, Rev. Isaac**
CONGREGATIONAL DEVELOPMENT CONSULTANT, The Anglican Diocese of Toronto, 135 Adelaide St. E., Toronto, ON M5C 1L8. Born: Uganda/ in Canada since: 1987.

▶ Rev. Kawuki-Mukasa is a consultant with The Anglican Diocese of Toronto, and responsible for program and congregational development. He describes his greatest contribution to the Anglican and United Churches in Canada as "helping to raise consciousness about the dimension of cultural racism in the two institutions." His work with the two has focused on promoting the values and wisdom of racial and ethnic minority groups and incorporating this knowledge arising from their experiences into the Church's life. Towards these goals, he writes (see below) and works with churches in the community; co-founded Uganda Martyrs Church of Canada; provided conflict resolution at a Tamil Anglican Church; has produced pedagogical resources for congregations; was program officer in Congregational Mission at the United Ethnic Ministries Council, 1996-2000; founded By Faith Sojourners' Network, an ecumenical network of Churches of people of African descent in Canada; was an instructor at the Centre for Christian Studies, 1992-95; served at Anglican-United Church in N. Manitoba, 1988-92. **VOLUNTEER ACTIVITIES:** Minister, Uganda Martyrs Church, since 1993; past VP and President of the Uganda N. American Assn. **WORKS:** in, *Toronto J Theology; Touchstone; Studies in Religion; The Clergy J.* Books: *Sojourner: Finding Faith Beyond Hope*, 2001; *In God's Presence*, 2000. **EDUCATION:** PhD candidate, Systematic Theology, Emmanuel College; MA, Religious Studies, U. of Zimbabwe, 1987; M.Div, Nairobi School of Theology, Kenya, 1984; BA/Hons., Makerere U., Uganda, 1980. **CONTACT:** mimukasa@sprint.ca

►KEENS-DOUGLAS, Richard
ACTOR/WRITER/DIRECTOR/STORYTELLER, c/o Core Group, Ste. 507-3 Church St., Toronto, ON M5E 1M2. Born: Grenada.

▶ Richard Keens-Douglas is a multi-talented writer/performer whose musical play *The Nutmeg Princess*, based on his book of the same title, won the Dora Mavor Moore Award for Outstanding New Musical, in 1999. He achieved national recognition in 1991-94 as the host of CBC Radio's storytelling talk show, *Cloud 9*. In this role he was the first Black to have his own network-wide program on CBC radio. He was also host of the CBC TV show, *Sunday Arts Entertainment*, for which he received a 1996 Gemini Award nomination for Best Host in an Arts Program. In the realm of theatre, his range includes drama, dance, comedy and musicals. He has performed in Canada, the US and the Caribbean, on stages such as Stratford, St. Lawrence Centre, and The Apollo. **THEATRE CREDITS:** *Candide; Ain't Misbehavin'; Sophisticated Ladies; The Threepenny Opera; Guys and Dolls; Smile Orange; Twelfth Night;* and, *Measure for Measure*. He wrote and starred in the play, *The Obeah Man,* 1985, and was nominated for a Dora Mavor Moore Award as Best Actor in a Musical. He has also had leading roles in films such as: *Zero Patience; Fields of Endless Day; Dance to Remember;* and has appeared in many radio dramas such as the solo reading of Cecil Foster's *No Man in the House,* for CBC Radio. **OTHER:** as a storyteller, RKD has performed across Canada, the US, the Caribbean and at international festivals; in 1991, he performed for Prince Charles and Princess Diana aboard the HMS Brittania. He is also the award-winning author of eight children's books, many of which have been translated into French, Spanish and Chinese. For a five-year period, RKD was the resident choreographer for the Children's Theatre of Montreal. As of 2002, he is the host of the new TV show, the Caribbean-version of *Who Wants to be a Millionaire*, which is to be broadcast throughout the Caribbean. He also delivers workshops at conferences around the world for teachers and students on self-esteem and the magic within. **HONS.:** several including, Dora Mavor Moore Award, for Outstanding New Musical (*Nutmeg Princess*), 1999; Sterling Award nominee for Best Touring Production for, *Once Upon an Island*, 1991. **WORKS:** selected: *The Nutmeg Princess; La Diablesse and the Baby; Freedom Child of the Sea; Anancy and the Haunted House; Mama God, Papa God; The Obeah Man.* **EDUCATION:** Dawson Professional Theatre School, Montreal; additional studies for mime, song, & dance in NY and the Caribbean. **CONTACT:** rkd38 @hotmail.com

►KEFENTSE, Dayo
JOURNALIST, CBC Radio, 205 Wellington St. W., Toronto, ON M5V 3G7. Born: Toronto, ON, 1974.

▶ Dayo Kefentse, in preparing to become a journalist, did what most would not consider: after graduating as an Ontario Scholar with a French Immersion Diploma, in 1993, she went to the Cave Hill Campus of UWI, in Barbados, to earn her BA. While completing subsequent studies at Humber College, she joined the Cdn Assn. of Black Journalists (CABJ), where she created the CABJ Mentorship Program, designed to assist Black students achieve excellence in the media. She spent three years hosting a talk show, The Cutting Edge, on CHRY Radio, 1997-2000; also in 1997, she joined Broadcast News, Canada's national radio news agency, as an audio editor. In 1999, she received an internship at CBC Radio as part of their New Voices Initiative; during the course of the internship, she was hired and promoted to the position of associate producer. Currently she is a reporter/editor, working primarily for CBC Radio's Metro Morning, both on-air and behind the scenes. **HONS.:** include: Best Print Feature, Cdn Ethnic Journalists & Writers Club

Award, 2000; Young Entrepreneur & Recognition Award, Black Enterprise Network, 1999. **WORKS:** articles/features: CBC Radio; Toronto Star; Pride. **EDUCATION:** Cert., Radio Broadcasting, Humber College, 1997; BA/Hons., UWI, Barbados, 1996. **HEROES/ROLE MODELS:** Fil Fraser; Avril Benoit, broadcaster. **MOTTO:** Love, and be grateful for life. **CONTACT:** dayo_kefentse@cbc.ca; dayo74@hotmail.com; Fax: 416-205-6336

▶**KELLY, Jude**
BROADCASTER/PUBLICIST, Versatile Communications. **WRITER,** Ontario Ministry of Public Safety and Security, 25 Grosvenor St., Toronto, ON. Born: USA/ in Canada since: 1962.

▶ Jude Kelly is active in the urban music scene throughout Canada. He is the former publisher/editor of *Glory* magazine; VP and Publicity Director, Urban Music Assn. of Canada; is a freelance contributor for CBC Radio; and, is President, Versatile Communications, an entertainment and music public relations firm, whose clients have included UMAC, Get Reel Film Festival, Reel Black Awards, and SOF Art House. **HONS.:** Hall of Fame, Brandon U., for men's basketball, 1999; Best Sports Story, Saskatchewan Reporters' Assn., 1985. **WORKS:** articles in most national newspapers, *Chart; Word; Your Time* magazines; urban music contributor for CBC Radio; web writer for *Umbrella Music*. **EDUCATION:** B.General Studies, Brandon U., 1983; Journalism, Grant MacEwan Community College, AB. **MOTTO:** Everything comes to he who hustles while he waits… **CONTACT:** sirjude@sympatico.ca

▶**KELLY, Paulette**
ASSOCIATE PROFESSOR, School of Fashion, Ryerson University, 350 Victoria St., Toronto, ON M5B 2K3. Born: USA/ in Canada since: 1975.

▶ Paulette Kelly has been teaching Industrial Pattern-making and Garment Construction in the

School of Fashion at Ryerson University, since 1975. Her research interests include ethnic clothing and clothing for people with special needs. Her students are consistent winners in provincial, national, and international design competitions, often garnering prizes in Men's Sportswear, Futuristic Design, International Young Designer, and Most Promising New Designer. **AFFIL/MBRSHP:** National Technical Committee, Women's Apparel Design, Skills Canada Competition; Chair, Technical Committee, Women's Apparel Design, Ont. Technological Skills Competition; past-President and Director of Community Services, Sunshine Club of Kiwanis International. **HONS.:** 25-yr. Club Award, Ryerson U., 2000. **WORKS:** forthcoming, a pamphlet on clothing preferences for people with Multiple Sclerosis and related illnesses, 2003. **EDUCATION:** MA, Clothing & Textiles, U. of Connecticut, 1975; BS, Vocational-Industrial Education, Central Connecticut State College, 1973; Assoc. in Applied Science Degree, Fashion Institute of Technology, NY, 1965. **CONTACT:** p2kelly@ryerson.ca

▶**KHENTI, Akwatu**
DIRECTOR, Education & Training Services, Centre for Addiction & Mental Health (CAMH), 33 Russell St., Toronto, ON M5S 2S1. Born: Trinidad & Tobago/ in Canada since: 1970.

▶ Akwatu Khenti has been an educator, front-line worker, and administrator for community-oriented initiatives. Currently he is the Director of Education and Training Services at CAMH, with responsibilities for planning and organizing a wide range of continuing professional education activities across the province and the country. **CAREER HIGHLIGHTS:** is credited with developing and managing a drug treatment program for youth, SAPACCY, based on Afrocentric principles, health promotion and prevention; community worker and executive director for the JCA; managed a joint national project entitled, Facilitating the Academic Success of Black Children in Canada; has been a researcher/writer with the North York Brd. of Education; developed and taught two 12-part courses on the Black Experience to educators in the Toronto and NY Brds. of Education. And, as a human rights activist, he developed the African Relief Committee in Canada (AFRIC), which raised awareness of the situation in southern Sudan. **WORKS:** including, "The History of Racism in Canada," in *Perspectives on Racism and the Human Services Sector*, 1995; booklet, *African Canadian Heritage in Historical Perspective*, North York Brd. of Education. **REVIEWED IN:** *Toronto Life; West Africa* magazine. **EDUCATION:** MA, Poli. Sci., U of T, 1988. **HEROES/ROLE MODELS:** Cheikh Anta Diop. **MOTTO:** Let earth and sky be your yardstick and eternity your measurement. (Marcus Garvey) **CONTACT:** bkbaya@netzero.net; Fax: 416-281-6041

►KIBUUKA, David

ARTIST, Oakville, ON. Born: Uganda/ in Canada since: 1983.

▶ David Kibuuka is a painter, originally from Uganda, who has been practising his craft since his childhood. His early education in art was influenced by his older brother, Henry Lumu, who introduced him to works by masters of traditional and contemporary Western art and whose techniques he began copying and combining with traditional African styles and images. In the 1970s, to avoid the political instability in Uganda, he spent six years studying art in Kenya, and there, began using the Maasai tribe as a favorite subject for his early works, executed in High Renaissance-styled realism. He was also exposed to the more modern Western styles of impressionism and surrealism, which have come to infuse his work. Although he is equally fluent in oils, acrylics, watercolors, pencil, and mixed media, his preference is acrylics. His works have been exhibited internationally and are found in public and private collections. **CONTACT:** lumu@kibuuka.com; www.kibuuka.com

►KILLINGBECK, Molly

ATHLETE SERVICES MANAGER/COACH, Canadian Sport Centre Ontario, Ste. 606A-1185 Eglinton Ave. E., Toronto, ON M3C 3C6. Born: Jamaica/ in Canada since: 1972.

▶ Molly Killingbeck is a three-time Olympian and multiple-medal-winning athlete who competed in 400m, 4x100m and 4x400m relays; since 1989, she has successfully moved into coaching. Her sports history includes the following: Cdn Olympic Team, 1980, 1984 (Silver Medal, 4x400m relay), 1988; Pan Am Games, 1983, 1987 (Silver Medal, 4x100m and 4x400m); Commonwealth Games, 1982 (Gold Medal, 4x400m), 1986 (Gold Medal, 4x400m, Silver Medal, 4x100m); World University Games, 1983 (Silver Medal, 400m, 4x100m, 4x400m), 1985 (Silver Medal, 4x400m). Since 1989, she has become increasingly involved in coaching and has now coached at all levels: Olympics, World Championships, Commonwealth Games, World University Games, and the Francophone Games. She successfully coached the men's 4x100m relay team (Esmie, Gilbert, Surin, and Bailey) to a Gold Medal at the 1996 Olympics in Atlanta. **OTHER:** former member of Toronto 2008 Olympic Bid team; motivational speaker through Athletes Motivating Excellence. Currently she is the Athlete Services Manager with the Canadian Sport Centre Ontario, in Toronto. **AFFIL/MBRSHP:** Commonwealth Games Canada; Athletics Canada Fdn.; ProAction (police helping children). **HONS.:** several including: Inductee, York U. Sports Hall of Fame, 2001; Merit Award, IAAF, 1998; Coaching Excellence Award, Coaching Assn. Canada, 1996; Ontario University–Coach of the Year, 1992, '94, '96; Sport Excellence Award, Govt. Ontario, 1980-89; Sport Excellence Awards, Govt. Canada, 1983, '85, '87; Cdn University–Athlete of the Year, , 1984, '85; Harry Jerome Award, 1984. **EDUCATION:** completing level IV of NCCP; BA, York U., 1986. **HEROES/ROLE MODELS:** Margie Schuett; Alex Gardiner;

Lynette Liburd. **MOTTO:** Find a way…to achieve! **CONTACT:** mollyk@cscontario.ca; www.cscontario.ca

▶**KING, Karen**
FILM PRODUCER, Special Mandate Team–Cultural Diversity, National Film Board of Canada (NFB), 150 John St., Toronto, ON M5V 3C3. Born: Trinidad & Tobago/ in Canada since: 1965.
▶ Karen King is a film producer and member of the NFB's Special Mandate Team for Cultural Diversity. She initiated the creation of the Reel Diversity Short Film Competition. **FILM CREDITS:** include, *Bollywood Bound*, chosen as Closing Night Film at *Hot Docs* film festival, 2002 and recipient of critical acclaim in NY, LA, and New Delhi (the film looks at actors returning to India in the hopes of succeeding in the film industry); *Raisin' Kane: A Rapumentary* (2001), looks at Canada's hip hop culture and won the HBO Documentary Prize at UrbanWorld Film Festival in New York; the Gemini Award-winning *Unwanted Soldiers* (1999), which tells the stories of Chinese-Canadian soldiers in WW I & II. Her most recent productions include *Film Club* (2000), a look at Trudeau's multicultural mosaic through the children affected; *Journey to Justice* (2001), which pays tribute to Black Canadians who challenged racist policies; *Some Kind of Arrangement* (1998), looks at arranged marriages among young Indo-Canadians; and, *Black, Bold, and Beautiful* (1999), looking at Black (people's) hair. Prior to joining the NFB, KK produced commercials, short films and the first Black full-length feature film, *Rude*, by Clement Virgo (*see: Virgo, Clement*), becoming the first Black woman to produce a theatrically released feature in Canada. She is the founding vice-president of the Black Film and Video Network (BFVN). **HONS.:** *Raisin' Kane*: Documentary Prize, Reel World Film Festival and UrbanWorld Film Festival, 2001; Best Documentary, for *Journey to Justice*, Reel Black Award. *Unwanted Soldiers*: Canada Award,

Gemini Awards, 2000; Best History Documentary, Hot Docs; Int'l Documentary Festival, 2000; Chris Award, Best Social Issue Documentary, 2000. Special Jury Citation, for *Rude,* TIFF, 1995. **EDUCATION:** BA, SFU; Canadian Film Centre. **HEROES/ROLE MODELS:** Claire Prieto; Cynthia Reyes. **CONTACT:** k.king@nfb.ca; www.nfb.ca

▶**KLAASEN, Lorraine**
SINGER/PERFORMER, Montreal, QC. Born: South Africa/ in Canada since: 1979.
▶ Lorraine Klaasen is a well-known singer and performer who is originally from South Africa, and daughter of the famous Thandie Klaasen, known as the "Ella Fitzgerald of S. Africa." Popular with jazz and African music lovers across N. America, the Caribbean, and Europe, LK sings in several languages, including English, French, Swahili, Zulu, Xhosa, Greek, and Hebrew. She has performed with Patti LaBelle, Roberta Flack, Al Jarreau, Charlie Biddle, Ray Charles, and many others. **HIGHLIGHTS:** her recordings include: *African Connexion*, 2000; *Free at Last*, 1997; *Soweto Groove*, 1988. She has been performing in musical theatre for many years including productions of: *Hair*, 1974; *Black Mikado*, 1976; *Jesus Christ Superstar*, 1976; *Sola Sola*, 1977. She performs regularly at the following: Montreal Int'l Jazz Festival, since 1993; Toronto Beaches Jazz Festival; Harbourfront Festivals; Halifax and PEI Jazz Festivals; as well as Jazz Festivals in Barbados, St. Lucia, Jamaica, and Grenada. She has also been a host on CBC Radio, *In Good Company with Lorraine Klaasen*, 2000, 2001; has appeared in several documentaries on Bravo, Vision TV, and CBC. **OTHER:** she is working on a documentary, *Madiba Legends*, about the lives of five legends of song from S. Africa: Thandie Klaasen, Dolly Rathebe, Dorothy Masuku, Sophie MgCina, and Abigail Kubeka. **HONS.:** include, Outstanding Artist of the Year, Mtl, 1998; Martin Luther King Jr. Award, BTW, 1997; Outstanding Performance Award, Beaches Jazz

Festival, 1996 & 1997; Award for Achievement, Contribution to Culture, Music, and Entertainment, Mtl, 1996. **CONTACT:** lklaasen@aei.ca; www.aei.ca/~lklaasen

▶**KLY, Yussuf, PhD.**
PROFESSOR, POLITICAL SCIENCE, University of Regina, Wascana Dr., Regina, SK S4S 0A2. Born: USA/ in Canada since: 1960.
▶ Dr. Yussuf Kly states, "I have focused my academic and human service efforts towards engendering socio-economic, political, and legal understandings and orientations that may assist the acceptance and societal integration of new concepts, paradigms and intuitions…to peacefully obtain an adequate societal response to present and future global challenges." **CAREER:** he is an invited Law Professor, U. of Durban-Westville, S. Africa, since 2001; International Legal Consultant to the Saskatchewan Dept. of Justice; professor of international law, justice studies, and social policy, at U. of Regina, since 1989; Consultant Professor, National RCMP Academy, 1994-98; also lectured or conducted research at universities and institutes across Canada, in the US, and Algeria. **AFFIL/MBRSHP:** founder and chair, Int'l Human Rights Assn. of American Minorities (IHRAAM)/SK since 1988; since 2000, member, Brd. of Governors, National Institute for Social Work, Orissa, India. **HONS.:** Inspiring Teacher Award, U. of Regina, 2000; Outstanding Book on Human Rights in the US, for *A Popular Guide to Minority Rights*, Gustavus Myers Center, 1995, and for *International Law and the Black Minority in the US*, 1990. **WORKS:** books include: *International Law and the Black Minority in the US*, 1985; *The Anti-Social Contract*, 1979; *Societal Development & Minority Rights*, 1997. Articles in: *The Black Scholar; Can J of Native Studies; NGO Bulletin; Can J of Peace Research; Can Review of Social Policy; Sociology Review*. Occasional Papers: pub. by Social Policy Research Unit, U. of Regina. **EDUCATION:** candidate, LLD,

Int'l Law, U. of Durban-Westville, S. Africa; Hague Academy of Int'l Law, Netherlands; PhD, U. Laval, 1980; DES, U. of Algiers, 1973; MA, U. of Montreal, 1970; BA, U. of Iowa, 1960. **HEROES/ROLE MODELS:** W.E.B. Dubois; Martin Luther King Jr. **CONTACT:** yussuf.kly@uregina.ca; www.ihraam.org

▶**KNIGHTS, Travis**
TAP DANCER/STUDENT, Dollard-des-Ormeaux, QC. Born: Montreal, QC, 1983.
▶ Travis Knights began tap dancing in 1993, at the age of ten, at the Ethel Bruneau Dance Studio, in Montreal (*see: Bruneau, Ethel*). Since then he has won many awards and danced at venues in Canada and the US. **HIGHLIGHTS:** dancing with Gregory Hines at the Montreal International Jazz Festival (1995); appearing in the movie, *Bojangles*, with Gregory Hines and Savion Glover (2000); performing at the half-time show between the Chicago Bulls and the Toronto Raptors (1996); being critiqued by the Tour Choreographer for the Broadway show, *Bring In Da' Noise, Bring In Da' Funk* in NYC (1999); and, winning the Gold Medal for Canada in the International Dance Competition held in Germany (1999). In 2000, he was featured in a CFCF TV documentary about dance, *Variations on a New Generation* in which he represented the art of tap across the country. **OTHER:** TK is a student in the Commerce Program at John Abbott College and aspires to be a film director. **HONS.:** include, The Victor Phillips Scholarship, 2002; Golden Reel Award, 2000; Gold Medal, small group, tap, World Dance Championship, 1999; Artist of the Year, Sound of Blackness Award, 1999; YTV Achievement Awards, Specialty Award–Tap Dance, 1997; Toastmasters Award, Public Speaking, 1996. **REVIEWED IN:** *Montreal Gazette; Chronicle; Spectator; Suburban*. **HEROES/ROLE MODELS:** Parents; Sammy Davis Jr.; Gregory Hines; Savion Glover; Ethel Bruneau. **MOTTO:** My excuses are my own. **CONTACT:** jocelyn.crawley@uhn.on.ca

►KOTASKA, Audrei-Kairen

PLAYWRIGHT/ACTOR/SINGER, c/o Playwrights Union of Canada. Born: USA/ in Canada since: 1991.

▶ Audrei-Kairen Kotaska is a playwright, actor, and singer, originally from the US; she now resides in both Canada and the US. Her most recent work, *Big Mama: The Willie Mae Thornton Story*, was performed at Calgary's Lunchbox Theatre in 1999, and starred Jackie Richardson. The subject of the play, Willie Mae Thornton, was a powerful female blues singer who was popular in the '50s and '60s, and is best known for having first recorded *Hound Dog*, in 1953; it was then re-recorded and released by Elvis Presley in 1955, becoming one of his signature songs. **HIGHLIGHTS:** AKK is also an actor with many credits from stage and film including: *Hair; Jesus Christ! Superstar; Showboat; Ain't Misbehavin'*; on film she has appeared in *Streetsmart*, with Morgan Freeman and Christopher Reeves; *Bright Lights, Big City* with Michael J. Fox; and, *An Act of Vengeance*, with Charles Bronson; she has also appeared in a number of commercials. **OTHER:** founder, Jazz-A-Matazz!, Edmonton's annual jazz benefit for breast cancer research; Director, Theatre/Dance of the San Diego Community Outreach Program. **HONS.:** BAASA, Professional Performing Artist; Outstanding Humanities Alumna award, San Diego Mesa College. **WORKS:** *Big Mama: The Willie Mae Thornton Story*, 1999. **EDUCATION:** Grant MacEwan Arts Administration; The American Conservatory Theater; Colorado Women's College. **HEROES/ ROLE MODELS:** Parents; John Cooper, director. **CONTACT:** audrei_kairen@hotmail.com; Fax: 702-838-7711

►KUEHN, Sadie

WRITER/HUMAN RIGHTS ACTIVIST, Sadie Kuehn Consulting, Vancouver, BC. Born: USA/ in Canada since: 1969.

▶ Sadie Kuehn is a writer, educator, and lecturer who works as a consultant in the areas of policy development, diversity, human rights, and mediation. For the past 30 yrs., she has worked across Canada and internationally on anti-hate, human rights, youth, and women's issues. In the mid-1980s, she became the first Black person and only the second visible minority person to be elected as a trustee to the Vancouver School Board; she introduced a number of important initiatives including a hot lunch program for inner-city schools. And, based on her earlier experiences in international development, she provided the impetus for agencies like CUSO and OXFAM to review the invisibility of Aboriginal and other racially diverse people in the staffing of their offices in Canada and the need for anti-racism training in the sector. **HIGHLIGHTS:** during her nine yrs. as the Managing Editor/Curriculum Developer at the Legal Services Society of BC, she produced the first comprehensive high school and college resources on Aboriginal rights and land claims, and *Women and the Law*; she also developed the first widely distributed historical resource on Black people in Canada and in BC, for the Black History Committee. In 1998, she became the first Black to be elected to chair the 19-yr. old Vancouver Family Court Youth Justice Committee for the City of Vancouver. During her tenure she has worked to raise the community's consciousness about the plight of young people on the street, the lack of proper services for Aboriginal youth, and the situation faced by young women on the street. Under her direction, the Family Court Youth Justice Committee held a Street Youth Forum, which was successful in raising awareness in the general population of the situation of young people on the streets; it also generated more money for relevant programs from municipal, provincial, and federal levels of government. **OTHER:** she has also worked as an advisor or resource person to many entities including, the federal government, Cdn Teachers Federation, HR Commission, Cdn Council for Refugees, Battered Women Support Services, Cdn Status of Women,

AMSSA. She is the past- chair of the BC and Yukon Citizenship and Immigration Advisory Committee for the Dept. of Citizenship and Immigration Canada; was named to the UNWCAR Advisory Committee; and in 2000, was instrumental in forming a new women's group, Women's Quest and was involved in setting up the Pacific Anti-Racism Institute of Canada. **HONS:** Martin Luther King Jr. Award, National Black Coalition; Award of Recognition, Black Educators of BC; also from National Congress of Black Women, West Coast Coalition Against Racism, BC Teachers' Federation, AMSAA and others. **WORKS:** in, *Globe and Mail*; *Vancouver Sun*; *Legal Perspectives* magazine, *Kinesis*; *AMSAA Bulletin*. **CONTACT:** sadiekuehn@hotmail.com

► **KUMSA, Martha Kuwee**
WRITER, c/o Harper Collins, Ste. 2900-55 Avenue Rd., Toronto, ON M5R 3L2. Born: Ethiopia/ in Canada since: 1991.

▶ Martha Kuwee Kumsa was a journalist in Ethiopia who was imprisoned for nearly ten yrs. by the Ethiopian military regime because of her writing, her ethnic origin, and her political beliefs. She was released in 1989 with the help of PEN Canada, Amnesty International and Human Rights Watch, and came to Toronto with her children in 1991; her husband followed in 1996. Since then, she has published essays, articles, prose and poetry. In 2000, MKK was the recipient of one of the first two new fellowships offered, through the Scholars at Risk Programme. This initiative resulted from efforts by John Fraser, long-time member of PEN Canada and Master of Massey College, and is designed to provide short-term university positions to support exiled writers financially while introducing them to the literary and academic community. In addition to working towards completing her doctorate in Social Work, MKK also reaches out to others by telling of her own experiences and advocating for the release of other writers who

have been wrongfully imprisoned. **OTHER:** member of the Faculty of Social Work at Wilfrid Laurier University, Waterloo, since Fall 2002. **HONS.:** Social Sciences and Humanities Research Council of Canada (SSHRC) fellowship, for her doctoral research on "Negotiating Identity and Cohesion: the Mundane Experiences of Young Oromo Refugees Living in Toronto," 2002. **WORKS:** articles/essays in: *Affilia, J of Women & Social Work; J of Oromo Studies; PEN Canada Newsletter; Fiery Spirits*. Poems include: "The Day I Forget," in *Canadian Centre for Victims of Torture Newsletter*; "My People" & "Massacre in Arsi" in *Qunnamtii*. **REVIEWED IN:** "Martha & the Minder," in *Paper Guitar*, 1995; *Blue is the Colour of Hope*, CBC Radio documentary, 1993 & '96. **EDUCATION:** completing PhD; MSW, 1997, U of T. BSW, 1996; BA, Sociology, 1995, York U. **HEROES/ROLE MODELS:** Timothy Findley: minder, friend. **MOTTO:** Love the life you live to live the life you love. **CONTACT:** m.kumsa@utoronto.ca; Fax: 416-975-9884

► **KURANTSIN-MILLS, Joseph,** PhD.
RESEARCH SCIENTIST & PROFESSOR, MEDICINE, PHYSIOLOGY, & EXPERIMENTAL MEDICINE, George Washington University, Washington, DC; Associate Professor, Biophysics & Physiology, and Research Scientist, Center for Sickle Cell Disease, Howard University College of Medicine, Washington, DC. Born: Ghana/ in Canada since: 1966.

▶ Dr. Joseph Kurantsin-Mills is a member of a team of scientists, at Howard University, investigating the genetics and molecular regulation of iron metabolism in sickle cell disease. His other responsibilities are at the George Washington University (GWU) Medical Center and include teaching health science students. He served as Principal Investigator (PI) & Supervisor, Blood Research Laboratory, 1986-96, responsible for developing and executing options for basic & clinical-related research programs. **OTHER**

CAREER HIGHLIGHTS: Project Director and PI, National Heart Lung Blood Institute (NHLBI), National Institutes of Health (NIH) Sickle Cell Disease Study, 1992-1995, where he coordinated and directed a nation-wide health assessment study to evaluate the current status of screening and treatment of newborns for hemoglobinopathies; Project Director and Senior Business Consultant, Hi-Tech International Inc., Arlington, VA, 1993-96; Assistant Professor (Research), Medicine and Physiology, GWU Medical Center, 1984-89, responsible for teaching medical & bio-engineering students, and developing & conducting biomedical research. In the Dept. of Biochemistry at The Research Institute, Hospital for Sick Children, U of T, he was a Staff Scientist, 1982-1984, where he was responsible for developing an *in vitro* model for immunochemically-targeted treatment for multiple sclerosis; from 1980-82, he was a Research Fellow, responsible for studies on membrane structure & function in multiple sclerosis using various biophysical and biochemical techniques. From 1979-80, he was a Post-doctoral Research Associate, Div. of Hematology and Oncology, Dept. of Medicine, GWU Medical Center, responsible for developing an *ex vivo* rheological technique for assessing drugs that inhibit the polymerization of hemoglobin S & hemoglobin C. Developed hemotopoietic stem cell culture for pre-leukemia studies. **RESEARCH INTERESTS:** pathophysiology and molecular biological aspects of sickle cell disease. **CONSULTANT APPOINTMENTS:** in Washington, DC: National Institutes of Health; National Science Foundation; Chemical Manufacturer's Assn.; Howard U. Women's Health Institute; Gambro Healthcare Inc.; and, several other medical and technology businesses in the National Capital Area (Washington, DC). **AFFIL/MBRSHP:** Brd., Sickle Cell Assn. of the National Capital Area, Washington, DC (past Chair, 1999-2001); co-founder, Brd., Ghana Health Fdn. (USA), Washington, DC; past Brd. member and Medical Liaison, Sickle Cell Assn. of Ontario, 1980-84. **HONS.:** several including: Principal Investigator, grant awards from the National Institutes of Health, 1987-95; Research Fellow, Multiple Sclerosis Society of Canada, grant award, 1980-82; Biomedical Sciences Scholar, WHO medical research fellowship, Geneva, research grant, 1974-79. **WORKS:** selected in: *J of Biochemical Toxicology; Am J Kidney Diseases; The European J of Clinical Investigations; Am J Physiology; Blood; British J Hematology.* Chapters in: *Basic Science of Vascular Diseases,* 1997; *Handbook of Pattern Recognition and Computer Vision,* 1993; *Textbook of Internal Medicine,* 1988. **EDUCATION:** Post-Doctoral Studies, Hematology, Biochemistry/Immunology, 1982; MSc, Physiology, 1971, U of T. Post-Doctoral Studies, Cell Biology, 1980; PhD, Cell Biophysics & Physiology, 1979, GWU, Washington, DC. BSc, Chemistry/ Biology, U. of Guelph, 1969. **HEROES/ROLE MODELS:** Dr. Cecil Yip, U of T; Dr. Lawrence Lessin, Washington Hospital Center, Washington, DC. **MOTTO:** Maintain a positive attitude in every situation. **CONTACT:** nkurantsin@hotmail.com; jkurantsin-mills@howard.edu

▶LAMPKIN, Vibert, The Hon. Mr. Justice. **JUDGE,** Ontario Court of Justice, 50 Eagle St. W., Newmarket, ON L37 6B1. Born: Guyana/ in Canada since: 1967.

▶ The Hon. Mr. Justice Lampkin began practising law in Guyana in 1959. He became a judge with the Ontario Court of Justice in 1982, a position he holds currently. **CAREER HIGHLIGHTS:** practised in partnership with Sir John Carter, QC, in Guyana, 1959-67; after articling in Toronto, 1967, and being called to the bar, 1969, he practised as a barrister and solicitor with Rosenfeld, Schwartz, and Brown, 1969-73; 1973-82, he was a partner with this firm, now Rosenfeld, Schwartz, Malcomson, Lampkin, and Levine; in 1982, he was appointed to the Provincial Bench. From 1994-96, he was a Commissioner, Ontario Law Reform Commission. **AFFIL/MBRSHP:** Toronto Junior Brd. of Trade, 1967-73; Director, OXFAM Canada, 1970-78; Police Complaints Commission; Director, New Leaf: Living and Learning Together, 1988-94. **EDUCATION:** LLM, York U., 1977; Final Exam, Law Society of England, 1958; LLB, U. of London, 1957. **HEROES/ROLE MODELS:** Sir John Carter, QC, uncle; Lord Denning, British judge. **MOTTO:** Do the best you can. **CONTACT:** Fax: 905-853-4832

◆LAPIERRE, Myrtha

PROFESSEURE (Ret.)/**CONSULTANTE**, GSF, Aylmer, QC. Née: Haiti/ au Canada depuis: 1956.

▶ Myrtha Lapierre était Professeur en sciences infirmières pendant 36 ans, 1961-97. **ACTIVITÉS PRINCIPALES**: pendant ses 36 ans d'enseignement (incluant 5 ans de coordination clinique), elle a travaillé dans le système hospitalier, puis dans le système collégial, à Ottawa, Kingston, et à Toronto). Ses objectifs était la promotion de l'apprentissage qui vise la réussite, et promotion de la sensibilisation ethnoculturelle. En 1982 et en 1988, elle était chargée de cours de soir à l'UQAH (Hull); 1993-96, elle a donné des ate-

liers de sensibilisation ethnoculturelle aux étudiants, professeurs, et aux personnels de soutien de premier ligne (Cité Collégiale); elle a fait la formation des formateurs en relation interculturelles au personnel des centres de santé et de ressources communautaires, Collège Algonquin. Depuis 1998, elle travaille dans la préparation de femmes immigrantes et réfugiées afin qu'elles apprennent à prodiguer des soins aux personnes âgées à domicile ou dans des résidences. **VIE ASSOCIATIVE:** membre exécutif de plusieurs comités pour des levées de fonds en matière de santé pour Haïti: Assn. culturelle Haïti-Canada; CPHSO (professionnels haïtiens de la santé); AQANU (ONG QC-Haiti); ICC (Int'l Child Care). Aussi membre de comités pour rehausser l'oeuvre des noirs: Harambee (*Carrie Best collection of books & videos by Black authors*) ou pour aider des jeunes souffrant d'une maladie surtout trouvée parmi les noirs: Anémie falsiforme ou *Sickle Cell Anemia of* Ottawa. **PRIX:** Plaque de la communauté haïtienne, reconnaissance de 25 ans de contribution, 2000; Cert. d'honneur pour les bénévoles en alphabétisation, 1993; Vœux du Ministre d'Etat, Multiculturalisme et à la Citoyenneté, pour le lancement de la collection *Carrie Best* de Harambee, 1988. **ŒUVRES:** sélection: co-auteur, ESL & Labour Market, guide curriculaire, 2000; « A la rencontre de deux solitudes, » revue *Reflets, Travailleurs Sociaux en Ontario*, 1998; co-auteur, « L'Adaptation dans un milieu collégial francophone devenu pluriethnique, » *Revue du Nouvel Ontario*, 1996; Rapport d'une recherche, « Vers une education en matière antiracisme et d'équité ethnoculturelle, » 1994; coauteur, *Initiation à la vie canadienne*, 1994; Manuel de gérontologie & de gériatrie selon le modèle de Roy, Collège Algonquin, 1986. **OEUVRES À SON PROPOS:** *Some Black Models in Ottawa*, 2000; « Un Triple Anniversaire pour Myrtha Lapierre Peters, » Collège Algonquin, 1986. **FORMATION:** Cert., ESL, 2000; Formation en TPN#1, résolution de conflit, U. St. Paul, 1998; Formation en sensibilisation ethnoculturelle, Collège Algonquin, 1993; Cert. Géronto-logie, U. de Montréal, 1980. M.Ed, Psychopéda-gogie, 1975; BSc, N.Ed (Bac en science de l'éd-ucation des infirmières), 1961; Dipl. Sciences infirmières, 1959, U. d'Ottawa. **MENTORS:** Dr Huguette Labelle, Margot Félix, Dr Marie Josée Berger: des collègues et des amies. **MOTTO:** A vaincre sans péril, on triomphe sans gloire. **CONTACT:** mlconsultants@videotron.ca

▶**LARBI, Madonna Owusuah**
EXECUTIVE DIRECTOR, MATCH International Centre, Ste. 1102-200 Elgin St., Ottawa, ON K2P 1L5. Born: Ghana/ in Canada since: 1985.
▶ Madonna Larbi is the Executive Director of MATCH International Centre, an international development organization that works in Africa, Asia, the Caribbean, and Latin America by fos-tering the efforts of women's groups to bring about equality, dignity, opportunity and better living standards in these regions of the world. In Canada, MATCH aims to increase awareness among Canadians of the issues facing women in the global south and how these impact on the lives of Canadians. **CAREER HIGHLIGHTS:** Admin-istrative and Liaison Consultant, UN Fund for Population Activities, and Public Affairs Consul-tant, World Bank Office, both in Ghana, 1980-81; Communications Assistant, Amnesty Internatio-nal, 1988-90; Executive Director, Nat'l Org. of Immigrant and Visible Minority Women of Canada, 1990-91; and, Program Officer, MATCH International Centre, 1991-92. Since becoming Executive Director of MATCH in 1993, she has participated in a number of international assign-ments including consultations for CIDA and other international organizations. **AFFIL/MBRSHP:** African Women's Development Fund, since 2000; North-South Institute, 1996-98; YWCA of Canada, 1994-96; SOS Children's Villages of Canada, 1993-99; UNESCO, Status of Women Committee, 1993-2000; Media Watch, 1992-94. **WORKS:** has written articles, chapters in books,

and book reviews. **REVIEWED IN:** *WWCW; WW Among Top Executive in NA*; *Outstanding People of the 20th Century.* **EDUCATION:** ongoing manage-ment & development training; Human Rights Research & Ed. Centre, U. of Ottawa, 1989; Dipl. Journalism, Ghana Institute of Journalism, 1975. **CONTACT:** matchint@magma.ca; Fax: 613-238-6867

▶**LARMOND, Londa**
SINGER/PERFORMER, c/o Richard Picart, Mekehla Music Group, Toronto, ON. Born: Toronto, ON.
▶ Londa Larmond is a gospel singer whose debut album, *Love Letters*, has been receiving interna-tional acclaim, and was nominated for the 2001 Juno Awards. Her musical style is described as "Pop and Jazz-influenced, R&B-flavoured brand of Gospel." Raised in a gospel musical environ-ment by her Jamaican parents, LL began singing in church at age seven and performing by age 14, as a featured member of Toronto's Youth Out-reach Mass Choir. From there she became a member of the Gospel Soul Sisters before joining the well known, Sharon Riley & Faith Chorale in 1995. Her involvement with the Faith Chorale led to an appearance in the movie, *Blues Brothers 2000*. She recorded on the movie's Grammy-nominated soundtrack, which also included recordings by Aretha Franklin, Erykah Badu, James Brown, Isaac Hayes, Eric Clapton, and many others. She also appeared in the HBO film, *Light to the Power of Two*, 1998. **OTHER:** has appeared at a number of gospel and Christian concerts and on a number of programs featuring gospel, including *Bobby Jones Gospel, 100 Hunt-ley Street,* Gospelfest, at the Ottawa Blues Festi-val, and at the Montreal Gospelfest; also sang for the heads of state and dignitaries at the Summit of the Americas, held in 2001. **HONS.:** include, nominee, Artist of the Year, and, Female Artist of the Year, VIBE Awards, 2002; nominee, Best Gospel Album of the Year, Juno Awards, 2002; Best Gospel Recording, UMAC, 2001; nominee, Urban Album of the Year, Dove Awards. And, as

the lead vocalist with Sharon Riley & Faith Chorale: Best Gospel Album, for *Life Is*, Juno Award, 1999; nominee, Best Gospel Album, for *Caught Up*, 1998; Best Gospel Album, for *Caught Up*, UMAC, 1997. **CONTACT:** c/o richard@mekehla.com

▶**LAROCHE, Maximilien, PhD, CH.**
PROFESSEUR DE LITTÉRATURE/ÉCRIVAIN, Université Laval, Cité Universitaire, Ste. Foy, QC G1K 7P4. Né: Haïti/ au Canada depuis: 1960.
▶ Dr Maximilien Laroche enseigne à l'Université Laval depuis 1971; il est spécialisé en littérature française, québécoise, et de la Caraïbe francophone. **ACTIVITÉS PRINCIPALES:** Professeur adjoint, 1971-74; Professeur agrégé, 1974-79; Professeur titulaire, 1979-97; et depuis 1997, il est Professeur honoraire. Comme écrivain il a publié des livres, des articles, et a contribué aux ouvrages collectifs. **AFFIL/MBRSHP:** Jury du prix Carbet de la Caraïbe; l'Union des écrivains québécois. **PRIX:** Chevalier de l'Ordre national Honneur et Mérite, Haïti (CH), 1999; Médaille du Conseil général de la Martinique, 1990; Membre de l'Ordre des francophones d'Amérique, Québec, 1988. **ŒUVRES:** sélective, y compris les livres: *Téké*, 2002; *Bizango*, 1997; *Dialectique de l'Américanisation*, 1993; *La découverte de l'Amérique par les Américains*, 1989; *La littérature haïtienne*, 1981; *Marcel Dubé*, 1970. Les articles dans: *Francophonie et dialogue des cultures; Panorama de la Littérature québécoise contemporaine; L'année francophone internationale.* **FORMATION:** Doctorat, Toulouse, 1971. Dipl. d'études supérieure, 1968; Maîtrise en-arts, 1962; Licence en-lettres, 1962, U. de Montréal. Licence en droit, U. d'Haïti, 1958. **MENTORS:** Jean-Jacques Dénoliner (détermination sans faille). **MOTTO:** Ce que vous ignorez, vous dépasse. **CONTACT:** maximilien.laroche@sympatico.ca; Fax: 418-681-5832

▶**LAROSE, Winston W.**
COMMUNITY VIDEOGRAPHER, African Canadian Communications & Broadcasting Corp., 1 York-Gate Mall Blvd., Unit F 4.1, Box 29 Toronto, ON M3N 3A1. Born: Guyana/ in Canada since: 1964.
▶ Winston LaRose is most notable for his collection of videotaped material on events concerning Blacks in Toronto and around the world. This includes interviews with cricketer Garfield Sobers, lawyer Johnnie Cochrane, anthropologists Dr. Molefe Asante and Dr. Maulana Karenga, boxer Muhammad Ali, Maroons of Jamaica; coverage of the 1995, Million Man March in Washington; Caribana events; a travel tour to Ghana with students from Jamaica and Canada; Tiger Woods playing in Canada, and many others. Some of this material will be archived at York University to ensure its availability for future research activities. His most significant project to date is the preparation of a millennium documentary depicting the legacy and contributions of Africans to world civilization over the past 2,000 years; filming has occurred in several countries including Ghana, Senegal, Cuba, Jamaica, Mexico, and others. **COMMUNITY INVOLVEMENT:** OBHS; Toronto Black Leadership Coalition; Jane-Finch Concerned Citizens Org.; Ebony Group Community Homes. **EDUCATION:** BA, Sociology, 1987; Real Estate Admin., 1977, McMaster University. RN courses: Guyana, 1959; UK, 1961; Canada, 1964. **CONTACT:** Fax: 905-853-4623

▶**LAURENT, Alix**
DIRECTEUR GÉNÉRAL, Images Interculturelles, bur. 401-430, Ste-Hélène, Montréal, QC H2Y 2K7. Né: Haïti/ au Canada depuis: 1971.
▶ Alix Laurent est le Directeur Général d'Images Interculturelles depuis 1991. La structure est une entreprise à but non lucratif créée par les membres fondateurs de la revue *Images*; son rôle principal est de publier des informations sur les com-

munautés culturelles et et de maintenir le dialogue sur les relations interculturelles. **RÉALISATIONS PRINCIPALES:** « la Semaine d'actions contre le racisme, » 2001, 2002; les conférences internationales, « La ville, lieu d'inclusion, lieu d'exclusion » et « Le racisme, comprendre pour agir » 2001, 2002; conférence/exposition, « Encre noire, littératures et communautés noires, » 2001; forum, « Marquez des points contre le racisme, » 1999; forum, « Citoyens jeunes et pouvoir politique, » 1997; l'exposition, Negripub, 100 ans d'images des Noirs dans la publicité, 1998; création du magazine, *Images Interculturelles*, 1991-99 (dont il était fondateur et éditeur); depuis, 1994, il est responsable pour l'organisation et la réalisation du MHN; depuis 1994, il est aussi Directeur les *Editions Images* et a supervisé les productions sur la culture et les langues patrimoniales. **AUTRES ACTIVITÉS:** Comité aviseur sur les relations interculturelles de Montréal (CARIM); Comité sur les relations interculturelles et interraciales de la CUM; La Maisonnée, Service d'aide aux immigrants et aux réfugiés. **PRIX:** Mention d'excellence en communication, Prix du rapprochement Interculturel, gouv. du Québec (MAICC), 1993. **ŒUVRES:** publications supervisées à titre de directeur des *Editions Images: L'autorité pastorale dans les églises haïtiennes, 2002; L'appartenance ethnique et les langues patrimoniales au Canada*, 2000. **FORMATION:** Maîtrise, Administration Publique, ENAP, en cours. Cert., Droit, 1990; Bac Spécialisé, Sciences économiques, 1988, U. de Montréal. **MOTTO:** If it is to be done, it is up to me! **CONTACT:** images@biz.videotron.ca; Fax: 514-842-5647

▶**LAURENT, Weber**

ARCHITECTE, Laurent + Vaccaro Architectes, bur. 305-911 Jean-Talon Est, Montréal, QC H2R 1V5. Né: Haïti/ au Canada depuis: 1971.

▶ Weber Laurent est un partenaire dans une des premières firmes d'architectes noires à s'établir à Montréal. Depuis 1980, il oeuvre dans plusieurs projets auprès d'agences d'architecture à titre de concepteur-designer, de chargé de projet; de plus, son expérience s'est développée par une étroite collaboration depuis 1993, avec l'architecte Félice Vaccaro. Il maintient des collaborations ponctuelles avec d'autres architectes sur des concours et d'autres réalisations. Son expérience professionnelle s'est développée auprès des institutions comme la Ville de Montréal, réglementation du bâtiment et zonage, le Ministère de l'éducation, section aménagement d'écoles, la Société Immobilière du Québec, et l'U. de Montréal. **ACTIVITÉS PRINCIPALES:** Il a réalisé des projets résidentiels, commerciaux, institutionnels et industriels. On trouve entre autre, divers projets d'aménagement d'école et de locaux universitaires, des projets de construction et de rénovation de bâtiments publics tel que le Palais de justice de Montréal, des bureaux ministériels, des caisses populaires, l'U. de Montréal, etc. Dans le domaine résidentiel, ses réalisations s'étendent des résidences privées cossues aux coopératives d'habitation, des maisons de ville en rangées aux tours d'habitation. Il est aussi le concepteur et chargé de la gérance de plusieurs projets de construction et de rénovation d'églises protestantes. En 2000, il a reçu le mandat de la Ville de Montréal, de restaurer un bâtiment classé « patrimoine historique » afin d'y aménager le premier musée Montréalais, entièrement consacré à la communauté afro-canadienne. Il siège actuellement comme conseiller professionnel pour le Conseil Consultatif d'Urbanisme de la ville de Montréal. **VIE ASSOCIATIVE:** il participe à plusieurs colloques sur la problématique du logement social, en plus d'agir de consultant auprès de plusieurs organismes culturels et sociaux à but non-lucratifs, au sein de la communauté noire de Montréal. Il est membre de la Jeune Chambre de Commerce; l'Assn. des gens d'affaires Haïtiens; CA, de FITHAC (un fond d'investissement). Une de ses préoccupations est « la transmission du savoir aux générations à venir et la nécessité de leur léguer un héritage constructif. » **AFFIL:** Ordre des Architectes de Québec; Institut Royal d'Architecture du Canada; Institut de Gestion de Projets, Montréal; Conseil de l'Enveloppe du Bâtiment, Québec; membre fondateur de l'Assn. des Ingénieurs et Architectes d'origine Haïtienne au Canada (AIHC). **PRIX:** y compris, Prix d'excellence, Fondation Haïtiano-Canadienne pour l'avancement des arts et de la culture, 2000; Prix Orange, pour l'Écomusée du Fier-Monde, 1996; Mention de la Ville de Montréal, dans le cadre des projets « Habiter Montréal », ainsi que pour la conception de petits bâtiments résidentiels de type « maison de ville », appelés « maison évolutive », et des projets d'habitation sélectionnés dans le cadre de l'Opération, 20,000 logements de la ville de Montréal. **ŒUVRES À SON PROPOS:** plusieurs: *Haïti-Observateur*; *calendrier Mois de l'Histoire des Noirs*, 1996; *La Presse; Habitat.* **FORMATION:** Maîtrise en Gestion de projets, UQAM, 1995; Bac, Architecture, U. Laval, 1982; DEC, Sciences pures et appliquées, Collège Bois de Boulogne, Mtl, 1977. **MENTORS:** Parents; René Exumé, premier professeur de dessin. **CONTACT:** Tél: 514-270-1621; wla@lauvac-architect.com; weberl@total.net

►LAW-BANCROFT, Carole

MUSIC TEACHER/EXAMINER, Royal Conservatory of Music, 273 Bloor St. W., Toronto, ON M5S 1W2. Born: Jamaica/ in Canada since: 1965.
▶ Carole Law-Bancroft has been a faculty member at the Royal Conservatory of Music (RCM) in Toronto, since 1968. She is also a member of the College of Examiners for RCM examinations since 1976 and has adjudicated extensively on behalf of organizations including the Ontario Registered Music Teachers' Assn., and serves as a workshop clinician. **BACKGROUND:** she studied piano with Clifford Poole and Margaret Parsons and has attended master classes with Leon Fleisher, Anton Kuerti, and Fanny Waterman; also studied violin and organ and won competitions in both piano and violin. Before leaving

Jamaica to pursue studies at the RCM, 1965, she was a violinist with the Jamaica Philharmonic Orchestra. She has performed in Canada and the US and has appeared several times in concert for the Jamaica Broadcasting Corp. **OTHER:** she is a member of the advisory board of the Chopin Society of Toronto, a former consultant for the Harry Jerome Music Award, and a member of Prime Mentors of Canada. **HONS.:** in addition to her own awards, over the years, several of her students have won first place and trophies in various music festivals. **EDUCATION:** Trinity College of Music, London, England: Fellow, 1977; Licentiate, 1974. ARCT, Royal Conservatory of Music, Toronto, 1968. **HEROES/ROLE MODELS:** Clifford Poole & Margaret Parsons, piano teachers; Dr. George W. Bancroft, husband. **MOTTO:** Desire is not enough to make your goals–you also need persistence.

►LAWRENCE, Delores

PRESIDENT & CEO, NHI Nursing & Homemakers Inc., 2347 Kennedy Rd., Toronto, ON M1T 3T8. Born: Jamaica/ in Canada since: 1968.
▶ Delores Lawrence is the President and CEO of NHI, a company she started in 1985. NHI provides home care, and supplies nursing staff to health-care facilities; over 1,200 nurses are employed in a combination of full- and part-time positions. NHI was listed on *Profit 2000*'s list of "Top 100 Women Business Owners" for the second consecutive year in 2001. **AFFIL:** Chair, Board of Governors, Seneca College; formerly, Director, Toronto 2008 Olympic Bid team; Chair, African Canadian Society on Health Care; President, African Canadian Entrepreneurs. In 1996, she was a member of the first Canadian Businesswomen's delegation to the US. **HONS.:** African-Canadian Woman of the Year Award, for business, 1994. **REVIEWED IN:** *Chatelaine's* "Top 100 Canadian Businesswomen," 2000 & 2001; interviewed on radio, profiled in various newspapers & magazines. **EDUCATION:** MBA, U. of New

Hampshire, 1994; Business Admin., Harvard U., 1990; BA, York U., 1980; RN, Ont. College of Nurses, 1975. **MOTTO:** The sky is the limit! **CONTACT:** lawrence@nhihealthcare.com; www. nhihealthcare.com

▶**LAWRENCE, Errol A.,** D.Min.
CHAIR/ASSOCIATE PROFESSOR, Dept. of Religious Studies, Canadian University College, 235 College Ave., Lacombe, AB T4L 2E5. Born: Jamaica/ in Canada since: 1995.
▶ Dr. Errol Lawrence is an Associate Professor of Religious Studies, and Chair of the Department of Religious Studies at the Canadian University College (CAUC) in Alberta. He is also an ordained minister in the Seventh-day Adventist Church (SDA). **CAREER HIGHLIGHTS:** six-week mission with Adventist Development and Relief Agency (ADRA) and CAUC, to Nicaragua, with 12 students, constructing toilets in a remote area, 2000; missionary to Liberia (held positions of Special Asst. to Mission President, Hospital Chaplain, Stewardship Director, Health and Temperance Director, Communications Director), 1983-90; Pastor/Evangelist in London, England, 1975-83; Pastor, Apple Creek Seventh-day Adventist Church, Toronto, 1995-98. He joined the CAUC in 1998 and teaches on Homiletics, Pastoral Practicum, Pastoral Counseling, Worship, Pastoral Ministry, History and Theology. **HONS.:** include, Distinguished Pastoral Service Award, Metro Toronto Ministerium SDA Church, 1999; Special Recognition for services to the WHO and the AIDS Program in Liberia, 1989-90; Special Recognition, for conducting Breathe Free Stop Smoking Programs in Liberia, Liberia Cancer Society, 1985-90. **WORKS:** many conference papers & presentations; chapter in, *100 Years of Adventism in Ontario*, 1999; forthcoming, *Marketing the Church for Growth in the Twenty-first Century.* **REVIEWED IN:** *Adventist Jamaicans Abroad.* **EDUCATION:** D.Min, 1995; M.Div, 1992, Andrews U., Michigan. BA, New

England College, 1975. **HEROES/ROLE MODELS:** Doris Lawrence, mother; Pastor O.E. Gordon, former colleague. **MOTTO:** It is not enough to dream about what you want to do; you must begin to do something about what you have spent so long dreaming about. **CONTACT:** ErrolLawrence@cauc.ca; Fax: 403-782-3170

▶**LAWRENCE, Raymond C.,** CPO1, MMM.
CHIEF PETTY OFFICER FIRST CLASS (Ret.), Royal Canadian Navy, Dartmouth, NS. Born: Fredericton, NB.
▶ Raymond Lawrence joined the Royal Canadian Navy in 1953 and served on many ships during a career which lasted over 32 years. In 1974, he was promoted to the rank of Chief Petty Officer First Class (CPO1), thus becoming the first Black to reach this rank. In 1976, he was posted to the HMCS Annapolis as a Coxswain, becoming the highest ranking non-commissioned officer on the ship, and again, the first Black to hold such a position. In 1980, he organized a Gun Run for the NS Tatoo, an event which had not been held since 1967. Due to his efforts, the event was a huge success and is now held annually; it is described by Maritime Command as, "one of the most important competitive events in the Royal Canadian Navy." In 1986, after 32 and a half years of service, RL retired from the Navy, then served for seven years as a Deputy Sheriff. **HONS.:** including, Member of the Order of Military Merit, 1976; Queen Elizabeth II Jubilee Medal, 1977; Canadian Forces Decoration & Clasp; Special Service Medal with NATO bar. **CONTACT:** cpolawrence@hotmail.com

▶**LAWS, Dudley**
CIVIL RIGHTS/COMMUNITY ACTIVIST, Black Action Defense Committee (BADC), 944A St. Clair Ave. W., Toronto, ON M6C 1C8. Born: Jamaica/ in Canada since: 1965.

▶ Dudley Laws is best known as a civil rights and community activist who has been at the forefront of advocating for an end to discriminatory practices against Blacks, for many decades. Born in Jamaica, and trained as a welder and machinist, he first became involved in community organizing in England through the Brixton Neighbourhood Assn., in response to acts of violence by local youth. He came to Canada and continued his community involvement in the JCA, UNIA, and the Marcus Garvey Movement. His primary concerns over the years have been policing, immigration, education, and the criminal justice system. During this time, he has formed, co-founded, or actively participated in the following: Black Action Defense Committee (BADC); Black Inmates and Friends; Justice for Albert Johnson Committee; Black Youth Community Action Project. More recently, his efforts have been directed to within the Black population, speaking to youth and advocating for more dialogue and an end to the violence which has resulted in the loss of several young lives. **HONS.:** including, Marcus Garvey Memorial Award; JCA Community Award; Pan African Award; Cdn Black Achievement Award; Bob Marley Memorial Award; Spirit of the Community, Dinthill Alumni Assn. **REVIEWED IN:** community, local, regional publications; *Some Black Men*, 1999. **CONTACT:** Tel: 416-656-2232; Fax: 416-656-2252

LEACOCK, Emile
COMMUNITY ACTIVIST/SENIORS ADVOCATE, Council for Black Aging Community of Montreal, 3007, rue Delisle, Montreal, QC H4C 1M8. Born: Montreal, QC.
▶ Emile Leacock is a community elder who has devoted a lifetime to unionism and community development in the Montreal area. **BACKGROUND:** born in 1929, he grew up playing all the sports (i.e. hockey, golf, football, baseball, boxing) and was good at several; he began working at the age of 12, first with the City Mission, until 1943, then with the Army Bugle Band, where he was a drummer with the fifth medical regiment, until 1946; he was involved with the University Settlement while boxing in the middleweight division; 1955-63, he worked as a porter with the CNR; afterwards, he worked at Steinberg, 1963-88, during which time he became the Union Workers' representative and was instrumental in negotiating better wages and improved working conditions for employees. **COMMUNITY INVOLVEMENT:** he was particularly involved with the Negro Coloured Centre (NCC), from 1955, volunteering on many committees and playing a major role in welcoming newly arrived immigrants and assisting them with finding housing and employment. Since retiring in 1988, he devotes himself on a full-time basis to volunteering within the Black community. He is a founding member of the Council for Black Aging, begun in 1988, which works as an advocate for the needs of Black seniors, undertaking activities designed to advance the interests of Black elders, keeping Black seniors better informed of issues relating to the availability of health and social services, and developing a unique day centre and a nursing home for Black elders. And, in its advocacy role, the Council for Black Aging works to ensure that all levels of government are made aware of the particular and changing needs of Black seniors in Montreal. He is also involved with the Sports Centre at Little Burgundy, Centre Research Action on Race Relations, and is a mentor at Lasalle Primary School. **HEROES/ROLE MODELS:** Father. **CONTACT:** counb@total.net; Fax: 514-935-8466

▶LEBEANYA, Charity
EXECUTIVE DIRECTOR, Heritage Skills Development Centre (HSDC), Ste. 303-1071 King St. W., Toronto, ON M6K 3K2. Born: Nigeria/ in Canada since: 1992.
▶ Charity Lebeanya is the Executive Director of HSDC, an organization she co-founded in 1993 which promotes the economic self-sufficiency

and well-being of immigrant women and their families. HSDC's services include: micro-enterprise development, computer training, Internet access, life skills and employment training; under her leadership, HSDC has received recognition from all levels of government and some international bodies, including the Society for the Study of Social Problems, which awarded them the Social Action Award, 1997. Prior to this, CL worked in a voluntary capacity with 761 Queen Street Community Centre in Toronto, as Assistant Manager in its economic development division. There, she developed a self-sufficiency program for disadvantaged people in Toronto, which was later expanded to other parts of the province. **COMMUNITY:** Cdn Feed the Children; Harriet Tubman Organization; Cdn Women Executives; Nigerian-Cdn Assn. of Ontario; Nelson Mandela Children's Fdn.; African Community Health Services; she has also provided mentoring support to at-risk youth and recently arrived immigrant women. **HONS.:** include, Community Service Award, 2001; Appreciation Cert., Cdn Alliance & Manufacturers' Export, 2000; Continental African Award, for community service, 1998; Cert., for contributions & participation in PM's Task Force on Youth Entrepreneurship, 1999; Black Achievement Award, 1998. **REVIEWED IN:** *African Profile; Toronto Star; Share; AfriCanadian J.* **EDUCATION:** MBA; post-graduate Dipl., Marketing, U. Strathclyde, Scotland. Dipl., Marketing, Chartered Institute, UK. **MOTTO:** We sow seeds for the present and future generations. **CONTACT:** info@hsdconline.org; www.hsdconline. org

▶**LEE, Ranee**
JAZZ PERFORMER, c/o Justin Time Records, Ste. 101-5455, rue Paré, Montreal, QC H4P 1P7. Born: USA/ in Canada since: 1972.
▶ Ranee Lee is a jazz performer who sings, acts and dances, and who has become well known for her conception, development and performance of *Dark Divas, The Musical*, a musical tribute to seven Black female jazz greats: Josephine Baker, Billie Holiday, Ella Fitzgerald, Sarah Vaughan, Pearl Bailey, Lena Horne, and Dinah Washington. **BACKGROUND:** RL began her stage career as a dancer, but also played the drums and tenor saxophone and toured with a number of groups throughout N. America before moving to Montreal in the '70s. In 1987-88, she starred in *Lady Day at Emerson's Bar and Grill*, a musical portrayal of Billie Holiday, for which she won a Dora Mavor Moore Award. In 1995, she headlined a Western Canadian Jazz Festival tour and a tour of the US; in 1996, she was the featured artist in The Canadian Jazz Greats, a month-long South African tour. **OTHER HIGHLIGHTS:** acted with Billy Dee Williams in the 1991 movie, *Giant Steps;* opened for George Burns, 1993, at Montreal's *Place des Arts*; hosted the TV series, *The Performer* for BET; performed with jazz masters, Oliver Jones, Bill Mayes, Herbie Ellis, Milt Hinton, Clark Terry and many others. She has released seven albums with Justin Time Records since 1984 (including: *Dark Divas*, 2000; *Seasons of Love*, 1997; *Live at Bijou*, 1984); regularly appears at international Jazz Festivals. RL is also an educator and has been teaching voice in the Faculty of Music at McGill U. for over 14 yrs. **HONS.:** include, Best Female Jazz Vocalist Award, American Federation of Int'l Musicians, 1998; nominated for Juno Award, for *I Thought About You*, 1995; Top Canadian Female Jazz Vocalist Award, 1994 & 1995, *Jazz Report Magazine*; Int'l Assn. of Jazz Educators Award, for outstanding service to jazz education, 1994. **CONTACT:** www. justin-time.com

▶**LEE-CHIN, Michael**
CHAIRMAN & CHIEF INVESTMENT OFFICER, AIC Limited, 1375 Kerns Rd., Burlington, ON L7R 4X8. Born: Jamaica/ in Canada since: 1971.
▶ Michael Lee-Chin is the Chairman & Chief Investment Officer of AIC Ltd., Canada's largest,

privately-held, mutual fund company, servicing close to one million investors and managing assets exceeding $14-billion. **BACKGROUND:** after completing a degree in civil engineering at McMaster U., and trying a number of different jobs, he joined the financial services industry in 1977. Working first with the Investors Group as a financial advisor, he left in 1979, to work with Regal Capital Planning Ltd., becoming a regional manager of one of their most successful branches. In 1983, he invested $500,000 in the Mackenzie Financial Corp.; two years later he founded his own financial services company, the Berkshire Group. In 1986, MLC bought a small Hamilton-based investment firm, Advantage Investment Counsel (AIC), which offered, at the time, only one fund, the AIC Advantage Fund, and held assets of about $800,000. **HIGHLIGHTS:** by 1990, AIC had holdings of $9-million; by 1993, these valued $100-million; by 1996, holdings valued over a billion dollars; and, by 1998, AIC had holdings of over $12-billion. Using his investment principle of "Buy, Hold, and Prosper" and from investing in the wealth management industry, MLC has added more than 40 funds to the company's portfolio. Avoiding the dot-com craze of the 1990s, he chose instead to invest in businesses in strong, long-term growth industries, thereby ensuring his investors long-term prosperity over time. The AIC Advantage Fund today stands among the top-performing Cdn equity funds, having delivered steady returns to investors over the past 15 yrs. AIC and its Funds have won a number of awards over the years: AIC Advantage Fund won the Analysts' Choice Award in 1996; the AIC Value Fund won the Analysts' Choice Award in 1996 and 1997; and, in 2002, the AIC American Balanced Fund was named "best global balanced fund" at the Cdn Mutual Fund Gala. AIC itself was named Investors Choice Fund Company of the Year in 1997 and 1998. The company won the Dalbar Mutual Fund Service Award in 2000. And, in January 2002, MLC purchased 75% ownership of one of Jamaica's leading banks, the National Commercial Bank (NCB). **OTHER:** as a benefactor, he supports a number of charities and recently made a donation of $5-million to McMaster U., the largest in the institution's history, to establish an AIC institute for Strategic Business Studies at the DeGroote School of Business. MLC is ranked by *Can Business* magazine and Forbes among the world's most financially successful business owners. **HONS.:** Entrepreneur of the Year, 1997 (sponsored by Ernst & Young, BMO Nesbitt Burns, Air Canada, & *Can Business*). **EDUCATION:** Civil Engineering, McMaster U., 1974. **CONTACT:** cwhite@aicfunds.com; www.aic.com

▶**LEGON, Jeni, Dr.**
PERFORMER/TAP DANCER/ACTOR, Vancouver, BC. Born: USA/ in Canada since: 1969.
▶ Jeni LeGon, singer, dancer, actor, was known as "Hollywood's Chocolate Princess" to those who saw her on screen or on stage, and was named "The Million-Dollar Personality Girl" by the Hollywood press for her winning smile and personality. Born in 1916 in Chicago, she got her big break at age 13, after auditioning for Count Basie's band, but, too undeveloped to wear the usual chorus line outfit, he allowed her to wear pants, which became her trademark for her tap-dancing routines. **CAREER HIGHLIGHTS:** she danced at the leading national and international clubs and theatres including the Apollo, Howard, Paramount, *Café de Paris*, Lincoln Theaters, and many others. At the age of 17, she became the first Black woman to be signed to a multi-year contract with MGM studios, in 1933 (slated to earn from $1,250 to $4,500/wk. over a five-year period). Over the course of her Hollywood acting career, she appeared in 23 films including *Easter Parade; While Thousands Cheer; Hi-De-Ho; Double Deal; Stormy Weather*; and *Hooray for Love*, which starred Bill "Bojangles" Robinson and featured the music of Fats Waller. She appeared with stars like Lena Horne, Cab Cal-

loway, Fred Astaire, Dorothy Dandridge, Carole Lombard, Harry Belafonte, Jimmy Durante and many others. However, because of her colour and the practice of segregation in the US she was not cast in the roles which would have made full use of her talents. Except for the few all-Black films made, she usually appeared in the role of maid or servant of one nationality or another. In 1936, she was dropped by MGM before the filming of *Broadway Melody* when she outperformed the film's lead in a stage performance. She continued to act and appeared in other films and on a number of TV variety shows, including the *Amos and Andy* series. During the '50s, she also began teaching tap and other forms of dance and later toured with her group, Jazz Caribe. While touring Canada in the late '60s, she visited Vancouver and decided to stay, opened a dance studio and gave lessons to hundreds of students over the following 25 yrs. In addition to teaching, she choreographed works, sang and performed locally as a jazz singer; she also appeared in three Canadian films, *Nobody's Child*, *Home is Where the Heart Is*, and *Cold Front*. In 1999, she was the subject of an NFB film, *Jeni LeGon: Living in a Great Big Way*, a celebration of her life, her accomplishments, and her zest for living. **HONS.:** several, including: Doctor of Performing Arts, and, Living Treasure Award, School of American Dance & Arts Management, Oklahoma U., 2002; Honorary Lifetime Member, Vancouver Ballet Society, 2001; Heritage Award (re-named the Jeni LeGon Heritage Award), New Orleans Jazz Dance Festival, 2001; Beacon of Freedom Award, Underground Railroad Forum, 2000; Bill "Bojangles" Robinson Award, Mary Collins Production, 2000; Lifetime Achievement in the Arts, National Congress of Black Women, 1999; Los Angeles Tap Hall of Fame, 1993; Micheaux Award, and Black Filmmakers Hall of Fame, 1987. **WORKS:** co-authored the song, *The Spring*, performed by Lena Horne in, *Panama Hattie*, 1942. **REVIEWED IN:** several nat'l & int'l publications, including: *Hope & Heroes: Portraits of*

Integrity, 2001; *Some Black Women*, 1993. **CONTACT:** jazz1@oanet.com

▶**LEWIS, Daurene, Dr.**
PRINCIPAL, HALIFAX CAMPUSES, Nova Scotia Community College, 1825 Bell Rd., Halifax, NS B3H 2Z4. Born: Annapolis Royal, NS.
▶ In 1979, Daurene Lewis became the first Black woman in Canada elected to municipal office. She served as councillor, Annapolis Royal 1979-84, and was also Deputy Mayor from 1982-84. In 1984, she became the first Black in NS and the first Black woman in N. America elected as Mayor and served until 1988. She then became the first Black woman in NS to win nomination for a major political party and to run in a provincial election. Since 2002, she is in her current position as Principal of the Halifax Campuses of the NS Community College. She is the first Black in Nova Scotia to hold the position of College Principal. **BACKGROUND:** a nurse by training, she has over 30 yrs. experience in health care (from staff nurse to educator, to administrator) in positions held in Nova Scotia and Ontario. And, for several years, she operated her own weaving business; her products were sold in a number of countries around the world. From 1998-2001, she was the Executive Director of the Centre for Women in Business at MSVU, responsible for assisting women entrepreneurs start and develop their business activities. **AFFIL/MBRSHP:** Advisory Council, Dalhousie U. Law School Prog. for Indigenous Blacks and Mi'kmaq; Chair, Women's Enterprise Fund, Cdn Women's Foundation; Vice-Chair, Federal Judicial Appointments Advisory Committee; Cdn Race Relations Foundation; BBI; Brd. of Governors, Dalhousie U. (Chair, Audit Cmtee); Queen's Counsel Appointment Advisory Committee; Annapolis Regional Community Arts Council. Previously served on Boards of: YMCA; Metro United Way; CNIB (NS and PEI region); National Leadership Committee, James Robinson Johnston Chair,

Black Cdn Studies; Gerontology Assn. /NS; Brd. of Governors, NS College of Art and Design. **HONS.:** several including: Outstanding Volunteer Recognition Award, YWCA, 2002; Volunteer Services Award, CNIB, 2001; Woman of Excellence, Public Affairs & Communication/Progress Club of Canada, 1998; Global Citizen Award/UN 50th Anniv.; BCC, Wall of Honour, 1994; Hon. Doctorate, MSVU., 1993. **REVIEWED IN:** *Chatelaine; Maclean's; Globe and Mail; Chronicle Herald;* etc. Film/TV: *Rhythm Stick to Freedom,* on the History Channel, 1998; NFB film *Black Mother, Black Daughter,* 1988. **EDUCATION:** MBA, Saint Mary's U., 1997; DTSN, Dalhousie U., 1968; RN, Halifax Children's Hosp. **MOTTO:** Better to burn out rather than rust out. **CONTACT:** lewisde@nscc.ns.ca; Fax: 902-491-4800

►LEWIS, Glenn

SINGER/SONGWRITER, Sony Music, 1121 Leslie St., Toronto, ON M3C 2J9. Born: Toronto, ON.

▶ Glenn Lewis has been performing on the Toronto music scene for several years. In 2002, he won the Juno Award for Best R&B/Soul Recording for his single, *Don't You Forget It,* which was well received by audiences throughout NA. The song, which has overtones of Stevie Wonder in its vocalization, ranked as a top 10 single in the Canadian Top 40 radio charts. *Don't You Forget It,* released in October, 2001, is the first single from his debut album, *World Outside My Window,* released March, 2002. **HONS.:** Best R&B/ Soul Recording for, *Don't You Forget It,* Juno Award, 2002 and UMAC Award, 2002; had previously received three other Juno nominations: *Only Be in Love,* (with Baby Blue Soundcrew) 2001, *'Bout Your Love,* 1999, and, *The Thing to Do,* 1998. **CONTACT:** Tel: 215-533-6080; titocorrales@rockstarentertainment.tv; www.glennlewismusic.com

►LEWIS, Ray, CM.

OLYMPIC ATHLETE & RAILWAY PORTER (Ret.), Hamilton, ON. Born: Hamilton, ON.

▶ Ray Lewis, in 1932, became the first Black to become a member of the Canadian Olympic Track & Field team. He first drew attention in his home town of Hamilton in 1929, when he won four high school championships in running, on the same day, in the 100-yard, 220-yard, 440-yard, and the mile relay; his relay team placed first in the 4 x 400-yard High School Relay Championships of the USA, at the University of Pennsylvania, in both 1928 & 1929. At the Olympic Games in Los Angeles, 1932, he won a bronze medal in the 4x400 relay; in 1934, at the British Empire Games in London, England, he won a silver medal in the mile relay and ran a personal best of 47.5 seconds. These wins, however, did not come easily; at the time, he worked on the Canadian Pacific Railways (CPR) as a porter, since that was the only job that he and a large number of Black men could get; with little time to formally train, he would run alongside the train, competing with his shadow; he competed until 1938 and continued working for CPR until 1952, a career which spanned 20 yrs. He then operated his own custodial firm until 1968, when he joined the staff of the Province of Ontario as chauffeur for MPP George Kerr (Burlington), for ten yrs.; in 1978, he joined the Unified Family Court in Hamilton and remained there for ten yrs., retiring from active employment at age 78. Throughout his career and within his community, RL has been praised for his dignity and his affability; particularly noted has been his ability to rise above the indignities to which he and many other Blacks had been subjected. Devoted to family and community, in 1945, he and his wife, Vivienne, adopted two children, Anthony and Lawrence; in 1948, he joined the Masonic Lodge, with which he is still involved. In recent years, he has been a frequent speaker at schools and community events. In 1999, Ray Lewis' life story was chronicled in *Shadow Running,* by John Cooper, of the Bell Centre at Centennial College. **HONS.:** include, Order of Canada, 2001; ACAA, for contribution to Canadian sports, 1999; included on Hamilton Sports Wall of Fame, 1996; inductee, Hamilton Gallery of Distinction, 1992. **REVIEWED IN:** several, including: *Shadow Running: Ray Lewis, Canadian Railway Porter & Olympic Athlete,* 1999; *Some Black Men,* 1999.

▶**LEWIS, Ronald,** MD, FRCSC, FACS.
SURGEON, CHAIR, DIVISION VASCULAR SURGERY, McGill University Health Centre, 687 Pine Ave., Montreal, QC H3A 1A1. Born: St. Lucia/ in Canada since: 1968.

▶ Dr. Ronald Lewis is a surgeon at the McGill University Health Centre. He studied medicine at the University of the West Indies (UWI) and surgery at McGill University. He served as Lecturer in Surgery at the University of the West Indies, 1973-74, and then returned to McGill University. From 1987-1996, he was the Surgeon-in-Chief of the Queen Elizabeth Hospital in Montreal. Currently he is the Chair, Division of Vascular Surgery at McGill University. **WORKS:** several including: seven book chapters; articles in, *World J of Surgery; British J of Surgery; American J of Surgery; Archives of Surgery; J of the American College of Surgeons; American J of Obstetrics & Gynecology; Can J of Surgery.* **EDUCATION:** FRCSC; FACS; MSc, Experimental Surgery, McGill U; MB BS, London, 1966. **HEROES/ROLE MODELS:** Alan Butler; Francis Moore; Fraser Gurd; Campbell Derby. **MOTTO:** Nothing beats a trial. The past does not equal the present. **CONTACT:** ronaldlewisa@sympatico.ca; Fax: 514-486-2317

▶**LEWIS, Roy**
ACTOR, Brampton, ON. Born: England/ in Canada since: 1968.

▶ Roy Lewis immigrated to Canada from England in his mid-teens. He studied Fine Art and Art History at McMaster U. before venturing into the theatre; has performed in many theatres throughout Ontario and Quebec, including the Shaw and Stratford Festivals. He is best known at Shaw for his work as Sandy Tyrell in Noel Coward's *Hay Fever;* at the Stratford Festival for the roles of Morocco in *The Merchant of Venice,* Capulet in *Romeo and Juliet,* and Norfolk in a *Man for All Seasons.* Other non-Festival, stage work includes: *Lambton, Kent and Other Vistas* for Volcano Productions; *Travels with My Aunt* at the National Art Centre; *The Taming of the Shrew* at the Canadian Stage Company; and *All Fall Down* at the Grand Theatre of London. After several years of performing, he returned to school and obtained his MFA at York U. His work now extends to film and TV, where his credits include a multitude of roles in mainstream TV programs such as *Top Cops; La Femme Nikita; Street Time; Counterstrike; ENG; Secret Service; War of the Worlds;* and *The Associates.* His film work includes roles in features such as *Tommy Boy; The Last Witness; The Taking of Pelham 1-2-3; Laughter on the 23rd Floor; Race to Freedom;* and most recently, Sidney J. Furie's *Partners in Action.* He is a founding member of the Obsidian Theatre Company and lectures on theatre and Elizabethan text at Concordia University. **HONS.:** Multicultural Award; Tyrone Guthrie Award. **EDUCATION:** MFA, York U.; BA, McMaster U. **HEROES/ROLE MODELS:** Marti Maraden, director/actor; Aron Tager, actor/artist; Henry Gomez, actor/academic. **MOTTO:** Do something because nothing comes of nothing! **CONTACT:** roylewis45@hotmail.com; Fax: 905-454-9710

▶**LEWIS, Sharon**
ON-AIR HOST, ZedTV, CBC Television, 250 Front St. W., Toronto, ON. Born: Toronto, ON, 1965.

▶ Sharon Lewis is a writer, performer and on-air TV host. From the Fall of 2001 to mid-2002, she was the host of CBC TV's current affairs talk show, *Counterspin;* is currently hosting the show

ZedTV on CBC TV. In a career in the arts which only began in 1992, she has accomplished the following: co-author with maxine bailey (*see: bailey, maxine*) of the play *Sistahs*, 1998, which was nominated for a Dora Mavor Moore Award; played the title role in Clement Virgo's (*see: Virgo, Clement*) first full-length feature film, *Rude*, 1994; her first principal role was in the Canadian production of *Imperceptible Mutabilities in the Third Kingdom*; co-founded Sugar 'n Spice Productions, 1993, to promote works by and for ethno-racially diverse women; hosted a 12-part series on TVO; played a principal role in the Showtime movie, *Mr and Mrs Loving*; since 1997, is the artistic director of Soulzstyle Productions, which produces films, books, and art by and for women of ethno-culturally diverse backgrounds. Most recently, she appeared in the film *Maple*, which she wrote and executive produced and which won the award for Best Director at the 2001 Reel Black Awards. In addition to performing, she has written fiction and non-fiction pieces, some of which have been published. **WORKS:** several including: *Sistahs*, 1998; articles in *Word; Fuse Magazine; Plural Desires; Revue Noir.* **EDUCATION:** BA/Hons., U of T, 1989. **MOTTO:** Whatever you think you can do or believe you can do, begin it. Action has magic, grace, and power in it. (Goethe) **CONTACT:** soulzstyling@yahoo.com; www.urbansoulspace.com

LISTER, Celya
INDEPENDENT TV PRODUCER/CEO, Caribbean Television Quebec, Montreal, QC. Born: Trinidad & Tobago/ in Canada since: 1972.
▶ Celya Lister has worn many hats throughout the course of her life and been involved in a wide range of activities. She is best known, however, for her time at Caribbean Television Quebec, as Executive Producer from 1992-97; she produced three shows: *Caribbean Sizzle, Hallelujah–A Soulful Celebration*, and, *GAMEDAZE*. At the time, these shows were fairly new to Montreal's

TV-watching audience (having only previously seen Betty Riley's *Black Is* in the 1970s), and catered primarily to the interests of the large African and Caribbean population. **AFFIL/MBRSHP:** 1991-97, Sec-Gen. Assn. of Third World Scientists; former Secretary of SPATEQ/CSN (TV producers of ethnic shows in Quebec). **EDUCATION:** studies in Biology, Chemistry, London U., UK, 1962; Biotechnology, U. of Montreal, 1992. **HEROES/ROLE MODELS:** Maya Angelou; David Suzuki. **MOTTO:** The impossible I can do immediately; miracles take a little longer. **CONTACT:** spateq@hotmail.com; www.spateq@blackplanet.com

▶LONGE, Winfield E., Capt.
FLEET CAPTAIN, Upper Lakes Group, Toronto, ON. Born: Guyana/ in Canada since: 1964.
▶ Captain Winfield Longe is a Fleet Captain with the Upper Lakes Group, a Canadian company whose major business activity is the transportation of bulk commodities on the Great Lakes, the St. Lawrence Seaway and the Atlantic Ocean. **CAREER HIGHLIGHTS:** appointed Captain, 1975; in 1976, he was Captain of the largest dry bulk carrier in Canada (800 ft. x 116 ft.); became Fleet Captain, 1981; was appointed Commodore, 1998-2000. In 1985, he was selected, from among 35 captains, to coordinate mooring arrangements of ships to the concrete platforms of the drilling rigs in the North Sea; taught Ship Master's Business at Georgian College; and, was consulted on the preparation of the "Atmospheric Environmental Program Alternative Service Delivery Study." According to the Union, he is the first Black sea captain in Canada or on the Great Lakes, Canadian or American. In 1984 and 1993, he was elected President of the Ship Masters' Assn. of Niagara. **EDUCATION:** George Brown College, Marine Institute; Montreal Marine & Electronics Navigational School. **HEROES/ROLE MODELS:** Captain Percy Smith, friend. **MOTTO:** You are only as good as your last successful voyage. **CONTACT:** captain1 @sprint.ca; Tel: 416-920-7610

▶**LOPES, Blair**
ADJUNCT PROFESSOR, Dalhousie University/ **PRESIDENT,** Added Dimension Consulting Services, Lake Charlotte, NS. Born: Halifax, NS.
▶ Blair Lopes is an Adjunct Professor, in the Faculty of Management, School of Public Administration, at Dalhousie University, since 1996. He is also President of his own consulting firm specializing in HR Management issues, and a Certified Human Resource Professional, since 1996. His major clients include the Government of Canada and the Government of Nunavut. **BACKGROUND:** spent 26 yrs. in the Federal Public Service where he held many senior positions; represented Canada internationally with the UN, the British Commonwealth Secretariat, and with the Gambia Government; last position was as Regional Director of the Atlantic Provinces for the Public Service Commission. **AFFIL/MBRSHP:** served on executive boards, Institute of Public Administration of Canada; the Black Educators Assn., NS; the Federal Institute of Management; Brd. of Governors, NS College of Arts and Design; Advisory Cmtee, School of Public Administration, Dalhousie U.; Black Employees Network of Federal Public Servants; was a provincial appointee to the Council on African Canadian Education (CACE), 1999; federal appointee, Steering Advisory Brd., Career Development/Technical Skills Training Program /Offshore Canada/NS Development Fund, 1998. **EDUCATION:** BA, Saint Mary's U., 1969; also studies completed at Alberta, Dalhousie, & Quebec universities; Cdn Centre for Mngmt Development. **HEROES/ROLE MODELS:** Dr. W.P. Oliver, minister & youth leader. **MOTTO:** Don't let someone else's negative perception of you become your reality. **CONTACT:** blair.lopes@dal.ca; Tel: 902-845-2179

▶**LORD, Richard M.**
ENGINEER/IMMIGRATION CONSULTANT/COM-MUNITY ORGANIZER, Montreal, QC. Born: Montreal, QC.
▶ Richard Lord is a pioneer who has had many successes in his life including: Engineer with Expo '67, Immigration Consultant and Adjudicator, and political party official. In addition, he has been extensively involved with a number of community organizations and community initiatives. Before beginning his professional life, he was the first Black to play in the American college hockey league, 1949, while he was studying engineering at Michigan State U. (MSU) **CAREER HIGHLIGHTS:** Process Engineer, Dominion Tar and Chemical (now Union Carbide), 1954-55; Engineer, to Team Engineer, Public Works Dept., City of Montreal, 1955-66; seconded from the City of Montreal to the Cdn Corp. 1967 World Exhibition, where he was Project Engineer, responsible for Communications, 1964-67. He was then Assistant to the President, with the engineering company of F.C. Hume and Co. Ltd., 1967-69. From 1968-69, he was appointed to the Special Senate Committee on Poverty as a Research Consultant and Community Liaison Officer; then worked with the Vanier Institute of the Family, 1969-72, eventually becoming Administrator. He was appointed to the Immigration Appeal Brd. of Canada, after which he enrolled in law school, 1975-76. In 1975, he created Canafric Development Corp., promoting Canadian engineering in Africa, until 1993, and, from 1978-93, he operated, Richard Lord Int'l Immigration Consultants, 1994-96. **COMMUNITY INVOLVEMENT:** has been extensive including, founding member MABBP; Brd., St. Leonard's House (Rehab. Centre); Cdn Bible Society; past President, Royal Commonwealth Society; Council for Black Aging; Westmount Historical Society. Featured in *Too Colourful for the League,* 2000, a documentary about his campaign to have Herbert Carnegie, one of Canada's best hockey players (*see: Carnegie, Herbert*) inducted into the Hockey Hall of Fame. **AFFIL/MBRSHP:** member, Immigration and Refugee Board of Canada; Order of

Engineers of Quebec, since 1955; American Institute of Chemical Engineers, since 1955; Westmount High School Old Boys' Assn.; Michigan State University Engineering Alumni; Liberal Party/Quebec, VP, 1966-68, and President, 1968-70; member, Kappa Alpha Psi Fraternity Inc. **HONS.:** including: Volunteer Citizen of the Year, Westmount Municipal Assn., 2002; Distinguished Alumnus Award, Michigan State U., 1998; Award for Contribution to the Community, Council for Black Aging, 1992; Award for Special Service, Barbados House, 1991; Award, MABBP, 1991; Award for Excellence as a Professional, Mtl Black Community, 1976 & '89. **WORKS:** in, *Community Contact; The Quebecer.* **REVIEWED IN:** *Detroit Tribune; The Westmount Examiner; Expo '67 Journal; Le Devoir; Vancouver Sun; Toronto Star.* **EDUCATION:** Civil Law, McGill U., 1972; BSc, Chemical Engineering, Michigan State U., 1953. **HEROES/ROLE MODELS:** Archdeacon Gower-Rees, St. George's Anglican Church, Mtl; Dr. John Hannah, President MSU, 1950s. **MOTTO:** God likes a cheerful giver. **CONTACT:** maisoncrossroads@qc.aibn.com; Fax: 514-932-6668.

◄ LORIMER, Edith, MD.
FAMILY PHYSICIAN, Rosedale Medical Centre, Ste. 412-600 Sherbourne St., Toronto, ON M4X 1W4. Born: Jamaica/ in Canada since: 1968.
▶ Dr. Edith Lorimer is a Family Physician and, through her extensive community involvement, a youth advocate for a number of groups. **CAREER HIGHLIGHTS:** during the course of completing her doctorate in mathematics, she decided to switch to the field of medicine. After obtaining her MD, she was a Research Fellow in Respiratory Diseases at St. Paul's Hospital in Vancouver, then at Sunnybrook Hospital, in Toronto, 1978. She first worked with *Le Partage* Medical Practice, 1990-95, and has been with the Rosedale Medical Centre since 1995. She has also been a Guest Emergency Physician to Jamaican Tourist Board Dele-

gations from Rome, Singapore, and Budapest. **COMMUNITY:** as a youth advocate, she supported the following: U of T Student Mentorship Program; Camp Jumoke, for Sickle Cell afflicted African Canadians; Toronto East SDA Church; Eastern Commerce College Professional Day. Other community activities: mentor and math tutor, Afro-Caribbean Cdn groups, 1980-95; member OBHS, since 1980; Women for PACE, since 1994. And, since 1997: Harambee Centres; Toronto East SDA Youth; the JCA; the St. Paul's Anglican Church; AABHS. **HONS.:** several including: North York Community African Cdn Achievement Award, 2000; ACAA, Medicine, 2000; Community Award, York U. Black Students Assn., 2000; Advocate Award, PACE, 2000. **EDUCATION:** MD, 1974; PhD, Mathematics Program (course work & comprehensive), 1970; MSc, 1968, McMaster University. BSc, Mathematics, Edinburgh U., Scotland, 1967. **HEROES/ROLE MODELS:** Parents & teachers. **MOTTO:** "Perseverance and Genius: genius, the power that dazzles mortal eyes, is often perseverance in disguise. So, persevere!" **CONTACT:** Fax: 416-929-6281

▶ LOWE, Keith D., PhD.
INTERNATIONAL EDUCATION CONSULTANT, Inter Cultural Associates Inc., Toronto, ON. Born: Jamaica/ in Canada since: 1979.
▶ Dr. Keith Lowe is an international education consultant with expertise in project planning, curriculum design, and human resources development. He has worked with the Min. of Education in Ontario and Jamaica, and has completed consulting or conference assignments in Belize, Bermuda, Trinidad, the UK, and Venezuela. Since 1997, he has been a Senior Policy Analyst, Ont. Min. of Education. **CAREER HIGHLIGHTS:** Assistant Professor, U. of California/San Diego, 1967-69; Director of Curriculum, Head of Research, Min. of Education, Jamaica, 1969-79; Community Development Officer, Ont. Min. of Citizenship and Culture, 1985-89; Policy Ana-

lyst, Human Resources Secretariat, Ontario, 1989-97. He has also held term teaching appointments with: Howard U., Washington, DC; Faculty of Education, U of T, and Ryerson University. He is the editor of a teacher's manual on remedial reading, Min. of Education, Jamaica; and, co-editor/editor of the education journal, 1995-98, of the Cdn Council on Multicultural and Intercultural Education. **OTHER:** in 2000, he coordinated and co-chaired Canada's first Conference for Hakkas, people of Chinese descent who had been distanced from their heritage as a result of being scattered over the world for generations, through voluntary or involuntary migration. **HONS.:** Boylston Speaking Prize, Harvard U., 1959, 1960. **EDUCATION:** Dipl. Ed, UWI, 1970. PhD, 1969; MA, 1966, Stanford University. BA, Harvard U., 1960; plus courses in curriculum development & cross-cultural communication. **CONTACT:** ica@ interlog.com; www.interlog.com/~ica

▶**LY, Aoua Bocar, PhD.**
CHERCHEURE/SOCIOLOGUE-ENVIRONNEMEN-TALISTE, Femmes, Environnement Viable & éducation interculturelle (FEM En Vie), 5819, av Cool Brook, Montréal, QC H3X 2M3. Née: Sénégal/ au Canada depuis: 1989.
▶ Dr Ly est sociologue et chercheur en sciences sociales, humaines, et environnementales; elle est spécialiste de questions de Genre/Égalité des sexes (femmes et développement), d'environnement et d'études interethniques et interculturelles. Elle a déjà travaillé pour des agences de développement international telles que l'ACDI, le Fonds européen de développement (FED), l'Agence américaine de développement international (USAID) et pour des organismes des Nations Unies comme l'UNIFEM, le PNUD, la FAO. Elle est aussi l'une des spécialistes de la question des mutilations sexuelles féminines (MSF) à travers le monde. Elle a mené dans ce domaine des études, des interventions, animé des sessions, organisé des rencontres (séminaires, colloques...)

accordé des entrevues aux médias et initié des documentaires, en vue de l'éradication des MSF. Après avoir été chercheure associée à la Chaire en relations ethniques (1997-1999), elle est depuis 2000 associée à l'Institut d'études des femmes de l'Université d'Ottawa. Elle dirige également un cabinet d'expert-conseil, Fem En Vie. Elle est souvent interviewée sur des questions sociologiques, touchant, en particulier les femmes et l'Afrique par des chaînes de radios et de télévisions (RDI, RFI, Radio Canada, néerlandaise, du Sénégal, ...) et par plusieurs journaux. **VIE ASSOCIATIVE:** présidente-fondatrice, Femmes Africaines, Horizon 2015, un réseau qui œuvre pour l'intégration positive des africaines au Canada; membre, Féderation des Femmes du Québec, de l'Assn. Canadienne des Etudes Africaines; elle est aussi membre fondateur de plusieurs organisations féminines, écologiques, culturelles et de recherches. **PRIX:** Flambeau d'excellence 2001, Gala de reconnaissance communautaire, catégorie académique; Prix Femmes de mérite, 2000, YWCA (1ère femme africaine à recevoir ce prix en Amérique du nord); Bourse d'excellence du Programme canadien de bourses de la Francophonie, 1989; Bourse d'excellence de la Coopération technique belge au Sénégal, 1981. **ŒUVRES À SON PROPOS:** *calendrier, MHN,* 2001; *J de Montréal*; *Diaspora*; *Afrique Tribune*; *La Renaissance, la Gazette des femmes*; *Femmes Plus; Châtelaine*, etc. **FORMATION:** Doctorat, sociologie de l'environnement, U. de Montréal, 1996. Maîtrise, en sociologie, 1980; Lic. en lettres, 1977; Dipl. d'études littéraires, 1976 , U. Cheikh Anta Diop de Dakar, Sénégal. **MOTTO:** Léguer aux générations futures un monde de paix et de justice sociale entre les races, les pays et les sexes. **CONTACT:** Tél: 514-739-5574; aoua.bocar.ly @vl.videotron.ca; www.pleiades.cdn-ndg.com

▶MACFARLANE, Anthony, MD.

MEDICAL PRACTITIONER, Private Practice, Ste. 705-1Young St., Hamilton, ON L8N 1T8. Born: Jamaica/ in Canada since: 1959.

▸ Dr. Anthony MacFarlane is a general practitioner who has been in private practice in Hamilton since 1969; he taught first-year medical students at McMaster U., from 1970-1980. He is also a member of the Temple Anshe Sholom and is a past-President of the Board of Trustees. **WORKS:** in *The Hamilton Spectator.* **EDUCATION:** MD, U of T, 1965; BA, McMaster U., 1961. **MOTTO:** The body thrives on regularity. **CONTACT:** tony.mac@mcmaster.ca

▸MAKEDA, Donna

REGGAE/DANCEHALL PERFORMER/CO-PUBLISHER, *Uprising International,* 17-238 Galloway Blvd., Scarborough, ON M1E 5H2. Born: Guyana/ in Canada since: 1990.

▸ Donna Makeda is well known as a "multi-award-winning reggae dancehall DJ performer." Since debuting on the Canadian Reggae scene in 1990, she has won eight awards, and has performed at many festivals in Canada and the Caribbean. Her first album, *Who Can Endure,* was well received, and, in 1999, she was awarded a licensing deal for a track, *Life Story,* in Italy. Some of her singles have reached No.1 in the US, including *South Africa, Jah Great Woman,* and *Sweet Victory.* She has also made three music videos, performed with many of the leading international reggae artists and has many TV appearances to her credit. She is also featured in the documentary film *Roots Daughters,* along with Judy Mowatt. She is also co-publisher of the newspaper *Uprising International.* **HONS.:** include, Recognition Award, Guyana Cdn Musical Awards, 2001; since 1993 has won several awards from the Cdn Reggae Music Awards including: three awards as Top Female Reggae Dancehall/ DJ; Top Reggae Newcomer, 1993. **EDUCATION:**

Dipl., Recorded Music Production, Trebas Institute, 1997. **CONTACT:** Tel: 416-287-9484; makongo @idirect.com

▶MANLEY, Rachel

WRITER, c/o Random House, Ste. 300-1 Toronto St., Toronto, ON M5C 2V6. Born: England/ raised in Jamaica/ in Canada since: 1985.

▸ Rachel Manley is a writer who has produced works of poetry and non-fiction; she has also edited a number of collections. **HONS.:** Gugghenheim Fellow, 2001-02; Rockefeller Fellow, 2000; Bunting Fellow, Radcliffe U., 1998-99; GG Award, non-fiction for *Drumblair,* 1997; Jamaica Centennial Medal, for Poetry, 1979. **WORKS:** include, *Slipstream: A Daughter Remembers,* 2000; *Drumblair: Memories of a Jamaican Childhood,* 1996; *A Light Left On,* collected poems, 1992; *The Edna Manley Diaries,* ed., 1980; *Poems 2,* 1978; *Poems,* 1972. **EDUCATION:** BA/Hons, UWI/Mona, 1969. **MOTTO:** Trust Life! **CONTACT:** c/o Tel: 416-957-1566

▶MANNING, George

REGULATORY ANALYST, ESBI (Alberta) Ltd., Calgary, AB. Born: Barbados/ in Canada since: 1969.

▸ George Manning is a Regulatory Analyst with ESBI (Alberta) Ltd., Alberta's independent transmission administrator for electricity, and is responsible for developing tariff applications and revenue requirements for approval by the Alberta Energy and Utilities Board. **CAREER:** he has over 20 yrs. experience in the utility environment, including telecommunications, water, wastewater, and electricity. From 1994-2001, he worked with the City of Calgary as a Financial and Rates Analyst; worked with AGT Ltd., 1979-93 in a number of positions including Corporate and Business Planner, Sr. Economist, and Marketing Research Specialist. From 1983-86 he was on secondment to Telecom Canada, in Ottawa, as a Supervising Analyst in the Revenue Estimates

Div. He has also represented AGT on a Federal/Industry Task Force on Productivity in the Telecommunications industry. **COMMUNITY:** volunteers for several charities, including Caribbean Associations. **EDUCATION:** MA, Economics, SFU, 1976; BA, Economics & Statistics, U. of Manitoba, 1973. **HEROES/ROLE MODELS:** Abraham Lincoln, for his resilience. **MOTTO:** I am my own expert; I am not affected by the negative attitudes and opinions of others. **CONTACT:** george.manning@eal.ab.ca; Fax: 403-705-5295

►MARK, Kirk

ADVISOR, RACE & ETHNIC RELATIONS, Multiculturalism Dept., Toronto Catholic District School Board (TCDSB), 80 Sheppard Ave. E., Toronto, ON M2N 6E8. Born: Trinidad & Tobago/ in Canada since: 1968.

► Kirk Mark is an Advisor/Coordinator of Race and Ethnic Relations with the Toronto Catholic District School Board, a position he has held since 1996. Previously, he was a Community Relations Officer with the TCDSB, 1991-95. During that mandate he assisted in the development of the *Antiracism and Ethnocultural Equity: Policy and Guidelines* for the school board. **OTHER:** since 1980, he has been the Founding Director of the Toronto Basketball Assn., and has been involved in the production of three videos on basketball and the African-Caribbean Diaspora. **COMMUNITY:** founding member, Willowdale Community Legal Services; Brd., Urban Alliance on Race Relations; former Vice-Chair, Caribbean Cultural Committee; Vice-Chair, Canadian Alliance of Black Educators. **HONS.:** several, including: Hon. Ghanaian Citizenship, Ghanaian Canadian Assn., 2001; Race Relations African Heritage Award, City of Toronto, 2001; Race Relations Harmony Award, City of Toronto, 1999; Cert. of Achievement, Urban Alliance on Race Relations, 1999. **EDUCATION:** doctoral candidate, Education, OISE/U of T. M.Ed, 1999; BA, 1978, York University. Dipl. Social Sciences,

Dawson College, QC, 1976. **HEROES/ROLE MODELS:** Spouse; parents; Bob Proctor, motivational speaker. **MOTTO:** You are your only problem and you are your only solution. (Raymond D. Stanford) **CONTACT:** kirkmark@rogers.com; Fax: 905-831-4249

►MARKHAM, The Reverend Dr. Jean J. Burke

MINISTER-IN-CHARGE & PASTOR, Peel Methodist Church (BME), 3535 South Common Crt., Mississauga, ON L5L 2B3. Born: Barbados/ in Canada since: 1957.

► The Reverend Dr. Jean Markham began her professional life as a teacher followed by several years in business including, real estate, owner and publisher of *Rainbow* magazine, owner and manager of her own secretarial service and employment agency. Since 1995, she has been the Minister-in-Charge and Pastor of Peel Methodist (BME) Church. Previously, she was the founder and Pastor of the Alexander S. Markham Memorial Methodist Episcopal Church, 1990-95. She is the first woman to found a BME church in its 145-yr. history, and the second woman to be ordained within its ranks. She is presently writing the history of the BME church from 1856 to the present. She is also the first woman Minister nominated to seek the highest office in the BME Church, that of Bishop and Superintendent. Her late husband, The Rt. Rev. Dr. Alexander S. Markham had served as General Superintendent and Bishop of the BME Church for 20 yrs. (five consecutive terms). **HONS.:** including, Hon. Doctor of Humane Letters, Virginia U., 1998; Cert. of Recognition, City of Mississauga, 1995; Plaque and inducted into Hall of Fame, Int'l Assn. of Ministers' Wives & Widows, 1997; President Emeritus & Founder, Canada Assn. Ministers' Wives & Widows, 1982; BME Church Ministers' Wives & Widows; various real estate awards incl. Million Dollar Club, 1978. **WORKS:** in, *Apostle* BME magazine; has edited several booklets honouring women in the church and community, 1975-89. **REVIEWED IN:** local and community publications; BME newsletters & publications; *WWCW*; *Some Black Women*; *Leading the Way: Black Women in Canada.* **EDUCATION:** MTS, Ont. Theological Seminary, 1998; BA, U of T, 1972; Bus. Admin. Dipl., Albert College, 1958. **HEROES/ROLE MODELS:** Bishop A.S. Markham. **MOTTO:** I seek truth, justice and order in all my undertakings; trying always to set a good example for others, especially children.

▶**MARSHALL, Amanda**
SINGER/SONGWRITER, c/o Erin Smyth, Sony Music, 1121 Leslie St., Toronto, ON M3C 2J9. Born: Toronto, ON.
▶ Amanda Marshall is a singer who has released three albums since 1996. Her debut album, *Amanda Marshall*, included seven top 10 singles, sold over two million copies worldwide and achieved gold certification in Germany, Norway, Holland and Australia. Her second album, *Tuesday's Child*, released in 1999, produced three top 20 singles, and surpassed triple platinum status in Canada. Following release of her second album, she embarked on a worldwide tour as the opening act for Whitney Houston, performing in more than 25 European cities. Her third album, *Everybody's Got a Story*, was released in the Fall of 2001 in Canada, the US, and Europe and has received positive reviews from critics and members of the listening public. **OTHER:** in addition to recording, AM has also appeared on TV on *The Rosie O'Donnell Show*, *Late Night with David Letterman*, and others; her songs are included in film soundtracks (*My Best Friend's Wedding, Tin Cup*). **BACKGROUND:** born to a Trinidadian mother and a Canadian father, AM was enrolled in a toddler's music program at a local conservatory at age three when her parents detected her musical aptitude. She began piano lessons and was singing publicly by the time she was in kindergarten; she joined her first band at 17 and was soon performing in clubs and theatres. **HONS.:** Gemini Award, 1998, for her TV special, *Amanda Marshall.* **REVIEWED IN:** major publications including *Rolling Stone* magazine. **CONTACT:** erin_smyth @sonymusic.com; www.amandamarshall.com

▶**MARSHALL, Clem**
EDUCATOR/DIVERSITY TRAINER, MangaCom Inc., Toronto, ON. Born: Guyana.
▶ Clem Marshall is an educator who specializes in aspects of language, culture and race. Through his company, he provides a range of equity-enhancing services in education, organizational change and the arts. His present work takes him across Canada and the USA as a consultant to public school boards and independent schools in developing anti-racist and diversity curricula. With his colleague, educator Enid Lee, he co-authored *Kaleidoscope of Health*, a training manual on cultural competence for the Ont. Hospital Assn. He wrote and directed *All Eyes On Africa*, an educational documentary video on African art, in English and French. He was a lecturer in the prize-winning Ontario Science Centre program, A Question of Truth, in 1997. He was invited to give a series of lectures on African Art by the Art Gallery of Ontario in January 2002. His experience as an anti-racist trainer has won him contracts with the Ont. Min. of Education, the Toronto YWCA, the Faculty of Medicine at U of T, and COSTI (a large, multicultural and immigrant service organization in Toronto). He has also designed and facilitated sessions for OPSEU and the Canadian Pharmacy Assn. as well as a range of other agencies serving diverse populations. **HONS.:** Teacher of the Year, Sociology, Atkinson College, York U. **WORKS:** co-author, *Kaleidoscope of Health*, 1997; *All Eyes on Africa* (video), 1993; column in *Share*; articles in *Panache; Catholic New Times.* **CONTACT:** clem@mangacom.com; Fax: 416-862-2194

▶MARSHALL, Valin G., PhD.

SOIL ZOOLOGIST, Royal Roads University, 2005 Sooke Rd., Victoria, BC V9B 5Y2. Born: Grenada/ in Canada since: 1955.

▸ After 31 years of service with the Canadian Forest Service, Dr. Valin Marshall retired in 1996 as a Senior Scientist and is currently a Research Associate in the Centre for Economic Development and Applied Research at Royal Roads University. He is a Canadian pioneer in soil zoology, focusing on impacts of environmental changes on biological diversity of forest ecosystems. During a short stay with Agriculture Canada, as a recent graduate in 1959, he gained his first experience in fertilizer research, which he continued to develop in forestry, using 15-N techniques. He has supervised visiting scientists from the Czech Republic, Finland, Japan, and Norway, and has co-authored major works with colleagues from the US and Russia. **HIGHLIGHTS:** he has described many soil animal species, while other species have been named in his honour in arthropod groups such as the Acari, Collembola, Pauropoda and Protura. For 15 years starting in 1985, he was an Adjunct Professor in the Soil Science Department at UBC. During that time he also lectured at the Silvicultural Institute of BC, the ecology program of Western Universities, and the University of Victoria. Currently, his research is focused on studying the taxonomy and ecology of Canadian soil fauna, and involves three projects: native and introduced earthworms of BC; biology of the yew mite, *Cecidophyopsis psilaspis* (Nalepa); and, the impacts of forest clearing on soil fauna. **AFFIL/MBRSHP:** holds membership in many scientific societies dedicated to Acarology, Entomology, Ecology, and Soil Science; in the 1980s, he served two terms as chairperson of the Victoria Branch of the Professional Institute of the Public Service of Canada. **OTHER:** the BC Black History Awareness Society (BCBHAS) grew out of a special Black History Event hosted by the BC Provincial Museum in 1993. He and others from that guiding committee became the founding members of BCBHAS; he was its first vice-president from 1994-95, and continued to be active in the society, holding various positions on the executive and in programs dealing with education and cemetery tours of BC Black pioneers. **WORKS:** articles in numerous scientific journals including, *Pedobiologia; Northwest Science; Can Entomol; Can J Forest Research; Forest Ecology and Management; Annu. Rev. Ecol. Syst.* **REVIEWED IN:** *Entomologists of BC*, 1991; *Victoria Times Colonist,* 1992. **EDUCATION:** PhD, 1964; MSc, 1963; BSc, (Agr.), 1959, McGill U. **HEROES/ROLE MODELS:** Dr. Keith Kevan, introduced him to Soil Zoology; Dr. Ernest M. Duporte, developed Dept. of Entomology, Faculty of Agriculture, at McGill U., 1915. **MOTTO:** Most problems are opportunities in disguise. **CONTACT:** valin.marshall@royalroads.ca; www.royalroads.ca

▶MARTIN, Eugenie, Dr.

DIRECTOR OF COSMETOLOGY, Topaz College of Aesthetics & Hair, 1553 Geta Circle, Pickering, ON L1V 3B5. Born: Guyana/ in Canada since: 1965.

▸ Dr. Eugenie Martin is the founder, President and CEO of Topaz Hairstyling Academy. She opened her first school in 1979 after recognizing the need for properly trained professionals who could cater to the specialized needs of Blacks. She has been in the aesthetic field for over 30 yrs. and the owner of Topaz for over 20 yrs. Since 1997, she has been the head of the Ontario Black Hair Assn.; she is also head of the Cdn National Barber Stylists Assn. She has served on many cultural committees including Miss Black Ontario and Miss Black Canada Beauty Pageants. From 1998-2001, she was a member of the Canada Customs and Revenue Agency's Southern Ontario Small Business Advisory Committee (SOSBAC). **HONS.:** several including, Hon. Doctorate, National Black Culturists League (NBCL) in the US, 1999; inducted into the Madam CJ

Walker Hall of Fame, 1998; nominated in East York business category awards for Business of the Year and Outstanding Turnaround; Outstanding Education Contribution Award, from *Hair News* magazine, 1995; and Achievement Award, from *Beauty Business.* **EDUCATION:** studied hair & aesthetics in the UK, the US, and Canada. **HEROES/ROLE MODELS:** Dr. Wanda Nelson, President, NBCL. **MOTTO:** Strong reasons make strong actions. (Shakespeare) **CONTACT:** Phone/ Fax: 905-426-7601

▶**MASSIAH, Thomas,** PhD, CChem., FCIC. **RESEARCH CHEMIST** (Ret.), Toronto, ON. Born: Montreal, QC.

▶ Dr. Thomas Massiah completed his studies in Organic Chemistry then carried out post-doctoral research for 22 yrs., primarily in the pharmaceutical area. He also taught chemistry, as an evening-division lecturer at SGWU (now Concordia U.), 1949-64; and, from 1985-91, was a faculty member at Seneca College (Toronto), teaching chemistry, pharmaceutical science and mathematics. He was appointed to the Ont. Min. of Health's Drug Quality and Therapeutics Committee (DQTC), serving from 1986-89. From 1985-99, he worked as a consultant in the pharmaceutical field. **COMMUNITY INVOLVEMENT:** in 1953, was founder and first President of the Montreal Negro Alumni Group (MNAG), dedicated to furthering post-secondary education among Blacks. The MNAG gave more than $30,000 in scholarships and bursaries during its 15 yr. existence. In 1968, he served as president of UNAC (University Negro Alumni Club), a Toronto-based group with similar objectives. Also, he liaised extensively with the Toronto Police, as chair (on behalf of the National Black Coalition) during 1973-74, attempting to improve police/community relations. **AFFIL/MBRSHP:** served as President of the Assn. of The Chemical Profession of Ontario (ACPO) from 1979-81. **HONS.:** elected Fellow of the Chemical Institute of Canada (FCIC) in 1988; Cert. of Appreciation, ACPO, 1986; Chartered Chemist (CChem.) of Ontario, 1984. **WORKS:** contributor to science publications, including *Canadian Chemical News.* **EDUCATION:** PhD, Organic Chemistry, U. of Montreal, 1962; MSc, Organic Chemistry, McGill U., 1956; BSc, Chemistry, SGWU (now Concordia U.), 1947. **MOTTO:** The only place where "success" comes before "work," is in the dictionary. **CONTACT:** tomclema@interlog.com

▶**MAULE, Josa Linda** **EDUCATOR,** Montreal School of Performing Arts, Ste. 201A-3480 Décarie, Montreal, QC H4A 3J5. Born: Montreal, QC, 1966.

▶ In 1992, Josa Linda Maule founded the Montreal School of Performing Arts (MSOP), which provides training to actors of all ages and skill levels to develop their talents under the tutelage of professional instructors. Through a variety of classes, workshops and professional training seminars, the MSOP provides training for on-stage or in front of the cameras. Since 1995, the school has trained over 1,000 aspiring actors and produced 38 shows, giving actors the opportunity to perform and providing affordable theatre to the community. In addition to her responsibilities as president, she has been the casting director for over 27 independent and student films (15 films on the Film Festival Circuit, three on CBC Reflection Series). **HONS.:** include, Young Entrepreneurs for the Arts, Alliance Quebec, 1995; Duke of Edinburgh Award, 1983; Citizen Award, 3rd Field Engineer Cadet Corp. **REVIEWED IN:** *Community Contact; Montreal Gazette; The Suburban; The Monitor; The Chronicle.* **EDUCATION:** American Academy of Dramatics; DEC, Early Child Care, Vanier College, 1985. **HEROES/ROLE MODELS:** Barbara Boatswain, mother; J. Boatswain & C. Braithwaite, uncles. **MOTTO:** If you fall down, if you can look up, you can get up. **CONTACT:** Fax: 514-483-1070; msopa2000@hotmail.com; www. msopa.iwarp.com

►MAYES, Rueben

ASSISTANT ATHLETIC DIRECTOR, WSU Athletic Foundation, Washington State University, Pullman, WA 99164. Born: North Battleford, SK, 1963.
▶ In 1986, Rueben Mayes became the first Canadian to be named NFL Rookie of the Year, he was also named NFL All-Pro and was a two-time All-Pro Selection. He spent seven years in the League, most of which were spent with the New Orleans Saints and two years in Seattle. His football career began at Washington State U. (WSU), where he was a two-time MVP, NCAA record holder, a two-time PAC-10 MVP, and Heisman Trophy candidate; in 1984 he set two NCAA records; rushed for a record 357 yards at Oregon and in consecutive games gained a record 573 yards, 216 at Stanford and 357 at Oregon. During the off-season of his professional career, 1986-93, he was a financial consultant with Merrill Lynch and throughout his professional playing career represented Pony International, Imperial Fitness, the National Assn. of Street Schools, Southern Baptist Hospital and WSU. Following his pro football career, RM became vice-president and Executive Director for CRISTA Ministries for three and a half years. In 1998, he served as an academic counsellor for WSU, assisting transfer students. While completing his MBA at WSU, he worked for the college of business and management information services, developing their website along with technology gift-in-kind procurement, simulation and corporate giving integration, and donor cultivation. Since 2001, he is the Assistant Athletic Director of the WSU Athletics Foundation and is responsible for overseeing all annual giving programs. **OTHER:** he is the subject of a 1989 NFB film by Selwyn Jacob (*see: Jacob, Selwyn*), *The Saint from North Battleford.* **HONS.:** include, Best Practices Award, in higher education information resources, Educause, 1999; Athlete of the Year, Saskatchewan, 1984, 1985. **EDUCATION:** MBA, 2000; BA, Social Sciences & Business, 1992, WSU. **CONTACT:** www.wsu.edu

►MBULU, Chief Emmanuel

PRESIDENT & CEO, Tone-A-Matic International, Ste. 18-145 Traders Blvd. E., Mississauga, ON L4Z 3L3. Born: Nigeria/ in Canada since: 1973.
▶ Chief Emmanuel Mbulu is the founder and President of Tone-A-Matic International, a company which manufactures and sells health and fitness products. He is also the CEO of TAMTEC Medical International, which markets health and fitness products overseas. As a result of his business success he has been active in the community supporting a number of development initiatives in Igbodo, Delta State in his native Nigeria, these include: helping to provide electricity; built a primary school and two dormitories; re-built St. George's Anglican Church and built a two-storey structure for the Bishop; donated musical instruments to the boys' brigade; and established scholarship funds. **AFFIL/MBRSHP:** serves on various boards; Patron, Assn. of Nigerians in Canada (ANIC); Chair, Nigeria Independence Committee. **HONS.:** include, Recognition for contribution to Anglican Church & community, from the Bishop of Delta State, 2001; Award of Recognition, for building school & dormitories, Min. Education, Nigeria; Cert. of Excellence, in recognition of business contribution, Nigerian-Canadian Assn., 2000; Cert. of Recognition, Anglican Grammar School Old Boys' Assn., 2000. **REVIEWED IN:** local & Nigerian publications: *AfriCanadian J.* **EDUCATION:** MBA, South Eastern U., Washington; BA/Hons., Economics, York U. **HEROES/ROLE MODELS:** Father. **MOTTO:** God is in charge. **CONTACT:** Fax: 905-501-9290

►MCCLAIN, Washington

BAROQUE OBOIST, McGill University & Indiana University. Born: USA/ in Canada since: 1992.
▶ Washington McClain is a native of Ouachita Parish, Louisiana and holds a bachelor's degree in musicology from Northeast Louisiana University and a master's degree in oboe performance

from Northwestern University. He has played with a number of symphony orchestras in the Chicago area, including the Chicago Symphony Orchestra (as extra), the Symphony of the Shores, the Chicago Symphonietta and the Aire Crown Theatre Orchestra. He has also played with the Chicago Chamber Orchestra and has been a featured soloist many times with the orchestra in the US, Europe and Asia. As an oboist performing on period instruments, he has performed on baroque and classical ones with The City Musik and Basically Bach baroque orchestras (Chicago), the Philharmonia Baroque Orchestra (San Francisco), the Early Music Consort (Kansas City), the Lyra Concert (Minneapolis), the Seattle Baroque Orchestra, Apollo's Fire (Cleveland) and various other early music ensembles in the United States. In 1992, WM moved to Toronto to play with the Tafelmusik Baroque Orchestra, where he remained a core member for seven years. In Canada, he has also performed with the Pacific Baroque Orchestra, l'Ensemble Arion, The Aradia Ensemble and various early music chamber and orchestral ensembles. He has recorded for the Sony Classical, ATMA, Analekta, CBC, Naxos and Centaur labels. He is also the first period instrument performer to be featured in *Windplayer* magazine. In addition to performing, his remaining time is divided between teaching at McGill and Indiana universities. **REVIEWED IN:** major newspapers & periodicals including, *Windplayer.* **EDUCATION:** MA, Oboe performance, Northwestern U.; BA, Musicology, Northeast Louisiana U. **CONTACT:** washmcc@attglobal.net; Fax: 514-522-2174

MCCURDY, Howard D., PhD.
FORMER MP, Government of Canada. **PROFESSOR, BIOLOGY** (Ret.), University of Windsor. Resides in LaSalle, ON. Born: London, ON.
▶ Dr. Howard McCurdy, has had two very successful careers in 34 years: he was Professor of Biology at U. of Windsor from 1959-84, then went on to a career in politics from 1979-93. **TEACHING HIGHLIGHTS:** he joined the Dept. of Biology at U. of Windsor in 1959-61 as a Lecturer; was Asst. Prof., 1961-63; Assoc. Prof., 1963-69; full Prof., 1969-84; he taught general and medical Microbiology, Microbial Physiology, and Ecology; he was also Acting Head of Dept., 1971-72 and 1974-79. He served on many professional bodies including: American Society for Microbiology; Cdn Society of Microbiologists; founder and first President of Cdn College of Microbiologists, 1976-80; also served on the editorial board of *Bacteriological Reviews*, 1973-76, and as assoc. editor (1977-78), then section editor (1978-84) on the *Can J of Microbiology.* **POLITICAL HIGHLIGHTS:** in reality, the political career of HM began in his youth when, in his teens, he led a campaign for an anti-discrimination by-law in his home town of Amherstburg; and, while at Michigan State U., was the founding President of the NAACP chapter there; later he was the founding President of the National Black Coalition of Canada. In his professional political career, he accomplished the following: was elected to the Windsor City Council in 1979, serving two terms until 1984; in 1984 was elected as Member of Parliament (NDP) for Windsor-Walkerville, then re-elected in 1988 for Windsor-St. Clair; in 1989, he contested the leadership of the NDP; while not successful in his bid, he is credited with having raised the level of awareness regarding the participation of visible minorities in politics. Now retired formally from politics and from teaching, he continues to consult, write and do research. He is the President of the Windsor Black Coalition, a group he founded in the 1960s and which was originally known as the Guardian Club. **HONS.:** including, Harry Jerome Award for Community Service, BBPA, 2002; J.S. Woodsworth Award, for Human Rights, 2001; Community Achievement Award, North American Black Historical Museum, 2001; Person of the Year, 1986; Black Achievement Award for Politics, 1976; Queen's Silver Jubilee Medal,

1977; Centennial Medal, 1967. **WORKS:** over 50 scientific publications in the field of biology; over 10 publications in the areas of politics & human rights. **REVIEWED IN:** all major local and nat'l publications; *Some Black Men*, 1999. **EDUCATION:** PhD, Microbiology & Chemistry, 1958; MSc, Microbiology & Physical Chemistry, 1955, Michigan State University. BSc, Microbiology, U. of Windsor, 1954; BA, U. of Western Ontario, 1953. **MOTTO:** Be the best at what you like best and success will follow. **CONTACT:** hdmccurdy @cogeco.ca; Fax: 519-734-6746

▶**MCCURVIN, Donna**
CO-PUBLISHER, *Word* Magazine, 6-295 Queen St. E., Brampton, ON L6W 4S6. Born: England/ in Canada since: 1972.

▶ Donna McCurvin and partner, Phil Vassell, are the founders and publishers of *Word*, Toronto's first and leading urban culture magazine, which they started in 1992 and publish ten times per year. The magazine is distributed across Canada, with local editions in Detroit and New York. *Word* magazine also provides training for students in media, through co-op programs; and, they initiated the Minority Media Training Program in partnership with the province of Ontario and the Southern Ontario Newspaper Guild. In 1997, the two co-founders started the Toronto Urban Music Festival, a showcase for new and emerging urban artists. **HONS.:** Best Publication, UMAC/Urban X-posure, 2002 & 2001; Harry Jerome, business, 2000; Special Recognition Award, UMAC, 2000. **WORKS:** *Word* magazine, published 10x/yr. **CONTACT:** info@wordmag.com; www.wordmag.com

▶**MCDONALD, Jasse (JC)**
JOURNALIST/RADIO & TV BROADCASTER. Distribution & Publications Manager, *Share* Newspaper, 658 Vaughan Rd., Toronto, ON M6E 2Y5. Born: Trinidad & Tobago/ in Canada since: 1971.

▶ Jasse (JC) McDonald, also known as "the Man with the Golden Voice" has been in the broadcasting business for over 25 yrs. as host, newscaster, voice-over announcer, and actor. **CAREER HIGHLIGHTS:** produced and narrated video in tribute to Canadian Olympian, Ray Lewis; produced and narrated video, *Caribana: The Legend*; selected as the "voice of space" for Citytv's Space Channel, which aired during 1998; hosted TV series, *Bachannal*, for three yrs. on CFMT/ channel 47; guest appearances on education broadcaster, TVO; lead role in productions in Trinidad, *Right and Wrong* and *Caribbean Fox*. On radio, he appeared in a number of programs; hosted *The J-McD Show*, CHIN-FM, for 11 yrs. and interviewed personalities from the realms of politics, entertainment, and government; previously, was a senior broadcaster on Radio Trinidad. **HONS.:** Award of Merit, Cdn Reggae Music, 2000. **REVIEWED IN:** *Toronto Star; Caribbean Camera.* **HEROES/ROLE MODELS:** Sir Trevor McDonald, brother. **CONTACT:** share@interlog.com

▶**MCFARLANE, Ivan,** PhD.
ADJUNCT LECTURER, Trinity College, University of Toronto/**ASSOCIATE GRADUATE FACULTY,** College of Graduate Studies, Central Michigan University, MI. Born: Jamaica/ in Canada since: 1961.

▶ Dr. McFarlane retired after a 29-yr. career teaching political science and sociology at Centennial College, where, for 13 of those years, he was Chair of the Social Science Dept. He is now an Adjunct Lecturer at Trinity College, U of T, and an Associate Graduate Faculty member of the College of Graduate Studies, Central Michigan University. Over the years, he has been involved with a number of community initiatives: the Black Community Centre Project, 1970-72, which documented strategies for achieving mutual respect and acculturation of newcomers; the United Way of Greater Toronto; and the BBPA. **AFFIL/MBRSHP:** Director, Canadian Club of

Toronto; member, Quadrangle Society, Massey College; and, member, Diversity Roundtable, TVO. He has also participated in the Caribbean Anglican Consultation Conferences. **HONS.:** Arbor Award, for outstanding personal service by alumni volunteers, U of T, 1998; Cert. Appreciation, BBPA, 1996. **WORKS:** include, "Ontario CAATS: Thoughts about Teaching in One," in *Int'l Mico J*; "Environmental Concerns: Possible Approaches for Future Canada-Africa Cooperation." **REVIEWED IN:** *Massey College Yearbook*, 1997-98; *U of T Magazine*, 1995; *Toronto Life*, 1981. **EDUCATION:** PhD, 1995; MA, 1982; BA/Hons., 1964, U of T. MES, Faculty Environmental Studies, York U, 1972; MA, Carleton U., 1969. **HEROES/ROLE MODELS:** Stanley Grizzle, friend. **MOTTO:** *Fortis cadere cedere non potest* –The brave may fall but cannot yield. **CONTACT:** imcfarlane@globalserve.net; Fax: 416-932-1200

▶MCINTOSH, Yanna

ACTOR & TEACHER, Toronto, ON. Born: Jamaica/ in Canada since: age 2.

▶ Yanna McIntosh is a professional theatre artist whose work is often described in superlatives by critics and audience members alike. She won early critical acclaim for her work in U of T student productions and for her portrayal of Medea in *The Impossible Can Happen* (The Other Theatre of Toronto, 1988). After completing her studies at U of T, she taught elementary school before receiving professional theatre training at the American Repertory Theatre at Harvard. Stage credits include: title role in *Belle*, Factory Theatre, Toronto, 2000 (re-mounted in 2002, Factory Theatre, Toronto and at the National Arts Centre, Ottawa), earning Dora Mavor Moore Award nominations for both performances; Kyra in *Skylight*, Tarragon Theatre, 2001; Petruchio in *The Taming of the Shrew*, 2000 and Helena in *A Midsummer Night's Dream,* 1995, both for CanStage; Dr. Mtubu in Andrei Alexis', *Lambton Kent*, Summerworks Festival, 2000, and at the Edinburgh

Festival, 2001; Veronica in *Valley Song,* New Globe Theatre, 1997. She performed at the Stratford Festival, 1992-94, in: *The Illusion*; *Cyrano de Bergerac*; *Antony and Cleopatra*; *A Midsummer Night's Dream*; *Two Gentlemen of Verona*; and, *Twelfth Night*. She has also appeared in *A Fertile Imagination*; *Jacob Two-Two Meets the Hooded Fang*; *The Song of Songs*; and *Tartuffe*. In 1997, her one-woman show, *Trace*, which she co-wrote and performed, was a hit at the Toronto Fringe Festival. In addition to her stage work, she has had principal roles in radio, TV, and feature films including, *Due South*; *True Blue*; *Atomic Train*; *Acceptable Risk*; *Deliberate Intent*; *John Q*, with Denzel Washington; and played Jenni, in CBC's *Riverdale*. **OTHER:** as an emerging director, she has assisted on *The Glass Menagerie* and *The Designated Mourner*; in 2001, she directed the Humber College second-year acting class' productions of *Macbeth* and *Julius Ceasar*, 2002. **HONS.:** Dora Mavor Moore Awards: Female Performance in a Principal Role, for *Skylight* (2002), and, Outstanding Performance, for *Valley Song*. Dora nominations for *A Midsummer Night's Dream* and *Belle*. **REVIEWED IN:** local, nat'l, and US publications since 1988. **EDUCATION:** American Repertory Theatre for Advanced Theatre Training, Harvard University. BA, B.Ed, U of T. **HEROES/ROLE MODELS:** Uta Birnbaum; Rod MacLennan; Bonnie Raphael.

▶MCLAREN, Headley

PRINCIPAL/SPECIAL EDUCATION TEACHER (Ret.), Federal Government/Winnipeg School District No. 1, Winnipeg, MB. Born: Jamaica/ in Canada since: 1962.

▶ Headley McLaren began his teaching career in Jamaica in 1957; by the time of his retirement in 1995, he had also served as a principal and as a Special Education Teacher. **CAREER:** taught elementary school in Jamaica, 1957-62; was appointed principal at four Federal Schools in Manitoba, with the Federal Dept. of Indian and

Northern Affairs, 1966-77; from 1978-95, he taught Special Education to students with severe behavioural disorders at three Winnipeg Schools. During this time, he designed a highly structured primary classroom behaviour modification program, based on a points system for observed positive and negative student behaviours. Based upon the progress shown by the students, the program was considered very successful and was subsequently the subject of many reviews by other educators and psychology students. Since his retirement in 1995, HM now devotes more time to his family, assisting his children in the realization of their academic and professional goals, and, is actively developing his knowledge and skills in oil painting. **EDUCATION:** Cert. Special Education; Cert. Principal; pre-M.Ed & B.Ed, U. of Manitoba; Cert. GCE (Eng. & Ec.), U. of London; Cert. Teacher's, Mico Teachers College, Jamaica, WI. **MOTTO:** The Lord is my shepherd, I shall not want. **CONTACT:** headleymclaren@shaw.ca

▶MCLEOD, Donald
BARRISTER & SOLICITOR/PARTNER, Hinkson, Sachak, McLeod, Ste. 1201-67 Yonge St., Toronto, ON M5E 1J8. Born: UK, 1968/ in Canada since: 1970.

▶ Donald McLeod is a lawyer and a partner in the firm Hinkson, Sachak, McLeod, and has been practising since 1996, in the areas of criminal and entertainment law. In 2001, he appeared in the Supreme Court of Canada, in the landmark case of R. v. Golden, which he subsequently won. This case (which involved the police conducting a strip search, in public, of a Black male who had been apprehended) was significant because the Supreme Court agreed with the presenting argument that race had been a substantial factor in the mistreatment of the individual and, as a result, the related charges laid by the police were subsequently dismissed. **AFFIL/MBRSHP:** Brd., African Cdn Legal Clinic, and Chair, Legal Cmtee; Brd., Cdn University College, Lacombe, AB; VP, Fed-

eration of Seventh-day Adventist Youth; President, 100 Strong (group formed to support initiatives benefitting young Black men); made submissions to the CRTC on behalf of Milestone Entertainment; currently a member of the Advisory Brd. for FLOW 93.5FM, the Urban Radio station for which Milestone received CRTC approval. **OTHER:** outside of his legal practice, DM is also a professional gospel singer, with the group Selections; 1993-94, he recorded with MCA/Attic Records; since 1999, he records with 4Ever Records. **HONS.:** include, UMAC Award, Best Gospel Album, for *Our Message*, 2000; nominee, Juno Award, for the album *Our Message* by Selections, 2000. **EDUCATION:** LLB, Queen's U., 1995; BA, McMaster U., 1991. **HEROES/ROLE MODELS:** Mother. **MOTTO:** A voice without a vision is a whisper. **CONTACT:** bwhour@ idirect.ca; Fax: 416-363-9917

▶MCNAB, The Reverend Canon Dr. John
DIRECTOR OF PASTORAL STUDIES (Ret.), Montreal Diocesan Theological College. Resides in Pickering, ON. Born: Jamaica/ in Canada since: 1973.

▶ The Reverend Canon Dr. John McNab was the Director of Pastoral Studies at the Montreal Diocesan Theological College, affiliated with McGill University, until his retirement in 2000. Earlier in his career, he was appointed Canon of the Cathedral Chapter, Jamaica, 1976; then, appointed Diocesan Canon, Diocese of Montreal, 1982, where he served until his retirement. **HONS.:** include, Hon. D.Div, United Theological College, Montreal, 2000; Reading Room named in his honor, Board of Governors, Montreal Theological College, 2000; Award of Appreciation, for contribution to Jamaicans & the community in the field of religion, Hon. Consul for Jamaica in Montreal, 2000; Award for contribution to "the development of the Caribbean community in N. America," 5th Caribbean Anglican Consultation,

1999. **WORKS:** articles in, *United Theological College J*; *Theological J*; *Montreal Anglican*; paper, "Christian Marriage in the 1990s." **EDUCATION:** PhD, 1972; M.Div, 1964, McGill University. B.Div, King's College, London U., 1958; Cert., St. Peter's Theological College, Jamaica, 1956. **HEROES/ROLE MODELS:** Rev. Daniel I. McNab; Canon John Wippell; Bishop Percival Gibson. **MOTTO:** It is easy to stand outside and criticize; it is a far more challenging and rewarding exercise to enter in and try to understand the other person's point of view. **CONTACT:** mcnab@netrover.com

▶**MCTAIR, Roger**
WRITER/FILMMAKER/LECTURER, Toronto, ON. Born: Trinidad & Tobago/ in Canada since: 1967.
▶ Roger McTair is a poet, short-story writer, and filmmaker. In the 1980s and '90s he made a number of films in collaboration with Claire Prieto (*see: Prieto, Claire*), which were screened in film festivals in Canada and the US including *Vues d'Afrique*, Atlanta Third World Film Festival, and the Chicago International Film Festival. **HIGHLIGHTS:** credits for documentaries and instructional videos: *Journey to Justice*, on the legal battles fought to combat discrimination in Canada, NFB, 2001; *Jane Finch Again!*, for Vision TV, 1997; *End the Silence*, 1996; *Employment Equity*, 1995 and *Voices of Change*, 1994, for the CAW; *Hymn to Freedom*, TVO, 1994; *Children are not the Problem*, for the Congress of Black Women, 1991; *Jennifer Hodge: The Glory and the Pain*, 1991; *Accommodating Abilities*, CBC, 1989; *The Challenge of Diversity*, CBC and Atomic Energy Canada, 1989; *Home to Buxton*, TVO, Vision TV, PBS, 1987; *It's Not an Illness*, 1979; *Some Black Women*, 1976. **OTHER:** he has been a lecturer in the School of Communications, Seneca@York since 1997, teaching courses such as Writing, Media Ethics and Issues, Media/Film as an Art Form; he was a panelist on *Arts Express*, Vision TV, 1991-94; wrote for the *Toronto Star*, 1992-94; and, contributed to

Caribbean publications, 1970-77 (*Contrast, Trinidad Express, The Nation, Caribbean Contact*). **AFFIL/MBRSHP:** founding member BFVN; Black Filmmakers Foundation, NY; Factory Theatre. **HONS.:** several including: Outstanding Achievement, for *Journey to Justice*, BFVN, 2001; Award of Merit, City of Toronto, 1993; Honourable Mention, for *Home to Buxton*, Gemini Awards, 1988; nominee, Golden Sheaf Award, for *Different Timbres*, 1981; nominee, for *It's Not an Illness*, Genie Awards, 1980. **WORKS:** including, "Just a Lark," in *Whispers from the Cotton Tree Root*, 2000; "Visiting," in *Critical Strategies*, 1998 & *Faber Book of Caribbean Short Stories*, 1997; *Passage to Canada*, 1986. **EDUCATION:** Cert., TV Production, 1980; BAA, Motion Picture Studies, 1976, Ryerson Polytechnic; workshops in screenwriting, theatre, film directing, and mime (NY, Ottawa, and Toronto). **MOTTO:** Dream big dreams; small dreams have no magic. **CONTACT:** thunderstone36@hotmail.com

▶**MCWATT, Faye E.,** The Hon. Madam Justice
JUDGE, Superior Court of Ontario, 361 University Ave., Toronto, ON M5G 1T3. Born: Guyana/ in Canada since: 1963.
▶ The Hon. Madam Justice Faye McWatt has been practising law since 1986, and, in 2000, was appointed to the Ontario Superior Court of Justice. **CAREER:** Assistant Crown Attorney, Ont. Min. of the Attorney General, 1986-89; in private practice from 1989, but also served on two Royal Commissions as Counsel (Royal Commission, Niagara Regional Police, 1989-92; Deployment of Canadian Forces to Somalia, 1995); appointed as a director on the Ontario Heritage Foundation, 1992-94, by Order-In-Council. At the end of 1995, she was appointed Standing Agent for the Attorney General for the Toronto/Brampton Regions. **AFFIL/MBRSHP:** Ontario Legal Aid Plan Area Committee; Criminal Lawyer's Assn.; CABL. **WORKS:** in, *Can Police College J; Can Police*

Chief. **EDUCATION:** LLB, 1984; MA, Criminology, 1981, U. of Ottawa. BA/Hons., U. of Western Ontario, 1978. **CONTACT:** Fax: 416-327-5417

▶**MGBEOJI, Ikechi, JSD.**
ASSISTANT PROFESSOR, Faculty of Law, University of British Columbia, 1822 East Mall, Vancouver, BC V6T 1Z1. Born: Nigeria/ in Canada since: 1998.

▶ Dr. Ikechi Mgbeoji is an Assistant Professor in the Faculty of Law at UBC. His areas of expertise include: Intellectual Property Law; International Environmental Law; International Trade Law; Maritime Law; Torts; and International Law on Traditional Knowledge. He was the recipient of the prestigious Killam Scholarship, with which he completed his graduate studies at Dalhousie University. Prior to arriving in Canada, IM practised and researched law in Nigeria, 1992-98; was a Carl Duisberg Fellow, Germany, 2000-01; and, is a consultant to the World Conservation Union, Bonn, Germany. **HONS.:** several including, Killam Fellow, 1999-2002; GG of Canada Gold Medal, for highest academic standing at the graduate level, Dalhousie U., 1999-2000 (possibly the first Black at Dalhousie U. to achieve this distinction). **EDUCATION:** JSD (Doctor in the Science of Law), 2001; LLM, 1999, Dalhousie University. LLB, Nigeria, 1992. **HEROES/ ROLE MODELS:** Dr. Obiora Okafor & Prof. Hugh Kindred. **MOTTO:** Be still and know that I am God. **CONTACT:** mgbeoji@law.ubc.ca; Fax: 604-822-8108

▶**MIGHTY, E. Joy, PhD.**
ASSOCIATE PROFESSOR, Faculty of Administration, University of New Brunswick, Fredericton, NB. Born: Guyana/ in Canada since: 1987.

▶ Dr. Joy Mighty is an Associate Professor in the Faculty of Administration at the University of New Brunswick (UNB). She also occupies the following positions: Coordinator of the UNB Teaching and Learning Centre, and Faculty Pro-

gram Coordinator of the UNB/ROYTEC BBA Partnership Program. She is a management educator, researcher, and consultant in organizational behaviour, with a special interest in the management of workforce diversity. She has made numerous presentations at regional, national, and international conferences; has several publications in conference proceedings, journals, and books; provides consultation (primarily on managing diversity, inter-cultural communication, and organizational change) to private, public, and not-for-profit organizations in the Caribbean, the US, and Canada. She is also editor of two publications, including *Teaching Voices.* **HONS.:** Excellence in Teaching Award, Faculty of Administration, UNB, 1994; Doctoral Fellowship, SSHRC, 1991; Beta Gamma Sigma inductee for Scholastic Excellence in Business Administration in the USA, 1987. **WORKS:** in, *Omega: Int'l J of Management Sciences; Can Women Studies; Can J of Higher Education; Can J of Administrative Sciences*; and book: *Managing the Organizational Melting Pot: Dilemmas of Workplace Diversity.* **EDUCATION:** PhD, Organizational Behaviour, York U., 1992; MBA, Howard U., 1987. Post-grad Dipl., Mngmt. Studies, 1986; MA, Ed, 1983; post-grad. Dipl., Ed, 1975; BA, 1971, UWI. **HEROES/ROLE MODELS:** Parents. **MOTTO:** *Ubuntu:* I am because we are and because we are, therefore I am. **CONTACT:** mightyj@unb.ca; Fax: 506-453-3561

▶**MILLAR, Harvey, PhD, P.Eng.**
PROFESSOR/JAZZ GUITARIST/CONSULTANT.
Faculty of Commerce, Saint Mary's University, 923 Robie St., Halifax, NS B3H 3C3. Born: St. Lucia/ in Canada since: 1982.

▶ Dr. Harvey Millar is Professor of Operations Management in the Frank H. Sobey Faculty of Commerce at Saint Mary's U. (SMU) in NS, where he began teaching in 1988. He is also an accomplished jazz guitarist and leader of the Freedom Jazz Band, a quartet specializing in jazz/hip hop fusion. In February, 2002, he won an

East Coast Music Award, for Best Urban Recording. **CAREER HIGHLIGHTS:** began teaching in 1988 as a lecturer of Operations Management; Assistant Professor, 1990-94; Associate Professor, 1994-2002; full Professor from 2002; from 1996-97, was Director of the MBA Program; teaches courses in Operations Management and Strategy, Simulation of Management and Industrial Systems, and the Use of Scientific Methods in Management Decision Making; is an avid researcher and has published several articles in a variety of academic journals. **RESEARCH INTERESTS:** the design and management of manufacturing systems; managing operations in health care systems; scheduling of manpower and work crews; allocating flights to gates at airports; the design and planning of industrial fishing operations; and, disaster recovery planning. In addition to teaching and research, he is a Management/ Engineering consultant with Logix Consultants, a firm helping businesses and organizations run cost-efficient and profitable operations through the use of scientific management practices. He has conducted projects for a number of agencies in the Caribbean and Canada including the Federal Govt. The projects spanned strategic planning to improvement of organizational performance. **OTHER:** as a musician, his first CD was released in the Fall, 2001, and won an East Coast Music Award, 2002; previously, 1984-88, he led a jazz quartet called Friends and Music; in the late 1980s and early '90s, he led a reggae group called Umoja. **AFFIL/MBRSHP:** Production Operations Management Society; Cdn Operational Research Society; Information and Operations Research Society; Society for Computer Simulation; African Cdn Education Project (founding member); African Nova Scotian Music Assn. **WORKS:** several including articles in: *Fisheries Research; J Operational Research Society; Computers & Operations Research*; opinion column, "Take Five," *St. Lucia Mirror*, 1995-2001; *Black to Business.* **EDUCATION:** PhD, Industrial Engineering, 1990; MSc, Industrial Engineering,

1984, Technical U. of NS. BSc/Hons., UWI/Trinidad, 1982. **MOTTO:** When spider webs unite, they can tie up a lion. (African proverb) **CONTACT:** harveymillar@yahoo.com; www.harveymillar.com

▶**MILLER, Earl Anthony**
FORMER DIRECTOR, Employment Relationships, Scotiabank Group, 12th Fl., 44 King St. W., Toronto, ON. Born: Montreal, QC.

▶ Earl Miller was Director, Employment Relationships with the Scotiabank Group and a leading practitioner of workplace diversity and employment equity. His team provided corporate leadership for diversity planning, employment equity compliance, workplace harassment policies, flexible workplace programs and diversity leadership education. He joined the bank in 1996, as the first Director of Diversity, responsible for bank-wide strategies and programs to attract, develop and retain a diverse workforce. Currently he is in a sales management development program with Scotiabank Group. Prior to banking, he worked in social policy research, city planning, the public sector, teaching and consulting. **BACKGROUND:** began his career with the Ontario Public Service, administering housing and community renewal programs in Eastern Ontario; joined the Ontario Social Development Council (OSDC) as a writer and researcher on employment and income security issues; joined City of Toronto, Planning and Development Dept. as a community planner, was involved in planning for group homes, workplace child-care centres, affordable housing projects and services for disabled and elderly persons; while with the City, he was the first coordinator of the Mayor's committee on Community and Race Relations; returned to the Ontario Public Service to lead a project on access to professions and trades for foreign-educated immigrants; was later appointed Executive Coordinator of the Ontario Race Relations Directorate, Ont. Min. of Citizenship, responsible for provincial anti-racism policies, community programs, public education and partnerships with local agencies and groups; was later appointed Director of Leadership and Education, responsible for executive development and appointments; then became Director of the Employment Equity Branch, and led the implementation of workplace equity programs covering provincial employees. He has been a lecturer on urban planning, at U of T, and in the School of Urban and Regional Planning at Ryerson; also taught in the Queen's U. program for Public Executives. **AFFIL/MBRSHP:** United Way of Greater Toronto; Harbourfront Corp.; Cdn Bankers Assn.; Institute for Public Admin. in Canada; Urban Alliance on Race Relations; Social Planning Council, Toronto. **HONS.:** Award for Community Service, Rotary Int'l; Volunteer Recognition Award, United Way of Greater Toronto. **WORKS:** in, *Can Human Resources Reporter; Profiles in Diversity J;* while with OSDC, co-authored, "…And the Poor Get Poorer," and, "Employing People with Disabilities." **REVIEWED IN:** *Workplace Diversity Update.* **EDUCATION:** MES, Urban Planning, York University. MA, Poli. Sci.; BA, McMaster U. **MOTTO:** Leave things better than the way you found them. **CONTACT:** millerearl@rogers.com; Fax: 416-933-1221

▶**MOISE, Claude**
HISTORIEN, Montréal, QC. Né: Haïti.
▶ Claude Moïse, historien et enseignant à la retraite, est co-fondateur et l'ancien rédacteur en chef de la revue *Collectif Paroles,* éditée à Montréal de 1979 à 1986. Il est membre d'Initiatives Démocratiques, en Haïti, et président de la Fondation Mémoire (Haïti). À titre de conférencier invité, il participe depuis plusieurs années à des rencontres, séminaires, colloques organisés en Haïti et en plusieurs lieux de concentration de la communauté Haïtienne émigrée. **ŒUVRES:** plusieurs, y compris: *Le Projet National de Toussaint L'Ouverture et la Constitution de 1801,* 2001; *Le pouvoir Législatif dans le système politique*

haïtien, 1999; *Une Constitution dans la Tourmente,* 1994; co-auteur, *Repenser Haïti,* 1992; co-auteur, *Colonisation et Esclavage en Haïti,* 1990; co-auteur, *Haïti, Quel développement?,* 1975. **CONTACT:** frimo@cam.org; Fax: 514-336-1993

▶**MONTAGUE, Kenneth,** DDS.
DENTAL SURGEON/GALLERY OWNER, Dr. Kenneth Montague & Associates, Ste. 503-800 Bathurst St., Toronto, ON M5R 3M8. Born: Windsor, ON, 1963.
▶ Dr. Kenneth Montague is a dental surgeon who was rated Best Dentist in Toronto for two consecutive Years by *NOW* magazine. A graduate of U of T's Class of '87, he has been in private practice since 1992. His practice is popular for its ambiance of friendly professionalism and "hip cool," as well as the production of a high-quality seasonal newsletter, *Word of Mouth.* He is also the owner of a private art gallery, The Wedge, dedicated to the exhibition and promotion of works by international Black photographers; the gallery, specially designed and located in his home, has already exhibited the works of Michael Chambers, James VanDerZee, Seydou Keita, and Okhai Ojeikere. **COMMUNITY:** volunteer mentor with AABHS, since 1995; member of school co-op programs; member of ODA, chaired the in-house advertising group which produced the 2000 TV/print/ advertising campaign; The Coloured Development Fund, a scholarship program for young achievers in the art and design fields; contributing editor to *Word* magazine, since 1992, introducing and organizing the publication's health section; in 1986, organized a professional excursion to Jamaica to initiate a rural dental program providing dental care to disadvantaged children. **OTHER:** he has appeared on TV in a number of features: *Diagnosis MD,* 2001; interviews on WTN to promote awareness of dental health issues, 1995; *The New Music* on Citytv describing his use of music as a means of relaxation for his clients. **HONS.:** several includ-

ing, U of T's list of *Alumni 40 & Under Taking the World by Storm*, 2001; Best Dentist in Toronto, *NOW* magazine, 1995, 1996; "Extra" Creative Award, for producing an original advertising campaign, 1994; Citizenship Award, Faculty of Dentistry, U of T, 1987. **WORKS:** editor/publisher seasonal newsletter, *Word of Mouth.* **REVIEWED IN:** *National Post*, 2002*; Toronto Life*, 1998; *U of T Alumni Magazine*, Summer 2001; *Maclean's; Flare; Who's Who of Executives & Professionals of NA.* **EDUCATION:** DDS, Faculty of Dentistry, U of T, 1987. **HEROES/ROLE MODELS:** Parents: "They gave me unconditional love and constant support." **MOTTO:** It can be done! **CONTACT:** montague @wedgegallery.com; www.wedgegallery.com

▶MOODIE, Andrew

ACTOR/PLAYWRIGHT, c/o Noble Caplan Agency, 1260 Yonge St., 2nd Fl., Toronto, ON, M4T 1W6. Born: Ottawa, ON, 1967.

▶ Andrew Moodie is an Ontario-based actor/playwright. His first play, *Riot,* premiered in 1995 and won the Chalmers Award. His subsequent plays include: *Oui,* 1998; *A Common Man's Guide to Loving Women*, 1999; *The Lady Smith*, 2001. As an actor he has appeared on stage and TV in: *Our Country's Good*, Ottawa; *Macbeth*, Vancouver; and, *Whale*, YPT, Toronto. He also acted in *Riot* when it was performed, in 1998, by Black Theatre Workshop (Montreal); *Alice*, YPT, 2000; and, *Macbeth,* Toronto, 2001. **HONS.:** Chalmers Award, for *Riot*, 1995. **WORKS:** *Riot*, 1995; *Oui*, 1998; *A Common Man's Guide to Loving Women*, 1999; *The Lady Smith*, 2001. **HEROES/ROLE MODELS:** Layne Coleman, "Canada's Marlon Brando." **MOTTO:** *Tabarnac, ça marche!* **CONTACT:** andrewtanya@sympatico.ca

MOODY, Benjamin H., PhD.

SCIENCE ADVISOR, FOREST PEST MANAGEMENT, Canadian Forest Service, Natural Resources Canada, 580 Booth St., Ottawa, ON K1A 0E4.

Born: Belize/ in Canada since: 1964.

▶ Dr. Ben Moody is a Science Advisor for Forest Pest Management, with the Canadian Forest Service (CFS), of Natural Resources Canada. He joined the federal public service in 1977, as a Research Scientist in insect population dynamics with the CFS and was soon involved with research on the spruce budworm, which was in outbreak conditions in Newfoundland and Labrador. **CAREER:** from 1980-87, he was Head of Forest Insect and Disease Survey Unit (FIDS) at the Northern Forestry Centre, and dealt with the first major outbreak of the Mountain Pine Beetle in Alberta and outbreaks of jack pine and spruce budworms in Saskatchewan, Manitoba and the NWT. In 1987, he was transferred to Ottawa as the Science Coordinator of the Forest and Disease Survey Program, and later became the CFS Scientific Advisor–Federal Partnerships, Pest Management, Ecology, and Biological Control. He has been involved in the implementation of activities under agreements with the Pest Management Regulatory Agency, the Canadian Food Inspection Agency (Plant Protection Branch), and the interdepartmental Federal Biosystematics Partnership; he has acted as Director within the Science Division on several occasions from 1988 to 1998. Internationally, he is a CFS delegate to the N. American Forest Commission, Insect and Disease Working Group, and the N. American Plant Protection Organization, and has responsibility for pest science and technology activities under agreements with the USA and China. **BACKGROUND:** he has work experience in forestry from the UK, Central America, and Africa; in 1993-96, he was a technical monitor of a CIDA project on the Biological Control of the exotic insect pest, the Cypress Aphid, which was killing cypress trees in high-value cypress plantations in eastern and southern Africa. At the beginning of his career, BM was a forester and Division Forest Officer in Belize, Central America, responsible for the linking of the southern highway in Belize, thereby providing the only road access to the southern part of the country; was also responsible for the establishment of mahogany plantations, pine regeneration, fire prevention, allspice production, recreation facilities development, and forest management. **HONS.:** several including, Head of the Public Service Award, for excellence in addressing the Asian Long-Horned Beetle threat, 1999; Dept. Merit Award, Natural Resources Canada, 1999; Merit Award, Canadian Forest Service Sector, 1999. **WORKS:** has authored several reports and publications on forest pest conditions, pest surveys and management, and pest impacts/damage. **EDUCATION:** PhD, Forest Entomology UBC, 1977. MSc Forestry, 1971; BSc Forestry, 1968, U. of New Brunswick. Forester's Certificates from England and Wales. **CONTACT:** bmoody@nrcan.gc.ca; Fax: 613-947-9090

▶MORGAN, Carlos

SINGER/SONGWRITER/PRODUCER, SolRoc Music, Toronto, ON. Born: Toronto, ON, 1967.

▶ Carlos Morgan is one of Canada's leading award-winning urban music performers; his style of music presents a new form of R&B, infused with gospel, jazz, rock, and hip hop. He has been the lead vocalist with a number of Canadian and American bands; has toured extensively in both countries; has 14 years experience as a session vocalist; released his debut album, *Feelin' Alright*, in 1996, which rose to No. 3 on the independent charts within two weeks of its release. His second album, *We're Gonna Make It*, is scheduled for release in 2003. **HONS.:** include, Best R&B video, *Give it to You*, UMAC Awards, 1998; Urban Artist of the Year, SOCAN, 1998; Juno Award, Best R&B/Soul Recording, 1997; Best R&B Video Award, for *Give it to You*, MuchMusic, 1997; Best Male Vocalist, UMAC Awards, 1997; Best Urban Songwriter, Cdn Cultural Committee, 1997. **REVIEWED IN:** *Billboard; Canadian Musician; Word; National Post; Toronto Star.* **MOTTO:** Keep your head up! **CONTACT:** carlos.morgan@solrocmusic.com; www.carlosmorgan.com

▶MORGAN, Christopher J., DC.

CHIROPRACTOR, OWNER/DIRECTOR, Morgan Chiropractic & Wellness, Toronto, ON. Born: Toronto, ON, 1970.

▶ Dr. Christopher Morgan is a chiropractor, and the owner/director of Morgan Chiropractic and Wellness (MCW), a family-oriented, multidisciplinary health centre, with health professionals in chiropractic, nutrition, nursing, personal training, therapeutic massage, and psychotherapy. He began his chiropractic career as an associate at the Wiles Centre for Chiropractic and Wellness, 1997-2001, and opened his own facility later in October 2000. **COMMUNITY:** his involvement with youth, community organizations, and the community as a whole, began in his teen years and continues today. As an undergraduate, he was featured in the campus magazine for his involvement in school activities and volunteer community endeavours; during his chiropractic studies, he was featured in the college's newspaper for his ongoing volunteer community work, particularly with children. Since his graduation in 1997, he continues to be on the Board of the Malvern Family Resource Centre, a mentor to the Malvern Youth Club, team doctor for the national Malvern Soccer Club and the community liaison for the Association for the Advancement of Blacks in Health Sciences (AABHS). **OTHER:** in 1999, he and other AABHS members organized the AABHS Heart and Soul Restaurant Food Skills Programme, designed to address the high incidence of hypertension and diabetes in the Black community. This initiative concluded with a popular, informative and interactive Food Expo, which has now become an annual event. He then spearheaded the formation of the Black Health Alliance, a network of community-based organizations advocating through research, awareness and treatment, for the improvement of the individual and collective health and well-being of the Black community. He is completing his fellowship program with the College of Chiropractic

Sports Sciences (2002). **HONS.:** include, Male Athlete of the Year, Cdn Memorial Chiropractic College, 1997; John Brooks Award & Scholarship Fund, 1989; many academic & athletic awards during high school & university. **WORKS:** writes bi-weekly column on health & well-being in *Share* newspaper. **REVIEWED IN:** *Millennium Minds*, 2000; *Profiles, Erindale College*, 1993. **EDUCATION:** D.Chiropractic, Cdn Memorial Chiropractic College, 1997; BSc, U of T, 1993. **HEROES/ROLE MODELS:** Mother. **MOTTO:** Watch your thoughts, for they become your words… develop your character, for it becomes your destiny. **CONTACT:** Tel: 416-447-7600; www.mcw4life.com

MORGAN, Dwayne

EXECUTIVE DIRECTOR/SPOKEN WORD ARTIST, Up From the Roots, Toronto, ON. Born: Toronto, 1974.

▶ Dwayne Morgan, poet and spoken word artist, has been performing since 1994. He founded Up From the Roots (UFTR) to promote the positive artistic contributions of African-Canadian youth while contributing to Toronto's growing urban entertainment scene. Since then, UFTR has produced over 40 events, including the AfriCanadian Arts and Music Festival at Ontario Place, the Talking Aloud Spoken Word series for Harbourfront Centre, SoulJazzFusion for the du Maurier Jazz Festival, and the annual, When Brothers Speak, and When Sisters Speak, events. DM has appeared on CBC news, TSN's *Off the Record,* and MuchMusic. In addition to two recordings of poetry, he has also self-published four books of poetry, and has appeared on-stage in *Memphis: the Life and Death of Martin Luther King Jr.*; in the radio play *Calabash Alley*; the movie *Hendrix*; and in the nationally televised TV commercial for the CRRF's *See People for Who They Really Are* campaign. **HONS.:** recipient of inaugural Best Spoken Word Recording Award, *The Evolution*, Urban Music Award, 2001; Harry Jerome Award, for Excellence in the Arts, 1998; ACAA/Youth, 1998; featured in the *Men on the Move* calendar by *Ebony*, 1998. **WORKS:** books of poetry*: The Man Behind the Mic; Long Overdue; The Revolution Starts Within; Straight From the Roots.* **REVIEWED IN:** *NOW*; *National Post*; *Toronto Sun*; *The Toronto Star.* **EDUCATION:** BA/Hons., York U., 1997. **MOTTO:** You can't sow seeds and reap a harvest in the same season. **CONTACT:** uftr@hotmail.com; www.upfromtheroots.ca

▶MORRISON, Rev. Eva May

SENIOR PASTOR, Toronto New Covenant Cathedral /COGOP, 255 Blantyre Ave., Toronto, ON M1N 2S2. Born: Jamaica/ in Canada since: 1968.

▶ Rev. Eva May Morrison is the first Caribbean-Canadian woman of the Pentecostal religion to achieve the status of Certified Specialist and Provisional Teaching Supervisor with the Cdn Assn. for Pastoral Education, at U of T. She has worked as an educator, supervisor, pastoral counsellor/therapist for families, couples and individuals, and currently serves as Adjunct Professor of Bible and Theology, Emmanuel Bible College in Kitchener. Since 1995, she is the Senior Pastor of a multi-ethnic Pentecostal congregation at Church of God of Prophecy (COGOP); Director of the Morrison-Ricketts Counselling Centre, COGOP; founder/director, School for Advanced Biblical Studies, COGOP, 1984; member, Ont. Society of Psychotherapists. And, since 1975, she has been a motivational speaker with the Int'l Women's Ministries, and has addressed groups in Israel, England, Europe, the Caribbean and parts of Africa. **HONS.:** include, honoured by COGOP, for years of service as National Women's Ministry Director. **WORKS:** articles in COGOP publications including: *White Wing Messenger; National Church Magazine.* **REVIEWED IN:** COGOP publications: *White Wing Messenger; The Maranatha Church News.* **EDUCATION:** M.Div, Tyndale Seminary, 1998; M.Relig. Ed, Central Baptist Seminary, 1984; BA, York U./Trinity

Western U., 1981. **HEROES/ROLE MODELS:** Mother; sister; Rev. Elva Howard, Int'l Dir. Women's Ministries. **MOTTO:** I am born to win, for no storm can uproot the tree that God plants. **CONTACT:** emaymorr@rogers.com; Fax: 905-479-6565

▶**MORRISON, Wilma L.**
COMMUNITY VOLUNTEER & LOCAL HISTORIAN, Nathaniel Dett Chapel BME, 5674 Peer St., Niagara Falls, ON L2G 1X1. Born: London, ON.

▶ Wilma Morrison is an important member of the Niagara Falls community for her efforts to preserve Black history and secure recognition for the contributions of Blacks to the region's development, for more than 40 yrs. Her extensive volunteer work encompasses history, culture, heritage preservation, tourism, genealogy and education. She is a dedicated educator who frequently speaks to schools and other groups on Black history; she was the driving force that saved the historic Nathaniel Dett Chapel (built in 1836) from destruction and had it officially designated as a National Historic Site, 2000. Earlier, in 1991, she created the Norval Johnson Heritage Library, which, along with the Chapel, has become an important tourist attraction; the library houses more than 1,000 volumes related to Black history and is a centre of research for students and educators interested in Black Canadian history or their own genealogical background. In 1994, she initiated the Niagara Falls Freedom Trail Tours, to accommodate the many visitors from the US who wanted to know more about the history of Blacks in the area. **HONS.:** include, Outstanding Achievement for Volunteerism in Ontario, Ont. Min. of Citizenship, 2001; George Siebel Award for preservation of Black History in Niagara Falls, 2001; John C. Holland Award of Merit, Hamilton, 2000; Human Rights Award, OFL, 1997; Paul Harris Award, Rotary Club, 1997. **HEROES/ROLE MODELS:** Mabel Miller, mother; Mary McLeod Bethune; Rev. John C. Holland. **MOTTO:** When pointing fingers, remember that three are aimed back at you. Get busy, you can make a difference. **CONTACT:** Tel: 905-358-9957; Fax: 905-358-8976

▶**MORTEN, Marvin G.,** The Hon. Mr. Justice
JUDGE, Ontario Court of Justice, 7755 Hurontario St., Brampton, ON L6W 4T6. Born: Toronto, ON.

▶ The Hon. Mr. Justice Morten was appointed to the Bench as a Provincial Court Judge in 1993. Previously, he served as an Assistant Crown Attorney, 1974-92, first with the Toronto Courts then with the Peel Courts. In 1993, he assisted in the development and presentation of Diversion Court in Peel. **COMMUNITY:** member, RESQ (a non-profit organization providing support to Black youth in crisis), Youth Justice Organizing Committee, Region of Peel; honorary patron, Marvin Morten Centre for Youth and Families, 1994-2000; United Achievers Celebrity Cooking Events, 1995-2000; Oware Centre for Youth, since 1998; Rotary Club, Brampton. MGM is also a mentor with Big Brothers, speaks regularly to schools and organizations, and, has a third degree Black Belt in tae kwon do. **HONS.:** Malton Black Development Assn., for contribution, field of Law, 2000; United Achievers Black History Makers, 1998; Positive Image Award, JCA, 1994. **REVIEWED IN:** *Toronto Star.* **EDUCATION:** LLB, Osgoode Hall, York U., 1971; BA, U. of Western Ont., 1968. **HEROES/ROLE MODELS:** Wife; Dr. R.J. Grey, Professor. **CONTACT:** marvin.morten@jus.gov.on.ca; Fax: 905-456-4899

▶**MOSE, Kenrick E.A.,** PhD.
PROFESSOR EMERITUS, Spanish Studies, University of Guelph, Guelph, ON. Born: Trinidad & Tobago/ in Canada since: 1969.

▶ Dr. Kenrick Mose is, since 1998, Professor Emeritus at the University of Guelph, with a specialization in Spanish and Latin American Studies. **CAREER HIGHLIGHTS:** began his teaching career in the Caribbean; Master and Instructor at St. George's College in Trinidad, 1959-61; Lecturer, UWI, Jamaica, 1964-67; Milton Buchanan and Canada Council Fellow, Uruguay and Argentina, 1967-69; Lecturer, Acadia U., 1969-70; then at U. of Guelph where he was Assistant Professor, 1970-77; Associate Professor, 1977-89; then full Professor from 1989. Administratively, he held a number of positions: Chair, Ontario Cooperative Program, Latin American and Caribbean Studies (OCPLACS), 1976-78; and at U. of Guelph, Coordinator of Spanish Studies, 1977-79, 1983-85, and 1988-90; Acting Chair, Dept. of Languages and Literature, 1978-79 and 1992-93. He is the author of many books, articles and over 30 reviews; his area of research has been the contemporary Colombian novel, and social problems in Spanish American Literature. **WORKS:** including: book of poetry, *Shades of Darkness*, 1993; *Defamiliarization in the work of Gabriel Garcia Marquez, 1947-1967*, 1989; *Enrique Amorim: The Passion of a Uruguayan*, 1973. **EDUCATION:** PhD, 1969; MA, 1962, U of T. Dipl. Ed, UWI-London, 1959; BA/Hons., UWI, 1958. **CONTACT:** kmose@uoguelph.ca

MOTIKI, Joseph
PERFORMER/TV & RADIO HOST, c/o Characters Talent Agency, 150 Carleton St., Toronto, ON M5A 2K1. Born: Toronto, ON, 1972.

▶ Joseph Motiki became one of the most-recognized faces on children's TV through the program he co-hosted at TVO from 1995-1999, *the crawlspace*. While completing his studies in radio and television at Ryerson University, he became the host of *What*, a late-night phone-in program for youth on TVO; the show was nominated for a Gemini for Best Youth Program. In 1995, he became co-host of *two kids' the crawlspace*, TVO's after-school block of children's programs. During his four yrs. on the show, *crawlspace* became number one in after-school

programming, surpassing YTV, CBC, and Fox. During this period, JM made over 200 appearances at children's events across the province; hosted the Alliance for Children and TV Awards of Excellence, 1995; co-hosted UNICEF's International Children's Day of Broadcasting on many occasions, including the TVO broadcast which won an International Emmy Award, 1997; he was an Ontario Spokesperson for UNICEF, 1997 and 1998; he and his fellow co-hosts were recognized by UNICEF for their work. After leaving TVO in 1999, he hosted an on-air feature, *Workplace Fun Patrol*, on EZRock 97.3FM; hosted the 1999 Golden Marble Awards for excellence in children's advertising in NY; he has also starred in a number of animated programs. His acting credits include *Doc, Blue Murder*, and, *The Other Me*; currently he is hosting the youth and sports quiz show, *Kidzone*; is the voice of Metabee on *Medabots;* and is the host of the high school quiz program, *Reach for the Top*. **HONS.:** nominee, Golden Sheaf Award & Gemini Award for Best Youth Program in Canada, for *What*, 1995. **EDUCATION:** BAA, Radio & Television Arts, Ryerson U., 1995. **MOTTO:** Stay cool; never settle, and never waste the skills you've been given. **CONTACT:** joe@joe4life.com; www.joe4life.com

MOTION
SPOKEN WORD POET/HIP HOP ARTIST. Toronto, ON. Born: Toronto, ON.

▶ Motion, a.k.a. Wendy Brathwaite, is a spoken word poet and hip hop artist, based in Toronto, who began writing poetry at an early age and song lyrics by the age of 12; soon thereafter she was performing with local rap and hip hop artists. Already known for her distinctive sound and socially conscious lyrics, she has many accomplishments to her credit, including: winner of the CBC Poetry Face-Off, Spring 2002, a Canada-wide competition of spoken word poets whose live performances were rated by listeners from across the country; published her first volume of poetry, *Motion in Poetry,* co-founded *The Masterplan Show,* in 1990 (a showcase for emerging urban music and hip hop artists), which airs on CIUT 89.5FM, and which won the Urban Music Award for Best Radio Show, 2000; co-founded Blacklist Music (1995), an independent record label under which her own music is released; has been a regular feature of PhemPhat Productions' annual Honey Jam, a showcase for Canada's emerging female urban artists. After rapping and MC'ing for several years, she debuted as a solo artist in 1997 with the release of her single and video, *Use What U Got,* which received a MuchMusic Video Award nomination and appeared on the Beat Factory *Rap Essentials Compilation;* has performed across Canada and parts of the US; and, has collaborated with a number of artists including Tara Chase, Butta Babees, and others. **OTHER:** was an instructor with the Fresh Arts Music Program (1992-96), within the Toronto Public School System and which contributed to the emergence of a number of talented young musicians; is active in a number of community initiatives. **HONS.:** Phenomenal Woman Award, for contribution to the Cdn music scene. **WORKS:** single recordings: *Man in Motion* and *Feelin' It,* 2002; *Trilogy,* 2001; *Use What U Got,* 1997; included on several CD anthologies (e.g. *Phem Phat Honey Drops,* 2002; *Blu Magazine Collection vol. 6; WoRDLIFE: Tales of the Underground Griots*); book: *Motion in Poetry,* 2002; also writes for a number of publications. **EDUCATION:** B.Ed, York U., 1999. **CONTACT:** motionlive@yahoo.ca; www.motionlive.com

▶**MUHTADI**
PERCUSSIONIST/ARTISTIC DIRECTOR, Muhtadi International Drumming Festival, Markham, ON. Born: Trinidad & Tobago/ in Canada since: 1974.
▶ Muhtadi began his musical career in Trinidad, at an early age, learning to play a number of percussion instruments. Since then, he has become a self-taught musician, playing professionally for over 30 yrs.; his music is described as a fusion of jazz, pop, African and Caribbean rhythms. He has performed with a number of leading Calypsonians, including Lord Kitchener, Duke, Sparrow, Super Blue, Shadow and others; has been a long-time member (over 20 years) of the Desperadoes Steel Orchestra from Trinidad; has performed at Caribana and a number of jazz and folk festivals including, Mariposa, du Maurier, Havana, Zacatecas Festival in Mexico, the 9th Annual Music Festival, Santiago, Chile, and at the Nan Ying Festival in Taiwan, 1998. In addition, his group, Muhtadi and the World Drummers, composed of professional and amateur drummers has performed at a number of venues in Toronto. He has performed in a number of Theatre Fountainhead productions including: *The Obeah Man; Swamp Dwellers; Africa in the Caribbean;* and *Anansi.* His first album, *Age Don't Matter,* was released in 1993; and, he has conducted a number of workshops in schools and universities. **CONTACT:** Fax: 905-294-0988

▶**MUNFORD, Clarence Joseph,** PhD.
PROFESSOR EMERITUS, Dept. of History, University of Guelph, ON. Born: USA/ in Canada since: 1966.
▶ Dr. C.J. Munford is Professor Emeritus of Black Studies and History at the University of Guelph. In a teaching career which began in 1959, he has taught at universities in Nigeria, Europe, and the US. Arriving at U. of Guelph in 1966, he taught there for 35 yrs. until 2001, when he retired. He is credited with, in 1969, introducing the first courses in Black history in an Ontario university. He is a scholar and activist who has authored numerous articles, addresses, and essays, and a three-volume autopsy of early Black enslavement in the West Indies. He is the lead developer of "civilizational historicism," the theory of human history from a Black vantage point. He is also active in the N'COBRA, a campaign for reparations to African Americans for

the ills of slavery. **HONS.:** Edward Blyden Book Award, for *Race and Civilization*, African Heritage Studies Association (AHSA), 2002; Book Award, for *Race & Reparations*, AHSA, 1997; honoured by the students at U. of Guelph with the opening of the Munford Centre, an anti-racism & race relations resource centre, 1995. **WORKS:** author of many publications including: *Race and Civilization: The Rebirth of Black Centrality*; *Race and Reparations: A Black Perspective for the 21st Century*; and, *Black Ordeal*. **EDUCATION:** PhD, U. of Leipzig, Germany, 1962. MA, 1959; BA, 1958, Western Reserve U., Cleveland, OH. **HEROES/ROLE MODELS:** Prof. W. Markov, dissertation supervisor. **CONTACT:** cjm@continuum.org; Tel: 519-824-7929; Fax: 519-767-0469

▶MUTUNGI, Allyce B.

LAWYER, Private Practice, Ste. 203A-419 King St. W., Oshawa, ON L1J 2K5. Born: Uganda/ in Canada since: 1988.

▶ Allyce B. Mutungi is a lawyer in private practice in the City of Oshawa. Her areas of specialization are Family Law, Construction Law, Real Estate, and, Wills and Estates. Previously, 1998-2002, she was an associate with Mazar & Associates, a firm in Oshawa; 1994-98, she worked as a sole practitioner, with a focus on Family Law, Real Estate, Wills and Estates. **COMMUNITY INVOLVEMENT:** Legal Advisor to Women's Rights Action Coalition and to women at the Ajax-Pickering Women's Resource Centre, shelter being constructed and which will provide a refuge to women and their children who have been the victims of domestic violence and/or abuse; Brd., Durham Legal Clinic; Ontario Bar Assistance Program; Uganda Martyrs Church of Canada; founding member, Friends of Makerere (Ugandan university) in Canada; founding member, Generation Africa (youth organization); Anglican Church of Canada, Toronto Diocese; speaker on custody and access, and estate planning. **EDUCATION:** Bar Admission, LSUC, 1994; LLB,

Cdn Equivalency, U. of Manitoba, 1992; Bar Admission, Law Society of Uganda, 1996; LLB, Makerere U., Kampala, Uganda, 1984. **HEROES/ROLE MODELS:** Laura Legge; Margaret Nganwa. **MOTTO:** Always reflect on yesterday, for it shapes today and tomorrow. **CONTACT:** Tel: 905-571-3057; Fax: 905-571-3548; amutungi@bellnet.ca

▶MUYINDA, Estella Namakula

LEGAL POLICY ANALYST, Court Challenges Program of Canada, Ste. 616-294 Portage Ave., Winnipeg, MB R3C 0B9. Born: Uganda.

▶ Estella Muyinda began her law career in Uganda where she practised as a Legal Officer, 1984-87. She is a member of the bar in Manitoba, the Northwest Territories, and Uganda. Since 1998, she has worked as a Legal Policy Analyst with the Court Challenges Program of Canada, a national non-profit organization set up in 1994 to provide financial assistance for important court cases that advance language and equality rights guaranteed under Canada's Constitution. **BACKGROUND:** she was the Executive Director, Beaufort Delta Legal Services Clinic, 1995-97, in Inuvik, where she represented clients as a criminal defence attorney, and managed the first Legal Aid Clinic in the MacKenzie Delta region of the NWT. There, she also developed training for court workers in the Beaufort Delta Region. From 1993-95, she had a general practice as a barrister and solicitor in Winnipeg, specializing in criminal defence work and family law. **COMMUNITY ACTIVITIES:** Ugandan-Canadian Assn., Manitoba; African Assn.; LEAF; AIDS Shelter Coalition Manitoba; Women's Health Clinic; Equity Committee, Law Society of Manitoba; Folklorama; Friends of Makerere. **WORKS:** conference papers include: "Equality Charter Challenges: How to identify & litigate the cases"; "Bridging the Generation Gap: Girls & Women, can they talk the same language?"; "Introduction of the Cdn Legal System to the new Immigrant"; article in *Can J Women & the Law*, 1993; "Violence against Women –

Zero Tolerance (from an African context)"; "An Introduction to the Canadian Charter of Rights and Freedoms." **EDUCATION:** LLB, Cdn Accreditation, U. of Manitoba, 1992; LLB, Makerere U., Uganda, 1983. **HEROES/ROLE MODELS:** Father. **MOTTO:** Never give up! **CONTACT:** emuyinda@ccppcj.ca; Fax: 204-946-0669

▶NANCE, Marcus

OPERA SINGER/BASS-BARITONE, Toronto, ON. Born: USA/ in Canada since: 1993.

▶ Marcus Nance is a singer, with a big voice and stage presence. Since switching from being a symphonic clarinetist, he has become an award-winning opera singer. Some of his opera performances include: Porgy, in *Porgy and Bess,* with the TSO; Alidoro, in *Cenerentola,* with the NYC Opera; Sparafucile in *Rigoletto,* with Tacoma Opera; Ali, in *L'Italiana in Algeri,* with Hawaii Opera; as Compere, in *Four Saints in Three Acts,* with Chicago Opera Theatre; he has also appeared with the Santa Fe and Glimmerglass Operas. In 1999, he starred as Malcolm in the world premiere of Atom Egoyan's opera, *Elsewhereless,* and received rave reviews; in 1998, he performed in another new opera, George Elliott Clarke's, *Beatrice Chancy (see: Clarke, George Elliott).* He has also performed with several symphonies and orchestras including: Fresno Philharmonic; Austin Civic Orchestra; Victoria Symphony; Fairbanks Alaska Festival Orchestra; he also performs in recitals throughout the US and Canada with pianist/conductor, Franklin Brasz. **HONS.:** several including: nominee, Dora Mavor Moore Award, for Most Outstanding Male Performer in an Opera; winner at the Metropolitan Opera National Council Regional Auditions; Clifford E. Blair Endowment Award, National Opera Assn. Vocal Competition. **REVIEWED IN:** arts columns & publications; *Musicworks; Chicago Defender; The Wholenote; Honolulu Advertiser.* **EDUCATION:** grad. studies, U. of Illinois & U. of Texas; BA, Fresno State U., CA, 1988. **HEROES/ROLE MODELS:** Franklin Brasz; Leyontine Price. **MOTTO:** Love and respect every person no matter what differences there are! **CONTACT:** steinwayFB@aol.com

▶NATION, Karlene

TV REPORTER, CFTO TV, PO Box 9, Stn. O,

Toronto, ON M4A 2M9. Born: Jamaica/ in Canada since: 1976.

▶ Karlene Nation is a reporter, writer, and producer with CFTO TV in Toronto, an affiliate of the CTV network. In 2001, she was appointed Diversity Producer/Reporter for CFTO and CTV, responsible for increasing representation of diverse communities in local and national newscasts. **CAREER:** joined the CFTO news team in 1992; previously worked at CBC and CTV; had been a reporter for the *Globe and Mail*'s *Report on Business* and covered spot news and business for the *Toronto Star*; spent six years at the Toronto Stock Exchange as a media and public relations officer. **HONS.:** include, *Vox Magazine* Award, for journalism; ACAA, media; Reel Black Award, journalism. **WORKS:** in *Globe and Mail*; *Toronto Star*. **EDUCATION:** Dipl., Journalism, Humber College; BA, Poli. Sci., U of T. **CONTACT:** Tel: 416-332-7100; Fax: 416-299-2273

▶**NDUBUBA, Edward O.**
CO-FOUNDER/DIRECTOR OF OPERATIONS, SS8 Networks Inc., Kanata, ON. Born: Nigeria/ in Canada since: 1979.

▶ Edward Ndububa is an electrical engineer and Director of Operations at SS8 Networks. As co-founder engineer and the first Director of Product Management, he initiated and proposed the idea of IPSTP and IPSCP as the business model and the Network topology for next generation signaling and services architecture of IP Telephony networks. Today, this foresight puts SS8 Networks at the forefront of the IP Signaling and the IP AIN Services market segment. Prior to co-starting SS8 Networks, he spent close to 11 years at Nortel Networks where he held a variety of engineering and management positions including Product Manager and Project Manager for the high-profile High-Speed SS7 signaling links. At Nortel, he was recognized as one of the best project managers in the New Product development group of the DMS product family. In addition, he was VP,

then President, of NPM Inc. **COMMUNITY INVOLVEMENT:** assisting non-profit organizations by serving on the Board of the Canadian African Newcomers Aid Centre of Toronto (CANACT). **WORKS:** in, *EETimes*. **EDUCATION:** MSc, Electronics & Robotics, Indiana State U., IN, 1988. BSc, Electrical Engineering, 1986; B.Ed, 1985, U. of New Brunswick. Dipl., Electronics Engineering Technology, George Brown College, Toronto, 1982. **HEROES/ROLE MODELS:** corporate CEOs like John Monty & John Roth. **MOTTO:** If at first you don't succeed, dust yourself off and try again. **CONTACT:** endububa@rogers.com; Fax: 905-460-9239

▶**NELSON, Amy**
HEAD SURGICAL NURSE (Ret.)/ **VOLUNTEER,** JCA/ Medical Mission International, Toronto, ON. Born: Jamaica/ in Canada since: 1959.

▶ Amy Nelson trained as a nurse in Jamaica; after graduating in 1951, she practised in a number of rural hospitals; she later returned to Kingston to work at the Jubilee Maternity Hospital; during this time, she also worked with local doctors, doing community work with the poorer members of the local population, including caring for children when their parents lacked the financial means. In 1959, she immigrated to Canada and obtained a nursing position at the Toronto General Hospital; over the years she worked in various capacities before becoming Head Surgical Nurse in the Ophthalmology Dept.; she retired from nursing in 1986. **COMMUNITY ACTIVITIES:** since retiring, her time has been fully devoted to the volunteer activities, locally and internationally, she had been pursuing over the preceding years; as a founding member of the JCA, in 1962, AN has served in most voluntary capacities; in 1971, she began volunteering with Medical Mission Int'l (a voluntary, self-help group whose volunteers pay their own way to visit other countries in order to assist the needy with medical, physical, social, economic and spiritual support), going to countries in Latin America, the Caribbean,

Africa, Asia, and parts of Europe, an initiative in which she is still active. In Toronto, her activities include the well-being of senior citizens; she was active in the founding and sustaining of the Caribbean Seniors Assn., since its creation, 1986. In this capacity, she has served on a number of committees including: Mayor's Committee on Aging and Elder Abuse; Senior Ethnic Women's Group; Ont. Coalition of Senior Citizens Organization; Sisters on the Move; Caribbean Youth Assn.; North York Health Centre for Seniors; Hurricane Relief and other disasters. She is also actively involved in her church. **HONS.:** several including, Community Award, Sisters on the Move; Volunteer Award, Honduras & El Salvador Relief; Lifetime Achievement Award, JCA; Caribbean Seniors Award, Women's International Network, 2001. **REVIEWED IN:** community papers, *Share; Weekly Gleaner; Shoppers' Drug Mart Magazine.* **EDUCATION:** Cert. Nursing Management; Nursing, Kingston Public Hospital. **HEROES/ROLE MODELS:** Dr. Douglas Harper. **MOTTO:** If you are not there to do something, do not expect results or expect anyone else to do it for you. **CONTACT:** c/o JCA, 416-746-5772

▶**NELSON, Anthony R.**
SENIOR VICE-PRESIDENT, Credit, SottoBank of Canada, 1106 Dundas St. W., Toronto, ON M6J 1X2. Born: USA/ in Canada since: 1961.
▶ Anthony Nelson has over 20 years experience in the banking industry. After completing his MBA at Concordia University, he was recruited by the Bank of Montreal; in a career which spanned 21 years, he worked primarily as a corporate and commercial lender, as a portfolio manager and a team leader. In 2001, he moved to SottoBank where he is Senior Vice-President, Credit. His responsibilities include managing the credit risk exposure for SottoBank and serving on the Bank's Executive Committee. **OTHER:** he represented Canada at the 1972 Olympics as a member of the Track & Field Team. **EDUCATION:** MBA,

Finance & Marketing, Concordia U.; BA, Eastern Michigan U. **MOTTO:** Life is determined by the lines we have the foresight to stand in. **CONTACT:** anelson@sottobanksbc.com; Fax: 416-588-1416

▶**NELSON, Kathleen**
NURSE & CLINICAL TEACHER, Toronto Rehabilitation Institute/Ryerson University, 350 Victoria St., Toronto, ON M5B 2K3. Born: Jamaica/ in Canada since: 1978.
▶ Kathleen (Kathy) Nelson completed her early training in nursing in the UK and has been practising in Canada since 1979. She is also the founder and President of the Caribbean Diabetes Chapter of the Canadian Diabetes Assn. **CAREER:** Staff Nurse, Toronto Rehabilitation Institute since 1979; Nurse Clinician on a part-time basis at Mount Sinai Hospital, since 1980; and in 2000, was appointed Clinical Teacher in the School of Nursing at Ryerson University. **COMMUNITY INVOLVEMENT:** extensive involvement in education related to diabetes since 1992, and began the Caribbean Diabetes Chapter given the high incidence of diabetes-related illnesses within the Black population. The Chapter's purpose is to raise awareness and teach prevention for those at risk of developing diabetes, and educating those with diabetes on how to manage this chronic illness. To meet these objectives, the Chapter holds information fairs in shopping malls and convenes information sessions in churches across the Greater Toronto Area. The Chapter comprises healthcare professionals knowledgeable in diabetes and also acts as a support group to those with this illness. KN also co-facilitates outreach sessions for Stroke Survivors and their caregivers, and is a member of the Heart and Stroke Foundation. **HONS.:** several including, first recipient of Valerie Fine Award, for nursing excellence, Mount Sinai Hospital, 1999; plaque for outstanding work & commitment, Toronto Rehabilitation Institute, 1998. **WORKS:** co-authored article in *Rehabilitation J;* articles in *Share.* **EDUCATION**

MHSc Nursing, Charles Sturt U., Australia, 1998; BSc Nursing, Ryerson U., 1996; Dipl. RN, Weston Supermare School of Nursing, UK, 1964; Dipl. Midwife, state certified, Bristol Maternity Hospital School of Nursing, UK, 1962. **MOTTO:** I can do with God's help. **CONTACT:** kahn@sprint.ca

▶NELSON, Ron
RADIO DJ/CONCERT PROMOTER/CEO, Ron Nelson Productions, Toronto, ON.

▶ Ron Nelson has been described as visionary and a trailblazer for his contributions to the urban music scene in Canada. **HIGHLIGHTS:** he is among the first DJs in Canada to promote rap music and rap artists, beginning in 1983 (until 1992) at CKLN 88.1FM on his *Fantastic Voyage* program. Through him, artists like Salt 'n Peppa, LL Cool J, Run DMC, Public Enemy, and others were presented to a Canadian audience; the artists' acknowledgement of RN's contribution to their promotion and success on the Cdn scene is noted in many album liner notes. He also became active in producing events which brought local artists (like Maestro and Michie Mee) to public attention through his Monster Jams, hip hop Battles, and Showdowns. In 1993, he worked in the US, hosting *Advance Remix*, which aired for two yrs. on WBLK and featured R&B and hip hop. Following this period in the US, he initiated *Friday Night Reggaemania* on CKLN and, while maintaining his awareness of the hip hop scene, became more involved in promoting reggae. His program is the only reggae radio show to secure regular and ongoing live-to-air broadcasts in Toronto clubs; during this time, he interviewed some of the most popular artists, including Beenie Man, John Holt, Dennis Brown, Shaba Ranks, Marcia Griffith, Baby Cham, and others. In 1997, he launched *Reggaemania Magazine*, the first publication of its kind in Canada to feature news and views on dancehall and reggae happenings, on a quarterly basis. **OTHER:** in addition to broadcasting, he produces radio commercials and jingles; through his multi-media production company, he is also a consultant and resource to the artists on the Urban Music scene. **HONS.:** include, Lifetime Achievement Award, Flava Record Pool, 2002; Lifetime Achievement Award, UMAC, 2001; Reggae DJ of the Year, 1998, '99, 2000, '01; Award for excellence in broadcasting, CKLN. **REVIEWED IN:** *NOW; eye Weekly; Word; Share; Pride.* **EDUCATION:** BAA, Radio & TV Arts, Ryerson U., 1985. **CONTACT:** rnelson@ reggaemania.com; www.reggaemania.com

▶NEWKIRK, Reginald
HUMAN RIGHTS, RACE & LABOUR RELATIONS SPECIALIST/MOTIVATIONAL SPEAKER, Parity Consulting, PO Box 962, Lumsden, SK S0G 3C0. Born: USA/ in Canada since: 1968.

▶ Reggie Newkirk is considered to be among Canada's leading human rights and race relations experts. Following completion of his studies at the University of Lethbridge, he worked for 15 yrs. in the area of human rights protection with various levels of government; he has also worked in the area of Native rights, labour relations and family violence prevention, occupying a number of positions. **CAREER HIGHLIGHTS:** Executive Director, Napi Friendship Assn., AB, 1971-72; Human Rights Officer, AB Human Rights Commission, 1972-75; Assistant Director, Human Rights Branch, Min. of Labour, BC, 1975-77; for the next nine yrs. he was Director, Western Region (BC, Yukon, AB, and NWT) of the Cdn Human Rights Commission; Executive Director, BC Institute on Family Violence, 1989-90; Executive Director, Yukon HR Commission, 1990-91. From 1992-99, he held the position of Secretary-General of the National Spiritual Assembly of the Baha'is of Canada. **OTHER:** since 1999, he has devoted himself full-time to running "healing racism workshops" with a colleague and developing his consulting business, featuring training programs, youth development, harassment prevention, and conflict resolution. They have facilitated over 40 two-day workshops in the US (Michigan, Maine, and New York) and throughout Canada (BC, Saskatchewan, Ontario, and Nova Scotia). During this time they have provided training to an estimated 1,500 individuals, including educators, clergy, police, and firefighters. **EDUCATION:** History/Philosophy, U. of Lethbridge, AB, 1972. **CONTACT:** r.newkirk@sasktel.net

▶**NICHOLAS, Everton S., MD, FRCPC.**
ENDOCRINOLOGIST, Toronto East General Hospital, Ste. 214-840 Coxwell Ave., Toronto, ON M4C 5T2. Born: Antigua/ in Canada since: 1983.
▶ Dr. Everton Nicholas has been an Endocrinologist at Toronto East General Hospital, since 1995. After completing his studies in medicine at UWI in Jamaica, 1985, and interning at the Princess Margaret Hospital in the Bahamas, he entered the residency program in Internal Medicine at U of T; from there he specialized in endocrinology and metabolism at U. of Western Ontario. By 1995, he was certified by the RCPC of Canada, to practise internal medicine, endocrinology, and metabolism. **OTHER:** in addition to his staff position at Toronto East General Hospital, he is active in the community, particularly with diabetic education programs, promoting awareness of the disease, along with measures to prevent its complications. **AFFIL/MBRSHP:** several professional bodies, including Endocrine Society, Canadian Diabetes Assn. (clinical and scientific section). **HONS.:** ACAA, Medicine, 2001; John H. Fowler Award, for Excellence in Teaching, Toronto East General, Family Practice Residents, 2001. **WORKS:** in, *Tetrahedron Letters; J Chemical Society, Perkin Transaction II; J Chemical & Engineering Data.* **EDUCATION:** Fellow, RCPC: Endocrinology & Metabolism, 1995; Internal Medicine, 1994. MB BS, UWI/ Jamaica, 1985; MSc, Organic Chemistry, Queen's U., 1980; BSc, Saint Mary's U., NS, 1979. **HEROES/ROLE MODELS:** Dr. L.R. Wynter. **MOTTO:** Heights reached and kept by great men were not attained by sudden

flight. But they, while their companions slept toiled upwards in the night. (Longfellow) **CONTACT:** Tel: 416-463-6280; Fax: 416-463-9480

▶**NICHOLLS-KING, Melanie**
ACTOR, Toronto, ON. Born: England/ in Canada since: 1972.
▶ Melanie Nicholls-King is an actor and co-founder of the theatre company, Sugar 'n Spice Productions, 1993, (with Sharon Lewis and maxine bailey), which produced the sold-out play, *Sistahs* (written by Sharon Lewis and maxine bailey), as well as *The Stockholme Syndrome,* and *Afrocentric.* At the time, Sugar 'n Spice was the only theatre company in Ontario operating specifically to produce works by, for, and about women of ethno-racially diverse backgrounds. As an actor, she has appeared on TV (*Traders; The Famous Jett Jackson*), stage (*Sistahs; Midsummer Night's Dream; NoonDay Sun*), and film (*Rude; Skin Deep*). She has worked with directors Helen Shaver, Norman Jewison, Sidney Lumet, Clement Virgo, and Clark Johnson. Upcoming projects include the HBO series, *The Wire,* and episodes on *Law and Order.* **COMMUNITY:** career mentor, Each One Teach One. **HONS.:** include, Best actress in a TV performance (*Traders*), Reel Black Award, 2000; rated among Best of Theatre Artists for 1995, *NOW* magazine; Dora Mavor Moore Award nominee for Best Female Performance in Small Theatre (*Sistahs*), 1994; Jessie Award, Best Ensemble Cast (*Love and Anger*), 1992. **EDUCATION:** Vancouver Playhouse Theatre School, 1989. **MOTTO:** FEAR is: False Evidence Appearing Real. **CONTACT:** loxinlove@aol.com

▶**NIMROD, Carl, MD, FRCSC.**
PROFESSOR, CHAIR, Dept. of Obstetrics & Gynecology, Faculty of Medicine, University of Ottawa, Ottawa, ON. Born: Guyana/ in Canada since: 1975.
▶ Dr. Carl Nimrod has been Chair of the Dept. of

Obstetrics and Gynecology at the University of Ottawa, since 1996 and Professor since 1989. **ACADEMIC HIGHLIGHTS:** Head, Division of Maternal-Fetal Medicine, Ottawa General Hospital (OGH), 1989-99; was Director, Fellowship Training Program Maternal-Fetal Medicine, U. of Ottawa, 1989-92. From 1980-88, he was in Alberta as an Assistant then an Associate Professor, U. of Calgary. At the same time he was Director of Residency Training, OB/GYN, then Director, Fellowship Training Program, Maternal-Fetal Medicince. **MEDICAL APPOINTMENTS:** Perinatologist, Southern Alberta Regional Perinatal Program, 1980-88; Director, Div. of Perinatology, Dept. of OB/GYN, OGH, 1989-99; Associate Clinical Scientist at the OGH Research Institute, 1998. Since 1992, he has been the Chief, Dept. of Obstetrics and Gynecology at the OGH. **AFFIL/MBRSHP:** Society of Obstetricians and Gynecologists of Canada, 1981-87; Examiner, Royal College of Physicians and Surgeons of Canada, 1986-91, 1994; American Institute of Ultrasound in Medicine, 1992-94; Ottawa Pregnancy Distress Centre, since 1997. **OTHER:** reviewer for several periodicals including: *CMAJ; American J of Obstetrics and Gynecology; J of Maternal-Fetal Investigation; J of Clinical Ultrasound.* **WORKS:** has written abstracts, chapters in books, edited books and articles; published in, *West Indian Medical J; CMAJ; J of Reproductive Medicine; Le J Can des Sciences Neurologiques.* **EDUCATION:** ARDMS, OB/GYN, 1997; Fellowship, Maternal-Fetal Medicine, 1980; FRCSC, OB/GYN, 1979, McMaster University. MB BS, UWI, 1974. **HEROES/ROLE MODELS:** Sid Effer, senior colleague. **MOTTO:** It's only in the dictionary that "success" comes before "work." **CONTACT:** cnimrod@ottawahospital.on.ca

▶NJOKU, William C.
COORDINATOR/ENTREPRENEUR, Will2Win Sports, 2065 Brunswick St., Halifax, NS B3K 5T8. Born: Ghana, 1972/ in Canada since: 1976.

▶ Will Njoku is a former professional basketball player who, through his company, Will2Win Sports, teaches young people about goal setting and individual development, while also assisting them to develop their athletic abilities. As a basketball player, he was a member of the Canadian National Basketball Program from 1989-98. He competed in three World Championship tournaments (1991, 1994, and 1998); in 1995 and '96 he competed in the US Basketball League, and was recognized as a CIAU All-Canadian in 1993 and '94. In 1994, he was drafted by the Indiana Pacers. He later played professionally in Europe and Asia. Will2Win was formed in 1999 and conducts workshops and youth camps throughout Atlantic Canada. **EDUCATION:** BA, Psychology, Saint Mary's U., NS, 1994. **MOTTO:** Success is a journey, not a destination. **CONTACT:** will@ will2winsports.com; www.will2winsports.com

▶NKANSAH, Peter, DDS, FADSA.
DENTIST-ANAESTHETIST, Pleasant Boulevard Dentistry & Anaesthesia, 39 Pleasant Blvd., Toronto, ON M4T 1K2. Born: Toronto, ON.

▶ Dr. Peter Nkansah is a dentist-anaesthetist and a co-owner of Pleasant Boulevard Dentistry and Anaesthesia. He is a Clinical Demonstrator and Lecturer at the Faculty of Dentistry, U of T; and, a staff dentist-anaesthetist at the Toronto General Hospital. **HIGHLIGHTS:** graduating from the Dental Anaesthesia postgraduate program in 1996, he is the first Black dentist-anaesthetist in Canada; is a member of the Dental Continuing Education teaching staff with U of T and the University of Western Ontario; co-initiator of the Advanced Cardiac Life Support course for dentists in Ontario; Team dentist for the Toronto Raptors; is also a spokesperson for the East Toronto Basketball Assn. **AFFIL/MBRSHP:** Vice-President, Ontario Dental Society of Anaesthesiology; past-President, Camp Jumoke (camp for children with sickle-cell anemia); co-founder of Summer Dreams (a charitable foundation for camping). **HONS.:**

Award for article, "Asthma, diabetes, & hypertension," Academy of General Dentistry, 1996; Hoskin Award, 1993. **WORKS:** in, *Ontario Dentist; U of T Dental J; Oral Surgery; Oral Medicine; Oral Pathology; Oral Radiology; Endodontics.* **REVIEWED IN:** *Toronto Star*, 2001; RCDSO dispatch to Ontario dentists, 2001; publication by AABHS, 1997. **EDUCATION:** Fellow, American Dental Society of Anesthesiology, 1997. Dipl., Dental Anaesthesia, 1996; DDS, 1993; MSc, Community Health, 1993, U of T. BSc, Biology, U. of Western Ontario, 1986. **HEROES/ROLE MODELS:** Parents; Dr. David Isen, friend. **CONTACT:** enkay @sympatico.ca; Fax: 416-927-9328

▶**NNADI, Joseph,** PhD.

PROFESSOR, Dept. of French Studies, University of Winnipeg, 515 Portage Ave., Winnipeg, MB R3B 2E9. Born: Nigeria/ in Canada since: 1988.
▶ Dr. Joseph Nnadi is Professor of French Studies at the University of Winnipeg; he became a full Professor in 1998. **CAREER HIGHLIGHTS:** Administrative Intern, Advanced Education Dept., Alberta; Dean of Arts, College of Education, U. of Nigeria, 1984-88; Consultant, Manitoba Assn. for Multicultural Education; co-editor, Manitoba Assn. for Rights and Liberties. **COMMUNITY:** actively involved with the Franco-Manitoban community, as well as the African and Afro-Caribbean communities; Manitoba Interfaith Immigration Council; African Pavilion; Manitoba Assn. of Rights and Liberties; Manitoba Assn. for Multicultural Education; Afro-Caribbean Assn. of Manitoba; Nigerian Assn. of Manitoba; Dinamba (Igbo) Cultural Assn. of Manitoba; nominated for Manitoba Ethnocultural Advisory and Advocacy Council. **HONS.:** several academic awards: Commonwealth Scholar, 1971; Prov. of AB, Graduate Scholar, 1973. **WORKS:** *Les Négresses de Baudelaire*, 1994; ed. *The Humanities in Contemporary Nigerian Education*, 1988; *Visions de l'Afrique dans l'oeuvre de Baudelaire*, 1980. **REVIEWED IN:** *Les Écrivains francophones de l'Ouest-Canada*, 1998; *Alumni Directory*, U. of AB, 1996. **EDUCATION:** M.Ed, 1991; PhD, 1978; MA, 1973, U. of AB. **HEROES/ROLE MODELS:** Prof. Charles Moore, "my academic godfather"; Dr. Okechukwu Ikejiani, a living encyclopedia of Igbo cultural heritage. **MOTTO:** Don't just let it happen, make it happen! **CONTACT:** j.nnadi@ uwinnipeg.ca; Fax: 204-774-4134

▶**NOEL, Asha**

YOUTH LEADERSHIP REPRESENTATIVE, Canadian Ethnocultural Council, Toronto, ON. Born: Trinidad & Tobago, 1977/ in Canada since: 1977.
▶ Asha Noel was born in Trinidad, raised in Fredericton, NB, and now lives in Toronto. She has been active in raising the profile of issues as they pertain to youth, especially in the areas of anti-racism, education, and reparations, and is involved with a number of organizations as a youth representative. She is chairperson to the Youth Forum of the Canadian Ethnocultural Council. She was a member of the International Youth Committee, one of three youth representing the Americas, who helped to facilitate the First Youth Summit to occur with a UN Conference; this Summit occurred with the UNWCAR, which took place in Durban, SA, 2001. She is a founding member of Black Youth United. **WORKS:** "Youth at WCAR," in *Connect, Speak Out*; "Young Women Connect–Violence, Poverty and Racism," *Tiny Giant* magazine, 2002; "Ideal Beauty: Cross-Cultural Assimilation" for Canadian Multicultural Health Council, 2000; "Drum Beat" in *Black Girl Talk: The Black Girls*, 1995. **EDUCATION:** MA, Adult Education & Community Development, OISE/U of T, 2002; BA, U of T, 1999. **HEROES/ROLE MODELS:** Father: "[He] gave me the skills I needed to survive in this world." **CONTACT:** asha_noel@hotmail.com

▶**NOEL, Dexter**

COORDINATOR INTERDISCIPLINARY STUDIES,

University of New Brunswick, Box 4400, Fredericton, NB E3B 5A3. Born: Trinidad & Tobago/ in Canada since: 1962.

▶ Prof. Dexter Noel has been an Associate Professor of Spanish at the University of New Brunswick (UNB), since 1987. He is also the Coordinator of Interdisciplinary Studies, and Director of International Development Studies. His program at the university studies the relationship between the developed and the developing world and their interconnectedness. His own areas of focus are Africa, Latin America, and the Caribbean. He is active both in the university and the larger community, working to foster greater unity amongst the various members of the Black population. He is a founding member of U of NB's Caribbean Circle and the Fredericton Caribbean Assn., organizations that aim to increase awareness and appreciation of Caribbean culture. He was a member of the 1967 Steering Committee for Caribana (Toronto); 1st vice-president, with the Credit Union Central of NB; Executive Committee, *Int'l Fiction Review* since 1977; executive member, Cdn Consortium of University Programs in Int'l Development Studies (CCUPIDS). **HONS.:** including, 25-yr. Plaque, 1998 & 20-yr. Plaque, Caribbean Circle, 1993; nominee, Award for the UNB Stuart Excellence in Teaching, 6 times since 1994. **WORKS:** "Perceptions as Reality: (Mis) Representation of Blacks in the New World," in *Re/Visioning: Canadian Perspectives on the Education of Africans in the late 20th Century*, 1998. **EDUCATION:** Cert., Intercultural Studies, UBC, 1999; Cert., Proficiency French, UNB, 1987; MA, U of T, 1966; BA, McGill U., 1965. **MOTTO:** Strive for excellence and always set a good example. **CONTACT:** de3055@unb.ca; Fax: 506-447-3166

▶NOLAN, Faith
MUSICIAN/ACTIVIST, PO Box 690, Stn. P., Toronto, ON M5S 2Y4. Born: Halifax, NS.

▶ Faith Nolan is a musician and a social activist who has introduced a number of initiatives in women's prisons and other communities across Canada. She has been conducting Black History Month workshops in Toronto schools, since 1983. She also offers free workshops to women in jails and shelters across Canada; is the founder and director of a number of women's choirs (P4W Women's Choir, Eastdale Collegiate young Black women's choir, Imani Freedom); and, is the organizer of Multicultural Women in Concert. She is also very involved as a social activist who supports Lesbian, Gay, Bisexual, & Transgendered (LGBT) Pride days across the country. In 1983, she recorded her first musical collection of Black History in Canada entitled, *Africville*. **HEROES/ROLE MODELS:** Angela Davis, activist; BME church. **MOTTO:** We all have the power to change the world; most people just fear using their power to do it. (Nelson Mandela). **CONTACT:** faith@nexicom.net; www.nexicom.net/~faith

▶N'SINGI, Vita M. Sébastien
LEGAL COUNSEL & NOTARY PUBLIC, Dept. of Justice, Office of the Associate Deputy Minister, Ste. 5005-275 Sparks St., Ottawa, ON K1A 0H8. Born: Angola/ in Canada since: 1984.

▶ Vita Sébastien N'Singi is a lawyer and a notary public; he is the Interim EA to the Assoc. Deputy Minister (ADM) of Justice, in the Federal Dept. of Justice, and Special Advisor to the ADM on issues of multiculturalism, human rights, and social justice, for the workplace and the community. **HIGHLIGHTS:** completed his articling with the CAS of Ottawa-Carleton, and in the Dept. of Justice in the Legal Excellence Programme (incl. analysis of the Income Tax Act and Regulations for the purpose of harmonizing it with the Civil Code of Quebec). **COMMUNITY:** narrated French version of the documentary, *Hate and Hate Crimes*, produced by the Toronto Police, 1995; co-produced the film, *Le Quatuor de l'Exil*, NFB, concerning immigrant Black Francophone youth and their challenges in the Cdn school system and the community, 1995; featured in the commercial, *Les Gens d'Ici,* by SRC, as a role model for Black youth in the community and schools, through a joint pilot project by the French School Board and the Anti-racism Secretariat, Ont. Min. of Citizenship, 1993, dealing with anti-racism and drop-out in the school system. Also is a freelance radio broadcaster on CIUT's *Pot-pourri.* Founder and first Director, Canada-Angola Chamber of Commerce, 1998; in partnership with INAC (Angolan National Institute for children, victims of war), carried out international outreach to children in war zones. **HONS.:** Tom Wilcox Memorial Bursary & The St-Lewis Bursary, for community work, Cdn Bar Assn., 2000; Award for leadership, All Nations Full Gospel Church, Toronto & Ottawa, 1998; Award for leadership and for *Le Quatuor de l'Exil,* NFB, 1993; Community Award, Toronto Police, for Youth and Police relationship, 1993. **EDUCATION:** LLL (Civil Law), 1999; LLB, 1998, U. of Ottawa. BA, Math for Comm., York U., 1988. Studies in medicine, 1988; Dipl., Luso-African Lit. & Portuguese, 1981, U. of Lisbon, Portugal. **HEROES/ROLE MODELS:** Rev. Dr. Samuel Donkor; Rev. Veronica Adu-Bobie. **CONTACT:** snsingi@justice.gc.ca

▶NUNES, Neville

TEACHER (Ret.), Hamilton Board of Education, ON. Born: Jamaica/ in Canada since: 1965.

▶ Neville Nunes began his teaching career in Jamaica as a "pupil" teacher in 1946 at Providence Elementary School; after graduating from Mico College in 1953, he returned to Providence in 1954 before teaching at Cornwall College in Montego Bay, where he remained until 1965. His first position in Canada was as a principal's assistant in 1965. In 1967, he began teaching with the Hamilton Board of Education, and taught Special Education at elementary and secondary schools (1970-86). He continued as a consultant in ESL until his retirement in 1995. **HIGHLIGHTS:** he is

credited with having introduced Black History Month to Hamilton-area schools; he is most proud of The Underground Railway Project, a cultural/educational exchange with the Buffalo School Board, as well as his role in founding Black Youth Achievement, a group promoting excellence in schools. He established a mentorship program in which members of the African Canadian Assn., at McMaster U., worked with at-risk students to improve their school performance. **COMMUNITY:** Black History Committee; John Howard Society/ Hamilton; Ontario Black Heritage Network; Kiwanis; Heart-Health Hamilton; Cdn Alliance of Black Educators, Steering Committee; African Canadian Workers Project. **HONS.:** include, Award for "dedication & contribution to Continuing Education," 1999; Community Service Award, Settlement & Integration Services, 1997; John Holland Award, Education, Black History Month Committee, 1995; Award, for dedication to the needs of exceptional children, Council for Exceptional Children, 1993; nominee, World Citizenship Award, 1993. **WORKS:** in, *The Hamilton Spectator; The Weekly Gleaner.* **REVIEWED IN:** *The Hamilton Spectator; West Hamilton J; Jamaica Weekly Gleaner.* **EDUCATION:** MSc, Education, Niagara U., 1975; BA, McMaster U., 1962; Cert., Teaching, Mico College, Jamaica, 1953. **HEROES/ROLE MODELS:** E.A. Barrett; O.A. Black. **MOTTO:** Organize to maximize; educate to liberate. **CONTACT:** nsnunes@sympatico.ca

▶NYOKA, Gail

PLAYWRIGHT, c/o Canadian Association of Professional Playwrights, Toronto, ON. Born: Trinidad & Tobago/ in Canada since: 1971.

▶ Gail Nyoka is a playwright whose play, *Mella Mella,* won the prestigious Chalmers Canadian Play Award, in the Theatre for Young Audiences category, in 2000. This play was the first by a Black woman to be presented on the mainstage at Young People's Theatre, in Toronto; the play has also been translated into French and toured southern Ontario. *Mella Mella* is also published in an anthology of five plays for young audiences. Her previous play, *Demeter and the Bird's Song* was shown at Groundswell Festival of Works in Progress, 1992. She is inspired by the poetry of Langston Hughes. **HONS.:** Chalmers Award, Canadian Play: Theatre for Young Audiences, for *Mella Mella*, 2000. **EDUCATION:** BA, Communications, U. of Ottawa. **CONTACT:** Tel: 416-703-0201

OCHEJE, Paul D., Dr.

ASSISTANT PROFESSOR, Faculty of Law, University of Windsor, 401 Sunset Ave., Windsor, ON N9B 3P4. Born: Nigeria/ in Canada since: 1991.

▶ Dr. Paul Ocheje is an Assistant Professor in the Faculty of Law at the University of Windsor since 2000. He completed his doctorate in jurisprudence in 1999, but his career in law began several years earlier. **BACKGROUND:** State Counsel, Min. of Justice, Nigeria, 1983-84; lecturer in Business Law at the University of Benin, 1984-91; was also Assistant Director of the LLB program, 1987-90. From 1991 to 1999, he completed a second LLM and his doctorate in jurisprudence at York University. **AFFIL/MBRSHP:** Nigerian Bar Assn.; International Bar Assn.; International Third World Legal Studies Assn.; Cdn Assn. of University Teachers. **HONS.:** many academic including, Rockefeller Dissertation Award, 1996 & 1997. **WORKS:** in, *J of African Law; J of African & Asian Studies; Windsor Yearbook of Access to Justice;* chapter in *Legitimate Governance in Africa*, 1999. **REVIEWED IN:** several citations, including Abstract of doctoral thesis in *McGill Law J.* **EDUCATION:** D.Jur, 1999; LLM, 1994, York University. LLM, U. of Benin, Nigeria, 1990; LLB/Hons., Ahmadu Bello U., Nigeria, 1982. **HEROES/ROLE MODELS:** Father; Chief O. Awolowo, politician. **MOTTO:** All things are possible for all who believe in God. **CONTACT:** pocheje@uwindsor.ca; www.uwindsor.ca

▶ODULANA-OGUNDIMU, A. Oluremi, MD, FRCPC, FAAP.

PEDIATRICIAN, Laurentian Hospital, 1486 Regent St., Sudbury, ON P3E 3Z6. Born: Nigeria/ in Canada since: 1978.

▶ Dr. Oluremi Ogundimu is a Pediatrician who began her medical career in Nigeria and, since 1985, is practising in Sudbury at the Sudbury Regional Hospital. **CAREER:** Clinical Lecturer,

Dept. of Pediatrics, University of Ottawa, since 1993; Chief, Dept. of Pediatrics, Laurentian Hospital, 1991-94; Medical Director, Children's Treatment Centre, Laurentian Hospital, 1987-90; and, Medical Officer in rural Nigeria under the National Youth Services Corp, 1975-76; pursued her medical studies and career while raising a family of four. **AFFIL/MBRSHP:** Cdn Pediatric Society; American Academy of Cerebral Palsy and Developmental Medicine; American Academy of Pediatrics; OMA; CMA. **EDUCATION:** FRCPC, FAAP, 1983; Pediatrics Residency, Dalhousie U., 1978-81; Pediatrics Resident, U. College Hospital, Ibadan, Nigeria, 1976-78; MB BS, U. of Ibadan Medical School, Nigeria, 1974. **HEROES/ROLE MODELS:** Parents; Dr. Awoliyi, first female OB/GYN in Nigeria. **CONTACT:** Fax: 705-523-5240

▶OFFISHALL, Kardinal

HIP HOP ARTIST/MC/PRODUCER, Toronto, ON. Born: Toronto, ON, 1975.

▶ Kardinal Offishall (a.k.a. Jason Harrow) has been described by his peers as the MC/Producer who has "raised the hip hop stakes and will continue to set them higher." His style of music blends reggae and hip hop into something unique; he has been writing lyrics since the age of ten; a childhood highlight was performing for Nelson Mandela; he has since performed across NA and overseas with the Beastie Boys, Run DMC, Outkast, and Roots. In 1997, he became one of the first urban artists to sign a publishing deal, with Warner Chappell. **HIGHLIGHTS:** singles *Husslin', Money Jane, BaKardi Slang, Ol' Time Killin'* received extensive play on MuchMusic; in 2000, he was signed to MCA; his first of three albums: *Firestarter Vol. 1: Quest for Fire,* was released in Spring, 2001 to positive response; *Firestarter Vol. 2* is scheduled for release, Fall, 2002. **OTHER:** his production company SHAG produced Choclair's Gold album, *Ice Cold.* **HONS.:** UMAC Awards, 2002: for *Heaven Only Knows,* Best Hip Hop/Rap Recording & Best Songwriting; Best Music Video, for *Ol Time Killin';* UMAC Awards, 2001: for *BaKardi Slang,* Best Hip Hop/Rap Recording; Best Music Video; Best Songwriting. Won two Juno Awards: Best Rap recording, for *Northern Touch* by the Rascalz; Best Rap Recording, for *Let's Ride* by Choclair; has been nominated for two MuchMusic Video awards; won a SOCAN award for *Husslin';* nominated for Juno Awards for Best Rap Recording (*Money Jane & Husslin'),* 2000 & (*BaKardi Slang*) 2001. **CONTACT:** lani.fumerton@umusic.com; Fax: 416-718-4213

▶OFOSU, Cottie, Ed.D.

ASSISTANT PROFESSOR, School of Nursing, McMaster University, 1200 Main St. W., Hamilton, ON L7N 3Z5. Born: Jamaica/ in Canada since: 1964.

▶ Dr. Cottie Ofosu is an Assistant Professor in the School of Nursing at McMaster University where she has taught since 1993; her area of specialization is Problem-Based Learning. **OTHER:** provides mentoring to Black students at McMaster University, to encourage them to pursue graduate studies in professional sectors. **HONS.:** nominee, President's Award for Excellence in Instruction, 2000 and 2002; nominated for Excellence in Teaching, 2002 and for Cert. of Excellence, 1997, by the McMaster Students' Union Teaching Awards Committee. **WORKS:** articles in: *J of Nursing Education; International J of Nursing Studies; Registered Nurse; The Can Nurse.* **EDUCATION:** Ed.D, 1993; Public Health Nurse, 1975, U of T. M.Ed, Brock U., 1986; BA, Sociology, McMaster U., 1982; RN, Canada, 1965. Midwife, 1964; RN, 1963, England. **HEROES/ROLE MODELS:** Dr. Fred Ofosu, spouse. **MOTTO:** Mother may have, father may have, but God bless the child who has his/her own. **CONTACT:** ofosuc@mcmaster.ca; Fax: 905-633-9426

▶OFOSU, Frederick A., PhD.

PROFESSOR, Dept. of Pathology & Molecular Medicine, McMaster University/ **SENIOR SCIENTIST,** Canadian Blood Services, Hamilton. Born: Ghana/ in Canada since: 1963.

▶ Dr. Frederick Ofosu is a Professor in the Dept. of Pathology and Molecular Medicine at McMaster University; he is also a Senior Scientist with Canadian Blood Services in Hamilton. Previously, he worked at the University of Ghana Medical School, and at the Hospital for Sick Children in Toronto. His current research focus is on abnormalities in the blood-clotting process that lead to excessive bleeding, or to heart attacks and strokes. He has published close to 200 articles in professional journals, reporting new findings made by his research group. **OTHER:** for over ten years, was a member of the various committees setting policies for Graduate education and participated in the selection of faculty members and students in Medical Sciences Graduate Programmes at McMaster U. Concerned by the low number of Black university students enrolled in graduate studies or pursuing education in the professions, particularly in medicine, nursing, engineering, and law, he and his wife, Dr. Cotilda Ofosu (a professor in the School of Nursing at McMaster U.; *see: Ofosu, Cottie*) began actively mentoring Black students at McMaster U. By advising students on suitable course selection and the academic requirements (and individual effort) necessary to attain these goals, the options of these students and their success rates have been increased. In turn, several of these students have become mentors and role models to others as volunteers at the Diverse Community Achievement Centre (DCAC), a Hamilton community organization assisting minority youth. **COMMUNITY:** President, Prince Hall Foundation; Vice-Chair, ACLC; past-President, DCAC. **AFFIL/MBRSHP:** several professional organizations, including: Factor VII, Factor IX, Heparin sub-committees, Int'l Society of Thrombosis and Haemostasis (1983-90); Expert Advisory Panel of Health Laboratory Services, WHO, since 1990; Expert Committee on Biological Standardization, WHO, since 1992 (this Committee institutes the international standards used to assess the quality, safety, and suitability of vaccines, and other biological drugs; it also approves the requirements vaccines and other biological drugs must meet on behalf of WHO). **EDUCATION:** PhD, Biochemistry, U of T, 1971. BSc, Biochemistry, McMaster U., 1967. **MOTTO:** Our actions and deeds, and not our words or beliefs, are what guide sensible people to judge who we are. **CONTACT:** ofosuf@mcmaster. ca; Fax: 905-521-2613

▶OFOSU-NYARKO, Helen, PhD.

TEAM LEADER/PSYCHOLOGIST, Overseas Operations Division, Dept. of Foreign Affairs & International Trade, Ottawa, ON. Born: Toronto, ON, 1969.

▶ Dr. Helen Ofosu-Nyarko completed her doctorate in psychology in 1999 and is in her second position, as an Industrial/Organisational Psychologist. Since Fall, 2001, she has been leading a team responsible for developing competency profiles, recruitment and selection tools, and a revised performance appraisal system for Foreign Service Officers and locally-engaged trade staff (i.e. local staff hired at Canadian Embassies abroad). Previously, 1999-2001, she was a psychologist in the R&D division of the Personnel Psychology Centre with the Public Service Commission of Canada (PSC). There she developed competency-based assessment tools for the selection and/or promotion of economists, policy researchers, computer scientists, middle managers, and executives in the Federal Public Service. While completing her doctorate in psychology, she also completed internships with the following units of the PSC: the Assessment, Counselling and Testing Directorate, 1998; the Psychometric Unit, Staffing Policy and Program Development Directorate, 1997. **COMMUNITY:** Visible Minority Recruitment Advisory Cmtee; Asst. Editor, Sankofa-Habari; Student Senator, U. of Windsor. **HONS.:** recipient of many awards & scholarships including: Head of the Public Service Award, for development of a recruitment process to assess applicants for the Policy Research Development Program; PSC Excellence Award, for development of tools to assess Diversity in Leadership Program participants for acceptance into the Career Assignment Program, 2001. **WORKS:** in, *Personality & Individual Differences; Feminism and Psychology.* **REVIEWED IN:** *Millennium Minds,* 2000. **EDUCATION:** PhD, Applied Social Psychology, 1999; MA, Applied Social Psychology, 1995, U. of Windsor. BSc, McMaster U., 1992. **CONTACT:** Tel: 613-859-8440; helen@ghawaco.com

▶**OGILVIE, Lana**

MODEL/ON-AIR HOST, c/o Ford Models (Canada) Inc., 385 Adelaide St. W., Toronto, ON. Born: Toronto, ON.

▶ Lana Ogilvie is an internationally recognized model who, in 1992, became the first Black model to sign a multi-year contract with the cosmetics company, Cover Girl. She has modeled for magazines such as *Sports Illustrated; Elle; Vogue; Glamour; Flare; Mademoiselle; Essence; Harpers Bazaar;* and others. She has appeared in advertisements for clients which include Gap, Guess Jeans, Victoria's Secret, John Galliano, and Katherine Hamnett. In 2000, she was featured in the campaign for Banana Republic. As a runway model, she has represented designers such as Karl Lagerfield, Christian Lacroix, Issey Miyake, Gianfranco Ferre, Isaac Mizrahi, and many others. Most recently she has become an on-air co-host of *The Review,* and a segment contributor on *This Week in Fashion,* both on the Fashion TV channel in Toronto. **CONTACT:** lanao @ftchannel.com

▶**OGUNDELE, Gabriel,** PhD.

SENIOR RESEARCH SCIENTIST, Kinectrics Inc., 800 Kipling Ave., Toronto, ON M8Z 6C4. Born: Nigeria/ in Canada since: 1978.

▶ Dr. Gabriel Ogundele is a Senior Research Scientist at Kinectrics Inc. (formerly, Ontario Hydro Research Division), since 1988. He is responsible for conducting fundamental and applied research on the integrity of engineering materials, and providing solutions to materials' degradation under various environmental and operational conditions. Specific activities include: performing tests in corrosion fatigue and stress corrosion cracking of carbon steel and nickel alloys, for input into "fitness-for-service" guidelines; developing specialized testing apparatus; conducting failure analysis on damaged components in thermal and nuclear plants. **BACKGROUND:** 1984-88, he was a Post-Doctoral Fellow and Research Associate at U of T; there he developed the "low pH test solution" currently used for the assessment of the stress corrosion cracking of underground gas transmission lines, and carried out experiments on stress corrosion cracking; also taught courses in fatigue and fracture engineering, and, dynamics. Since 1986, he has been a staff lecturer at U of T, in the Dept. of Mechanical and Industrial Engineering, teaching a graduate course on direct energy conversion and corrosion. From 1997-2000, he was an Adjunct Professor at Ryerson U., in the School of Mechanical Engineering. **AFFIL/MBRSHP:** NACE, since 1979; Knights of Columbus; co-founder, Society of Cdn-Nigerian Engineers. **COMMUNITY:** Advisory Council, St. Francis Xavier Catholic Secondary School; Organizing Committee, Black History Month Event, Ontario Science Centre; Dixie Soccer Club; attends and speaks at school events and Career Days. **HONS.:** including: co-winner, Paul Cohen Memorial Award, for most precise & innovative paper on Power Systems Water Technology, International Water Conference, 1993; Dissertation Fellowship & A. Wayne Dingman Scholarship, U.

of Calgary. **WORKS:** articles in, *Microstructural Science*; *Corrosion*; *J Testing Evaluation*; and, numerous conference papers. **EDUCATION:** PhD, Mechanical Engineering (Metallurgy & Corrosion), 1984; MSc, Mechanical Engineering (Metallurgy & Corrosion), 1980, U. of Calgary. Higher Dipl., Mechanical Engineering, The Polytechnic, Ibadan, Nigeria, 1977. **HEROES/ROLE MODELS:** Dr. Bill White. **MOTTO:** Do what needs to be done; do not worry about what should have been done. **CONTACT:** gabriel.ogundele@kinectrics.com

▶**OJO, Oluremi, Dr.**

PHARMACIST, Corporate Pharmacy, 78 Corporate Dr., Toronto, ON M1H 3G4. Born: Nigeria/ in Canada since: 1987.

▶ Dr. Oluremi Ojo is a pharmacist and a joint owner of Corporate Pharmacy, located in east Toronto. He is also a partner in the company, Island Dialysis, which, as a division of Atlantis Healthcare Group Inc., has developed international dialysis facilities in Jamaica, St. Lucia, Barbados and Puerto Rico, to provide vacationers needing dialysis with access to quality treatment in some of the most popular Caribbean vacation locations. **HONS.:** ACAA, Business, 2002. **WORKS:** *Rheological Properties of Viscosity: Increasing Macro Molecular Adjuvants*, Doctoral thesis, Hungary, 1987. **EDUCATION:** Pharm.D., 1987; MSc, Pharmacy, 1984, Szeged Medical University, Hungary. **HEROES/ROLE MODELS:** Delores Lawrence, business. **MOTTO:** If you can put your mind to it, you can do it! **CONTACT:** corporate.gdn @dt.pharmassist.ca; Fax: 416-279-0821

▶**OKAFOR, Obiora, PhD.**

ASSISTANT PROFESSOR, Osgoode Hall Law School, York University, 4700 Keele St., Toronto, ON M3J 1P3. Born: Nigeria/ in Canada since: 1994.

▶ Dr. Obiora Okafor is an Assistant Professor at Osgoode Hall Law School. He began his law career in Nigeria, where he practised as a junior partner, 1990-94; he also lectured in the Faculty of Law at U. of Nigeria while completing his LLM. In Canada, he was a lecturer in the Faculty of Law at UBC, 1996-98; was a Visiting Scholar with the Human Rights Program, Harvard Law School, 1999 and 2001; was Assistant Professor in the Dept. of Law at Carleton University, 1998-2000; and, since 2000, is in his current position at Osgoode Hall Law School, at York U. He is on the Editorial Advisory Board of the *Osgoode Hall Law Journal*. **HONS.:** include, Teaching Excellence Award, Osgoode Hall Law School, York U., 2001-02; GG Gold Medal for "best university-wide doctoral student at UBC," 1999. **WORKS:** including, *Re-Defining Legitimate Statehood: Int'l Law and State Fragmentation in Africa*, 2000; five chapters in books, 14 articles in refereed journals. **REVIEWED IN:** *West Africa Magazine*, 2000. **EDUCATION:** PhD, Law, 1998; LLM, 1995, UBC. LLM, 1994; LLB, 1989, U. of Nigeria. **HEROES/ROLE MODELS:** Parents. **CONTACT:** ookafor @yorku.ca; Fax: 416-736-5736

▶**OKELU, Chinwe Pete**

COORDINATOR, Alberta Municipal Affairs, Edmonton, AB. Born: Nigeria/ in Canada since: 1972.

▶ Chinwe Okelu has been in the employ of the Alberta Government since 1975, and has worked with a number of Ministries including Housing; Municipal Affairs; and, International and Intergovernmental Relations. Currently he is a Coordinator with the Ministry of Municipal Affairs. Over the years, partially through his work and partially through personal interest, he has had extensive involvement with a number of community organizations and initiatives. **COMMUNITY INVOLVEMENT:** Knottwood Community League, where he assisted in the identification of community needs and the development of relevant programs; U. of Alberta Community Day Care, which he re-structured to eliminate the operating deficit; Mill Woods Multicultural Brd., where he set the goal of improving relations within Edmonton's ethnically diverse community, by introducing a number of initiatives (localized citizenship ceremonies, workshops, seminars and other community events); founding President, Nigeria Assn. of Alberta; Chair, Mill Woods Community Leagues Presidents' Council, where he formed committees to deal with impact of government initiatives such as changes to health care, increased dialogue and better working relations amongst various community groups and businesses; Quality of Life Commissioner, one of eight, mandated to address the limited amount of information available on government restructuring and its impact on the disadvantaged members of the community; member of City of Edmonton, Transportation Master Plan, and responsible for ensuring community input from SE Edmonton; first Chair of Community Health Council for Mill Woods; member, Edmonton Community Lottery Brd., appointed in 1998, responsible for ensuring distribution of funds allotted to the city by the provincial government, from lottery earnings, to arts, culture, sports, and recreation organizations, and other social service agencies. He has also presented himself as a candidate in two municipal elections. **HONS.:** including, Award for service to community, BAASA, 1997; Board Award, Edmonton Federation of Community Leagues, 1996; Salute to Excellence, City of Edmonton, 1996; Citation for Citizenship, Govt. Canada, 1995; Cert. Appreciation, Int'l Year of the Family, Govt. Canada, 1994; GG 125th Anniv. Medal, 1993. **EDUCATION:** MBA, Idaho State U., 1982; MA, U. of Alberta, 1974; BA/Hons., U. of Nigeria, 1971. **HEROES/ROLE MODELS:** Nelson Mandela. **MOTTO:** Believe in yourself. **CONTACT:** chinwe.okelu@gov.ab.ca; Fax: 780-422-8624

▶**OLATUNBOSUN, Olufemi,** MD, FRCSC. **PROFESSOR & CHAIR, OBSTETRICS, GYNECOLOGY, & REPRODUCTIVE SCIENCES,** University of Saskatchewan, Saskatoon, SK. Born: Nigeria/ in Canada since: 1977.

▶ Dr. Olufemi Olatunbosun is Professor and Chair, Dept. of Obstetrics, Gynecology, and Reproductive Sciences at the University of Saskatchewan, a position he has held since 1999. **BACKGROUND:** after completing his studies in Canada, he returned to Nigeria and was a Lecturer at the University of Ife, 1982-85; he was Director of the Assisted Conception Unit, at St. Nicholas Hospital, Lagos, 1985-89; and, Clinician at the King Saud University, in Riyadh, Saudi Arabia, 1989-92. He returned to U. of Saskatchewan in 1992 where he held the following positions: Assistant Professor, 1992-95; Associate Professor, 1995-99; Director, Residency Training Program, 1998-2000; Professor & Chair, 1999; and, Chief of Obstetrics & Gynecology at Saskatoon District Health, since 2000. **HIGHLIGHTS:** has been responsible for a number of discoveries and innovations in his field of medicine: early in his career, OO pioneered the use of the emergency cervical cerclage in advanced cervical dilation; this is now known as the "Olatunbosun technique"; he did pioneering work in the delay of delivery interval in multiple gestation using cervical cerclage; this has now become an established procedure for prolonging the gestation of multi-fetal pregnancy and increasing fetal salvage rates. And, his most recent study (*see Obstetrics and Gynecology*, 2001) has led to a recommendation that Human Papilloma Virus (HPV) DNA testing be performed on prospective sperm donors so that the risk of cervical cancer in the recipient can be reduced. **OTHER:** OO continues to pursue his interest in the refinement of surgical interventions; his recent research focuses on assisted reproduction, hormone contraception, menopause, International Women's Health, and Curriculum Reforms in Medical Education. **HONS.:** several including: Award of Excellence; Excellence in Teaching Award, College of Medicine, U. of Sask., 2000; Excellence in Teaching Award, Professional Assn. of Interns & Residents of Sask., 2000; Clinical Teacher of the Year Award, College of Medicine, U. of Sask., 1994; Excellence in Resident Education, Council on Resident Education in OB/GYN, 1994 & 1995. **WORKS:** in, *Obstetrics & Gynecology*; *J Society of Obstetricians & Gynecologists of Canada*; *Obstetrics & Gynecology*; *African J of Reproductive Health*; *British Medical J*; *British J of Family Planning*; *Int. J Gynecol Obstet.* **REVIEWED IN:** nat'l and int'l medical publications. **EDUCATION:** FRCSC, U. of Sask., 1981. FACOG; RCPSC, 1977; MD, 1973, U. of Lagos, Nigeria. **HEROES/ROLE MODELS:** Wole Soyinka, Nobel Laureate, Literature; Nelson Mandela. **MOTTO:** My mission in life is to live with integrity and make a difference in the lives of others. **CONTACT:** olatunbosun@sask.usask.ca; Fax: 306-966-8040

►**OLIVER, A. Pearleen (Borden),** Dr.
ACTIVIST/HISTORIAN/COMMUNITY LEADER.
Born: Cooks Cove, NS.
▶ Dr. Pearleen (Borden) Oliver is a significant figure in Nova Scotia for providing over 60 years of active leadership and community involvement as a religious and human rights leader, researcher, author, youth leader, choir director, historian and noted public speaker. She was the first Black graduate of the New Glasgow, NS High School; was married to the renowned Rev. Dr. William Pearly Oliver (minister, social activist and educator; minister of Cornwallis Street Baptist Church, 1937-62, then the Beechville Baptist Church until 1989; founding member NS AACP, BUF, BCC), from 1936 until his death in 1989. As an activist, PO fought hard to remove barriers of discrimination, which restricted education and employment opportunities for Blacks and other minorities in the 1940s and 1950s. She is a founder of the NS AACP and, in 1947, crusaded successfully for the admission of Black women to nursing schools in Canada. She organized youth training groups, summer camps and women's groups and was responsible

for obtaining continuing education and music classes for several Black communities. She served on civic and regional youth boards such as the Maritime Religious Education Council and the NS Training School for Girls; mentored hundreds of girls in the process, helping them to choose and work towards achieving goals for a fulfilling life. As a historian, she wrote and published on the history of Blacks in NS (see below). In her lifelong involvement with the Baptist Church, PO has held many positions and served in many roles. In 1976, she became the first woman Moderator of the African United Baptist Assn. of NS. Now, at age 85, she remains an active community leader and serves as organist and choir director at Beechville United Baptist Church. **HONS:** several including, Hon. Doctor of Humane Letters, MSVU, 1993; Hon. Doctor of Letters, SMU, 1990; Woman of the Year Award, 1981 (first recipient) and 1991. **WORKS:** *Song of the Spirit*, 1994; *From Generation to Generation*, 1985; *A Root and a Name*, 1977; *A Brief History of the Coloured Baptists of Nova Scotia, 1782-1953*, 1953. **REVIEWED IN:** *Journey: African Canadian History*, 2000; *Millennium Minds*, 2000.

►**OLIVER, Leslie H.,** PhD.
PROFESSOR, Jodrey School of Computer Science, Acadia University, Wolfville, NS. Born: Halifax, NS.
▶ Dr. Leslie Oliver is a Professor of Computer Science at Acadia University, specializing in medical digital image processing research and development. Since 1989, he has been the Director of the Jodrey School of Computer Science (JSCS). **AFFIL/MBRSHP:** since 1990, he has been leading a math camp for local Black youth, through Dalhousie U.; since 2001, is the National President, Canadian Information Processing Society (CIPS), has been the NS Provincial President, since 1998; co-Chair, National Professional Certification Council, 1995-97. **HONS.:** include, Teacher of the Year, JSCS, 1999; C.C. Gotlieb

Award, for service to the profession, CIPS, 1999; inducted into Acadia U., Sports Hall of Fame, 1999; Recognition Award, Society of Black Student Engineers/U. of Florida, 1984; Award for Teaching Excellence, Confederation College, 1974. **WORKS:** include, *Proceedings of 10th Int'l Medical Signal Processing Conference BIOSIGNAL '90*. **EDUCATION:** PhD, Computer Science, McGill U., 1979. MSc, Math, 1966; BSc, Math, 1962, Acadia U. **HEROES/ROLE MODELS:** William and Pearleen Oliver, parents. **CONTACT:** Tel: 902-585-1331; Fax: 902-585-1067; leslie.oliver@acadiau.ca

▶OLIVER, Sharon, Dr.

PRESIDENT & CEO, Oliver Management Connexus Inc., Wolfville, NS. Born: Montreal, QC.

▶ Sharon Oliver is a retired health care executive who provides strategic planning and management expertise through her company, Oliver Management Connexus. Working with government agencies, community groups, and not-for-profit organizations she provides corporate strategies and plans, meeting client needs. For private corporations, she develops strategies and plans for recruitment and retention of racially and culturally diverse employees. Community clients include: HRDC; Black Loyalist Heritage Society, Birchtown, NS; Community Enhancement Assn., Truro, NS; Lucasville/Upper Hammonds Plains Development Assn. **OTHER:** lectures to university students in areas of African Canadian history and heritage; through writings and public addresses, she works to raise awareness of African-Nova Scotian history and the need for heritage-diversity recognition. **AFFIL/MBRSHP:** Chair, Order of NS Advisory Council; Council on African Cdn Education; NS Black Business Women's Network; Atlantic Provinces Economic Council; Brd. of Governors, Dalhousie U.; Brd. of Governors, Mount Saint Vincent U. **HONS.:** including, luncheon with Hilary Clinton, G-7 Summit, Halifax, 1995; Progress Women of Excellence Award,

Health Category, Cdn Progress Club, 1992. **WORKS:** articles in *Chronicle Herald*; Connexus publications. **REVIEWED IN:** several local and regional publications including: *Chronicle Herald; Black to Business; The Coast Guard; Sunday Daily News.* **EDUCATION:** JD (Juris Doctor), College of Law, U. of Florida, 1983. BN, 1965; Dipl. PH.N, 1963, McGill University. RN, Montreal General Hospital, 1962. **HEROES/ROLE MODELS:** Emily & Stanley Clyke, parents; husband; children. **MOTTO:** People change when the fear of change is *less* than the fear of staying the same. **CONTACT:** sharon.oliver@ns.sympatico.ca; Fax: 902-542-4846

▶OLIVER, The Hon. Donald H.

SENATOR, Senate of Canada, Ottawa, ON. Born: Wolfville, NS.

▶ Senator Donald H. Oliver, QC, self-describes as a lawyer, farmer, politician, author, teacher, and businessman. He has been active in politics with the Progressive Conservative Party for more than 40 yrs., including serving as Director, Legal Affairs in six consecutive general elections from 1972-88; also served in many executive offices with the PC: as national VP (Atlantic region); Director of the PC Canada Fund and as a member of the Audit Committee of this fund. In 1990, he was appointed to the Senate under then–Prime Minister, Brian Mulroney. In the Senate he is Deputy Chair, Standing Committee on Transport and Communications; member, Standing Committee on Banking, Trade, and Commerce; Standing Committee on Agriculture and Forestry. **BACKGROUND:** practised law in Halifax, 1965-90, primarily in Civil Litigation with Stewart McKelvey Stirling Scales and, taught at Dalhousie University, part-time for 14 yrs. He is President of Glen Moir Holdings Ltd. and Pleasant River Farms Ltd.; and is consultant, advisor, and director of other companies. He is a former member of the Canada Council Investment Committee, and former Director on the Advisory Brd.,

AT&T/Canada. **AFFIL/MBRSHP:** past Governor, Technical U. of NS; past Chair, Halifax Children's Aid Society; founding Chair, Metro Volunteer Resource Centre; founding President and first Chair of Brd., Society for the Protection and Preservation of Black Culture/NS; founding Dircctor BUF; founding Chair, Cdn Assn./Visible Minorities; Patron, National Council /Black Educators of Canada. **HONS.:** include: Hon. Life Member, BCC/NS, 1999; Harry Jerome Award for Community Services, 1996; President's Award, BCC/NS, 1990; Metro Volunteer Res. Centre Appreciation Award, 1990. **WORKS:** Report: *The Nova Scotia Black Community & Diaspora: Models of Upward Mobility.* **REVIEWED IN:** *Journey: African Canadian History*, 2000; *Some Black Men*, 1999. **EDUCATION:** LLB, Dalhousie U., 1964; BA/Hons., Acadia U., 1960. **HEROES/ROLE MODELS:** Lincoln Alexander; Nelson Mandela; Martin Luther King Jr. **MOTTO:** Hard work is the foundation of success. **CONTACT:** olived@sen.parl.gc.ca; www.sen.parl.gc.ca/doliver

▶**OLLIVIER, Émile,** PhD, CQ, CF.
PROFESSEUR ÉMÉRITUS, ÉCRIVAIN, Université de Montréal, QC. Né: Haïti/ au Canada depuis: 1968.

▶ Exilé d'Haïti depuis 1965, Dr Émile Ollivier a terminé ses études en France et au Canada. Il a effectué des séjours au Mexique, à Cuba, et au Japon. Il écrit des romans, des essais, des nouvelles, et des articles. Il a passé sa carrière à l'Université de Montréal: en 1977, il devient professeur au faculté des sciences et de l'éducation; 1980, professeur adjoint; 1985, professeur agrégé; en 1989, professeur titulaire; en 2002, professeur émérite. **PRIX:** Doctorat (Hon.), Collège Saint-Michaels, 2001; élu à l'académie de lettres québécoises, 2000; décoré de la ville de Paris, 1999; Chevalier de l'Ordre des Arts & des Lettres (CF), Rép. Française, 1997; Prix Carbet de la Caraïbe, 1995; Chevalier de l'Ordre national du Québec (CQ), 1993. **ŒUVRES:** romans prin-cipaux: *Mille Eaux*, 1999; *La Discorde aux cent voix*, 1987; *Mère-Solitude*, 1995. Essais: « Repenser Haïti, » 1992; « Haïti, quel développement? » 1976; « 1946/1976: Trente ans de Pouvoir Noir en Haïti, » 1976. Nouvelles: *Regarde, regarde des lions*, 2001; *Paysage de l'aveugle*, 1977. Articles aux journaux inclus: *Liberté; Les écrits; Tribune Juive; Collectif Paroles; Nouvelle Optique.* **ŒUVRES À SON PROPOS:** y compris, *Québec Studies; Chemins Critiques; Afrique Littéraire et Artistique.* **FORMATION:** PhD, 1980; Maîtrise, 1974, U. de Montréal. Bac, Paris, 1965; Dipl., Haïti, 1961. **CONTACT:** emileollivier@hotmail.com; Fax: 514-481-5641

▶**OLWENY, Charles Lwanga Mark,**
MD, FRACP.
PROFESSOR, University of Manitoba/ **MEDICAL ONCOLOGIST,** Cancer Care Manitoba/Winnipeg Regional Health Authority, St. Boniface General Hospital, Winnipeg, MB. Born: Uganda/ in Canada since: 1990.

▶ Dr. Charles Olweny is a Cancer Care Specialist who occupies the following positions: Professor, University of Manitoba; Medical Oncologist, CancerCare Manitoba and Winnipeg Regional Health Authority; Site Coordinator, Haematology/ Oncology, St. Boniface General Hospital; Associate Staff, Health Science Centre. **BACKGROUND:** he began his medical career in Uganda, taught at Makerere University in Kampala, in the Faculty of Medicine, 1969-84, as a Tutorial Fellow (1969-70), Lecturer (1970-73), Sr. Lecturer (1973-75), Associate Professor (1975-79) and Professor, 1979-84. He was Director of the Uganda Cancer Institute, 1973-84; was a consultant with the World Health Organization (WHO), and Visiting Professor of Medicine, U. of Zambia, and WHO Consultant at the Tropical Disease Research Center, Ndola, Zambia, 1982-83; was WHO Visiting Professor of Medicine, U. of Zimbabwe, 1984; was Senior Director, Medical Oncology, Royal Adelaide Hospital and Clinical Professor, Dept. of Medicine and Surgery, U. of Adelaide, South Australia, 1985-90. He relocated to Canada in 1990, to assume a position as Co-Director of WHO Collaborating Center for Quality of Life in Cancer Care, a position he held until 1997, in addition to his position as Professor, U. of Manitoba and Medical Oncologist at St. Boniface General Hospital. **AFFIL/MBRSHP:** Fellow, Royal Australasian College of Physicians; American Society of Clinical Oncology; New York Academy of Sciences; Editorial Brd., *Oncology*, 1977-90 and 1995 to present; Editorial Brd., *J of Experimental and Clinical Cancer Research*, 1983-90. **COMMUNITY:** founder & President, Friends of Makerere in Canada; Rotary Club (in Uganda and Australia); Ugandan Cdn Assn. of Manitoba; Council of African Organizations of Manitoba. **HONS.:** include, Achievement Award, Uganda Medical Assn., 2001; Fellowship Award, Int'l Cancer Research Technology Transfer Project, 1976. **WORKS:** publications on: Hodgkin's disease; Kaposi's sarcoma; Burkitt's lymphoma; Hepatocellular carcinoma; Quality of Life; Bioethics. Articles in: *Int'l J Cancer*; *Brit J Cancer*; *Cancer Chemotherapy*; *Oncology*; *Surgery*; *Eur J Cancer*; *J Psycho-Oncology*; *J Palliative Care*; *CMAJ*; *J Trop Med & Hygiene*; *J Med Ethics*. **EDUCATION:** MD, 1978; M.Med, 1970; MB, ChB (Medicine/Surgery), 1966, Makerere Medical School, Uganda. **MOTTO:** Never leave till tomorrow what you can do today. **CONTACT:** charles.olweny@cancercare.mb.ca; Fax: 204-896-3830

▶**O'REE, William (Willie)**
HOCKEY/DIRECTOR, YOUTH DEVELOPMENT,
National Hockey League, 1251 Avenue of the Americas, 47th Fl, NY, NY, 10020 1189, USA. Born: Fredericton, NB.
▶ Willie O'Ree, in 1958, became the first Black to play in the NHL. Born and raised in New Brunswick, he was an outstanding athlete as a youngster, excelling at hockey, rugby, soccer, basketball, track and baseball. His abilities in baseball were so good that in 1956, he was invited to training camp with the Milwaukee Braves. But he declined, choosing to pursue his hockey career. Though he lost 95% of the sight in his right eye during a Junior A game in the 1955-56 season, he was not deterred from pursuing his goal. In 1957, he turned professional and signed with the Quebec Aces, a minor league team affiliated with the Boston Bruins; that year the Aces won their league championship. **CAREER HIGHLIGHTS:** January 18, 1958, WOR was called up to play for the Boston Bruins, thereby becoming the first Black to play in the NHL; this was ten yrs. after Jackie Robinson broke the colour bar in baseball; however, it would be another 25 yrs. before the next Black hockey player would play in the NHL. Following his debut with the Bruins for two games in the 1957-58 season, WOR played 43 more games with them, 1960-61, then was traded to the Montreal Canadiens; two months later he was traded to the LA Blades of the Western Hockey League where he played for six seasons; in 1964, he won the league scoring title with 38 goals; when this team folded, he signed with the San Diego Gulls in 1968 and won the league scoring title again with 39 goals. After a long professional career of 21 seasons, he retired from hockey in 1980. Throughout his career WOR had been known for his exceptional speed and his checking ability. **OTHER:** late in the 1990s WOR began to receive recognition for what he had accomplished in the late 1950s at a time when hockey and hockey fans were reluctant to accept non-whites, regardless of their talent. The NHL created an all-star game for young minority hockey players and named it in WOR's honour: the Willie O'Ree All-Star Game is held every year in an NHL city. And, in 1998, prior to the NHL All-Star Game, the NHL honoured him for his pioneering efforts and named him the Director of Youth Hockey Development. A documentary of WOR's career entitled, *Echoes from the Rink: The Willie O'Ree Story*, was shown at

the Toronto International Film Festival in 1998. **HONS.:** several including WHL scoring title, 1964 & 1968; Willie O'Ree All-Star Game played annually. **REVIEWED IN:** *Journey: African Canadian History*, 2000. **CONTACT:** Tel: 212-789-2000; Fax: 212-789-2020

▶OSAMUSALI, Sylvester, PhD.
SENIOR NUCLEAR DESIGN ANALYST, Ontario Power Generation, 700 University Ave., Toronto, ON M5G 1X6. Born: Nigeria/ in Canada since: 1983.
▶ Dr. Sylvester Osamusali is a Senior Nuclear Design Analyst at the Ontario Power Generation (OPG); he has over 13 yrs. experience in nuclear reactor safety analysis and has published and presented over 20 papers to peers on "Two-Phase flow and Nuclear Reactor Thermal Hydraulics." At the OPG, his responsibilities include: performing thermal hydraulic analysis of postulated loss of coolant accidents in OPG reactors using advanced computer codes; developing advanced methods and techniques for thermal hydraulic analysis of the reactor heat transport systems and components to improve the code predictions; and, conducting system thermal hydraulic analysis to support the safe operation of the reactors and provide responses to comments and questions by the Canadian Nuclear Safety Commission (CNSC). **BACKGROUND:** after completing his doctorate in Nuclear Engineering, he was awarded a Post-Doctoral Research Fellowship, 1988-90, completed at the University of Ottawa and Atomic Energy Canada, Chalk River. **COMMUNITY ACTIVITIES:** is an accomplished soccer player in S. Ontario and Renfrew County; Brd., Nigerian-Canadian Assn.; Society of Nigerian Cdn Engineers. **HONS.:** many academic awards including: NSERC Post-Doctoral Research Fellowship, 1990; McMaster U. departmental Scholarship, 1985-88; U. Ife (Nigeria) Post-Graduate Scholarship Award, 1983-85; Best Nuclear Engineering Student Prize, U. Ife (Nigeria), 1981. **WORKS:** over

20 technical papers on "Two-Phase flow & Nuclear Reactor Thermal Hydraulics," published & presented; some found in proceedings from Conferences on Simulation Methods in Nuclear Engineering; Canadian Nuclear Society and American Nuclear Society*; Heat and Technology J.* **EDUCATION:** PhD, Nuclear Engineering, 1988; M.Eng, Engineering Physics, 1985, McMaster University. BSc, Engineering Physics, U. of Ife, Nigeria, 1981. **HEROES/ROLE MODELS:** Father. **MOTTO:** Whether you think you can or you think you can't, you are right. (Gerald Ford) **CONTACT:** sylvester.osamusali@opg.com

▶OWOLABI, Titus, MD, FRCSC.
CHIEF, OBSTETRICS/GYNECOLOGY, and, PROGRAM MEDICAL DIRECTOR OF MATERNAL NEWBORN, North York General Hospital, 4001 Leslie St., Toronto, ON M2K 1E1. Born: Nigeria/ in Canada since: 1964.
▶ Dr. Titus Owolabi has been in his present position as Chief of Obstetrics and Gynecology, and Program Medical Director of Maternal Newborn at the North York General Hospital, since January, 2000. After completing his medical studies at U. of Toronto in 1976, he began a consultancy practice in Obstetrics and Gynecology at Chaleur Regional Hospital in Bathurst, NB. He returned to Toronto in 1978 as a staff Obstetrician/Gynecologist at St. Michael's Hospital and Lecturer in the Faculty of Medicine at U of T. **HIGHLIGHTS:** wanting to give back to his country of origin, he returned to Nigeria from 1981 to 1987 where, with a colleague, he set up a private hospital providing specialty care in Obstetrics, Gynecology, General Surgery, and General Medicine. He returned to his previous positions in Canada, in 1987, and was also appointed Assistant Professor. One of his most outstanding accomplishments grew from his interest in laparoscopic gynaecology surgery, which he learned in the US and brought to St. Michael's Hospital in 1991. This procedure, which he taught to colleagues and stu-

dents, was innovative for reducing the operating and recovery time for women undergoing certain gynaecological procedures. In 1992, he set up the Laparoscopic Laser Unit at St. Michael's Hospital. He was appointed Obstetrician and Gynecologist-in-Chief at St. Michael's Hospital, in 1994. In addition to his practice and his teaching, he has authored or co-authored relevant clinical guidelines for Canadian Obstetricians and Gynecologists. **HONS.:** including, ACAA, for "innovations in medicine & service to the community," 1999; Departmental Award, for teaching excellence, U of T. **REVIEWED IN:** *Toronto Star*; *CMAJ*. **EDUCATION:** FRCSC, 1976; MD, 1971; BSc/Hons., 1968, U of T. **HEROES/ROLE MODELS:** Walter Hannah, Prof. Emeritus, U of T. **MOTTO:** Make life better and happier if you can, for each person that comes your way. **CONTACT:** towolabi@nygh.on.ca; Fax: 416-756-6406

▶**PACHAI, Bridglal, CM, PhD.**
ADJUNCT PROFESSOR, Saint Mary's University & Dalhousie University, Halifax, NS. Born: South Africa/ in Canada since: 1975.
▶ Dr. Bridglal Pachai is currently an Adjunct Professor with Saint Mary's & Dalhousie universities. During the course of his career, he has worked in a number of African countries as well as in Canada. **HIGHLIGHTS:** Equity Consultant and Ombudsman, NS Power Corp., 1994-95; Executive Director, NS Human Rights Commission, 1989-94; Director, BCC/NS, 1985-89; Dean, Faculty of Arts and Islamic Studies, U. of Nigeria, 1979-85; Director, International Education Centre, Saint Mary's U., 1977-79; Sr. Killam Prof., History, Dalhousie U., 1975-77; Dean, Head and Prof. of History, U. of Malawi, 1965-75. **AFFIL/MBRSHP:** Director, Vision TV, 1995-2000; Founding Chair, Literacy NS, 1988-89; Member, Cdn Human Rights Tribunal, 1989-92. **HONS.:** Order of Canada, 2000; BCC Wall of Honour, 1997; Hon. Doctorate, 1994, Saint Mary's U.; GG 125th Anniv. Medal, 1992. **WORKS:** selected: *Blacks in the Maritimes*, 1987; *A Documentary History of Indian South Africans, 1860-1982*, 1984; *Beneath the Clouds of the Promised Land, vol. 1 & 2; My Africa, My Canada*, 1989; *Education in Nova Scotia: The African Nova Scotian Experience*, 1997. **REVIEWED IN:** many publications, including: *International Authors and Writers*; *Dictionary of African Biography*. **EDUCATION:** PhD, U. of Natal, 1963. BA, 1956; MA, 1958, U. of S. Africa. **HEROES/ROLE MODELS:** Rev. Dr. William P. Oliver; Dr. Fred MacKinnon. **MOTTO:** Acknowledge and advance the dignity and worth of every human person. **CONTACT:** b.l.pachai@ns.sympatico.ca; Fax: 902-455-1467

▶**PARIS, Brenda**
EXECUTIVE DIRECTOR, Black Community Resource Centre, 6767 Côte-des-Neiges, Montreal, QC. Born: Montreal, QC.

▶ Brenda Paris is Executive Director of the Black Community Resource Centre (BCRC), which was founded in 1996 and designed to identify and address the needs of Montreal's English-speaking Black community (aged 0-35 yrs.). The Centre offers programs with a holistic approach that deal with the well-being of young children, their parents, development programs for youth, and an entrepreneurship program for young adults. It also offers diversity training to the English school boards and leadership programs for young women with an emphasis on gender-based analysis. BP is an educator, administrator, and community worker who has served on various provincial government committees and was recently appointed to the Board of Directors of the *Société de Transport de Montréal* (STM). **CAREER:** Coordinator, Student Development, Dawson College, 1986-97; Director, Shastri-Indo Cdn Institute, McGill U., 1985-87; Education and Training Consultant, as Director for Language Schools. **COMMUNITY:** Quebec Provincial Govt. appointee to *Conseil des Relations Interculturelles*, 1993-98; Special Advisory Committee, Montreal Urban Police; Congress of Black Women; Coloured Women's Club, and others. **REVIEWED IN:** *BHM Calendar*, Montreal, 2001; *Community Contact*. **EDUCATION:** BA; Cert. Family Life Educator, Concordia U. **HEROES/ROLE MODELS:** Iris McCracken; Juanita Westmoreland-Traoré; Angela Davis. **MOTTO:** *a lutte continua*: the struggle continues. (Samora Machel). **CONTACT:** brenda. paris@sympatico.ca

▶PARIS, David Ronald, MWO, MB.

MASTER WARRANT OFFICER, Canadian Forces, National Defence HQ, 101 Colonel By Dr., Ottawa, ON K1A 0K2. Born: New Glasgow, NS.
▶ Master Warrant Officer (MWO) David Paris is a career soldier who has been with the Canadian Forces since 1967. He has served on international missions in Cyprus, Damascus, Somalia, Germany, and Albania, and has garnered a number of medals in the process, including the Order of Military Merit and a Medal for Bravery, (1988, for rescuing two people from a burning house). He began his career as an Infantryman and subsequently held a number of Operational and Administrative positions both in Canada and while posted to UN and NATO duties. Since 2001, and his return to Canada from Germany, he has been a member of staff to the Deputy Chief of Defence. **HONS.:** include, Member, Order of Military Merit, 1997; Medal of Bravery, 1988; Somalia Medal; Special Service Medal; Cdn Peacekeeping Medal; UN Medal (Cyprus); UN Medal (Middle East); NATO Medal (Albania); CF Decoration (2nd Clasp); has received several commendations. **HEROES/ROLE MODELS:** Patience Paris, mother; Sparky & Herb Paris, uncles; James Wasson, friend. **MOTTO:** Lead or follow, but do something! **CONTACT:** dave-marty-paris@ rogers.com

▶PARIS, Henderson

COMMUNITY ORGANIZER, Run Against Racism (Annual Ultra Marathon), New Glasgow, NS. Born: New Glasgow, NS.
▶ Henderson Paris is best known in Nova Scotia as the founder of the Run Against Racism, a 38-mile ultra marathon which is held on March 21st each year, The International Day to Eliminate Racism and Discrimination, as decreed by the UN. Through this event he has "become a symbol of the fight against racism in the northeast region of NS." **BACKGROUND:** his involvement with athleticism began in his youth when he was active in baseball and track events; after leaving school he continued to run, play baseball and broomball; in 1984 he helped form, and became president of, the Pictou Roadrunners Club; he also started the Tartan 10K Road Race. He has been the head coach of the New Glasgow High School Track & Field Team since 1994 and reintroduced district track meets in 1996, for the first time in 20 yrs., with an increasing number of

schools participating each year. In 1989, he and his wife became managers of the NS Provincial Legion T&F Team (which meets annually with other regional Legion T&F teams); in 1994, they were promoted to Head Chaperones for the National Meet, positions they still hold. In 1990, he began the Run Against Racism, to raise awareness of the problem of racism as it exists in Canada and around the world. The motto of this program is: "Together... we can make a difference." Each year there are hundreds of school children who participate in this event. In addition to running in many marathons, HP is also a torchbearer for the Special Olympics, on behalf of Michelin, his employer of 25 yrs. **HONS.:** many, including, National Race Relations Award, "for fostering Cultural Diversity & Racial Harmony," Federation of Cdn Municipalities, 2000; Human Rights Citizenship Award, 1999; YW-YMCA Canada Peace Medal, 1996. **HEROES/ROLE MODELS:** Mother. **MOTTO:** Together we can make a difference. **CONTACT:** Fax: 902-752-3764

▶PARRIS, Jean Veronica

LABOUR RELATIONS CONSULTANT, Federation of Nurses of Quebec (FIIQ), 2050, Bleury, 4 étage, Montreal, QC H3A 2J5. Born: Barbados/ in Canada since: 1974.

▶ Jean Parris is a Registered Nurse by training, and has been working as a Labour Relations Consultant since 1985. She completed her nursing training in England, then came to Canada in 1974 and worked at the Jewish General Hospital for 11 yrs. before becoming a Labour Relations Consultant with FIIQ. A workplace situation experienced by nurses in 1989 which had clear racial overtones led her to become an agent for change on their behalf. To address that situation, she collaborated with the Quebec Human Rights Commission, the Committee for Research and Action on Race Relations (CRARR), and representatives from the hospital's union. And, to raise the level of awareness at FIIQ itself to racially charged sit-

uations encountered by some of its members, she ensured that educational sessions were held for staff. Subsequently her employer agreed to set up a committee of Black nurses to document and report complaints of racist attitudes and incidents in the workplace. FIIQ also initiated an awareness campaign on racism and violence. As a result, behaviours which had been accepted before or which had never before been discussed, were now out in the open. In 1993, there was a decision from the arbitration tribunal concerning the original 1989 incident: it held the employer responsible for maintaining a safe and harassment-free workplace. Subsequently, mechanisms were put in place for hospitals in the province to set up policies and procedures, with mechanisms for dealing with complaints of racism, violence and harassment of any form. **HONS.:** several including, Cert. of Honour, for four yrs. of service on the intercultural and interracial Advisory Committee, City of Montreal, 1996. **REVIEWED IN:** Montreal's first *Black History Month Calendar*, 1994; articles in local and nat'l publications including, *Montreal Gazette*; *Maclean's*. **EDUCATION:** Cert., Human Resource Management, McGill U., 1988; Cert., Midwifery, Plymouth, UK, 1969; RN, Isle of Wight, 1968. **HEROES/ROLE MODELS:** Hélène Wavroch; Glenda Sims; Juanita Westmoreland-Traoré. **MOTTO:** I can do all things through Christ who strengthens me. **CONTACT:** jeanvparris@yahoo.ca; Fax: 514-987-7273

▶PARSON, Patrick

EXECUTIVE/ARTISTIC DIRECTOR, Ballet Creole, 300 Bloor St. W., Toronto, ON M5S 1W3. Born: Trinidad & Tobago/ in Canada since: 1988.

▶ Patrick Parson is the founder of Ballet Creole, which he began in 1990. He is also the principal choreographer and musical director. Since its creation, the company has gained local and national acclaim, and tours extensively presenting educational and general entertainment performances. Previously, PP toured internationally as principal dancer with the Astor Johnson Rep. Dance Theatre of Trinidad; his dance experiences include Caribbean, African, East Indian, Jazz, and modern dance styles. Currently, he conducts dance/music workshops and lecture demonstrations for educators and student bodies in schools and universities across Ontario. He is also a Professor in the Faculty of Fine Arts at York University. **OTHER:** has served as cultural advisor to the Toronto Arts Council, Metro Cultural Affairs, Ont. Arts Council, Harbourfront Centre, and Arts Advantage; has also served on the boards of Kalinka Russian Dance Co. and the Black Canadian Congress. **HONS.:** Entrepreneurial Award of Merit, African-Caribbean Chamber of Commerce; New Pioneers Award, Skills for Change. **EDUCATION:** MA, Dance Ethnology, York U.; graduate School of the Toronto Dance Theatre; also studies at Ryerson U., the Caribbean School of Dance & the Dance Academy of T&T. **HEROES/ROLE MODELS:** Katherine Dunham; Danny Grossman; Astor Johnson. **MOTTO:** Diversity in harmony creates a new energy! **CONTACT:** Tel: 416-960-0350; Fax: 416-960-2067; bcreole @on.aibn.com

▶**PATTERSON, H. Keith**
TAX PARTNER, Deloitte & Touche, Ste. 1400-181 Bay St., Toronto, ON M5J 2V1. Born: Jamaica/ in Canada since: 1962.
▶ Keith Patterson is a Partner in Taxation with Deloitte & Touche, and has been with the firm since 1973, first in Montreal and now in Toronto. **AFFIL/MBRSHP:** Chair, University Health Network (US) Foundation; Chair, Toronto Eglinton Rotary Charitable Foundation; Director, The Toronto Hospital Crown Foundation; founding member and past-President, MABBP; former Chair, Race Relations in Business Committee, Toronto Board of Trade; former Director, Canadian Club; past-President, Toronto Eglinton Rotary Club; past-Treasurer, Rotary International, district 7070. **HONS.:** including, 20-year Partner Distinguished

Service Award, Deloitte & Touche, 2001; Jackie Robinson Special Achievement Award, MABBP, 2001; Paul Harris Fellowship Award, Rotary International, 1994. **WORKS:** including: "US Charities raising funds in Canada," *Tax Management International J,* 2001; "Tax on Capital," *Can Tax Fdn J,* 1977. **EDUCATION:** LLB/Hons., U. of London, UK, 1972; B.Comm, McGill U., 1966. **MOTTO:** *Fortes fortuna juvat*–Fortune favours the brave. **CONTACT:** Fax: 416-601-6480; kpatterson@deloitte.ca

▶**PATTERSON, Pat**
TEACHER, Toronto District School Board (TDSB)/ **LOCAL HISTORIAN,** Underground Railroad Descendants of North America (UGRD), Toronto, ON. Born: Toronto, ON.
▶ Pat Patterson is co-founder and president of the community organization, Underground Railroad Descendants of N. America, which was formed to "promote and preserve the history of the UGRR and its descendants." PP is an Aboriginal person of First Nations and African ancestry, and a fifth-generation descendant of the UGRR. A teacher by training, she is currently the Program Head of Cdn World Studies and Social Sciences at Northview Heights Secondary School, TDSB; was formerly Supervisor Human Resources and Employment Equity for the City of North York and Executive Director for the Ontario Native Council on Justice, as well as Principal at Sandy Bay School, Sandy Bay Indian Reserve, Manitoba. **COMMUNITY INVOLVEMENT:** she has worked with several organizations including, the Harry Gairey Scholarship Cmtee; Conflict Mediation Services of Downsview; Grand Chapter Order of the Eastern Star; the Black Educators' Working Group; and, the Native Canadian Centre. She has appeared on radio and TV, giving interviews on her historical research with the UGRD. **HONS.:** nominee, GG Award for excellence in teaching Cdn History, 2001. **WORKS:** co-wrote revisions for *Black Studies Guide,* Ont. Min. of Education,

1995; articles in, *Akili Newsletter; Canadian Images Poster Series*, 1993; *Confronting the Stereotypes*, Dept. of Education, Winnipeg, 1985. **REVIEWED IN:** *Toronto Star; Houston Sun Press; Pride; Share; Community Role Models Inventory*, 2000. **EDUCATION:** B.Ed (in-service), York U., 1994. M.Ed, 1985; B.Ed, 1989; BA, 1979, U. of Manitoba. **HEROES/ROLE MODELS:** Charlotte McGruder Patterson, mother; Walter Jay McGruder, grandfather. **MOTTO:** Be yourself. **CONTACT:** www.ugrd.com

▶PENNANT, Kevin
EXECUTIVE PUBLICIST, The Publicity Group, Ste. 300-438 Parliament St., Toronto, ON M5A 3A2. Born: Toronto, ON, 1974.

▶ Kevin Pennant is an Executive Publicist and co-founder of The Publicity Group, a publicity and marketing firm specializing in working with the entertainment sector. He has worked in entertainment publicity and promotions since 1993. His career began at Warner Bros. where he spent six years, starting as an intern, and advancing through the Theatrical Marketing Dept. to become Campus Representative, Canadian Div., targeting the 18-30-yr.-old market. During this time he organized film premieres, PA tours, cross promotions, and post-screening parties; he has worked with celebrities such as Leonardo DiCaprio, Neil Jordan, and Tom Cruise. By 1995, he was publicizing and promoting films at the Toronto International Film Festival; he also free-lanced locally by creating publicity campaigns for local musicians. Recognizing a mutual desire to create a publicity and promotions firm for Black-focused events and individuals, he, Tonya Lee Williams, and partners began The Publicity Group in 1998. **EDUCATION:** Int'l Business Marketing, Seneca College. **HEROES/ROLE MODELS:** Parents; Tonya Lee Williams. **CONTACT:** kpennant @thepublicitygroup.com; www.thepublicitygroup. com

▶PEREZ, John "Jayson"
STEEL PAN PERFORMER/COMPOSER/INSTRUCTOR, Toronto, ON. Born: Trinidad & Tobago.

▶ John "Jayson" Perez began playing in the steel-band in Trinidad at the age of 15; there he played and arranged for bands like Esso Tripoli, the National Steelband, Starlift, and the Coast Guard Steelband. He began singing calypso in 1983 and winning awards and competitions from the same period. In 1984, he won the Cdn Calypso Monarch competition, and repeated the feat in '86, '87, and '88. He wrote the winning song for the Cdn Calypso Monarch in 1993, '96, '98, and 2001; most significantly, he won a Juno Award, 1990, for the song, *Soldiers We are All.* He has performed in Canada, the US, and the Caribbean; he taught steelband music at the Lewis S. Beattie Secondary School for seven yrs.; currently, he is VP of the Organization of Calypso Performing Artists. **HONS.:** winner, first Canadian road march, 1992; Juno Award, for *Soldiers We are All,* 1990; nominee, Juno Award, for *Free South Africa,* 1986; winner, Calypso Monarch, NYC, 1986. **CONTACT:** thejayse@hotmail.com

▶PETERS, David J., CCdC.
CHEF/EDUCATOR (Ret.), PRUDE Inc., Saint John, NB. Born: Saint John, NB.

▶ David Peters is a founding member of Pride of Race, Unity & Dignity through Education, (PRUDE), a local organization which began in 1980; he has been active in a number of this group's activities over the years. Professionally, he is a Certified Chef de Cuisine (CCdC), an international designation accorded following eight yrs. training, and teacher. **CAREER HIGHLIGHTS:** designed and administered the first Hospitality Training Course for New Brunswick, which is still being taught in the community colleges; taught cooking at the NB Community College for over 20 years; in 1976, opened Saint John's first elegant dining room, The Iron Duke, which was the forerunner of local heritage inns; the restaurant was situated in a building dating to 1878, with Victorian architecture and design. In 1978, The Iron Duke, with its menu of Creole cuisine, was included in *Where to Eat in Canada*. The establishment closed in 1981, when the city bought the site to create a parking lot. He retired from teaching in 1983, but returned to teach French Immersion, 1990-92; 1992-2002, he worked with the Saint John Regional Correctional Centre, providing counselling to inmates. **COMMUNITY:** active within PRUDE, in 1983, he designed and coordinated an educational program which contained seven federally financed training programs for the local Black community; the courses included commercial cooking, day care assistance, office administration, management and visual media; the program operated until 1990. He is also the founder of the local annual celebration, Polungo Days; hosted and produced a local TV show, *Afro Vision*, which dealt with Black history, food, and local Black achievements; coordinated and obtained federal funding (1992) to produce a kit to promote and teach Black history in the local school system. **AFFIL/MBRSHP:** Saint John Tourism Committee; NB Teachers Assn.; NB Kennel Club; National and Provincial Federation of Chefs; Chef de Cuisine and co-coordinator of food services, Canada Games, 1985; 4th Degree of Knights of Columbus. **OTHER:** DP is a descendant of Thomas Peters, one of the leaders of the Black exodus to Sierra Leone, in 1792. **HONS.:** several including, Cert. of Appreciation Award, for years of outstanding service, NB Civil Service (upon retirement), 2002; Award of Appreciation, for Cultural Diversity Works, Multicultural Assn. of the Greater Moncton Area (MAGMA), 1997; GG 125th Anniv. Medal, 1992; selected, New Brunswick's Chef of the Year, 1982; Iron Duke restaurant ranked in *Where to Eat in Canada*, 1978. **WORKS:** *My World of Cooking New Brunswick Style*, 1974. **EDUCATION:** French Studies, 1990; Cert. Life Skills Coach, 1986; CCdC,

1976; Teacher's Cert., 1965; Hotel, Restaurant, Resort Admin., Ryerson Polytechnic, 1960. **HEROES/ROLE MODELS:** Dr. Clifford (Nick) Skinner. **MOTTO:** Don't look back and always strive for new things. **CONTACT:** peterso@nbnet.nb.ca; Fax: 506-634-6080

▶**PETERS, Walter W.**
AVIATION CONSULTANT, Bombardier Aerospace NFTC, Orleans, ON. Born: Lichtfield, NS.
▶ Walter Peters has been an Aviation Consultant with Bombardier Aerospace, working on the development of a Ground-Based Training System for NATO Pilot Training in Canada, since 1999. A pilot by training, he was a member of the RCAF and has the distinction of having been a member of the Snowbird Aerobatic Team, before joining Transport Canada. **CAREER HIGHLIGHTS:** Canadian Military/RCAF, 1963-84, served as a Senior Officer in a variety of Air Force squadrons; Flight Safety Officer, at the Military College; member of the Snowbirds Aerobatic Team; Instrument Check Pilot; Squadron Commander; and, Operational Pilot. From 1983-84, he was the Air Advisor to the Secretary General of the UN, New York. In 1984, he joined Transport Canada Aviation, and was responsible for Safety Programs; he was Director of Safety Programs, 1991-96, and Director General, Systems Safety, 1996, until his retirement in 1998. **OTHER:** he has completed several international consulting assignments; represented Canada in the Air India accident investigation; was advisor to the Nation-Air accident in Saudi Arabia; chairs the International Data Exchange Aviation Safety, with membership from 20 countries; plans and conducts reviews of organizational structures, including that of Pearson International Airport; developed and implemented risk management training programs and acted as coach to colleagues during career assignments. **COMMUNITY:** founding member and first President of the NB AACP. **HONS.:** include, Minister Award of Merit, Transport

Canada, 1994; UN Medal, 1983; CF Decoration, 1975; Flying Trophy, City of Moose Jaw; Flying Trophy, Prov. Sask.; Birk Medal Winner, Academic Achievement; Half Century All-Star Football Team, Mount Allison U., 1980; several scholarships & academic awards (including Sharpe Scholarship, 1955). **WORKS:** include, *Risk Management in Aviation Safety*; ICAO Safety publications; articles on accident prevention. **REVIEWED IN:** *Atlantic Advocate*; military publications; *Transport Canada newsletter*; Bombardier publications. **EDUCATION:** Executive Management Training, Harvard U.; Civil Engineering, Mount Allison U.; Psychology, Collège Militaire; postgraduate studies, Aviation Safety, U. of S. California. **MOTTO:** If you can dream it, you can do it! **CONTACT:** wwpeters@cyberus.ca

▶PETERS, Wilfrid E.D., QC.

LEGAL COUNSEL to the Chief Election Officer of Ontario, Toronto, ON. Born: Montserrat/ in Canada since: 1953.

▶ Wilfrid Peters worked in the Crown Law Office-Civil Law of the Ontario Ministry of the Attorney General, from 1981-96, and has been Legal Counsel to the Chief Election Officer of Ontario, since 1996. **CAREER:** 1981-96, as Senior Counsel, in the Crown Law Office, his responsibilities included providing legal advice to ministers of the Crown as well as appearing before committees of the legislature on behalf of the AG, and appearing before all levels of courts and administrative tribunals on behalf of the Province of Ontario; 1972-81, Senior Solicitor, Legal Services, Ont. Min. of Natural Resources; and, 1964-72, he was a Solicitor, with the Ont. Dept. of Lands and Forests. **AFFIL/MBRSHP:** elected member, Queen's University Council (term to 2007); appointed member, Queen's Faculty of Law Advisory Council, 1994-99; sustaining member, Osgoode Society; member, Executive of Queen's Toronto Law Alumni Assn. **HONS.:** appointed Queen's Counsel, 1985. **EDUCATION:** LLB,

Queen's U., 1962; BA, SGWU (now Concordia U.), 1959. **CONTACT:** Fax: 416-483-1790; wilfridp@rogers.com

▶PETERSON, Oscar, Dr., CC, CQ.

JAZZ PIANIST/COMPOSER, Regal Recordings Ltd., 2421 Hammond Rd., Mississauga, ON L5K 1T3. Born: Montreal, QC.

▶ Oscar Peterson, born in Montreal in 1925, is world renowned as a jazz pianist and composer; he has been acknowledged in Canada and around the world with awards including 16 honorary doctorates, eight Grammy Awards, inducted into the American Jazz Hall of Fame, and designated a Companion of the Order of Canada. **BACKGROUND:** like his siblings, he began playing piano from an early age, under his father's instruction; as he grew older and his abilities improved, he trained under the Hungarian classical pianist, Paul de Marky. In his early teens and at his sister, Daisy's, urging, he entered and won a CBC amateur competition, which led to appearances on local and national radio shows, including *The Happy Gang* and *The Light Up and Listen Hour*. By 1942, he was playing at clubs around Montreal, and by 1947, he had formed his first trio. After being heard by jazz-producer Norman Granz, during a live broadcast from the Alberta Lounge, he was invited to make a guest appearance at Carnegie Hall with the all-star Jazz at the Philharmonic; this appearance took place in 1949 and a year later he joined the group as a member and began recording for Granz under his Verve label. **CAREER HIGHLIGHTS:** OP formed his first US trio with Ray Brown and Herb Ellis, touring extensively in NA, Europe and Asia, and making many live and studio recordings. In 1958, Ellis retired from the group and was replaced by Ed Thigpen; this trio would remain together until 1965, making many more live and studio recordings. In 1960, OP and a number of like-minded musicians, opened the Advanced School of Contemporary Music in Toronto, which attracted students from around the world. The year 1962 was considered the most gruelling as OP and his trio, in addition to touring, recorded seven studio and four live albums. In 1964, the *Canadiana Suite* was composed and released. Over the years, he has recorded with jazz greats including Count Basie, Louis Armstrong, Ella Fitzgerald, Dizzy Gillespie, Charlie Parker, Coleman Hawkins, and many others. By 1965, the trio had disbanded, and OP went on to tour and record, spending more time composing. His *Hymn to Freedom* became one of the anthems used during the Civil Rights Movement in the US. He composed for films such as *Big North* and *Silent Partner,* and for the NFB he composed for *Begone Dull Care* and *Fields of Endless Day* (a story of the UGRR); he was commissioned by *Les Ballets Jazz du Canada,* to produce a ballet and included a special waltz for Toronto, which he entitled *City Lights.* He is composing *A Suite called Africa,* and completed a commission marking the 300th birthday of Johann Sebastian Bach, which was performed at Roy Thomson Hall in Toronto. **OTHER:** Over the years, OP has starred in a number of TV specials and has hosted at least six where he interviewed guests like Anthony Burgess, Andrew Lloyd Webber, former UK PM Edward Heath, and many others. He has played at many Cdn and European jazz festivals such as the *Festival international de jazz de Montréal* and the Montreux Festival in Switzerland; he continues to record, to perform, and to attend public events. **HONS.:** several including: eight Grammy Awards; DownBeat Award, Best Jazz Pianist, 13 times; Keyboard Award, best jazz pianist, five times; inducted into the Hall of Fame for UCLA, the Junos, Cdn Jazz & Blues, American Jazz; Chancellor Emeritus, York U.; Oscar Peterson Day proclaimed in Florida & Baltimore; Companion & Officer, Order of Canada; Order of Ontario; Chevalier, Order of Quebec; Oscar Peterson Scholarship established, Berklee School of Music, Boston; Officer, Order of Arts & Letters, France; GG Lifetime Achievement Award; Harry

Jerome Award; Lifelong Contribution Award, BTW, Mtl; Genie Award for *The Silent Partner*; Lifetime Achievement Award, UMAC. **WORKS:** over 200 recordings; compositions include, *Canadiana Suite*; *African Suite*; *Hallelujah Time*; *Blues for Big Scotia*; *Blues for Smedley*; *The Smudge*; *Bossa Beguine*; and *Hymn to Freedom.* **REVIEWED IN:** several including: *Oscar Peterson, The Will to Swing*; NFB documentary, *In the Key of Oscar*; profiled in, *Some Black Men*; *Millennium Minds; WWIC.* **HEROES/ROLE MODELS:** Norman Granz; Paul de Marky; Art Tatum. **CONTACT:** Fax: 905-855-1773

▶**PHIDD, Richard Wesley,** PhD.

PROFESSOR, Dept. Political Science, University of Guelph, ON. Born: Jamaica/ in Canada since: 1961.

▶ Dr. Richard Phidd is a Professor of Political Science at the University of Guelph. **CAREER:** he began teaching in the Faculty of Administrative Studies, Regina Campus, U. of Saskatchewan, 1970; was a Visiting Assistant Professor at U. of Guelph, 1972-73; assumed a regular appointment in 1973; Associate Professor, 1977-78; Visiting Associate Professor, School of Public Administration, Carleton U., 1978-79; promoted to full Professor in 1986 at U. of Guelph. He teaches courses in Canadian and comparative public policy, and public administration, with an interest in development administration. **RESEARCH INTERESTS:** economic policy-making and management; public-private sector relations and management; public sector organization behaviour; and, public sector organizational development and change in Canada; is also interested in comparative public administration and development. **WORKS:** *Public Sector Management in Canada: Development, Change and Adaptation,* 2001; co-author: *Canadian Public Policy: Ideas, Structure and Process,* 1983, 2nd ed., 1992; *The Politics and Management of Canadian Economic Policy,* 1978; chapters in: *Public Service Reform,* 1999; *Policy Stud-*

ies in Canada: The State of the Art, 1996; *Public Enterprise Management,* 1996; *Public Administration in a World Perspective,* 1990; *Issues in Canadian Public Policy,* 1974; *The Structures of Policy-Making in Canada,* 1971. **EDUCATION:** PhD, Poli. Sci./Public Admin., Queen's U., 1972. MA, Public Admin., 1966; Dipl., Public Admin., 1965, Carleton University. BA, Econ. & Poli. Sci., SGWU (now Concordia U.), 1964. **CONTACT:** Tel: 519-824-4120; Fax: 519-837-9561

▶**PHILIP, Dan**
PRESIDENT, Ligue de Noirs du Québec/Black Coalition of Quebec, 5201, boul. Décarie, Montreal, QC H3W 3C2.

▶ Dan Philip is the President of the Black Coalition of Quebec and has been working for the promotion of human rights and social justice for over 30 yrs. He joined the Black Coalition in 1977, and became its president in 1980. The Coalition was formed after the riot at Sir George William University (SGWU) in 1969, in order to defend the rights of those who were charged in the incident; since then it has been the moral conscience of the Black Community. Under the presidency of DP, the Coalition became more proactive, holding demonstrations protesting the apartheid regime in S. Africa, fighting for the liberation of Nelson Mandela from prison, and against injustice and racial discrimination in Quebec, particularly in cases of police brutality and the frequent shootings of Blacks in that province at the time. Through demonstrations, court cases, presentations to parliamentary commissions and other measures, the situation improved. The education and awareness-raising continues through conferences, addresses to churches and to schools. The Coalition is active in teaching about basic human rights and the need to fight against all forms of discrimination. It now has the support of all levels of government for its activities and works closely with both the Cdn and the Quebec Human Rights Commission on issues of racism

and discrimination. Prior to joining the Black Coalition, DP was the Director of the NCC in Montreal. **HONS.:** *Hommage-bénévolat Québec,* 2001; Rosa Parks Award, Cdn Human Rights Commission, 2000; honoured by the Round Table on Black History, 2000; GG 125th Anniv. Medal, 1992. **CONTACT:** danphilip@liguedesnoirs. org; www.liguedesnoirs.org

▶**PHILIP, M. NourbeSe**
POET/WRITER, c/o Mercury Press, Toronto, ON. Born: Tobago/ in Canada since: 1970.

▶ M. NourbeSe Philip is a writer and poet who has produced several published works. Her first play, *Coups and Calypsos,* was produced in both the UK and in Toronto, 1999; a stage adaptation of *Harriet's Daughter,* her popular novel for young adults, was successfully workshopped in both 2000 and 2001. She has also been a lecturer at U of T (1992-97) and at the Ontario College of Art and Design (1993-94). A lawyer by training, she practised, from 1973-82, with the Parkdale Community Legal Services, then with Jemmot and Philip and as a sole practitioner. **HONS.:** include, Woman of Distinction Arts Award, YWCA, 2001; Rebel for a Cause Award, Elizabeth Fry Society; Dora Mavor Moore Award finalist, for *Coups and Calypsos,* 1999; Toronto Arts Award finalist, for *Harriet's Daughter,* 1995; Guggenheim Fellow, Poetry, 1990-91; Casa de las Americas Prize, for *She Tries her Tongue,* 1988. **WORKS:** include, *Coups and Calypsos* (play), 1999; *A Genealogy of Resistance* (collected essays), 1997; *She Tries Her Tongue; Her Silence Softly Breaks,* 1988; *Frontiers: Essays & Writings in Racism & Culture,* 1993; *Harriet's Daughter,* (novel), 1988. **REVIEWED IN:** *WWCW; WWIC; Mango Season,* 2000; *Africana Encyclopaedia.* **EDUCATION:** LLB, 1973; MA, 1970, U. of Western Ontario. BSc, Econ., UWI, Jamaica, 1968. **CONTACT:** nourbese@nourbese.com; www. nourbese.com

▶**PICART, Richard**
MANAGER/INDUSTRY CONSULTANT, Mekehla Music Group, 56 Muirhead Rd., Toronto, ON M2J 3W4. Born: Toronto, ON, 1971.
▶ Richard Picart is the founder of Mekehla Music Group, a Toronto-based management company specializing in music and consultation. In Canada, he is recognized as an authority on Gospel music and the convergence of Christian content with non-traditional mainstream music forms. He has worked with Sony Music Canada, Attic Music, and Snap Media, and has served as an on-air personality for the *Gospel Music Machine* on CIUT 89.5FM. He has successfully managed the careers of Sharon Riley and Faith Chorale, winners of Juno and Grammy awards, and currently represents EMI Gospel artist, Londa Larmond and Mark Masri. **OTHER:** speaker, Tyndale College's Music and Arts Seminar; Gospel Music Assn. (Canada); Int'l Urban Music Conference, 2002; Christian Music Industry Workshop; Brd., Toronto Mass Choir; established Canada's first gospel networking forum, Industry Black. **HONS.:** include, UMAC Award, (Juno & Dove nominations) Artist & Repertoire Consultation (A&R), for Londa Larmond's *Love Letters*, 2001; Juno Award nomination for, Executive Production on, Sharon Riley & Faith Chorale's *Caught Up* album, 1999; Juno Award nomination for, A&R Consultation, on Hiram Joseph's *Speak Lord.* **EDUCATION:** Dipl./Hons., (Richard Hahn Scholarship) Recording Arts Management, Harris Institute for the Arts, 1997; Arts Admin., Humber College, 1995; Dipl., Civil Engineering Technology, Seneca College, 1994. **HEROES/ROLE MODELS:** Pastor Orim Meikle; Ken Pennell, colleague. **MOTTO:** Anticipate excellence! **CONTACT:** richard @mekehla.com

PIERRE, Jean
FOUNDER, PRESIDENT, Jean Pierre Aesthetics & Spa, 530 Yonge St., 2nd Fl., Toronto, ON M4Y 1X8. Born: Jamaica/ in Canada since: 1977.
▶ Jean Pierre, aesthetician and entrepreneur, is the creator of Obsidian skin care line and owner of two salon/spas which bear her name; her clientele includes sports personalities and celebrities. A nurse by training, she took time to observe health and beauty care practices in Germany, France, and Switzerland, during 15 yrs. living and working in the UK. Shortly after coming to Canada in 1977, she completed studies in Aesthetics at Seneca College, and in 1983, she left her full-time nursing career to open her first spa on campus at York U. Within two yrs., and, in order to respond to her growing list of clients, she moved to a larger location in downtown Toronto; she later opened a second one in North York. She has made numerous appearances on radio and TV both in the Caribbean and in Canada, including Citytv, CFTO, CBC; she speaks internationally on skin care, marketing, and succeeding in business. Within the Black community she often acts as an advisor, educator, and lecturer; speaks on industry trends, and hosts workshops on skin care and make-up application. **COMMUNITY INVOLVEMENT:** mentor, Youth Entrepreneurship Training Assistance Program for the Cdn Centre on Minority Affairs; Advisory Committee, Sheridan College for Aesthetics Training; regularly addresses North York and Toronto Boards of Education. **HONS.:** several, including: ACAA, for business, 2001; Entrepreneur of the Year, Caribbean & African Chamber of Commerce, 1998; Harry Jerome Award for Excellence in Business, 1997; Women on the Move Award, *Toronto Sun,* 1988. **WORKS:** in, *Skin Inc.*; *Beauty News*; *Pride.* **REVIEWED IN:** community newspapers and *Toronto Star*; *Toronto Life*; *IBM Insight*; *Essence*; *Toronto Business Times.* **EDUCATION:** Degree, Aesthetics, Seneca College, 1980; Nursing, Midwifery, UK. **HEROES/ROLE MODELS:** Mother. **MOTTO:** Luck is when preparation meets opportunity. **CONTACT:** jpierre@interlog.com; www.jeanpierrespa.com

▶PIETERS, Gary

EDUCATOR, Toronto Public School System. Born: UK/raised in Guyana/ in Canada since: 1987.

▶ Gary Pieters was born in the UK and raised in Guyana before moving to Canada. He currently teaches within the Toronto Public School system, and had previously taught in the Los Angeles County Public School System, 1996-99. Prior to teaching, he worked at Human Resources Development Canada (HRDC) with the Canada Employment Centre for Students. He has been involved with a large number of community groups and organizations. A significant contribution to date has been the creation and maintenance of a highly educational website, Canadian Black Heritage in the Third Millennium: fcis.oise.utoronto.ca/~gpieters/blklinks.html, which covers all sectors of Black involvement and which was created to promote awareness of resources pertaining to Canadians of African descent, equity initiatives and inclusive education. He has been an invited speaker at equity, human rights, and inclusive schooling events. **HONS.:** Website of the Month, Operation Dialogue, 2001; Cert. Merit, Victoria College, U of T, 1995; Literacy Volunteer Award, Frontier College, 1994. **REVIEWED IN:** *Globe and Mail*; *Toronto Sun*; *Caribbean Camera*; *Share*; *Toronto Star*; and others. **EDUCATION:** M.Ed in progress; B.Ed, 1996; BA/Hons., 1993, U of T. **HEROES/ROLE MODELS:** Selwyn Pieters, brother; Isiah Thomas. **MOTTO:** If you can imagine it, you can achieve it. If you can dream it, you can become it. **CONTACT:** gary_pieters@hotmail.com; www.fcis.oise. utoronto.ca/~gpieters/

▶PIETERS, Selwyn

REFUGEE CLAIMS OFFICER, Immigration & Refugee Board of Canada/Toronto, Ste. 400-74 Victoria St., Toronto, ON M5C 3C7. Born: UK/ in Canada since: 1987.

▶ Selwyn Pieters is, since 1999, a Refugee Claims

Officer; he is also an activist for anti-racism and has challenged the judicial system on racism as it pertains to Blacks, particularly in the area of racial profiling by police officers and customs officials. He has argued that racial harassment is a workplace health and safety hazard, and has issued challenges on the admissions policies of law schools in Ontario. **HONS.:** nominee, JS Woodsworth Award, 2000; nominee, OPSEU Human Rights Award, 1999. **REVIEWED IN:** *Globe and Mail*; *Toronto Star*; *Toronto Sun*. **EDUCATION:** law degree in progress; BA, Criminology, U of T, 1997. **HEROES/ROLE MODELS:** Gary Pieters, brother. **MOTTO:** Whatever the mind can conceive and believe it can achieve. **CONTACT:** selwyn.pieters@ utoronto.ca

▶PINNOCK, Nicole C.N.

ASSISTANT ATHLETIC TRAINER, Indiana Pacers, Indianapolis, Indiana. Born: Trinidad & Tobago, 1977/ in Canada since: 1977.

▶ Nicole Pinnock is an Assistant Athletic Trainer with the NBA team, the Indiana Pacers, since September 2001. **VOLUNTEER ACTIVITIES:** Special Olympics, Washington, 1996-2000; Circle K(iwanis) International, Howard U., 1997-2000; Our Lady of Good Counsel, since 1990; St. Joseph's Hospital, 1990-96. **HONS.:** Award for community service, Our Lady of Good Counsel, 2001; Bison Academic Award, Howard U., 2000; Outstanding Future Professional Award, American Alliance of Health, 1999. **EDUCATION:** MSc, Kinesiology (specializing in Athletic Training), Indiana U., 2001; BSc, Phys. Ed, Howard U., 2000. **HEROES/ROLE MODELS:** Parents; aunts. **MOTTO:** Do unto others as you would have them do unto you. **CONTACT:** Fax: 416-781-4556; npinn00@aol.com

▶PITT, Romain W.M., The Hon. Mr. Justice

JUDGE, Ontario Superior Court of Justice, 361 University Ave., Toronto, ON M5G 1T3. Born Grenada/ in Canada since: 1954.

▶ The Hon. Mr. Justice Romain Pitt was appointed to the Superior Court of Ontario, in 1994. He had been practising law in Ontario since 1965, first with Blaney, Pasternak until 1967, then in the first Black law partnership in Ontario (and possibly in Canada), with E. Lindsay (now also a judge). That partnership continued until 1976, after which he maintained a sole proprietorship until 1992; he then worked in association with Victor Burke until 1994. With his appointment to the bench in 1994, he became the first Black lawyer to be appointed from private practice in Ontario (and possibly in Canada) to a Superior Court. **COMMUNITY INVOLVEMENT:** founding director, Caribana; assisted with the creation of the BBPA; assisted in the formation of the Sickle Cell Assn. of Ontario; served briefly on the Brd. of Urban Alliance for Race Relations; contributor to seat endowment, Massey Hall, for Paul Robeson Row; mentored Grade 12 and 13 students planning to pursue law careers through U of T. **AFFIL/MBRSHP:** Ont. Superior Court Judges Assn.; Cdn Institute for Administration of Justice (Director, 1996-2000); Delos Davis Law Guild; worked on many *ad hoc* committees on civil liberties issues; Trustee, Art Gallery of Ontario; Trustee, The Toronto Hospital. **HONS.:** include, Caribana Award for "cultural contribution, community development & awareness," 1984; GG 125th Anniv. Medal, 1992. **WORKS:** include, "Conduct of Wrongful Dismissal File," *View from the Bench*, LSUC, 2002; *Pet Peeves*, LSUC, 2001; *A View of Pleadings from the Court Room*, LSUC, 2000. **REVIEWED IN:** *WWIC*; major community & nat'l newspapers. **EDUCATION:** LLB, 1963; BA/Hons., Economics, 1959, U of T. **HEROES/ROLE MODELS:** "Parents, uncles, brothers, and one incredible sister, Martha." **CONTACT:** Fax: 416-920-8737

POWELL, Juliette
PRESIDENT & CEO, Powell Entertainment International Inc., Toronto, ON. Born: USA/ in Canada since: 1978.

▶ Juliette Powell is an entrepreneur whose company, Powell Entertainment International, was incorporated in 1999. One of her largest clients is CHUM TV, for whom she has been hosting and producing shows since 1992. Since 2000, she has been the anchor and finance reporter for three CP24 News shows (*MoneyLine, Opening Bell*, and *MoneyFlow*), while concurrently acting as Producer/Host for specialty shows on MuchMusic; 1996-2000, she hosted and produced four shows on MuchMusic (*FAX, FrenchKiss, Electric Circus, RapidFax)*. In 2002, E! (a TV entertainment network in the US) also signed on as one of her clients. **BACKGROUND:** her career in broadcasting began in Montreal: from 1992-96 she was a VJ with MusiquePlus TV; was also a radio host and produced for Mix 96. Her company, Powell Entertainment Int'l, was created to assist clients launch new products or ideas; clients include Microsoft, Nokia, Bell, YWCA, the Govt. of Canada (i.e. Heritage Canada, Dept. of Justice); also produces educational videos on topics concerning youth. In 2000, in addition to her role as financial host and reporter for *MoneyFlow*, she was hired by CHUM to produce and host 200 French language TV programs. **OTHER:** is also known for her philanthropy and community involvement; in 1999, JP was chosen to host "Mandela and the Children" at Skydome, in Toronto; has worked with ABC to promote literacy; hosted breast cancer benefits; worked with the YWCA on sexual assault prevention videos; addresses teens on the importance of staying in school; and participates in the national Stop Racism project. In her brief but successful career to date, JP counts as highlights: hosting events for Nelson Mandela, Prince Charles, and Prime Minister Jean Chrétien; being a delegate to the UNWCAR, 2001; interviews with Sir Richard Branson, Puff Daddy, Janet Jackson, Destiny's Child, Tina Turner, and many others. She also has the distinction of being the first (and, to date, only) Miss Canada of mixed heritage. **EDUCATION:** currently studying Economics, U of T; Finance &

Int'l Business, McGill U., 1996; Computer Programmer Assistantship, Dept. Mechanical Engineering, Concordia U., 1988. **HEROES/ROLE MODELS:** Bran Ferren (technologist), created Imagineering for Disney International. **CONTACT:** c/o bperry@icmtalent.com

▶PRIETO, Claire

FILM PRODUCER, C+C Films Inc., Ste. 328-133 Wilton St., Toronto, ON M5A 4A4. Born: Trinidad & Tobago/ in Canada since: 1971.

▶ Claire Prieto began making films in the mid-1970s as a partner in Prieto-McTair Productions; she has been a producer, director, researcher, and narrator on a number of documentaries that explore the lives of Blacks in Canada. **CAREER HIGHLIGHTS:** *Some Black Women*, 1977, the first film made by independent Black filmmakers in Canada; *It's Not an Illness*, 1979; and, *Children are Not the Problem*, 1991. She produced and co-directed, *Home to Buxton*, 1987, which looks at the southern Ontario community settled by Blacks fleeing slavery in the US; it aired on TVO, CBC, Vision TV, and PBS stations in the US. Independent of her production company, from 1988-90, she co-directed *Black Mother, Black Daughter*, and directed *Older, Stronger, Wiser*, for the NFB, both of which were broadcast and screened at festivals internationally. Other works produced include: *Jennifer Hodge: The Glory and the Pain*; *Survivors*, a short drama on AIDS; she then joined the NFB as Producer for New Initiatives in Film, a professional development program for Aboriginal Women and Women of Colour filmmakers; she subsequently became the Diversity Producer at NFB-Ontario; in 1999, she co-produced *Love Songs*, for Showtime Networks. She also production-managed *Raizin' Kane* for the NFB, and *Exhibit A–Secrets of Forensic Science*, a documentary series for the Discovery Channel; line-produced *Lord Have Mercy* for Leda Serene Films. She is a founding member and past-President of the Black Film and Video Network (BFVN). **HONS.:** include, Golden Sheaf Awards (Yorkton Film Festival) & Chris Statuette (1st place, Columbus Int'l Film Festival) for *Survivors*; Woman of Distinction, for arts/entrepreneurship, YWCA, 1992; Award of Merit, City of Toronto, 1992; Honourable Mention, Int'l Film Festival, California, 1991 & Kathleen Shannon Award, Yorkton Film Festival, 1990 for *Black Mother, Black Daughter*; Red Ribbon, for *It's Not an Illness*, American Film & Video Festival, 1980. **EDUCATION:** BA, Radio & TV, Ryerson Polytechnic. **MOTTO:** It is important that we tell the stories–painful, funny, positive–of our history and our reality; we must continue to create images that represent us in all our complexities. **CONTACT:** ccfilms@sympatico.ca

▶PROCTOR, Hazel

JAZZ SINGER, Calgary, AB. Born: Edmonton, AB.

▶ Hazel Proctor is described as "a jazz legend" in Calgary. She began singing in public at the age of ten, and performing professionally since age 16 with her father, Bert Proctor and his Proctor's Swingsters Show Band, which was very popular at the time in Calgary. They made regular appearances on the TV show, *Uncle Tom's Cabin*; appearing solo, she sang on the weekly TV program, *Soft Sounds of Jazz*; she sang with Bill Galliardi for six yrs. then for eight yrs. with Big Daddy and the Dixiecats (and performed with them at jazz festivals in California, Montana, and BC). From 1985-89, she was the vocalist with the Dixieboppers and with Southport Jazz, 1990-94, performing at various locations around Calgary. Since 1994, she has been performing with the Wild Rose All Stars, locally and at jazz festivals. For 15 yrs. she modeled at the Beta Sigma Phi annual fashion show; has appeared on film and TV; in addition to performing at a number of festivals and local venues, she has also participated in recordings of *Anything Goes,* with Southport Jazz, *Ain't no Thorns Here*, *Go Wild*, *Jazz Gospel*

Favourites, and others, with the Wild Rose All Stars Diexieland Band. In addition to singing and performing, HP worked in administration for CP Rail, Ogden Shops, 1965-92, in Calgary, Alberta. **HONS.:** include, Performing Arts Professional Award, BAASA, 1995; Woman of the Year Award, six-time winner, Beta Sigma Phi Women's Organization. **REVIEWED IN:** local publications, *Seniors World.* **HEROES/ROLE MODELS:** Bert & Idabelle Proctor, parents; Eleanor Collins & Pearl Brown, cousins. **MOTTO:** I can do that!

▶PROVIDENCE, Edford McConnie

CONDUCTOR/COMPOSER/PIANIST, c/o TESC/ Different Faces, Toronto, ON. Born: St. Vincent/ in Canada since: 1968.

▶ Edford Providence began studying music through piano in St. Vincent; he continued his musical studies in Canada, in 1968, at the Royal Conservatory of Music and later studied in the US and Germany. He describes his orchestral works as reflecting the influences of the Caribbean in all of its diversity. He has written a number of works including concertos for flute, cello, and piano; and, an opera, *Mutesa,* based on the life of Sir William Mutesa of Uganda; he has also written a number of musicals, a ballet, and several orchestral, choral, and solo works. In 1995, his musical drama, *Viadorsha,* set in the Caribbean and NY, was performed at the Ford Centre in Toronto. He has made many recordings including: *Viadorsha*; *Remembered Rhythms,* vol. I and II; *West Indian Rhapsodies and Dances*; *Tales of Anansi.* He has lectured in the field of ethnomusicology, musicology, and other musical concepts. In recent years, he spends an increasing amount of time touring and conducting in Europe, particularly the Czech Republic, Germany, Holland and Belgium. Through his organization, Black Cultural Arts, he has devoted much time to assisting young Black classical musicians further their education and gain exposure for their talents. **EDUCATION:** Conducting

studies with Eugene Kash, RCM, 1996-98; MA, Music Ed. & Admin., Florida State U., 1992. MA, Music, 1983; BA/Hons., Music, 1978, York University. Studies in Germany, 1970-73; RCM, UK, 1968. **HEROES/ROLE MODELS:** Prof. George W. Bancroft; Prof. John A.B. McLeist. **MOTTO:** Serve not sell. **CONTACT:** Tel: 416-410-6612; Jmonteith@ntc.on.ca

▶PUGH, Kevin

DIRECTOR/BALLET TEACHER, Dance-TEQ, 470 Queen's Quay W., Toronto, ON. Born: USA, 1960/ in Canada since: 1973.

▶ Kevin Pugh is a former principal dancer with the National Ballet of Canada (NBC); he was described by Clive Barnes of the *NY Post* as "a young dancer of outstanding style and technique." He joined the NBC in 1978, after completing his studies at the National Ballet School. He was promoted to second soloist in 1979, to first soloist in 1980, and to principal dancer in 1984. He received accolades for many of his roles, namely as Basilio in *Don Quixote,* the Neapolitan dance in *Swan Lake,* Oberon and Puck in *The Dream,* Solor in *La Temperaments,* and Anubis in *Sphinx.* In frequent demand as a guest artist, KP has performed with such international companies as London Festival Ballet, 1985, and the Toulouse Opera Ballet, 1989. During the NBC's 1990 season, he created a role in the World Premier of James Kudelka's *Pastorale.* Since 1993, he has been in demand as an instructor, and has been a guest teacher at Ballet BC and the Indianapolis Ballet Theatre. Currently, he teaches with the NBC, guest teaches at the National Ballet School, and Opera Atelier. Most of his time is devoted to teaching classes through Dance-TEQ, a company he formed in 1997. **HONS.:** Harry Jerome Award for Outstanding Achievement, 1984; Silver Medal, Sr. Men's category, 4th Int'l Ballet Competition, Moscow, 1981. In 1979, after a brilliant performance as the Bluebird in *Sleeping Beauty,* at the NY State

Theatre, Rudolf Nureyev presented him with his own bouquet during the curtain calls. **EDUCATION:** National Ballet School of Canada, 1978. **HEROES/ ROLE MODELS:** Parents; Rudolph Nuryev; Erik Bruhn. **CONTACT:** danceteq@sympatico.ca; www3. sympatico.ca/danceteq

▶**QUAMINA, Odida T.,** PhD.
SOCIOLOGIST/EDUCATOR/WRITER/COMMUNITY ORGANIZER, Toronto, ON. Born: Guyana/ in Canada since: 1972.

▶ Dr. Odida T. Quamina is a researcher and writer who has worked in the public and private sectors. From 1997-2002, he served as the first Ombudsperson at Seneca College of Applied Arts and Technology, responsible for designing and establishing the Ombuds Office, its policies, procedures, and practices. **CAREER:** served three consecutive terms, as a Vice-Chair, Social Assistance Rev. Brd. with the Govt. of Ontario, heard appeals of decisions of municipal and provincial administrators under the General Welfare Assistance Act, Family Benefits Act, and Vocational Rehabilitation Services Act, 1987-96; Research Coordinator, UN Research Institute for Social Development, Caribbean Area, 1979-84; Researcher, Guyana Mining Enterprises (formerly, ALCAN), 1976-80. Also taught in the part-time faculty at Atkinson College, York U., McMaster U., and at U of T. **OTHER:** in the afterword of *All Things Considered: Can We Live Together,* Austin Clarke wrote: "There is in Canada no body of black analytical writing touching on community life, touching on the political interaction of the host society and the black citizenry and the sociological conclusions that may be drawn. That vacuum has now been filled… with essays that have the immediacy of their moment and the universality of their concerns." **AFFIL/MBRSHP:** University and College Ombuds Assn.; The Ombudsman Assn.; Writers' Union of Canada; founding member, North York Black Ed. Cmtee; Chair, Black Inmates and Friends Assembly. **HONS.:** Community Service Award, Alliance of Cdn-Guyanese Organizations; Guyana Ex-Police Assn. of Canada; Guyana Heritage & Cultural Assn.; Harambee Centres; Pearl of St. Jago Lodge No. 17. **WORKS:** include, *All Things Considered: Can We Live Together,* 1996; *Mineworkers of Guyana: The Making of a Working Class,*

1987; *Growing up in Plantation Mackenzie*, 1979; columnist for *Share*, 1985-96. **REVIEWED IN:** *Some Black Men*, 1999. **EDUCATION:** Cert., Alternative Dispute Resolution, U of T, 1997. PhD, Industrial Sociology, 1980; MA, Sociology, 1976; BA/Hons., 1975, York University. Cert., Inter-University Centre of Post-graduate studies, Dubronvik, Yugoslavia, 1979. **HEROES/ROLE MODELS:** Father; Malcolm X. **MOTTO:** That which does not destroy me will make me stronger. (Nietzsche) **CONTACT:** otquamina@sympatico.ca; Fax: 416-656-9147

▶**QUAMMIE, Arsinoée Salomon**
EDUCATOR/CIVIL & HUMAN RIGHTS ACTIVIST,
Lester B. Pearson School Board, Roxboro, QC. Born: Haiti.

▶ Arsinoée Quammie is a human rights and anti-racism activist, active in the Montreal and Ottawa Conference of the United Church of Canada (UCC) on social justice concerns. She was co-chair of the National Anti-Racism Task Group within the UCC, and assisted in developing and implementing an anti-racism policy for the entire church; organized and facilitated an ecumenical consultation on the diversity of God's people, 1999; project director, Church Council on Theological Education in Canada (re: cross-cultural and global theological understanding valuing theological perspectives from overseas colleges); was the official Human Rights Rep., UCC's Mission division, at the North-South dialogue and fair missionary partnership, Kenya, 1994. She taught French at John Grant High School, 1984-99, was Dept. Head, 1990-97. Currently she teaches in the French Immersion Program with the Lester B. Pearson School Board, and is a member of the Coalition for the Advancement of Aboriginal Studies. **HONS.:** Award of Excellence, French Dept. Team Leader, Protestant School Board, Mtl, 1998; profiled in *BHM Calendar*, City of Mtl. **EDUCATION:** MA, Moral Philosophy; Dipl., Ed., French as a 2nd Language, McGill University. BA/Hons., Queen's U.; Lay Preacher, UCC; Cert., Human Rights & Race Relations, Cdn Human Rights Foundation. **MOTTO:** Be the best that you can be. **CONTACT:** myrlande@hotmail.com

▶RAEBURN-BAYNES, Gemma

SENIOR AUDITOR, Corporate Audit Dept., Bank of Montreal, 3rd Fl., 120 Bloor St. E., Toronto, ON. Born: Grenada/ in Canada since: 1964.

▶ Gemma Raeburn-Baynes is a Senior Auditor with the Bank of Montreal (BMO), where she has worked since 1973. In addition to her banking career, she has also been active in business, community development and charitable initiatives. During the course of her banking career with the BMO, GRB has held a number of managerial positions and made significant contributions to the bank's development, particularly in the areas of equity and diversity. These contributions have allowed the BMO to foster closer ties with Black and other cultural communities. **CAREER HIGH-LIGHTS:** 1990, Advisor to the Task Force on the Advancement of Women; 1993, was responsible for the research of the Task Force on the Advancement of Visible Minorities, also held the position of Research Coordinator, then Manager, Workplace Equality; 1995, initiated the Trans-Canadian, Possibilities Internship Scholarship Program, a BMO education and work experience partnership with local school boards and community organizations, aimed at visible minority and aboriginal youth, as well as youth with disabilities, encouraging them to achieve academic success. This program now operates in NS, Quebec, Ontario, Manitoba, Alberta, and BC. In 1996, she managed the Leadership for Tomorrow Today program, an internship program aimed at encouraging and assisting at-risk visible minority high school students in Ontario to stay in school, graduate, and build job skills; 1997, initiated the Excel Minority Youth Group, a non-profit organization sponsored by BMO to instill leadership and management skills in young people; 1998, implemented and managed the Career Edge Program, enabling university and college graduates to intern at BMO; 1999, initiated the first Minority Youth Conference entitled, EXCEL '99, at McGill U., which attracted over 2,000 minority students over a three-day period; many high-profile Black Achievers were there including, Dr. Mae Jamieson, the first Black female astronaut to fly in space, who was the keynote speaker. **OTHER:** 2000, founded Playmas 2000 to enhance the Mtl Carnival; on executive of James Robinson Johnston Chair in Black Canadian Studies at Dalhousie U.; 1986, founded African Dynasty, an organization raising funds for Sickle Cell Anemia; 1985, created Safari Cosmetiques Inc., first Black-owned cosmetic business in Quebec (business offers training, self-development and employment to low-income women); 1980, founder of Miss Black Quebec Pageant, instilling pride and self-confidence in young Black women; 1979, founded the Montreal Ebony Models, which raises money for charity through fashion shows; 1973, founding member of the Montreal Carnival, now called Carifesta. **COMMUNITY:** Children's Wish Fdn.; Cdn Cancer Society; Jewish General Hospital, Hope and Cope; Negro Community Centre; Friends for AIDS; Grenada Assn. of Mtl. She is affectionately described by her son as "the Energizer bunny because she never stops!" **HONS.:** include, Mtl Carifesta Trophy, Band of the Year, 2001; Champion of Diversity, Applaud Award, BMO, 2000; Mentor of the Year, Career Edge Program, 2000; Entrepreneurship Award, BMO, 1999; Woman of Achievement Award, Business & Professional Women's Club of Mtl, 1998; YWCA, Woman of Distinction Award, 1997; Honored by Mtl's Black Community for 25 yrs of dedicated community service, 1997; GG 125th Anniv. Medal, 1992; Role Model Award, Côte-des-Neiges Black Community, 1987; Miss World Canada Award, 1980. **WORKS:** several, writes for *Community Contact*; *Caribbean Camera*; and others. **REVIEWED IN:** many banking, local, & nat'l publications; *Millennium Minds*, 2000; *BHM Calendar*, 2000. **EDUCATION:** Public Relations Management, McGill U.; Psychology/ Humanities, Dawson College; Cosmetology, Dynique International. **HEROES/ROLE MODELS:** Johanne Totta, friend;

Brenda Rowe, friend. **MOTTO:** Just do it! **CONTACT:** graeburn@yahoo.com; Fax: 514-620-8404

▶**RAMSANKAR, Stephen R.,** Dr., CM. **CITIZENSHIP JUDGE/EDUCATIONAL CONSUL-TANT/ PRINCIPAL** (Ret.), Alberta Learning, Government of Alberta, 11160 Jasper Ave., Edmonton, AB T5K 062. Born: Trinidad & Tobago/ in Canada since: 1954.

▶ Dr. Stephen Ramsankar has been the recipient of the highest honours the governments of Alberta and Canada have to offer, for his contributions to the field of education. His proposals for reform in support of more caring schools have also been well received internationally. **CAREER HIGHLIGHTS:** after teaching students with developmental disabilities for eight yrs. in two inner-city schools, he was made principal of one of Edmonton's most challenging primary schools, the Alex Taylor, situated in one of the city's most marginalized areas; he remained there from 1970-98. Described as "one of the most unorthodox and influential educators in Canada," he transformed this school into "a haven for skid-row kids, troubled parents, destitute elderly, and new immigrants," through the introduction of programs such as Nutrition, Police Liaison, ESL for students and adults, a senior citizens drop-in centre and an in-school child care centre. Several of the programs he started have been either adopted or studied in other Canadian and US cities. Over the course of his 28 yr. career at Alex Taylor School, he was offered promotions, university fellowships and government appointments, all of which he declined, calling this school his "second home." He was motivated by the belief that "children learn best if they have food, warm clothing, respect, love and security." And, by introducing programs which benefitted their parents and others in the community, he ensured that these children were growing up in a warm and nurturing environment. He has addressed conferences throughout NA, Japan, Holland, the Caribbean,

Egypt and India, sharing his concept of the school as a caring place for building students' self-esteem. In 1998, he was appointed Judge of the Citizenship Court and has received numerous honours locally (from the Vietnamese, Native, Trinidad, and business communities), nationally, and internationally. His efforts and accomplishments have been profiled on CBC's *Man Alive*, 1986; and, he is the subject of an NFB co-production, *Alex Taylor Community School: Learning with Love*, 1991. Since retiring from Alex Taylor in 1998, SR works with the AB Min. of Education in their Open and Caring Schools Project; using components from the Alex Taylor School model, the program focuses on safe and caring schools, native education and poverty. **HONS.:** several including, named Servant of the Rep. of Trinidad & Tobago, 2000; identified as Global Citizen by the UN, 1995; Great Canadian Award, 1992; Hon. LLD, U. of Alberta, 1989; Citizen of the Year, Edmonton Jaycees, 1988 & 1978; Alberta Achievement Award & Premier's Award for Excellence, 1987; named as one of Canada's 50 Men of Influence, *Influence* magazine, 1986; Member, Order of Canada, 1983; Fellow, Cdn College of Teachers, 1983. **WORKS:** in *J of Curriculum & Supervision*, 1992; *Informing Educational Policy & Practice through Interpretive Inquiry*, 1992. **REVIEWED IN:** local & regional publications; *Reader's Digest*, 1987; *Influence* magazine, 1986. **EDUCATION:** Graduate Studies; B.Ed, 1960; BSc, 1958, U. of Alberta. **MOTTO:** You can become/achieve anything you wish in Canada. **CONTACT:** sramsankar@edc.gov.ab.ca; Fax: 780-422-2039

▶**RAWLINS, Micheline,** The Hon. **Madam Justice** **JUDGE,** Ontario Court of Justice, 200 Chatham St. E., Level 7, Chatham, ON N9A 2W3. Born: Montreal, QC.

▶ The Hon. Madam Justice Micheline Rawlins was appointed to the Ontario Court of Justice in

1992, and became the first Black woman in Ontario to receive such an appointment. Prior to that, she was Assistant Crown Attorney in Kent County, Chatham, 1986-1992. **AFFIL/MBRSHP:** Windsor Board of Education, 1982-84; Board of Governors, 1985-87 and since 1995, U. of Windsor; Ont. Court of Justice representative on National Judicial Council Advisory on Education, since 1998; co-chaired Ont. Court of Justice Conference on Race Relations, 1996. **OTHER:** President, Chatham Youth Soccer Assn., 1990-93; she is also a qualified hockey trainer. **HONS.:** several including: ACAA, Law, 1997; Recognition Award, NA Black Historical Museum & Cultural Centre, 1994; Distinguished Service Award, Chatham Youth Soccer Assn., 1994; Service Award, Trinidad & Tobago Assn., 1993; Recognition Award, National Council of Jamaicans & Supportive Org. in Canada, 1993. **REVIEWED IN:** *Some Black Women*, 1993. **EDUCATION:** LLB, U. of Windsor, 1978; BA, McGill U., Montreal, 1974. **MOTTO:** Do unto others as you would have them do unto you. **CONTACT:** Fax: 519-973-6671

▶**REGIS, Gregory,** The Hon. Mr. Justice
JUDGE, Ontario Court of Justice, 242 King St. E., Oshawa, ON L1H 3Z8. Born: St. Lucia/ in Canada since: 1974.

▶ The Hon. Mr. Justice Gregory Regis was appointed to the Ontario Court of Justice in 1999, and presides in the Durham Region. He began his professional life in St. Lucia, first as a teacher, lab technician, then as a photo and broadcast journalist. After completing a degree in journalism at Ryerson U., 1977, he worked with the CBC in both radio and TV. After completing his law degree, he was admitted to the Ontario bar in 1985; he is also a member of the bar in Grenada. He was the Executive Director of the Jane-Finch Legal Clinic for four yrs. before joining the Ont. Min. of the Attorney General as an Assistant Crown Attorney. **COMMUNITY:** has served on the boards of many community organizations; regularly participates in workshops and community outreach; former Chair, Caribana. **HONS.:** including, ACAA, 2000. **EDUCATION:** LLB, Osgoode Hall, York U., 1983; BAA, Ryerson U., 1977. **CONTACT:** gregory.regis@jus.gov.on.ca

▶**REYES, Cynthia**
EXECUTIVE PRODUCER/VICE-PRESIDENT, ProMedia International Inc., Ste. 202B-260 Carlaw Ave., Toronto, ON M4M 3L1. Born: Jamaica/ in Canada since: 1974.

▶ Cynthia Reyes is VP of ProMedia International, a TV production and consulting firm, and President of Innoversity. A TV journalist and executive producer, she also has several years experience training journalists and consulting with senior managers. She is now an executive producer, trainer and organizational development consultant. Her projects have taken her across Canada and to all continents. **HIGHLIGHTS:** from 1994-96, she led a CBC initiative designed to change S. African journalists from being journalists of the state to becoming journalists in a democracy. Earlier she led a research, training and development project that helped to launch The Windsor Experiment, the CBC's first multiskilled TV station. At the CBC, she was known as a "change leader." **BACKGROUND:** she began her career as a journalist while still a student in Jamaica where, from the age of 15, she was already writing for local newspapers. While studying journalism at Ryerson, in Toronto, she was hired by the CBC; a series of reporting and production positions followed, including three yrs. as Executive Producer of *What's New*, the acclaimed news show for teenagers. CR left the CBC in 2000 to launch ProMedia International and co-founded Innoversity, aimed at bridging the gap between the mainstream media and Canada's multicultural population. In 2000, she helped UNESCO develop the work of film and TV professionals in the Caribbean and to showcase their work in the international film and TV industry. **AFFIL/MBRSHP:** has included, President, BBPA; Advisory Board, Ryerson U.'s Journalism School; BFVN; Secretary-General of INPUT, the int'l public television board; chair, INPUT 2000 screening conference; director, WTN Foundation. **HONS.:** several including, ACAA, 1997; CBC's President Award, 1995, for her work with S. African journalists & the Windsor Experiment; named Broadcaster of the Future, 1994, by the Cdn Assn. of Broadcasters/ CanWest Global. **WORKS:** *SCAN*; short stories and essays in *Toronto Life*; *Toronto Star*; anthologies of short stories. **REVIEWED IN:** *Excellence* magazine; *Share*; *Pride*; *Toronto Star.* **EDUCATION:** BA, Journalism, Ryerson U., 1979. **HEROES/ROLE MODELS:** Louise Reid, mother; Les Lawrence; Beverly Mascoll; Lincoln Alexander. **MOTTO:** If you want something you've never had, do something you've never done. **CONTACT:** promedia@innoversity.com; www. innoversity.com

► RICHARDS, Lloyd, Dr.
THEATRE DIRECTOR/PROFESSOR EMERITUS, Yale University. Resides in New York, NY. Born: Toronto, ON.

▶ In 1959, Lloyd Richards became the first Black, since 1907, to direct a play on Broadway, by and about Blacks. The play, *A Raisin in the Sun*, was written by Lorraine Hansberry, the first Black woman to have her work produced on Broadway. The play won the New York Drama Critics' Circle Award (selected over plays by Eugene O'Neill and Tennessee Williams) and opened the eyes of America to real-life, working-class Black Americans. The play's leading actors, Sydney Poitier, Ruby Dee, Diana Sands, and Claudia McNeil became stars of theatre and film, and Lloyd Richards would later become first the Dean of African-American Stage Directors and then, Dean of the Yale University School of Drama. **BACKGROUND:** he was born in Toronto, in 1919, and soon thereafter, his family moved to Detroit,

in search of better opportunities. He later enrolled at Wayne University in Detroit to study law, but switched to drama. He served in the US Army Air Force, 1943-44, and was one of the first Black pilot-trainees. Following the war, he completed his studies in drama. **CAREER HIGHLIGHTS:** in 1966, he became a Master Teacher in the actor training program at NY University's School of the Arts; was Prof. of Theater and Cinema at Hunter College in NY before he was made Dean of Yale University School of Drama, 1979 (first Black Dean in the Ivy League Schools); at the same time he became Artistic Director of the Yale Repertory Theater; he held both positions for an unprecedented 12 yrs. While at Yale and even before, he worked to make regional theatres centres for new writing, not merely places to present the classics and off-Broadway hits. Of his contributions to Yale, a *NY Times* reporter wrote that "he cemented the standing of the school by transforming it into the most prestigious professional drama training program in the country... increased the number of minority students and faculty members and reoriented the repertory theater from an avant-garde, director-dominated company into a writer's theater with a commitment to social concerns." A number of famous plays debuted at the Yale Repertory Theater under his direction, including Athol Fugard's *Master Harold ... and the Boys* and two Pulitzer Prize-winning works by August Wilson; these plays later went to Broadway for long and lucrative runs. **ACCOMPLISHMENTS:** throughout his career, Lloyd Richards sought to discover and develop new plays and playwrights; he was key in furthering the careers of playwrights like August Wilson, Athol Fugard, Charles Fuller, David Henry Hwang, and others; he was able to do so as Artistic Director of the National Playwrights Conference at the Eugene O'Neill Memorial Theater Center for 38 yrs., as a member of the playwrights' selection committee of the Rockefeller Foundation and of the New American Plays program of the Ford Foundation. His search for a major new American playwright bore fruit with the 1984 production of *Ma Rainey's Black Bottom* by August Wilson; he directed seven successive instalments of Wilson's multi-part chronicle of African-American life, including *Fences, Joe Turner's Come and Gone, The Piano Lesson.* He also has a number of TV credits including, *Roots: the Next Generation.* **HONS.:** several including: inducted into the Theater Hall of Fame, 1990; Tony Award, best director, *Fences,* 1986; Emmy Award nominee, for *The Piano Lesson;* Professor Emeritus, Yale U.; holds 18 honorary degrees, (17 honorary doctorates); National Medal of Arts, President Clinton; Christopher Award, for *Paul Robeson;* Frederick Douglas Award; National Black Theater Festival Award; Audelco Pioneer Award... and many others. **EDUCATION:** MFA, Yale U., 1980; BA, Wayne U., 1944. **MOTTO:** There is no substitute for work; there is no substitute for commitment; you've got to commit to something that you love. **CONTACT:** Fax: 212-749-9861

▶RICHARDS, Vanessa

ARTISTIC DIRECTOR, Mannafest, 27 Links Yard, Spelman St., London, E1 5LX, UK. Born: Vancouver, BC, 1964.

▶ Vanessa Richards is a writer, performing artist, producer, and workshop facilitator, residing in the UK since 1992. She is a founder and Joint Artistic Director of Mannafest, an interdisciplinary performance company creating and producing works at: Royal Albert Hall, Royal Festival Hall, the Notting Hill Carnival, and the Golden Jubilee. As an artist and former lead singer of Vancouver group, Bolero Lava, she has performed throughout Canada, parts of the US, Trinidad, the UK, and Western Europe. As a writer and poet, her works have been included in a number of anthologies. **COMMUNITY:** mentors emerging writers and producers; Arts Advisor for London Arts. **WORKS:** in anthologies including: *Bluesprint: an Anthology of Black British*

Columbian Literature and Orature, 2002; *West Coast Lines: New African-Canadian Writing,* 1997; *Bittersweet: Contemporary Black Women's Poetry,* 1998; *Mating Rituals,* 1995; *The Fire People, Anthology of Contemporary Black British Poetry.* **EDUCATION:** completing M.Phil, Cardiff U., Wales. **CONTACT:** vanessa@mannafest. net; www.mannafest.net

▶RICHARDSON, Doug

SAXOPHONIST/ACTOR/TEACHER, Toronto, ON. Born: Toronto, ON.

▶ Doug Richardson, jazz musician, is known in Toronto and across the country as a "saxophonist par excellence." He studied at the Oscar Peterson School of Music and under the tutelage of Sonny Rollins and Roland Kirk. A veteran of jazz, live theatre, movies and TV, his talents and experience include arranging, composing and scoring for live theatrical productions, films, and commercial jingles. He has performed around the world and at major jazz festivals. He has toured with the O'Jays, Stephanie Mills, Johnny Nash, Dick Clark's Rock 'n Roll Review, and others. And, he has played backup to the Platters, Percy Sledge, Ben E. King, The Drifters, Mary Wells, Salome Bey, and many others. In the early '80s he released his own album, *Night Talk,* which sold well in the Chicago, Baltimore, and New York areas. He made his theatrical debut as the lead in George Boyd's play, *Shine Boy,* at the Neptune Theatre in NS, in 1987. Since then he has been the musical director for several theatrical presentations including *Coming Through Slaughter, Lord Buckley's Finest Hour* and has been actor and musician in a number of film and TV productions, including a role in *The Contract,* with Billy Dee Williams. When he's not playing or composing, DR is teaching saxophone or flute, something he has been doing professionally for nearly 40 yrs. He is also co-leader, with Archie Alleyne, of the Afro-Canadian jazz band, Kollage. ****Doug's father, Samuel Richardson, was also quite famous: in 1934 at age 15, he won a gold medal for Canada at the Commonwealth Games and set a record in long jump of 24ft. 11in., which stood until 1965. He and Jesse Owens became friends after meeting at the 1936 Olympics; in 1978, Richardson was recognized by the Canadian Amateur Hall of Fame for his accomplishments** **EDUCATION:** Arranging & Orchestration (2yrs.), Humber College; Oscar Peterson School of Music; Dick Grove School of Music, Los Angeles; and, under Sonny Rollins & Roland Kirk. **HEROES/ROLE MODELS:** Sonny Rollins; Gene Ammons. **CONTACT:** Fax: 905-527-1392

▶**RICKARD-BON, Sharon,** PhD.
NUTRITION CONSULTANT/RESEARCH COORDINATOR, Dynalife Health Services, 35 Algoma St. N., Thunder Bay, ON P7B 5G7. Born: Toronto, ON, 1968.
▶ Dr. Sharon Rickard-Bon is a Nutrition Consultant at St. Joseph's Care Group, and Research Coordinator for Dynalife Health Services, in Thunder Bay. She completed her studies in Nutritional Sciences at U of T and did research on the role of flax seed in the treatment of breast cancer. She has authored six book chapters and 11 published articles on this research. In her new posting, she makes nutrition education presentations for adults recovering from drug and/or alcohol abuse and for older adults in the community; she also works as a research coordinator examining the link between nutrition and disease. **OTHER:** involved with the AABHS, 1996-99, and was particularly active in the affiliated Health Science Summer Mentorship Program. **HONS.:** include, Gordon Cressy Student Leadership Award, 1998; A. Laird Graduate Fellowship, Nutritional Sciences, 1998; Am. Assn. Cereal Chemists Graduate Fellowship, 1998; Open Doctoral Fellowship, 1996-98; Mitchell Scholarship in Cancer Research, 1993 & '95; Merit Award, Society of Chemical Industry, 1991. **WORKS:** articles in, *J Nutrition*; *Latin American Arch Nutri-*

tion; *Carcinogenesis*; *Cancer Lett.* Book chapters in*: Flax, The Genus Linum,* 2001; *Complex Carbohydrates,* 1999; *Antinutrients & Phytochemicals in Foods,* 1997. **EDUCATION:** PhD, Nutritional Sciences, 2000; MSc, Nutritional Sciences, 1994; BSc, 1991, U of T. **HEROES/ROLE MODELS:** Parents. **CONTACT:** srickard-bon@shaw.ca

▶**RILEY, Betty**
TELEVISION PRODUCER/COMMUNITY ORGANIZER, Windsor, ON. Born: Montreal, QC.
▶ Betty Riley is a pioneer in TV production featuring Blacks in Canada, and has been honoured by the cities of Montreal and Windsor as well as various levels of government for her important contributions. **HIGHLIGHTS:** she began her career in TV by producing her own program, *Black Is*, in 1970, which provided news and views by and about Blacks in Montreal and from around the world, as well as Black history, politics, and culture. This made her the first Black woman TV producer in Canada and, her program was unique both for its content and for being bilingual. In 1973, she founded and directed the first ever Black Youth Television Network (BYTN), teaching Black youth, aged 17-21, to work with TV equipment and allowing them to acquire training by producing *Black Is* (many who had left school prematurely, subsequently returned to further their education in this field). She also produced a radio program at McGill U., in 1972, *Black Speaks*, which provided hands-on training for youth in this medium. She was the co-founder and Executive Director for the Black Community Communication Media Inc., 1975, and in 1977, organized the first national Black media conference in Canada. In 1980, at the age of 50, she decided to upgrade her grade seven education by returning to school; she graduated in 1984 from U. of Windsor with a degree in Communication Studies (minor in Organizational Skills). Following her studies, she remained in Windsor becoming involved in a number of activities; created a

TV program which ran for three years, *Building Together*, and which provided a hands-on training opportunity for youth of diverse cultural backgrounds to work with TV equipment and production. **COMMUNITY INVOLVEMENT:** in Montreal, had been involved with the National Black Coalition; was active in the Union United Church, wrote history for the 65th Anniversary, and prepared a three-part documentary on this institution. In Windsor: Executive, Windsor Black Coalition; President, Windsor Urban Alliance (coordinator of the first provincial conference held in Windsor); appointed to a Mayor's Committee on Race Relations; became active in issues related to immigrants and women. **OTHER:** she has lectured in universities and other institutions across Canada and the US; is the subject of a CBC Radio documentary, 1974, in honour of International Year for Women. **HONS.:** several, including: GG 125th Anniv. Medal, 1992; Woman of the Year (first Black recipient), City of Windsor, 1987; Ontario Volunteer Award; Award, for "having the longest running show of excellence by an ethnic group," Cable TV Ltd., Mtl, 1979; Citation and Silver Jubilee Award, 1977; honoured as "one of the leading Black women of the century in Quebec," National Congress of Black Women, Mtl, 1974. **REVIEWED IN:** a number of publications; *Some Black Women*, 1993; *Identities*; *Canada and Its People of African Descent*, 1977. **EDUCATION:** BA, Communications, U. of Windsor, 1984. **HEROES/ROLE MODELS:** Harriet Tubman. **MOTTO:** Aim high, it doesn't cost any more! **CONTACT:** Tel: 519-253-9929

▶**ROACH, Charles**
LAWYER/BARRISTER/SOLICITOR, Roach, Schwartz, & Associates, 688 St. Clair Ave. W., Toronto, ON. Born: Trinidad & Tobago/ in Canada since: 1955.

▶ Charles Roach is a civil rights lawyer and activist in Toronto. He began his law career at the legal department of the City of Toronto, in 1961.

In 1968, he left the civil service to open his own practice, now a law office of seven lawyers. Working to advance and defend the cause of racial minorities, his law firm specialized in wrongful dismissals, police brutality, labour and immigration law, and civil rights. In 1985, he convened the International Conference of Black Lawyers and Jurists in Toronto. Since the mid-'80s he has been leading a national campaign to remove the pledge of allegiance to the Queen from the Oath of Canadian Citizenship. Since 1998, he has been lead defence counsel at the International Criminal Tribunal for Rwanda. **COMMUNITY:** his involvement over the years has been extensive including: Deputy leader of World Pan African Movement, 1993; founder, Martin Luther King Jr. Day Commemorative Cmtee, 1987; Co-Chair of the International Committee Against Racism; co-founder, BADC, 1988; founding member and first Chair of Caribana, 1966; musician and band leader, 1955-71. **HONS.:** several including, Badagry Pilgrim, 1992; Lawyer of the Year, NCBL, 1985. **WORKS:** several articles, interviews on radio & TV re: civil rights cases; poetry in *Root for the Ravens* and *Canada in Us Now*. **REVIEWED IN:** *PanAfrican View of Global Warming*; *PanAfrican Spirituality*; *Canada's Aboriginals*; *Some Black Men*, 1999; *WWIC*. **EDUCATION:** JD (LLB), U of T, 1961; BA, U. of Sask., 1958. **HEROES/ROLE MODELS:** Jan Carew; Lennox Hinds; Phil Taylor. **MOTTO:** It is up to you, it is up to me, we can change the world. **CONTACT:** www.roachschwartz.com; charoa @sympatico.ca; Fax: 416-657-1511

▶**ROBBINS, Juneau Kipola, DC.**
CHIROPRACTOR/AUTHOR, Cultural Chiropractic, Minneapolis, Minnesota. Born: Toronto, ON, 1970.

▶ Dr. Juneau Robbins is a chiropractor and an author. Originally from Toronto and raised in Chatham, he now lives in Minneapolis and maintains his multiple practices in the Twin Cities area. After completing his studies in chiropractic, he and a former classmate, also originally from Canada, opened their first clinic, Urban Chiropractic in 1996, in North Minneapolis; they opened a second clinic in St. Paul, 1997; and, in 1999, he opened a clinic by himself in S. Minneapolis, Cultural Chiropractic. Through word of mouth and his reputation for community involvement (led church youth group, Big Brother for over ten yrs.), their practices became extremely popular. **OTHER:** JKR is a strong advocate of youth achievement and self-empowerment through self-responsibility; was the keynote speaker at the annual scholarship banquet for the African Cdn Society of Kent County and is frequently invited to speak to groups (classrooms, church, health care clinics) in order to share his message of reaching for goals. Towards this end, he collaborated with his father, Larry Mansfield Robbins, to write the book, *121 Tips on Raising a Child of Colour*, 2000. **REVIEWED IN:** *First Fridays* magazine, Minneapolis; *Black Enterprise* magazine. **EDUCATION:** D.Chiropractic, 1996; BSc/Hons., Human Biology, Northwestern Health Sciences U., Minnesota. BA, Kinesiology, U. of Windsor, 1993. **CONTACT:** drjuneaurobbins @aol.com; www.gmnetwork.cc/drjunea

▶ROBBINS, Larry Mansfield

COUNCILLOR, Municipality of Chatham-Kent, 315 King St. W., Box 640, Chatham ON N7M 5K8. Born: North Buxton, ON.
▶ Councillor Larry Mansfield Robbins is serving his second term as a Councillor in the Municipality of Chatham-Kent. A retired teacher from the Kent County Board of Education, he was the Business Studies Director at Lambton-Kent Composite School in Dresden. He was first elected Councillor in 1994; after serving the first term of three years, he ran for Mayor and placed second in a field of six candidates. He was re-elected to Council in the year 2000, and, as a result of the death of the incumbent, he ran for Mayor in 2001 and placed third out of six candidates. **COMMUNITY:** Chair, Kent Restructuring Transition Brd.; Chatham-Kent Tourism Brd.; Industrial Development Committee; Chatham-Kent Museum and Cultural Centre Brds.; Parks and Recreation Advisory Committee; Moderator, Amherstburg Baptist Assn.; Coach, Minor Baseball and Basketball; Brd., United Way; Family Service Kent Brd. **WORKS:** co-authored, with son Juneau Robbins, *121 Tips on Raising a Child of Colour*, 2000. **EDUCATION:** M.Ed, U. of Windsor; BA, York U. **HEROES/ROLE MODELS:** Verlyn Ladd; Arthur Alexander Sr. **MOTTO:** Continuing to do what you have always done, will get you the same results. **CONTACT:** larrym.robbins@sympatico.ca; Fax: 519-351-2503

▶ROBERTS, Kim

ACTOR, c/o Noble-Caplan Agency, 2nd Fl., 1260 Yonge St., Toronto, ON M4T 1W6. Born: Toronto, ON.
▶ Kim Roberts is a Toronto-based actor who has performed extensively in film, TV, radio and on stage. **SELECTED CREDITS:** film and TV: *The Tuxedo*; *Soul Food*; *Get a Clue*; *The Associates*, series regular; *All That Glitters*; *One Special Night*; *The Agency*; *Down in the Delta*; *Blues Brothers 2000*; *Extreme Measures*. As the doctor in a popular Benelyn commercial, she became the first Black female lead in a speaking role in a national Canadian commercial. Stage: *Sistahs*; *...and the Girls in Their Sunday Dresses*; *dark diaspora...in dub*. **OTHER:** KR has worked with a variety of artists including Jackie Chan, Julie Andrews, Maya Angelou, Wesley Snipes, and Deborah Cox; has been directed by Sydney Lumet, Peter Bogdanovitch, and Robert Townsend. She appeared on *Entertainment Tonight,* during filming of *The Agency*, with Tom Berenger. She is the longest-serving host of Harbourfront Centre's Summer concert series (Toronto), since 1995. **COMMUNITY:** founding member, Obsidian Theatre Co.; former board member, BFVN; Nubian Disciples of

Pryor; mentor, Each One Teach One. **HONS.:** Harold Award, theatre, 1996. **EDUCATION:** Poli. Sci., U. of Western Ont.; Theatre, York U. **MOTTO:** Just believe: it will come! **CONTACT:** kimmyonline @yahoo.com

▶**ROBINSON, Frank Price,** PhD.
ASSISTANT DEAN, Arts & Science (Ret.)/ **ASSOCIATE PROFESSOR EMERITUS,** Dept. Arts & Science, University of Victoria, BC. Born: USA/ in Canada since: 1957.

▶ Dr. Frank Price Robinson is Associate Professor Emeritus of the University of Victoria in BC. During his career, he was an Associate Professor of Chemistry for 37 yrs. and was one of the longest-serving professors this university had ever had, 1963-2000. His area of specialization was organic synthesis and physical organic chemistry; from 1990-2000, he was Assistant Dean, Arts and Science, responsible for managing the Arts and Science Advising Centre. Upon his retirement, June 2000, he was made Associate Professor Emeritus. **HONS.:** include, Honorary Alumni, U. of Victoria, 1999; Rhodes Scholarship candidate, 1956; Alpha Chi Sigma (Nat'l Chemical Honor Society), U. of Kansas, 1956; Beta Kappa Chi (Nat'l Scientific Honor Society), Fisk U., 1955. **WORKS:** articles in, *J Chemistry*; *Applied Spectroscopy*; co-authored chemistry lab manual, 1964 & '65. **REVIEWED IN:** *Alumni Magazine*, U. of Victoria, 2001. **EDUCATION:** PhD, Organic & Physical Chemistry, U. of Alberta, 1963; MSc, U. of Kansas, 1956; BA, Chemistry & Math, Fisk U., 1955. **MOTTO:** If I can be here at 08:30, so can you! **CONTACT:** fprob@uvvm.uvic. ca; Fax: 250-477-5753

▶**ROBINSON, Gwendolyn**
LOCAL HISTORIAN/AUTHOR, Chatham WISH Centre, 177 King St. E., Chatham, ON N7M 3N1. Born: Chatham, ON.

▶ Gwendolyn Robinson, a local historian and author, is the driving force behind the WISH Centre's Heritage Room. A great-grand niece of Mary Ann Shadd, she began researching Black history to help her son find information for a school project. Then, realizing that information about the history of African-Canadians in the Chatham area was almost non-existent, she set out to learn and share the history, accomplishments, and contributions of local Blacks, with the city. The result of her endeavour was *Seek the Truth*, a book that helped to restore a valuable part of Chatham's history. The book has two purposes: to provide young Black students with information on the roles played by Kent County's Black population in the development of Chatham, and thereby instill a sense of pride in their heritage; and, to give young white students a more accurate rendering of the history of Chatham. In addition to providing lectures and presentations on Black history in the region, GR has also written and produced the script for a video, *Celebrating the Legacy: The History of Chatham's Black Community*, 2001. **HONS.:** include, Women of Excellence Award, Chatham-Kent YMCA, 2002; Service to Mankind, District Award, Sertoma Int'l, 2001; Int'l Year of Older Persons Award, Province of Ontario, 2001; GG 125th Anniv. Medal, 1993. **WORKS:** *Seek the Truth*, co-authored with John Robinson, 1989; reprinted 1994. **HEROES/ROLE MODELS:** Arlie Robbins; Vivian Robbins Chavis. **MOTTO:** To live in the presence of great truths and eternal laws, that is what keeps a man patient when the world ignores him, calm and unspoiled when the world praises him. (Balzac) **CONTACT:** Tel: 519-354-4248

▶**ROBINSON, Karen**
ACTOR, c/o Lefeaver Talent Management, Ste. 202-2 College St., Toronto, ON M5G 1K3. Born: UK/ in Canada since: 1984.

▶ Karen Robinson has achieved high acclaim, locally and nationally for her work, since embarking on her professional acting career in 1993. Her internship at the Citadel Theatre in Edmonton was spent under the tutelage of renowned director Robin Phillips; there she appeared in a variety of his productions, including *Hamlet, Caesar and Cleopatra,* and *Man of La Mancha.* **CAREER HIGHLIGHTS:** her Toronto breakthrough came in 1995, in Factory Theatre's production of Andrew Moodie's *Riot* (earned a Dora Mavor Moore Award for the role of Grace); the play was also produced in Ottawa, Halifax and at the du Maurier World Stage Festival. Other stage credits: Demetrius and Flute in *A Midsummer Night's Dream,* at Theatre Passe Muraille, 2001; *The Vagina Monologues,* 2001/02; Billie, in Djanet Sears' *Harlem Duet,* Neptune Theatre, 2000; *The Play's the Thing,* and *Endgame,* Soulpepper Theatre Company; the title character in Lorena Gale's *Angelique,* Alberta Theatre Projects (ATP), 1998, earning her a nomination for a Betty Mitchell Theatre Award; and three plays from George F. Walker's series, *Suburban Motel: Problem Child* (ATP, 2000), *Adult Entertainment,* and *End of Civilization,* Factory Theatre, 1997/98. **FILM AND TV CREDITS:** *Owning Mahowny,* 2002; *Two Against Time,* 2002; *Interviews with my Next Girlfriend,* 2001 (Emmy Winner, Outstanding Children's Special); *Mr. and Mrs. Loving,* and, *My Louisiana Sky,* 1996/2001; *They Call me Sirr,* 2001 (Emmy nominee, Outstanding Children's Special); *Dangerous Evidence,* 1999; *Booty Call,* 1997; and, *We The Jury,* 1996, along with guest appearances on several series including: *Soul Food; Blue Murder; The Associates; PSI Factor;* and *The Famous Jett Jackson.* **HONS.:** include, nominee, Betty Mitchell Theatre Award, for Outstanding Female Performance, *Angelique,* 1999; Dora Mavor Moore Award, for Outstanding Female Performance, *Riot,* 1996. **REVIEWED IN:** *Edmonton J; Sunday Gleaner; NOW; Toronto Star; Chronicle-Herald; WWIC; WWCW.* **EDUCATION:** BFA, U. of Calgary, 1992; Dipl. Theatre Arts, Mount Royal College. **HEROES/ROLE MODELS:** Parents. **MOTTO:** We are born to make manifest the glory of God that is within us. (Nelson Mandela)

▶ROGERS, George, The Hon.

MAYOR, City of Leduc, 1 Alexandra Park, Leduc, AB T9E 4C4. Born: Jamaica/ in Canada since: 1975.

▶ Mayor George Rogers is in his second term as mayor of Leduc, Alberta. First elected to city council in 1992, as a Councillor, he was re-elected in 1995, and served a second term. In October 1998, he made his first bid for mayor and won by a three-to-one margin; in 2001 he was re-elected to serve a second term, again with a resounding victory. Since occupying public office with the City of Leduc (10 minutes from Edmonton), GR has been active in many capacities; he is currently serving as President, after serving four years as Vice-President of the Alberta Urban Municipalities Assn. (AUMA). In this capacity, he has represented the AUMA on several committees, most notably as co-chair of a task force with the Urban Development Institute and other entities, reviewing development levies in Alberta in conjunction with Alberta Municipal Affairs. He also sits on the Board of the Federation of Canadian Municipalities. **OTHER:** in his life before politics, he worked in the oil industry in various accounting positions until he became Assistant Controller; in 1986, he joined the City of Leduc as Assistant Treasurer; after three years he moved to Redcliff, Alberta, where he was Municipal Administrator and also handled the roles of Secretary-Treasurer and Assistant Town Manager. **EDUCATION:** Cert., Local Government Studies, U. of Alberta, 1989; Dipl., Business Administration, Northern Alberta Institute of Technology, 1980. **HEROES/ROLE MODELS:** Hal Rogers, father. **MOTTO:** If you want good, you nose ha' fi run! **CONTACT:** grogers@city.leduc.ab.ca; www.city.leduc.ab.ca

▶ROMILLY, Selwyn R., The Hon.

JUDGE, British Columbia Supreme Court, 800 Smithe St., Vancouver, BC V6Z 2E1. Born: Trinidad & Tobago/ in Canada since: 1960.

▶ The Hon. Judge Romilly was appointed to the Provincial Court of British Columbia in 1974, and thereby became the second Black person to be appointed to any court in Canada. In 1995, he was appointed to the British Columbia Supreme Court and became the first Black in BC to occupy such a position. **HONS.:** CABL, 1997; Congress of Black Women, 1996; Harambee Foundation, 1996; Black Law Students' Assn. of Canada; voted "one of the four best judges in the Provincial Courts of BC," by the BC Lawyers Assn., 1991. **EDUCATION:** LLB, 1966; BA, 1963, UBC. **CONTACT:** Tel: 604-660-3448

▶**ROSEMAY, Vibert T.,** The Hon.
Mr. Justice
JUDGE, Ontario Court of Justice, 7755 Hurontario St., Brampton, ON L6W 4T6. Born: Guyana/ in Canada since: 1959.
▶ The Hon. Mr. Justice Rosemay was appointed to the Ontario Court of Justice in 1991; he was appointed as a Queen's Counsel in 1983 and was called to the bar in 1971. **COMMUNITY:** co-founder, Delos Davis Law Guild, 1977; Chair, National Black Awards Committee, 1972-73; Legal Advisor to National Black Coalition of Canada, 1973-78; Legal Advisor to Black Community Centre Project, 1972-75. **EDUCATION:** LLB, Dalhousie U., 1969; BA, U. of PEI, 1963.

▶**ROSS, Christopher,** PhD.
ASSOCIATE PROFESSOR, Dept. of Marketing, Concordia University, 1455, boul. de Maisonneuve W., Montreal, QC H3G 1M8. Born: Trinidad & Tobago/ in Canada since: 1974.
▶ Dr. Christopher Ross is an Associate Professor in the Dept. of Marketing at the John Molson School of Business at Concordia University, where he has the distinction of having been the first Black Dean of a major Canadian Business School. He was Acting Dean (1988; 1990-92) and Dean from 1992-95. While Dean, and in conjunction with IATA (Int'l Air Transport Assn.), the first Aviation MBA was established. In addition, with funding from the Quebec Government and other institutions, he established the Minority Entrepreneurship Institute in the Faculty. He also oversaw the establishment of the student co-op program (work-study) in the Faculty. **CAREER HIGHLIGHTS:** he began his teaching career as a lecturer in Jamaica at UWI, in the Dept. of Management Studies, 1974-77; taught at the St. Augustine Campus of UWI, in Trinidad, 1980-81; joined the Faculty of Commerce and Administration at Concordia as an Assistant Professor, 1981-84; became an Associate Professor in 1984; from 1984-88 he was Assistant then Associate Dean, for the Research and PhD Program, then Associate Dean, Graduate Studies and Research. This was followed by his appointment to Acting Dean, then Dean. In addition to his teaching experience in Canada and the Caribbean, he has also taught MBA level courses on Marketing and International Marketing, in China. He researches and publishes in the areas of: marketing and economic development; marketing education in developing countries; the transfer of management technology to developing countries; and, minority entrepreneurship. He is the author of several papers and articles. **COMMUNITY:** member, Advisory Brd., Aurora Business Project for Women. **HONS.:** Best Paper Award, for the article, "Growth & Ethnic Enterprises," Administrative Science Assn. of Canada, 2001; Merit Award, Faculty of Commerce & Admin., 2000, 1989, 1985; Award of Excellence: Best Paper, for the article "Promotional Activities of Black Entrepreneurs," 1998; Charles C. Slater Award of Excellence, *J of Macromarketing*, 1991. **WORKS:** several conference papers & articles published in: *J of Small Business Management*; *J of Global Maketing*; *J of Macromarketing*; *Possibles* (fr.); *Marketing Educator*. Contributing editor to *Community Contact*. **REVIEWED IN:** *BHM Calendar*, 1998. **EDUCATION:** PhD, Business Admin., 1982; MBA, 1974, Ivey Business School, U. of Western

Ontario. BSc, Management Studies, UWI/ Trinidad, 1972. **CONTACT:** caross@vax2.concordia. ca; Fax: 514-848-4554

▶**ROSS, Joyce L., Dr., CM.**
FOUNDER/EXECUTIVE DIRECTOR, East Preston Day Care Centre, 1799, #7 Highway, East Preston, NS B2Z 1E9. Born: East Preston, NS.
▶ Dr. Joyce Ross has been active in her community of East Preston since her childhood and was the driving force behind the creation of the East Preston Day Care Centre, which she has been running as Executive Director since 1975. In 1969, while working on a community health program sponsored by the Black United Front (BUF), she completed a survey of the local population to identify means of improving the community; a day care facility was often mentioned. In 1974, JLR and a small committee secured land from a community resident and erected a facility to be used for a day care. Since then, the East Preston Day Care Centre has been expanded four times to include four additional classrooms, a library, gym, and an off-site infant unit. It accommodates 115 children, aged six months to ten yrs.; offers half-day, full-day and after-school programs; and, employs 25 staff. Services are also offered for adults: family education and planning programs; pre- and post-natal classes sponsored by Health Canada. The Centre has also conducted a two-year pilot project in women's health, wellness and prevention. For its many innovations and high service-delivery ratings, the Centre has been honoured by many organizations, including a nomination by the Cdn Child Care Federation as one of the top ten child care centres in NS. **OTHER:** extensive community involvement, including organizing Girl Guides movement and being first District Commissioner for the area; BUF; NS Home for Coloured Children; BCC NS; Dartmouth YMCA; and many others. **HONS.:** several including, Hon. LLD, Dalhousie U., 2002; Order of Canada, 2002; Plaque,

for 20 yrs. of service of Spiritual Ministry to prison inmates, Corrections Canada; Plaque, Black Loyalists Assn.; Plaque, BCC; Plaque, BUF; Plaque, Metro United Way; Cert., Black Educators Assn.; two Cert., Congress of Black Women; BCC Wall of Fame; GG 125th Anniv. Medal; recognition dinner by Health Services. **REVIEWED IN:** *Black to Business*; *National Child Care Exchange*; *Business & Professional Women's Calendar*, 1986. **CONTACT:** epreston. daycare@ns.sympatico.ca; Fax: 902-462-5744

▶**ROSS, Sandi**
ACTOR/DIRECTOR/CULTURAL ACTIVIST, Toronto, ON. Born: USA/ in Canada since: 1978.
▶ Sandi Ross has been a professional actor since 1969, both in the US and in Canada. While making her living as an actor on stage, in film and TV, in 1986, she also became involved in arts organizations, their unions, and in the promotion of cultural diversity within the performing arts in Canada. **HIGHLIGHTS:** she is the founding Editor of *Into the Mainstream*, a talent directory for ACTRA and Equity members who are visible minorities, audible minorities or disabled performers. In 1994, she became the first woman and the first person from a visible minority group to be elected President of ACTRA, Toronto Branch (the largest in the country). She has served on arts juries for the Canada Council, the Ontario Arts Council, Toronto Arts Council, Laidlaw Performing Arts Committee, and others. As a performer, she has appeared on stage, radio, film, and TV; performed during three seasons at the Stratford Theatre Festival; and, appeared on most stages in Toronto. **SELECTED CREDITS:** *The Little Foxes; Much Ado About Nothing; Sweet Bird of Youth; The Vagina Monologues; Ain't Lookin'; Joe Turner's Come and Gone; The Crucible; Coming Through Slaughter; The Sea Horse;* and, *Tartuffe.* Film credits: *Adventures in Babysitting; Suspect; Guilty as Sin; Trial by Jury; Down in the Delta* (directed by Maya Angelou),

and, *Blues Brothers 2000*. TV credits: *Trailer Park Boys*; *Twice in a Lifetime*; *Blue Murder*; *The Natalie Cole Story*; *10,000 Black Men Named George*; *Ready or Not*; *Moonlight Becomes You*; and, *Forever Knight*. **COMMUNITY:** involved in a number of theatre companies and community organizations; founding member of Obsidian Theatre Co., she was also the Resource Development Officer. **HONS.:** New Pioneers Award, for work on *Into the Mainstream*, Skills for Change, 1993. **REVIEWED IN:** most local, nat'l publications: *Toronto Star*; *NOW*; *eye Weekly*; *WWCW*. **CONTACT:** ross4068@rogers.com; Fax: 416-535-3974

▶**ROSSI, Miriam F., MD, FRCPC, FAAP.**
STAFF PHYSICIAN, Division of Adolescent Medicine, Hospital for Sick Children (HSC), 555 University Ave., Toronto, ON M5G 1X8. Born: USA/ in Canada since: 1976.

▶ Dr. Miriam Rossi earned her first medical degree in the US, in 1970; when this degree was not fully recognized in Italy, where she was living in 1973, she repeated the medical program, in Italian, graduating in 1975. Currently, a Professor in the Dept. of Paediatrics, Faculty of Medicine, U of T, she specializes in the medical care of adolescents. **CAREER HIGHLIGHTS:** was Assistant then Associate Dean of Student Affairs, Faculty of Medicine, U of T, 1988-2001; joined U of T, 1981, as Assistant Professor (to 1995); Associate Professor, 1995-2001; has been with the Div. of Adolescent Medicine at HSC, since 1981. Since 1985, she has been on cross appointment with the Div. of Studies in Medical Education, Faculty of Medicine; since 1987, on cross appointment to Div. of Community Health (now Public Health Sciences), Faculty of Medicine. **BACKGROUND:** MFR began her career as a Therapeutic Dietician and Clinical Instructor, Boston, 1961-63; Public Health Nutritionist and Health Educator, New York City Dept. of Public Health, 1963-66. **RESEARCH ACTIVITIES:** Cdn street youth and an examination of HCV risk factors and behaviours;

dietary and health beliefs and practices in the Afro-Cdn community; STD surveillance in Cdn street youth; and, the learning environment in the medical school project. **COMMUNITY:** involvement has been extensive; has been particularly active as co-founder and Faculty Advisor to the Assn. for the Advancement of Blacks in Health Sciences (AABHS), since 1993. Designed initially to provide mentoring support to encourage Black students to enter the health sciences, AABHS then expanded to develop outreach through U of T, boards of education, and community agencies. It initiated the Summer Mentorship Program for high school students at U of T; has conducted educational programs at the Ontario Science Centre, and was co-founder (with the Sickle Cell Assn.) of Camp Jumoke, a unique camp for children with sickle cell anemia. **OTHER:** MFR has been on the Boards of the Donwood Institute and CAMH; currently serves on the Program Advisory Committee of SAPACCY. She has served on provincial councils and working groups dealing with health issues concerning children and youth. **HONS.:** include, ACAA, 2002; Vision Award, YMCA/Young Black Achievers Program, 1999; Harry Jerome Award, Excellence in the Professions, BBPA, 1997; Community Service Award, Ontario Psychological Foundation, 1991. **WORKS:** *J of Women's Health*; *CMAJ*; *American J of Clinical Nutrition*; *J Paediatrics*. **REVIEWED IN:** several, including, *U of T Alumni News,* 2001; local & community publications. **EDUCATION:** Fellow, RCPC, 1981; Fellow, American Academy of Pediatrics, 1981; Clinical & Research Fellowship, Paediatric Gastroenterology, HSC/U of T, 1979-81; MD, State U., Milan, Italy, 1975; MD, Mount Sinai School of Medicine, NY, 1970; Reg. Prof. Dietitian & MSc, Nutritional Sciences, U. of Iowa, 1961; BSc, Simmons College, Boston, 1958. **CONTACT:** miriam.rossi@utoronto.ca

▶**ROWE, Brenda F.**
EDUCATOR/COORDINATOR, Learning Centre,

John Abbott College, Dollard-des-Ormeaux, QC. Born: USA/ in Canada since: 1981.

▶ Brenda Rowe is a career educator who has worked with the public and private sectors, designing and delivering workshops in learning skills, life skills and human development for community organizations and businesses in both the US and Canada. **CAREER:** designed Career Focus job re-entry programs for women, to build confidence and job search skills, 1982-98; established BFR Human Development Consulting, providing counselling and workshops to companies, educational institutions, churches and community organizations, 1985; joined Faculty of Women Studies, Simone de Beauvoir Institute, Concordia U., 1994, and taught courses on Black Women's Culture, Intro to Women's Studies, and Feminist Research Methods; 1998, co-founder and VP, Excel Youth and Visible Minority Group, and was a key organizer of the 1999 Science Technology Fair; in 1999, served as Coordinator, Centre for Native Education, Concordia U. In 2000, BR became Coordinator of the Learning Centre at John Abbott College, where she is responsible for its administration and is involved with assessment and implementation of programs and strategies to assist students with learning disabilities, physical disabilities, and students in need of academic support. In this capacity, she has also been instrumental in establishing The Cultural Diversity Office at the College. **COMMUNITY INVOLVEMENT:** Black Community Council, Quebec; Black Community Resource Centre; West Island Black Community Assn.; Youth in Motion; N-D-G Black Community Centre; Jamaica Assn. of Montreal; Minority Apprenticeship Program; provincial and national committees for the Seventh-day Adventist Church. **HONS.:** include, Award, for services rendered, Excel Youth Science & Technology Conference, 1999; Outstanding Service Award, Westmount, SDA, 2000. **EDUCATION:** M.Ed, Iowa State U., 1977; BSc, Psychology & Sociology, Oakwood College, 1974. **HEROES/ROLE MODELS:**

Mother; Dean Ruth Green & Dean Rita Jones, former supervisors. **MOTTO:** Move on up a little higher. **CONTACT:** brendarowe@johnabbott.qc.ca; Fax: 514-457-6091

▶**ROWE, Ebonnie**
CEO, PhemPhat Productions/ **COMMUNITY ORGANIZER.** Toronto, ON. Born: Montreal, QC.
▶ Ebonnie Rowe can claim success for initiating and developing two programs which have had significant impact on the Black population, particularly in Toronto. She is the co-founder and former director of the highly successful mentoring program, Each One Teach One (EOTO); she is also the founder and CEO of PhemPhat Productions, an all-female production company for young women interested in urban music. **EOTO:** began in 1992 and was designed as a profession-based mentoring program, linking Black youth with Black professionals working in trades or professions which were of interest to the youth; the program was highly successful having a positive impact on hundreds of youth and garnering much praise and recognition from the media and the larger community. Since 2001, the EOTO program is operated through the community organization, Tropicana. **PHEMPHAT PRODUCTIONS:** began in 1995 to provide young women interested in developing their talent in urban music with the opportunity to do so in a supportive, constructive, and non-male-dominated environment. The company produced a series of events allowing young women to showcase their talents in urban music including Honey Jams, Women on Wax, seminars on the urban music sector (making, producing, promoting, and selling their products), and a poetry/spoken word event, Brown Girls in Da Ring. **HONS.:** include, Special Achievement Award, UMAC, 2000; Achievement Award, Onyx Lions Club, 1999; Volunteerism Award, Prov. Ontario, 1997; Phenomenal Woman Award, Xclusive Entertainment, 1997; Community Service Award, Ryerson African-

315

Cdn Org., 1996; Women on the Move Award, *Toronto Sun*, 1995. **EDUCATION:** U of T; Queen's College, Barbados. **HEROES/ROLE MODELS:** Mother; Beverly Mascoll. **MOTTO:** When all is said and done, more should be done than said. **CONTACT:** www.phemphat.com

▶ROWE, Owen De Vere
WWII VETERAN & CARIBBEAN DIPLOMAT (Ret.). Resides in Montreal, QC. Born: Barbados/ in Canada since: 1942.

▶ Owen Rowe came to Canada in 1942 to join the war effort and to "fight for victory." He served in the Canadian Army, 1942-44. When a strange set of circumstances prevented him from going overseas on three separate occasions, he joined the Air Force (RCAF), 1944-46, where he attained the commissioned rank of Flying Officer. After the war he briefly re-visited Barbados, then returned to reside permanently in Canada, where he built a professional career which included teaching, consular work, diplomacy and corrections. **HIGHLIGHTS:** first served as Assistant Commissioner and then as British Caribbean Student Liaison Officer, in the former West Indies Commission in Montreal, 1955-60; served as Eastern Caribbean Commissioner in Canada, 1961-66; then, with the independence of Barbados in 1966, he served as Counsellor, at the Barbados High Commission in Ottawa, 1967-70. He returned to Barbados for a year, serving as Chief of Protocol in the Min. of External Affairs in Barbados, before returning to Canada where he worked with the Federal Corrections Service as Chief of Case Management, then Head of Social Development at the Kingston Federal Prison for Women, 1972-87. **OTHER:** over the years he has advocated for greater recognition of the contributions by West Indians to the war effort in Canada. In 1982, he spearheaded the founding of the West Indian World War II Veterans Assn. of Montreal; he has written several newspaper articles and participated in radio and TV interviews to document the

Canada/Caribbean military connection in WWII. Largely through his efforts, as of November 11th, 2000, a wreath is now laid annually at the Cenotaph at the National War Memorial in Ottawa "in honour of the West Indian WWII Veterans"; he laid the wreath in 2000 and 2001, accompanied by the Hon. Senator Anne Cools. **COMMUNITY INVOLVEMENT:** St. Paul's Anglican Church; Heritage Committee, Union United Church; Black Theatre Workshop; Council of Black Aging; and, Toastmasters. **HONS.:** several including: Plaque, presented by Barbados House (Montreal) at banquet held in his honour, 2001; Plaque from Correctional Service of Canada, for "contribution to the social development of Inmates." **WORKS:** several articles and photographs in local publications. **REVIEWED IN:** several, including *BHM Calendar*, 1999. **EDUCATION:** Course in diplomacy, Geneva, 1968. MSW, 1955; BSW, 1951, McGill University. BA, SGWU (now Concordia U.), 1950. **MOTTO:** Life is what you make it! **CONTACT:** Fax: 514-738-5983

▶RUCK, The Hon. Calvin W., CM.
SOCIAL WORKER & SENATOR (Ret.), Senate of Canada, Ottawa, ON. Born: Sydney, NS.

▶ The Hon. Calvin Ruck was appointed to the Senate of Canada by Prime Minister Jean Chrétien and served from 1998-2000; he was also awarded the distinction of Member of the Order of Canada, 1994, for his many years of serving the community. **HIGHLIGHTS:** born in 1925 in Nova Scotia, he worked with the Dominion Steel and Coal Corp., 1942-45; then with the CNR as a sleeping car porter, 1945-58; was a Community Development Worker, 1968-81 with the NS Civil Service; was appointed a Commissioner of the Supreme Court of NS, 1971; was a Human Rights Officer with the NS Human Rights Commission, 1981-86; was a Community School Coordinator, 1986-90. CWR is best known though for his civil rights activities in NS: he was a member of the NS AACP and chaired the Employment Committee, which examined and sought to remedy the situation faced by Blacks when seeking employment in certain non-traditional sectors; the NS AACP held public meetings in the '50s and '60s to inform residents of their rights and methods to obtaining those rights; mounted campaigns against local Dartmouth businesses, including barber shops, which refused to provide service to Blacks; initiated a Stay in School Project for Black students. One of his most significant accomplishments was achieved through his research and publication of the story of the No. 2 Construction Battalion, *Canada's Black Battalion: 1916-1920: Canada's Best Kept Secret*, which brought attention to the experiences of Blacks in the military in WWI, the opposition they faced from the government, the discrimination they experienced from members of the military and their determination to serve their country, even though in a segregated unit. **COMMUNITY INVOLVEMENT:** has been extensive over the years, including, Preston and Area Lions Club; BCC NS; North Preston Medical Daycare Society; NS Assn. Social Workers; Advisory, Maritime School of Social Work, Dalhousie U. Now retired, CWR continues his research on military history. **HONS.:** several including: Hon. LLD, University of King's College, 1999; Member, Order of Canada, 1994; Hon. LLD, Dalhousie U., 1994; GG 125th Anniv. Medal, 1993; Plaque, BCC NS, 1993; Outstanding Individual, Cultural Life Awareness, 1993; Plaque, Federal Secretary of State, 1987; Harry Jerome Award, BBPA, 1987; Black Wall of Fame Society, 1981. **WORKS:** *Canada's Black Battalion: 1916-1920: Canada's Best Kept Secret,* 1987. **REVIEWED IN:** *Some Black Men*, 1999. **EDUCATION:** Human Rights Cert., U. of Ottawa, 1984; Dipl., Social Work, Maritime School of Social Work, Dalhousie U., 1979; several other courses in Public Relations, Sociology, Paralegal, Small Business Management. **HEROES/ ROLE MODELS:** Martin Luther King Jr. **CONTACT:** www.sen.parl.gc.ca/cruck

▶**RUCK, Douglas G.,** QC.
VICE-CHAIR, Canada Industrial Relations Board, 4th Fl.-240 Sparks St. W., Ottawa, ON K1A 0X8. Born: Halifax, NS.
▶ Douglas Ruck is a lawyer and former consultant in labour negotiations, mediation and dispute resolution. In June 2001, he was appointed to a five-year term as Vice-Chair of the Canada Industrial Relations Board (CIRB), whose role is to be an independent, representational, quasi-judicial tribunal responsible for the interpretation and administration of certain provisions (industrial relations, occupational safety and health) of the Canada Labour Code. **HIGHLIGHTS:** previously, DGR served a five-year term as the Ombudsperson for the province of Nova Scotia; he has expertise in the fields of labour, human rights, civil litigation and administrative law. While a managing partner for the private law practice of Ruck and Mitchell, he served on a number of boards and tribunals: Vice-Chair, the NS Labour Relations Brd.; Chair, the Labour Standards Tribunal; the Civil Service Employee Relations Brd.; Public Sector Compensation Brd.; Brd. of Inquiry, Human Rights Commission; Premier's Task Force on Employment Equity in the NS Legal Profession. He was instrumental in the creation and implementation of the Children's Ombudsman for the province of NS, and is a founding director of the Cdn Ombudsman Assn. **COMMUNITY INVOLVEMENT:** East Preston Day Care; BCC NS; Dartmouth Lakes Advisory Brd.; Rotary Club; Board, U. of King's College; Change Canada Foundation; Duke of Edinburgh Awards. **EDUCATION:** Mediation Training, Harvard Law School. Negotiation & Conflict Management Programme; LLB, 1977, Dalhousie University. Graduate studies, Poli. Sci., SFU; BA, U. of King's College, 1972. **HEROES/ROLE MODELS:** Parents; Frederick Douglass.

▶**RYAN, Theodore (Ted) P.,** CGA.

CERTIFIED ACCOUNTANT/PRESIDENT, ACCTAX Services, 1355 Kingston Rd., Pickering, ON L1V 6V4. Born: Trinidad & Tobago/ in Canada since: 1987.

▶ Ted Ryan is a Certified Accountant who established an accounting firm in 1993. With no capital and 600 clients at the time, his company has now grown to 3, 000 clients. **HONS.:** Recipient of Best Accounting Firm Award, Readers' Choice Award, *News Advertiser*, 2000. **EDUCATION:** CGA, Self-Study, Canada, 1993; ACCA ATII, College of Commerce, Leeds U., 1970. **MOTTO:** Success is always in direct proportion to effort. **CONTACT:** Tel: 905-837-0564; Fax: 905-837-5089

▶**SADLIER, Rosemary,** MSW.

AUTHOR/PRESIDENT, Ontario Black History Society, Ste. 202-10 Adelaide St. E., Toronto, ON M5C 1J3. Born: Toronto, ON.

▶ Rosemary Sadlier is the author of three books dealing with Black history in Canada. Since 1993, she is President of the Ontario Black History Society (OBHS), whose objectives are to preserve and promote the contributions of Blacks to Canadian history, and to promote the inclusion of such material in school curricula. Under her leadership, the OBHS was instrumental in: persuading Ottawa to declare Black History Month a national event in Canada, 1996; having August 1st declared Emancipation Day by the cities of Toronto and Ottawa; having Dec. 26th officially recognized as the beginning of Kwanzaa by Toronto; developing the bus tour, Discover Black History in Toronto, which is included in the *Guide's Guide to the UGRR*; securing political and public support for the creation of a Museum of African Canadian History. A frequent speaker and panelist, she has appeared on radio, TV, at schools, conferences, and community events. In 1994, she hosted six episodes of *Blacks in Ontario* on Rogers TV; was the executive producer for five Public Service Announcements, *Black History Bytes*, shown on many TV stations (incl. YTV and CBC); and, was featured as a *Local Hero* on Global TV, 1992. **OTHER:** RS has worked in education, social work, and with the Women's Bureau (Office of the Ont. Deputy Minister); was a member of the Ont. Min. of Education Advisory Panel examining the new curriculum. **COMMUNITY:** is involved with a number of organizations; volunteers with developmentally delayed adults, emotionally disturbed children, and new Canadians; Brd., Obsidian Theatre. **HONS.:** include, Black History Makers Award, United Achievers of Brampton, 2001; William P. Hubbard Race Relations Award, City of Toronto, 2000; Salute to the City Award, Toronto Eaton Centre, 1997; Hon. Colonel, Kentucky, US; Women for PACE award; Black Links Award; 10 yr. Volunteer Service Award, Ont. Min. Citizenship & Culture, 1994. **WORKS:** including, *Tubman, Harriet Tubman and the Underground Railroad*, 1996; *Mary Ann Shadd*: *Publisher, Editor, Teacher, Lawyer, Suffragette*, 1995; *Leading the Way: Black Women in Canada*, 1994. **REVIEWED IN:** *Toronto Star*; *Share*; *Pride*; *WWCW*. **EDUCATION:** MSW; B.Ed, U of T. BA/Hons., York U. **CONTACT:** jeejeec@aol.com; www.blackhistorysociety.ca

▶**SADU, Itah**
AUTHOR/STORYTELLER, A Different Booklist, 746 Bathurst St., Toronto, ON M5S 2R6. Born: Toronto, ON.
▶ Itah Sadu is a master storyteller and best-selling author of children's books; in the oral tradition of the Caribbean, Africa, and N. America, she tells stories which incorporate history, tradition, and strong visual images to which children can relate. She frequently speaks in schools, at workshops and presents at many international festivals and conferences. She has appeared on radio, TV, and stage. She is the co-owner of A Different Booklist, an Afrocentric bookstore in Toronto, which also carries a wide selection of academic and children's books. **WORKS:** several including: *Christopher, Please Clean Up your Room*; *Name Calling*; *How the Coconut got its Face*; *Christopher Changes his Name*. **EDUCATION:** Poli. Sci., York U. **HEROES/ROLE MODELS:** Edna Walcott, grandmother. **MOTTO:** If you can help someone along the way, then your living shall not be in vain. **CONTACT:** adibook@idirect.com; Tel: 416-538-0889

▶**SALMON, Beverley,** Dr.
PUBLIC HEALTH NURSE/MUNICIPAL COUNCILLOR (Ret.), Metropolitan Toronto. Born: Toronto, ON.
▶ Dr. Beverley Salmon trained as a nurse and practised as a Public Health Nurse in Toronto and Detroit for several years. During this time she became aware of the needs of those from various ethno-cultural backgrounds; she was a founding member of the Toronto Urban Alliance on Race Relations and was a supporter of the National Black Coalition of Canada. In 1979, she became the first Black female Commissioner on the Ontario Human Rights Commission, serving until 1985. In 1985, she was elected as a Councillor for the City of North York; from 1988-97, was re-elected as Councillor for Metropolitan Toronto, and served on several committees and advisory boards. **COMMUNITY INVOLVEMENT:** Black Heritage Education Program; Black Liaison Committee; United Way; North York Symphony; OBHS; National Action Committee for the Status of Women. **HONS.:** several including: Hon. LLD, Ryerson U., 1999; Harry Jerome Award, 1998; Award of Excellence, Cdn Centre for Police Race Relations, 1996; Onyx Lions Award, 1995; Canada Day Achievement Award, 1992; Outstanding Achievement, Assn. Black Women. **REVIEWED IN:** local & community publications; *Some Black Women*, 1993. **EDUCATION:** Cert., Dispute Resolution, Faculty Law, U. of Windsor; Public Health, U of T; Wellesley Hospital School of Nursing. **CONTACT:** bevsalm@hotmail.com; Fax: 416-447-6666

▶**SALMON, John Douglas,** MD, FRCSC.
CHIEF OF GENERAL SURGERY (Ret.), Scarborough Centenary Hospital, ON. Born: Toronto, ON.
▶ Dr. J. Douglas Salmon completed his degree in Medicine, at U of T, in 1955 (was also class president). After interning at the Toronto Western Hospital, he completed his general surgical residency, 1956-60, at Detroit Receiving, Providence, and Children's Hospitals. Afterwards, despite being offered an established practice in Detroit, he chose to return to Toronto. In 1967, he joined the General Surgical staff at Centenary Hospital; he later became President of the Medical Staff, then Chief of General Surgery, for

seven years. He retired from active practice in 1997. In addition to his medical studies and subsequent medical practice, he was very active in the community; in the 1940s he was a member of an *ad hoc* group opposing discriminatory practices at the Palais Royale dance hall which showcased Black performers (like Duke Ellington, Count Basie, Cab Calloway) but would not allow local Blacks to attend as patrons. **HONS.:** include, Cdn Black Achievement Award, Medicine, *Pride*, 1986-94. **EDUCATION:** FRCSC; FACS. MD, 1955; BSc, Physiology & Biochemistry, 1951, U of T. Piano, RCM. **HEROES/ ROLE MODELS:** Dr. Paul McGoey, former Chief of Surgery at Centenary Hospital. **MOTTO:** Always do your best! **CONTACT:** Fax: 416-447-6666

▶**SALMON, Warren**

CEO, Black Board International/First Fridays, Box 114, 123 Queen St. W., Toronto, ON M5H 3M9. Born: Toronto, ON.

▶ Warren Salmon is the founder of Black Board International (1990), Canada's first Black on-line service and Afrocentric software development company. In 1994, he became the owner and founder of First Fridays (a networking event for Black professionals), the first of its kind in Canada. First Fridays is held across N. America on the first Friday of each month, providing an opportunity for African-Canadian entrepreneurs, professionals, organizations, artists and individuals to network and share information. He recently started a new company, focused on developing and providing a wireless service to the mainstream marketplace. **COMMUNITY INVOLVEMENT:** Brd., The Brothers' Keepers Network (TBKN), established in October 2001, to foster the development of at-risk youth and community-based businesses; former Brd. member, Caribbean and African Chamber of Commerce. **HONS.:** Business Award, Men of Excellence, 1996. **REVIEWED IN:** *Silicon Valley North*; *Essence*; *Toronto Sun*; *Toronto Star.* **EDUCATION:** B.Technology, Computer Science, Ryerson U., 1985; Bus. & Tech., UBC & York U. **HEROES/ROLE MODELS:** Beverley & J. Douglas Salmon, parents. **MOTTO:** If at first you don't succeed, try, try, again. **CONTACT:** Tel: 416-441-0792; www.ashaware.com; www.firstfridays.ca

▶**SAM, Francis B.,** MD, FRCSC, FACOG.

OBSTETRICIAN/GYNECOLOGIST, Private Practice, Ste. 305-360 College St., Toronto, ON M5T 1S6. Born: Ghana/ in Canada since: 1964.

▶ Dr. Francis Sam is a medical practitioner specializing in Obstetrics and Gynecology, with a particular interest in infertility. After completing his medical training in Alberta, 1968, he returned to Ghana and was a Medical Officer of Health with the Ghanaian Army, 1968-72, then returned to Canada and completed his residency in Obstetrics and Gynecology in Alberta. Following his Surgical Research Fellowship, 1976, he moved to Toronto where he has been practising. **COMMUNITY INVOLVEMENT:** Etobicoke Liberal Party, since 1978; Ghanaian Business & Professional Assn. of Canada, since 1992; Urban Alliance on Race Relations, since 1992; Advisory Council on Multiculturalism and Citizenship of Ontario, 1988-93; Advisory Committee on Health and Culture, 1989-93; BBPA. **AFFIL/MBRSHP:** American Laparoscopists; American Fertility Society; Ghanaian Medical and Dental Club; Society of Obstetrics and Gynecologist of Canada. **HONS.:** Award of Excellence, Ghanaian-Cdn Assn., 2001. **EDUCATION:** Dipl., Pelviscopic Surgery, 1991; FACOG, 1980. FRCSC, 1976; Surgical Research Fellow, 1976; MD, 1967; BSc, 1966, U. of Alberta. **CONTACT:** Tel: 416-967-0761; Fax: 416-967-0882

▶**SAMUELS-STEWART, Victorine (Viki)**

COORDINATOR, Race Relations/Affirmative Action, NS Human Rights Commission, Box 2221, 1690 Hollis St., 6th Fl Halifax, NS B3J 3C4. Born: Sudbury, ON.

▶ Viki Samuels-Stewart was raised in Sudbury, where her father worked in the mines; she returned to her family's home province of NS after completing her studies as a social worker, at Ryerson Polytechnic. Since 1994, she has been in her present position as Coordinator of Race Relations and Affirmative Action with the NS Human Rights Commission. **CAREER HIGHLIGHTS:** counsellor at Bryony House, 1978, the first shelter for battered women, east of Montreal; Parole Officer with the John Howard Society; Executive Director of a half-way house for male adult offenders, St. Leonard's Society; in 1986, she joined the government as one of the first Employment Equity Officers in Nova Scotia, hired to work on the Black Employment Program and introduced a successful summer employment program; from 1992-94, she worked in the private sector as the first Equity Manager, Atlantic Region, for the Bank of Nova Scotia. In her current position, she promotes positive relations between people from different cultures and ethnic backgrounds; she also addresses issues of systemic discrimination. **COMMUNITY ACTIVITIES:** President and member of the NS Mass Choir which has travelled throughout Canada and the US singing gospel music and winning many awards. **HONS.:** GG 125th Anniv. Medal, 1993. **REVIEWED IN:** *Black Focus* magazine, 1990. **EDUCATION:** Mediator, U. of Windsor, 1998; Social Worker, Ryerson Polytechnic, 1975. **HEROES/ROLE MODELS:** Mother; Mayann Francis, ED, NS HRC. **CONTACT:** samuelvj@gov.ns.ca; Fax: 902-424-0596

SANDIFORD, Keith A.P., PhD.
PROFESSOR EMERITUS, History Dept., University of Manitoba. Born: Barbados/ in Canada since: 1960.

▶ Professor Keith Sandiford taught history at the University of Manitoba from 1966-1998. He is one of the pioneers of the historical sociology of sports and has published extensively in this field. He is considered one of the leading cricket sociologists and statisticians in the world and has written extensively on this as well as other topics ranging from Victorian politics and diplomacy, to Barbadian culture and education. Within the university, he served two terms as Chair of the Graduate Studies Program/History; chaired the Teaching Advisory Cmtee, 1986-93; and, was appointed the first Chair of the President's Advisory Council on Human Rights, 1991. **COMMUNITY:** has served as President of the Nat'l Council of Barbadian Assn. in Canada; executive council of the Nat'l Council of Black Educators; Cdn Ethnocultural Council; the Cdn Labour Force Development Brd., and others. **HONS.:** several including, Community Service Award, Caribbean Millennium Cmtee, 2001; Lifetime Achievement Award, MB Black History Month Cmtee, 2000; Meritorious Service Plaque, Afro-Carib. Assn., 1993; Merit Award, for excellent teaching and for outstanding service, U. of Manitoba, 1991 & '92; Plaque, for contribution to the sport as one of its leading historians, Barbados Cricket Assn. **WORKS:** selected: *At the Crease with Gary Sobers,* 2001; *Cassius: From Wharf Boy to Role Model,* 2001; *Cricket Nurseries of Colonial Barbados,* 1998; *Cricket and the Victorians,* 1994. Articles on cricket in: *Albion; British J Sports History; Can J History; Historical Reflections; J Sport History; Int'l J History of Sport; Our Voice.* Non-cricket articles in: *Bulletin of Eastern Caribbean Affairs; J Caribbean Studies;* contributed to *Victorian Britain: An Encyclopedia,* 1989. **EDUCATION:** PhD, 1966; MA, 1961, U of T. BA, UWI/London, 1960. **CONTACT:** sandifo@ms.umanitoba.ca

▶SANDOVAL, Dolores, PhD.
PROFESSOR EMERITA, University of Vermont. Resides in Montreal, QC. Born: Montreal, QC.

▶ Dr. Dolores Sandoval taught at the University of Vermont from 1971-99 in the areas of Education, Race and Culture, Africa, Middle East and Latin American Studies. In 1972, she was appointed Assistant to the President for Human

Resources (the university's first affirmative action officer). Later, her responsibilities expanded to being part of the staff of the VP for Academic Affairs, as much of the work involved faculty hiring, retention and promotion, and admissions requirements for undergraduate and graduate students. In 1997, she was appointed Director of the campus-wide University Race and Culture Course program; 1992-97, was the co-Chair, Middle East Studies Program. Now retired, she continues her career as a consultant to academic institutions and government on multicultural programming and diversity issues. **AFFIL/MBRSHP:** was extensive including, chaired Faculty Senate; Public Access Channel 17; Brd., Rhode Island School of Design; National Advisory Cmtee, Conference for Black Administrators at Predominantly White Universities; presented at, and moderated, many national and international conferences and panels. Elected President, 2002-04, St. James Literary Society, Mtl; Cdn Authors Assn., Mtl Chapter. **OTHER:** ran in 1988 and was elected in 1990 as the Democratic candidate for the US House of Representatives. As President of the Vermont/Honduras Partners of the Americas, undertook fundraising for emergency relief to the Honduras following Hurricane Mitch; represented Partners of the Americas at the International Landmine Treaty Conference, Ottawa, 1997; Liaison Officer for Sierra Leone Minister at the International Conference for Foreign Ministers on War Affected Children, Winnipeg, 2000. **HONS.:** include, 2002 Convocation Speaker, Plymouth State College, New Hampshire. Fellowships: Netherlands & Belgium, 1995; Costa Rica, 1993; Jordan, Israel, Palestine, 1992; Tunisia, 1989; Award, for speeches at Duke Ellington Concert series, CUNY & Black American Heritage Fdn.; Lifetime Award, President's Fellow, Rhode Island School of Design. **WORKS:** Author/ Illustrator, *Be Patient Abdul*, 1996; numerous presentations & papers, articles/essays in: *Black Issues in Higher Education*; guest editorial byline, *Rutland VT Herald*. **EDUCATION:** Post-gradu-

ate study, Institute for Ed. Mngmt., Harvard University. PhD, Curriculum & Fine Arts; MS, Elementary Education, Indiana University. Studies at Art Institute Chicago; BA, Interior Design & S. Asian Studies, U. of Michigan, 1960. **MOTTO:** It takes only one to… **CONTACT:** dssandoval@ earthlink.net

▶**SANGSTER, Peggy Ann**

COORDINATOR, Quality & Risk Management, Montreal Children's Hospital, 2300, rue Tupper, Montreal, QC H3H 1P3. Born: Jamaica/ in Canada since: 1966.

▶ Peggy Ann Sangster is the Coordinator of Quality, Risk and Utilization Management at the Montreal Children's Hospital (MUHC), since 1999. Prior to that she held the following positions: Director of Nursing Staff Development at the Montreal General Hospital, 1984-99; since 1980, she has held a joint appointment with the School of Nursing, McGill U., as a Faculty Lecturer; she was Clinical Instructor at the Montreal General Hospital, 1979-82; and a Staff Nurse at the Ongwanada Hospital in Kingston, ON, 1972-74. Her nursing career began in Jamaica when she was Operating Room Nurse, in charge of Anaesthesia. **AFFIL/MBRSHP:** Chair, Isobel MacLeod Conference Planning Committee, 1982-99; *L'Ordre des infirmiers et infirmières du Québec*; Brd., St. James United Church; Centre for Literacy, Dawson College; *Centre des Femmes de Montréal*. **HONS.:** Marion Lindeburgh Scholarship, McGill U., 1976. **EDUCATION:** MSc, Nursing, 1979; BN, 1977, McGill University. Post-Graduate Dipl., Operating Room Techniques, Montreal Hospital, 1970; Nursing, UWI, 1965. **MOTTO:** I can do all things through Christ who strengthens me. **CONTACT:** peggy.sangster @muhc.mcgill.ca

▶**SARSFIELD, Mairuth Hodge, CQ.**
WRITER, Parksville, BC. Born: Montreal, QC.

▶ Mairuth Sarsfield, is a writer, former diplomat, published author, TV host and community activist. Born and raised in Montreal, she completed her post-secondary education in Canada, New York, and Ghana. In apprenticing for her professional career, she wrote for TV, film and magazines. **CAREER HIGHLIGHTS:** she became a research writer for *The New Generation* with CBC TV, 1962-66, and was involved with Expo '67 as coordinator of The People Tree Exhibit. Following that success, she was sent to develop a theme for the Canadian Pavilion at Expo '70 in Osaka, Japan (1967-70), for which the Canadian team won an award. She was the co-host of *Hour Glass* with CBC TV, 1970-71. She then joined the Dept. of External Affairs in Ottawa, as an Information Officer, 1971-80; then served as a Sr. Information Officer with UNEP, in Nairobi, Washington and New York, 1980-84. Returning to Canada she became Director of Development Communicators Inc., 1985-2001, as well as co-hosting the *Senior's Report,* 1992-93, and *Literati* on PBS TV, 2001. **AFFIL/MBRSHP:** has been extensive, including Board of Governors, CBC Radio, 1984-89; Board of Governors, Carleton U., 1997-99; organization of Harambee Black Orpheus fundraising galas, Ottawa, 1989 and 1991; past-President of MATCH International. **COMMUNITY:** spearheaded development of the Carrie Best Collection for Equatoria of culturally sensitive books and book lists for racial enlightenment; actively participated in Literacy in the Prisons. **HONS.:** include, ACAA, for Community Service, 2000; Literary Award (first recipient), National Congress of Black Women Fdn., 1997; *Chevalier de l'ordre national du Québec*, 1985; Mairuth Sarsfield Day, Oct. 22nd each year in Cleveland, Ohio; Int'l Arbor Day Award, Nebraska, 1982. **WORKS:** first published novel, *No Crystal Stair*, 1997, is now part of the curriculum at Brock and Carleton universities, and at the University College of Cork, Ireland (10,000 copies have been reprinted to date). **REVIEWED IN:** nat'l & int'l publications; *WWIC; Millennium Minds*, 2000; *Some Black Women,* 1993. **EDUCATION:** MA, U. of Ghana; Post-Grad Journalism, Columbia U., NY; BA, SGWU (now Concordia U.). **CONTACT:** Fax: 250-248-8073

▶**SAUL, Ras. Leon**
PUBLISHER/EDITOR/WRITER/PRODUCER/ PERFORMING ARTIST, *Uprising International,* 17-238 Galloway Blvd., Scarborough, ON M1E 5H2. Born: Guyana/ in Canada since: 1986.
▶ Ras Leon Saul is the publisher and editor-in-chief of *Uprising International*, a monthly cultural entertainment newspaper; he is also Artistic Director of the Caricom Cdn Cultural Centre. He is described as "an accomplished playwright, producer, performing artist and musician." His artistic career began in Guyana in the early '80s when he was commissioned by the government to write a radio serial, which became *For Better…For Worse* and its sequel, *Beyond the Dream*; since then he has also written *Berbice Uprising* and *Repatriation*. His career as a journalist also began in Guyana, where he was Information Officer in the Min. of Information, and a senior reporter at the *Chronicle* newspapers. In Canada, he was assistant editor at *Contrast*, then editor of *Equality* and *Rainbow* newspapers. As an actor, he has many film and TV credits: *Three Men and a Baby*; *Cocktail*; CBC's *The Twins*; and the 1988 Coca-Cola Olympic commercial. He is also a writer and performer of dub poetry. And, he is the producer of reggae dancehall recording artist, Donna Makeda (*see: Makeda, Donna*), on the Uprising Int'l music label. **HONS.:** include, Peter Tosh Memorial Award, Cdn Reggae Music Awards, 1999; *Ujaama* Award, Afri-Can Food-Basket, 1998; Bob Marley Memorial Day Award, 1993. **WORKS:** in community newspapers such as *Uprising International*; *Share*; *Contrast*; *Caribbean Camera.* **EDUCATION:** Dipl., Film & TV, Trebas Institute, Toronto, 1997; Dipl., Public Communications, U. of Guyana, 1977. **CONTACT:** Tel: 416-287-9484; makongo@idirect. com

▶SCARLETT, Vivine
DANCER/CHOREOGRAPHER/INSTRUCTOR, Dance Immersion, Toronto, ON. Born: UK/ in Canada since: 1962.

▶ In 1994, Vivine Scarlett founded Dance Immersion and is its Program Director and Curator. The company promotes dancers and dances of the African Diaspora. And, from 1996-2001, she was the Community Development Coordinator, Dance Umbrella of Ontario; completed an apprenticeship with CAN: BAIA, 1995-96; completed an apprenticeship with DanceWorks, 1994-95. She is also an independent choreographer, instructor of adult and children's African dance programs, and is the producer and artistic director for *Danceology*, a video of African-Cdn Artists in Ontario. **HONS.:** Dora Mavor Moore Award, Choreography, for *The Adventures of a Black Girl in Search of God*, 2002. **EDUCATION:** Humber College, 1980; dance studies in Guinea with *Les Ballets Africains*; add'l dance studies in Toronto & New York. **HEROES/ROLE MODELS:** Safiyatou Tsekani, friend. **CONTACT:** info@danceimmersion.ca; Tel: 416-203-0666

▶SCOTT, Gilbert H., OD(JM).
PERMANENT SECRETARY, Ministry of National Security, Government of Jamaica. Born: Jamaica/ in Canada since: 1968.

▶ Gilbert Scott retired from the Government of Canada in 1997 after a career in the public service sector. He then joined the Government of Jamaica, first as a Senior Advisor to the Cabinet Office and Office of the Services Commissions, 1997-2001. His responsibilities included advising on policy formulation, government decision-making processes, and human resource management policies. In November, 2001, he was appointed to his present position as Permanent Secretary for the Min. of National Security. **CAREER HIGHLIGHTS:** Consultant/Executive Director, Canadian Secretariat, UNWCAR, responsible for Canada's preparations for the UN Conference, S. Africa (May 2000 to September 2001); Regional Executive Director, Dept. of Cdn Heritage, Ont. Region, 1994-97; Commission, Public Service Commission of Canada, was one of three Commissioners responsible for implementing legislation governing employment in the Federal Public service, 1988-94; Director-General, Multiculturalism, Dept. Secretary of State, 1985-88; from 1975-85 occupied other positions with the Dept. Secretary of State. **OTHER:** worked as a meteorologist, 1960-68 with the Meteorological Service of Jamaica, then from 1968-75 with Environment Canada; 1994, member of six-person Cdn team to advise the African National Congress (ANC) on public service policies and structure, in preparation for governance; Waterloo Advisory Council, 1989-95. **COMMUNITY:** United Way; Black History Ottawa Cmtee; CODE; Real Opportunity for Prisoner Employment; National Council of Jamaicans. **HONS.:** include, Officer, Order of Distinction, Govt. of Jamaica, 1989. **EDUCATION:** Programs at CCMD, 1993, 1991; Carleton U.; Dipl. Computer Programming, Analysis & Design, Algonquin College, 1971. **CONTACT:** gill.scott@mnsj.gov.jm; Fax: 876-962-5105

▶SEALY, Joe
JAZZ PIANIST/COMPOSER, Blue Jade Productions, 43 Summerhill Gardens, Toronto, ON M4T 1B3. Born: Montreal, QC.

▶ Joe Sealy is one of Canada's leading award-winning jazz musicians; he is an internationally renowned pianist, composer and music director. He has performed with a wide variety of artists ranging from Sammy Davis Jr., to jazz legends, Joe Williams and Milt Jackson, to Blood, Sweat & Tears. He has performed throughout Canada, the US, and Europe, and is best known for his Juno Award-winning recording, *Africville Suite*, an original composition paying tribute to the historical Black community in Nova Scotia. His other recordings include: *Blue Jade*; *Dual Vision*; *Double Entendre*; *Live at Errol's*; and, *Clear Vision*. He has also scored numerous works for film, TV, and radio. He recently wrote and recorded a new theme for TVO's book program, *Imprint*. His music direction credits include: *The Evolution of Jazz*; *Arts Against Apartheid*; and, *Ain't Misbehavin'*, for which he won a Dora Mavor Moore Award. He has also appeared in a number of TV shows and films including: *Brown Bread Sandwiches,* and *I'll Take Manhattan*. As a stage actor he was featured in *Ma Rainey's Black Bottom,* and, *Lady Day at Emerson's Bar and Grill.* JS is the president of his own recording label, Seajam Recordings, and collaborates with his long-time musical partner, bassist Paul Novotny. He has performed in concert as a soloist, with a quartet, and with the Nathaniel Dett Chorale. His most recent endeavour is the musical revue, *The Nearness of You.* **HONS.:** many including, four Juno nominations and a Juno Award for *Africville Suite*; Dora Mavor Moore Award for musical direction of *Ain't Misbehavin'*; Gemini nomination for film score of the documentary, *The Road Taken*; Socan Award, for Best Original Jazz Composition; *Jazz Report* Award, for Composer of the Year; Cdn Black Achievement Award, for entertainment. **REVIEWED IN:** local, nat'l and int'l publications; *Some Black Men*, 1999. **EDUCATION:** SGWU (now Concordia U.); Berklee College of Music; studied contemporary classical music at Dalhousie U.; studied technique with Darwin Aitkin, course in Music in Media, York U. **CONTACT:** blue.jade@sympatico.ca

►SEARLES, Edsworth McAuley, QC.

LAWYER (Ret.), Toronto, ON. Born: Toronto, ON.
▶ Edsworth M. Searles has the distinction of being the first Black person called to the bar and admitted to practice as a solicitor in BC; this occurred in 1957. **HIGHLIGHTS:** born in Toronto, he spent his early years and had his pre-university education in Barbados. He worked in Curaçao, at

CPIM Oil Refinery for two years. Returning to Canada he worked as a sleeping car porter with the CNR. He resigned in 1950, then worked as a postal clerk, during which time he also attended U of T and obtained his LLB degree. He articled in BC where he was called to the Bar. He worked as a solicitor with the Dept. of Veteran Affairs; 1959, he was called to the Ontario Bar and admitted as a solicitor. In 1961, he opened a private practice which he operated until his retirement in 1991. In 1971, he was appointed Queen's Counsel; and in 1984, he was appointed to the Toronto Police Complaints Commission. **COMMUNITY ACTIVITIES:** founding member and first President, Delos Davis Law Guild; Harry Jerome Awards Committee; executive member, Home Services Assn.; Universal Negro Improvement Assn.; Toronto United Negro Improvement Assn.; Toronto Negro Credit Union; founding and executive member, Negro Citizenship Cmtee; Progressive Conservative Assn.; member and general counsel, British Methodist Episcopal Church. **OTHER:** he provided free legal services to many Black community organizations; and, in the 1950s, along with his wife, opened their home twice weekly to receive foreign students studying at the university and women from the Caribbean who worked as domestics, to facilitate their integration into Canadian life. **HONS.:** several including: ACAA, 1997; Award of Excellence, Barbados Planning & Coordinating Committee, 1996; Honoured by Delos Davis Law Guild; and received awards from the British Methodist Episcopal Church. **REVIEWED IN:** *Toronto Star*; *Pride*; *Excellence* magazine. **EDUCATION:** LLB; BA, U of T. **CONTACT:** c/o sylvia.searles@sympatico.ca

►SEARLES, Sylvia E.

PRESIDENT, Searles Success Systems, Toronto, ON. Born: Toronto, ON.
▶ Sylvia Searles operates her own health and nutrition business and is a founding director and independent distributor with the Symmetry Corp.

In 2000, her business grossed in excess of $1.5-million in retail sales. She turned to private enterprise after a successful and varied career in public service. **CAREER HIGHLIGHTS:** worked with the City of Toronto and the Municipality of Toronto over a 16-yr. period; held senior positions in Human Resource Management, Corporate Training and Development, Equity, and Race Relations; developed internationally recognized management training programs, including the Kingswood Program; and, under the direction of Dr. Zanana Akande (*see: Akande, Zanana*) (then Parliamentary Asst. to then-premier, Bob Rae), created and implemented the jobsOntario Youth Program. She established Access Metro, the public service centre for the amalgamated city government, which used multilingual staff and technology to enable the public to obtain information on access to municipal services; also developed and implemented multicultural programming for teachers and students through TVO, the Min. of Education, and various school boards; was the Associate Producer of the NFB's history of Blacks in Canada, *Fields of Endless Day*; also helped to develop race and ethnic relations policies for several school boards. She was appointed by the provincial government to develop race relations training programs for Ontario's 116 police services; was the first Executive Director of the North York Committee on Community Race and Ethnic Relations (the first such in Canada). **AFFIL/MBRSHP:** founding director Scarborough Community Legal Services; Brd., Urban Alliance on Race Relations; Brd., BBPA; Friends of Scarb.; Brd., Centenary Health Centre; former Vice-Chair, Rouge Valley Health Systems; Chair, Advisory Board, FLOW 93.5FM. **HONS.:** several including, Race Relations Award, Scarborough. **REVIEWED IN:** *Chatelaine*; *Toronto Star*; *Share*. **CONTACT:** sylvia.searles@sympatico.ca

▶**SEARLES, Sylvia Kathleen (Kathy)**
COMMUNITY VOLUNTEER (Ret.), Toronto, ON.

Born: Barbados/ in Canada since: 1947.
▶ Sylvia Kathleen Searles arrived in Canada in 1947 from Barbados and over the following decades served the Black community through a wide range of organizations and activities. These included: Toronto United Negro Assn.; Toronto Negro Credit Union; UNIA; Home Service Assn.; founded the Cdn Ebonite Assn., 1966, to provide social, cultural and educational programs for Black youth, and, in 1968, held the first Black Cotillion Ball in Toronto; founding member of Caribana, 1967-68; active member of the British Methodist Episcopal Church since 1948; founding member, St. Michael's Alumni Assn.; active in the Black Heritage Assn., which provided an educational upgrading program for Black youth in Scarbourough. As a result of the success of this program, the Scarborough School Board hired Black teachers selected by SKS to tutor students in an after-school program in eight schools, involving over 200 children; she also sponsored parent education meetings to help parents better understand the school system; and, operated Saturday morning educational and cultural programs for Black youth in Toronto, Scarborough, and North York. **OTHER:** in the 1950s, SKS and her husband opened their home twice a week to women from the Caribbean who worked as domestics in Toronto and to foreign students studying at local universities, to facilitate their integration into Canadian life. In addition to her community activities, SKS also served on the Selection Committee of the Transitional Year Program at U of T. **HONS.:** several, including: Award of Excellence, Barbados Planning & Coordinating Committee, 1996; profiled in the North York Brd. of Education poster series on Black Achievers, 1993; GG 125th Anniv. Medal, 1992; scholarship established in her name by the Barbados St. Michael Alumni in Toronto, for a deserving Black university student, 1988; received 2nd Kay Livingstone Award, Congress of Black Women, 1988; Volunteer Service Award, Province of Ontario, 1986; several from

BME Church. **REVIEWED IN:** *Black Women in Canada*; *Some Black Women*; *Chatelaine* & *Excellence* magazines. **CONTACT:** c/o sylvia.searles @sympatico.ca

▶SEARS, Djanet

WRITER/DIRECTOR/ACTOR, c/o WCA Film & TV, 94 Harbord St., Toronto, ON M5S 1G4.

▶ Djanet Sears is an award-winning playwright, director, and actor. She is best known for the plays she has written and is a recipient of the 1998 GG Literary Award. Her plays include: *Afrika Solo*, 1989 (a one-woman show in which she initially performed; staged in Toronto, Montreal, Ottawa and aired on CBC Radio); *Harlem Duet*, 1997 (produced in both Toronto and Halifax; she also directed the first two Toronto productions, which won four Dora Mavor Moore Awards, and is now being adapted for the screen). Her most recent work, *The Adventures of a Black Girl in Search of God*, launched the 2002 inaugural season for the Obsidian Theatre Co. and played to critical acclaim. Other directing credits: *The Wonder of Man*; *dark diaspora...in dub*; *Princess Pocahontas*; and, *A Streetcar Named Desire*. **FILM AND TV CREDITS:** selected: Clement Virgo's *One Heart Broken Into Song* (written by George Elliott Clarke); *Love Songs*; *Call for Help*; *In His Father's Shoes*; *Escape Clause*; *Personals*; *Childsaver*; Canadian feature films, *Milk and Honey*; *April 01*, and over 25 other works. **ACTIVITIES:** is the driving force behind the AfriCanadian Playwrights' Festival, a celebration & examination of African diasporic writing for the stage in Canada, at the du Maurier World Stage, since 1997; founding member of the Obsidian Theatre Co., a repertory theatre company created to explore works by and about Africans on the continent and in the diaspora. She was the Barker Fairly Visiting Professor, University College, U of T, 1999-2000; Visiting Lecturer in the University College Drama Program, U of T, where she teaches playwriting,

since 2000; Playwright-in-Residence, Factory Theatre, 2001-02; Playwright-in-Residence, Can-Stage, 1999-2000; Int'l Playwright-in-Residence, Joseph Papp Public Theater (NYC), 1995-96; Playwright-in-Residence, Nightwood Theatre, 1994-95. **HONS.:** include, Reel Black Award, Outstanding Achievement in Film & TV, Best Supporting Actress for *One Heart Broken Into Song*, 1999-2000; GG Literary Award, for *Harlem Duet*, 1998; Chalmers Award, Outstanding New Cdn Play, *Harlem Duet*, 1998; Harry Jerome Award, Excellence in the Cultural Industries, 1998; Dora Mavor Moore Awards, Outstanding New Play & Outstanding Direction, *Harlem Duet*, 1997; Phenomenal Woman of the Arts Award, 1997; Nominee, Gemini Award, for guest appearance in *Side Effects*, 1996; Gold Prize, Int'l Major Armstrong Awards, *Afrika Solo*, 1992. **WORKS:** *Harlem Duet*, 1997 and in, *Adaptations of Shakespeare*, 2000, and in Modern Canadian Plays, 2001; *Afrika Solo*, 1990. Non-fiction & essays: "Can I get a Witness?" in *Testifyin': Contemporary African Cdn Drama*, 2000; "Naming Names: Black Women Playwrights in Canada," in *Women on the Cdn Stage*, 1991. **EDUCATION:** Cdn Film Centre; Cert. Film, New York U.; BFA, York U. **CONTACT:** Literary: 416-944-0475; Others: 416-928-0299

▶SEIVERIGHT, Archbishop Dr. Deloris Devan

ARCHBISHOP, Shouters National Evangelical Spiritual Baptist Faith, 447 Birchmount Rd., Toronto, ON M1K 1N6. Born: Jamaica/ in Canada since: 1969.

▶ Archbishop Dr. Deloris Seiveright is the founder, president and Archbishop of Shouters National Evangelical Spiritual Baptist Faith (NESBF)/Canada and overseer, since 1988, for the Archdiocese, which comprises five churches. She became Archbishop in 1996, and is co-founder of St. Frederic's Cathedral. **ACTIVITIES:** introduced a youth mentorship program and a special project for older persons, in 1999; operates a summer career placement for youth; launched a scholarship fund in 2000. As an Evangelist, she speaks at seminars, conferences, and workshops about Spiritual Baptists. She also serves on many community organizations. **HONS.:** Service Award, NESBF/Trinidad & Tobago, 2001; Racial Harmony, City of Toronto, 2000; ACAA, 1999; Hon. Doctorate, St. Andrew Theology, UK, 1997. **WORKS:** authored a hymnal, *Hymnal & Trumpets*, 2001; book of devotions, *Thoughts and Prayers from the Heart*, 2001; CD, *Rhythm for the Soul.* **EDUCATION:** BA, Relig. Education, Tyndale College, 1993; degrees in Theology, London & Caribbean Academy, 1981; Business Admin., Ryerson Polytechnic, 1972. **CONTACT:** nesbf@shouterbaptist.org; www.spiritualbaptist. ca

▶**SEIVRIGHT, Lloyd, O.Ont.**
GRAND MASTER, Independent United Order of Solomon/Canada, 2040 Weston Rd., Weston, ON M9N 1X4. Born: Jamaica/ in Canada since: 1969.

▶ Lloyd Seivright's charitable work and community involvement spans over 40 yrs. He is the founder and President of the Independent United Order of Solomon/ Canada, and coordinator of charitable gifts through Pride of Toronto, an Ontario charity created in 1978. **HIGHLIGHTS:** organized millions of dollars worth of wheelchairs, medical supplies and equipment, computers and educational material for distribution to individuals, hospitals and other institutions in Canada, the Caribbean and other parts of the world. Through his efforts, three medical scholarships were established in 1989, 1992 and 1999 for Caribbean third year medical students attending UWI, who are in need of financial assistance to complete their studies. To date there have been 22 recipients of these scholarships; in 1998, he established a scholarship in Computer Sciences, at U of T. Since 1978, LS organizes an annual Christmas Treat for needy families, through the food bank and the churches; those in need receive dinner, a food basket, gifts of clothing and toys for each child. He has devoted most of his nonworking hours to charitable work and is known to be a major promoter of volunteerism, and firmly believes in the motto, "Out of many, one people." **HONS.:** several including: Order of Ontario, for charitable works, 1997; Voluntary Award, Easter Seal Society, 1989; his works have also been recognized and acknowledged by the Mayor of Toronto, Toronto City Council, various governments from the Caribbean (including Jamaica, Grenada, Trinidad). **REVIEWED IN:** *Toronto Sun*; *Share*; *Jamaica Gleaner.*

▶**SEWELL, J. George, MD.**
OPTOMETRIST, Private Practice, Ste. 215-1333 Neilson Rd., Scarborough, ON M1B 4Y9. Born: Jamaica/ in Canada since: 1974.

▶ Dr. George Sewell is an optometrist whose practice, according to OHIP (1994), is among the ten largest in Ontario. He is also an Adjunct Clinical Professor at the University of Waterloo and was the first Black optometrist to practise in Nova Scotia (1984-90). And, committed to giving back, he is the Ophthalmic Director at the Princess Margaret Eye Clinic in Jamaica. **WORKS:** has written for journals and contributed monthly articles on eye care; for the NS Assn. of Optometrists; *Black Pages.* **REVIEWED IN:** *Jamaica Gleaner*; *Share.* **EDUCATION:** Dipl. Ocular Therapeutics, North Eastern State U., Oklahoma, 1994. MD, Optometry; BSc, OD; BSc, 1984, U. of Waterloo. **HEROES/ROLE MODELS:** Dr. Renn Holness, friend. **MOTTO:** Nothing is hard; just your head. It's all learnable! **CONTACT:** g_sewell@sympatico.ca

▶**SHAQQ, Hameed**
STEEL PAN MUSICIAN/COMPOSER, Toronto, ON. Born: Trinidad & Tobago/ in Canada since: 1978.

▶ Hameed Shaqq is also known as "The Pan Piper,"

a steel pan musician and composer who plays jazz, blues, classical, calypso and religious music. While he works primarily as a solo performer, he also performs with a group known as the Pan Piper Ensemble, which incorporates string, wind and percussion instruments. **HIGHLIGHTS:** 1972-75, he toured Europe, performing at the Zurich World Fair and Spain's Music Festival. Since settling in Toronto, he performs regularly at the Beaches Jazz Festival, Harbourfront Centre and other local venues. He has released a CD, *Planet Pan*, and an audio cassette, *Life on the Line*. He has performed on radio and TV including: TVO, Citytv, CBC Radio, and CHRY. And, in an effort to introduce the pan as a musical interest, he has been teaching steel pan music and composition in primary and secondary schools in Toronto and Etobicoke Boards of Education. **CONTACT:** hameed_shaqq@hotmail.com; www.thepanpiper.com

▶SHAW, Sherene

COUNCILLOR, Toronto City Council, 100 Queen St. W., Toronto, ON M5H 2N2. Born: Guyana/ in Canada since: 1970.

▶ Councillor Sherene Shaw has been elected to municipal office since 1988, first in the municipality of Scarborough and, since 1997, represents the riding of Scarborough-Agincourt in the amalgamated Toronto City Council. She has a special interest and expertise in community development and economic development initiatives, and plays an active role in international alliances and municipal city partnerships. She is Toronto's first appointed Diversity Advocate, whose role is to promote the principles of harmony and equality in the city; she has served on committees for business development; recreation, parks and culture; race relations; Ryerson School of Nursing; and, Scarborough Grace Hospital. She is Vice-President of the International Union of Local Authorities (IULA) and President of the N. American section. **OTHER:** developed and admin-

istered policies for the Ont. Min. of Citizenship and Culture and the Office of Disabled Persons; local CBC TV broadcaster and researcher; teaches at the School of Business at Centennial College, and is a panelist on the weekly talk show, *Megacity Free-for-all* on CFRB radio. Her volunteer work has included Girl Guides of Canada, Local Lions Club, and, the Rotary Club. **HONS.:** include, Gold Medal, for her work in the area of Diversity, Human Rights & Race Relations Centre, 2002; REH'MA Foundation Award, for outstanding public service and dedication to the community, 2002; Alumni of Distinction, Centennial College School of Business, 2000. **REVIEWED IN:** *Some Black Women*, 1993. **EDUCATION:** completing graduate degree, U. of Waterloo. Cert., Teacher of Adults; Dipl., Business Admin., Centennial College. BA, U of T. **CONTACT:** councillor_shaw@city.toronto.on.ca; Fax: 416-392-7431

▶SHERWOOD, Anthony

FILMMAKER/PRODUCER, Anthony Sherwood Productions, 122 Muirland Cres., Brampton, ON L6X 4G2. Born: Halifax, NS.

▶ Anthony Sherwood is a fifth-generation Canadian, born in Halifax and raised in Montreal. He is an actor, writer, producer, and director who has been in the entertainment business for over 25 yrs. He is one of Canada's most successful actors having performed in more than 30 feature films including: *Guilty As Sin*; *Closer and Closer*; *Eddie And The Cruisers, II*; *Switching Channels*; *Deadbolt*; *The Guardian*; and, *Physical Evidence*. He has worked with such actors as Henry Fonda, Burt Reynolds, Sidney Poitier, and Lou Gossett Jr. He has written and directed original musical productions for the stage: *Ain't Got No Money*; *Once Upon A Stage*; *Razz M' Jazz*; and, *But I Was Cool*. He has recently written a new musical play with Cdn music legends Oscar Peterson and Oliver Jones entitled, *Rockin' in Paradise*. **FILM:** he has created and produced a number of documentaries. The most recent is *Honour Before Glory*, which aired on CBC TV in November, 2001 and is based on Canada's first and only all-Black military unit, the 2nd Construction Battalion. *Music–A Family Tradition*, CBC, won a Gemini Award in 1997; he created, developed, and co-wrote a half-hour dramatic series for the CBC entitled, *Playin' 4 Keeps.* In 1998, he wrote, produced and directed a series of heritage minutes for Black History Month called, *Paths of Glory*; these vignettes were aired in February 1998 on CBC, YTV, and TVO. In the US, he is remembered as "Jason Locke" from the popular American TV series, *Airwolf II.* **TV:** For six successful seasons, he portrayed the character of Dillon Beck on CBC's award-winning television drama, *Street Legal* and received a Gemini nomination for his performance. He has also guest-starred in more than 40 TV shows including: *Night Heat*; *Outer Limits*; *Earth: Final Conflict*; *PSI Factor*; *Black Harbour*; *Due South.* For five years, he hosted and narrated the TV series, *Forbidden Places,* on the Discovery Channel, which was nominated for best documentary series on Canadian TV two years running. **AFFIL/ MBRSHP:** has served on the Boards of ACTRA, OBHS, and the Academy of Cdn Cinema and Television; has been an advisor for the YTV Achievement Awards. **HONS.:** ACAA, Arts, 2002; Gemini Award, for *Music–A Family Tradition*, 1997; Dr. Martin Luther King Jr., Lifetime Achievement Award; 25th Anniv. Award, Urban Alliance on Race Relations; Arts Acclaim Award, Brampton. **CONTACT:** asherwood49@aol.com

▶**SIMON, Kenneth**
DEAN, School of Social and Community Services/ **ASSOCIATE PRINCIPAL,** Humber College of Applied Arts & Technology, 205 Humber College Blvd., Mississauga, ON. Born: Trinidad & Tobago/ in Canada since: 1968.
▶ Ken Simon is both Dean of the School of Social and Community Services and Associate Princi-

pal of the Lakeshore Campus of Humber College. **CAREER:** he began teaching at Humber College in 1977, then moved into management; he later became Program Coordinator for the business programs; after being responsible for these School of Business programs for several years, he was appointed to the Chair of the School of Manufacturing, Technology, and Design, in 1998. In this capacity, he participated in a program which took computers to the island of St. Vincent, and which included installation and training of faculty members and students. He has also traveled to Cuba to explore business opportunities for Canadians and in Jamaica, he has provided training particularly in the hotel industry. **COMMUNITY:** Hawks; Mississauga Caribbean Assn.; National Council of Trinidad & Tobago. **HONS.:** Kellog Fellowship, attended League for Innovation (leadership training) with 16 other Black community college administrators from the US. **EDUCATION:** pursuing Ed.D, Education in Community Colleges; M.Ed, U of T, 1987; BA, Economics, York U., 1977. **HEROES/ROLE MODELS:** Father; Dr. Roy Giroux, colleague. **MOTTO:** Recognize opportunities and always strive to capitalize on them. The results will be quite satisfying. **CONTACT:** simon @admin.humberc.on.ca; Fax: 416-252-2371

▶**SIMPSON, Denis**
SINGER/ACTOR/PERFORMER, Vancouver, BC. Born: Jamaica/ in Canada since: 1958.
▶ Denis Simpson is a multi-talented, award-winning actor, singer, writer, songwriter, dancer, and TV host, with a career spanning 35 yrs. **HIGHLIGHTS:** appeared in the original Canadian productions of *Hair*; *A Chorus Line*; *Little Shop of Horrors*; *Five Guys Named Moe*; *The Colored Museum*; *Ain't Misbehavin'* (won Dora Mavor Moore Award), *Indigo!* Other theatre credits include: Broadway productions of *DUDE*; *Jesus Christ Superstar*; *Angels in America* (1 & 2); *Two to Tango*; *Godspell*; *A Funny Thing Happened on the Way to the Forum*; *Spring Thaw*; *Lend me a*

Tenor; and, his one-man show, *Denis Anyone?* (now being adapted for radio by the CBC and which, along with *Five Guys Named Moe,* and *Blowin' on Bowen,* earned him a Jessie Award, for his body of work). He is the creator and director of *Wang Dang Doodle,* which will be included in the 2002-03 season of the Grand Theatre in London, Ontario. Sept. 2002, new Live Eye guy on citytv's Vancouver *Breakfast Show.* **OTHER:** He has appeared in many TV productions as an actor, singer, host: *All for One* (nominated for an ACTRA); hosted six seasons of TVO's *Polka Dot Door.* He has also written songs including *It's Christmas and I Miss You,* and several children's songs. He is a founding member of the *a cappella* singing group, The Nylons (1979). **COMMUNITY:** engages in a lot of charity work for AIDS organizations in his newly adopted home of Vancouver. **HONS.:** include, BC Entertainment Hall of Fame; Star on the BC Walk of Fame; Dora Mavor Moore Award, for best performance by an actor in a musical, *Ain't Misbehavin';* Jessie Award, for his body of work, for *Denis Anyone?* (along with *Five Guys Named Moe* and *Blowin' on Bowen);* nominee, ACTRA Award for TV Variety, *All For One.* **MOTTO:** May there always be love, forgiveness, and music. **CONTACT:** dbelize98@hotmail.com

SINTIM-ABOAGYE, Kofi

PRESIDENT, Premex Courier, 5651 Ferrier St., Montreal, QC H4P 1N1. Born: Ghana/ in Canada since: 1980.

▶ Kofi Sintim began his courier company in 1991 and now has offices in Montreal, Ottawa, and Toronto; the company also ships worldwide. Concluding that a master's degree in economics might not enable him to pursue his dream of being an entrepreneur, he left his studies to find a business opportunity responding to his interests. Premex Courier has succeeded because of its prompt service and because it has found and capitalized on a few niche markets. One such innovation is MedicRush, which specializes in delivering prescription drugs from wholesalers to over 1,500 pharmacy outlets in the Quebec-Ontario area. **COMMUNITY:** in 1994, KS held his first community charity drive, raising funds for a local charity or institution; in 1995, the beneficiary was the Montreal Children's Hospital; the drive is now held annually. **HONS.:** Jackie Robinson Award, Business Person of the Year, MABBP, 2001. **EDUCATION:** BA/Economics, Concordia U., 1982. **HEROES/ROLE MODELS:** Parents. **MOTTO:** The quality of a man's life is in direct proportion to his commitment to excellence, regardless of his chosen field of endeavour. (Vince Lombardi) **CONTACT:** kofi.sintim@premex.com; www.premexcourier.com

▶SLOLY, Peter

POLICE INSPECTOR, Toronto Police Services, 31 Division, 40 Norfinch Dr., Toronto, ON M3N 1X1. Born: Jamaica/ in Canada since: 1976.

▶ Inspector Peter Sloly joined the Toronto Police Services (TPS) in 1988 and has already been promoted to the rank of Inspector (2001). He is one of the youngest senior police officers in Canada and has been particularly active in promoting equity and diversity within the TPS with the development and implementation of a Policing and Diversity course. In August 2001, he participated in the UN Peacekeeping mission to Kosovo for a period of nine months. **OTHER:** is a former member of the Canadian National Soccer Team; participated in over 30 international competitions; played in the 1985 World Youth Cup in the former USSR; played professionally with the Toronto Blizzard and the North York Rockets. **AFFIL/MBRSHP:** member, ABLE and has introduced recruiting, mentorship and professional development programs for youth, women, and minorities. **REVIEWED IN:** *Share*; *Pride.* **EDUCATION:** MBA, York U., 2000; Ont. Police College, 1991; BA, McMaster U., 1989. **MOTTO:** "Family values, education and work ethic are the foundation upon which I have built highly successful careers as a

professional athlete and as a police officer."
CONTACT: cephas_777@hotmail.com

▶SMITH, Craig

AUTHOR/HISTORIAN/CONSTABLE, Royal Canadian Mounted Police (RCMP), Yarmouth, NS. Born: Halifax, NS.

▶ Constable Craig Smith has been a member of the RCMP since 1996, but is best known for his activities on behalf of youth and Black history, prior to joining the police force. In 1992, while working as Director of the YMCA, he was on the Diversity Committee, which created the YMCA's first policy on Race Relations, Multiculturalism, and Affirmative Actions. In 1993, he and his wife produced a poster featuring 28 outstanding Black Nova Scotians; in 1996, he produced another poster, *African Canadians of Achievement* highlighting eight African Canadian "firsts"; and, while working as a Library Youth Worker, he created programs which raised awareness on Black achievements and key historical figures; in addition he created a program which brought together black male youth and members of the Halifax Police Dept., to discuss issues of common concern. In 2000, he produced an educational resource for students: *Journey: African Canadian History* and the study guide for teachers. **COMMUNITY INVOLVEMENT:** Concerned Citizens Against Drugs; Police Multicultural Liaison; Black History Month Assn.; Inner-City Education Advisory Committee; HRDC Black Community Work group. **HONS.:** many including: Cert. of Appreciation, Black Educators Assn. of NS, 2001; inducted into the W.P. Oliver Wall of Honour, BCC/NS, 1999; Cert. of Appreciation, RCMP H-Div. Commanding Officer, 1998; Cert. of Appreciation, Cdn Centre for Police Race Relations, 1993. **WORKS:** including, *Journey: African Canadian History*, study guide & instructional guide, 2000; *African Canadians of Achievement*, poster, 1996; *Black Firsts*, poster, 1993. **REVIEWED IN:** *Halifax Daily News*; *Halifax Chronicle Herald*. **EDUCATION:** Cert., Community Development, Henson College, Halifax, 1994. **HEROES/ROLE MODELS:** Father; Terry B. Symonds. **CONTACT:** cra458@hotmail.com; Fax: 902-742-4590

▶SMITH, Ifeyironwa F., PhD.

NUTRITIONIST & DIETICIAN, Nosi Smith Food & Nutrition Consultants, 51 Hackett St., Ottawa, ON K1V 0P6. Born: Nigeria/ in Canada since: 1997.

▶ Dr. Ifeyironwa Smith is an author, teacher, researcher and expert in foods and nutrition. She is a former Senior Lecturer in Foods and Nutrition in the Faculty of Health Sciences, Obafemi Awolowo University in Nigeria. She was also during this time, Consultant and Head of the Dietetic Unit of this University's teaching hospitals. Over the course of her career, she has concentrated on: finding solutions to problems of hunger and malnutrition, particularly for children; the rational utilization of locally available food resources for the proper nutrition of all groups in the community, to ensure food security in families and communities; defining the nutritional status and requirements of school-age children in Nigeria. She was also involved in the formulation of Nigeria's Food and Nutrition Policy, in 1989. Since 1990, she has focused on food security issues and has advocated for the integration of women as effective food producers, processors and distributors within the food and agriculture sector in the West African sub-region. Currently, she works as a food and nutrition consultant, and is also a Scientific Advisor in Foods and Nutrition to the International Foundation for Science (IFS). In this capacity she has provided consultancy services to CIDA, IDRC, UNESCO, the UN Development Fund for Women (UNIFEM), the West African Women's Assn., CARE Canada, the Cdn Assn. of Parliamentarians on Population and Development, and the Micronutrient Initiative. **HONS.:** Fellowship for post-doctoral work, Royal Society of England, 1985. **WORKS:** several including: *Foods of West Africa: Their Origin & Use*, 1998; *Nutrition & Diet Therapy for Health Care Professionals in Africa*, 1995. Articles in: *Food & Nutrition Bulletin*; *Nigerian J Nutritional Science*; *Eur. J Clinical Nutrition*; *Nutrition in Clinical Practice*; *Nutrition Research*; several conference papers & consultancy reports; co-authored monograph, "Towards more effective programs & policies for improving human nutrition," Food Policy Research Institute, 1982. **EDUCATION:** PhD, Nutrition, Cornell U., NY, 1979; MSc, Nutrition, U. of Guelph, 1975; BSc, Nutrition & Dietetics, U. of Nigeria, 1966. **HEROES/ROLE MODELS:** Jean Augustine, MP. **CONTACT:** Tel/Fax: 613-247-0578; nosismith@rogers.com

▶**SMITH, Olanrewaju B., PhD, DVM, DVTM.**

SENIOR PROGRAMME SPECIALIST, International Development Research Centre (IDRC), 250 Albert St., Ottawa, ON K1G 3H9. Born: Nigeria/in Canada since: 1996.

▶ Dr. Olanrewaju Smith is a livestock production and health specialist with nearly two decades of field-based research experience. He has worked in various capacities as a veterinary practitioner, a researcher, a professor and a research manager. His responsibilities at IDRC are in the development, management and evaluation of research projects in the areas of natural resources management, biological diversity, participatory research, development approaches, and capacity building. He has been with the IDRC since 1989, was previously the Regional Representative for the West and Central Africa Regional Office, and is now based at HQ in Ottawa. **ACTIVITIES:** he has participated in formulating the following programs to assist the IDRC in identifying opportunities for future programming: Sustainable Agricultural Production in High Potential Ecosystems; Community Management of Fragile Ecosystems; Food

Security and Environmental Sustainability; Desertification and Land Regeneration; Urban Agriculture; and Sustainable Utilization of Biodiversity. He managed a number of projects related to these programs, and others dealing with agro-forestry, integrated crop-livestock systems, biodiversity and research methodologies in several countries including: Mali, Senegal, Ghana, Gambia, Sierra Leone, Burkina Faso, Cameroon, and Kenya. **CAREER:** 1979-89, became Professor of Animal Production and Health at Abafemi Awolowo University in Nigeria. During that time, he served at different periods as Head of two of the University's units, Radiobiology Div., Centre for Energy Research and Development, and, the Dept. of Animal Science of the Faculty of Agriculture. At the beginning of his career, 1971-73, OBS was a Veterinary Research Officer with the National Veterinary Research Institute in Nigeria. **AFFIL/MBRSHP:** FAO Regional Task Force, for the manufacture and utilization of molasses urea blocks; Brd., and Sr. Scientific Advisor International Foundation for Science; Millennium Ecosystem Assessment and the West Africa Rural Foundation; Int'l Trypanosomiasis Centre. **HONS.:** including, Int'l Atomic Energy Agency Fellowship, 1985; Commonwealth Scholar, 1973-78. **WORKS:** in, *Animal Reproduction Science*; *Tropical Agriculture*; *J Animal Physiology & Animal Nutrition*; *Animal Feed Science & Technology*. **EDUCATION:** PhD, Animal & Poultry Science, 1978; MSc, Animal & Poultry Science, 1975, U. of Guelph. DVTM (Doctor, Tropical Vet. Med.) & Dipl., Parasitology, Institute, Tropical Medicine, Belgium, 1971; DVM, U. of Liege, Belgium, 1970. **CONTACT:** osmith@idrc.ca; Fax: 613-567-7749

▶**SMITH, Robert (Mark)**

SOFTBALL COACH/DIRECTOR OF SPORT DEVELOPMENT, Sport Nova Scotia; **PROVINCIAL COORDINATOR,** 3M Fair & Safe Play Program, 5516 Spring Garden Rd., Box 864, Halifax, NS B3J 2V2. Born: Halifax, NS.

Mark Smith enjoyed a softball career which lasted nearly 25 yrs. and which allowed him to become one of the most successful softball players in Canada and the world. **HIGHLIGHTS:** four Pan American Games Gold Medals (1979, '83, '91, and '99); three World Championships (1992, '96 and 2001); Canadian Championship; and 17 provincial championships. He spent 15 yrs. as a member of Canada's Senior Men's National Team, and was named an ISC All-World Selection five times. Coaching: he retired as an athlete in 1998 and turned his focus to coaching; he was the Sr. Men's Assistant Coach in 1998; since 2001, he is the Sr. Men's Head Coach of the National Team; he was also the Head Coach of Canada's Junior Men's National Team program, which attended the Junior World Championships in Sydney, Australia in 2001. **CURRENTLY:** serves as a member of Softball Canada's National Coaching Committee; sits on Softball Nova Scotia's Board of Directors and is chairman of their Canada Games Technical Committee. He also makes presentations and delivers workshops on a variety of topics including, Sport Builds Character, Leadership is Coaching, among others. **OTHER:** he is a supervisor with the NS Dept. of Justice, working with Young Offenders at the NS Youth Centre in Waterville. For the past 18 months MS has been on secondment from the Youth Centre to serve as the Provincial Coordinator for the 3M Fair & Safe Play program. **HONS.:** include, Inductee, Softball Canada Hall of Fame, 1999; named one of Nova Scotia's Top 10 Male Athletes of the Century. **REVIEWED IN:** local, regional, nat'l publications, sports features; *Journey: African Canadian History*, 2000. **HEROES/ROLE MODELS:** Terry Baytor, former Men's National Team Head Coach. **MOTTO:** Good things happen to good people! **CONTACT:** rmarksmith@ns.sympatico.ca; Fax: 902-585-1702

▶**SMITH, Rohan**

FINANCIAL ADVISOR, Laurentian Financial Services, Ste. 130-100 Cawdray Crt., Scarborough, ON M1S 5C8. Born: Jamaica, 1964/ in Canada since: 1978.

▶ Rohan Smith is a Financial Advisor with Laurentian Financial Services and a former athlete who competed four times in the World Deaf Games (WDG). At Gallaudet University in Washington, the only university in the world for the deaf, he pursued his passion for Track & Field, competing in the 100m and the 200m sprints. He was captain of the university's track team for three years; was ranked among the top ten for the 100m in regional division; broke numerous records during competition. In 1997, after the WDG in Denmark, RS retired from Track & Field competition; he still coaches and was an Assistant Coach in track for the WDG in Italy, 2001. **COMMUNITY:** involved in many activities; President of the Ontario Deaf Sports Assn. **HONS.:** many including: Silver Medal, 100m, WDG, LA, 1985; set Cdn & Gallaudet U. 100m record, 1987; Silver Medal, 100m, WDG, NZ, 1989; Most Valuable Athlete twice, at Gallaudet U.; Sportsmanship Award & Most Improved Athlete Award from his North York Track Club; many awards & recognition from the City of Brampton. **WORKS:** in, *Deaf Canada Today.* **REVIEWED IN:** most local and nat'l newspapers; also appeared on major radio & TV stations. **EDUCATION:** pursuing CFP; BSc Accounting, Gallaudet U., Washington, 1991. **MOTTO:** My deafness will not prevent me from pursuing my dreams. In fact, it pushes me to strive harder. **CONTACT:** rohan.smith@sympatico.ca; Fax: 416-297-6015

▶**SMITH, Shirley,** MSW, CSW.

SERVICE MANAGER, Centre for Addiction & Mental Health (CAMH), 175 College St., Toronto, ON M5T 1P7. Born: Jamaica/ in Canada since: 1971.

▶ Shirley Smith is a career social worker with extensive experience and training from Canada and the US in the field of Addiction and Mental Health. Since 1998, she has served as the Service Manager for the Metro Addiction Assessment Referral Service (MAARS), a program of CAMH, Toronto's sole community-based assessment and referral service for the Min. of Health and Long Term Care. She is responsible for program planning, development, administration and evaluation, training and supervision of clinical staff and students. **CAREER HIGHLIGHTS:** 2002, member of a four-member team, designed and taught the first certificate course in Concurrent Disorders: Working with Special Populations, York U., School of Social Work; 1996-98, Director, Specialty Programs (Women, Youth, Family and Evening Health Out-patient Programs), at the Donwood Institute (Canada's only public hospital for alcohol and drug addiction), responsible for the development of programs and services for women, family and youth in the Health Recovery Program; 1993-94, Manager, Women and Family Programs, Donwood Institute, designed and implemented model programs for women and children with alcohol and other drug addictions; 1994, designed and taught the first Social Work and Addiction course at York U. From 1990-92, she was a Senior Counsellor at the Alcoholism and Fellowship Center of Greater New York, responsible for managing and directing the Regular Population Prevention Unit, she also worked with the NY State Div. of Parole and Probation and other public and private social service agencies, to design and implement Relapse Prevention and Recovery Training Programs; 1989-90, Social Work Supervisor, Project Enable, The City University, NY, developed and managed the Personal Social Services Unit model project for homeless and formerly homeless students attending the university; 1974-80, member of a four-member team to design and implement the Professional Fee Billing Dept. at the Memorial Sloan Kettering Cancer Center, in NYC. Clinic Coordinator, Hospital for Sick Children, coordinated and administered activities for 14 outpatient clinics. **AFFIL/MBRSHP:** representative, Toronto Region Addiction Services Implementation Cmtee; Brd., Street Haven Services for Women; Brd., JVS (formerly Jewish Vocational Services); Social Work Council, CAMH (plus, Diversity Steering Cmtee, HR Cmtee); YMCA, Youth Substance Abuse Program Advisory Cmtee, 1995-97; Brd., Cdn Centre on Minority Affairs; National Assn. of Black Social Workers (NABSW); National Assn. Social Workers (NASW); Ont. College of Social Workers and Social Service Workers. **HONS.:** include, Alumni of the Year Award, most Distinguished Social Work student, York U., 2000; Award, for contribution to the development of SAPACCY, Ont. Min. of Health, Community Health Div., 1997. **WORKS:** in *CAMH Newsletter*, 2000. **REVIEWED IN:** *Toronto Star*, 1994. **EDUCATION:** Forensic Law & Mental Health, Centennial College, 2001; MSc, Clinical Occupational Social Work, Columbia U., New York, 1989. BSW, 1983; BA, Social Science, 1982, York University. Cert., Social Services Admin., Ryerson Polytechnic, 1978. **HEROES/ROLE MODELS:** Linda Joseph-Messiah; Larry Johanson; Oliver Martin. **MOTTO:** *Tentanda via*: The way must be tried. **CONTACT:** shirley_smith@camh.net; Fax: 416-535-8501

▶**SMITH, Winsome E., DDS.**
DENTIST, Specializing in Children/Youth, Private Practice, 852 Bathurst St., Toronto, ON M5R 3G1. Born: Jamaica/ in Canada since: 1964.
▶ Dr. Winsome Smith is a dentist who specializes in Pediatric Dentistry; since completing her studies in 1972, she has been in private practice; she operates two offices of dentistry for children and youth, in Toronto and Etobicoke. She also has her qualifications in Orthodontics and has completed part of her fellowship for the Royal College of Dental Surgeons. Her community involvement spans 25 yrs., with a strong emphasis on youth; she has mentored and assisted with remedial academic skills and has served with many organiza-

tions. **AFFIL/MBRSHP:** Royal College of Dental Surgeons; Ontario Society of Pediatric Dentists; Marcus Garvey Homes for emotionally disturbed youth; West Indian Christian Fellowship Int'l (WICFI); BBPA; Board of Governors, Humber College; Sky Dome Corp.; currently, Chair of Governance, Ontario Council of Regents. **OTHER:** she is also a qualified musician, having obtained her LRSM (London, England); she plays the piano and organ for her church, and accompanies soloists and choirs in the city. **HONS.:** several including, Hon. Dipl. (1996) and a Scholarship Fund named in her honour (2001), Humber College; 10-yr. Volunteer Service Award, 1995, Ont. Min. of Citizenship & Culture. **EDUCATION:** Dipl. Pedodontics, U of T, 1972. DDS, 1970; BSc, 1966, Dalhousie U. **MOTTO:** Aim high: she who aims at the stars falls higher than she who aims at the trees. **CONTACT:** Tel: 416-534-2316; Fax: 416-534-6665

▶ SOLOMON, Adam

MUSICIAN, Adam Solomon & Tikisa, Toronto, ON. Born: Kenya/ in Canada since: 1992.

▶ Adam Solomon, a.k.a. "The Professor," is a well-known musician who incorporates a number of African sounds and rhythms into his musical style. He sings in six languages, plays bass and rhythm guitar, and plays the keyboard. He formed his world beat band, Tikisa, in 1995 and their first CD, *Safari,* was released in 1996 to popular acclaim and led to a cross-country tour; their second CD, *Tabia,* was released in 2001. Performance highlights include Folk and Jazz Festivals in Montreal, the Atlantic, Vancouver, Guelph, and Winnipeg. In 1992, he was a co-founder of the pan-African Afro-Nubians band; he collaborated on two CD releases *Tour to Africa,* 1994, and *The Great Africans,* 1995. Coming from a musical family in Kenya, he began playing early and performed with many of Kenya's most popular bands. Now, in addition to performing, he is also developing a reputation as a teacher of music

and is a valuable contributor to programs on African Heritage education. **HONS.:** Best Release, for *Safari,* Toronto African Music Awards, 1996. **CONTACT:** prof_tikisa@hotmail.com; Fax: 416-483-5484

▶ SOLOMON, Damian

ASSISTANT DIRECTOR, Professional & Development Services, Canadian Teachers' Federation, 2490 Don Reid Dr., Ottawa, ON K1H 1E1. Born: Trinidad & Tobago/ in Canada since: 1959.

▶ Damian Solomon is the Assistant Director, Professional and Development Services with the Canadian Teachers' Federation (CTF). Since joining the CTF, 1987, he has held a number of positions: Acting Director, 2000-early 2002; Assistant Director, 1991-2000; Assistant Director, International Programs, 1987-1991. Prior to joining the CTF, he was a specialist in French and Spanish studies and was the French as a Second Language Coordinator, Huron County Board of Education, 1982-85; member of the Ontario Secondary School Teachers' Federation (OSSTF) Provincial Professional Development Committee, 1982-87, and was Chairperson, 1986-87. **OTHER:** organized, since 1996, what is now the Mathieu Da Costa Challenge; this program invites elementary and secondary students to explore the contributions of Aboriginals and other people of diverse ethnocultural backgrounds, to the building of Canada. In 1992, he compiled a collection of essays on *Racism and Education,* for a CTF conference. **AFFIL/MBRSHP:** Coalition for the Advancement of Aboriginal Studies; represented CTF at the UNWCAR, in S. Africa, 2001; Brd., OBHS; N. American Assn. for Environmental Education; Canadian Network for Environmental Education and Communication. **HONS.:** Provincial Professional Development Award, OSSTF, 1982. **WORKS:** compiled, *Racism and Education: Different Perspectives and Experiences*, CTF, 1992. **EDUCATION:** BA/Hon., Modern Languages, U of T, 1963. **CONTACT:** dsolo@ctf-fce.ca; www.ctf-fce.ca

▶SOSA, Thomas (Tom) G.

EXECUTIVE DIRECTOR, Sosa & Associates, Ste. 500-160 Eglinton Ave. E., Toronto, ON M4P 3B5. Born: Trinidad & Tobago/ in Canada since: 1958.

▶ Tom Sosa is a former Vice-President of Ryerson Polytechnic Institute (now Ryerson University), 1977-89, and Ontario Deputy Minister in the Ministries of Energy, and Skills Development, 1989-93, and was one of the first Blacks to hold such a senior position. **HIGHLIGHTS:** 1989-93: led Ontario's provincial government team in its negotiations with the federal government, and coordinated the strategy which resulted in a joint $1.6-billion three-year training agreement with a federal funding increase of 83%; directed and promoted a program with school boards to reduce the number of unskilled entry level employees in Ontario's workforce. Following his time in government, from 1993-98, he was VP, Student Services, Community Relations and Human Resources at Centennial College; developed and introduced a Headstart program for the graduating class (primarily Black students and new immigrants) at Warden Ave. Public School in Scarborough (joint project with Centennial College). A key component of this program was the ongoing mentoring relationship of the students throughout their secondary school career with college staff and faculty. **BACKGROUND:** began his professional life at Ryerson Polytechnic, as a member of the Faculty of Arts, 1964-71; from 1971-77, he was Director of Student and Academic Services; then served as Vice-President of Ryerson, 1977-89, possibly the first Black in Canada to hold such a position. **AFFIL/MBRSHP:** appointed Bencher, Law Society of Upper Canada, 1987-89; Chair, Canada Employment and Immigration Advisory Council, 1981-86; Director, Cdn Labour Market and Productivity Centre, 1984-89; Director, Ont. Training Corp., 1988-89; Director, Progress Career Planning Centre, 1993-98; Arbitration and Mediation Institute of Canada; Cdn Bar Assn. (ADR section); Society for Conflict Resolution in Ontario. **COMMUNITY INVOLVEMENT:** extensive, including: Afropan Steelband (Toronto's oldest and "winningest" community steelband); Black Achievers Program; Subway Academy One Alternative School; co-Chair, School Council, Subway Academy; West Rouge Community Assn.; West Indies United Soccer Club; Boy Scouts of Canada; Ont. Soccer Referees Assn. **HONS.:** include, ACAA, outstanding contribution in education & community service, 1998; Excellence Award, for Headstart Program, Nat'l Inst. Staff & Organizational Development, U. of Texas, 1998; Chaconia Gold Medal, national award, Rep. of Trinidad & Tobago, for meritorious service in education & community service, 1983; Province of Ontario Award, for leadership in the Black community, 1973. **WORKS:** papers: "A Balance between Professional & Private life," Law Society Call to the Bar address, 1990; "Women's Access to non-traditional occupations," 1992; "Collaborative Leadership," 1986. **REVIEWED IN:** local & nat'l publications *Who's Who in Toronto: A Celebration of the City*, 150th anniv. edition. **EDUCATION:** Cert., Educational Mngmt., Harvard U., 1986; Cert., Mngmt. & Organizational Development, U. of Michigan, 1981; M.Ed, U of T, 1977; MA, BA/Hons., U. of Manitoba, 1963; BA, U. of Winnipeg, 1961. **MOTTO:** My world becomes intelligible for me through caring and being cared for…as I become responsible for the growth and actualization of others. (Milton Mayeroff) **CONTACT:** tsosa@ican.net

▶SOUTHWELL, Gracey, CMA.

DIRECTOR, Systems Support and Operations, Aliant Telecom Broadband Services, 1505 Barrington St., Halifax, NS B3J 2W3. Born: Curaçao/ in Canada since: 1976.

▶ Gracey Southwell is the Director of Systems Support and Operations at Aliant Telecom Broadband Services. As a Certified Management

Accountant, she has more than 21 yrs. of experience in a variety of areas within MTT and Aliant Telecom (including, most recently, Controller of Consumer Broadband and Wireless). She is responsible for directing the customer care and service delivery development for High Speed Internet and Interactive Digital Television services, which are Aliant Telecom's emerging Internet-based businesses. **COMMUNITY:** has served on several boards; Treasurer, Metro United Way; executive member, (Chair, Communications), St. Ignatius Parish Catholic Women's League (Bedford, NS). **AFFIL/MBRSHP:** VP, Finance and Admin., Metropolitan Halifax Chamber of Commerce; former member and Alumni Representative, Board of Governors, Saint Mary's U. **EDUCATION:** CMA; B.Comm, Saint Mary's U. **CONTACT:** gracey.southwell@aliant.ca; Fax: 902-429-1099

▶**SOUTHWELL, Rustum**
EXECUTIVE DIRECTOR, Black Business Initiative, 1575 Brunswick St., Halifax, NS B3J 2G1. Born: St. Kitts/ in Canada since: 1972.

▶ Rustum Southwell was appointed founding Executive Director of the Black Business Initiative (BBI), in 1996. The BBI was created as a business development enterprise, funded by the Federal and Provincial levels of government, and aimed at improving the economic and business opportunities available to the African-Nova Scotian community. This initiative resulted from a Task Force Report highlighting the limited business-creation opportunities available to Blacks in NS and the ongoing barriers to economic prosperity presented by systemic racism. The BBI now has a team of 11 employees which delivers services province-wide from the Canada/Nova Scotia Business Service Centre; services provided include training and development for new and existing businesses as well as funding support. Initiatives introduced and contributing to the group's success include: an effective communication and trade strategy; a high-quality periodical, *Black to Business*; the *BBI Business Directory*; regular Trade missions; the Black Business Summit, with participants from across Canada and the US; and, the Business is Jammin' youth program. Prior to joining the BBI, RS was the Executive Director of the African Canadian Business Development Centre; owned and operated a Harvey's franchise; and, served as Chair of the Harvey's Atlantic Franchise Assn. **AFFIL/MBRSHP:** National Steering Committee, which responds to potential opportunities of the Africa Direct Trade mission; Sable Gas Community Benefits Advisory Committee; Atlantic representative on the Brd. of Directors for the Canadian Council on Africa; Preston Area Board of Trade. **OTHER:** RS further contributes to African Nova Scotia community initiatives through volunteer membership on the HRDC-sponsored Black Employment Partnership committees; is past Chair of the African Heritage Month Cmtee; and, a member of the Black Cultural Society. He has presented extensively on the state of Black businesses to organizations and agencies; voluntary planning, African Canadian Services Div.; Task Force on the Future of the Financial Services Sector; Dept. of Foreign Affairs for Investment and Trade; Cdn Manufacturers and Exporters International Development Days; and, many private and public sector operations. **HONS.:** MVP, NS Cricket Team, Canadian Tournament, 1978. **WORKS:** in, *Black to Business.* **REVIEWED IN:** *Atlantic Progress*; *Daily News*; *Chronicle Herald*; *Mail Star*; *Business Voice*; *Business J.* **EDUCATION:** holds several business & training certificates; Dalhousie U. **HEROES/ ROLE MODELS:** C.A. Paul Southwell, father and former prime minister of St. Kitts-Nevis. **MOTTO:** It will get done! **CONTACT:** southwell.rustum@ cbsc.ic.gc.ca; www.bbi.ns.ca

▶**SPARKS, Corrine E., The Hon.**
JUDGE, Nova Scotia Family Court, Ste. 200-277 Pleasant St., Dartmouth, NS B2Y 3S2. Born: Halifax, NS.

▶ The Hon. Judge Corrine Sparks was appointed to the Nova Scotia Family Court in 1987 and thereby became the first Black Nova Scotian to be appointed to the bench and Canada's first Black woman judge. Born and raised in Nova Scotia, she studied law at Dalhousie U.; upon graduation she worked as a Human Rights Officer with the NS Human Rights Commission; was a corporate manager with Turbo Resources in Alberta; then maintained a private practice as a barrister and solicitor. Since being appointed to the bench in 1987, she has also been a lecturer with the National New Judges Training Program, and a lecturer with the Commonwealth Judicial Education Institute. **COMMUNITY:** involvement while still a lawyer, was extensive and diverse; she served on many Boards ranging from the NS Home for Coloured Children to the Canadian Mental Health Assn. **HONS.:** including, CABL, 2001; Frances Lillian Fish Award, 1998; National Award, Congress of Black Women; Wall of Fame Inductee, NS Society for the Protection of Black Culture. **REVIEWED IN:** *WWIC*; *Millennium Minds*, 2000. **EDUCATION:** LLM, 2001; LLB, 1979, Dalhousie Law School. BA, Mount Saint Vincent U., Halifax, 1974. **CONTACT:** sparksce@gov.ns.ca

▶SPENCE, Alwin C., Dr.

PROFESSOR/SENIOR LECTURER, Dept. of Psychology, John Abbott College, Montreal, QC. Born: Jamaica/ in Canada since: 1961.

▶ Dr. Alwin Spence has been teaching psychology at John Abbott College since 1975, and was Chair of the Psychology Dept., 1997-99. **CAREER HIGHLIGHTS:** lecturer, Concordia U., since 1976; lecturer, School of Social Work, McGill U., 1992-94; Consulting Psychologist with the Protestant School Board of Greater Mtl, 1974-75; Assistant Professor, Graduate School of Education, Vermont U., 1974-75; lecturer, Rutgers U., 1972-74. He has conducted several workshops with teachers, administrators, and social welfare workers on: counselling the minority student; motivation

through positive regard; building positive self-concept; and, stages in the development of Black awareness. He has also held parenting workshops in Montreal, Toronto, Ottawa, Winnipeg, and Vancouver. **COMMUNITY INVOLVEMENT:** past-Secretary, Quebec Cricket Federation; Wanderers Cricket Club; VP, Black Studies Centre; past-President (1984-91), MABBP. As President of the MABBP, he initiated the following: annual vocational seminars for Black youth; annual Black Business Week; the Black Business and Professional Directory; Seminar for Black Women; and, two Annual Graduate Scholarships to Black scholars. **AFFIL/MBRSHP:** past member, American Assn. for Counselling and Development. **HONS.:** Harry Jerome Award for Professionalism, 1992; Cert. Merit, Govt. of Canada, 1988; member, Kappa Delta Pi, 1976; Quebec Govt. post-graduate scholarship, 1972. **WORKS:** a number of articles in newspapers & magazines, including *Sentinel*; *Focus Omojo*; booklets: *Toward an Understanding of the Culturally Different Black Youth*, 1978; *Psychologically Speaking–Jamaica is just another Adolescent*, 1980. **EDUCATION:** Ed.D, Counselling Psychology, Rutgers U., NJ, 1974; MS, Ed. Admin., State U. of New York, 1971; BA, SGWU (now Concordia U.), 1967; Dipl. Teaching, Mico Teachers College, Jamaica, 1958. **MOTTO:** I cannot be OK until we are all OK. **CONTACT:** alwin@johnabbott.qc.ca; Fax: 514-457-4730

▶SPENCE, Christopher, PhD.

SUPERINTENDENT OF SCHOOLS, Borden/Maplewood/West Hill Family of Schools, 4th Fl.-140 Borough Dr., Toronto, ON M1P 4N6. Born: England/ in Canada since: 1969.

▶ Dr. Chris Spence is a Superintendent with the Toronto District School Board. He is an educator with a strong record of community service and is recognized as providing leadership in developing policies, programs, and procedures involving all relevant stakeholders in the educational process. **HIGHLIGHTS:** one of his greatest successes was the transformation at Lawrence Heights Middle School where, under his leadership, and with the support and participation of teachers, students and parents, the school was transformed from a "problem school" with a reputation for violence and low academic results, to one which, in 2000, scored above the city and provincial averages in reading, writing, and math. This success led to a Canada Award for Excellence for the school from the National Quality Institute. In addition to his senior administrative responsibilities, CP lectures on issues of race, equity, sport, and education at York University. He is a motivational speaker for Masterpiece Corp.; the President of CMS Productions, which develops and produces educational resources; and, is the President of the International Star Search Basketball and Life Skills Development Camp. Previously, after completing his BA at Simon Fraser U. in 1985, he was drafted by the BC Lions and remained with the CFL until 1988. **OTHER:** he is also a filmmaker and views films as a powerful tool for educating; his film credits include *No "J"* and, *SkinGames and Football's Pioneering Duo*, both of which he wrote, directed and produced. He also wrote the AIDS education film, *Teammates*, which premiered on CBC, 1996; the film was used as part of World AIDS Day that year, and is being used by boards of education and libraries in Canada, the US, and the Caribbean. He has also written *The Skin I'm In*, responding to the concerns and experiences of Black student athletes. **HONS.:** recipient of many for community service: Outstanding Alumni Award, Simon Fraser U., 2002; ACAA, education, 2002; joint winner of the Children's Advocate Award for his Boys to Men program, 2001. **WORKS:** forthcoming, *Passion and Purpose: Schooling in the Heights; The Skin I'm In: Racism, Sport, and Education.* **REVIEWED IN:** local and nat'l newspapers & magazines, *Reader's Digest.* **EDUCATION:** PhD, Education, OISE/U of T, 1996; M.Ed, U of T, 1993; B.Ed, York U., 1991; BA, Simon Fraser U., 1985. **HEROES/ROLE MODELS:** Parents. **MOTTO:** Believe you can

achieve. **CONTACT:** chris.spence@tdsb.on.ca; Fax: 416-396-4281

▶**SPICER, Vincent A.**
CAPTAIN (Ret.), Canadian Armed Forces, Dept. National Defence. Resides in London, ON. Born: Jamaica/ in Canada since: 1948.
▶ Captain Vince A. Spicer was a career soldier who joined the Canadian Forces (CF) in 1954, serving until his retirement in 1989. During that time, he garnered several medals and secured a permanent place in history for his achievements, becoming the first Black in the history of the Canadian Forces to be promoted to the rank of Chief Warrant Officer (CWO) and appointed as Regimental Sergeant Major (RSM) of an active regular infantry battalion. **CAREER HIGHLIGHTS:** after enlisting, he served as an NCO Instructor with the Regiment of Guards, and was posted with the 1st Battalion of the Canadian Guards to NW Europe for two tours with NATO (1959-62; 1968-71). He served three tours of UN duty in Cyprus (1964; 1974; 1978), during which time he was promoted to the rank of Master Warrant Officer (MWO). On reduction to nil strength of the Regiment of Canadian Guards in 1968, he transferred to the Royal Canadian Regiment. He served as an Instructor on Military Staff at Royal Roads Military College (1978-80), at which time he was promoted and posted to the 1st Battalion of the Royal Cdn Regiment as the Regimental Sergeant Major. In 1981, he was appointed Regimental Chief Warrant Officer (RCWO) and Base Chief Warrant Officer (BCWO); commissioned in the rank of Captain, in 1984, he served as the Unit Support Officer (USO) with the Royal Regiment of Canada, before his retirement in 1989. **HONS.:** include, Canadian Peacekeeping Service Medal, 2000; Special Service Medal, NATO, 1992; Canadian Decoration, 1970; UN Medal, Cyprus, 1964. **REVIEWED IN:** *Afro-Can*, June, 1987. **MOTTO:** Let's get on with it!

▶STANFORD, C. Lloyd, PhD.

PRESIDENT, Le Groupe Stanford Inc., Ottawa, ON. Born: Jamaica/ in Canada since: 1959.

▶ Lloyd Stanford is a former senior public servant and now President of Le Groupe Stanford, a consulting firm specializing in matters of governance, human resources, administration of justice, bilingualism, biculturalism, Cdn social and cultural policy, and int'l development issues. **CAREER HIGHLIGHTS:** policy development, Min. of Education, Govt. of Jamaica; organizational analysis, Budget Bureau, Govt. of Saskatchewan; research on the Canadian power elite (for, *The Vertical Mosaic*); research and management of research for the Royal Commission on Bilingualism and Biculturalism; research grants administration, humanities and social sciences division, The Canada Council; direction of special studies, Office of the Commissioner of Official Languages; management of policy development and review at the UI Commission; policy development in the Federal-Provincial Relations Office and provision of advice to the PM and Ministers of State on social and cultural issues; led work on the establishment of the Canadian Human Rights Commission, Dept. of Justice; management of program evaluation and internal audit, Labour Canada; research and writing for the parliamentary committee on the "participation of visible minorities in Cdn society" (reported in *Equality Now!*); feasibility study for the establishment of the Cdn Race Relations Foundation; served on the Cdn Human Rights Tribunal Panel, the Ont. Grievance Settlement Board, and the Ont. Min. of Communications and Culture Cmtee, to review heritage legislation; teaches at Carleton U.'s School of Public Administration and U. of Ottawa's Faculty of Administration. **COMMUNITY:** co-founder, Third World Players; Rothwell Heights Property Owners' Assn.; BBPA; Community-Police Cmtee of Gloucester; Media Resources Advisory Group. **AFFIL/MBRSHP:** past member Brd. of Governors and Senate, Carleton U.; Cdn Ethnocultural Council; National Visible Minority Council on Labour Force Development; Royal Commonwealth Society; Institute of Public Administration of Canada; Commonwealth Assn. Public Admin. & Management. **HONS.:** CAT Productions Award, for "outstanding contribution to the Canadian community," 1991; National Heroes Day Award, for Arts & Culture, Jamaica (Ottawa) Community Assn., 1991. **WORKS:** several including: co-ed. *Canada 2000: Race Relations & Public Policy;* co-author, *Visible Minorities and the Public Service of Canada,* and *Reaching our full potential: Prior learning assessment and recognition for foreign-trained Canadians.* **EDUCATION:** doctoral studies, Poli. Sci., Queen's University. MA, Public Admin.; Dipl. Public Admin., Carleton U.; BA/Hons., UCWI (London). **HEROES/ROLE MODELS:** Bishop Percival Gibson & Douglas Forres, Kingston College; F.A. Robotham, Greenwich Town Elementary School. **MOTTO:** *Mens sano in corpore sano*: A sound mind in a sound body. **CONTACT:** stanford@ncf.ca

▶STEPHENS, Dell, CFP.

CHARTERED FINANCIAL PLANNER, CIBC Wood Gundy, Bow Valley Square IV, Calgary, AB T2P 3H7. Born: Jamaica/ in Canada since: 1974.

▶ Dell Stephens is an Investment Advisor with CIBC Wood Gundy. She is a certified Financial Planner with 20 yrs. experience in financial planning, investment management and inter-generational wealth transfer. She has given seminars and workshops on behalf of the Education Dept. of the Investment Dealers Assn.; provides workshops on financial planning to the general public; and, writes financial advice columns for local newspapers. **COMMUNITY INVOLVEMENT:** she has also used her financial background to support several community initiatives: currently serving a second term on Senate, U. of Calgary; served on Calgary Region Arts Foundation Brd. for eight yrs.; Congress of Black Women, Calgary chapter, served as president, four yrs. and three yrs. as national treasurer; served as president, Calgary Caribbean Council, which organized the annual Carifest festival; served as president, Calgary Multicultural Centre, and was Advisor/Facilitator for West African culture exhibit displayed at Glenbow Museum; president, Brd., Calgary Distress Centre, 1994-97; sponsor and organizer of Unique Lives Forum, held in 2000, which featured successful women such as Canada's first female astronaut, Roberta Bandar, Ann Margaret, Olivia Dukakis, and Coretta Scott King; volunteered at the 1988 Calgary Olympics; participated in 1992 Honolulu marathon; 1995, attended the UN conference on women in Beijing and facilitated a working session. **HONS.:** include, Award, Congress of Black Women, 1996; Awards for performance, including outstanding achievement, Merrill Lynch (then Midland Walwyn), 1993, 1995. **WORKS:** wrote financial articles for *Calgary Sun*, 1995 & 1997-98; financial articles for community newspapers, 1995-2001. **EDUCATION:** UWI. **HEROES/ROLE MODELS:** Father. **MOTTO:** Treat people with respect. **CONTACT:** dell.stephens@cibc.ca

▶**STEVENS, Vida,** MSc.
PUBLIC HEALTH NUTRITIONIST, Toronto Public Health. Markham, ON. Born: Antigua/ in Canada since: 1968.

▶ Vida Stevens is a Public Health Nutritionist and a Manager with the Peer Nutrition Program, Toronto Public Health. This program in nutrition education and food skills awareness is designed for the ethno-cultural communities, which are often missed by traditional nutrition programs. She is also involved in research on the food habits of first and second generation Blacks in Canada. **HIGHLIGHTS:** developed a Multicultural Nutrition and Food Skills program using the "Train the Trainer" model; chaired Seniors Nutrition Advisory Cmtee and facilitated the development of Congregate Dining Programs for Seniors in Toronto; coordinated activities of the First Int'l

Breast Feeding Week celebrations, 1994; advocated for policies to improve nutritional health of the population (e.g. Welfare Pregnancy Allowance, and enrichment of cornmeal); partnered with the AABHS to develop a program for African and Caribbean restaurant owners to reduce fat and salt in foods on their menus; served on a National Food Security Cmtee to review and advise the Federal Food Security Bureau on domestic and international food security/food access issues; consulted on the development of the African Food basket, a cost-efficient way to purchase fresh, local and imported fruit and vegetables. **OTHER:** she has co-authored nutrition teaching manuals for ethno-racial and ethno-cultural communities; developed *Healthy Eating in Every Culture*, North York Brd. of Education; co-chaired first international education symposium on Health and Research Bridge Building between African N. Americans; has also presented papers on reducing obesity in Blacks; nutrition promotion for seniors; developed a model to reach Blacks with Healthy Eating messages; prenatal nutrition programs for high-risk groups. **AFFIL/MBRSHP:** American Dietetic Assn.; College of Dietetics and the Ont. Society of Nutritional Professionals in Public Health; Caribbean Diabetes Chapter; Nat'l Org. of Blacks in Dietetics and Nutrition; AABHS, USA; Organization of Parents of Black Children; The Black Secretariat. Has mentored many students, and provided them with opportunities to develop skills and relevant experiences necessary for writing the dietetics registration exam. **HONS.:** several including, Outstanding Volunteer, Canadian Diabetes Assn., 2002; Leadership Award, Nat'l Org. of Blacks in Dietetics & Nutrition, USA, 1996; Volunteer Award, Ont. Min. Citizenship & Culture, 1995. **WORKS:** published abstract, "Using the Community Development Model to Promote Nutrition with Multicultural Groups," 1995; co-authored, *A Nutrition teaching manual for Ethno-cultural & Ethno-racial communities*. **REVIEWED IN:** *Share*; *Pride*; *Gleaner*; *Toronto Star*; *Canadian Living*.

EDUCATION: MSc, Food, Nutrition, & Dietetics, NYU, 1988; BA, Food & Nutrition, Ryerson, 1980. **HEROES/ROLE MODELS:** Dr. Sarah Wilder, Prof. & ED, Blacks in Dietetics & Nutrition. **MOTTO:** Too blessed to be stressed. **CONTACT:** vida.stevens@attcanada.net; Fax: 416-294-3593

▶**STEWART, Esme**

FACULTY ADVISOR, University of Manitoba, Rm. 227, Education Bldg., Winnipeg, MB R3J 2N2. Born: Trinidad & Tobago/ in Canada since: 1962.
▶ Esme Stewart has been working in education since 1959, beginning as a primary school teacher, in Trinidad, then teaching in Montreal and Winnipeg before becoming a Vice-Principal in 1976. In 1977 she became Principal at Pinkham School, then Machray School, 1979-92. She was the first member of the Black community to be appointed Principal in the Winnipeg School Division No. 1. Since 1992, she has been a Faculty Advisor at the University of Manitoba. **OTHER HIGHLIGHTS:** Summer School Lecturer, Brandon U., Dept. of Education, 1970-80; CIDA Instructor for U. of Manitoba's Special Education Project in Trinidad, 1987; initiated and organized parenting programs over the years; in 1994, she presented a series on parenting, called *Caribbean Echoes*, broadcast on community TV; from 1991-96, she organized a number of youth conferences and symposiums to help youth cope with the conflict of living in two cultures; organized many community workshops and conferences to help new immigrants develop a better understanding of Canadian culture, as well as their rights and responsibilities. **COMMUNITY:** initiated a Youth Excellence Award, 1996, for youth aged 18-24; in 1985, helped to establish Caribbean Carnival, CARIPEG, which has become an important cultural festival in Manitoba. **AFFIL/MBRSHP:** Black Educators' Assn., Manitoba; Congress of Black Women, Manitoba; Trinidad & Tobago Society; Caribbean Canadian Assn., Manitoba; UN Platform for Action. **HONS.:** include, Dedication &

Leadership Award, Immigrant Women's Assn., 2001; Premier's Volunteer Service Award Cert., Prov. Manitoba, 2000; Millennium Professional Distinction Award, Council of Caribbean Assn.; Nominee, Women of Distinction Award, YM-YWCA, 1992. **REVIEWED IN:** *Community News*, 1994; *Our Voices*, 1990; *The Black Experiences in Manitoba*, Winnipeg School Div., 1989. **EDUCATION:** M.Ed, 1973; B.Ed, 1970; BA, 1968, U. of Manitoba. Teachers' Cert., Trinidad, 1959. **HEROES/ ROLE MODELS:** Mother. **MOTTO:** Perseverance seldom fails. **CONTACT:** Fax: 204-253-0427

▶**STEWART-MORGAN, Gloria**

COORDINATOR/LECTURER/WRITER, Dept. Surgery, McGill University, QC. Born: Trinidad & Tobago/ in Canada since: 1967.
▶ Gloria Stewart-Morgan has been with McGill U. since 1968 in a variety of administrative positions and as a lecturer in computer courses. Since 1991, she has been the Coordinator, Surgical Undergraduate Education Program in the Dept. of Surgery; 1992-94, she developed and taught a course for the Faculty of Education's Distance Education program, Graphic Design for Instruction Materials; since 1992, she is an Instructor in the deKuyper Computerized Instruction Unit, Dept. Surgery; and since 2000, is a lecturer of computer courses in the General Studies Dept., Centre for Continuing Education. **OTHER:** she is an aspiring writer who has written a number of short stories and published a book on the life of her father, *No Ordinary Man*, with two others underway. **COMMUNITY:** active within her church and is Asst. editor of the church newsletter; executive member of the Charles Drew Society Mentorship Program, where health and education professionals provide support and assistance to Black medical students. **WORKS:** co-author, "Problems of Implementing problem-based learning for teaching surgical oncology to 2nd year medical students," *Annals*, RCPSC, 2001; book, *No Ordinary Man: Memoirs of My Father*, 1997. **EDUCATION:**

B.Ed, 1993; Quebec Teaching Cert., 1986, McGill U. **MOTTO:** I can do all things through Christ. **CONTACT:** gloria.morgan@muhc.mcgill.ca

▶**SUTHERLAND, Tony**
URBAN MUSIC PROMOTER/PROGRAM HEAD, Trebas Institute, 410 Dundas St. E., Toronto, ON M5A 2A8. Born: St. Vincent/ in Canada since: 1974.

▶ Tony Sutherland has been promoting and advocating on behalf of Canada's urban music sector since 1980, using local, regional, national, and international initiatives including educational workshops, music showcases, and networking functions. He was the first Black from Canada to work as a Marketing and Promotions Manager for a major record label, A&M/Island/Motown Records, Canada (PolyGram). **HIGHLIGHTS:** advocated for, and assisted in, the inclusion of the Dance Music and Reggae Music categories in the Juno Awards; participated in the lobbying of the CRTC for the licensing of Canada's first urban music station, which was granted to FLOW 93.5FM and to a second station in Calgary; is President and founding member of the Urban Music Assn. of Canada (UMAC); and, has been the catalyst and chair of the Annual Cdn Urban Music Awards, since 1997. **OTHER:** Program Head, Music Business Administration Program and Senior Manager of Career Services, Trebas Institute; Professor, Entertainment Scene, Durham College; Chair, R&B/Soul Cmtee, Juno Awards since 1993; former on-air radio host at CKFM and CIUT. He is also a founding member of the National Black Alliance (umbrella group for CABJ, BBPA, BFVN, UFSC, UMAC, AABHS). **WORKS:** *RPM* magazine; *Your Time*; *The Bridge*; *UpFront*; *Share.* **CONTACT:** sutherland_t@hotmail.com; Tel: 416-966-3066

▶**SUTTON, Nicola**
LEGAL COUNSEL, Supreme Court of Canada, Ottawa, ON K1A 0J1. Born: Jamaica, 1965.

▶ Nicola Sutton has been working at the Supreme Court of Canada since 1995, as Legal Counsel . Her position entails conducting legal research and writing legal memoranda; she completed a sabbatical in the Dept. of Justice where she represented the Canadian delegation at the 2000 Council of Europe convention on computer crime. **COMMUNITY:** CABL; Bereaved Families of Ottawa-Carleton; Pastoral Care Committee, First United Church. **EDUCATION:** LLM, 1996; LLB, 1992, U. of Ottawa. BA, U of T, 1988. **HEROES/ROLE MODELS:** Shawn Sutton. **MOTTO:** A setback can only set you back if you fail to recognize how it can push you forward. **CONTACT:** snsutton@sympatico.ca

▶**SUTTON, Shawn, CA.**
DIRECTOR, BUSINESS PLANNING & ANALYSIS, Mitel Networks, Gloucester, ON. Born: Toronto, ON, 1967.

▶ Shawn Sutton has been working at Mitel Networks since June 2001, as Director, Business Planning and Analysis. Previously, he worked at Nortel Networks (1995 to 2001), in the position of Manager, Business Development and Investments, and where he was designated as Top Talent (1999, 2000, and 2001), an award for outstanding contribution. In 1998, when completing the American Institute of Certified Public Accountants Reciprocity exam, he scored in the 98th percentile. He also finished in the 95th percentile of his MBA graduating class. **COMMUNITY:** Bereaved Families of Ottawa-Carleton; First United Church. **EDUCATION:** CPA, American Institute of Certified Public Accountants, 1998; MBA, U. of Ottawa, 1995; CA, Cdn Institute of Chartered Accountants, 1994; B.Comm, McMaster U., 1991. **HEROES/ROLE MODELS:** Nicola Sutton; David Clark. **MOTTO:** Failure is not an option! **CONTACT:** shawn_sutton@mitel.com

▶**SUTTON, Winston, Prof.**

ACTOR/DIRECTOR/THEATRE PROFESSOR, Dawson College, 3040, rue Sherbrooke O., Westmount, QC H3Z 1A4. Born: St. Kitts/ in Canada since: 1969.

▶ Winston Sutton is a theatre professional who has been an actor and director, and is currently a Professor of Theatre at Dawson College in Montreal. In 1974, he became the second Black to be accepted at the National Theatre School (Ardon Bess was the first; *see: Bess, Ardon*); in his third year, he attended a workshop at Stratford given by Robin Phillips, Martha Henry, and Maggie Smith. **CAREER HIGHLIGHTS:** in 1977, he was invited to join the Stratford Theatre Company, where he stayed for three seasons, appearing in: *Henry IV; Julius Caesar; Antigone; The Merry Wives of Windsor; As You Like It*; understudied for *Titus Andronicus* and *Othello*. From 1980-85, he freelanced across Canada; participated in a public reading for Amnesty Int'l, 1981, with R.H. Thompson, Martha Henry, Barbara Gordon, and others. Key productions: *Mattie and Rose*, Persephone Theatre, Saskatoon; *A Lesson from Aloes*, Globe Theatre, Regina; *Othello*, Magnus Theatre, Thunder Bay; *Rum an' Coca Cola*, BTC; *River Niger, Nevis Mountain Dew*, and *The Shelter*, BTW; appeared in his first film in 1977, *Fields of Endless Day*; debuted as a director with *Smile Orange*, 1983, BTW. In 1985, he received a Dean Scholarship to the Masters Directing Program at Boston U.; while there he assisted in teaching improvisational classes; also assistant directed, *A Streetcar Named Desire*; directed, *Look Back in Anger, Cloud 9, The Golden Fleece*, and *Hedda Gabler*. From 1988-92, he was Artistic Director of Black Theatre Workshop, and sought to create programs connecting the company more closely to the community. With his wife, Maxine Banton, he introduced Spring Extravaganza and the BTW Summer Fair. He also initiated Second Stage Productions (training for local actors), and the Victor Phillips Award, named in honour of BTW's long-time supporter and the (generally considered) founder of Black theatre in Montreal. During his tenure, WS directed, *The Coloured Museum, The Dragon Can't Dance*, and *Smile Orange*. **OTHER:** He was also a part-time Professor of Theatre, Concordia U., 1988-93, and taught part-time at Dawson College, 1992-95. Since 1995, he has been a tenured Professor of Theatre at Dawson College, and was co-chairman, 1997-98. Since then, he has directed: *Much Ado About Nothing; Blood Relations; Cards On the Table; The Rimers of Eldritch; The Miracle Worker; The Hands of Its Enemy*; and, *All My Sons*. WS wrote, *Our Lost Heroes*, a play commissioned by BTW, and which had successful tours across Canada. **HONS.:** include, Best Actor Award, Quebec Drama Festival, Montreal, 1989; Ester B. Khan Award (awarded to the top 10 graduates of the Fine Arts dept.), Boston U., 1988. **WORKS:** play, *Our Lost Heroes*. **EDUCATION:** MFA, Boston U., 1988; Dipl., National Theatre School of Canada, 1977. **HEROES/ROLE MODELS:** Robin Phillips, former Artistic Director, Stratford; Jacques Cartier, Theatre Prof., Boston U. **MOTTO:** You can only create in a vulnerable state; everything else is merely a repetition of what you already know. **CONTACT:** winmax20@hotmail.com

▶**SYMONDS, Nelson**

JAZZ GUITARIST, Montreal, QC. Born: Halifax, NS.

▶ Nelson Symonds is a highly respected, self-taught jazz guitarist who began performing at the age of 13. At the age of 17, he moved from his home in Nova Scotia to Sudbury, joining his uncle to play in local venues. In 1955, the two joined a carnival, touring for three years in Canada and the US; in 1958, NS moved to Montreal, and, outside of a few short stays in the US, made his career in this city he calls home. He has appeared at clubs such as *Le Vieux Moulin*, The Black Bottom, Rockhead's Paradise, *L'Air du Temps*, Club 2080, and Biddle's. A former member of the legendary Montreal band, The Stablemates, Symonds has also worked with the likes of Rahsaan Roland Kirk, Blue Mitchell, George Coleman, Jimmy Heath, Booker Ervin, Thad Jones, Pepper Adams, Art Farmer, Benny Golson and Brother Jack McDuff. Though well-known and well-regarded on the Montreal jazz scene, it is felt that despite his obvious talent, he did not get the exposure he deserved and that opportunities, which would have increased his visibility, were not seized. Since 1964, NS has led his own groups; he is the subject of two documentary films and has released five recordings. **REVIEWED IN:** *Jazz in Canada: Fourteen Lives,* 1982.

▶**TALBOT, Alan W.**
OPERATIONS MANAGER, Steelcase Canada Ltd., One Steelcase Rd., W., Markham, ON L3R 0T3. Born: Windsor, ON.

▶ Alan Talbot is the Operations Manager at Steelcase Canada, the largest office furniture design and manufacturing company in the world. He joined Steelcase in 1979 as a materials analyst, and, due to his prior work experience and educational background, in three months was promoted to PIC Planner. Within a year he was again promoted and became Senior Expediter. Soon thereafter he became Second Shift Supervisor, responsible for Plant Operations, then was moved to the first shift, in a similar capacity. His career at Steelcase now spans more than 20 years. During that time, and through the various positions held, he has added value to the organization. One of his many accomplishments was in leading the Core Team for World Class Manufacturing, in Markham. AT returned to the operations side of the business as Operations Manager in the Seating division, which includes successful product lines such as Player, Trilogy, Snodgrass, and Ally. Currently, he is responsible for the product engineering, database engineering, supply chain management, and central quality departments in the Markham Plant. As the first Black person to move into management, at Steelcase Canada, he believes that similar opportunities exist for others provided they identify their goals then work towards them with hard work, dedication, and continuous education. **EDUCATION:** Productions & Operations Management Program, Centennial College; Capacity Planning, Seneca College. Currently pursuing CIM (Certified Industrial Manager) certification. **CONTACT:** atalbot@yahoo.com

▶**TAYLOR, Garth Alfred,** MB BS, FRCSC, FACS.
OPHTHALMOLOGIST/ASSOCIATE PROFESSOR,

Dept. Ophthalmology, Queen's University, Kingston, ON. Born: Jamaica/ in Canada since: 1971.

▶ Dr. Garth Taylor is an Ophthalmologist and a Cornea Specialist. He is Chief of the Department of Ophthalmology, Cornwall General Hospital (CGH) and Hotel Dieu Hospital since 1984, and, Associate Professor, Dept. of Ophthalmology, at Queen's University, where he conducts Resident seminars and clinics in cornea and external diseases. He has been on staff at Hotel Dieu Hospital, Cornwall, since 1977, and is a Clinical Associate at Kingston General Hospital and Kingston Hotel Dieu. **OTHER:** Hon. Professor at Hunan Medical University, Hunan Province, China; Chief of Staff, Cornwall General Hospital; was President, Medical Staff, 1995-99, CGH; Clinical Consultation Editor, *Ophthalmic Practice J.* He is Director, co-founder, and volunteer surgeon with Canadian Surgical Eye Expeditions (CAN SEE), a voluntary organization that provides eye services to those in developing countries. He is also a member of ORBIS, an international humanitarian organization which provides practical, hands-on training to local eye doctors, nurses, technicians and health care workers and restores sight to thousands in developing countries; he has completed more than 90 missions since 1982. **AFFIL/MBRSHP:** Cdn Ophthalmic Society; Cornea and External Disease Society, Canada; Cdn Society of Cataract and Refractive Surgery; Ophthalmologic Society West Indies; American College of Surgeons; American Board of Ophthalmology. **HONS.:** include, Meritorious Service Medal (MSM), Cdn Govt., 2001; Lifetime member, Islamia Eye Hospital, Bangladesh, 2000; Cert. Appreciation, Int'l Agency for the Prevention of Blindness, China, 1999; Paul Harris Award, Rotary Club, 1994; Harry Jerome Award, for professional excellence, 1993; Commander, Order of Distinction (CD), Jamaican Govt., 1992; Humanitarian Award, Rosicrucian Order, 1992; Jackie Robinson Special Humanitarian Award, MABBP, 1991. **WORKS:** several conference papers & publications. Articles in: *Can J Surgery*; *American J of Ophthalmology*; *Current Can Ophthalmic Practice.* **EDUCATION:** Fellow, American College of Surgeons, 1982; FRCSC, Ophthalmology, 1976; E.A. Baker Fellow, Bascom Palmer Eye Institute, Florida, 1977; Dipl., American Brd., Ophthalmology, 1977; Specialist, Ophthalmology, Queen's U., 1976; MB BS, UWI, Jamaica, 1970. **HEROES/ROLE MODELS:** Dr. Herbert Morrison: physician, surgeon, godfather. **MOTTO:** The harder I work, the luckier I get! **CONTACT:** greglea@cnwl.igs.net; Fax: 613-938-6763

▶**TAYLOR, Ronald A.**
DANCER/CHOREOGRAPHER/ARTISTIC DIRECTOR, Canboulay Dance Theatre, 201-286 Major Mackenzie Dr., Richmond Hill, ON L4C 8T3. Born: Trinidad & Tobago.

▶ Ronald Taylor is a dancer, choreographer and founder of Canboulay Dance Theatre, where he serves as Artistic Director. In describing his fusion of ballet, modern and ethnic dance, the *Globe and Mail* wrote, "Taylor's dances are characterized by indigenous movements that, while rooted in tradition, make room for improvisatory displays of virtuoso dancing." **CAREER:** he received his early training in Trinidad with the Tesoro Dance Co., then later studied with Astor Johnson. Under Johnson's tutelage, RT toured the Caribbean, Mexico, the US and Haiti. Following his studies in New York, he was a member of the Lincoln Center Touring Program; he also danced with the Dance Theatre of Harlem. Since founding Canboulay Dance Theatre in 1993, he has created over 15 works for the company; one of his creations, *MAS*, premiered in 1998 at the du Maurier Theatre, Toronto; this piece, depicting his journey from Christianity to Buddhism, was received with high acclaim and led to him being featured in Vision TV's program, *Skylight.* As a solo performer, RT particpated in the 1997 and '98 Dance Immersion performances at the du

Maurier Theatre; he also performed at the 1997 Black Dance Conference in S. Africa, S. Carolina, and in New York. As a dance educator, he has taught in the Youth Program at the Royal Conservatory of Music/Toronto; UWI's School of Continuing Studies; and, in the Faculty of Fine Arts at York U. **EDUCATION:** MA, Fine Arts, York U.; Juilliard School, NY; Dance Theatre of Harlem, NY; early training with the Tesoro Dance Co., Trinidad. **CONTACT:** canboulaydt@ netscape.net

▶**TAYLOR, Sheldon,** PhD.
WRITER/RESEARCHER/HISTORIAN, Toronto, ON. Born: St. Kitts/ in Canada since: 1966.
▶ Sheldon Taylor is a writer, researcher and historian who works to capture the African-Canadian experience and present it as a learning tool for all Canadians. **HIGHLIGHTS:** Curator, *400 Years: African Canadian History and Many Rivers to Cross*; Historical Consultant, NFB film, *Journey to Justice*; has taught at York U., and U of T; editor, *Akili: Journal, African-Canadian Studies.* **HONS.:** Race Relations Award, City of North York, 1996; Service Award, Onyx Lions Club, 1995; 10-yr. Volunteer Service Award, Ont. Min. of Citizenship & Culture, 1992. **WORKS:** selected: co-author, *Bromley: Tireless Champion for Just Causes*, 2000; columnist, *Share;* editor, *Akili: Journal, African-Canadian Studies.* **EDUCATION:** PhD, History, U of T, 1994; MA, History, McMaster U., 1988; BA, York U., 1986. **HEROES/ROLE MODELS:** Malcolm Streete; Harry Gairey; Beverly Mascoll. **CONTACT:** sheldtaylor @netscape.net

▶**TELFER, Norma**
PRESIDENT, TelCam Training & Consulting, 4550 Moccasin Trail, Mississauga, ON L4Z 2W4. Born: Jamaica/ in Canada since: 1976.
▶ Norma Telfer is a professional speaker and the founder and President of TelCam Training and Consulting, a firm which designs, develops and conducts workshops in customer service, team building, presentation, and networking skills. Her clients include: Ontario Workers' Compensation Board, Inroads Canada, Nortel, AGF Financial, Canada Trust, Eli Lilly, YMCA of Greater Toronto, and Caribana. **OTHER:** member, Ontario Liberal Party, was elected to the executive and served as chair and VP, Policy, 1988-91; member, Ontario Society of Training and Development (OSTD) and served as Chair, Corporate Consultant Committee for three yrs.; has been interviewed by CBC, TVO, Channel 47 and the print media on a number of political issues. **AFFIL/ MBRSHP:** Mississauga Board of Trade; Cdn Women in Communications; Cdn Assn. of Professional Speakers. **HONS.:** Volunteer of the Year Award, 2001; Award, Community Service, Congress of Black Women/ Durham Chapter. **REVIEWED IN:** *Toronto Star; Share.* **EDUCATION:** BA, Admin. Studies, York U.; Dipl., Teaching, Church Teachers' College, Jamaica. **HEROES/ROLE MODELS:** David Peterson; Durcy Burton; Lawrence Telfer. **MOTTO:** You can do it if you try. **CONTACT:** nh@telcamtraining.com; Fax: 905-502-0164

▶**TERRELONGE, Del**
GRAPHIC DESIGNER/DIRECTOR, Rhed Corporation, Ste. 306-477 Richmond St. W., Toronto, ON M5V 3E7. Born: England/ in Canada since: 1963.
▶ Del Terrelonge is a designer whose award-winning studio, Terrelonge, has specialized in graphic, interior, and product design since 1986. This array of design services has been used by clients such as travel and modelling agencies, a sound recording studio, a loft space/art gallery, photo finishing lab, a theme-inspired restaurant, and many others. Since 1994, he has lectured at a number of international venues including: Yale University School for the Arts, 1998; Atlanta Designers Assn., 1997; DDD Gallery, Osaka, 1997. His works have been exhibited in the US, France, and Japan and have been published in a

number of international design publications. His latest initiative is the formation of "rhed," a multi-disciplinary design firm specializing in architecture, interior, graphic, new media, and product design. **HONS.:** many industry-related awards, including New York Art Directors Club, 1996 & '97; AIGA, 1997, '93, '92. **REVIEWED IN:** several publications including: *Interior Design*; *AIGA J of Graphic Design*; *Globus Communication*; *Diseno Interiors*; *Graphis Magazine.* **EDUCATION:** Advertising & Graphic Design, Humber College. **CONTACT:** mail@terrelonge.com; Fax: 416-504-5239

▶THOMAS, H. Nigel, PhD.

PROFESSOR/WRITER, Université Laval, Cité Universitaire, Laval, PQ G1K 7P4. Born: St. Vincent/ in Canada since: 1968.

▶ Dr. Nigel Thomas is a Professor of Literature at Université Laval and an author of many publications including short stories, critical studies, poems and novels. He is one of the few authors to openly write and/or talk about being gay in the Caribbean. He spearheaded many initiatives in Montreal, where he lived from 1968-88, including co-founding the Free South Africa Committee, and founding the literary magazine, *KOLA.* Much of what he writes comes out of a need to explore, via the imagination, what it is to be human. Previously he taught English and French for several years at what is now the Montreal English School Board. **HONS.:** Jackie Robinson Professional of the Year, MABBP, 2000; short-listed for Hugh MacLennan Fiction Award, QSPELL, 1994. **WORKS:** include, *Behind the Face of Winter*, 2001; *Moving Through Darkness*, 1999; *How Loud Can the Village Cock Crow?*, 1996; *Spirits in the Dark*, 1993; *From Folklore to Fiction: A Study of Folk Heroes and Rituals in the Black American Novel*, 1988. **REVIEWED IN:** *Callaloo*; *KOLA*; *South Atlantic Review*; *J West Indian Literature*; *Commonwealth*; *Times Literary Supplement*; *Caribbean Writer*; *Montreal*

Gazette; *Globe and Mail*; *Quill & Quire*; *Writers' Monthly.* **EDUCATION:** PhD, U. de Montréal, 1986. MA, 1975; BA, 1974, Concordia U. **HEROES/ROLE MODELS:** John & Hester Dickson, maternal grandparents. **MOTTO:** Time passes without our control, but we can control how we pass time. **CONTACT:** jan08@sympatico.ca; Fax: 418-656-2991

▶THOMAS, Sandra

COUNSEL, Criminal Prosecutions, Dept. of Justice, Federal Prosecution Service, Ste. 3400-130 King St.W., Toronto, ON M5X 1K6. Born: Halifax, NS.

▶ Sandra Thomas is Counsel with the Criminal Prosecutions Section of the Federal Dept. of Justice. Having first studied law in the US, she was called to the bars of Pennsylvania in 1987, New Jersey in 1988, and Ontario in 1992. She is former Counsel to Governor Thomas Kean of New Jersey, 1986-89. **COMMUNITY:** founding President, CABL; initiated establishment of N. Thomas Foster Scholarship, at Rutgers U. School of Law; established on behalf of CABL and in collaboration with the class of 1990, the Michael Kelly Award, U of T's Faculty of Law, for a deserving Black student studying law at U of T; also mentors many high school and law school students; former member Brd., Toronto Dance Theatre, 1992-94. **HONS.:** Vision of Justice Award, from Black Law Students Assn., 2000. **REVIEWED IN:** *Who's Who of American Law Students*, 1985; *inter pares*, Dept. of Justice, 1997. **EDUCATION:** JD, Rutgers U., NJ, 1986; BA/Hons., York U., 1982. **HEROES/ROLE MODELS:** Dr. & Mrs. Ferdinand Thomas, parents; Hon. Julius Isaac. **CONTACT:** sthomas9110@rogers.com

▶THOMAS, Sharlene

MOTIVATIONAL SPEAKER/EVENTS PRODUCER, Sharlene Thomas Productions, 1531 Scotia Place II, 10060 Jasper Ave., Edmonton, AB T5J 3R8. Born: Trinidad & Tobago/ in Canada since: 1974.

▶ Sharlene Thomas is the founder and Artistic Director of Movements: the Afro-Caribbean Dance Ensemble which began in 1990, at the request of local leaders in the Black community in Edmonton. This award-winning company, which specializes in African and Caribbean theatre, has performed across Canada and throughout the Caribbean. **HIGHLIGHTS:** in addition to her work as a choreographer, ST is a popular motivational speaker and often addresses schools, corporate meetings, and women's groups across Canada, the US, and Africa; was a keynote speaker at the World Conference of Mayors in Bermuda. She came to Canada in 1974 and, after a successful career as a model pursued her own corporate interests from which both Movements companies, Edmonton and Trinidad, were launched. As a special events organizer, she has produced the Black Achievement Awards, the Carifest Festival, and worked with the 1999 Miss Universe Pageant held in Trinidad & Tobago. **COMMUNITY:** Consular Advisory Cmtee, Trinidad & Tobago in AB; Edmonton Multicultural Council Steering Cmtee; Advisory Council, Heritage Artists Development Project; Victoria School for the Arts Society; Western Carnival Development Assn. **HONS.:** include, Wall of Fame Honour & City of Edmonton Poster, Edmonton Arts Council, 2000; Telus Award for Community Relations, 1998; Woman of Vision Award, Global TV, 1998; Excellence in the Performing Arts Award, BAASA, 1997; Fil Fraser Award, for excellence in the performing arts, National Black Coalition of Canada, 1993. **REVIEWED IN:** *Edmonton Woman* magazine; *Black Diaspora* magazine; *Edmonton J*; *Edmonton Sun*; *Trinidad Guardian*. **EDUCATION:** Academy of Learning Business Career College, 1998. **HEROES/ROLE MODELS:** Mother, for her wisdom; Nelson Mandela, for his indomitable spirit. **MOTTO:** If you don't climb the mountain, you won't see the view! **CONTACT:** info@sharlenethomas.com; Fax: 780-424-3505

▶**THOMAS OSBOURNE, Marlene**
COMMUNITY & OUTREACH DEVELOPMENT CONSULTANT, Kujichagalia (self-determination), 181 Maplewood Ave., Hamilton, ON L8M 1X6. Born: Dominica/ in Canada since: 1974.

▶ Marlene Thomas Osbourne is an Empowerment Specialist and Motivational Speaker, with a special interest in human rights, mediation, conciliation, and conflict resolution. For the past 25 yrs., she has been active in the community as a business owner, social activist, and humanitarian. She has worked with many diverse groups, particularly youth, educating them in the benefits of social democracy and justice for all. **HIGHLIGHTS:** founder, Hamilton Cultural and Ethnic Mosaic Assn.; founder, Kujichagalia (self-determination); developed the Youth-at-Risk Project Impact; co-founder, John C. Holland Awards Banquet; past co-chair, Mayor's Committee Against Racism and Discrimination. **AFFIL/MBRSHP:** Govt. of Ontario Advisory Group on Racism; Hamilton Health Sciences Corp.; Black Women's Business and Professional Assn.; Immigrant Advocacy and Research Centre; Robert Gentles Action Cmtee for Justice. **HONS.:** include, Cert. of Appreciation, Govt. of Ontario, 1993; Woman of the Year in Community & Public Affairs, City of Hamilton, 1994 & 1995; Cultural Awareness Cert. of Recognition, Victorian Order of Nurses, 1997; Community Services Award, Hamilton-Wentworth Police, 1995. **REVIEWED IN:** local & community newspapers, including *The Hamilton Spectator*. **HEROES/ROLE MODELS:** Grandmother; Amah Harris, teacher. **MOTTO:** The world I want, begins within me. **CONTACT:** marleneto@sympatico.ca

▶**THORNHILL, Esmeralda, LLD.**
PROFESSOR, Dalhousie Law School, Dalhousie University, 6061 University Ave., Halifax, NS B3H 4H9. Born: Barbados.

▶ Dr. Esmeralda Thornhill is a lawyer, linguist,

lecturer, writer, human rights advocate, and professor of law; 1996-2002, held the James Robinson Johnston Endowed Chair in Black Canadian Studies, at Dalhousie U. Teaching-Research Areas: Critical Race & Legal Theory, International Human Rights Law, Human Rights, Discrimination, Black History. Fluently trilingual in English, French, and Spanish; longstanding community advocate. Founding member: Congress of Black Women of Canada, 1977; Congress of Black Lawyers-Jurists of Quebec, 1986; *La Maisonnée*, 1979; Int'l Resource Network for Women of African Descent, 1982. Served on many governmental cmtees; supervised/co-authored multiple reports/ studies. Published scholar and authority on "Race"; has written and lectured extensively on "material reality" of Racism in Law, Education, and Public Services, to judicial, legal, academic, government, public, and grassroots audiences; pioneered first Cdn university-accredited course in Black Women's Studies (Concordia, 1983); writings constitute core readings for academic courses. **CAREER:** Second Language Teacher; Human Rights Anti-Racist Educator. First woman from a racialized group appointed to Quebec Council Status of Women, Montreal Public Service Commission; Advisory Panel, National Human Genome Centre (Howard U.); Ugandan Constituent Assembly Elections Observer Mission, 1994. **AFFIL/MBRSHP:** Quebec Bar, 1987; NS Barristers' Society, 1998; Ed. Brd., *Can J of Women & the Law*; Black Lawyers' Assn. of NS; Racism and the Black World Response Society; Brd. of Governors, Quebec Bar, 1981-83; Panel of Brd. of Inquiry Chair, NS Human Rights Commission; Brd. of Governors, NS Law Foundation. **HONS.:** Hon. LLD (Concordia U., 1997; City University, NY, 1996); Arts & Science Convocation Address, Concordia U., 1997; Testimonial Dinner Honoree, Coloured Women's Club of Montreal, 1996; Woman of the Year Award, Humanitarian and Social Action, Quebec Salon de la femme 1991. **WORKS IN:** *Racism and the Black World Response*

Symposium Proceedings; Can J of Women & the Law/ Revue femmes et droit; *La Revue québécoise de droit international*; *Alberta Law Review*; *J of Intergroup Relations*; *Currents*; *Can Bar Assn; Nat'l Parole Board Conference Proceedings*; *Fireweed*; *US Congressional Record*; *UNESCO Institute for Ed. Review*; *National Judicial Institute Training Manual for Judges*; *Le Devoir*; *The Issue is –Ism*; *Multicultural Education and Policy.* **REVIEWED IN:** *Those 350 Women Who Built Montreal*, 1993; *L'Agenda des femmes du Québec*, 1993; *La gazette des femmes*; *The Lawyers' Weekly*; *Dalhousie News*; *Community Contact*; *Spear*; *Share; Mtl Gazette; Mtl Star.* **EDUCATION:** Dip. Int'l Law, San Diego, CA & Paris, France. MA, U. de Montréal; LLB, UQAM. Dip. Ed.; BA/Hons., McGill U. **HEROES/ROLE MODELS:** Hilda Doreen Brathwaite Thornhill, mother. **MOTTO:** It's left to us. **CONTACT:** esmeralda.thornhill@dal.ca; http://as01.ucis.dal.ca/ law/people

▶**THORPE, Carl**
EXECUTIVE DIRECTOR, Multicultural History Society of Ontario, 43 Queen's Park Cres., Toronto, ON M5A 2S3. Born: Guyana/ in Canada since: 1959.
▶ Carl Thorpe served as Chief of the Heritage Administration Branch of the Ont. Min. of Citizenship and Culture, 1982-90, and was Executive Secretary of the Ontario Heritage Foundation during four of those years. His responsibilities included implementing the historical aspects of the Ontario Heritage Act, as well as managing Ministry of Culture financial assistance programs, related to the preservation of the built and the natural environment. In his present position, as Executive Director of the Multicultural History Society, he has, in partnership with others, restructured the organization into a self-sufficient academic/community organization. A former treasurer of the Ontario Black History Society, he was instrumental in the design and management

of a lectureship, Arts in a Pluralist Society, established at the University of Toronto's Scarborough campus. He is a member of the Cultural Pluralism and the Arts Network, which manages a program set up to assist arts managers to live, learn, and work in a multiracial and culturally diverse society. **WORKS:** articles in *Compass;* co-editor, *Polyphony* magazine; ed., *Teacher's Guide to the Encyclopedia of Canada's Peoples*; produced research papers on Blacks in Ontario, & brochures on heritage promotion. **EDUCATION:** MA, U. of Manitoba; BA, U. of Winnipeg. **MOTTO:** Serving, not excelling, makes us truly human. **CONTACT:** Tel: 416-979-2973; Fax: 416-979-7947

▶**TIDLUND, Mary A.**
OIL INDUSTRY CEO/HUMANITARIAN, Mary A. Tidlund Charitable Foundation, PO Box 75091, Calgary, AB T3H 3B6. Born: Calgary, AB.

▶ Mary Tidlund worked for 15 yrs. in the oil industry, later becoming President and CEO of Williston Wildcatters Oil Corp., a publicly traded oil and gas exploration and service company in Alberta. Later, she and her partners relocated the company to Arcola in eastern Saskatchewan, and expanded its operations to include drilling and trucking companies. MT owned a clothing store, an art gallery, and a restaurant, establishments which greatly benefited the local population. All of these businesses together employed more than 250 people. Following an industry downturn in 1996, MT left the oil and gas sector and turned her attention towards helping others from a humanitarian perspective. In 1998, she founded the Mary A. Tidlund Charitable Foundation, which supports and participates in medical, dental, and educational programs in Canada and overseas. Some completed projects include: Operation Eyesight, India; Meals for the Homeless, Calgary; water filtration, Haiti; medical projects in Peru and Ecuador. **OTHER:** MT was adopted at the age of seven by a Calgary couple

with three other adopted children; over the years they were foster parents to nearly 40 foster children; she attributes her interest in helping others to this early experience. **HONS.:** Award for Humanitarianism, BAASA, 2000; Ms. Black Alberta, 1995; Award of Appreciation, for having the most impact on the community, Town of Arcola; finalist in the Cdn Women Entrepreneur Awards, 1993. **REVIEWED IN:** *Calgary Herald; Edmonton J; Ottawa Star; Daily Oil Bulletin;* featured on CBC's *Venture* Program; *Canadian Business; Alberta Report; Business Edge.* **EDUCATION:** BSc, U. of Calgary. **MOTTO:** It's all about caring, sharing, and receiving. **CONTACT:** info@tidlundfoundation.com; www.tidlundfoundation.com

▶**TOLBART, Gwen**
TV BROADCASTER, FOX 5/WTTG, 5151 Wisconsin Ave. NW, Washington, DC 20016, USA. Born: Montreal, QC.

▶ Gwen Tolbart began her professional life before the camera, as an actress (commercials, CBC's *Degrassi High*, several films). After appearing as a guest on Montreal's Black community TV news magazine show, *Black Is*, she became the host, interviewing Jesse Jackson, Burning Spear, and others. She went on to work for Canada's Weather Network, anchoring weather and news; her next move was to Montreal's CFCF 12,where she worked as a weather anchor, reporter for *Fighting Back* and host on *Travel Travel*, all of this without any formal broadcast training. She returned to school and completed a Journalism degree at Concordia U., and in 1997, after attending a convention of the National Assn. of Black Journalists in Chicago, she secured a position as a Weather Anchor at CBS-11 in Dallas. Her role was later expanded to reporter and talk show host. On her talk show, *Positively Texas*, some of her guests included Buck O'Neil (1st Black baseball coach for a major league team), Amy Grant, John Walsh, Stedman Graham, and others. Since August, 2002, she is the Weather Anchor with

FOX 5/WTTG in Washington, and also does some feature reporting. **OTHER:** GT is also a motivational speaker, and finds time to serve her community by mentoring teens and volunteering. **HONS.:** include, Woman of Distinction, Metro Business & Professional Women, TX, 2002, 2001; Commendation from Texas Governor Rick Perry & Congresswoman Kay Granger, 2002; Recognition, NS House of Assembly, 2002; Best On-Air Performance, NABJ, 2002; Best Anchor Weather, Best Anchor News, NABJ, 2001, 2000; Emmy Award, Weather Special, 1999; US National Community Service Award, NABJ, 1998; Concordia U. billboard Role Model Image campaign, 1997 & '98; Award, NS Mayflower Assn., 1996. **REVIEWED IN:** *Concordia U. Magazine*, 2001; *Mtl Gazette*; *Trend*; *Community Contact*; *Jet.* **EDUCATION:** BA, Concordia U., 1995; DEC, Dawson College. **HEROES/ROLE MODELS:** Mother; grandmother; aunts. **MOTTO:** We can achieve our goals if we unwrap and utilize the gifts we have within ourselves. **CONTACT:** gwentolbart@mindspring.com

▶TOURÉ, A. Lamine
AGENT DE RECHERCHE ET DE PLANIFICATION, Ministère de l'Industrie et du Commerce, 710, pl. d'Youville, 4ᵉ étage, Québec, QC G1R 4Y4. Né: Côte d'Ivoire, 1967/ au Canada depuis: 1993.

▶ Lamine Touré est analyste du commerce extérieur au Min. de l'Industrie et du Commerce (MIC) au gouv. du Québec. Il est chargé de fournir aux autorités du MIC et aux directions géographiques et sectorielles des analyses et des études sur l'économie et le commerce mondial, le commerce extérieur du Québec ainsi que sur les politiques gouvernementales en matière de développement des marchés et proposer des politiques, stratégies et programmes en vue de stimuler le commerce extérieur en tenant compte des plus récents développements au plan commercial. En plus, il examine l'évolution du commerce du Québec avec les autres provinces canadiennes

afin de proposer des pistes de solutions pour accroître la pénétration des produits et services québécois sur ces marchés. **PRIX:** académique, y compris, Bourse d'Excellence, Rép. Côte d'Ivoire, 1993-96; 1997-98, 1998-99. **ŒUVRES:** co-auteur, « Gestion stratégique des projets de privatisation en contexte africain: le cas de la Côte d'Ivoire, » *Rev. Internationale en Gestion et Management de Projets.* **FORMATION:** en cours, Doctorat en Études Urbaines, UQAM; Maîtrise en Sciences et Gestion de Projets, UQATrois-Rivières, 1996. Maîtrise d'Éc. Appliquée, 1991; Bac d'Éc. Appliquée, 1990, U. de Côte d'Ivoire. **MENTORS:** Koffi Anan, secrétaire-général des Nations Unies. **MOTTO:** Quelque soit la durée de la nuit, le soleil apparaîtra. **CONTACT:** lamineman @hotmail.com; Fax: 418-646-6435

▶TOWNSEND, Beverly
PRINCIPAL, Dalkeith Elementary School, 9751 Dalkeith, Anjou, QC, H1K 3X6. Born: Jamaica/ in Canada since: 1966.

▶ Beverly Townsend is the Principal of Dalkeith Elementary School in Anjou. Her work with economically disadvantaged families in the Côte-des-Neiges area began in 1972 with the establishment of a day care for single parents. As an administrator for the former Protestant School Board of Greater Montreal, she transformed an English inner city school in Côte-des-Neiges into a thriving French Immersion school. At her current school she has successfully facilitated the merger of Dalkeith with Tara Hall, where different philosophies and backgrounds have come together. **BACKGROUND:** served as the principal of Coronation Elementary School for seven yrs. prior to moving to Dalkeith; vice-principal at Lachine High School from 1989 to 1992; previously taught computer science, math, English and business education. Using a hands-on approach with youth, as well as the professionals who work with them, she has organized and implemented workshops on a wide range of topics for the past 16 yrs.; these included presentations for the Mcgill Undergraduate Society for new teachers and workshops with youth leaders from the Côte-des-Neiges Black Community Assn. Throughout her career, she has worked to encourage a positive self-image among Black students and their parents, and, has always promoted a culturally diverse curriculum. **OTHER:** member, Brd. of Directors, ERS Youth Development Corp., and the T.R.E.E. Foundation for Youth Development, where she has been actively involved in projects such as youth exchange programs which incorporate a work-study component; developed and implemented programs towards augmenting and updating work-related and technical skills for students entering the labour force as well as adult learners. **HONS.:** Woman of the Year, Mtl Council of Women, 2000. **WORKS:** in, *McGill Daily*, 1993; "Black History," *Mtl Teachers' Assn.* magazine, 1978. **REVIEWED IN:** *The Mtl Gazette*, other local publications. **EDUCATION:** M.Ed, 1984; Dipl., Ed, 1975, Mcgill University. BA, Concordia U., 1970. **HEROES/ROLE MODELS:** Parents. **MOTTO:** Not to know is bad, not to want to know is worse; not to hope is unthinkable, not to care is unforgivable. **CONTACT:** btownsend@emsb.qc.ca

▶**TROTMAN, Gene Thornton T.,** QC.
GENERAL COUNSEL, Federal Dept. of Justice, assigned to Dept. of Natural Resources, Government of Canada, 580 Booth St., Ottawa, ON K1A 0E4. Born: Trinidad & Tobago/ in Canada since: 1956.

▶ Gene Trotman has been working with the Federal Government since 1963. At the time, he was the first person from a visible minority to be hired by the Department of Justice and would, in 1970, become the first promoted to the position of Director of the Legal Branch. **CAREER HIGHLIGHTS:** since 1970, he has held the following positions: Director, Legal Branch, Dept. of Justice, attached to National Revenue and Excise; 1975, appointed

Director, Legal Branch, Dept. of Justice, attached to Dept. Supply and Services, and Legal Advisor to the Royal Cdn Mint, Cdn Commercial Corp., and Crown Assets Disposal Corp.; 1978, appointed General Counsel and Corporate Secretary to the Cdn Commercial Corp., and Royal Cdn Mint; 1993, appointed General Counsel, Special Commercial Law Projects; and, since 1996, is with the Dept. of Natural Resources. **OTHER:** in 1989, he was appointed Chair of the newly formed Advisory Committee on Visible Minorities in the Dept. of Justice, a position he held until 1993. **COMMUNITY:** has been involved with the National Alliance for Race Relations; Cdn Alliance for Visible Minorities; and the Shakuntule Benevolent Foundation. **HONS.:** include, Group Achievement Award, Dept. of Justice, 1993; Gold Pin & Citation, for 15-yrs. volunteer community services, Ont. Min. of Citizenship, 1992; GG 125th Anniv. Medal, 1992; appointed Queen's Counsel, 1985. **EDUCATION:** National Defence College, 1975; LLM, U of T, 1963. LLB, 1962; BA, 1958, U. of Manitoba. Inter. BSc Economics, U. of London, 1955. **MOTTO:** You either stand for something or fall for anything. **CONTACT:** trotman48@rogers.com; Fax: 613-995-2598

▶**TUCKER, Elrie C.,** MD, CM, FRCSC.
OBSTETRICIAN & GYNECOLOGIST, Private Practice, Ste. 101-1822 Sherbrooke St.W., Montreal, QC H3H 1E4. Born: Trinidad & Tobago/ in Canada since: 1953.

▶ Dr. Elrie Tucker is a successful medical specialist and business person whose innovativeness resulted in new medical services being made available in breast cancer detection. **HIGHLIGHTS:** after completing his studies at McGill U., 1961, and his residency at the Queen Mary Veteran's Hospital, 1962-63, and at the Royal Victoria Hospital (RVH), 1963-66, he held a number of positions: Clinical Fellow, RVH, using Lymphangiography as an aid in cancer diagnosis, 1966-67; McLaughlin Travelling Fellow, Gynecologic

354

Endocrinology, Guy's Hospital and Chelsea Hospital for Women, 1967-68. Since 1968, he has maintained a private practice and is Asst. Obstetrician/ Gynecologist at the RVH. From 1972-80, he was the co-founder and president of the Breast Centre Group, which was Canada's largest group of breast cancer detection clinics; nine diagnostic centres were equipped with thermography and mammography systems. In 1978, he founded (and operated until 1983) the Carolyn Birthing Centre, Canada's first medically supervised location for non-hospital births. In 1989, in Barbados and in Montreal, he launched *In Vivo Spectroscopy*, as a new diagnostic tool in the fight against breast cancer. **OTHER:** 1973, founded Tropical Air Services Ltd., a charter air service for the Caribbean islands which had a fleet of ten light aircrafts; sold his majority interest in 1979, but remained involved in the company until 1986. **COMMUNITY INVOLVEMENT:** co-founder and President, Quebec Black Medical Assn.; *Centraide*; Negro Community Centre; Marine Biology Div., Bellairs Research Institute; Air Dale Ltd. (Regional Airline of N. Ontario). **HONS.:** several including, Award, 30-yrs of service, RVH, 1996; Award, Prov. of Quebec, for exceptional contribution to Quebec Black Medical Assn., 1994; Quarter Century Club Member, RVH, 1991; Person of the Year Award, MABBP, 1989. **WORKS:** in, *American J of Obstetrics & Gynecology; CMAJ; J of Obstetrics & Gynecology of the British Commonwealth.* **EDUCATION:** FRCS Canada & Quebec Certified Specialist, 1966-67. MD, CM, 1961; BSc, 1957, McGill University. Cdn Officers Training Corp. (2nd Lieutenant RC Artillery), 1956. **CONTACT:** Tel: 514-937-8432

TUCKER, Margaret Y.

COMMUNITY ORGANIZER, Nepean, ON. Born: Jamaica/ in Canada since: 1972.

▶ Margaret Tucker has been actively involved in a variety of community and charitable organizations in the Ottawa area for many years: National Institute of Jamaican-Canadians; Nepean Lions Club; Barrhaven Lions Club; Rich Little Endowment Fund; former Director, Canadian Ethnocultural Council; National Council of Jamaicans and Supportive Org.; she has also coordinated visits to Ottawa by the National Dance Theatre Co. of Jamaica. **CAREER:** worked with the Govt. of Canada for 17 yrs. in Human Resources; as Employment Equity Officer with Revenue Canada, she led sessions on cultural awareness and workplace harassment for management and employees. In 1993, she was appointed to the Treasury Board's Interdepartmental Visible Minorities Committee and participated in organizing the first Aboriginal Career Symposium, which attracted over 300 Aboriginal youth from across the country. She was also a member of the 1993 Cdn NGO delegation to the UN World Conference on Human Rights in Austria and participated in the presentation of amendments to the Articles of the Human Rights Charter. **HONS.:** 2000 Medal, for contributions to community life, City of Nepean; Lion of the Year, 1996-97; Recognition by the RCMP for community work. **MOTTO:** You'll never walk alone. **CONTACT:** yomar@cyberus.ca

▶TURENNE, Joujou

CONTEUSE, Joujou – Amie du Vent, Montréal, QC. Née: Haïti/ au Canada depuis: 1969.

▶ Joujou Turenne a reçu une formation en psychologie et récréologie de l'Université d'Ottawa et en danse thérapeutique de l'Ottawa Dance Centre. Professeur de théâtre et de danse à l'Université de Montréal 1985-93, et à l'École Internationale de Montréal, 1990-93, elle est maintenant, co-fondatrice d'une compagnie de danse afro-antillaise et d'un camp d'été pour les jeunes d'origine haïtienne à Ottawa. Elle a choisi les arts pour exprimer sa vision du monde. Elle est, tour à tour, comédienne, chorégraphe, conteuse et auteur, surtout de contes et de récits poétiques. Depuis 1990, elle travaille davantage comme conteuse à travers le Canada, aux Antilles, en Europe et en Afrique. Elle est comédienne et co-scénariste du film *Tabala, rythmes du vent*, 1997; et a aussi participé à la série pour enfants, *Mon ami Maya*, TFO, 1992, et dans l'émission pour enfant, *Passe-Partout* de Radio-Québec, de 1987 à 1989. **PRIX:** plusieurs, y compris: Personnalité, détermination et engagement: témoins actuels, 2000; Prix Cator, pour l'ensemble de son travail, 1998; Prix Gémeau: Multiculturalisme, 1988. **ŒUVRES:** y compris: *Ti Pinge*, 2000; *Joujou, amie du Vent*, 1998; « La Mort, » dans, *La grande nuit du conte,* 2000; « Lune dansera pour Soleil » dans, *Tout un monde à raconter*, 1995. **ŒUVRES À SON PROPOS:** y compris: *La Presse*; *Le Devoir*; *La Nouvelliste*; *La Dauphine*, France; *The Native J* (Yukon); *Livresplus.com*; magazine *D'ici et d'ailleurs*; Personnalité, *calendrier MHN*, 1996. **FORMATION:** Voix et mouvement, Groupe de la Place Royale, Ottawa; Pol Pelletier, Dojo for actors, Montréal; Stage, danse africaine et orientales (France, Brésil, Canada); Danse moderne, jazz, & danse thérapeutique, Ottawa Dance Theatre; BA, Psychology, U. d'Ottawa. **CONTACT:** amieduvent@hotmail.com; Fax: 514-369-6808

▶**TURNER-BAILEY, Marjorie**
PRACTICAL NURSE, Roseway Hospital/ **GENEALOGICAL RESEARCHER,** Black Loyalist Society, Box 317, Lockeport, NS B0T 1L0. Born: Lockeport, NS.
▶ Marjorie Turner-Bailey, in her youth, was an Olympic sprinter who qualified for three Olympic Games (1968, '72, and '76). From 1963 to 1977, she won medals in the Pan Am and Commonwealth Games and competed in track events all over the world. In 1966, she played in the Cdn Senior League Basketball Championships, and was a member of the winning Winnipeg team. Professionally, she trained as a Practical Nurse in Manitoba and, after a year in Jamaica, returned to BC and began working at the Vancouver General Hospital. **COMMUNITY:** acts as a presenter for local schools; is active with the Black Loyalist Heritage Society. She has also written articles on her genealogical research. **HONS.:** Wall of Honour, BCS/NS, 2000; Marjorie Turner-Bailey Award, established and named in her honour, Black Loyalist Heritage Society, 1999; Hon. Member inductee, Black & Gold Wall of Fame, Dalhousie U., 1985; NS Sports Hall of Fame, 1984; BC Sports Hall of Fame, 1976; NS Athlete of the Year, 1964. **WORKS:** publications on the descendants of the Turner Family for the Shelburne Genealogical Society, 2001; and for the Black Loyalist Heritage Society, 2001. **REVIEWED IN:** papers & magazines across Canada including: *Maclean's*; *The Coast Guard*; *Vancouver Sun*; *Globe and Mail*. **EDUCATION:** Practical Nurse, Manitoba Institute of Technology, 1968. **CONTACT:** blackloyalist@auracom.com; www. blackloyalist.com

▶UPSHAW, Fred

LABOUR UNION LEADER & ACTIVIST (Ret.), Ontario Public Service Employee's Union (OPSEU). Resides in Oshawa, ON. Born: Halifax, NS.

▶ Fred Upshaw has had many chapters in his life but is best known as: a student activist, leading his first strike at age 17 over the introduction of mandatory school uniforms without consultation with the student body; a singer, with the Bellaires, then the Lincolns (but declined an offer to join the Mills Brothers); a lacrosse coach, for over 20 yrs. and winner of many championships; an orator, winning many speaking contests with the Oshawa Jaycees and preparing him for his future role as leader of one of Ontario's largest and most powerful unions, OPSEU. **CAREER:** he joined the Whitby Psychiatric Hospital (WPH) in 1971, and worked his way up from attendant to nurse once his courses at Durham College were completed in 1974; at WPH, he became active in the union and was soon elected Chief Steward, then president of local 331, representing over 1,000 employees; 1980, he was elected to the OPSEU executive board; 1984, he was elected First Vice-President and treasurer for the 90,000 strong membership across Ontario. In 1990, he became President of OPSEU and served until 1995, becoming the first Black in Canada to lead a major union. **HIGHLIGHTS:** during his involvement with the union there were many successes: at WPH, he advocated for Employee Assistance Programs to assist staff with personal problems; he negotiated bargaining unit reform and human rights language; he won the right to strike for provincial civil servants; won joint control over the pension plan in the OPS and colleges; secured political rights for Crown employees; won bargaining for BPS ambulance officers; promoted employment equity within the OPSEU membership and in the union's hiring. In 1991, he held a summit to foster closer relations with Indian Reserves and Native Friendship Centres. During his second term as President he successfully fought to reverse a number of decisions by the NDP government of the day. On completion of his second term in 1995, he was not re-elected, but continued as an executive board member and VP of region 3, until his retirement in 1998. He has also been an active member of the Coalition of Black Trade Unionists. **HONS.:** numerous awards over the years including: OFL Honour Roll, 2001; OPSEU Human Rights Award, 1999; Lifetime membership in OPSEU, 1998; Outstanding Commitment, Onyx Lions Club, 1998; Outstanding Leadership, WPH, 1997; Alumnus of Distinction, Durham College, 1994; 30 yrs. dedication, CBTU, 1993. **REVIEWED IN:** major newspapers, magazines, radio and TV interviews; *Some Black Men*, 1999. **EDUCATION:** Durham College, 1974; Malvern Collegiate, 1953; declined scholarship offered by NAACP to attend university in Texas, opting instead to work to help his mother support the family. **CONTACT:** fred.upshaw@sympatico.ca; Fax: 905-721-7573

▶UPSHAW, Robert Graham (Ted)

INSPECTOR, Royal Canadian Mounted Police (RCMP), Cole Harbour Detachment, Cole Harbour, NS. Born: NS.

▶ In 1999, Ted Upshaw became the first Black commissioned officer in the RCMP, attaining the rank of Inspector, and was given charge of Cole Harbour Detachment. He joined the RCMP in 1981; after training, he was posted to BC until 1993; was promoted to the rank of Corporal and was an Instructor at the Training Academy in Regina, SK, 1993-96; promoted to Sergeant and served in Ottawa; 1997, transferred to NS as Support Operations NCO. **OTHER:** he excelled in basketball while in high school and university; 1976-81, was a member of the national basketball program; while at Acadia University was a three-time all-Canadian player. **COMMUNITY:** TU supports a number of community initiatives and has a particular interest in being a role model to youth. **HONS.:** Inductee, Acadia Sports Hall of Fame, 2002; Award of Excellence, Cdn Centre for Police Race Relations, 1999. **REVIEWED IN:** *Journey: African Canadian History*, 2000. **EDUCATION:** BA, Acadia U.; Windsor Regional High School. **MOTTO:** You'll always miss 100 per cent of the shots you don't take. **CONTACT:** Ted.Upshaw@rcmp-grc.gc.ca

▶USHER, Harold

COUNCILLOR, London, ON. **ENGINEER/AUTHOR/PRESIDENT,** "Adventures in…" Seminars & Speeches, 718 Chiddington Ave., London, ON N6C 2W8. Born: Belize/ in Canada since: 1963.
▶ Harold Usher is a Councillor in London, Ontario who, with his election in 2000, became the first Black elected to London City Council. He is a 1972 Civil Engineering graduate of Concordia U. and worked for Bell Canada for 24 yrs. During that time he became a motivational speaker, personal development trainer and author. He is an advocate for human rights issues, equity, and anti-racism; has been a mentor to many and encouraged others to become mentors and role models. **AFFIL/MBRSHP:** past: Brd., Fanshawe College; Brd., London Library; Toastmasters Int'l; current: Commissioner, London Transit Commission; Vice-Chair, Joint Board of Management, Lake Huron Primary Water Supply System; Brd., Elgin Middlesex Oxford Local Training; Ont. Society of Professional Engineers; Telephone Pioneers of America. **OTHER:** founder and president of "Adventures in…" Seminars and Speeches, a company offering HR development workshops to individuals and organizations for learning, leading and performing in the workplace. **HONS.:** GG 125th Anniv. Medal, 1992. **WORKS:** include, *Prostate! Prostate! Prostate! A Problem of Men*; *Communicating with Impact.* **EDUCATION:** B.Eng, Civil, Concordia U., 1972. **MOTTO:** Lots of people believe in you, make sure you are one of them. **CONTACT:** Tel: 519-661-4879; Fax: 519-661-5933; husher@wwdc.com

▶VANCOL, Frantz

PRESIDENT & CEO, Jeunes Romantiques/Drula Fabrik, PO Box 355, Stn. R, Montreal, QC H2S 3M2. Born: Haiti/ in Canada since: 1976.
▶ Frantz Vancol was born in Port-au-Prince, Haiti but left in 1969 due to the political situation. He joined relatives in Liberia, then moved to the US to study Civil Engineering; in addition, he studied Business Administration and Cosmetology. Soon after, Holiday Magic Cosmetics recruited him as their general distributor and marketing instructor, a position that involved teaching sales techniques worldwide. In addition, he established NYC's Young Romantic Beauty Salons. In 1976, he moved to Canada and launched a chain of three beauty shops, *Les Jeunes Romantiques*, wherein he introduced the Canadian market to some of the most popular hair and skin care products specifically tailored for Blacks. He founded Tropico Inc., a wholesaler of tropical consumer products, and New York-New York, a retailer of food and cosmetics, and became the exclusive distributor of many specialized products. With a loan from the Mathieu Da Costa BDC, he fulfilled a lifelong dream when he started to manufacture Quisqueya-Boyo, a tropical flavoured soft drink. **COMMUNITY:** has supported many community activities which foster closer relations between the anglophone and francophone Blacks in Montreal; has tutored students with learning difficulties, taught languages to new immigrants, and organized and spoken at seminars and conferences on hairstyling and cosmetology. A past member of the Organizing Committee of Quebec's Caribbean Festival, he has regularly supported the Miss Black Quebec Contest. He is also Vice-President of the Racing Soccer Club of Montreal-North. **HONS.:** include, Award, for extraordinary contribution to the business world, Muhammad's Mosque of Montreal, 1996; Jackie Robinson Award, Businessman of the Year, MABBP, 1995. **REVIEWED IN:** *Montreal Gazette*; *BHM Calendar*, 1998; *Commerce*, 1997; *Les*

Affaires, 1996. **EDUCATION:** Cosmetology, Wilfred Academy, NY; Bus. Admin., Geneva Business School; Civil Engineering, NY Staten Island College. **CONTACT:** Tel: 450-963-9817; Fax: 450-963-9817

▶VASSELL, Phillip

CO-PUBLISHER, *Word* Magazine, 6-295 Queen St. E., Brampton, ON L6W 4S6. Born: Jamaica/ in Canada since: 1975.

▶ Phil Vassell and partner, Donna McCurvin, are the founders and publishers of *Word*, Toronto's first and leading urban culture magazine which they started in 1992 and publish ten times per year. The magazine is distributed across Canada, with local editions in Detroit and New York. *Word* magazine also provides training for students in media, through co-op programs; and, they initiated the Minority Media Training Program in partnership with the province of Ontario and the Southern Ontario Newspaper Guild. In 1997, the two co-founders started the Toronto Urban Music Festival, a showcase for new and emerging urban artists. **HONS.:** Best Publication, UMAC/ Urban X-posure, 2002 & 2001; Harry Jerome, business, 2000; Special Recognition Award, UMAC, 2000. **WORKS:** *Word* magazine, published 10x/yr. **CONTACT:** phil@wordmag.com; www.wordmag.com

VEECOCK, June

DIRECTOR, Human Rights, Ontario Federation of Labour, Ste. 202-15 Gervais Dr., Toronto, ON M3C 1Y8. Born: Guyana.

▶ June Veecock has been an active trade unionist for many years. Since 1986, she has been the Director, Human Rights at the Ontario Federation of Labour (OFL), with responsibility for the organization's anti-racism and equity programs. In this capacity, she advises the OFL on policy matters relating to human rights and the workplace; she works with affiliates of the OFL by assisting in the development of anti-racism, human rights policies, and training materials for their members; she also facilitates human rights and anti-racism workshops for labour and community groups. Her trade union roots in Canada began with Local 79 of CUPE where, during her years of service at the Riverdale Hospital, she was a shop steward, member of the health and safety committee, and deputy chair of the women's committee. **COMMUNITY:** founding member and two-time President of the Coalition of Black Trade Unionists (CBTU); Congress of Black Women of Canada, working primarily with Black nurses to challenge racism in health care facilities across the province. **HONS.:** include, 25th Anniv. Award, Urban Alliance on Race Relations, 2001; Award of Distinction, Harmony Movement, 2000; Leadership, 1999, Humanitarian, 1998, CBTU; Kay Livingstone Award, Congress of Black Women, 1997; Community Award, Town of Markham, 1997; Community City Award, Ont. Min. of Correctional Services, 1997. **REVIEWED IN:** local, community, labour publications; *Millennium Minds,* 2000. **CONTACT:** jveecock@ofl-fto.on.ca; Fax: 416-441-0772

▶VIEIRA, John F.

EDUCATOR (Ret.), City of York Board of Education. Resides in Mississauga, ON. Born: Guyana/ in Canada since: 1968.

▶ John Vieira spent 25 yrs. as a teacher with the York Board of Education. His most significant contribution to the community has been the introduction of a Saturday morning tutorial program for Black youth at Vaughan Rd. Collegiate, which ran from 1982 to 2001. Under the supervision of the Cdn Alliance of Black Educators, the program was designed to offer remedial support in Math, English, Science, and History to students of Caribbean heritage. This program had the distinction of being one of the longest-running community tutorial programs, helping hundreds of youth over the years, many going on to attend and complete university. Since his retirement, JV continues to provide education and training through the introduction of the Each One Teach One program in his native Guyana. **HONS.:** include, Award, City of York Board of Education, 1996; Charles Moody Award, National Alliance of Black School Educators (US), 1995, the only Black from Canada to receive this honour. **REVIEWED IN:** *Globe and Mail*; *Share*; *NOW*; *Weekly Gleaner.* **EDUCATION:** M.Ed; B.Ed, U of T. BA, York U.; London U., UK, 1966. **MOTTO:** You pass here but once; this is no trial run. **CONTACT:** johnvieira@sympatico.ca; Fax: 905-896-2064

▶**VIRGO, Clement**
FILMMAKER/DIRECTOR, c/o BFVN, Toronto, ON. Born: Jamaica/ in Canada since: 1976.
▶ Clement Virgo is one of Canada's emerging new feature filmmakers. His first feature, *Rude*, had its world premiere in 1995, at the Cannes International Film Festival and was the opening Canadian feature at the 1995 Toronto International Film Festival (TIFF); it was invited to 25 other film festivals and received three Best Film citations. His second feature film, *Love Come Down*, premiered at the TIFF, 2000; it later won three Genie Awards; was shown at the Berlin Film Festival, 2001, and won prizes at Urbanworld, Jamerican, and Acapulco Film Festivals, including Best Film prize at the London, UK Black Filmmakers Festival. In 1997, he completed production of a TV feature for the CBC, *The Planet of Junior Brown*, which premiered at the TIFF and for which he received an Emmy nomination; the film has also been shown internationally winning a number of prizes including Grand Prize, Urbanworld FF, and the Silver Nymph for innovative screenwriting, Monte Carlo Festival. He also has several other TV credits, including episodes for *Soul Food.* **OTHER:** his first short film produced at the Cdn Film Centre, 1993, won prizes at the Toronto and Chicago film festivals; it also won the Paul Robeson Award at the 1995, Pan African Film Festival. His other shorts, made in 1991 and '92 have been sold for TV broadcast in the UK, Australia and Canada; he also directed a music video for the Warren Beatty movie, *Bulworth.* **EDUCATION:** Canadian Film Centre, 1991 & '92. **CONTACT:** pjvirgo@rogers.com

▶WADE, Jan

VISUAL ARTIST, Vancouver, BC. Born: Hamilton, ON.

▶ Jan Wade is a visual artist, originally from Hamilton, Ontario, now residing in Vancouver BC. Her work: drawings, altars, and cross icons, reflects her roots in the African Methodist Church and the Southern Black American aesthetic (her father's family is from Danville, Virginia), which greatly influenced her formative years. "I am very interested in the spiritual practices formed by new world slave cultures, notably, Afro- Christianity, Vodoun, and Santeria, and their power to adapt symbols of dominant culture and transform them into symbols of survival, self-reflection and empowerment." She spent several summers as a travelling visual artist with Lilith Fair and has exhibited widely across Canada and abroad as both artist and lecturer. She has been the recipient of several Canada Council grants and was one of two artists selected to represent Canada at the first international art biennial in Johannesburg, South Africa. **CONTACT:** soultonepoem@yahoo.ca

▶WALKER, Phyllis

EDUCATOR/ENAMELLIST/STORYTELLER, Enamel-on-copper murals & holloware, Toronto, ON. Born: Jamaica/ in Canada since: 1965.

▶ Phyllis Walker is a teacher, storyteller, and artenamellist. She is the founder and past-President of the Canadian Enamellist Assn. In this capacity she represented Canada in China, 1999, at the Enamellist Society Delegates Convention. She is the winner of the former City of North York's Award for Art in Public Places, for the 19-foot mural honouring Garrett A. Morgan, inventor of the traffic signals, and which is permanently housed at the Maria Schucka Library (Toronto). As a storyteller, she has participated in many storytelling events including the gala opening of *The Lion King*, 2001, and the GG's first Christ-

mas Concert in Toronto, 1999. She was the first Black talk show host on CFRB radio, 1991-93. **COMMUNITY:** JCA; Chair, Arts York, 2001-02; Storyteller's School of Toronto. **AFFIL/MBRSHP:** Cdn Enamellists' Assn.; American Enamellists' Assn. **HONS.:** winner of the Toronto Outdoor Art Exhibition for Original Art, 1998 & '99; Award for Art in Public Places, City of North York, 1998. **WORKS:** wrote for *Glass on Metal*, 1988-90. **EDUCATION:** M.Ed, 1997; ESL/D Specialist, 1993; BA, 1982, U of T. B.Ed, York U., 1991. **HEROES/ROLE MODELS:** Beverly Mascoll, friend. **MOTTO:** If you have no confidence in yourself, you are twice defeated in the race of life. With confidence you have won even before you have started. (Marcus Garvey) **CONTACT:** llanoka@aol.com

▶WALL, Carol

HUMAN RIGHTS DIRECTOR, Communications, Energy & Paperworkers Union/Canada, Ste. 1900-350 Albert St., Ottawa, ON K1R 1A4. Born: Toronto, ON.

▶ Carol Wall is the first Human Rights Director with the Communications, Energy and Paperworkers Union of Canada (CEP), a position she has held since 2000. She first joined CEP in 1995, as a national representative, responsible for negotiating collective agreements, presenting arbitrations, facilitating educational courses, etc. CEP is one of the largest private sector unions in Canada, representing workers in pulp and paper mills, telephone companies, in the oil, gas, chemical and mining industries. It also includes printers, journalists/technicians in print and broadcast, hotel workers, truck drivers, and nurses. While working with the *Toronto Star* for 17 yrs., she was a union representative and occupied a number of volunteer positions, from Steward to Local Officer, Union Counsellor to the Union's representative on various labour bodies. **OTHER:** she has served on the Women's Committee of the Ontario Federation of Labour; works with the

Human Rights Committee of the Canadian Labour Congress (CLC); is a member of the CBTU; and, was an executive brd. member of the Pay Equity Advocacy and Legal Services Clinic. She represented the CEP as a member of the CLC delegation at the UNWCAR, 2001. **CONTACT:** cwall@cep.ca; Fax: 613-230-5801

▶**WALLS, Bryan Edmond,** DDS, O.Ont. **DENTAL SURGEON,** Private Practice/ **LOCAL HISTORIAN/ AUTHOR,** Essex, ON. Born: Windsor, ON.

▶ Dr. Bryan Walls was born in Windsor and raised in Puce, Ontario, a small farming community outside of Windsor. He began his studies at the University of Detroit and completed them at the University of Windsor and U of T, graduating with a Doctor of Dental Surgery degree in 1973. Along with his dental practice, he is also well known for his work in researching and documenting the history of the UGRR. **ACTIVITIES:** founder and co-curator of the John Freeman Walls Historic Site and Underground Railroad Museum in Puce, Ontario; a noted historian and lecturer on how the UGRR can teach math and science, anti-bullying, and little-known African diaspora history; a deacon of the historic First Baptist Church Puce, founded by his ancestors in 1846; author of *The Road That Led to Somewhere,* based on a true story, of the UGRR; and, has co-authored an educational study unit for teachers and students. **AFFIL/MBRSHP:** past-President, Essex County Dental Society; past Brd. Secretary, Ont. Heritage Foundation; past-President, Ont. Historical Society, founded in 1888; cmtee member, Metropolitan Toronto Police Services Recruiting Unit. **HONS.:** several including: Chancellor's Award, Iona College, U. of Windsor, 2002; Order of Ontario, 1994; Outstanding Achievement Award, for Volunteerism, Govt. of Ontario, 1992; Lamp of Learning Award, OSSTF, 1989; Hon. Doctor of Humanities, Urban Bible College, Detroit, 1982. **WORKS:** *The Road*

that Led to Somewhere, concept album, 2002; book, 1980. **EDUCATION:** screenwriting, Ryerson U., 1998; D.Dental Surgery, 1973, U of T; BSc, 1969, U. of Windsor. **HEROES/ROLE MODELS:** Clifford Walls, father; Earl Walls, uncle. **MOTTO:** Never, never, never give up! **CONTACT:** Tel: 519-727-4866; Fax: 519-727-5793

▶**WALTER, Paul L.,** QC. **LAWYER/PARTNER,** Waterbury Newton, Box 98 Kentville, NS B4N 3V9. Born: Antigua/ in Canada since: 1974.

▶ Paul Walter is a partner in the law firm of Waterbury Newton, where he began his practice as an associate lawyer in 1982; he became a partner in 1987. His areas of practice were general, 1982-86; since 1986, he has specialized in the area of civil litigation with emphasis on personal injury claims, criminal defence, and administrative law. He has represented clients at all levels including Provincial, Family, County, Supreme Courts, Court of Appeal, as well as the Supreme Court of Canada. In addition, he has represented clients before several boards and tribunals, Workers' Compensation Board, Workers' Compensation Appeals Board/Tribunal, and the Canada Pension Plan Review Tribunal. **AFFIL/MBRSHP:** NS Barristers' Society, since 1982; founding member, Black Lawyers' Assn. of NS; BBI; Brain Injury Assn. of NS. **OTHER:** has made many presentations on the practice of law to elementary and secondary school classes, as well as to members of the Dalhousie Black Law Students' Assn.; represents the legal profession at Career Day Workshops; has mentored a number of junior associates and articling clerks; coaches "Mini" Soccer, 1989-99. **HONS.:** appointed QC, 1998. **EDUCATION:** LLB, Dalhousie U., 1981; BA, Saint Mary's U., 1978. **MOTTO:** Look, listen, learn, strategize and execute. If a task is worth doing, always strive to do it to the best of your ability. **CONTACT:** pwalter@waterburynewton. ns.ca; Fax: 902-678-7727

► **WALTERS, Ewart L.**
JOURNALIST/COMMUNICATIONS CONSULTANT,
Boyd McRubie Communications, 473 View-mount Dr., Ottawa, ON K2E 7P3. Born: Jamaica/ in Canada since: 1964.

▶ Ewart Walters is a writer, poet, and award-winning journalist. He is credited with launching Ottawa's Black community newspaper, *The Spectrum*, in 1984. He also produced the book, *Jamaican Canadians–A Commitment to Excellence,* 1987, for the Toronto-based, JCA. Trained as a journalist, he worked for many years as a public servant in Jamaica and Canada; he was Sr. Advisor in the office of the President of CIDA; more recently was appointed Sr. Advisor Employment Equity, and elected Executive Secretary of the National Council of Visible Minorities in the federal public service. **BACKGROUND:** earlier in his career, he was a member of Jamaica's Foreign Service, serving in Ottawa as Counsellor and in New York as Consul and Director of Information at the Consulate-General, with responsibilities for the Permanent Mission to the United Nations. Before coming to Canada, he occupied senior positions with the *Daily Gleaner* and the *Jamaica Daily News*. **COMMUNITY:** executive positions in several organizations, including the West Indian Assn. of Ottawa; Nat'l Council of Jamaican and Supportive Organizations in Canada; Ontario Cricket Assn.; Black History Ottawa; Ottawa-Carleton Immigrant Services Organization. **HONS.:** citations from several groups including the Ottawa Police, Jamaica-Ottawa Community Assn., Bel Air Cricket Club, the *Ottawa Citizen*, the Federal Govt. of Canada. **EDUCATION:** MA, Journalism, 1979; BA, Journalism, 1968, Carleton U. **CONTACT:** spectrum@storm.ca; Fax: 613-226-8984

► **WALWYN, Frank E.**
LAWYER, PARTNER, WeirFoulds LLP, Ste. 1600-130 King St. W., Toronto, ON M5X 1J5.

▶ Frank Walwyn is a partner at WeirFoulds LLP, a full-service law firm in Toronto. His practice area is civil litigation; he appears before all courts and tribunals. A member of the Law Society of Upper Canada, he was also called to the bar of St. Kitts and Nevis and is qualified to practise in the Caribbean. While the majority of his practice focuses on litigation in Ontario, he also currently advises Canadian clients on matters involving their activities in the Caribbean. **AFFIL/MBRSHP:** Advocate's Society; CABL; Queen's Business Club; Organization of Commonwealth Caribbean Bar Assn.; St. Kitts and Nevis Bar Assn. **WORKS:** contributing editor to *Credit and Banking Litigation J.* **EDUCATION:** Cert., Legal Education, Eugene Dupuch Law School, Nassau, 2000; LLB, Queen's U., 1993; BA, U of T, 1987. **CONTACT:** Tel: 416-365-1110; fwalwyn@weirfoulds.com

► **WARREN, Rev. Brian**
MINISTER/EXECUTIVE DIRECTOR, Canada in Prayer, 1295 North Service Rd., Burlington, ON L7R 4M2. Born: USA/ in Canada since: 1987.

▶ Rev. Brian Warren played with the Toronto Argonauts for eight yrs. before leaving professional football, in 1994, to enter into full-time ministry. He was ordained in 1997, in the African Methodist Episcopal Church (AME, founded in 1816 in the US by Richard Allen, an ex-slave), and served as Associate Pastor at the Grant AME chapel in Toronto. **ACTIVITIES:** since 1994, he has been actively involved with Promise Keepers, a Christian men's ministry; in 1995, he and seven colleagues, established Promise Keepers Men's Ministry in Canada. In 1997, he founded Canada in Prayer (CIP), an evangelical movement which uses popular media like the Internet and TV to increase the number of Christians in Canada through prayer-driven ministries. CIP falls under the umbrella organization, Connect Family of Ministries, which is also responsible for the following: Canadian Prayer Assembly (sponsored by the Cdn Council of Churches and the Evangelical Fellowship of Canada), which brings together over 8,000 participants annually; Kids Fest Canada, which assists children living in poverty (national ratio is one in five) through literacy programs and purchase of school supplies; Canada for Christ tours; Market Place, which provides mentoring support to business leaders across the country. In addition, he is Chaplain to the Toronto Phantoms football team and works with the Toronto Argonauts football team, and has been signed to commentate their games for the 2002-03 season. He appears as a regular host on *100 Huntley Street*, the TV magazine program. **EDUCATION:** completing M.Theology, Tyndale College; BA, Arts, Science & Communication, U. of Arizona. **HEROES/ROLE MODELS:** Father; David Eaton; Ed Trexler. **MOTTO:** It's hard to stumble on your knees. **CONTACT:** prayer@ canadainprayer.com; www.canadainprayer.com

▶WASHINGTON, Jackie

JAZZ & FOLK MUSICIAN/PERFORMER, Borealis Recording Co., Ste. 19-225 Sterling Rd., Toronto, ON M5R 2B2. Born: Hamilton, ON.

▶ Jackie Washington was born in Hamilton in 1919 and made his musical debut in 1924. He came from a musical family: his father played the fiddle and accordion, his mother sang, his uncle played the guitar. **BACKGROUND:** by 1930, he and three of his brothers were playing around Hamilton as the Four Washingtons. He played guitar and later the piano. In the late '30s, he joined the CPR as a sleeping car porter before he was drafted into the army. After the war and his discharge, he became the first Black in Canada to become a DJ with Hamilton's CHML. He continued to perform locally and with visiting jazz performers (including Duke Ellington, Lionel Hampton and later with folk performers Gordon Lightfoot, Joni Mitchell, and others); but as music could not provide an adequate living, he continued to juggle jobs as a CPR sleeping car attendant, factory worker, washroom attendant and as operator of a shoeshine stand at the old Woodbine Racetrack. He also continued to develop his growing repertoire of songs, which is now estimated at over 1,260. **HIGHLIGHTS:** JW's musical career was greatly advanced in 1964 at age 45, when folk music promoter Bill Powell introduced him to Toronto's Yorkville music scene. In 1976, he released his first album, *Blues and Sentimental*; in 1983, he made his film debut, appearing in Sneezy Waters' movie *Hank Williams–The Show He Never Gave*; he has also performed on CBC Radio and TV. Since the '70s, JW has become a regular feature at folk festivals across the country. His other recordings include: *Where Old Friends Meet*, 1991 (nominated for a Juno); *Keeping out of Mischief*, 1995; *Midnight Choo Choo*, 1998; and, his 1999 CD, *We'll Meet Again,* is a compilation of concert recordings made with Mose Scarlett and Ken Whitely, accomplished musicians with whom he has collaborated over the years. **HONS.:** include, inducted into Canadian Jazz & Blues Hall of Fame, 2002; Estelle Klein Lifetime Achievement Award, Ontario Council of Folk Festival, 2001; award created in his honour, Sudbury's Northern Lights Festival; Lifetime Achievement Award, Ontario Arts Council, 1991; inducted into Hamilton Gallery of Distinction; Blues with a Feeling Award, Maple Blues. **CONTACT:** Tel: 416-530-4288; Fax: 416-533-9988

▶WATERMAN, The Most Reverend Dr. Vincent

ARCHBISHOP, St. Philip's African Orthodox Church of Canada, 34 Hankard St., Sydney, NS B1N 2C2. Born: Barbados/ in Canada since: 1983.

▶ The Most Reverend Dr. Vincent Waterman has been the Archbishop of the African Orthodox Church (AOC) in Canada since 1994, and serves at St. Philip's AOC in Nova Scotia. **CAREER:** joined the AOC in 1967, and served in New York for seven yrs. before assuming the rectorship of St. Philip's AOC in 1983; became the Commissioner of Oaths for the province of NS in 1986; was instrumental in having the St. Philip's AOC site designated as a Heritage Property of NS; was consecrated to the office of Archbishop in 1994. **BACKGROUND:** prior to joining the Church, he was the first Black to work at the Brooklyn Union Gas Company; he rose from meter reader to inspector and, by his example, made it easier for other Blacks to gain employment in this company. He was first ordained a priest in the old Catholic Church before joining the AOC. **AFFIL/MBRSHP:** member, Council of Churches; past-President, John Howard Society; executive, Sydney City Home Makers; Brd., Black Employment Partnership Cmtee; previously on the Boards of the Red Cross Society, Cancer Society, Right to Life Society, Children's Aid Society, Sydney Boys and Girls Club. **HONS.:** include, Hon. D.Div., Int'l Reform U., Mississouri, 1999; Griot Merit Award, BCC/NS, 1999; GG 125th Anniv. Medal, 1992; Volunteer Service Award, Boys & Girls Club of Canada, 1988; Volunteer Service, Sydney City Council, 1988. **EDUCATION:** Dipl., Licentiate, Endich Theological Seminary, New York, 1978; Sheldon Bible College & St. James Evangelical Orthodox Church, 1958. **HEROES/ROLE MODELS:** Mother; Archbishop George Ford. **MOTTO:** With God, all things are possible. **CONTACT:** Tel: 902-567-1220

►WAVROCH, Hélène

PRÉSIDENTE, Conseil des aînés, 3e-10, P-O Chauveau, Québec, QC G1R 4J3. Née: Montréal, QC.

▶ Hélène Wavroch a commencé sa vie professionnelle comme infirmière avec une compétence importante pour les relations syndicales. Au cours de sa carrière, des formations en soins infirmiers, en relations industrielles, en droit, et en communication, l'ont amenée aux postes de porte-parole, conciliateur, procureur ou arbitre pour différents regroupements. **ACTIVITÉS PRINCIPALES**: Avant d'avoir 25 ans elle a été élue Présidente de la Fédération des Infirmières et Infirmiers Unis (devenue la FIIQ plus tard), composée de 10,000 membres, 1973-85; pendant son mandat elle a réussi à négocier une augmentation salariale de 44,8% en 1975, hausse jamais vue dans l'histoire syndicales québécoise. De 1974-80, elle a également été élue à la Présidence du Cartel des organismes professionnels de la santé (infirmier/e/s, travailleurs sociaux, radiothérapeutes, etc.), composé de 35,000 membres; en 1975, elle a représenté le Québec au Congrès International des femmes à Berlin-Est; lors de cette conférence, elle a été choisie comme rapporteur au nom de l'atelier, Femmes et travail, et elle a fait une présentation à ce sujet à l'ONU. De 1974-84, elle a été professeur à l'École des relations de travail des Maritimes où elle a enseigné un cours d'Administration et de Leadership. En 1985-98, elle a été nommée par l'Assemblée nationale du Québec, au poste de Vice-présidente de l'Institut de recherche et d'information sur la rémunération (IRIR), elle fut aussi directrice des relations patronales et syndicales; l'IRIR avait comme mandat d'informer le public de l'état et de l'évolution comparée de la rémunération globale des salariés du gouvernement et la rémunération globale des autres salariés québécois par la publication annuelle d'un rapport de recherche. Pendant six ans, 1991-97, elle a été aussi présidente du CRARR (Centre de recherche et d'action sur les relations raciales), un organisme à but non-lucratif, où elle a initié les premiers projets de développement de politiques visant à outiller les employeurs et les syndicats aux prises avec des problèmes de discrimination raciale dans le milieu de travail; elle a été membre fondatrice du Manoir Le Regain, une maison pour personnes âgées, regroupant surtout les infirmier/e/s à la retraite; depuis 1998, elle est Présidente du Conseil des aînés, un conseil consultatif pour le gouvernement provincial. Elle est aussi impliquée dans d'autres activités communautaires: Chambre du Commerce, Montréal Métropolitain; Conference Brd. Canada; et, une structure pour les jeunes défavorisés à Verdun. **PRIX:** plusieurs y compris: Plaque commémorative, Côte-des-Neiges Black Community Assn., 1998; mise en nomination, Femme de mérite, YWCA, 1996; Distinction Award, Social Order of Creative Arts, 1995; Trophée commémorative, CRAAR, 1994; mise en nomination, Femme de l'Année, Salon de la Femme, 1992; Plaque commémorative, Infirmier/e/s Unis; Plaque commémorative, Woman of the Year, Montreal Star, 1975. **ŒUVRES:** éditeur, *J Dialogue*; éd. *J Iota*. **ŒUVRES À SON PROPOS:** publications locales et nationales, y compris, *Montreal Gazette*; *Montreal Oracle*; *City Woman*; *J Le Devoir*; *Montreal Star*. **FORMATION:** Assoc. Conseillers en Relations Industrielle, 1980; Dipl., Broadcasting, Dave Boxer School of Broadcasting, 1977; Dipl., Nursing, Royal Victoria Hosp. School of Nursing, 1971. **MENTORS:** Adoptive parents, whose favourite expression was, "against all odds." **MOTTO:** If not, why not? **CONTACT:** hcorvaw@ hotmail.com; www.conseil-des-aines.qc.ca

► **WEBB, Rudy**
SINGER/ACTOR/PRODUCER, Overcoat Productions, Toronto, ON. Born: Bermuda/ in Canada since: 1960.
► Rudy Webb has had an extensive career as a singer and actor, appearing in the original Canadian productions of *Godspell*; *Indigo*; *Ain't Misbehavin'*; *Cats*; and *Tommy*, among others. For six years he was one of the hosts of the popular TVO children's series, *Join In*. After conceptualizing the late-night variety show, *Curtains Up*, he developed and produced it at the Ports Dinner Theatre; the show was such a success that Global TV had it adapted for television, resulting in 26 episodes of *Variety Tonite*. He was also a creative consultant on the CBC TV Gemini-award-winning special, *Music: a Family Tradition*. Other production credits include: *Fences* at the National Arts Centre and Theatre Calgary; *But I was Cool*, *Sophisticated Ladies*, and *Don't Dress for*

Dinner at the Limelight Dinner Theatre; *The Evolution of Jazz* at Young People's Theatre. He also produced the Mississauga Arts Awards for three yrs. and, *Amazing Journey*, narrated by Dr. David Suzuki. **HONS.:** Brenda Donahue Award, for "distinguished contribution & achievements within the Toronto Theatre Community," 1985; winner of the du Maurier Search for Talent, 1979. **EDUCATION:** Radio College of Canada, 1961. **CONTACT:** rudian76@hotmail.com; Fax: 416-265-9874

► **WEDDERBURN, Hobartson A.J. (Gus)**
BARRISTER/SOLICITOR/NOTARY PUBLIC, H.A.J. Wedderburn Law Office, Ste. 303-287 Lacewood Dr., Halifax, NS B3M 3Y7. Born: Jamaica/ in Canada since: 1952.
► "Gus" Wedderburn began his professional life in education before entering the legal profession in 1973. From 1957-71 he was a science and math teacher, Supervising Principal, and Principal in schools in the Halifax area; he also taught Latin at St. Mary's University. Since 1973, he has been a practising barrister, solicitor and notary public, and has been very active in community activities. **AFFIL/MBRSHP:** NS AACP, since 1959; Africville Relocation Cmtee; co-founder, BUF; candidate in provincial elections, 1968; founder, Black Educators' Assn.; Govt. of NS appointee to NS Human Rights Commission, 1965-81; Director and Solicitor, NS Home for Coloured Children, 1972-80; National Black Coalition of Canada; Moot Court Observer, Dalhousie U.; Advisor to the Black Businessmen's Consortium of NS, since 1989; Black Lawyers' Assn. of NS; St. John's Anglican Church. **HONS.:** include, Award, for outstanding contribution, City of Halifax, 2000; establishment of the HAJ Wedderburn Bursary at the Dalhousie Law School, 1998; inducted to W.P. Oliver Wall of Fame, BCC, 1998; Award of Recognition, CABL; Meritorious Award of Excellence, BUF, 1993; Award, for 30

yrs. of service, NS AACP, 1990; NS Human Rights Award, 1989; Education Recognition Award, Black Educators' Assn., 1989; Ebony Wall of Fame, 1980; Citation for Humanitarian Services, City of Halifax, 1980; Centennial Medal, 1967. **WORKS:** including, *From Slavery to the Ghetto, the History of the Negro in NS*, NS HRC, 1967. **REVIEWED IN:** *Millennium Minds*, 2000. **EDUCATION:** LLB, Dalhousie U., 1971; predoctoral studies, SS Administration, Columbia U., 1962-67; MA, Saint Mary's U., 1961; BA & B.Ed, Mount Allison U., 1957. **HEROES/ROLE MODELS:** Wife; children; sister. **MOTTO:** He that dwelleth in the secret place of the most high shall abide under the shadow of the Almighty. **CONTACT:** Fax: 902-443-5227

►**WEEKES, Kevin**
HOCKEY PLAYER/GOALTENDER, Carolina Hurricanes/ National Hockey League, c/o 1251 Avenue of the Americas, New York, NY 10020-1189, USA. Born: Toronto, ON, 1975.
▸ Kevin Weekes is a hockey player who plays in the position of goaltender, currently with the Carolina Hurricanes. Labeled the "Goalie of the Future" by various hockey teams, he began playing professionally in 1995 in the American Hockey League (AHL), after being drafted by the Florida Panthers. **CAREER HIGHLIGHTS:** played in the AHL until his first NHL game in October 1997; played 11 games that season and posted a 3.96 goals against average (GAA); traded to the Vancouver Canucks in January 1998, and posted a 3.83 GAA over 11 games; in the 1999-2000 season, he posted a 2.86 GAA over 20 games with the Canucks and registered his first shutout on October 24th; traded to the New York Islanders, December 1999, and posted a 3.41 GAA over 36 games; traded to the Tampa Bay Lightning, June 2000; in the 2000-2001 season, he played 61 games, posting a 3.14 GAA and four shutouts. In March 2002, he was traded to the Carolina Hurricanes, who became contenders for the Stanley

Cup and provided him an opportunity to play in his first Stanley Cup playoffs. Wearing jersey number 80, he is known to fans as "ShadyEighty" Weekes for his sharp and hard-to-anticipate goaltending strategies. During the 2001-2002 NHL playoffs, he was praised by fans and the media for improving the chances of the Carolina Hurricanes in their contention for the Stanley Cup. **OTHER:** born and raised in Toronto of Barbadian parentage, KW began playing hockey from an early age. Today, he is one of two Black goalies playing in the NHL. **HONS.:** shared James Norris Memorial Trophy, for fewest goals against, IHL, 1999; Harry Jerome Award, Athletics, 1994. **REVIEWED IN:** N. American publications including: *NY Times*; *The Washington Times*; *The Tampa Tribune*; *Toronto Star*; *Globe and Mail*, etc. **HEROES/ROLE MODELS:** Carl & Vadney Weekes, parents. **CONTACT:** info@nhl.com; www. nhlpa.com; Fax: 212-789-2080

►**WESTMORELAND-TRAORÉ, Juanita,** The Hon.
JUDGE, Court of Quebec, Palais de Justice, 1, Notre-Dame Est, Montreal, QC H2Y 1B6. Born: Montreal, QC.
▸ The Hon. Judge Juanita Westmoreland-Traoré is, since 1999, a member of the Court of Quebec and the first Black to be appointed to the judiciary in this province. She serves in the Criminal and Penal Division. Prior to this appointment, she was the Dean of the Faculty of Law, at the University of Windsor, as well as an Associate Professor, 1996-99. **CAREER HIGHLIGHTS:** Employment Equity Commissioner, Govt. Ontario, 1991-95, directed the creation of the first employment equity commission in Canada, which was set up to support and monitor the introduction of employment equity planning to 17,000 Ontario businesses; Professor, Dept. Legal Sciences, UQAM, 1976-91; Assistant Professor, Faculty of Law, U. of Montreal, 1972-76; Arbitrator, Human Rights Tribunal, Quebec, 1990; President, Coun-

cil on Cultural Communities and Immigration, Govt. Quebec, 1985-90, through extensive public consultations, research, public engagements and joint initiatives, increased public awareness of growing cultural diversity in Quebec; Commissioner, Canadian Human Rights Commission, 1983-85; Board, Consumer Protection Bureau, Govt. Quebec, 1979-83; maintained law practice, 1969-85. **OTHER:** Présidente, *Tribunal International contre la violence faite aux femmes haïtiennes*, 1997; Consultant, UN, seconded to National Commission on Truth and Justice, Haiti, 1995. **COMMUNITY:** Quebec Civil Liberties Union; Equality Rights Panel, Court Challenges Program of the Canadian Council on Social Development; Congress of Black Women of Canada. **HONS.:** including, Hon. Doctorates, UQAM, 2001 & U. of Ottawa Law Faculty, 1993; Alan Rose Award, Human Rights, Cdn Jewish Congress-Quebec Region, 2000; Woman's Pioneer Award, as 1st African-Cdn appointed to Bench in Quebec, Cdn Bar Assn.-Quebec, 1999; Medal for Achievement in the field of Human Rights, U. de Montréal, 1996; Chevalier, Ordre national du Québec, 1990. **WORKS:** including several conference & presentation papers; "Educational Equity: No Turning Back," in *Equity & How to Get It*, 1999. **REVIEWED IN:** *Millennium Minds*, 2000; *Some Black Women*, 1993. **EDUCATION:** Sr. Executives Program in Dispute Resolution, Harvard, MIT, Tufts Consortium, 1995. Doctorate in Public Law, 1972; *Dipl. d'études supérieures en sciences administratives*, 1968, U. Paris II, France. Lic. Droit (LL.1), U. de Montréal, 1966; BA, Marianopolis College, 1963. **MOTTO:** We are carried on the shoulders of those who went before us. **CONTACT:** jwestr@videotron.ca; Fax: 514-864-2465

▶WHITE, Carl A.

DEPUTY MAYOR, Saint John City Council; Human Rights Officer, New Brunswick Human Rights Commission, PO Box 5001, Saint John, NB E2L 4Y9. Born: Saint John, NB.

▶ Carl White is the Deputy Mayor of the City of Saint John, since 2001, and the first Black to occupy this position. He was first elected Councillor of the City of Saint John in 1998, serving until 2001; upon re-election, he was appointed to his current position. **CAREER:** has extensive experience in community development and race relations; since 1986 is a Human Rights Officer with the NB Human Rights Commission; was a member of the City of Saint John Committee on Race Relations and Multiculturalism, 1990-93; was Secretary of the Atlantic Multicultural Council, 1983-86; Delegate to the NB Multicultural Council, 1983-89; Vice-President and Secretary, Multicultural Assn. of Saint John, 1983-87. **COMMUNITY INVOLVEMENT:** he has been a member of PRUDE (the community organization working to enhance the quality of life for the Black population of Saint John) since the 1980s, was President, 1983-93, remained on the executive until 1995; member of the Human Rights Unit, Anglican Church of Canada, 1988-93; member of the NB Minorities Policing Committee (formed by the NB Assn. of Chiefs of Police and the RCMP to establish a better working relationship with racial and cultural minority communities in the province) since 1991; VP, Saint John Boys' and Girls' Club; Brd., Saint John Non-Profit Housing, since 1998. He has also had extensive involvement in athletics and coached or chaired committees for football, track & field, basketball, hockey, and golf. **HONS.:** recognition by PRUDE, for being first Black Deputy Mayor of Saint John, 2002; Volunteer Recognition, RCMP/Govt. of Canada, 2002; GG 125th Anniv. Medal; Recognition from Football New Brunswick, for outstanding contribution to Touch Football in NB, 1990. **EDUCATION:** Sociology & Psychology courses, U. of New Brunswick (Saint John); Human Rights and Relations course, National Training Institute; Human Rights Summer College, U. of Ottawa. **CONTACT:** cawhite@nb.sympatico.ca; Fax: 506-658-3075

▶WHITE, John Edgar (Jack)

LABOUR UNION ORGANIZER (Ret.), Canadian Union of Public Employees (CUPE), Toronto, ON. Born: Halifax, NS.

▶ Jack White is the son of Rev. William A. White who was the Chaplain and Honorary Captain of the No. 2 Construction Battalion, the only military unit in which Blacks were allowed to enlist in Canada in WWI. In 1949, JW was an early member of the Communist Party and spent the rest of his professional life fighting for greater rights for Blacks and all workers; he became known as, "Jack White, the Black Red." **CAREER HIGHLIGHTS:** in 1954, he became editor of *The Canadian Negro*, and one of the first to propose having a Charter of Rights for Canadians; he was invited to join the Iron Workers' Union as a Business Agent and was a delegate to the Labour Council; he was later with the Ontario Federation of Labour for two yrs., as Acting Director of Social Services; from 1970-90, he worked for CUPE and developed expertise in Workmen's Compensation appeals. Some of his most outstanding accomplishments include: winning the first heart attack case, proving that the condition, resulting in death, was caused by the intensity of the job; winning the first asbestos case, showing that contamination came from unsafe working conditions; he also won the first Fibra-Miyelda (back pain) case. Being the first Black to join these unions, JW realized that, in addition to advocating for greater respect of rights for workers, the unions themselves needed to be more inclusive of the diversity in their membership. Following retirement from CUPE, he worked, until recently, as a private Labour Consultant. **OTHER:** In addition to his labour activities he remained active in the community; was one of the advocates for the banning of *Little Black Sambo* from Ontario schools; founding member, Coalition of Black Trade Unionists; in 1963, ran as the NDP candidate for Dovercourt in the provincial elections. **HONS.:** several from the various Labour Councils: Lifetime Achievement Award, OFL, 1990; CBTU. **WORKS:** a number of pamphlets including, *Your Rights & the Employer's Obligations; Bill 99.* **REVIEWED IN:** local & nat'l publications, *Colour in the Union*, CUPE. **HEROES/ROLE MODELS:** Parents; Paul Robeson. **MOTTO:** Being Black, one must work twice as hard and be twice as good.

▶WHITE, Sheila

COMMUNICATIONS CONSULTANT, Words Media & Communications, 14 Murray Ave., Toronto, ON M1S 2A2. Born: Toronto, ON.

▶ Sheila White is a former community news specialist, newspaper columnist and editor; was Toronto Mayor Mel Lastman's Advisor and Community Resource Coordinator, from 1985-98, while he was mayor of North York. In that position, she dealt with issues pertaining to health, job creation, the disabled community, crime prevention, police-community initiatives, economic development, initiatives for seniors, and multiculturalism. She is now a senior advisor to Ontario provincial NDP Leader, Howard Hampton, and the NDP Caucus at Queen's Park in Toronto. **COMMUNITY INVOLVEMENT:** has been extensive, including musical performer; choir director; past President of CD Farquharson Community Assn.; founding Brd. member of Community Unity Alliance, formed to foster community unity within diversity and in partnership with groups like the police. **OTHER:** she is also the author of several children's books on anti-racist themes, and developed anti-racism questionnaires used by the Toronto Police and the Toronto Transit Commission. She has run twice for elected office, as a Toronto Councillor in a 2000 by-election and in the 2001 municipal elections. She is the owner of Words Media and Communications and provides services as a communications consultant. **HONS.:** several certificates of appreciation from the United Way, North York Harvest Food Bank, Toronto Police Services,

Toronto Fire Dept. **HEROES/ROLE MODELS:** Patricia Robbins, children's author. **MOTTO:** Remember your origins. **CONTACT:** Tel: 416-321-5294; words@rogers.com

▶**WHITEN, Grover (Tim)**
PROFESSOR/ARTIST/SCULPTOR, Dept. of Visual Art, York University, Rm. 246-4700 Keele St., Toronto, ON M3J 1P3. Born: USA/ in Canada since: 1968.

▶ Tim Whiten is a Professor at York University and former Chair of the Dept. of Visual Arts; he is also an internationally renowned artist whose works are included in many private, corporate, and public collections, including Canada's National Gallery, and the Art Gallery of Ontario. His works have been exhibited in major exhibitions of drawing and sculpture throughout N. America and Asia. Of his works it is said "Whiten creates his sculptural works by transforming familiar objects and materials, investing them with enigmatic presence." He began teaching at York U. in 1968; served as Director of Co-Curricular Art; Director, MFA Program; has been Artist-in-Residence in NY, 1977 and in Brazil, 2001/02. **HONS.:** Dean's Teaching Award, Faculty of Fine Arts, 1999/2000; Distinguished Leadership Award, for Extraordinary Service to the Arts, American Biographical Institute, 1989. **REVIEWED IN:** *Who's Who in American Art*; *5,000 Personalities of the World.* **EDUCATION:** MFA, U. of Oregon, 1966; BS, Central Michigan U., 1964. **HEROES/ROLE MODELS:** Oscar Oppenheimer, philosopher. **CONTACT:** Tel: 416-736-2100, ext. 77418; Fax: 416-736-5875

▶**WHITING, Sandra**
COMMUNITY ORGANIZER. Born: Jamaica.
▶ Sandra Whiting is best known for her years of community involvement in Toronto, both in the Caribbean and the wider community context. She was president of the Black Business and Professional Association (BBPA), 1995-2000 and played a key role in the development of the Harry Jerome Scholarship Fund. She also worked extensively with the Jamaican-Canadian Association and the Caribbean Cultural Committee; was also involved with many others, including the Ontario Black History Society. And, in the interest of ensuring that the perspective of the Caribbean community was known to the mainstream, she was also actively involved with: the Metro Toronto Convention Centre; the Performing Arts Development Fund; Empire Club of Canada; Ontario Regional Panel of the Canadian Broadcast Standards Council; former vice-chair Royal Bank Small Business Advisory Council (Ontario Region); member Brd. and Fundraising Chair, YWCA; in 1999, was a member of the planning committee which organized the Mandela and the Children rally for 40,000 attendees, at Toronto's SkyDome. **BACKGROUND:** has written for community newspapers *Contrast* and *Share*, and for *Excellence* magazine; Bank of Montreal, Loans Officer; is a performance artist, actor, storyteller, and was an event programmer at Toronto's Harbourfront Centre. **HONS.:** include, Community Leadership Award, BBPA, 2002. **MOTTO:** Nothing is impossible! **CONTACT:** s_whiting@sympatico.ca

▶**WICKHAM, Aisha**
DIRECTOR, Spoken Word & New Media, FLOW 93.5FM, Ste. 400-211 Yonge St., Toronto, ON M5B 1M4. Born: Toronto, ON.
▶ Aisha Wickham is the Director of Spoken Word & New Media at Toronto-based FLOW 93.5FM, Canada's first Black-owned urban music station. **PREVIOUS POSITIONS:** Sector Development Officer for IT and New Media for the City of Toronto's Economic Development Division, where she worked with public- and private-sector stakeholders to design and implement strategies supporting the advancement of the IT, telecommunications and new media sectors in Toronto; Man-

ager of Communications and Client Services for SMART Toronto, the city's leading business association for the technology sector. **COMMUNITY:** volunteer, African-Canadian Heritage Assn. **HONS.:** Canadian Woman in New Media Award, 1999; Harry Jerome Award, for leadership, 1993. **EDUCATION:** BA, Radio & Television, Ryerson U. **CONTACT:** aisha@flow935.com; Fax: 416-214-0660

▶WIGGAN, Albert

PRESIDENT & OWNER, Albert's Real Jamaican Foods, 542 St. Clair Ave. W., Toronto, ON M6C 1A5. Born: Jamaica/ in Canada since: 1978.

▶ Albert Wiggan is the owner of the popular Toronto restaurant, Albert's Real Jamaican Foods, which can now be found in two locations in Toronto. The first location opened in 1986, the second in 2000. He began developing his culinary skills from his childhood in rural Jamaica; the youngest of 15 children and having lost his father at age two, he accompanied his mother to the fields where she cultivated their crops for the market. Cooking the usual midday meal of yams led him to experiment with natural herbs to season and add variety to the taste. Later, as a result of his severe dyslexia and above-average IQ, he and his wife decided to utilize his self-taught skills in the culinary arts; this led to their decision to enter the restaurant business, which has proven quite successful. **COMMUNITY:** AW is active in the community and speaks regularly to groups and schools, encouraging youth, particularly those with learning disabilities, to overcome whatever obstacles may be in their path; he also speaks to youth about taking responsibility for their actions and the importance of celebrating their African heritage. He has been interviewed on radio (CBC, CFRB, and Talk 640) and TV, where he has appeared as a guest chef. **HONS.:** Black History Month Award, City of Toronto, 2001; Harry Jerome Award, for excellence in business, BBPA, 1999. **REVIEWED IN:** local & community papers including: *NOW*; *Toronto Star*; *Globe and Mail.* **HEROES/ROLE MODELS:** Carolyn Wiggan, wife. **MOTTO:** If I can do it, you can do it! **CONTACT:** Fax: 905-281-9662

▶WILKINSON, Evadne

EXECUTIVE DIRECTOR, Out of the Cold Resource Centre, PO Box 612, Stn. F, Toronto, ON M4Y 2L8. Born: Barbados/ in Canada since: 1969.

▶ Evadne Wilkinson has been the Executive Director of the Out of the Cold Resource Centre since 1997. It is a partnering organization of Out of the Cold, and is an interfaith charity providing food and shelter to the homeless, particularly during the winter months. Related to her work with Out of the Cold, she is also active with the following: Wellesley Central Health Corp. and the Wellesley Health Bus; YMCA; ABLE; Trellis Housing Initiatives, which will be building affordable housing under the City of Toronto's, Let's Build program; Toronto Drug Treatment Court; Provincial Synod Social Action Committee. **EDUCATION:** Dipl., Computer Programming & Systems Analysis, 1999; Dipl., Micro computers, 1989, Toronto School of Business. **HEROES/ROLE MODELS:** Muriel & James Wilkinson, parents. **MOTTO:** Trust in God and all things will be possible. **CONTACT:** Tel: 416-782-0122; Fax: 416-782-5822

▶WILLIAMS, Castor, The Hon.

JUDGE, Provincial Courts of Nova Scotia, 5250 Spring Garden Rd., Halifax, NS B3J 1E7. Born: Antigua/ in Canada since: 1970.

▶ The Hon. Judge Castor Williams was appointed to the bench as a Provincial Court Judge in Nova Scotia, in 1996. Prior to this, he had been a Crown Attorney, since 1992; before that had been practising independently. **CAREER:** had worked with the government of Antigua and Barbuda Civil Service (Govt. of UK Civil Service); served as a non-commissioned officer in the West India Regiment, and in the UK Armed Forces; had worked with the Bank of Scotland, UK, and served as Manager with the Seaview Credit Union, where he was involved in community development in the Halifax metropolitan area. **COMMUNITY:** founding member, Joint Consultative Committee, which brought together major Black organizations with a view to community economic development, in Nova Scotia; past-Chair of the Black Learners' Advisory Committee (BLAC); past-President of the Black Lawyers Association of NS. **OTHER:** was the Honorary Consul of Antigua and Barbuda for Atlantic Provinces of Canada. **HONS.:** GSM, with clasp "Borneo"; GG 125th Anniv. Medal, 1992. **WORKS:** include, *BLAC Report on Education*, 1994; "Sentencing Blacks in NS," Seminar paper, 1992. **EDUCATION:** LLB, 1976; BA, Poli. Sci. & Economics, 1973, Dalhousie U. **CONTACT:** williach@ns.sympatico.ca; Fax: 902-424-0603

▶WILLIAMS, Charlotte, DVM.

VETERINARIAN, Elrose Wildrose/Eston Veterinary Services, Box 581, Elrose, SK, S0L 0Z0. Born: North Battleford, SK, 1965.

▶ Dr. Charlotte Williams is a veterinarian in Saskatchewan with the Elrose Wildrose/Eston Veterinary Services. She maintains a mixed practice treating food-producing animals & companion animals (dogs, cats, horses). **HONS.:** Norman Pearle Scholarship, 1990. **REVIEWED IN:** local & regional publications: *Entrepreneurs*; *Western Producer*; *Western People*. **EDUCATION:** DVM, Western College of Veterinary Medicine, 1994; BSc, Agriculture, U. of Saskatchewan, 1990. **HEROES/ ROLE MODELS:** Rueben Mayes, brother (*see: Mayes, Rueben*); Dr. Wanda Mann, colleague. **MOTTO:** I can do all things through Christ who strengthens me. **CONTACT:** hortvet@sk.sympatico.ca; Fax: 306-378-2830

▶WILLIAMS, Denise

SOPRANO/CLASSICAL SINGER, c/o Anne Summers International, Box 188, Stn. A., Toronto,

ON M5W 1B2. Born: Antigua.

▶ Denise Williams is a soprano and classical performer who has appeared in concerts, operas and Broadway productions. She has performed as a soloist with the Toronto Symphony, Toronto Sinfonietta, the Concert Strings, the Etobicoke Centennial Choir, the Nathaniel Dett Chorale, and opened for featured artist, Kathleen Battle, in 1999. In 2000, she appeared again with the Toronto Symphony in a program, *Sophisticated Soul*, including excerpts from Gershwin's *Porgy and Bess* and *Spirituals*. As a recitalist she has appeared at Massey Hall, the St. Lawrence Centre, the Toronto Centre for the Performing Arts, and many other venues in Toronto, across Ontario and the Caribbean. She has created and performed a variety of unique solo concert programs, under the trade name *Sophisticated Soul*, which blend diverse cultural and musical traditions including: *Classical Steel*, opera and classics, with steel pan accompaniment; *Walk Together Children*, commonality in the music of Black and Jewish cultures; *Music in Times of Conflict*, portrays contrasts in the music of German composer, Richard Strauss and Jewish composer, Kurt Weill. Her Black and Jewish music has been presented at the Toronto Centre for the Performing Arts, the Glenn Gould Studio and broadcast on CBC's *Music Around Us*. She has also been a music educator and voice teacher for several years and has led workshops on Psychological Development Through Music and, Singing African American Spirituals. She is a member of the Royal Conservatory of Music Examiners. **HONS.:** include, Margaret Gardiner Laidman Scholarship for Voice, RCM; Jack Overhold Prize, U of T, Faculty of Music; The Four Seasons Festivals Award, Jackman Fdn. **EDUCATION:** ARCT, Singing Performance, RCM; BSc, U of T. **HEROES/ROLE MODELS:** Michael Warren & Evelyn Mandac, voice teachers; Kathleen Battle, soprano. **MOTTO:** If it is to be, it is up to me! **CONTACT:** dwstudio413@hotmail.com; www.denisewilliamssoprano.com

▶WILLIAMS, Dorothy W.

HISTORIAN/WRITER/EDITOR, Montreal, QC. Born: Montreal, QC.

▶ Dorothy Williams is a Montrealer who has been active collecting, documenting and sharing the history of Blacks in Quebec. She is the founder of Ethnocultural Diffusions, established to collect the oral history of Blacks in Montreal; in addition to sharing her findings with local groups, schools, universities and the media, she is also a resource to filmmakers. She consulted on the NFB's award-winning production of *Show Girls*; in 2000, did research for *Journey to Justice*; and in 2001, she assisted with *Black Soul*, an award-winning animation film. She is the author of two books (see below). The first, *Blacks in Montreal: 1628-1986, An Urban Demography*, was written at the request of the Quebec Human Rights Commission during their study of racism in Montreal's housing market. She also worked on the *Canadian Black Communities Demographics Project* produced in 1997 by the McGill Consortium for Ethnicity and Strategic Social Planning. And, during the initial planning for the creation of the NCC/Charles H. Este Cultural Centre (intended to be Montreal's first Black museum), she was the historical consultant on the Master and Vision Plan, helping the museum designers and architect in the conceptualization and historical rendering of their ideas. She was the historical contributor on, *Challenging Anti-Black Racism in Canada: an African Canadian Coalition Against Racism (ACCAR) Report*, 2002. Currently, she is completing her doctorate; her thesis entails the compilation and analysis of Black serials (broadsheets, periodicals, newspapers, etc.) in Montreal; she is also preparing a child's A-B-C of noted Black figures and events in Canadian history. **COMMUNITY:** NDG Anti-Poverty Group; Network of Black Business and Professional Women; McGill Centre for Research and Teaching on Women; *Black History Month Calendar*. **HONS.:** E.J. Josey Scholarship, Black Caucus of the American Library Assn., 2000-2001; Mathieu Da Costa Award, Black Coalition of Quebec, 1993. **WORKS:** several including: *The Road to Now: A History of Blacks in Montreal*, 1997; *Blacks in Montreal: 1628-1986, An Urban Demography*, 1989 (translated into French, 1998). **REVIEWED IN:** *Black History Month Calendar*, 1995-96. **EDUCATION:** PhD candidate, McGill University. MA, History, 1999; BA, 1984, Concordia U. **CONTACT:** dwill@accglobal.net

▶WILLIAMS, Eugene F., QC.

DIRECTOR, Federal Prosecution Service, Department of Justice, Ste. 2403-160 Elgin St., Ottawa, ON K1A 0H8. Born: Trinidad & Tobago/ in Canada since: 1959.

▶ Eugene Williams joined the Criminal Law Branch of the Federal Dept. of Justice in 1980, as a Federal Prosecutor and agent of the Attorney General of Canada; he worked primarily with cases relating to prosecutions under Canada's drugs, excise, competition, and income tax laws. From the late 1980s to early '90s he worked almost exclusively with applications to the Min. of Justice by those who, having exhausted all other judicial remedies against their conviction, were seeking either a new trial, an appeal or some other form of relief pursuant to section 690 of the *Criminal Code*. Since 1998, he has been Director of the Ottawa-Hull office of the Federal Prosecution Service. He began his career with the Bureau of Competition Policy, in 1976. **HONS.:** Team Achievement Merit Award (for development of dept. policy on conflict resolution & harassment prevention in the workplace), 1995; Deputy Minister's Award, Dept. of Justice, 1994; Queen's Counsel, 1993. **EDUCATION:** LLB, U. of Ottawa, 1974; BA, U of T, 1971. **HEROES/ROLE MODELS:** W.H. Corbett, former supervisor. **MOTTO:** You cannot give up just because you encounter hurdles. **CONTACT:** eugene.williams@justice.gc.ca

▶WILLIAMS, Georgina

CONCERT PIANIST/COMPOSER/SINGER/ SONG-WRITER, Edmonton, AB. Born: Edmonton, AB.

▶ Georgina (Gina) Williams is, by training, a concert pianist who is also an accomplished singer and composer. She has won many awards for her Bach performances, but has a preference for the works of Chopin, which she performed at her master's thesis recital. As a composer, she wrote the anthem, *Glory,* for the 25th anniversary of Grenada's Independence, for choir and reduced orchestra. She has also written music for orchestra, a string quintet, and solo piano (*Titanic, Prairie Winter,* and others). One of her piano works, *Look, I don't want to hurt again,* was performed by C. Athparia and aired on CBC (*Alberta Arts and Beyond*), and was also broadcast on national radio in Poland. As a singer/songwriter, she has performed in Canada, the US, and internationally; her song, *God is Real,* debuted at Edmonton's Jubilee Auditorium with a 300-voice choir. Since winning MusicCity TV's vocal talent search, she has appeared on a number of TV shows, and is the vocalist in a Capital City Savings TV commercial. She has debuted as an actor, first in the film, *The Jack Bull* (with John Cusack), then in the pilot for *The Beat,* which aired on CBC; and, she is featured in a video promoting the Fine Arts Degree at Cdn universities and colleges. **HONS.:** Silver Jubilee Grenada National Award, 1999; BAASA Award, 1998; Outstanding Musicianship Award, Berklee in LA; Clarence "Big" Miller Award; Bach Trophies; MusicCity TV Finals Cert., Best Song. **REVIEWED IN:** *Edmonton J*; *United Church Observer*; *Celebrating Women in the Arts* magazine; listed in *Who's Who in Professional & Business Women.* **EDUCATION:** MA, Music, U. of Alberta, 2000. **MOTTO:** I don't believe in "can't." **CONTACT:** georgina@musician.org; Fax: 780-444-1190

▶WILLIAMS, Mojo

PROPRIETOR/MUSICIAN (Semi-Ret.), Aries Gold, Ste. 228-339 50 Ave. SE, Calgary, AB T2G 2B3. Born: Calgary, AB.

▶ Mojo Williams is a goldsmith and jewellery designer who, in 1988, was awarded the contract to design a commemorative piece of jewellery for the wife of then-IOC President, Juan Antonio Samaranch, in honour of the Calgary Winter Olympics. Over a 40-year period, MW has been a professional musician who played with Bo Diddley, Red Sovine, the Country Scouts, and many others. He is a long-time member of the Alberta AACP which, in the 1950s, led protests until local clubs and restaurants stopped denying Blacks right of access to their premises. **REVIEWED IN:** *Calgary Sun,* 1988. **EDUCATION:** Gemological Institute of America, 1983; Lethbridge Community College, 1972. **MOTTO:** Don't let the problem grow; nip it in the bud! **CONTACT:** Fax: 403-243-0644

▶WILLIAMS, Raymond M.

BANKER/CONSULTANT, Derivative and Capital Markets, Toronto, ON. Born: Grenada/raised in the UK/in Canada since: 1991.

▶ Ray Williams was a principal in the Foreign Exchange Advisory, Global Markets Group, with the Bank of America from 1995 until early 2002. Currently he is a consultant for Derivative and Capital Markets. **OTHER:** organizer, International Black Summit (Toronto) and coordinator for Team Canada, 2002; since 2000 he has been a member of the Advisory Board to the Federal Govt. on Embracing Change within the Federal Public Service and the federally regulated industries; founding member of the National Black Alliance of Canada (umbrella group for CABJ, BBPA, BFVN, UFSC, UMAC, AABHS); past-President of UFSC (formerly NAUB), Toronto. **WORKS:** in *Profiles & Perspectives*; *Derivatives Weekly.* **EDUCATION:** MA, Regional Planning,

Lanchester U., UK, 1982; BA/Hons., North Staffs Polytechnic, UK, 1981. **HEROES/ROLE MODELS:** Susan Crocker. **MOTTO:** Matching the mission to the moment. (Earl Graves Sr.) **CONTACT:** raywilliams@sympatico.ca

▶WILLIAMS, Taly, P.Eng.

ENVIRONMENTAL ENGINEER, PRESIDENT, TM Williams LLC, Ste. 400-433 N. Camden Dr., Beverly Hills, CA 90210, USA. Born: Toronto, ON, 1970.

▶ Taly Williams is an environmental engineer, now based in California, who has received international recognition for his involvement in environmental remediation projects. In 1999, he designed and oversaw the construction of the first drinking water facility in US history to comply with the State Dept. of Health Services' requirement to remediate the toxic gasoline additive, MTBE. The award-winning current affairs TV program, *60 Minutes,* aired a special featuring his site and the issues related to MTBE contamination; this resulted in the Clinton Administration banning the additive in 2000. In 1997, he represented and directed all phases of an *ex-situ* bioremediation program, in London, England, which later won an award for, Environmental Cleanup of the Year. **BACKGROUND:** played professional football in the CFL with the Toronto Argonauts and the Hamilton Tiger-Cats, between 1994 and 1996. In 1994, he held the Toronto Argonaut record for longest rush from scrimmage. **REVIEWED IN:** nat'l and industry-specific publications. **EDUCATION:** BA/Hons., Co-op, Applied Science/ Civil & Environmental Engineering, U. of Waterloo, 1994. **HEROES/ROLE MODELS:** Dr. Jude Igwemezie, P.Eng (*see: listing under: Igwemezie, Jude*). **MOTTO:** If it ain't broke, break it! (Don't accept the status quo, do it your way.) **CONTACT:** tmw@tmwilliams.com

▶WILLIAMS, Tonya Lee

ACTRESS/PRODUCER, Wilbo Entertainment & ReelWorld Film Festival, Ste. 400-438 Parliament St., Toronto, ON M5A 3A2. Born: England.

▶ Tonya Lee Williams is best known for her role on *The Young and the Restless* as Dr. Olivia Winters, a role she has played since 1990. Her career in entertainment began nearly 20 years ago when she became well known for her role as "the milk girl" in the *Wear a Moustache* milk campaign of the 1980s. Since then she has appeared in many TV programs including: *Street Legal*; *Hill Street Blues*; *The Polka Dot Door*; *Matlock.* **OTHER:** TLW is President and founder of ReelWorld Film Festival, dedicated to featuring films from diverse ethno-cultural communities. She is also President and founder of Wilbo Entertainment and The Publicity Group, which seek to identify and provide opportunities for artists in the entertainment industry. She was a co-executive producer of the short film, *Maple,* which was awarded Best Short Film by the BFVN, 2001. **HONS.:** many including: NAACP Image Award, Best Daytime Actress, 2002, 2000; Daytime Emmy award nominee, Supporting Actress, 2000 & 1996; Dr. Bird Award; Positive Impact Award; Red Ribbon of Hope Award, TV Cares, 1999. **REVIEWED IN:** *Soap Digest*; *Soap Opera Weekly*; *Toronto Star*; *Toronto Sun*; *Flare*; *Essence*; *Toronto Life*; *JET*; *Hollywood Reporter*; *TV Guide,* and others. **EDUCATION:** Theatre Arts studies, Ryerson U. **MOTTO:** The only obstacle to overcome is yourself. **CONTACT:** wilboent2@aol.com; www.tonyaleewilliams.com

▶WILLIAMS, Vivienne

SINGER/PERFORMER, Vivienne Williams Enterprises, Toronto, ON. Born: England.

▶ Vivienne Williams is a singer of R&B, hip hop, and jazz; she is also an actor who has appeared on stage, TV and film. As a singer she has toured across Canada, the US, and throughout Asia. At the beginning of her career, she was a member of the vocal trio, Sway; in 1988, their single, *Hands Up* reached gold status and was nominated for a Juno Award. Her debut album, *My Temptation,* was released in 1992, and produced her Juno-nominated single *Infatuated.* She has appeared on various TV programs including Citytv's *Electric Circus, Breakfast TV, Anne Murray's Christmas Special*, and the *Jerry Lewis Telethon for Muscular Dystrophy*. VW has also performed with The Temptations, Percy Sledge, Corey Hart, George Benson, Bruce Cockburn and others. On the jazz scene, she has collaborated with Archie Alleyne, Joe Sealy, George Koller, and others. In addition to being a voice heard in popular commercials (Hershey's, Bank of Montreal), she has appeared on stage in *Ain't Misbehavin'* and the Canadian tour of *One More Stop on the Freedom Train*; and on screen in *The Natalie Cole Story* and *Sins of the Father*. **HONS.:** Juno Award nominee, Best Soul/R&B, for *Infatuated*, 1993 and Single of the Year, *Hands Up*, 1989; Gold Record, to Sway, for sales over 50,000 units, for single, *Hands Up*. **CONTACT:** info@vivienne williams.com

▶**WILLS, Dorothy Abike,** PhD, CM.
EDUCATOR, DEAN (Ret.), Faculty of Applied Technologies, Vanier College, Montreal, QC. Born: Dominica/ in Canada since: 1952.
▶ Dr. Dorothy Wills retired in June 2000 as Dean of the Faculty of Applied Technologies at Vanier College in Quebec. During her career, she worked as a social worker and later taught Business Education at John F. Kennedy High School, Special Care Counselling at Vanier College, and Andragogy at Concordia University. **HIGHLIGHTS:** in 1972, as one of the founding faculty members of the Special Care Counselling Program, she developed the program which she adapted in 1982 to meet the needs of the First Nations people on the Kahnawake Reserve, Quebec, thereby enabling the First Nations people to obtain a college diploma, as well as work with their own special populations. In 1983, she was a researcher with the Non-partisan Parliamentary Committee that looked into the "Participation of Visible Minorities in Canadian Society" and produced the report entitled, *Equality Now.* In 1987, as part of her work with the Quebec Board of Black Educators, she developed a mentoring program, which was aired on CBC Radio. It spoke of providing role models by pairing young people with professionals; this concept has been replicated many times since (ed. note: most notably as Each One Teach One). Beginning in 1988, she served for six years on the Immigration and Refugee Board of Canada, before returning to Vanier College, in 1994, as Dean of the Faculty of Applied Technologies, where she administered 15 programs. Over the course of her career she was appointed to several Federal, Provincial, and Municipal Committees, along with her extensive involvement in various Black community organizations, particularly as a founder and Executive Secretary of the National Black Coalition of Canada. **HONS.:** recipient of many awards including: Hon. LLD, Dalhousie U. (1996) and Concordia U. (1989); Order of Canada, 1989; Martin Luther King Jr. Award of Excellence; Mount St. Vincent U. Alumni Jubilee Award of Distinction; Minister's Award for Excellence in Race Relations; named Woman of the Year, by *Salon de la Femme du Québec*. **REVIEWED IN:** many publications including: *Millennium Minds*, 2000; *Some Black Women*, 1993. **EDUCATION:** PhD, Pacific Western U., California. MSW, McGill U.; MA, Concordia U.; BSc, Mount St. Vincent U. **MOTTO** There is no gathering the rose without being pricked by the thorn. **CONTACT:** dorothy.wills@ sympatico.ca

▶**WILLS, Roland,** MBA.
ASSOCIATE DEAN (Ret.)/**PROFESSOR EMERITUS,** John Molson School of Business, Concordia University, Montreal, QC. Born: Nigeria/ in

Canada since: 1948.

▶ Professor Emeritus Roland Wills served as Associate Dean of Academic and Student Affairs in the Faculty of Commerce and Administration at the John Molson School of Business at Concordia University for many years before retiring in 1993. The early part of his career was spent in the pharmaceutical industry as a Control Chemist; once he joined the academic field, he excelled as a teacher and as an administrator. As Associate Dean he was responsible for curriculum development and piloted many innovative pedagogical measures; he also conducted several curriculum revisions to ensure that programs reflected changes in the business world. His involvement in community organizations has been extensive and he was rewarded for his commitment and contributions by the Director General of Citizenship and Immigration Canada. **HONS.:** many including: several from student associations for program development and for his understanding of student life; students voted unanimously to name their computer lab, The Roland Wills Computer Lab; Jackie Robinson Award, for his contribution to the field of Business Education, MABBP; Cert. of recognition for "valuable contribution to Canadian society," Citizenship & Immigration Canada. **EDUCATION:** MBA, U. of Windsor, 1965; Cert., Civil Engineering, SGWU (now Concordia U.); BSc, Dalhousie U., 1952. **MOTTO:** "Kuumba," the seventh principle of Kwanzaa: "to do the best we can, in the way we can, to leave our community a better place than we inherited it." **CONTACT:** dorothy.wills@sympatico.ca

▶**WILSON, Anthony "Salah"**
MUSICIAN/STEEL PAN INSTRUCTOR, Salah's Steel Pan Academy, 3730 de Coutrai, Montreal, QC H3S 1C1. Born: Trinidad & Tobago/ in Canada since: 1973.

▶ Anthony "Salah" Wilson is a musician, composer and promoter of steel pan music in the Montreal area. Since 1987, he has introduced steel pan courses to the Black community in Montreal, for children and adults of all ages; 1988, he introduced his Family Steel Pan Group (including six children), which has since toured Canada and the US, made CD recordings, appeared on TV, radio, and in the press. In 1991, he introduced steel pan programs in the public school system in Montreal; currently it is taught in four public schools. In 1992, he established Pan Quebec for the cultural promotion of the instrument. He also pursued a degree in music using the pan as his principal instrument (this was a "first" at the university level). In 1996, he established Salah's Steel Pan Academy, a private school for teaching the instrument. His Family Group performed during the Montreal International Jazz Festival, 1997, and in 2001, he initiated Montreal's first International Steel Pan Festival. **HONS.:** several for steel pan competitions including: first place champions in 2001, 2000, and 1995 at Panorama competitions in Toronto & Mtl; third place in Panorama competition, Boston, 1997. **WORKS:** published textbook, *Steelpan Playing with Theory*, 1999; wrote steel pan musical arrangements for *Picture on my Wall*, 2000, and *Stranger*, 2001. **EDUCATION:** BFA, Music/Jazz Specialization using the steel pan, Concordia U., 1995. **HEROES/ROLE MODELS:** Malcom X, activist, humanist. **MOTTO:** Which one of the favours of my Lord can I deny? **CONTACT:** salahpan@videotron.ca; Fax: 514-696-9538

▶**WILSON, Sybil Fay E., PhD.**
PROFESSOR, Faculty of Education, Brock University, St. Catharines, ON. Born: Jamaica/ in Canada since: 1973.

▶ Dr. Sybil Wilson has been teaching at Brock University since 1973. She is a professor in the Faculty of Education; began the Secondary Teacher Education Program; began the Enterprise Education Program; teaches undergraduate, graduate, and teacher-education students. She teaches courses in curriculum, pedagogy, evaluation, and multicultural education. She has held several positions in the university, including Acting Dean of the Faculty of Education. **BACKGROUND:** her career began in Jamaica, first as a teacher and deputy principal, 1961-64; then as a lecturer and research editor at UWI, 1965-68; as a Research Officer, JA Min. of Education, 1971-72. She then worked at Western Michigan University, Faculty of Education, as a lecturer and teacher-education program coordinator, 1971-73; Education Officer with the Ontario Min. of Education, 1989-90. **AFFIL/MBRSHP:** Cdn Council for Multicultural Education; Cdn Society for Studies in Education; Cdn Assn. of Teacher Educators; International Society for Teacher Education. **COMMUNITY:** Niagara Black Historical Assn.; Ontario Multicultural Assn.; Women for PACE. **HONS.:** including: John C. Award, 2002; Woman of Distinction, YWCA/St. Catharines, 2001.**WORKS:** include, *Instructional Strategies for Adult Learners*, 1996; *Curriculum Theory & Design*, 1995; *Let's Stop Racism, Teacher's Guide*, 1994; articles in *J of the Int'l Society for Teacher Ed*; *J of Prof. Studies*; *Multicultural Education*; *Curriculum Directions*; *Pádagogisches Handeln*. **EDUCATION:** Cert. in Enterprise Education, 2002; Specialist TESL, 1988, Brock University. Teaching Cert. (Ont.), 1987. PhD, Curriculum/Educational Theory, U of T, 1972; MA, Educational Guidance & Counselling, Columbia U., NY, 1965; BA, U. of Western Michigan, 1961. **CONTACT:** swilson@ed.brocku.ca; Fax: 905-688-0544

▶**WILSON, Trevor**
PRESIDENT/GLOBAL DIVERSITY STRATEGIST, TWI Inc., 468 Queen St., 5th Fl., Toronto, ON M5A 1T7. Born: England/ in Canada since: 1964.
▶ Trevor Wilson is the founder and President of TWI Inc., a global consulting firm specializing in equity and diversity management. He began his career in the public sector advising Ontario's premier on issues of multiculturalism, race relations,

employment equity, affirmative action, and human rights. **HIGHLIGHTS:** Since its launch in 1995, TWI has evolved into one of N. America's leading consulting practices on issues of equity in the workplace; clients include IBM, Ernst and Young, Shell Oil, Nike, and Coca-Cola. The company's focus is global through work with business consortiums of leading multi-national corporations in N. America, S. Africa and in Europe with the European Network on Social Cohesion. In 1997, TW was instrumental in the creation of The Trinity Group, a group of global corporations dedicated to the development of standards in the measurement of diversity (has created a software tool that will measure issues relating to workplace diversity). In 1999, he was selected to sit on a newly established global advisory board, The Centre for Business and Diversity, based in England. **COMMUNITY:** City of Toronto's Committee on Race Relations; Ontario Council of Regents for the Colleges of Applied Arts and Technology; VP, Government Affairs for the African Canadian Entrepreneurs; Brd., the United Way; Inroads Canada. **HONS.:** nominated for Entrepreneur of the Year, *Can Business* Magazine, 1998. **WORKS:** *Global Diversity at Work: Winning the War for Talent*, 2002; *Diversity at Work: The Business Case for Equity*, 1996; monthly electronic newsletter, *Diversity at Work*. **REVIEWED IN:** *Financial Post Magazine*, feature stories on business news magazine shows, and various radio phone-in shows across N. America. **EDUCATION:** MA, Political Economy; BA/Hons.; Cert., Industrial Relations, U of T. **CONTACT:** twilson@diversityatwork.com; www.diversityatwork.com

▶**WINN, Paul A.**
LAWYER/HUMAN RIGHTS ACTIVIST, Paul A. Winn Law Corp., 1717 6th Ave., New Westminster, BC V3M 2C8. Born: Toronto, ON.
▶ Paul Winn is a lawyer, former civil servant, former broadcaster, and community and human

rights activist who describes himself as "just an ordinary man trying to make a difference." **CAREER:** prior to his most recent career as a lawyer, PW was Acting Director Federal/Provincial/Territorial Relations, National Literacy Secretariat, 1990-95, engaged in negotiations on cost-sharing with provinces and territories on jointly funded literacy activities; as Senior Policy Analyst, Multiculturalism Secretariat, 1988-90, assisted federal depts. and agencies to design and implement programs and activities as per the *Canadian Multiculturalism Act*, also worked with the CBC in drafting a program to train visible minority writers in TV drama and script writing; as Director, Office of Services for Visible Minority Groups, 1986-87, developed and wrote procedures and communication strategies for the affirmative action initiative; as TV writer/broadcaster/host, CBC Pacific Region, 1983-84, wrote and hosted *The Canadians*; as Regional Conciliator, Anti-Discrimination Directorate, 1981-83, investigated and mediated disputes in the Western Region. After completing his law degree in 1995, he was Staff Liaison, Multiculturalism Committee, Law Society of BC, until 1998; member of the BC Human Rights Tribunal, since 1997. In 1999, he opened his four-person law firm. **COMMUNITY:** Black History and Cultural Society, BC; BC Festival of the Arts Society; BBPA/BC; Chief Constable's Advisory Committee; CRRF; Black United Front, NS (1968-72); and many others. **HONS.:** include, Harry Jerome Award, Lifetime Achievement, BBPA. Cert. of Appreciation from: Chinese Community Enrichment Society; Black Historical & Cultural Society; Cdn Alliance for Visible Minorities; Cdn Centre for Police Race Relations; City/District North Vancouver. **EDUCATION:** LLB, UBC, 1995; Career Assignment Program, Govt. of Canada, Exec. Training Centre, 1986; TV & Radio Journalism, CBC, 1983; BSW, UBC, 1967. **HEROES/ROLE MODELS:** Mother; John Braithwaite. **MOTTO:** Don't talk about it, do it! **CONTACT:** paul@winnlegal.com; Fax: 604-519-1509

▶**WINSOM**
ARTIST/EDUCATOR. Toronto, ON. In Canada since: 1969.
▶ Winsom is a painter whose work is Afrocentric and described as being filled with spiritual symbolism; her works are often multi-media installations combining painting, textiles, sculptures, and video. She infuses her work with African and Arawak spirituality, in particular, the Orishas, which she has studied extensively and of which she is a Priestess. **BACKGROUND:** from an early age, she wanted to be an artist; as a child she made and sold "Jamaican" Christmas cards to family and friends; these were an alternative to the cards imported from the UK, which did not reflect the local environment. Her early influences for painting came from European artists and Canadian, Emily Carr. After her arrival in Canada, she studied traditional African textile design and dye technique from books. Subsequently, she made several trips to a number of W. African countries (e.g. Nigeria, Togo, Benin, Mali, Senegal, Ghana), where she studied with the older local artists. These visits also reflected a spiritual journey, which is conveyed in her works. With these different influences, it is said that "her work also displays an interest in landscape but from a symbolic angle and incorporates African and Caribbean religions of the Yoruba and Arawak." Her works have been exhibited across Canada, the US, and Caribbean. She lectures widely on African spirituality and art. Some recent exhibits are: *Kindred Spirit* (touring the US until 2004), *River of Life* (Chatham, 2000), *A Spiritual Dialogue* (AGO, 1997). Her works are in many private and public collections. **COMMUNITY:** teaching/workshop leader at Young Offenders Detention Centres; advisor and mentor for youth and emerging artists; volunteer artist/facilitator with Black female inmates in Kingston, Ontario facilities. **HONS.:** Marilyn Lastman Award, for promoting the arts and mentoring, City of Toronto, 2002. **REVIEWED IN:** newspapers & magazines,

and in museum and art gallery catalogues, including *Kindred Spirits*, 2000; *Draw it Black*, 2000; *River of Life*, 2000; many radio and TV interviews on CBC, TVO, CFMT. **EDUCATION:** Jamaica School of Art, 1968. **HEROES/ROLE MODELS:** Leonard Gardner, father; Odetta. **MOTTO:** I am beneath no one and superior to no one. **CONTACT:** winsom@winsomwinsom. com; www.winsomwinsom.com; www.collections.ic. gc.ca

▶WINT, Shirlette

SOCIAL WORKER, Côte-des-Neiges Black Community Assn., 6999, rue Côte-des-Neiges, Montreal, QC H3S 2B. Born: Jamaica/ in Canada since: 1991.

▶ Shirlette Wint is a social worker, former elementary school teacher and psychotherapist. Her work is founded on the principle of assisting Black parents and youth towards social integration and community building in Quebec society; this aim is achieved through workshops, individual consultations, and working collectively with other community organizations and departments of government. She began her teaching career in the South Bronx of NYC, and was selected Rookie Teacher of the Year by her colleagues, 1985. She also worked as a community liaison on the McGill Demographic study of Blacks in Montreal, 1999-2001. Since 1996, she has been in private practice as a psychotherapist; and, since 2001, she has been working with the Côte-des-Neiges Black Community Assn. as a social worker. **COMMUNITY:** Contemporary Afro-Canadian Art Assn., helping artists of African descent to find resources, network, exhibit and sell their work; member of intercultural association, Le Mosaïque; Tel-Aide, crisis intervention; Intercultural Consulting Committee, Catholic School Board; *Entraide Kouzin Kouzin*. Has contributed to articles on consumer affairs affecting the Black community in NY; currently collaborating on a book project with local historian, Dorothy

Williams (*see: Williams, Dorothy*), on the role of Island associations in the integration of Caribbean immigrants into Quebec society. **HONS.:** Rookie Teacher of the Year, Bronx, NY, 1985. **EDUCATION:** MSW, 2000; BSW, 1999, McGill University. BA, Brooklyn College, NY, 1982. **CONTACT:** swint67@hotmail.com; Fax: 514-849-2871

▶WITTER, Mervin

DIRECTOR, Ontario Regional Office, Canadian Human Rights Commission, S. Tower, 175 Bloor St. E., Toronto, ON M4W 3R8. Born: Jamaica/in Canada since: 1967.

▶ Mervin Witter is the Director of the Ontario Region of the Canadian Human Rights Commission, a position he has held since 1989. Previously, he was with the Ontario Human Rights Commission and from 1977-89, held the positions of Race Relations Officer, Investigator, Regional Manager, and, Acting Director of Compliance. He also spent a year on secondment to the Ont. Min. of Citizenship as Manager, Community Development and Race Relations. Prior to this, he had a career in policing and law enforcement, and rose to the rank of Sergeant of Police. **COMMUNITY INVOLVEMENT:** B'nai Brith Advisory Cmtee on Hate Propaganda and Hate Crimes; City of Toronto Access and Equity Advisory Cmtee; assisted in the establishment of the Chatham, Windsor, and Sarnia Human Rights committees; Advisor to the Kitchener-Waterloo Race Relations Cmtee, London Urban Alliance on Race Relations, the Community Dialogue on Racism; National Black Coalition (Windsor), and others; Hamilton and District Multicultural Council; served nine yrs. on Advisory Brd. for St. Clair College Law and Administration Program; founding member, Hamilton Mayor's Cmtee on Race Relations; volunteers as an official with the Ontario Track & Field Assn. and the Hamilton Olympic Track & Field Club. **HONS.:** several including, Award for Human Rights, North Halton Cultural Awareness Council; John C. Holland Professional Award; Award, for promotion of Human & Equity Rights, Assn. of Progressive Muslims of Ontario; Award for Community Service, Jamaica Fdn., (Hamilton); Cert. Recognition, for service on the Access & Equity Cmtee, from Mayor Mel Lastman, City of Toronto. **EDUCATION:** M.Ed; B.Ed, Counselling & Guidance, U. of Windsor. BA/Hons., U. of Western Ontario. **MOTTO:** Whatever the mind can conceive and believe, it can achieve. **CONTACT:** mervin. witter@chrc-ccdp.ca; Fax: 416-973-6184

▶**WIWA, Ken**
WRITER, Toronto, ON. Born: Nigeria, 1968/ in Canada since: 1999.

▶ Ken Wiwa is a journalist who contributes regularly to newspapers throughout Europe, N. America, and Africa. He came to international prominence in 1995 when his father, Ken Saro-Wiwa, civil and human rights activist for the Ogoni people of Nigeria, was arrested, sentenced to death, and subsequently executed. KW took his father's plight to the international forum but was unsuccessful in having the sentence changed. His book, *In the Shadow of a Saint: A Son's Journey to Understand His Father's Legacy*, was released in 2000 and discusses the campaign led by his father (against Shell Oil, for environmental rights and for economic improvement) and the expectations placed on the children of prominent figures. KW currently lives in Canada with his family, where he writes for the *Globe and Mail*. He is a Saul Rae Fellow in the Munk Centre for International Studies, at the University of Toronto. He travels to Nigeria several times a year, where he is Managing Director of Saros International. **HONS:** nominated for a National Newspaper Award (NNA), 2001. **WORKS:** articles in, *National Post*; *Toronto Life*; *Toronto Star*; *The Guardian* (UK); *The Observer* (UK); *Mail & Guardian* (S. Africa); book, *In the Shadow of a Saint*, 2000. **EDUCATION:** BA/Hons., U. of London, UK.

HEROES/ROLE MODELS: Parents. **MOTTO:** It's just as important to find out what you don't want to do as what you want to do. **CONTACT:** wiwa@dial. pipex.com

▶**WOODING, Marjorie Eglantine**
EDUCATOR (Ret.)/**ORGANIST/CHOIR DIRECTOR,** Church of Nativity, Malvern, ON. Born: Trinidad & Tobago/ in Canada since: 1987.

▶ Marjorie Eglantine Wooding began studying music at the age of three in Trinidad and has been a church organist since age 13. **HIGHLIGHTS:** she was a primary school teacher, 1955-59, then studied music at the Guildhall School of Music and Drama in England, 1959-62, where she graduated with the Guildhall Graduate School of Music (GGSM) Diploma in Teaching. She returned to Trinidad where she resumed teaching at St. Stephen's Anglican College; she became Vice-Principal, 1977-80, then Principal, 1980-83. She was also organist and choir director at St. Paul's Anglican Church and St. Clement's Anglican Church, as well as Lay Minister and Parish Counsellor. **OTHER:** in addition to teaching, she was often an Adjudicator at the Steel band festivals, Carnival Panorama, Best Village Competitions, and School Festivals. She composed the mass *Rejoice* for the Anglican Church of Trinidad & Tobago. **COMMUNITY:** in Canada since 1987, MEG was the organist at the Church of Nativity, Malvern, until 1998. Now, she is a part-time organist wherever needed. **AFFIL/MBRSHP:** ENOWAH; No Longer Strangers (group assisting church administration in welcoming church members from various parts of the world); Toronto Diocesan Bishop's Cmtee on Prayer; Lay Pastoral visitor, Scarborough General Hospital, 1997-99. **HONS.:** several including: Order of St. Clements, from St. Clement's Church, Trinidad, 2001; Plaque of Honour, ENOWAH, 2001. **EDUCATION:** Dipl. (Teacher's) Guildhall Graduate School of Music, London, UK, 1962; Teacher's Dipl., Board of Education, Trinidad & Tobago,

1957. **HEROES/ROLE MODELS:** Lisle E. McLear, father; Henrietta Shurland, grandmother; Canon Clive Griffith. **MOTTO:** Be still and know that I am God. **CONTACT:** Fax: 416-593-5095

▶**WOODS, Anne-Marie**
PERFORMANCE ARTIST & WRITER, Imani Enterprises, Toronto, ON. Born: England, 1968/ in Canada since: 1972.

▶ Anne-Marie Woods is an actor, dancer, playwright, poet, singer, storyteller, and community organizer. She developed her artistic skills in NS and is presently based in Toronto; has been Playwright-in-Residence at the Lorraine Kimsa Theatre for Young People (formerly YPT), since 2001. She is one of the New Creative Voices on CBC Radio. In 2001, she became the first African-Canadian to perform at the prestigious National Black Theatre Festival, held every two years in North Carolina; her latest work *Waiting to Explode* was performed there to critical and popular acclaim. **HIGHLIGHTS:** performed *Afrika Solo* (written by Djanet Sears), for BTW in Mtl, 2002; member of Four the Moment, *a capella* group in Halifax, NS for 12 yrs. (produced three CDs and a video); was the host and featured poet on CBC's *Live Poet Society*, June 2000; appeared in spoken word performance, *When Sisters Speak*, 2000 and 2002; wrote *Voices in the Dark* song for the film, *Them That's Not,* 1994; wrote and produced *Active Living* theme rap song, used for Participaction Fitness Week, by the NS Dept. of Health, 1990; director, Cultural Awareness Youth Group, 1994-96. **OTHER:** founded Imani Women's Artistic Project, 1996, which encourages young Black women to explore societal issues through drama, music, and movement. **HONS.:** Pioneer Award, 2000, & Artist of the Year, 1999, African NS Music Assn.; African-Cdn Artist of the Year (group, Four the Moment), East Coast Music Awards, 1998; Community Activism Award, Rebels with a Cause, 1998; First Place, YTV Vocal Spotlight, 1994. **WORKS:**

articles in: *Daily News*, 1998; *Dalhousie Gazette*, 1990. "Profile of an Artist," in, *And I will Paint the Sky* (anthology), 2001. **REVIEWED IN:** *Dalhousie Alumni Magazine*, 2001; *Mtl Gazette*; *Community Contact*; *Halifax Mail Star*; *Chronicle Herald.* **EDUCATION:** Internship, Freedom Theatre, Philadelphia, PA, 1997; BA, Theatre, Dalhousie U., 1993. **HEROES/ROLE MODELS:** Jackie Richardson; David Woods; Delvina Bernard; Sylvia Hamilton. **MOTTO:** God has definitely got my back, so there's nothing I can't do! **CONTACT:** awoods@attcanada.ca

▶**WOSU, Leonard,** PhD.
RESEARCH SCIENTIST/SCIENCE TEACHER, Greaves Adventist Academy, Montreal, QC. Born: Nigeria/ in Canada since: 1970.

▶ Dr. Leonard Wosu is a research scientist, who conducted research in the Thyroid Research Unit at Montreal General Hospital (1985-86), and in Rheumatic Diseases at Notre-Dame Hospital (1986-89) before leaving to teach science at Greaves Adventist Academy. After completing his studies in experimental medicine, at McGill U., he became a post-doctoral fellow at the Lady Davis Institute for Medical Research, in Montreal, researching the interaction of steroid hormones with mammary tissue in breast cancer. He has recently completed studies in environmental toxicology. At the Greaves Adventist Academy, he teaches courses in chemistry, physical science, human biology, and ecology to students in grades 7 through 11. **COMMUNITY:** initiated the Assn. of Black Scientists, which includes researchers, scientists and graduate students; its aim is to encourage more young people to pursue careers in the sciences. He is also well known in the Montreal area as the founder/director of a local choir; it began in 1986 while he worked at Montreal General Hospital and was named the Inter-Hospital Choir; since then it has become the Montreal Intercultural Choir, with 50-70 members and has performed at many venues around the city. **HONS.:**

include, Community Service Award, SDA Church, 2001; Award of Recognition, Mtl Assn. of School Administrators, 1999. **WORKS:** in, *Reflections & Visions*; *Can J Biochem*; *J Clin. Endo. Metab.*; *Atherosclerosis*; *J Steroid Biochem.* **EDUCATION:** Dipl. Ecotoxicology, Concordia U., 2000. PhD, Experimental Medicine, 1983; MSc, Animal Science, 1973, McGill University. BSc, Biological Sciences, U. of Aston, UK, 1969. **HEROES/ROLE MODELS:** Pastor R.O. Wosu, father & SDA minister in W. Africa. **MOTTO:** Whatever is worth doing, is worth doing well. **CONTACT:** illsay@msn.com

▶**WRIGHT, Cornell C.V.**

LAWYER, Torys LLP, Ste. 3000-79 Wellington St. W., Box 270, TD Centre, Toronto, ON M5K 1N2. Born: Toronto, ON, 1973.

▶ Cornell Wright is a lawyer practising a broad range of corporate and commercial law, including securities, corporate finance, and, mergers and acquisitions. **HIGHLIGHTS:** led student government bodies during secondary school and university; developed career awareness programs for minority students; worked as a policy and communications consultant; served as senior policy advisor to the CEO of Ontario's Education Quality and Accountability Office. Currently, he serves on the Board of Directors of Goodwill, and is an accomplished public speaker and public policy commentator. **HONS.:** Gordon Cressy, Student Leadership Award, U of T, 2000; Scarlet Key Award, McGill U., 1996; GG 125th Anniv. Medal, 1992; inaugural Harry Jerome Award for Leadership, in honour of Lincoln Alexander, 1992. **EDUCATION:** MBA, 2000; LLB, 2000, U of T. BA/Hons., McGill U., 1996. **CONTACT:** Tel: 416-865-7651; cwright@torys.com

▶**WRIGHT, Leebert A., PhD, FACB, FCACB.**

DIRECTOR, CLINICAL BIOCHEMISTRY (Ret.), Wellesley/ Princess Margaret Hospitals, Toronto, ON. Born: Jamaica/ in Canada since: 1951.

▶ Dr. Leebert A. Wright served as Director of Clinical Biochemistry at Wellesley/Princess Margaret Hospitals, and was Associate Professor of Clinical Biochemistry at U of T, until his retirement in 1993. Throughout his career, his goal was "to promote accuracy and professionalism in the development and delivery of diagnostic procedures in order to enhance the care and well-being of the patients." **CAREER:** His work began with early research into the re-absorption and excretion of amino acids and other amino compounds by the kidneys in order to diagnose and treat renal disorders (1963-68, he was a clinical chemist, Montreal General Hospital); later, as Associate Director of Clinical Chemistry at the Montreal General Hospital (1968-69) and as Director of Clinical Biochemistry at the Wellesley Hospital and later the Wellesley and Princess Margaret Hospitals, he led the laboratories, which provided a full range of diagnostic tests. As Associate Professor of Clinical Biochemistry in U of T's Faculty of Medicine, he taught medical and science students, conducted research and was able, thereby to promote the profession of clinical biochemistry. **HIGHLIGHTS:** as Chair of the Definitive and Reference Methods Cmtee of the Cdn Society of Clinical Chemists (CSCC), he and other colleagues developed a reference method for the accurate determination of cholesterol, useful in the management of patients with cardiovascular risks and reference methods for the determination of 17-hydroxyprogesterone and testosterone useful in the investigation of those patients with endocrine disorders; and, with the support of the National Health Research and Development Program of Health and Welfare Canada, he developed a national program for the standardization of clinical chemistry diagnostic tests in Canada. He also initiated a Toxicology and Therapeutic Drug Monitoring Centre, which provided in-house service for hospitals and reference service to several hospitals in Ontario and other provinces. The data and experience from this service formed the basis for a chapter on diagnostic clinical toxicology in a book entitled, *Applied Biochemistry of Clinical Disorders*, 1980 and 1986; this chapter set the standard and continues to be published in the *J of Clinical Biochemistry*. **OTHER:** 1972-79, he was Chair of the Education Cmtee of the CSCC and was instrumental in developing and promoting programs for the training, specialization and certification of clinical chemists in Canada. He also coordinated the post-doctoral program in Clinical Biochemistry at U of T, 1975-83. **AFFIL/MBRSHP:** many nat'l and int'l including: Cdn Society of Clinical Chemists, since 1968, President, 1971-72; European Cmtee for Clinical Laboratory Standards; founding member, Cdn Academy of Clinical Biochemistry. **HONS.:** several including: the Leebert A. Wright Lecture in Analytical Clinical Biochemistry, established by U of T, 1992; Fellow of the American Academy of Clinical Biochemists (FACB); Fellow of the Assn. of Clinical Scientists, US; Ames Award, for outstanding contributions in research, teaching, and professional development in clinical chemistry, 1979; Stuart Allan Hoffman Memorial Award, for his work on renal handling of amino compounds, U of T, 1962. **WORKS:** many scientific publications, with articles in: *Clinical Chemistry*; *Clinical Biochemistry*; *Lab World*; *Can J Physiology & Pharmacology*; *Can J Biochemistry & Physiology*. **REVIEWED IN:** several scientific publications including: *CSCC News*, 1979; *Lab World*, 1972. **EDUCATION:** Certified Clinical Chemist, 1973; PhD, Pathological Chemistry, U of T, 1963. MSc, Biochemistry, 1957; BSc/Hons., Biochemistry, 1955, McGill U. **HEROES/ROLE MODELS:** Albert & Susan Wright, parents; Iris Scarlet, aunt; Dr. James Dauphine & Dr. Fred Nicholson, professors. **MOTTO:** If it's worth doing, it's worth doing well!

▶**WRIGHT, Ouida Marina,** PhD, FCCT.
EDUCATOR/ASSISTANT DEPUTY MINISTER (Ret.), Ontario Ministry of Education, Toronto, ON. Born: Jamaica/ in Canada since: 1952.
▶ Dr. Ouida Wright, over the course of a lengthy professional career, held positions in teaching and administration in elementary and secondary schools in Jamaica, Ontario, and Quebec, as well as in universities in Quebec and Ontario. She also served as Assistant Deputy Minister in the Ont. Min. of Education and spearheaded or played a major role with various levels of educators, government, NGOs and community organizations, in the development and implementation of a wide range of policies. **CAREER HIGHLIGHTS:** Teacher/ Chair of English with Brds. of Education in Montreal (1953-57, 1963-64), Ottawa (1957-59), and North York (1959-63, 1970-72); Peel Brd., to develop an English Minimum Core Curriculum, K-13, 1972-74; elementary school principal, 1975-88; Assistant Superintendent, then Superintendent of Curriculum, Toronto Board of Education (now TDSB), 1977-92; contributed to the development of the Toronto Observation Project and its publications. The Project developed materials to meet the educational needs of Toronto students while reflecting their diversity. Two booklets from this project, on which she collaborated, were well received in Ontario, nationally, and internationally: *Observing Children in their Formative Years* and *Observing Adolescents in their Developing Years*. OW has also taught at the university level: at McGill U., was lecturer, 1964-65, then Asst. Prof., 1965-70, taught, did research and chaired the committee which developed the M.Ed degree; Sessional Lecturer, Faculty of Education, U of T, 1993, and Erindale Campus; Sessional Lecturer at OISE, 1970-71, 1980; was for several years a contributor and/or presenter at York U.'s annual reading conference. She was appointed Assistant Deputy Minister, Ont. Min. of Education and Training, 1993-95, responsible for establishing the Anti-racism, Access, and

Equity Division; was also responsible for overseeing the implementation of the provincial government's policies in these areas at elementary, secondary, and post-secondary institutions. **AFFIL/MBRSHP:** nat'l and int'l, several including: Phi Delta Kappa; Assn. for Sup. and Curriculum Development; National Alliance of Black School Educators; PACE; Cdn College of Teachers. **HONS.:** many including: PM's Commendation, for Contribution to Education, 1995; Recognition Award, Cdn Alliance of Black Educators, 1995; Citation in *International Leaders in Education*, 1991; The Colonel Watson Award for Curriculum Development, 1991; Cdn Women in Science Annual Award for Curriculum Development, 1991; Fellow of the Cdn College of Teachers, 1968. **WORKS:** has authored and co-authored many pamphlets; has written articles and chapters in books including: *Weaving Connections: Educating for Peace, Social & Environmental Justice*, 2000; *Re/Visioning Canadian Perspectives on the Education of Africans in the Late 20th Century*, 1998; *Reach for the Stars* (Grade Seven Reader), 1966. **REVIEWED IN:** *Focus on Equality*, 1993; *Curriculum Connections*, 1991; *McGill U. Report*, 1968. **EDUCATION:** PhD, Education, Cornell U., 1970; MA, Education, McGill U., 1956; BA/Hons., London U., 1950 (also, additional certificates & diplomas in education). **HEROES/ROLE MODELS:** C.C. Simms, father; Mary Avison, example of grace & humanity. **MOTTO:** Get on with it!

WRIGHT, Patrica (Pat) A. Pearson

EDUCATOR/EXECUTIVE DIRECTOR, Brampton, Mississauga and District Labour Action Centre, 969 Derry Rd. E., Mississauga, ON. Born: Jamaica/ in Canada since: 1975.

▸ Pat Wright is a chemist by background and training. After moving to Canada, she switched to the field of education, and has also been active in the representation of teachers within the OSSTF. She became active with the Teachers'

Federation in 1984. When elected in 1993 as a Provincial Executive Officer, she became the first Black to hold such a position, and served until 1997. She was then elected to fill one of the newly-created positions of Visible Minority VP on the executive of the OFL, and served in that capacity until 1999. Until early 2002, she coordinated a special project providing services for adults with learning disabilities for Accommodation Training and Networking (ATN), a not-for-profit agency. Currently, she is Executive Director, Brampton, Mississauga and District Labour Action Centre, a not-for-profit agency which provides employment-related assistance and services to a diverse client group. **BACKGROUND:** trained as a chemist in Jamaica, she worked primarily in the bauxite-alumina sector, as an x-ray specialist and lab supervisor in the analytical lab for the Alumina Partners of Jamaica; then was recruited by the Guyana Bauxite Company, 1973, as a bauxite chemist, responsible for the bauxite and alumina laboratories, and the development of new products. At the time, she was the only female manager and the only female chemist. After her arrival in Canada, she worked at the Princess Margaret Hospital in the Medical Bio-Physics Dept. Realizing though that education paid better than research, she moved to the secondary school system, teaching math, chemistry and biology from 1975 until her retirement from teaching in 2000. **COMMUNITY:** London Race Relations Advisory Cmtee; Brd. of Governors, Fanshawe College; Referee, Employment Insurance Brd. of Referees; London Chapter, Congress of Black Women; Instructor, Cdn Labour Congress. **HONS.:** including, Award of Merit, for service to District 3, OSSTF, 1998; Life Membership, for outstanding service to the Union, OSSTF, 1997; President's Award, for service to the teachers of Lambton County, 1992. **WORKS:** conference papers; articles in *Orbit*, 1994; *Education Forum*, 1992. **EDUCATION:** MSc, Education, U. of Western Ont., 1987; Hon. Specialist Teacher, Chemistry & Biology, U of T, 1981; Teacher's Cert., U of T,

1968; BSc, Chemistry & Botany, UWI, Jamaica, 1965. **MOTTO:** This above all, to thine own self be true, and it follows as the night the day, thou canst not then be false to any man. (Shakespeare) **CONTACT:** patw@sprint.ca; Fax: 519-246-9745

▶YAKIMCHUK, Clotilda A.

MENTAL HEALTH NURSE (Ret.), Cape Breton Regional Hospital, NS. Born: Sydney, NS.

▶ Clotilda Yakimchuk, despite many obstacles and with great determination, became a nurse in 1954, and thereby, the first Black Nova Scotian to graduate from the School of Nursing with a Nursing Diploma. She worked in Nova Scotia and Grenada before retiring 40 yrs. later, in 1994. **CAREER HIGHLIGHTS:** Head Nurse, Admissions Unit, NS Hospital, 1954-57; Director of Nursing, Psychiatric Hospital in Grenada (while there she established an outpatient psychiatric clinic), 1958-67; Staff Nurse at the Sydney City Hospital, 1967-68; Nursing Supervisor, Cape Breton Hospital, 1968-73; first Director of Staff Development, Cape Breton Hospital, 1973-92; Director of Education Services, 1992-94 at the Cape Breton Regional Hospital. Following her retirement in 1994, CY contributed her knowledge and expertise in the field of mental health to the development of the Community Residential Worker Program at the Marconi Campus of the NS Community College. This program was recognized by the province's Dept. of Community Services and has been adopted by them as the minimum standard of care for residential services in NS. She also worked with faculty at the Marconi Campus in the development and delivery of their Long-Term Care Program and has played a key role in the Alzheimers/Dementia course, and Non-Violent Crisis Intervention. **OTHER:** founding President, Black Community Development Organization whose focus initially was to improve housing for the community, then expanded to monitoring the educational system and the cultural development of the Black Nova Scotian community; represented her community at municipal, provincial, and national housing conferences; organized meetings between parents and the police to address the problem of youth and the law; was also active in community economic development initiatives through the New Dawn

Enterprises. **AFFIL/MBRSHP:** past-President of the Registered Nurses' Assn. of Nova Scotia (RNANS, was the first Black in their 83-yr. history to hold that position); NS Provincial Health Council; Brd., University College of Cape Breton; St. John's Ambulance; African Cdn Advisory Cmtee on Education; Brd., BCS/NS; NS Community College; Brd., NS Gerontology Assn.; Cape Breton Council of Seniors and Pensioners. **HONS.:** many from municipal, provincial and national, including: President's Achievement Award, for outstanding service to humanity, BCS/NS; Community Achievement Award, Sydney Bicentennial; Honorary Life membership, distinguished service and assistance to Nursing Profession, RNANS; Citation, Black Hall of Fame; Congress of Black Women; Harry Jerome Award, BBPA; Hon. Dipl., Marconi Campus, NS Community College (first time awarded by this college); Remarkable Senior Award, for community service. **EDUCATION:** Dipl., Adult Education, St. Francis Xavier U., NS, 1989; Post Graduate Psychiatric Nursing, NS Hospital, 1973; Post Graduate Midwifery Dipl., Grenada, 1958; RN Dipl., NS Hospital, School of Nursing, 1954. **HEROES/ROLE MODELS:** Parents; grade eight teacher. **MOTTO:** One's goal in life should be the improvement of one's self, one's neighbours, and one's environment. **CONTACT:** Tel: 902-562-3436

Appendices

In Memoriam

This section is dedicated to those individuals who died within the past ten years and whose contributions, whether to the community or in their professional lives, were significant.

Aylestock, Lloyd (b.1912; d.1997, ON): aircraft engineering with Avro Aircraft plant; production engineer, Pratt & Whitney, until retirement, then taught aircraft engineering to new recruits. ▶ **Aylestock, Viola** (b.1910; d.2002, ON): union activist, 1940s; correctional officer, 1964-73, Vanier Centre for Women, assisted in rehabilitation of previous offenders. ▶ **Barber, Jack** (b.1895; d.1993, ON): speed skater; involved with racing and organizing events (provincial, regional, and int'l) for over 60 years; president, Ottawa Speed Skating Club (1949-67) and Ontario Speed Skating Assn. (1950-68); credited with raising sport's profile; Ottawa Sports Hall of Fame, and other honours. ▶ **Barnes, Emery** (b.1929, US; d.1998, BC): elected MLA, BC, 1972, re-elected five times; voted Deputy Speaker of the legislature, 1994; previously played in NFL and CFL; promoted Black history and multiculturalism. ▶ **Benn, Andrew** (b. Guyana; d.1995, ON): Min. of Agriculture; developed hydroponics gardening (esp. for patios and balconies); developed national programs for vegetable sufficiency. ▶ **Best, Carrie** (b. 1903; d. 2001, NS): civil rights activist; journalist; founder/publisher (1946-56) *The Clarion* newspaper, later became the *Negro Citizen;* radio broadcaster. ▶ **Braithwaite, Daniel** (b. NS; d. 2002, ON): community organizer/activist; trade unionist; led campaign, 1950s, to have *Little Black Sambo* removed from Toronto Schools; co-founded and belonged to several community organizations. *See biography.* ▶ **Brooks, Wilson** (b.1924; d.1994, ON): WWII, navigator-bomber; became first known Black principal in Toronto (1971-86); community builder (OBHS, Urban Alliance on Race Relations). ▶ **Clarke, Edward** (b.1925; d.1998, ON): community builder; promoted diversity; founding director, National Black Coalition of Canada. ▶ **Clarke, Ernest** (b.1922; d.1993, ON): chemist, Dupont Canada for 35 yrs.; active member, Grant AME Church; lay member, Cdn Conference, 1964-92; facilitated purchase of church at 2029 Gerrard St. E., Toronto. ▶ **Coverley, Eric** (b.1911, Jamaica; d. 2002, ON): actor; comedian; impresario; career began in 1930s; member comedy duo, Eric and Flo; a.k.a. "Chalk Talk" for chalk drawings; known for skills as a calligrapher; honoured by Govt. of Jamaica; spouse, Louise Bennett *(see biography).* ▶ **Elliott, Lorris** (b.1931, Tobago; d.1999, QC): playwright; novelist; English professor, McGill U.; introduced Black and Caribbean literature to curriculum; 1980, organized conference, The Black Artist in the Canadian Milieu. ▶ **Gairey Sr., Harry Ralph** (b.1898, Jamaica; d.1993, ON): civil rights activist; community advocate; early member BSCP; founding member, Negro Citizenship Cmtee, lobbied Ottawa for changes to immigration laws which restricted entry of Blacks and other minorities; initiated first Black community centre (West Indian Federation Club). ▶ **Hamilton, Alfred** (b. AB; d.1994, ON): publisher *Contrast* newspaper, 1969-83; early advocate of rights for Blacks in South Africa. ▶ **Head, Wilson** (b.1914, US; d.1993, ON): academic; equal rights activist; director, Research & Planning for the Social Planning Council of Metro Toronto; founder, Urban Alliance on Race Relations, National Black Coalition of Canada; professor of social work, York U., 1970-82. ▶ **James, Ralph Eric** (b.1932; Trinidad; d. 1992, MB): taught for 26 yrs. (specialty, chemistry) at Winnipeg Adult Centre, served as judge for science fairs in Winnipeg School Div.1; was unofficial consultant to the English Dept.; encouraged emerging writers; co-founder, Black Writers' Assn., supported formation of Caribbean Theatre Workshop; extensive community involvement, community activist; certified cricket umpire. ▶ **Johnson, Leonard** (b.1918; d.1998, ON): along with wife, Gwen, opened Toronto's first Afrocentric bookstore, Third World Books & Crafts, in 1968; book-

391

store was also a meeting place for students, educators, and those interested in learning more about African heritage; the historic site closed shortly after LJ's death. ▶ **Langdon, Henry** (d.1997, QC): WWII veteran, RCAF, aircraft engineer; lifelong UNIA activist, historian, and community builder. ▶ **Lewsey, Marjorie** (b.1923; d.2001, ON): human rights activist. ▶ **Mascoll, Beverly** (b. NS; d.2001, ON): founder, Mascoll Beauty Supply Ltd.; philanthropist (Beverly Mascoll Community Foundation); mentor; community builder. ▶ **Mercury, Albert** (b. Toronto; d.1998, ON): first known Black member of Royal Cdn Military Institute; established Lions Clubs (esp. Toronto Onyx Lions Club). ▶ **Moore, Donald** (b.1891, Barbados; d.1994, ON): community advocate; along with others, persuaded Ottawa to modify discriminatory immigration rules to allow Black women to come to Canada (first as nurses then others as domestics); founding member of UNIA/Toronto and other organizations. ▶ **Packwood, Anne** (b.1898, Bermuda; d.2000, ON): lived most of her life in Montreal; community organizer; founding member, Coloured Women's Club of Montreal; foster parent, 1926-66; featured in film, *Fields of Endless Day.* ▶ **Packwood, Edward** (b.1898, Guyana; d.1994, ON): founder/publisher *The Free Lance,* 1932-38, a Black weekly newspaper, distribution of 8,000 across Canada; entrepreneur; community organizer. ▶ **Parris, Gerald** (b.1923; d.2001, NS): WWII veteran; RCAF, last surviving Black member of D-Day landing forces, Normandy, France, 1944. ▶ **Perry, Lloyd** (b. NS; d.1997, ON): lawyer, QC; staff, office of the Official Guardian of Ontario, 1950; became Deputy (1960) then Official Guardian, prov. of Ontario (1975-85), responsible for protecting the personal and property rights of children. ▶ **Ruggles, Clifton** (b. NS; d.1998, QC): teacher; activist; artist; photographer; social historian. ▶ **Smith, Eva** (b.1923, Jamaica; d.1993, ON): community service; activist for equity, rights of women and youth; advocated for access to education and greater parental involvement; bursary and youth shelter named in her honour. ▶ **Spence, Rudyard** (b. Jamaica; d.2000, BC): taught at BCIT; involved with many community organizations; advocated diversity and multiculturalism. ▶ **Streete, Malcolm D.** (b.1934, NS; d.1997, ON): worked with CPR, then CNR, then Via Rail; entrepreneur; appointed Ont. Justice of the Peace, 1989; supported youth and community development initiatives. ▶ **Walls, Earl** (b.1928; d.1996, ON): former heavyweight boxing champion; real estate broker; philanthropist. ▶ **Yearwood, Sylvia** (b. 1926, Barbados; d.2000, QC): long-standing member of Union United Church; over a 40-year period served on most committees, sang in choir, and was on pastor's advisory committee.

Compiled with information from: *Some Black Women; Some Black Men; Millennium Minds;* the Internet.

Index by Province

ALBERTA

ADAMS, John
Ministerial Dir., AB Conference of
Seventh-day Adventists

ALLEYNE, Brian C.
Clinical Epidemiologist/Lecturer,
U. of Alberta

BROWNIE, Edward
Biochemistry Research Technologist,
U. of Alberta

BRUCCOLERI, Claudette
Teacher, Calgary Board of Education

CHAMBERS, Juanita
Psychologist/Prof. Emeritus,
U. of Alberta

CHEESMAN, Sean
Dancer/Choreographer

FOGGO, Cheryl
Writer/Journalist/Film Director

FRASER, Felix (Fil)
Writer/Journalist/Filmmaker

FUHR, Grant
Frmr. Goaltender/Goaltending
Consultant, Calgary Flames

HARRIS, Claire
Author

HARRISON, Herman (Herm)
Frmr. Football Player/Philanthropist

HOOKS, Gwendolyn
Author/Teacher (Ret.), County of Leduc

IGINLA, Jarome
Hockey Player, Calgary Flames

JONES, Lionel L.
Judge (Ret.), The Court of Queen's
Bench of Alberta

KACELENGA, Ray
Principal Engineer,
General Dynamics Canada

LAWRENCE, Errol A.
Chair/Assoc. Prof., Dept. of Religious
Studies, Canadian U. College

MANNING, George
Regulatory Analyst, ESBI (Alberta) Ltd.

OKELU, Chinwe Pete
Coordinator, Alberta Municipal Affairs

PROCTOR, Hazel
Jazz Singer

RAMSANKAR, Stephen R.
Citizenship Judge/Educational
Consultant/Principal (Ret.),
Govt. of Alberta

ROGERS, George
Mayor, City of Leduc

STEPHENS, Dell
Chartered Financial Planner,
CIBC Wood Gundy

THOMAS, Sharlene
Motivational Speaker/Events Producer,
Sharlene Thomas Productions

TIDLUND, Mary A.
Oil Industry CEO/Humanitarian,
Mary A. Tidlund Charitable Fdn.

WILLIAMS, Georgina
Concert Pianist/Composer/Singer/
Songwriter

WILLIAMS, Mojo
Proprietor/Musician (Semi-Ret.),
Aries Gold

BRITISH COLUMBIA

ADAMS, James L.
Artist/Prof. (Ret.), Douglas/Kwantlen
University College

ALEXANDER, Norman E.
Reg. Prof'l Biologist (Ret.),
BC Inst. of Technology

ALEXANDER, Thérèse
Judge, Provincial Courts BC

ALLEYNE, John
Artistic Director, Ballet BC

ALLSOPP, W. Herbert L.
Fisheries Consultant, CEO,
Smallworld Fishery Consultants Inc.

BRAITHWAITE, John B.
Councillor, City of North Vancouver

BROWN, Rosemary
MLA (Ret.)/Rights Activist

CHRISTENSEN, Carole Pigler
Prof., School of Social Work &
Family Studies, UBC

COMPTON, Wayde
Writer/Editor

CROOKS, Charmaine
Olympian/IOC member, Int'l Olympic
Committee/NGU Consulting

DURITY, Felix
Prof./Head, Div. of Neurosurgery,
Dept. of Surgery, UBC

FOX, Lovena
Actor/Singer/Songwriter

GALE, Lorena
Actor/Playwright/Director,
Curious Tongue

GIBSON, Leonard (Len)
Dancer/Choreographer/Teacher

GIBSON-TOWNS, Thelma
Performer/Director, Afro Jazz Drum &
Dance Ensemble

GRIFFITH, Clyde
Recreation & Leisure Consultant (Ret.),
BC Provincial Govt.

IGALI, Daniel
Freestyle Wrestling Champion,
Landmark Sport Group

JACOB, Selwyn
Filmmaker/Producer, NFB

JONES, Roger B.
The Ability Market Consultant

KUEHN, Sadie
Writer/Human Rights Activist,
Sadie Kuehn Consulting

LEGON, Jeni
Performer/Tap Dancer/Actor

MARSHALL, Valin G.
Soil Zoologist, Royal Roads U.

MGBEOJI, Ikechi
Assistant Prof., Faculty of Law, UBC

ROBINSON, Frank Price
Asst. Dean, Arts & Science
(Ret.)/Assoc. Prof. Emeritus,
U. of Victoria

ROMILLY, Selwyn R.
Judge, BC Supreme Court

SARSFIELD, Mairuth Hodge
Writer

SIMPSON, Denis
Singer/Actor/Performer

WADE, Jan
Visual Artist

WINN, Paul A.
Lawyer/Human Rights Activist,
Paul A. Winn Law Corp.

MANITOBA

ASAGWARA, K.C. Prince
Researcher/Policy & Planning Analyst,
Education and Training
Dept. Govt. of MB
ATWELL, Frances
Pharmacist (Ret.)
ATWELL, George
Teacher (Ret.)/Commercial Beekeeper,
Winnipeg Sch. Brd.
ATWELL,Gerry
Performer/Visual Arts Curator
COOPSAMMY, Madeline F.
Writer/Poet
GORDON, Donald K.
Prof. (Ret.), U. of Manitoba
HARRIS, Jeffrey F.
Lawyer/Partner, Myers, Weinberg
HARRIS, Paul F.
Owner/Manager (Ret.), Supreme
Electric Manufacturing Ltd.
JAMES, June Marion
Consultant, Allergy and Asthma,
Winnipeg Clinic
JONES, Beryle Mae
Asst. Prof., U. of Winnipeg &
U. of Manitoba
JONES, Byron
Educator/Principal, Munroe Junior
High School
MCLAREN, Headley
Principal/Special Ed. Teacher
(Ret.)/Winnipeg Sch. Distr. No. 1
MUYINDA, Estella Namakula
Legal Policy Analyst, Court Challenges
Program of Canada
NNADI, Joseph
Prof., Dept. of French Studies,
U. of Winnipeg
OLWENY, Charles Lwanga Mark
Prof./Medical Oncologist, U. of
Manitoba/ Cancer Care Manitoba
SANDIFORD, Keith A.P.
Prof. Emeritus, History Dept.,
U. of Manitoba
STEWART, Esme
Faculty Advisor, U. of Manitoba

NEW BRUNSWICK/ NEWFOUNDLAND

BRUEGGERGOSMAN, Measha
Soprano/Opera Singer
MIGHTY, E. Joy
Assoc. Prof., Faculty of Admin.,
U. of New Brunswick
NOEL, Dexter
Coordin. Interdisciplinary Studies,
U. of New Brunswick
PETERS, David J
Chef/Educator (Ret.), PRUDE Inc.
WHITE, Carl A.
Deputy Mayor, Saint John City Council
ALGOO-BAKSH, Stella
Assoc. Prof., Dept. of English,
Memorial U. of Newfoundland

NOVA SCOTIA

ATUANYA, Tony I.
Executive Director, WADE Inc.
AYLWARD, Carol A.
Assistant Prof., Faculty of Law,
Dalhousie U.
BARTON, Brad
Educator/CEO, Bar Jun Consultants
BAYLIS, Françoise
Prof., Bioethics & Philosophy,
Faculty of Medicine, Dalhousie U.
BISHOP, Henry V.
Chief Curator, Director, Black Cultural
Centre for NS
BORDEN, George
Captain (Ret.)/ Poet-Songwriter/
Historian, RCAF/CF
BRUCE, Lawrence S.
Vice-President, Black Loyalist
Heritage Society
CALLISTE, Agnes
Assoc. Prof. & Black Student Advisor,
St. Francis Xavier U.
CLAYTON, Cyril A.
Chief Warrant Officer (Ret.),
Canadian Forces
CRAWLEY, Iona
Recruitment-Retention Cnsltant,
Sch. of Nursing, Dalhousie U.
EARLE, Gordon
Sr. Public Admin. (Ret.)/Frmr. MP,
Govt. of NS & Canada

EVANS, Doris
Volunteer & Senior Citizens Advocate
EWING, Brendon
Manager, Personal Financial Services,
RBC Financial Group
FARROW-LAWRENCE, Jacquie
Municipal Clerk, Municipality of
Annapolis County
FRANCIS, Mayann
Executive Director, NS Human Rights
Commission
FRASER, James H.
Chief Warrant Officer (Ret.),
Canadian Forces
GANNON, Louis
Exec. Dir., Better Business Bur.,
Maritime Provinces Inc.
GRANT, Sheryl
Assistant Managing Editor,
The Halifax Herald Ltd.
HAMILTON, Sylvia
Filmmaker, Maroon Films Inc.
HARTLEY, Max
Police Sergeant (Ret.),
Halifax Regional Police
HOLNESS, Renn O.
Prof., Neurosurgery/Dir. Surgical
Education, Dept. of Surgery, Dalhousie U.
IBHAWOH, Bonny
Killam Scholar/Lecturer,
Dept. of History, Dalhousie U.
INCE, Thelma Coward
Personnel Admin. (Ret.),
Dept. of National Defence
JOHNSON, Allister
Program Coordin./Comm'y Volunteer,
N. Preston Holistic, Cultural and
Academic Enrichment Program
JOHNSON, E. Bruce
Pharmacist/Co-owner,
City Drug Store Ltd.
JOHNSON, Kaye
Coordin., Race Relations,
Annapolis Valley Reg'l Sch. Brd.
JOSEPH, Richard (Rick)
Executive Director, NS Environmental
Industry Assn.
KAKEMBO, Patrick N.
Director, African Canadian Services,
NS Dept. of Education
LAWRENCE, Raymond C.
Chief Petty Officer First Class (Ret.),
Royal Canadian Navy

LEWIS, Daurene
Principal, Halifax Campuses,
Nova Scotia Community College

LOPES, Blair
Adjunct Prof./Dalhousie U., President,
Added Dimension Cnslting

MILLAR, Harvey
Prof., Faculty of Commerce,
Saint Mary's U.

NJOKU, William C.
Coordinator/Entrepreneur,
Will2Win Sports

OLIVER, Leslie H.
Prof., Jodrey School of Computer
Science, Acadia U.

OLIVER, Pearleen
Activist/Historian

OLIVER, Sharon
President & CEO, Oliver Management
Connexus Inc.

OLIVER, The Hon. Donald H.
Senator, Senate of Canada

PACHAI, Bridglal
Adjunct Prof., Saint Mary's U. &
Dalhousie U.

PARIS, Henderson
Community Organizer,
Run Against Racism

ROSS, Joyce L.
Founder/Executive Director,
East Preston Day Care Centre

SAMUELS-STEWART, Victorine (Viki)
Coordin., Race Relations,
NS Human Rights Commission

SMITH, Craig
Author/Historian/Constable,
Royal Canadian Mounted Police

SMITH, Robert (Mark)
Softball Coach, Dir. of Sport Dev't/
Prov. Coordin. Sport NS/3M Fair &
Safe Play Program

SOUTHWELL, Gracey
Dir., Systems Support and Operations,
Aliant Telecom Broadband Services

SOUTHWELL, Rustum
Executive Director,
Black Business Initiative

SPARKS, Corrine E.
Judge, Nova Scotia Family Court

THORNHILL, Esmeralda
Prof., Dalhousie Law School,
Dalhousie U.

TURNER-BAILEY, Marjorie
Nurse/Genealogical Res., Roseway
Hosp./Black Loyalist Society

UPSHAW, Robert Graham (Ted)
Inspector, Royal Canadian
Mounted Police

WALTER, Paul L.
Lawyer/Partner, Waterbury Newton

WATERMAN, Vincent
Archbishop, St. Philip's African
Orthodox Church of Canada

WEDDERBURN, Hobartson A.J. (Gus)
Barrister/Solicitor/Notary Public,
H.A.J. Wedderburn Law Office

WILLIAMS, Castor
Judge, Provincial Courts of Nova Scotia

YAKIMCHUK, Clotilda A.
Mental Health Nurse (Ret.),
Cape Breton Regional Hospital

ONTARIO

ABUKAR, Hassan
Youth Leadership Rep.,
Toronto Youth Cabinet

ACQUAAH-HARRISON, Kobèna
Musician/Producer, Ice Hut Production

ADAMS, Leonard
Prof. Emeritus, Dept. of French
Studies, U. of Guelph

ADIBE, Michael
Principal (Ret.), Office of the Auditor
General of Canada

AGINAM, Obijiofor
Assistant Prof., Dept. of Law, Carleton U.

AITCHESON, Adrian
Fashion Designer, Roots

AKANDE, Zanana L.
Educator (Ret.)/Frmr. MPP, Toronto
Dist. Sch. Brd./Govt. of Ont.

AKANO, Liz
Business Teacher,
Thames Valley Dist. Sch. Brd.

ALEXANDER, Siobhan
Legal Counsel, Bank of Montreal

ALEXANDER, The Hon. Lincoln M.
Lawyer, Lieutenant-Governor (Ret.),
Govt. of Ont.

ALEXIS, Horace C.
Physician/Philanthropist, Private Practice

ALLEN, Daniel H.
Director, Service Delivery Policy,
HRDC (NHQ)

ALLEN, Lillian
Writer/Poet/Creative Writing Prof.,
Ont. College of Art & Design

ALLEYNE, Archie
Musician/Drummer

ALLEYNE-NIKOLIC, Eucline Claire
Registrar, Ont. Institute for Studies in
Education (OISE), U of T

ANDERSON, Wolseley W. (Percy)
Prof. Emeritus and Senior Scholar,
Social Sciences, York U.

ANDRE, Irving
Lawyer/Author

ANNOR-ADJEI, Ellen
Concert Pianist

APPELT, Pamela
Citizenship Judge (Ret.),
Court of Canadian Citizenship

APPIAH, Yvonne
Executive Director, CODE

ARMSTRONG, Bromley
Labour & Civil Rights Activist (Ret.)

ARMSTRONG, Neil
Journalist/News Director,
CHRY Radio, York U.

ASANTE, Kabu
Employment Consultant/CEO,
D&S Personnel Services

AUGUSTINE, The Hon. Jean
MP, Secretary of State
(Multiculturalism & Women's Dir.),
Govt. of Canada

AZAN, Kemeel
Hair Stylist/Salon Owner,
Azan's Beauty Salon

BACCHUS, Natasha Cecily
Athlete/Medallist, World Deaf Games

BADOE, Adwoa
Author

BAILEY, Cameron
Film Critic/Broadcaster, *NOW*
Magazine/ Alliance Atlantis
Broadcasting

BAILEY, Daphne
Nursing Specialist (Ret.),
D&B Footcare Business

BAILEY, Donovan
Olympic Athlete

bailey, maxine
Manager, Public Affairs,
Toronto Int'l Film Festival

395

BAILEY, Nehemiah L.
Community Organizer/Educator (Ret.),
Toronto Dist. Sch. Brd.

BANCROFT, George W.
Prof. Emeritus, Scholarship, U of T

BANCROFT, Joseph (Dan)
City Auditor (Ret.), City of Toronto

BARCLAY, John V.
Deputy Grand Master, Indep. United
Order of Solomon/Canada

BARNES, Kofi
Sr. Counsel & Special Advisor, Dept.
of Justice, Fed. Prosecution Service

BARNES, Leesa
IT Manager/President, BITePRO

BATCHELOR, Barrington de Vere
Prof. Emeritus, Civil Engineering,
Queen's U.

BELL, David V.J.
Prof./Director, Centre for Applied
Sustainability (YCAS), York U.

BENNETT, Karl
Associate Prof., Dept. of Economics,
U. of Waterloo

BENNETT-COVERLEY, Louise Simone
Folklorist/Performer/Author

BENN-IRELAND, Tessa
Author/Senior Librarian,
Markham Public Libraries

BERGER, Marie-Josée
Doyenne, Faculté de l'Education,
U. d'Ottawa

BERNARDINE, Marion
Educator/Principal (Ret.),
Toronto Dist. Sch. Brd.

BERNHARDT, Kim
Lawyer, Grant & Bernhardt

BERRY, Ivan
President/Head, Int'l Div.,
Beat Factory/ BMG Music

BERTLEY, John N.
Physician/Internist/Respirologist,
Sir William Osler Health Centre

BESS, Ardon
Actor

BEST, J. Calbert
Civil Servant/High Commissioner
(Ret.), Federal Public Service

BEY, Salome
Singer/Actor

BLACKMAN, Craig
General Manager, Rehab. and Training,
COSTI Immigrant Services

BLACKWOOD, Yvonne
Banker/Author, Royal Bank of Canada

BLAIR, Ned
Community Activist/President,
Organization of Black Tradesmen &
Tradeswomen of Ont.

BLAKE, Ronald E.
Director of Studies, Higher Marks
Educational Institute Inc.

BLIZZARD, Stephen V.
Aviation Medicine Consultant

BLYDEN-TAYLOR, Brainerd
Founder/Artistic Director,
The Nathaniel Dett Chorale

BON, Trevor
Physician, Geriatrics and Internal
Medicine, St. Joseph's Care Group

BOVELL, Keith T.
MD, Gastroenterologist & Internist,
Private Practice

BOYD, Suzanne
Editor-In-Chief, *FLARE* Magazine,
Rogers Media

BRAITHWAITE, Daniel
Community Organizer/
Trade Unionist (Ret.)

BRAITHWAITE, F. Carlton
Economist/Entrepreneur/
Community Leader

BRAITHWAITE, Jack
Lawyer/Partner, Gatien◆Braithwaite

BRAITHWAITE, Leonard A.
Barrister, Solicitor, & Notary Public,
Private Practice

BRAITHWAITE, Rella Aylestock
Writer/Historian

BRATHWAITE, Keren Sophia
Associate Director, Transitional Year
Programme, U of T

BRATHWAITE, Shirley N.
Psychiatrist/Prof., Royal Ottawa
Hospital/ U. of Ottawa

BRIN, Derek
Music Producer/Composer,
Fierce Music Group

BROOKS, C. John
Humanitarian & Community Advocate,
The John Brooks Community Fdn.

BROWNE, Christene
Filmmaker,
Syncopated Productions Inc.

BUREY, Owen Leslie
Minister, Sandwich First Baptist Church

BUSH, Rochelle
Local Historian/Community Activist,
Harriet Tubman Centre for Cultural
Services

BUTTERFIELD, Joan
Artist

CADER, Eric
Agent d'Ed/Dir., program. française,
Interlink Consulting/ CIUT 89,5FM

CALLENDER, Chloe E.
Educator/Race Relations Consultant
(Ret), Waterloo Dist. Catholic Sch.
Brd.

CALLENDER, Murchison G.
Prof. Emeritus, School of Optometry,
U. of Waterloo

CAMPAYNE, Hazel
Diocesan Multicultural Consultant,
The Anglican Diocese of Toronto

CAMPBELL, Constantine A.
Soil Research Scientist Emeritus/
Consultant, Eastern Cereal & Oilseed
Research Centre

CAMPBELL, Denise Andrea
Youth Activist/Frmr. President, NAC

CARNEGIE, Herbert
Hockey Pioneer/Community Leader

CARTER, George E.
Judge (Ret.), Ont. Court of Justice

CARTER, Jean
Journalist, CBC Radio

CARTER, Rubin "Hurricane"
Frmr. Boxer/Activist, Assn. in Defence
of the Wrongfully Convicted

CARTER-HENRY LYON, Grace
Founder/Musical Director,
The Heritage Singers

CARTY, Donald
WWII Veteran, RCAF

CHAMBERS, Mary Anne
Senior Vice-President, Scotiabank

CHAMBERS, Michael
Photographic Artist/Publisher,
Nok Photo Publishing

CHARLES, Maurice A.
Judge (Ret.), Provincial Court of Ont.

CHUMPUKA, Florence
Legal Counsel, Federal Dept. of Justice

CLARK, Eugene
Performer/Singer/Songwriter/Producer

CLARKE, George Elliott
Prof./Poet/Author/Playwright,
Dept. of English, U of T

CLARKE, LaFerne
Executive Director, Family Services
Hamilton-Wentworth

CLARKE, Neville
Artist

CLARKE WALKER, Marie
Trade Unionist/ past VP National
Diversity, CUPE

COLLINS, David
Actor

COLLINS, Enid M.
Prof. Emeritus, Nursing, Ryerson U.

COLLINS, Erma B.
Prof. (Ret.)/Community Volunteer,
George Brown College

COMESEE, Auntie
Performer/Storyteller

COOK, Verda
Community Volunteer

COOLS, The Hon. Anne C.
Senator, Senate of Canada

COOPER, Afua
Prof. of Sociology/Poet, Ryerson U.

COOPER-WILSON, Jane
Historian/Artist/Writer,
TigerLily Enterprises

CRICHLOW, Wesley
Activist/Assistant Prof., Dept. of Law,
Carleton U.

CURLING, Alvin
Member Provincial Parliament,
Legislative Assembly of Ont.

DADSON SR., Joseph E.
Bio-medical Engineer/President/CEO,
Newsol Technologies

DALEY, Sandy
Actor/Entrepreneur,
Chocolate Dolls Productions

DANIEL, Juliet
Assistant Prof., Dept. of Biology,
McMaster U.

DAVIS, Erica
Minister, British Methodist Episcopal
Church

DAVIS, Rodney
Proprietor/CA, Nappy's Inc./Chartered
Accounting Practice

DAVIS, Wells
Owner & Managing Partner, Clarity/
Urban Engine Commun.

DAWKINS, Ettie E.
Director of Marketing, Ettie Dawkins
Fashion Sales Agency

deGRAFT-JOHNSON, Ama
Anaesthesiologist/Clinical Prof.,
Hamilton HSC/McMaster U.

DEI, George J.S.
Prof. & Chair, Dept. of Sociology,
OISE/ U of T

DEVERELL, Rita Shelton
Vice-President, New Concept
Development, Vision TV

DEVONISH, Terrie-Lynne
Vice-President, Legal Counsel, Corp.
Sec., HSBC Securities (Canada) Inc.

DICK, Emmanuel
Educator (Ret.)/Community Organizer,
Nat'l Council of T&T Organizations in
Canada

DOGBE, Julius
Justice of the Peace,
Min. of the Attorney General

DONKOR, Samuel
Senior Pastor,
All Nations Full Gospel Church

DORSEY, Robert Edward
President/Mngmt. Consultant, 3rd
Dimensions & Associates Ltd.

DOWNES, M. Peggy
Aide-de-Camp/Admin. Officer,
Canadian Forces Army Reserve

DUNCAN, Alvin
WWII Veteran, Royal Canadian Air
Force

DUNCAN, Carol B.
Assistant Prof., Dept. Religion &
Culture, Wilfrid Laurier U.

DUNCAN, George
City Manager, City of London

DWYER, Mike
Track and Field Coach

EDOGHAMEN, Robin
Executive Director, Metro Street Focus

EDWARDS, Haskell G.
Pastor, Seventh-day Adventist Church,
HQ

EDWARDS, Jacqueline
Recruitment Officer, Federal
Correctional Service of Canada

EDWARDS, Madeline
Community Organizer/Manager (Ret.),
Geriatric Psychiatric Outreach, CAMH

ELLIS, Keith A.A.
Prof. Emeritus, Dept. Spanish &
Portuguese, U of T

ELLISTON, Inez
Educator & Community Volunteer
Leader

EMERENCIA, Emerita
Multidisciplinary Artist & Educator,
Prologue to the Performing Arts

ENYOLU, Evans Rick A.
Publisher/Principal Consultant,
Multitech Consulting Int'l Inc.

ESHO, David
Realtor, Prudential Elite Realty

ESTRIDGE, Christopher
Artist, The Publicity Group

FALCONER, Julian N.
Barrister, Senior Partner,
Falconer Charney Macklin

FARRELL, Lennox
Teacher/Community Organizer,
Toronto Dist. Catholic Sch. Brd.

FARRELL, Vernon W.
Principal (Ret.)/ Educational
Consultant, InclusivEd Associates

FEARON, Gervan
Assistant Prof./Economics,
Atkinson College, York U.

FERNANDES, Lester
Geologist (Ret.), COMINCO Ltd.

FERRIER, Ross
Investment Advisor, CIBC Wood Gundy

FIELDS, Stephen
Incumbent, The Anglican Church of St.
Stephen

FITZ-RITSON, Don
Chiropractor/Dir.,
Advanced Therapeutic Centre

FORDE, Keith
Superintendent of Police,
Toronto Police Service

FRANCIS, Flora H. Blizzard
Author/Librarian (Ret.), U. of Guelph

FRANCIS, Ken K.
CEO & President, Ken K. Francis
Financial Services

FRANCIS, Pat
Senior Pastor, Founder,
Deeper Life Christian Ministries

FRANCIS, Verlyn F.
Lawyer, Law Office of Verlyn F. Francis

FRANCOIS, Pierre
Mechanical Engineer/Teacher (Ret.)

FRASER, Frank M.
VP Market Development (Ret.),
MDS Nordion

GALABUZI, Grace-Edward
Research Associate/Community
Activist, Centre for Social Justice

GAYLE-ANYIWE, Brenda Claire Hope
Prof., Faculty of Business,
Seneca College

GEORGE, Gbadebo Oladeinde
Nigerian Ambassador (Ret.),
Nigerian Min. of Foreign Affairs

GEORGE, Kenrick
President/CEO,
Aaron Multi-Tec Systems

GITTENS, Rudolph Ormsby
Orthopedic Surgeon/Sport Medicine
Consultant, Private Practice

GLANVILLE, Carlton R.W.
Chartered Accountant, Carlton R.W.
Glanville, MBA, CA

GLASGOW, Valerie
Clinical Nurse Educator/Faculty
Instructor, Mount Sinai Hosp./Ryerson U.

GOMEZ, Henry
Musician/Actor,
King Cosmos Entertainment

GOODING, Victor E.
Future Technology Development
Specialist, Telesat Canada

GRANGE, Hamlin
Journalist/ President,
ProMedia Int'l Inc.

GRANT, Gerald
Assistant Prof., Eric Sprott School of
Business, Carleton U.

GRANT, Rudolph W.
Prof. Emeritus, York U.

GRANT, Yola
Lawyer/Activist, Grant & Bernhardt

GRIMMOND, Claude N.
Mediator/Trainer/Facilitator,
Conflict Management Services

GRIZZLE, Stanley G.
Citizenship Judge (Ret.),
Court of Canadian Citizenship

GUDGE, Leyland
Consultant, Family Services &
Anti-racism/ Multicultural Organ'l
Change

GUY, Sol
Global Hip Hop Entrepreneur

GYLES, Carlton L.
Prof. of Bacteriology, Dept. of
Pathobiology, U. of Guelph

HALSTEAD, Joseph A.G.
Commissioner, Economic Dev't,
Culture, and Tourism, City of Toronto

HAMALENGWA, Munyonzwe
Lawyer, Private Practice

HAMIS, Ahmed R.
Environmental Coordin.,
Regional Municipality of Halton

HANSRAJ, Luther
Actor/Producer/Director

HAREWOOD, John L.
Academic Advisor/Prof. (Ret.),
U. of Ottawa

HARTY, Corita
Regional Director, HR, Ont. and
Nunavut Region, Health Canada

HERRERA JACKSON, Denise
Consultant/Technical Writer,
Farrell Haynes Associates

HEZEKIAH, Jocelyn
Nursing Education Consultant

HIBBERT JR., Leroy
Multicultural Outreach Coordin.,
LUSO Community Services

HILL, Dan
Singer/Songwriter/Producer,
Big Picture Entertainment

HILL, Lawrence
Writer, c/o Harper Collins

HILL III, Dan G.
Founder /President Emeritus (Ret.),
Ont. Black History Society

HINKSON, Steven
Lawyer/Partner, Hinkson, Sachak,
McLeod

HOLAS, Patricia W.
Creative Director/Author,
Pan-African Publications

HOPE, Jay
Chief Superintendent,
Ont. Provincial Police

HOPKINSON, Nalo
Author

HUDSON, Maurice
Secondary School Principal,
Peel Dist. Sch. Brd.

HUGGINS, Arleen
Barrister & Solicitor/Partner,
Koskie Minsky

HUGGINS, Dorette
Dir., Communications, Dept. of Justice
Canada, Ont. Reg'l Office

IEN, Marci
TV News Anchor, CTV NewsNet

IGWEMEZIE, Jude O.
Professional Engineer, CEO,
Applied Rail Research Technologies

IKEJIANI, Alexander O.
Barrister & Solicitor,
Dept. of Justice Canada

IKEJIANI, Charles
Orthopaedic Surgeon, Private Practice

IKEJIANI, Okechukwu
Pathologist (Ret.),
Duncan Professional Consultants

IMRIE, Kathy
Actor/Entrepreneur,
Imre Background Talent Agency

ISAAC, Julius Alexander
Federal Court Judge,
Federal Court of Appeal

ISAACS, Joy Enid
Human Resource Consultant (Ret.),
City of Toronto

ISAACS, Orin
Musician, Moca Music

JACKSON, Ovid
Member of Parliament,
Govt. of Canada

JACKSON, Richard Lawson
Prof. Emeritus, Spanish, Carleton U.

JAILALL, Peter
Teacher/Poet/Storyteller

JAMES, Carl E.
Associate Prof., Faculty of Education,
York U.

JARRETT, Carolyn Joyce
Optometrist, Private Practice

JARVIS, Michael
Filmmaker, Recfilm

JEMMOTT, Anthony
Incumbent, All Saints Anglican Church

JENNINGS, Marlene
Member of Parliament,
Govt. of Canada

JOHN, Dexter
Lawyer, Donahue Ernst & Young LLP

JOHNSON, Ben
Athlete/Coach

JOHNSON, Beverley C.H.
Human Rights Officer, OPSEU

JOHNSON, Lillie
Director of Nursing (Ret.), Leeds,
Grenville, Lanark Dist. Health Unit

JOHNSON, Molly
Singer/Songwriter/Philanthropist,
c/o EMI Music
JOHNSTON, Roy
WWII Veteran, Royal Canadian Air Force
JOLLY, Brandeis Denham
Business Owner, Flow 93.5FM
JONES, Ann
Clinical Nurse Specialist, Nephrology
JONES, Denise
President/Events Organizer,
Jones & Jones Productions
JONES, Robert William (Bud)
Bibliophile/Historian/Lecturer, Anne
Packwood Quebec Afro-Cdn. Res. Inst.
JULIEN, Stanley J.
Vice-President, BMO Nesbitt Burns
JUNOR, Kevin R.
Regimental Sergeant-Major,
Canadian Forces
KABUNDI, Marcel
Gestionnaire, Progr. ethnoculturels,
Service correctionnel du Canada,
Min. du Sol. Gén.
KADIRI, Yahaya Z.
Anaesthesiologist/Internist,
Southlake Regional Health Centre
KAFELE, Paul Kwasi
Director, Corporate Diversity, CAMH
KASSIM, Ola A.
Pathologist-in-Chief & Dir. of
Laboratory Services, West Parry Sound
Health Care Services
KAWUKI-MUKASA, Isaac
Congregational Development
Consultant, The Anglican Diocese
of Toronto
KEENS-DOUGLAS, Richardo
Actor/Writer/Director/Storyteller,
c/o Core Group
KEFENTSE, Dayo
Journalist, CBC Radio
KELLY, Jude
Writer, Ont. Min. of Public Safety
and Security
KELLY, Paulette
Associate Prof., School of Fashion,
Ryerson U.
KHENTI, Akwatu
Director, Education & Training
Services, CAMH
KIBUUKA, David
Artist

KILLINGBECK, Molly
Athlete Services Manager/Coach,
Canadian Sport Centre Ont.
KING, Karen
Film Producer, NFB
KUMSA, Martha Kuwee
Writer, c/o Harper Collins
LAMPKIN, Vibert
Judge, Ont. Court of Justice
LARBI, Madonna Owusuah
Executive Director, MATCH Int'l Centre
LARMOND, Londa
Singer/Performer
LAROSE, Winston W.
Videographer, African Cdn Comm. &
Broadcasting Corp.
LAW-BANCROFT, Carole
Music Teacher/Examiner,
Royal Conservatory of Music
LAWRENCE, Delores
President & CEO, NHI Nursing &
Homemakers Inc.
LAWS, Dudley
Civil Rights/Community Activist,
Black Action Defense Committee
LEBEANYA, Charity
Executive Director, Heritage Skills
Development Centre
LEE-CHIN, Michael
Chairman & Chief Investment Officer,
AIC Limited
LEWIS, Glenn
Singer/Songwriter, Sony Music
LEWIS, Ray
Olympic Athlete & Railway Porter
(Ret.)
LEWIS, Roy
Actor
LEWIS, Sharon
On-Air Host, ZedTV, CBC Television
LONGE, Winfield E.
Fleet Captain, Upper Lakes Group
LORIMER, Edith
Family Physician,
Rosedale Medical Centre
LOWE, Keith D.
International Education Consultant,
Inter Cultural Associates Inc.
MACFARLANE, Anthony
Medical Practitioner, Private Practice
MAKEDA, Donna
Reggae/DanceHall Performer/
Co-Publisher, *Uprising Int'l*

MANLEY, Rachel
Writer, c/o Random House
MARK, Kirk
Advisor, Race & Ethnic Relations,
Toronto Catholic Dist. School Brd.
MARKHAM, Jean J. Burke
Minister-in-Charge & Pastor,
Peel Methodist Church
MARSHALL, Amanda
Singer/Songwriter, Sony Music
MARSHALL, Clem
Educator/Diversity Trainer,
MangaCom Inc.
MARTIN, Eugenie
Director of Cosmetology,
Topaz College of Aesthetics & Hair
MASSIAH, Thomas
Research Chemist (Ret.)
MBULU, Emmanuel
President & CEO, Tone-A-Matic Int'l
MCCURDY, Howard D.
Frmr. MP/Prof., Biology (Ret.),
Govt. of Canada/U. of Windsor
MCCURVIN, Donna
Co-publisher, *Word* Magazine
MCDONALD, Jasse (JC)
Journalist/Radio & TV Broadcaster
MCFARLANE, Ivan
Adjunct Lecturer/Assoc. Graduate
Faculty, U of T/Central Michigan U.
MCINTOSH, Yanna
Actor & Teacher
MCLEOD, Donald
Barrister & Solicitor/Partner, Hinkson,
Sachak, McLeod
MCNAB, John
Director, Pastoral Studies (Ret.),
Montreal Diocesan Theological
College
MCTAIR, Roger
Writer/Filmmaker/Lecturer
MCWATT, Faye E.
Judge, Superior Court of Ont.
MILLER, Earl Anthony
Frmr. Director, Employment
Relationships, Scotiabank Group
MONTAGUE, Kenneth
Dental Surgeon/Gallery Owner,
The Wedge Gallery
MOODIE, Andrew
Actor/Playwright, c/o Noble Caplan
Agency

MOODY, Benjamin H.
Science Advisor, Forest Pest
Management, Cdn. Forest Service,
Nat. Res. Canada

MORGAN, Carlos
Singer/Songwriter/Producer,
SolRoc Music

MORGAN, Christopher J.
Chiropractor, Owner/Director,
Morgan Chiropractic & Wellness

MORGAN, Dwayne
Executive Director/Spoken Word Artist,
Up From the Roots

MORRISON, Eva May
Senior Pastor, Toronto New Covenant
Cathedral /COGOP

MORRISON, Wilma L.
Comm'y Volunteer/Local Historian,
Nathaniel Dett Chapel, BME

MORTEN, Marvin G.
Judge, Ont. Court of Justice

MOSE, Kenrick E.A.
Prof. Emeritus (Ret.), Spanish Studies,
U. of Guelph

MOTIKI, Joe
Performer/TV & Radio Host,
c/o Characters Talent Agency

MOTION
Spoken Word Poet/Hip Hop Artist

MUHTADI
Percussionist/Artistic Director,
Muhtadi Int'l Drumming Festival

MUNFORD, Clarence Joseph
Prof. Emeritus, Dept. of History,
U. of Guelph

MUTUNGI, Allyce B.
Lawyer, Private Practice

NANCE, Marcus
Opera Singer/Bass-Baritone

NATION, Karlene
TV Reporter, CFTO TV

NDUBUBA, Edward
Co-founder/Director of Operations,
SS8 Networks Inc.

NELSON, Amy
Head Surgical Nurse (Ret.)/Volunteer,
JCA/Medical Mission Int'l

NELSON, Anthony R.
Senior Vice-President, Credit,
SottoBank of Canada

NELSON, Kathleen
Nurse & Clinical Teacher,
Toronto Rehab. Inst./Ryerson U.

NELSON, Ron
Radio DJ/Concert Promoter/CEO,
Ron Nelson Productions

NICHOLAS, Everton S.
Endocrinologist,
Toronto East General Hospital

NICHOLLS-KING, Melanie
Actor

NIMROD, Carl
Prof., Chair, Dept. of Obstetrics &
Gynecology, Faculty of Medicine,
U. of Ottawa

NKANSAH, Peter
Dentist-Anaesthetist, Pleasant
Boulevard Dentistry & Anaesthesia

NOEL, Asha
Youth Leadership Rep.,
Canadian Ethnocultural Council

NOLAN, Faith
Musician/Activist

N'SINGI, Vita Sébastien
Legal Counsel & Notary Public,
Dept. of Justice

NUNES, Neville
Teacher (Ret.), Hamilton Brd. of
Education

NYOKA, Gail
Playwright

OCHEJE, Paul D.
Assistant Prof., Faculty of Law,
U. of Windsor

ODULANA-OGUNDIMU, A. Oluremi
Pediatrician, Laurentian Hospital

OFFISHALL, Kardinal
Hip Hop Artist/MC/Producer

OFOSU, Cottie
Assistant Prof., School of Nursing,
McMaster U.

OFOSU, Frederick A.
Prof., Dept. of Pathology & Molecular
Medicine, McMaster U.

OFOSU-NYARKO, Helen
Team Leader/Psychologist, Dept. of
Foreign Affairs & Int'l Trade

OGILVIE, Lana
Model/On-Air Host

OGUNDELE, Gabriel
Senior Research Scientist, Kinectrics Inc.

OJO, Oluremi
Pharmacist, Corporate Pharmacy

OKAFOR, Obiora
Assistant Prof., Osgoode Hall Law
School, York U.

OSAMUSALI, Sylvester
Senior Nuclear Design Analyst,
Ont. Power Generation

OWOLABI, Titus
Chief, Obstetrics/Gynecology, and,
Program Medical Dir. of Maternal
Newborn, NYGH

PARIS, David Ronald
MWO, Canadian Forces,
National Defence HQ

PARSON, Patrick
Executive/Artistic Director,
Ballet Creole

PATTERSON, Keith
Tax Partner, Deloitte & Touche

PATTERSON, Pat
Teacher/Local Historian,
Toronto Dist. Sch. Brd./UGRD

PENNANT, Kevin
Executive Publicist,
The Publicity Group

PEREZ, John "Jayson"
Steel Pan Performer/Composer/
Instructor

PETERS, Walter W.
Aviation Consultant,
Bombardier Aerospace NFTC

PETERS, Wilfrid E.D.
Legal Counsel,
Chief Election Officer of Ont.

PETERSON, Oscar
Jazz Pianist/Composer,
Regal Recordings Ltd.

PHIDD, Richard Wesley
Prof., Dept. Political Science,
U. of Guelph

PHILIP, M. NourbeSe
Poet/Writer, c/o Mercury Press

PICART, Richard
Manager/Industry Consultant,
Mekehla Music Group

PIERRE, Jean
Founder, President,
Jean Pierre Aesthetics & Spa

PIETERS, Gary
Educator, Toronto Public School
System

PIETERS, Selwyn
Refugee Claims Officer,
Immig. & Ref. Brd., Canada

PITT, Romain W.M.
Judge, Ont. Superior Court of Justice

POWELL, Juliette
President & CEO,
Powell Entertainment Int'l Inc.

PRIETO, Claire
Film Producer, C + C Films Inc.

PROVIDENCE, Edford McConnie
Conductor/Composer/Pianist

PUGH, Kevin
Director/Ballet Teacher, Dance-TEQ

QUAMINA, Odida T.
Sociologist/Educator/Writer/
Community Organizer

RAWLINS, Micheline
Judge, Ont. Court of Justice

REGIS, Gregory
Judge, Ont. Court of Justice

REYES, Cynthia
Executive Producer/Vice-President,
ProMedia Int'l Inc.

RICHARDSON, Doug
Saxophonist/Actor/Teacher

RICKARD-BON, Sharon
Nutrition Consultant/Res. Coordin.,
Dynalife Health Services

RILEY, Betty
Television Producer/Community
Organizer

ROACH, Charles
Lawyer/Barrister/Solicitor, Roach,
Schwartz & Associates

ROBBINS, Larry Mansfield
Councillor, Municipality of
Chatham-Kent

ROBERTS, Kim
Actor, c/o Noble-Caplan Agency

ROBINSON, Gwendolyn
Local Historian/Author,
Chatham WISH Centre

ROBINSON, Karen
Actor, c/o Lefeaver Talent Management

ROSEMAY, Vibert T.
Judge, Ont. Court of Justice

ROSS, Sandi
Actor/Director/Cultural Activist

ROSSI, Miriam F.
Staff Physician, Div. of Adolescent
Medicine, Hospital for Sick Children

ROWE, Ebonnie
CEO/Community Organizer,
PhemPhat Productions

RUCK, The Hon. Calvin W.
Social Worker & Senator (Ret.),
Senate of Canada

RUCK, Douglas G.
Vice-Chair, Canada Industrial Relations
Board

RYAN, Theodore P.
Certified Accountant/President,
ACCTAX Services

SADLIER, Rosemary
Author/President, Ont. Black History
Society

SADU, Itah
Author/Storyteller, A Different Booklist

SALMON, Beverley
Public Health Nurse/Councillor (Ret.),
Metro Toronto

SALMON, John Douglas
Chief of General Surgery (Ret.),
Scarborough Centenary Hospital

SALMON, Warren
CEO, Black Board Int'l/First Fridays

SAM, Francis B.
Obstetrician/Gynecologist,
Private Practice

SAUL, Ras Leon
Publisher/Editor/Performing Artist,
Uprising Int'l

SCARLETT, Vivine
Dancer/Choreographer/Instructor,
Dance Immersion

SEALY, Joe
Jazz Pianist/Composer,
Blue Jade Productions

SEARLES, Edsworth McAuley
Lawyer (Ret.)

SEARLES, Sylvia E.
President, Searles Success Systems

SEARLES, Sylvia Kathleen
Community Volunteer (Ret.)

SEARS, Djanet
Writer/Director/Actor,
c/o WCA Film & TV

SEIVERIGHT, Deloris Devan
Archbishop, Shouters National
Evangel. Spiritual Bapt. Faith

SEIVRIGHT, Lloyd
Grand Master, Indep. United Order of
Solomon/Canada

SEWELL, J. George
Optometrist, Private Practice

SHAQQ, Hameed
Steel Pan Musician/Composer

SHAW, Sherene
Councillor, Toronto City Council

SHERWOOD, Anthony
Filmmaker/Producer,
Anthony Sherwood Productions

SIMON, Kenneth
Dean, School of Social and
Community Services/ Assoc.
Principal, Humber College

SLOLY, Peter
Inspector, Toronto Police Service

SMITH, Ifeyironwa F.
Nutritionist & Dietician, Nosi Smith
Food & Nutrition Consultants

SMITH, Olanrewaju B.
Sr. Programme Specialist, IDRC

SMITH, Rohan
Financial Advisor,
Laurentian Financial Services

SMITH, Shirley
Service Manager, CAMH

SMITH, Winsome E.
Dentist, Specializing in Children/Youth,
Private Practice

SOLOMON, Adam
Musician, Adam Solomon & Tikisa

SOLOMON, Damian
Assistant Director,
Canadian Teachers' Federation

SOSA, Thomas G.
Executive Director, Sosa & Associates

SPENCE, Christopher
Superintendent of Schools, Borden/
Maplewood/West Hill Family of
Schools

SPICER, Vincent
Captain (Ret.), Canadian Armed Forces

STANFORD, C. Lloyd
President, Le Groupe Stanford Inc.

STEVENS, Vida
Public Health Nutritionist,
Toronto Public Health

SUTHERLAND, Tony
Urban Music Promoter/Program Head,
Trebas Institute

SUTTON, Nicola
Legal Counsel,
Supreme Court of Canada

SUTTON, Shawn
Director, Business Planning &
Analysis, Mitel Networks

TALBOT, Alan W.
Operations Manager,
Steelcase Canada Ltd.

TAYLOR, Garth Alfred
Ophthalmologist/Associate Prof.,
Dept. Ophthalmology, Queen's U.

TAYLOR, Ronald A.
Dancer/Choreog./Artistic Dir.,
Canboulay Dance Theatre

TAYLOR, Sheldon
Writer/Researcher/Historian

TELFER, Norma
President, TelCam Training &
Consulting

TERRELONGE, Del
Graphic Designer/Director,
Rhed Corporation

THOMAS, Sandra
Counsel, Criminal Prosecutions,
Fed. Dept. of Justice

THOMAS OSBOURNE, Marlene
Community & Outreach Dev't
Consultant, Kujichagalia

THORPE, Carl
Executive Director,
Multicultural History Society of Ont.

TROTMAN, Gene Thornton T.
General Counsel,
Federal Dept. of Justice

TUCKER, Margaret Y.
Community Organizer

UPSHAW, Fred
Labour Union Leader & Activist (Ret.),
OPSEU

USHER, Harold
Councillor/Engineer/President, London
City Council/"Adventures in…"
Seminars & Speeches

VASSELL, Phillip
Co-Publisher, *Word* Magazine

VEECOCK, June
Director, Human Rights,
Ont. Federation of Labour

VIEIRA, John F.
Educator (Ret.),
City of York Board of Education

VIRGO, Clement
Filmmaker/Director

WALKER, Phyllis
Educator/Enamellist, Enamel-on-
copper murals & holloware

WALL, Carol
Human Rights Dir., CEP Union/Canada

WALLS, Bryan
Dental Surgeon/Local Historian/Author,
Private Practice

WALTERS, Ewart
Journalist/Commun. Consltnt.,
Boyd McRubie Commun.

WALWYN, Frank E.
Lawyer/Partner, WeirFoulds LLP

WARREN, Brian
Minister/Executive Director,
Canada in Prayer

WASHINGTON, Jackie
Jazz & Folk Musician/Performer

WEBB, Rudy
Singer/Actor/Producer,
Overcoat Productions

WHITE, John Edgar (Jack)
Labour Union Organizer (Ret.), CUPE

WHITE, Sheila
Commun. Consltnt., Words Media &
Communications

WHITEN, Grover (Tim)
Prof./Artist/Sculptor,
Dept. of Visual Art, York U.

WHITING, Sandra
Community Organizer

WICKHAM, Aisha
Director, Spoken Word & New Media,
FLOW 93.5FM

WIGGAN, Albert
President & Owner,
Albert's Real Jamaican Foods

WILKINSON, Evadne
Executive Director,
Out of the Cold Resource Centre

WILLIAMS, Denise
Soprano/Classical Singer,
c/o Anne Summers Int'l

WILLIAMS, Eugene F.
Director, Dept. of Justice,
Federal Prosecution Service

WILLIAMS, Raymond M.
Banker/Consultant

WILLIAMS, Tonya Lee
Actress/Producer, Wilbo
Entertainment, ReelWorld Film Festival

WILLIAMS, Vivienne
Singer/Performer

WILSON, Sybil Fay E.
Prof., Faculty of Education, Brock U.

WILSON, Trevor
President/Global Diversity Strategist,
TWI Inc.

WINSOM
Artist/Educator

WITTER, Mervin
Director, Ontario Reg'l Office,
Canadian Human Rights Commission

WIWA, Ken
Writer

WOODING, Marjorie Eglantine
Educator (Ret.)/Organist/Choir
Director, Church of Nativity

WOODS, Anne-Marie
Performance Artist & Writer, Imani
Enterprises

WRIGHT, Cornell
Lawyer, Torys LLP

WRIGHT, Leebert A.
Dir., Clinical Biochemistry (Ret.),
Wellesley/Princess Margaret Hospitals

WRIGHT, Ouida Marina
Educator/Asst. Deputy Minister (Ret.),
Ont. Min. of Education

WRIGHT, Patrica (Pat) A. Pearson
Educator/Exec. Dir., Brampton, Miss.,
and District Labour Action Centre

QUEBEC

AGNANT, Marie-Célie
Écrivaine

ALCINDOR, Maryse
Dir., Dir. de l'éducation & de la
coopération, Commission des droits
de la personne et des droits de la
jeunesse

ALLICOCK, Robert L.W.
Salon Owner/Stylist,
Salon Robert Allicock Montreal

ANGLADE, Georges
Géographe-Écrivain,
ex-Prof. Titulaire, UQAM

ARCELIN, Andre
Médecin, Clinique Médicale

BAFFOE, Michael Kofi
Executive Director,
Black Star Big Brothers

BAYLIS, Gloria L.
Founder/CEO,
Baylis Medical Company

BAYNE, Clarence S.
Prof., John Molson School of
Business, Concordia U.

BEAUREGARD, Kettly
Ex-Conseillère municipale,
Ville de Montréal

BERTLEY, Frederic Marcus
Immunologist/Res. Scientist,
Harvard U. Med. School/Boston
Children's Hospital

BERTLEY, June A.
Educator/Director-General,
The Garvey Institute

BERTLEY, Leo W.
Author/Journalist/Educator/Prof.,
Vanier College

BIDDLE, Charlie
Jazz Musician, Justin Time Records

BIDDLE, Sonya
Actor/Frmr. City Councillor

BLACKETT, Adelle
Assistant Prof., Faculty of Law,
McGill U.

BLACKMAN, Gordon
High School Teacher (Ret.),
Lakeshore Sch. Brd., Montreal

BLACKMAN, Margot
Community Advocate/Nursing Teacher
(Ret.), Vanier College

BOATENG, Kwaku-Barima
Athlete/High Jumper,
Canadian Track & Field Team

BONNY, Yvette
Prof. Emérite/Hématologue,
Hôpital Maisonneuve-Rosemont

BOYD, George
Playwright/Journalist

BRAXTON, Evelyn
Community Organizer,
Coloured Women's Club

BROWN, Jeri
Jazz Performer/Prof. of Music,
Justin Time Records

BRUNEAU, Ethel
Master Tap Dance Prof.,
Ethel Bruneau Dance School

CARRENARD, Patrice
Dirigeant d'Entreprise/PDG,
VISICOM MEDIA

CARRINGTON-MCCRACKEN, Iris
Journalist/Social Activist (Ret.)

CHARLES, Bernadette
Poet/Storyteller, Kulanga Production

CIRIAQUE, Marie-Claudette
Organisatrice Communautaire,
EPMANDOK

CROOKS, Kipling
President/Owner,
K.K. Machine Products Inc.

DANIEL-LEWIS, Emily Louise
Admin. Asst./Social Worker (Ret.),
Negro Community Centre

de B'BERI, Boulou E.
Filmmaker/Activist

DIDY
Artiste/Peintre, Les Entreprises Didy

DILLON-MOORE, Patricia (Pat)
Publicist/Spoken Word Performer, NFB

DORSINVILLE, Max
Prof./Writer, Dept. of English, McGill U.

DORTELUS, Daniel
Juge, Cour du Québec,
Palais de justice

DOUYON, Emerson
Psychologue/Prof., Centre de
Psychologie René Laennec

DOWNES, Wray
Classical/Jazz Pianist,
Justin Time Records

DUPERVAL, Raymond
Prof./Chef du Service d'infectiologie,
Faculté de médecine, U. de Sherbrooke

EDEY, David
Vice-President, Advisor,
Tandem Financial Services

EDMONDS, Pamela
Artist/Writer/Curator

EDWARDS, Leeroy
Photographer/Poet

FÉQUIÈRE, Madeleine
Worldwide Dept. Dir., Treasury/Credit
Risk, Abitibi Consolidated Inc.

FLEGEL, Peter
Youth Advocate/Comm'y Organizer,
Black Youth in Action

FRITZBERG, Daleus
Organisateur Communautaire,
Centre d'Union Multiculturelle &
Artistique des Jeunes

GARNER, Linton
Reg'l Services Dir., Quebec,
Canadian MedicAlert Fdn.

GAYLE-BENEDEK, Theresa
Financial Consultant/President,
Benetheque Managerial Services

GODDARD, Horace
Director, Community Services,
English Montreal Sch. Brd.

GRANT, Otis "Magic"
Professional Boxer/Entrepreneur,
Stele Promotions; Otis Grant & Friends

GRANT STATES, Violet
Symphony/Music Teacher (Ret.),
Montreal Women's Symphony

GRAY, Darryl
Minister, Union United Church

GYLES, Shirley
President, The Coloured Women's
Club of Montreal

HOLDER, Peter Anthony
Radio Host/Broadcaster, Standard
Broadcasting– CJAD 800 AM

HUNTE, Wesley
Warrant Officer (Ret.), Canadian Forces

HUSBAND, Gwen
Church Volunteer & Community
Organizer, Union United Church

HYPPOLITE, Marc-Arthur
Warden, Regional Reception Centre/
Special Handling Unit

ISAACS, Camille Nicola
Manager, Market Strategy & Services,
Standard Life Investments Inc.

JEAN, Michaëlle
Journaliste-présentatrice,
Société Radio Canada

JEANTY, Bernard
Chartered Accountant/Partner,
Schwartz Levitsky Feldman

JEFFERS, Garvin
High School Principal (Ret.), Protestant
Sch. Brd. of Greater Montreal

JOHNSON, Errol W.Clive
Insurance & Financial Services
Executive, Clarica

JOHNSON, Veronica
Educator, Lester B. Pearson Sch. Brd.

JONES, Oliver
Jazz Pianist/Composer,
Justin Time Records

JOYETTE, Anthony
Painter/Writer

JUMELLE, Yolène
Sociologue et Juriste,
Tribunal Administratif du Québec

KAVANAGH, Anthony
Artiste/Showman,
Soulman Productions

KLAASEN, Lorraine
Singer/Performer

KNIGHTS, Travis
Tap Dancer/Student

LAPIERRE, Myrtha
Prof. (Ret.)/Consultante

403

LAROCHE, Maximilien
Prof. de littérature/Écrivain,
Université Laval, Cité Universitaire

LAURENT, Alix
Directeur Général,
Images Interculturelles

LAURENT, Weber
Architecte, Laurent + Vaccaro
Architectes

LEACOCK, Emile
Community Activist/Seniors Advocate,
Council for Black Aging Community of
Montreal

LEE, Ranee
Jazz Performer, Justin Time Records

LEWIS, Ronald
Surgeon, Chair, Div. Vascular Surgery,
McGill U. Health Centre

LISTER, Celya
Indep. TV Producer/CEO,
Caribbean Television Quebec

LORD, Richard M.
Engineer/Immigration Consultant/
Community Organizer

LY, Aoua Bocar
Chercheure/sociologue, Femmes,
Environnement Viable & éducation
interculturelle

MAULE, Josa Linda
Educator, Montreal School of
Performing Arts

MCCLAIN, Washington
Baroque Oboist, McGill U. & Indiana U.

MOÏSE, Claude
Historien

OLLIVIER, Emile
Prof. Éméritus, Écrivain,
Université de Montréal

PARIS, Brenda
Executive Director,
Black Community Resource Centre

PARRIS, Jean Veronica
Labour Relations Consultant,
Federation of Nurses of Quebec

PHILIP, Dan
Président, Ligue de Noirs du
Québec/Black Coalition of Quebec

QUAMMIE, Arsinoee Salomon
Educator/Civil Rights Activist,
Lester B. Pearson Sch. Brd.

RAEBURN-BAYNES, Gemma
Senior Auditor, Corporate Audit Dept,
Bank of Montreal

ROSS, Christopher
Associate Prof., Dept. of Marketing,
Concordia U.

ROWE, Brenda F.
Educator/Coordin., Learning Centre,
John Abbott College

ROWE, Owen
WWII Veteran & Caribbean Diplomat
(Ret.)

SANDOVAL, Dolores
Prof. Emerita, U. of Vermont

SANGSTER, Peggy Ann
Coordin., Quality & Risk Management,
Montreal Children's Hospital

SINTIM-ABOAGYE, Kofi
President, Premex Courier

SPENCE, Alwin C.
Prof./Sr. Lecturer, Dept. of Psychology,
John Abbott College

STEWART-MORGAN, Gloria
Coordinator/Lecturer/Writer,
Dept. Surgery, McGill U.

SUTTON, Winston
Actor/Director/Theatre Prof.,
Dawson College

SYMONDS, Nelson
Jazz Guitarist

THOMAS, H. Nigel
Prof./Writer, U. Laval, Cité Universitaire

TOURE, A. Lamine
Agent de rech. et de planif'n,
Min. de l'Industrie et du Commerce

TOWNSEND, Beverly
Principal, Dalkeith Elementary School

TUCKER, Elrie C.
Obstetrician & Gynecologist,
Private Practice

TURENNE, Joujou
Conteuse, Joujou - Amie du Vent

VANCOL, Frantz
President & CEO,
Jeunes Romantiques/ Drula Fabrik

WAVROCH, Hélène
Présidente, Conseil des aînés

WESTMORELAND-TRAORE, Juanita
Judge, Court of Quebec

WILLIAMS, Dorothy W.
Historian/Writer/Editor

WILLS, Dorothy Abike
Educator, Dean (Ret.), Faculty of
Applied Technologies, Vanier College

WILLS, Roland
Assoc. Dean (Ret.)/Prof. Emeritus,
John Molson School of Business,
Concordia U.

WILSON, Anthony (Salah)
Musician/Steel Pan Instructor,
Salah's Steel Pan Academy

WINT, Shirlette
Social Worker, Côte-des-Neiges Black
Community Assn.

WOSU, Leonard
Research Scientist/Science Teacher,
Greaves Adventist Academy

SASKATCHEWAN

BARRETT, Danny
Head Coach, Saskatchewan Roughriders

BRUCE, Ronald A.
Corporate Internal Auditor, SaskPower

EGUAKUN, George
Manager, Market Research & Analysis,
Sask. Power Corp.

EKONG, Chris
Clinical Prof., Surgery/Neurosurgery,
U. of Saskatchewan

ELABOR-IDEMUDIA, Patience
Assoc. Prof., Dept. of Sociology,
U. of Saskatchewan

KLY, Yussuf
Prof., Political Science, U. of Regina

NEWKIRK, Reginald
H. Rights, Race & Lab. Relations
Specialist, Parity Consulting

OLATUNBOSUN, Olufemi
Prof. & Chair, Obstetrics, Gynecology,
& Reproductive Sciences,
U. of Saskatchewan

WILLIAMS, Charlotte
Veterinarian, Elrose Wildrose/Eston
Veterinary Services

OUTSIDE OF CANADA

ANDERSON, Roy T.
Stunt Coordinator/Actor,
Action 4 Reel, US

ARCHER, Hutton Gilbert
Dir., External Relations,
Global Environment Facility, US

BATCHELOR, Wayne B.
Cardiologist,
Southern Medical Group, US

BLANCHETTE, Howard
Chair, Dept. of Obstetrics &
Gynecology, Danbury Hospital, US

CRAWFORD, Rachael
Actor, US

DAVIDSON, Patricia
Internist & Cardiologist,
Private Practice, US

ECHOLS, Edith McGruder
Social Worker (Ret.),
Women's Christian Alliance, US

EDEH, Rosey
Olympic Athlete (Ret.)/TV
Broadcaster, Cable News Network, US

ESTRIDGE, Winston
President, Enterprise Solutions NA,
Nortel Networks, US

GORDON, Kevin
Writer, US

HOOPER, Charmaine
Soccer Player,
Women's United Soccer Assn., US

JACKSON, D.D.
Jazz Pianist/Composer, US

JENKINS, Ferguson Arthur
Baseball Commissioner,
Canadian Baseball League, US

KOTASKA, Audrei-Kairen
Playwright/Actor/Singer, US

KURANTSIN-MILLS, Joseph
Res. Scientist & Prof., Medicine,
Physiology, & Exp'l Medicine,
GWU./Center for Sickle Cell Dis.,
Howard U. College, US

MAYES, Rueben
Asst. Athletic Dir., WSU Athletic Fdn.,
Washington State U., US

O'REE, William (Willie)
Hockey/Director, Youth Development,
NHL, US

PINNOCK, Nicole C.N.
Assistant Athletic Trainer,
Indiana Pacers, US

RICHARDS, Lloyd
Theatre Director/Prof. Emeritus,
Yale U., US

RICHARDS, Vanessa
Artistic Director, Mannafest, UK

ROBBINS, Juneau Kipola
Chiropractor/Author,
Cultural Chiropractic, US

SCOTT, Gilbert H.
Permanent Sec., Min., National
Security, Govt. of Jamaica

TOLBART, Gwen
TV Broadcaster, FOX 5/WTTG, US

WEEKES, Kevin
Hockey Player/Goaltender,
Carolina Hurricanes/NHL, US

WILLIAMS, Taly
Environmental Engineer, President,
TM Williams LLC, US

Index by Primary Activity

WALKER, Phyllis
Educator/Enamellist, Enamel-on-copper murals & holloware, Toronto

WHITEN, Grover (Tim)
Prof./Artist/Sculptor, Dept. of Visual Art, York U., Toronto

WINSOM
Artist/Educator, Toronto

 **ATHLETICS: Athletes; Coaches; Administrators...**

BACCHUS, Natasha Cecily
Athlete/Medallist, World Deaf Games, Toronto

BAILEY, Donovan
Olympic Athlete, Oakville

BARRETT, Danny
Head Coach, Saskatchewan Roughriders, Regina

BOATENG, Kwaku-Barima
Athlete/High Jumper, Canadian Track & Field Team, Montreal

CROOKS, Charmaine
Olympian/IOC member, Int'l Olympic Cmtee/NGU Consulting, Vancouver

DWYER, Mike
Track and Field Coach, Toronto

EDEH, Rosey
Olympic Athlete (Ret.)/TV Broadcaster, CNN, GA/US

FUHR, Grant
Frmr. Goaltender/Goaltending Consultant, Calgary Flames/NHL, AB

GRANT, Otis "Magic"
Professional Boxer/Entrepreneur, Stele Promotions; Otis Grant & Friends, QC

HARRISON, Herman (Herm)
Frmr. Football Player/Philanthropist, Calgary

HOOPER, Charmaine
Soccer Player, Women's United Soccer Assn., GA/US

IGALI, Daniel
Freestyle Wrestling Champion, Landmark Sport Group, BC

IGINLA, Jarome
Hockey Player, Calgary Flames/NHL, AB

JENKINS, Ferguson Arthur
Baseball Commissioner, Canadian Baseball League

JOHNSON, Ben
Athlete/Coach, Toronto

KILLINGBECK, Molly
Athlete Services Manager/Coach, Cdn Sport Centre Ont., Toronto

LEWIS, Ray
Olympic Athlete & Railway Porter (Ret.), Hamilton

MAYES, Rueben
Asst. Athletic Dir., WSU Athletic Foundation, Washington State U., US

NJOKU, William C.
Coordin./Entrepreneur, Will2Win Sports, Halifax

O'REE, William (Willie)
Hockey/Dir., Youth Development, National Hockey League, US

PINNOCK, Nicole C.N.
Asst. Athletic Trainer, Indiana Pacers, US

SMITH, Robert (Mark)
Softball Coach, Dir. of Sport Dev't, Sport NS/3M Fair & Safe Play Prog.

WEEKES, Kevin
Hockey Player/Goaltender, Carolina Hurricanes/NHL, US

BUSINESS: Entrepreneurs; Owners; Business Professionals; Administrators...

BLACKWOOD, Yvonne
Banker/Author, RBC, Toronto

BRAITHWAITE, F. Carlton
Economist/Entrepreneur/Comm'y Leader, Gloucester

BRUCE, Ronald A.
Corporate Internal Auditor, SaskPower, Regina

CHAMBERS, Mary Anne
Senior Vice-President, Scotiabank, Toronto

CROOKS, Kipling
President/Owner, K.K. Machine Products Inc., QC

DAVIS, Rodney
Proprietor/CA, Nappy's Inc./Chartered Accounting Practice, Pickering

DAVIS, Wells
Owner & Managing Partner, Clarity/Urban Engine Communications, ON

DORSEY, Robert Edward
President/Mngmt. Consultant, 3rd Dimensions & Assoc. Ltd., Ottawa

EDEY, David
VP, Advisor, Tandem Financial Services, QC

EGUAKUN, George
Manager, Market Res. & Analysis, Sask. Power Corp., Regina

ENYOLU, Evans Rick A.
Publisher/Principal Consultant, Multitech Consulting Int'l Inc., Pickering

ESHO, David
Realtor, Prudential Elite Realty, Brampton

ESTRIDGE, Winston
President, Enterprise Solutions NA, Nortel Networks, TX/US

EWING, Brendon
Manager, Personal Financial Services, RBC Financial Group, NS

FÉQUIÈRE, Madeleine
Worldwide Dept. Dir., Treasury/Credit Risk, Abitibi Consolidated Inc., QC

FERRIER, Ross
Investment Advisor, CIBC Wood Gundy, Thornhill

FRANCIS, Ken K.
CEO & President, Ken K. Francis Financial Services, ON

GANNON, Louis
Exec. Dir., BBB of the Maritime Provinces Inc., Dartmouth

GARNER, Linton
Regional Services Dir., Quebec Div., Canadian MedicAlert Fdn.

GAYLE-BENEDEK, Theresa
Financial Consultant/President, Benetheque Managerial Services, QC

GEORGE, Kenrick
President/CEO, Aaron Multi-Tec Systems, Toronto

GLANVILLE, Carlton R.W.
Chartered Accountant, Ancaster

HARRIS, Paul F.
Owner/Manager (Ret.), Supreme Electric Manufacturing Ltd., MB

ISAACS, Camille Nicola
Manager, Market Strategy & Services, Standard Life Investments Inc., QC

JEANTY, Bernard
Chartered Accountant/Partner,
Schwartz Levitsky Feldman, Montreal
JOHNSON, Errol W.Clive
Insurance & Financial Services
Executive, Clarica, QC
JOLLY, Brandeis Denham
Business Owner, Flow 93.5FM, Toronto
JONES, Denise
President/Events Organizer,
Jones & Jones Prod., Toronto
JOSEPH, Richard (Rick)
Exec. Dir., NS Environmental Industry
Assn., Halifax
JULIEN, Stanley J.
Vice-President, BMO Nesbitt Burns,
Toronto
LAURENT, Weber
Architecte, Laurent + Vaccaro
Architectes, Montreal
LAWRENCE, Delores
President & CEO, NHI Nursing &
Homemakers Inc., Toronto
LEE-CHIN, Michael
Chairman & Chief Investment Officer,
AIC Limited, Burlington
LONGE, Winfield E.
Fleet Captain, Upper Lakes Group,
Toronto
MANNING, George
Regulatory Analyst, ESBI (Alberta)
Ltd., Calgary
MARTIN, Eugenie
Dir. of Cosmetology, Topaz College of
Aesthetics & Hair, Pickering
MBULU, Emmanuel
President & CEO, Tone-A-Matic Int'l,
Mississauga
MILLER, Earl Anthony
Frmr. Dir., Employ't Relations.,
Scotiabank Group, Toronto
NELSON, Anthony R.
Senior VP, Credit, SottoBank of
Canada, Toronto
OLIVER, Sharon
President & CEO, Oliver Management
Connexus Inc., Wolfville
PATTERSON, Keith
Tax Partner, Deloitte & Touche, ON
PETERS, David J
Chef/Educator (Ret.), PRUDE Inc.,
Saint John

PIERRE, Jean
Founder, President, Jean Pierre
Aesthetics & Spa, Toronto
RAEBURN-BAYNES, Gemma
Sr. Auditor, Corporate Audit Dept.,
Bank of Montreal, QC
RYAN, Theodore P.
Certified Accountant/President,
ACCTAX Services, Pickering
SALMON, Warren
CEO, Black Board Int'l/First Fridays,
Toronto
SEARLES, Sylvia E.
President, Searles Success Systems,
Toronto
SINTIM-ABOAGYE, Kofi
President, Premex Courier, Montreal
SMITH, Rohan
Financial Advisor, Laurentian
Financial Services, Toronto
SOUTHWELL, Rustum
Exec. Dir., Black Business Initiative,
Halifax
STEPHENS, Dell
Chartered Financial Planner, CIBC
Wood Gundy, Calgary
TALBOT, Alan W.
Operations Manager, Steelcase
Canada Ltd., Newmarket
TELFER, Norma
President, TelCam Training &
Consulting, Mississauga
TERRELONGE, Del
Graphic Designer/Dir., Rhed
Corporation, Toronto
TIDLUND, Mary A.
Oil Industry CEO, Mary A. Tidlund
Charitable Fdn., Calgary
VANCOL, Frantz
President & CEO, Jeunes
Romantiques/Drula Fabrik, Montreal
WIGGAN, Albert
President & Owner, Albert's Real
Jamaican Foods, Toronto
WILLIAMS, Raymond M.
Banker/Consultant, Toronto
WILSON, Trevor
President/Global Diversity Strategist,
TWI Inc., Toronto

 **COMMUNITY
ORGANIZATIONS &
PHILANTHROPY:
Foundations; Associations;
National & Int'l
Organizations; Volunteers;
Administrators...**

APPIAH, Yvonne
Exec. Dir., CODE, Ottawa
ATUANYA, Tony I.
Exec. Dir., WADE Inc., Dartmouth
BAFFOE, Michael Kofi
Exec. Dir., Black Star Big Brothers,
Montreal
BARCLAY, John V.
Dep. Grand Master, Indep. United
Order of Solomon/Canada, ON
BLACKMAN, Craig
Gen'l Manager, Rehab. and Training
Services, COSTI, Toronto
BLAIR, Ned
Comm'y Activist/President,
Org. of Black Tradesmen &
Tradeswomen of Ont.
BRAXTON, Evelyn
Comm'y Organizer, Coloured
Women's Club, QC
BROOKS, C. John
Humanitarian & Comm'y Advocate, The
John Brooks Comm'y Fdn., Toronto
CARNEGIE, Herbert
Hockey Pioneer/Community Leader,
Toronto
CIRIAQUE, Marie-Claudette
Organisatrice Communautaire,
EPMANDOK, Montreal
CLARKE, LaFerne
Exec. Dir., Family Services Hamilton-
Wentworth, ON
COOK, Verda
Community Volunteer, Toronto
DANIEL-LEWIS, Emily Louise
Admin. Asst./Social Worker (Ret.),
Negro Community Centre, QC
DAWKINS, Ettie E.
Dir. of Marketing, Ettie Dawkins
Fashion Sales Agency, Toronto
ECHOLS, Edith McGruder
Social Worker (Ret.), Women's
Christian Alliance, PA/US

EDOGHAMEN, Robin
Exec. Dir., Metro Street Focus, Toronto

EVANS, Doris
Volunteer & Senior Citizens Advocate, Dartmouth

FRITZBERG, Daleus
Organisateur Communautaire, CUMAJ, Montréal

GUDGE, Leyland
Consultant, Family Services & Anti-racism, ON

GYLES, Shirley
President, The Coloured Women's Club of Montreal, QC

HUSBAND, Gwen
Church Volunteer & Comm'y Organizer, Union United Church, QC

JOHNSON, Allister
Program Coordin./Comm'y Volunteer, N. Preston Holistic, Cultural and Academic Enrichment Prog., NS

LARBI, Madonna Owusuah
Exec. Dir., MATCH Int'l Centre, Ottawa

LEACOCK, Emile
Comm'y Activist/Seniors Advocate, Council for Black Aging, Montreal

LEBEANYA, Charity
Exec. Dir., Heritage Skills Development Centre, Toronto

PARIS, Brenda
Exec. Dir., Black Community Resource Centre, QC

PARIS, Henderson
Comm'y Organizer, Run Against Racism (Annual Ultra Marathon), New Glasgow

ROSS, Joyce L.
Founder/Exec. Dir., East Preston Day Care Centre, NS

ROWE, Ebonnie
CEO/Comm'y Organizer, PhemPhat Productions, Toronto

SEARLES, Sylvia Kathleen
Comm'y Volunteer (Ret.), Toronto

SEIVRIGHT, Lloyd
Grand Master, Indep. United Order of Solomon/Canada, ON

THOMAS OSBOURNE, Marlene
Comm'y & Outreach Development Consultant, Kujichagalia, Hamilton

TUCKER, Margaret Y.
Comm'y Organizer, Nepean

WHITING, Sandra
Comm'y Organizer, Toronto

WILKINSON, Evadne
Exec. Dir., Out of the Cold Resource Centre, Toronto

WINT, Shirlette
Social Worker, Côte-des-Neiges Black Community Assn., Montreal

WRIGHT, Patrica (Pat) A. Pearson
Educator/Exec. Dir., Brampton, Mississauga and District Labour Action Centre, ON

EDUCATION: Primary; Secondary; Post-Secondary; Educators; Administrators...

ADAMS, Leonard
Prof. Emeritus, Dept. of French Studies, U. of Guelph, ON

AGINAM, Obijiofor
Asst. Prof., Dept. of Law, Carleton U., Ottawa

AKANDE, Zanana L.
Educator (Ret.)/Frmr. MPP, Toronto Dist. Sch. Brd./Govt. of Ont.

AKANO, Liz
Business Teacher, Thames Valley Dist. Sch. Brd., London

ALGOO-BAKSH, Stella
Assoc. Prof., Dept. of English, Memorial U. of Newfoundland

ALLEYNE-NIKOLIC, Eucline Claire
Registrar, Ont. Inst. for Studies in Education (OISE), U of T

ANDERSON, Wolseley W. (Percy)
Prof. Emeritus and Sr. Scholar, York U., Toronto

ANGLADE, Georges
Géographe-Écrivain, ex-Prof. Titulaire, UQAM

ATWELL, George
Teacher (Ret.)/ Commercial Beekeeper, Winnipeg Sch. Brd., MB

AYLWARD, Carol A.
Asst. Prof., Fac. of Law, Dalhousie U., Halifax

BAILEY, Nehemiah L.
Comm'y Organizer/Educator (Ret.), Toronto Dist. Sch. Brd.

BANCROFT, George W.
Prof. Emeritus, Scholarship, U of T

BARTON, Brad
Educator/CEO, Bar Jun Consultants, Dartmouth

BATCHELOR, Barrington de Vere
Prof. Emeritus, Civil Engineering, Queen's U., Kingston

BAYLIS, Françoise
Prof., Bioethics & Philosophy, Dalhousie U., Halifax

BAYNE, Clarence S.
Prof., Decision Sciences, John Molson School of Business, Concordia U., Montreal

BELL, David V.J
Prof./Dir., Centre for Applied Sustainability, York U., ON

BENNETT, Karl
Assoc. Prof., Dept. of Economics, U. of Waterloo, ON

BENN-IRELAND, Tessa
Author/Sr. Librarian, Markham Public Libraries, ON

BERGER, Marie-Josée
Doyenne, Fac. de l'Education, U. d'Ottawa, ON

BERNARDINE, Marion
Educator/Principal (Ret.), Toronto Dist. Sch. Brd.

BERTLEY, June A.
Educator/Dir.-General, The Garvey Institute, QC

BERTLEY, Leo W.
Author/Journalist/Educator/Prof., Dept. of History, Vanier College, QC

BLACKETT, Adelle
Asst. Prof., Fac. of Law, McGill U., QC

BLACKMAN, Gordon
High School Teacher (Ret.), Lakeshore Sch. Brd., Montreal

BLAKE, Ronald E.
Dir. of Studies, Higher Marks Educ'l Institute Inc., Toronto

BRATHWAITE, Keren Sophia
Assoc. Dir., Transitional Year Programme, U of T

BRUCCOLERI, Claudette
Teacher, Calgary Brd. of Ed., AB

CALLENDER, Chloe E.
Educator/Race Relations Consltnt (Ret.), Waterloo Dist. Catholic Sch. Brd.

CALLENDER, Murchison G.
Prof. Emeritus, School of Optometry, U. of Waterloo, ON

409

CALLISTE, Agnes
Assoc. Prof. & Black Student Advisor,
St. Francis Xavier U., NS

CHAMBERS, Juanita
Psychologist/Prof. Emeritus, U. of
Alberta

CHRISTENSEN, Carole Pigler
Prof., School of Social Work & Family
Studies, UBC

COLLINS, Enid M.
Prof. Emeritus, Nursing, Ryerson U.,
Toronto

COLLINS, Erma B.
Prof. (Ret.)/Comm'y Volunteer,
George Brown College

COOPER, Afua
Prof. of Sociology/Poet, Ryerson U.,
Toronto

CRAWLEY, Iona
Nurse/Recruitment-Retention
Consultant, School of Nursing,
Dalhousie U., NS

DANIEL, Juliet
Asst. Prof., Dept. of Biology,
McMaster U., Hamilton

DEI, George J.S.
Prof. & Chair, Dept. of Sociology,
OISE/U of T

DICK, Emmanuel
Educator (Ret.)/Comm'y Organizer,
Nat'l Council of T&T Organizations in
Canada, Toronto

DORSINVILLE, Max
Prof./Writer, Dept. of English,
McGill U., Montreal

DOUYON, Emerson
Psychologue/Prof., Centre de
Psychologie René Laennec, Montreal

DUNCAN, Carol B.
Asst. Prof., Dept. Religion & Culture,
Wilfrid Laurier U., ON

ELABOR-IDEMUDIA, Patience
Assoc. Prof., Dept. of Sociology,
U. of Saskatchewan

ELLIS, Keith A.A.
Prof. Emeritus, Dept. Spanish &
Portuguese, U of T

ELLISTON, Inez
Educator & Comm'y Volunteer Leader,
ON

FARRELL, Vernon W.
Principal (Ret.)/ Educational
Consultant, InclusivEd Assoc., ON

FEARON, Gervan
Asst. Prof./Economics, Atkinson
College, York U., Toronto

FRANCIS, Flora H. Blizzard
Author/Librarian (Ret.), U. of Guelph

GAYLE-ANYIWE, Brenda Claire Hope
Prof., Fac. of Business, Seneca
College, Toronto

GODDARD, Horace
Dir., Comm'y Services, English
Montreal Sch. Brd.

GORDON, Donald K.
Prof. (Ret.), U. of Manitoba

GRANT, Gerald
Asst. Prof., Eric Sprott School of
Business, Carleton U., Ottawa

GRANT, Rudolph W.
Prof. Emeritus, York U., Toronto

GRIMMOND, Claude N.
Mediator/Trainer/Facilitator, Conflict
Management Services, ON

HAREWOOD, John L.
Academic Advisor/Prof. (Ret.), U. of
Ottawa

HUDSON, Maurice
Principal, Peel Dist. Sch. Brd., ON

IBHAWOH, Bonny
Killam Scholar/Lecturer, Dept. of
History, Dalhousie U., Halifax

JACKSON, Richard Lawson
Prof. Emeritus, Spanish, Carleton U.,
ON

JAMES, Carl E.
Assoc. Prof., Fac. of Education, York U.,
Toronto

JEFFERS, Garvin
Principal (Ret.), Protestant Sch. Brd.
of Greater Montreal

JOHNSON, Kaye
Coordin., Race Relations,
Annapolis Valley Reg'l Sch. Brd., NS

JOHNSON, Veronica
Educator, Lester B. Pearson Sch. Brd.,
QC

JONES, Beryle Mae
Asst. Prof., U. of Winnipeg & U. of
Manitoba

JONES, Byron
Educator/Principal, Munroe Junior
High School, Winnipeg

KAKEMBO, Patrick N.
Dir., African Canadian Services, NS
Dept. of Education

KELLY, Paulette
Assoc. Prof., School of Fashion,
Ryerson U., Toronto

KLY, Yussuf
Prof., Political Science, U. of Regina

LAROCHE, Maximilien
Prof. de littérature/Écrivain, U. Laval,
Cité Universitaire, QC

LEWIS, Daurene
Principal, Halifax Campuses, Nova
Scotia Community College

LOPES, Blair
Adjunct Prof./President, Dalhousie
U./Added Dimension Consulting, NS

LOWE, Keith D.
Int'l Education Consultant, Inter
Cultural Assoc. Inc., Toronto

LY, Aoua Bocar
Cherch./sociologue, Femmes,
Environnement Viable…, Montreal

MARK, Kirk
Advisor, Race & Ethnic Relations,
Toronto Cath. Dist. Sch. Brd.

MARSHALL, Clem
Educator/Diversity Trainer, MangaCom
Inc., Toronto

MCCURDY, Howard D.
Frmr. MP/Prof., Biology (Ret.), Govt.
of Canada/U. of Windsor,

MCFARLANE, Ivan
Adjunct Lecturer/Assoc. Graduate
Fac., U of T/Central Michigan U.

MCLAREN, Headley
Principal/Special Ed. Teacher (Ret.),
Fed. Govt./Winnipeg School Dist. No. 1

MGBEOJI, Ikechi
Asst. Prof., Fac. of Law, UBC

MIGHTY, E. Joy
Assoc. Prof., Fac. of Admin., U. of
New Brunswick

MILLAR, Harvey
Prof., Fac. of Commerce, Saint Mary's
U., NS

MOSE, Kenrick E.A.
Prof. Emeritus (Ret.), Spanish
Studies, U. of Guelph

MUNFORD, Clarence Joseph
Prof. Emeritus, Dept. of History, U. of
Guelph

NNADI, Joseph
Prof., Dept. of French Studies, U. of
Winnipeg

NOEL, Dexter
Coordin., Interdisciplinary Studies,
U. of New Brunswick

NUNES, Neville
Teacher (Ret.), Hamilton Brd. of Ed.

OCHEJE, Paul D.
Asst. Prof., Fac. of Law, U. of Windsor

OFOSU, Cottie
Asst. Prof., School of Nursing,
McMaster U., Hamilton

OFOSU, Frederick A.
Prof., Dept. of Pathology & Molecular
Medicine, McMaster U., Hamilton

OKAFOR, Obiora
Asst. Prof., Osgoode Hall, York U.,
Toronto

OLIVER, Leslie H.
Prof., Jodrey School of Computer
Science, Acadia U., NS

PACHAI, Bridglal
Adjunct Prof., Saint Mary's U. &
Dalhousie U., NS

PATTERSON, Pat
Teacher/Local Historian, Toronto Dist.
Sch. Brd./UGRD

PHIDD, Richard Wesley
Prof., Dept. Political Science, U. of
Guelph, ON

PIETERS, Gary
Educator, Toronto Public School System

QUAMMIE, Arsinoee Salomon
Educator/Civil-Human Rights Activist,
Lester B. Pearson Sch. Brd., QC

RAMSANKAR, Stephen R.
Citizenship Judge/Educational
Consultant/ Principal (Ret.), Govt. of
Alberta

ROBINSON, Frank Price
Asst. Dean, Arts & Science (Ret.)/
Assoc. Prof. Emeritus, U. of Victoria

ROSS, Christopher
Assoc. Prof., Dept. of Marketing,
Concordia U., QC

ROWE, Brenda F.
Educator/Coordin., Learning Centre,
John Abbott College, QC

SANDIFORD, Keith A.P.
Prof. Emeritus, History Dept., U. of
Manitoba

SANDOVAL, Dolores
Prof. Emerita, U. of Vermont

SIMON, Kenneth
Dean, School of Social and
Community Services/ Assoc.
Principal, Humber College, ON

SOLOMON, Damian
Asst. Dir., Professional & Dev't Services,
Canadian Teachers' Fed., Ottawa

SPENCE, Christopher
Superintendent of Schools, Borden/
Maplewood/West Hill Family of
Schools, Toronto

STEWART, Esme
Faculty Advisor, U. of Manitoba

STEWART-MORGAN, Gloria
Coordin./Lecturer/Writer, Dept.
Surgery, McGill U., QC

SUTTON, Winston
Actor/Dir./Theatre Prof., Dawson
College, QC

THORNHILL, Esmeralda
Prof., Dalhousie Law School,
Dalhousie U., Halifax

TOWNSEND, Beverly
Principal, Dalkeith Elementary
School, Pierrefonds

VIEIRA, John F.
Educator (Ret.), City of York Brd. of Ed.

WILLS, Dorothy Abike
Educator, Dean (Ret.), Fac. of Applied
Technologies, Vanier College,
Montreal

WILLS, Roland
Assoc. Dean (Ret.)/Prof. Emeritus,
John Molson School of Business,
Concordia U., Montreal

WILSON, Sybil Fay E.
Prof. of Education, Brock U., ON

WRIGHT, Ouida Marina
Educator/Asst. Deputy Minister (Ret.),
Ont. Min. of Education

**GOVERNMENT: Canadian;
International; Elected
Officials; Appointees;
Administrators…**

ADIBE, Michael
Principal (Ret.), Office of the Auditor
General of Canada

ALEXANDER, The Hon. Lincoln M.
Lawyer, Lieutenant-Governor (Ret.),
Govt. of Ont.

ALLEN, Daniel H.
Dir., Service Delivery Policy, HRDC
(NHQ)

APPELT, Pamela
Citizenship Judge (Ret.), Court of
Canadian Citizenship

ARCHER, Hutton Gilbert
Dir., External Relations, Global
Environment Facility, US

ASAGWARA, K.C. Prince
Researcher/Policy & Planning Analyst,
Govt. of Manitoba

AUGUSTINE, The Hon. Jean
MP, Secretary of State
(Multiculturalism & Women's Dir.),
Govt. of Canada

BANCROFT, Joseph (Dan)
City Auditor (Ret.), City of Toronto

BEAUREGARD, Kettly
Ex-Conseillère municipale, Ville de
Montréal

BEST, J. Calbert
Civil Servant/High Commissioner
(Ret.), Federal Public Service

BRAITHWAITE, John B.
Councillor, City of North Vancouver

BROWN, Rosemary
MLA (Ret.)/Rights Activist, Vancouver

COOLS, The Hon. Anne C.
Senator, Senate of Canada

CURLING, Alvin
Member Provincial Parliament,
Legislative Assembly of Ont.

DUNCAN, George
City Manager, City of London

EARLE, Gordon
Sr. Public Administrator (Ret.)/Frmr.
MP, Govt. of Nova Scotia & Canada

FARROW-LAWRENCE, Jacquie
Municipal Clerk, Municipality of
Annapolis County, NS

FRANCIS, Mayann
Exec. Dir., NS Human Rights
Commission

GEORGE, Gbadebo Oladeinde
Nigerian Ambassador (Ret.), Nigerian
Min. of Foreign Affairs

GRIFFITH, Clyde
Recreation & Leisure Consultant
(Ret.), BC Provincial Govt.

GRIZZLE, Stanley G.
Citizenship Judge (Ret.), Court of
Canadian Citizenship

HALSTEAD, Joseph A.G.
Commissioner, Economic
Development, Culture, and Tourism,
City of Toronto

HARTY, Corita
Regional Dir., Human Resources, Ont.
and Nunavut Region, Health Canada

HUGGINS, Dorette
Dir., Communications, Dept. of
Justice Canada, Ont. Reg'l Office

ISAACS, Joy Enid
Human Resource Consultant (Ret.),
City of Toronto

JACKSON, Ovid
Member of Parliament, Govt. of Canada

JENNINGS, Marlene
Member of Parliament, Govt. of
Canada

OKELU, Chinwe Pete
Coordin., Alberta Municipal Affairs

OLIVER, The Hon. Donald H.
Senator, Senate of Canada

ROBBINS, Larry Mansfield
Councillor, Municipality of Chatham-
Kent

ROGERS, George
Mayor, City of Leduc, AB

RUCK, The Hon. Calvin W.
Social Worker & Senator (Ret.),
Senate of Canada

RUCK, Douglas G.
Vice-Chair, Canada Industrial
Relations Board

SALMON, Beverley
Public Health Nurse/Municipal
Councillor (Ret.),
Metropolitan Toronto

SAMUELS-STEWART, Victorine (Viki)
Coordinator, Race Relations, NS
Human Rights Commission

SCOTT, Gilbert H.,
Permanent Secretary, Ministry of
National Security, Govt. of Jamaica

SHAW, Sherene
Councillor, Toronto City Council

SOSA, Thomas G.
Executive Director, Sosa & Associates

STANFORD, C. Lloyd
President, Le Groupe Stanford Inc.,
Ottawa

TOURE, A. Lamine
Ag. de recherche/planification, Min.
de l'Industrie et du Commerce, QC

USHER, Harold
Councillor/Engineer, London City
Council/"Adventures in…"

WHITE, Carl A.
Deputy Mayor, Saint John City
Council, NB

WITTER, Mervin
Dir., Ontario Regional Office,
Canadian Human Rights Commission

✊ HISTORY & ACTIVISM: Historians; Curators; Activists; Members of Unions; Administrators…

ABUKAR, Hassan
Youth Leadership Rep., Toronto Youth
Cabinet

ARMSTRONG, Bromley
Labour & Civil Rights Activist (Ret.),
ON

BISHOP, Henry V.
Chief Curator, Dir., Black Cultural
Centre for Nova Scotia

BRAITHWAITE, Daniel
Comm'y Organizer/Trade Unionist
(Ret.), Toronto

BRAITHWAITE, Rella Aylestock
Writer/Historian, Toronto

BRUCE, Lawrence S.
Vice-President, Black Loyalist
Heritage Society, NS

BUSH, Rochelle
Local Historian & Comm'y Activist, H.
Tubman Ctre. for Cultural Services, ON

CAMPBELL, Denise Andrea
Youth Activist/Frmr. President, NAC,
Toronto

CARTER, Rubin "Hurricane"
Frmr. Boxer/Activist, Assn. in Defence
of the Wrongfully Convicted, Toronto

CLARKE WALKER, Marie
Trade Unionist/ past VP National
Diversity, CUPE, Toronto

COOPER-WILSON, Jane
Historian/Artist/Writer, TigerLily
Enterprises, ON

CRICHLOW, Wesley
Activist/Asst. Prof., Dept. of Law,
Carleton U., Ottawa

FARRELL, Lennox
Teacher/Comm'y Organizer, Toronto
Dist. Cath. Sch. Brd.

FLEGEL, Peter
Youth Advocate/Comm'y Organizer,
Black Youth in Action, Montreal

GALABUZI, Grace-Edward
Research Assoc./Comm'y Activist,
Centre for Social Justice, Toronto

HIBBERT JR., Leroy
Multicultural Outreach Coordin., LUSO
Community Service, London

HILL III, Dan G.
Founder /President Emeritus (Ret.),
Ont. Black History Society, Toronto

HOOKS, Gwendolyn
Author/Teacher (Ret.), County of
Leduc, AB

JOHNSON, Beverley C.H.
Human Rights Officer, OPSEU,
Toronto

JONES, Robert William (Bud)
Historian/Lecturer, Anne Packwood
Quebec Afro-Cdn Res. Inst.,
Brockville

JONES, Roger B.
The Ability Market Consultant,
Vancouver

KUEHN, Sadie
Writer/Human Rights Activist, Sadie
Kuehn Consulting, Vancouver

LAWS, Dudley
Civil Rights/Comm'y Activist, Black
Action Defense Cmtee, Toronto

MOISE, Claude
Historien, Montréal

MORRISON, Wilma L.
Comm'y Volunteer/Local Historian,
Nathaniel Dett Chapel BME, Niagara
Falls

NEWKIRK, Reginald
Human Rights, Race & Labour
Relations Specialist, Parity
Consulting, SK

NOEL, Asha
Youth Leadership Rep., Cdn.
Ethnocultural Council, ON

OLIVER, Pearleen
Activist/Historian/Comm'y Leader,
Halifax

PARRIS, Jean Veronica
Labour Relations Consultant,
Federation of Nurses of Quebec

PHILIP, Dan
President, Ligue de Noirs du Québec/
Black Coalition of Quebec

PIETERS, Selwyn
Refugee Claims Officer, Immig'n & Refugee Brd. of Canada, Toronto

QUAMINA, Odida T.
Sociologist/Educator/Writer/Comm'y Organizer, Toronto

ROBINSON, Gwendolyn
Local Historian/Author, Chatham WISH Centre, ON

SADLIER, Rosemary
Author/President, Ont. Black History Society, Toronto

SMITH, Craig
Author/Historian/Constable, RCMP, Yarmouth

TAYLOR, Sheldon
Writer/Researcher/Historian, Toronto

THORPE, Carl
Exec. Dir., Multicultural History Society of Ont., Toronto

TURNER-BAILEY, Marjorie
Nurse/Genealogical Researcher, Roseway Hospital/Black Loyalist Society, NS

UPSHAW, Fred
Labour Union Leader & Activist (Ret.), OPSEU

VEECOCK, June
Dir., Human Rights, Ont. Federation of Labour, Toronto

WALL, Carol
Human Rights Dir., CEP Union/Canada, Ottawa

WAVROCH, Hélène
Présidente, Conseil des aînés, QC

WHITE, John Edgar (Jack)
Labour Union Organizer (Ret.), CUPE, Toronto

WILLIAMS, Dorothy W.
Historian/Writer/Editor, Montreal

⚖ LAW: Lawyers; Judges; Administrators...

ALCINDOR, Maryse
Directrice, Dir. de l'éd. et de la coopération, Commission des droits de la personne et des droits de la jeunesse, Montreal

ALEXANDER, Siobhan
Legal Counsel, Bank of Montreal, Toronto

ALEXANDER, Thérèse
Judge, Provincial Courts BC

ANDRE, Irving
Lawyer/Author, Brampton

BARNES, Kofi
Sr. Counsel & Special Advisor, Dept. of Justice, Fed. Prosecution Service, Toronto

BERNHARDT, Kim
Lawyer, Grant & Bernhardt, Toronto

BRAITHWAITE, Jack
Lawyer/Partner, Gatien◆Braithwaite Law Firm, Sudbury

BRAITHWAITE, Leonard A.
Barrister, Solicitor, & Notary Public, Private Practice, Toronto

CARTER, George E.
Judge (Ret.), Ont. Court of Justice, Toronto

CHARLES, Maurice A.
Judge (Ret.), Provincial Court of Ont., Toronto

CHUMPUKA, Florence
Legal Counsel, Federal Dept. of Justice, Ottawa

DEVONISH, Terrie-Lynne
VP, Legal Counsel and Corp. Secretary, HSBC Securities (Can.) Inc., Toronto

DOGBE, Julius
Justice of the Peace, Min. of the Attorney General, ON

DORTELUS, Daniel
Juge, Cour du Québec, Palais de justice

FALCONER, Julian N.
Barrister, Sr. Partner, Falconer Charney Macklin, Toronto

FRANCIS, Verlyn F.
Lawyer, Law Office of Verlyn F. Francis, Toronto

GRANT, Yola
Lawyer/Activist, Grant & Bernhardt, Toronto

HAMALENGWA, Munyonzwe
Lawyer, Private Practice, Toronto

HARRIS, Jeffrey F.
Lawyer/Partner, Myers, Weinberg, Winnipeg

HINKSON, Steven
Lawyer/Partner, Hinkson, Sachak, McLeod, Toronto

HUGGINS, Arleen
Barrister & Solicitor/Partner, Koskie Minsky, Toronto

IKEJIANI, Alexander O.
Barrister & Solicitor, Dept. of Justice, Ottawa

ISAAC, Julius Alexander
Federal Court Judge, Federal Court of Appeal, Ottawa

JOHN, Dexter
Lawyer, Donahue Ernst & Young LLP, ON

JONES, Lionel L.
Judge (Ret.), The Court of Queen's Bench of Alberta

JUMELLE, Yolène
Sociologue et Juriste, Tribunal Administratif du Québec

KABUNDI, Marcel
Gestionnaire, Prog. ethnoculturels, Service correctionnel du Canada, Min. du Sol. Gén. du Canada, Ottawa

LAMPKIN, Vibert
Judge, Ont. Court of Justice, Toronto

MCLEOD, Donald
Barrister & Solicitor/Partner, Hinkson, Sachak, McLeod, Toronto

MCWATT, Faye E.
Judge, Superior Court of Ont., Toronto

MORTEN, Marvin G.
Judge, Ont. Court of Justice, Brampton

MUTUNGI, Allyce B.
Lawyer, Private Practice, Ajax

MUYINDA, Estella Namakula
Legal Policy Analyst, Court Challenges Prog. of Canada, Winnipeg

N'SINGI, Vita Sébastien
Legal Counsel & Notary Public, Dept. of Justice, Ottawa

PETERS, Wilfrid E.D.
Legal Counsel, Chief Election Officer of Ont., Toronto

PITT, Romain W.M.
Judge, Ont. Superior Court of Justice, Toronto

RAWLINS, Micheline
Judge, Ont. Court of Justice, Windsor

REGIS, Gregory
Judge, Ont. Court of Justice, Ajax

ROACH, Charles
Lawyer/Barrister/Solicitor, Roach, Schwartz & Assoc., Toronto

ROMILLY, Selwyn R.
Judge, BC Supreme Court

ROSEMAY, Vibert T.
Judge, Ont. Court of Justice

SEARLES, Edsworth McAuley
Lawyer (Ret.), Toronto

SPARKS, Corrine E.
Judge, Nova Scotia Family Court, Dartmouth

SUTTON, Nicola
Legal Counsel, Supreme Court of Canada, ON

THOMAS, Sandra
Counsel, Criminal Prosecutions, Dept. of Justice, Fed. Prosecution Service, Toronto

TROTMAN, Gene Thornton T.
General Counsel, Federal Dept. of Justice, Ottawa

WALTER, Paul L.
Lawyer/Partner, Waterbury Newton, NS

WALWYN, Frank E.
Lawyer/Partner, WeirFoulds LLP, Toronto

WEDDERBURN, Hobartson A.J. (Gus)
Barrister/Solicitor/Notary Public, H.A.J. Wedderburn Law Office, Halifax

WESTMORELAND-TRAORE, Juanita
Judge, Court of Quebec, Montreal

WILLIAMS, Castor
Judge, Provincial Courts of Nova Scotia, Halifax

WILLIAMS, Eugene F.
Dir., Dept. of Justice, Federal Prosecution Service, Ottawa

WINN, Paul A.
Lawyer/Human Rights Activist, Paul A. Winn Law Corp., BC

WRIGHT, Cornell
Lawyer, Torys LLP, Toronto

MEDIA & FILM: Radio; TV; Print; Film; Writers; Producers; Directors; Critics...

ARMSTRONG, Neil
Journalist/News Dir., CHRY Radio, York U., Toronto

BAILEY, Cameron
Film Critic/Broadcaster, *NOW* Magazine/ Alliance Atlantis Broadcasting, Toronto

BOYD, Suzanne
Editor-In-Chief, *FLARE* Magazine, Toronto

BROWNE, Christene
Filmmaker, Syncopated Productions Inc., Toronto

CADER, Eric
Agent d'Ed./Dir., program. française, Interlink Consulting/CIUT 89,5FM, Toronto

CARRINGTON-MCCRACKEN, Iris
Journalist/Social Activist (Ret.), QC

CARTER, Jean
Journalist, CBC Radio, Toronto

de B'BERI, Boulou E.
Filmmaker/Activist, Montreal

DEVERELL, Rita Shelton
VP, New Concept Development, Vision TV, Toronto

DILLON-MOORE, Patricia (Pat)
Publicist/Spoken Word Performer, NFB, Montreal

FRASER, Felix (Fil)
Writer/Journalist/Filmmaker, Edmonton

GRANGE, Hamlin
Journalist/ President, ProMedia Int'l Inc., Toronto

GRANT, Sheryl
Asst. Managing Editor, The Halifax Herald Ltd., NS

HAMILTON, Sylvia
Filmmaker, Maroon Films Inc., NS

HOLDER, Peter Anthony
Radio Host/Broadcaster, CJAD 800 AM, Montreal

IEN, Marci
TV News Anchor, CTV NewsNet, Toronto

JACOB, Selwyn
Filmmaker/Producer, NFB, Vancouver

JARVIS, Michael
Filmmaker, Recfilm, Toronto

JEAN, Michaëlle
Journaliste-présentatrice, Société Radio Canada, Montréal

KEFENTSE, Dayo
Journalist, CBC Radio, Toronto

KELLY, Jude
Writer, Ont. Min. of Public Safety and Security

KING, Karen
Film Producer, NFB, Toronto

LAROSE, Winston W.
Videographer, African Cdn Comm. & Broadcasting, Burlington

LAURENT, Alix
Directeur Général, Images Interculturelles, Montréal

LEWIS, Sharon
On-Air Host, ZedTV, CBC, Toronto

LISTER, Celya
Independent TV Producer/CEO, Caribbean TV Quebec

MCCURVIN, Donna
Co-publisher, *Word* Magazine, Brampton

MCTAIR, Roger
Writer/Filmmaker/Lecturer, Toronto

MOTIKI, Joe
Performer/TV & Radio Host, c/o Characters Talent Agency, Toronto

NATION, Karlene
TV Reporter, CFTO TV, Toronto

NELSON, Ron
Radio DJ/Concert Promoter/CEO, Ron Nelson Prod., Toronto

PENNANT, Kevin
Executive Publicist, The Publicity Group, Toronto

POWELL, Juliette
President & CEO, Powell Entertain't Int'l Inc., Toronto

PRIETO, Claire
Film Producer, C+C Films Inc., Toronto

REYES, Cynthia
Executive Producer/VP, ProMedia Int'l Inc., Toronto

RILEY, Betty
TV Producer/Community Organizer, Windsor

SAUL, Ras Leon
Publisher/Editor/Performing Artist, *Uprising Int'l*, Scarborough

SHERWOOD, Anthony
Filmmaker/Producer, Anthony Sherwood Prod., Brampton

TOLBART, Gwen
TV Broadcaster, FOX 5/WTTG, US

414

VASSELL, Phillip
Co-Publisher, *Word* Magazine,
Brampton
VIRGO, Clement
Filmmaker/Director, Toronto
WALTERS, Ewart
Journalist/Communications
Consultant, Boyd McRubie
Communications, Ottawa
WHITE, Sheila
Communications Consultant, Words
Media & Communications, Toronto
WICKHAM, Aisha
Dir., Spoken Word & New Media,
FLOW 93.5FM, Toronto
WIWA, Ken
Writer/Journalist, Toronto

**MEDICINE: Doctors;
Nurses; Dentists;
Chiropractors;
Researchers; Educators;
Administrators...**

BATCHELOR, Wayne B.
Cardiologist, Southern Medical
Group, FLA/US
BERTLEY, Frederic Marcus
Immunologist/Research Scientist,
Harvard U. Medical School/Boston
Children's Hospital, MA/US
BERTLEY, John N.
Physician/Internist/Respirologist, Sir
William Osler Health Centre, Toronto
BLACKMAN, Margot
Comm'y Advocate/Nursing Teacher
(Ret.), Vanier College, Montreal
BLANCHETTE, Howard
Chair, Dept. of Obstet. & Gynec.,
Danbury Hospital, CT/US
BLIZZARD, Stephen V.
Aviation Medicine Consultant, Nepean
BON, Trevor
Physician, Geriatrics and Internal
Medicine, St. Joseph's Care Group,
Thunder Bay
BONNY, Yvette
Prof. Emérite/Hématologue, Hôpital
Maisonneuve-Rosemont, QC
BOVELL, Keith T.
MD, Gastroenterologist & Internist,
Private Practice, Guelph

BRATHWAITE, Shirley N.
Psychiatrist/Prof., Royal Ottawa
Hospital/ U. of Ottawa, ON
DAVIDSON, Patricia
Internist & Cardiologist, Private
Practice, DC/US
deGRAFT-JOHNSON, Ama
Anaesthesiologist/Clinical Prof.,
Hamilton Health Sciences
Centre/McMaster U.
DUPERVAL, Raymond
Prof./Chef du Service d'infectiologie,
Faculté de médecine, U. de
Sherbrooke, QC
DURITY, Felix
Prof./Head, Division of Neurosurgery,
Dept. of Surgery, UBC
EDWARDS, Madeline
Comm'y Organizer/Manager (Ret.),
Geriatric Psychiatric Outreach, CAMH,
ON
EKONG, Chris
Clinical Prof., Surgery/Neurosurgery,
U. of Saskatchewan
FITZ-RITSON, Don
Chiropractor/Dir., Advanced
Therapeutic Centre, Toronto
GITTENS, Rudolph Ormsby
Orthopedic Surgeon/Sport Medicine
Consultant, Private Practice, Ottawa
GLASGOW, Valerie
Clinical Nurse Educator/Faculty
Instructor, Mount Sinai
Hospital/Ryerson U., ON
GYLES, Carlton L.
Prof. of Bacteriology, Dept. of
Pathobiology, U. of Guelph
HEZEKIAH, Jocelyn
Nursing Education Consultant, ON
HOLNESS, Renn O.
Prof., Neurosurgery/Dir. of Surgical
Education, Dept. of Surgery;
Dalhousie U., NS
IKEJIANI, Charles
Orthopaedic Surgeon, Private
Practice, Barrie
IKEJIANI, Okechukwu
Pathologist (Ret.), Duncan
Professional Consultants, Nepean
JAMES, June Marion
Consultant, Allergy and Asthma,
Winnipeg Clinic, MB

JARRETT, Carolyn Joyce
Optometrist, Private Practice, Toronto
JOHNSON, E. Bruce
Pharmacist/Co-owner, City Drug Store
Ltd., Yarmouth
JOHNSON, Lillie
Dir. of Nursing (Ret.), Leeds,
Grenville, and Lanark District Health
Unit, ON
JONES, Ann
Clinical Nurse Specialist, Nephrology,
Toronto
KADIRI, Yahaya Z.
Anaesthesiologist/Internist, Southlake
Regional Health Centre, ON
KAFELE, Paul Kwasi
Dir., Corporate Diversity, CAMH,
Toronto
KASSIM, Ola A.
Pathologist-in-Chief & Dir. of Lab.
Services, West Parry Sound Health
Care Services, ON
KHENTI, Akwatu
Dir., Education & Training Services,
CAMH, Toronto
KURANTSIN-MILLS, Joseph
Res. Scientist/Prof., Med., Phys'y, &
Exper'l Med., G. Washington U./Ctr.
for Sickle Cell Dis., Howard U.
College
LAPIERRE, Myrtha
Prof. (Ret.)/Consultante, QC
LEWIS, Ronald
Surgeon, Chair, Div. Vascular Surgery,
McGill U. Health Centre, QC
LORIMER, Edith
Family Physician, Rosedale Medical
Centre, Toronto
MACFARLANE, Anthony
Medical Practitioner, Private Practice,
Hamilton
MONTAGUE, Kenneth
Dental Surgeon/Gallery Owner, Dr. K.
Montague & Assoc./The Wedge
Gallery, Toronto
MORGAN, Christopher J.
Chiropractor, Owner/Dir., Morgan
Chiropractic & Wellness, Toronto
NELSON, Amy
Head Surgical Nurse (Ret.)/ Volunteer,
JCA/Medical Mission Int'l, Toronto

NELSON, Kathleen
Nurse & Clinical Teacher, Toronto
Rehab. Inst./Ryerson U., Toronto

NICHOLAS, Everton S.
Endocrinologist, Toronto East General
Hospital, ON

NIMROD, Carl
Prof., Chair, Dept. of Obstet. &
Gynec., Fac. of Medicine, U. of
Ottawa, ON

NKANSAH, Peter
Dentist-Anaesthetist, Pleasant
Boulevard Dentistry & Anaesthesia,
Toronto

ODULANA-OGUNDIMU, A. Oluremi
Pediatrician, Laurentian Hospital,
Sudbury

OFOSU-NYARKO, Helen
Team Leader/Psychologist, Dept. of
Foreign Affairs & Int'l Trade, Ottawa

OJO, Oluremi
Pharmacist, Corporate Pharmacy,
Toronto

OLATUNBOSUN, Olufemi
Prof. & Chair, Obstet. Gynec., &
Reproductive Sciences, U. of
Saskatchewan

OLWENY, Charles Lwanga Mark
Prof./Medical Oncologist, U. of
Manitoba/ Cancer Care Manitoba

OWOLABI, Titus
Chief, Obstet., Gynec., and, Program
Medical Dir. of Maternal Newborn,
NYGH

RICKARD-BON, Sharon
Nutrition Consultant/Research
Coordin., Dynalife Health Services,
Thunder Bay

ROBBINS, Ju..au Kipola
Chiropractor/Author, Cultural
Chiropractic, MN/US

ROSSI, Miriam F.
Staff Physician, Div. of Adolescent
Medicine, Hospital for Sick Children,
Toronto

SALMON, John Douglas
Chief of General Surgery (Ret.),
Scarborough Centenary Hospital,
Toronto

SAM, Francis B.
Obstetrics/Gynecology, Private
Practice, Toronto

SANGSTER, Peggy Ann
Coordin., Quality & Risk Mngmt.,
Montreal Children's Hospital

SEWELL, J. George
Optometrist, Private Practice, ON

SMITH, Ifeyironwa F.
Nutritionist & Dietician, Nosi Smith
Food & Nutrition Consultants, Ottawa

SMITH, Shirley
Service Manager, CAMH, Toronto

SMITH, Winsome E.
Dentist, Private Practice, Etobicoke

SPENCE, Alwin C.
Prof./Sr. Lecturer, Dept. of
Psychology, John Abbott College, QC

STEVENS, Vida
Public Health Nutritionist, Toronto
Public Health, ON

TAYLOR, Garth Alfred
Ophthalmologist/Assoc. Prof., Dept.
Ophthalmology, Queen's U., ON

TUCKER, Elrie C.
Obstetrician & Gynecologist, Private
Practice, Montreal

WALLS, Bryan
Dental Surgeon/Local
Historian/Author, Essex

WILLIAMS, Charlotte
Veterinarian, Elrose Wildrose/Eston
Veterinary Services, SK

WOSU, Leonard
Res. Scientist/Science Teacher,
Greaves Adventist Academy, Montreal

WRIGHT, Leebert A.
Dir., Clinical Biochemistry (Ret.),
Wellesley/Princess Margaret
Hospitals, Toronto

YAKIMCHUK, Clotilda A.
Mental Health Nurse (Ret.),
Cape Breton Regional Hospital, NS

MILITARY & POLICE:
Veterans; Officers;
Administrators...

BORDEN, George
Captain (Ret.)/Poet-Songwriter/
Historian, RCAF/CF, Dartmouth

CARTY, Donald
WWII Veteran, RCAF, Toronto

CLAYTON, Cyril A.
Chief Warrant Officer (Ret.), Canadian
Forces, NS

DOWNES, M. Peggy
Aide-de-Camp/Admin. Officer,
Canadian Forces Army Reserve, Toronto

DUNCAN, Alvin
WWII Veteran, RCAF, Oakville

EDWARDS, Jacqueline
Recruitment Officer, Federal
Correctional Service of Canada,
Kingston

FORDE, Keith
Superintendent of Police, Toronto
Police Service

FRASER, James H.
Chief Warrant Officer (Ret.), Canadian
Forces, NS

HARTLEY, Max
Police Sergeant (Ret.), Halifax
Regional Police, NS

HOPE, Jay
Chief Superintendent, Ont. Provincial
Police, Orillia

HUNTE, Wesley
Warrant Officer (Ret.), Canadian
Forces, Montreal

HYPPOLITE, Marc-Arthur
Warden, Regional Reception
Centre/Special Handling Unit, QC

INCE, Thelma Coward
Personnel Administrator (Ret.), Dept.
of National Defence, Dartmouth

JOHNSTON, Roy
WWII Veteran, RCAF, Toronto

JUNOR, Kevin R.
Regimental Sergeant-Major, Canadian
Forces, Toronto

LAWRENCE, Raymond C.
Chief Petty Officer First Class (Ret.),
Royal Canadian Navy, Dartmouth

PARIS, David Ronald
Master Warrant Officer, Canadian
Forces, National Defence HQ, Orleans

PETERS, Walter W.
Aviation Consultant, Bombardier
Aerospace NFTC, Orleans

ROWE, Owen
WWII Veteran & Caribbean Diplomat
(Ret.), Montreal

SLOLY, Peter
Inspector, Toronto Police Service, ON

SPICER, Vincent
Captain (Ret.), Canadian Armed
Forces, London

UPSHAW, Robert Graham (Ted)
Inspector, Royal Canadian Mounted Police, NS

 **MUSIC: Performers; Producers; Composers; Administrators...**

ACQUAAH-HARRISON, Kobèna
Musician/Producer, Ice Hut Prod., Toronto

ALLEYNE, Archie
Musician/Drummer, Toronto

ANNOR-ADJEI, Ellen
Concert Pianist, Toronto

BERRY, Ivan
President/Head, Int'l Div., Beat Factory/ BMG Music, Toronto

BEY, Salome
Singer/Actor, Toronto

BIDDLE, Charlie
Jazz Musician, Justin Time Records, Montreal

BLYDEN-TAYLOR, Brainerd
Founder/Artistic Dir., The Nathaniel Dett Chorale, Toronto

BRIN, Derek
Music Producer/Composer, Fierce Music Group, Toronto

BROWN, Jeri
Jazz Performer/Prof. of Music, Justin Time Records

BRUEGGERGOSMAN, Measha
Soprano/Opera Singer

CARTER-HENRY LYON, Grace
Founder/Musical Dir., The Heritage Singers, Toronto

DOWNES, Wray
Classical/Jazz Pianist, Justin Time Records, Montreal

FOX, Lovena
Actor/Singer/Songwriter, Vancouver

GOMEZ, Henry
Musician/Actor, King Cosmos Entertainment, Toronto

GRANT STATES, Violet
Symphony/Music Teacher (Ret.), Montreal Women's Symphony

GUY, Sol
Global Hip Hop Entrepreneur, ON

HILL, Dan
Singer/Songwriter/Producer, Big Picture Entertainment

ISAACS, Orin
Musician, Moca Music, Toronto

JACKSON, D.D.
Jazz Pianist/Composer, Justin Time Records

JOHNSON, Molly
Singer/Songwriter/Philanthropist, c/o EMI Music, Toronto

JONES, Oliver
Jazz Pianist/Composer, Justin Time Records, Montreal

KLAASEN, Lorraine
Singer/Performer, Montreal

LARMOND, Londa
Singer/Performer, Toronto

LAW-BANCROFT, Carole
Music Teacher/Examiner, Royal Conservatory of Music, Toronto

LEE, Ranee
Jazz Performer, Justin Time Records, Montreal

LEWIS, Glenn
Singer/Songwriter, Sony Music

MAKEDA, Donna
Reggae/DanceHall Performer, *Uprising Int'l,* ON

MARSHALL, Amanda
Singer/Songwriter, Sony Music

MCCLAIN, Washington
Baroque Oboist, McGill U. & Indiana U.

MORGAN, Carlos
Singer/Songwriter/Producer, SolRoc Music, Toronto

MUHTADI
Percussionist/Artistic Dir., Muhtadi Int'l Drumming Festival, ON

NANCE, Marcus
Opera Singer/Bass-Baritone, Toronto

NOLAN, Faith
Musician/Activist, Toronto

OFFISHALL, Kardinal
Hip Hop Artist/MC/Producer, Toronto

PEREZ, John "Jayson"
Steel Pan Performer/Composer/Instructor, Toronto

PETERSON, Oscar
Jazz Pianist/Composer, Regal Recordings Ltd., ON

PICART, Richard
Manager/Industry Consultant, Mekehla Music Group, Toronto

PROCTOR, Hazel
Jazz Singer, Calgary

PROVIDENCE, Edford McConnie
Conductor/Composer/Pianist, Toronto

RICHARDSON, Doug
Saxophonist/Actor/Teacher, Toronto

SEALY, Joe
Jazz Pianist/Composer, Blue Jade Productions, Toronto

SHAQQ, Hameed
Steel Pan Musician/Composer, Toronto

SOLOMON, Adam
Musician, Adam Solomon & Tikisa, Toronto

SUTHERLAND, Tony
Urban Music Promoter/Program Head, Trebas Institute, ON

SYMONDS, Nelson
Jazz Guitarist, Montreal

WASHINGTON, Jackie
Jazz & Folk Musician/Performer, Toronto

WILLIAMS, Denise
Soprano/Classical Singer, c/o Anne Summers Int'l, Toronto

WILLIAMS, Georgina
Concert Pianist/Composer/Singer/Songwriter, Edmonton

WILLIAMS, Mojo
Proprietor/Musician (Semi-Ret.), Aries Gold, Calgary

WILLIAMS, Vivienne
Singer/Performer, Toronto

WILSON, Anthony (Salah)
Musician/Steel Pan Instructor, Salah's Steel Pan Academy, QC

WOODING, Marjorie Eglantine
Educator (Ret.)/Organist/Choir Dir., Church of Nativity, Toronto

NATURAL RESOURCES: Forestry; Soil; Agriculture; Administrators...

ALEXANDER, Norman E.
Registered Professional Biologist (Ret.), BC Institute of Technology, Chilliwack

ALLSOPP, W. Herbert L.
Fisheries Consultant, CEO, Smallworld Fishery Consultants Inc., N Vancouver

CAMPBELL, Constantine A.
Soil Res. Scientist
Emeritus/Consultant, Eastern Cereal &
Oilseed Res. Centre, Ottawa

MARSHALL, Valin G.
Soil Zoologist, Royal Roads U.,
Victoria

MOODY, Benjamin H.
Science Advisor, Forest Pest Mngmt.,
Cdn Forest Service, Natural
Resources Canada, Ottawa

SMITH, Olanrewaju B.
Sr. Programme Specialist, Int'l
Development Research Centre, Ottawa

RELIGION: Ministers; Pastors; Educators; Administrators...

ADAMS, John
Ministerial Dir., Alberta Conference of
Seventh-day Adventists

BUREY, Owen Leslie
Minister, Sandwich First Baptist
Church, Chatham

CAMPAYNE, Hazel
Diocesan Multicultural Consultant,
The Anglican Diocese of Toronto

DAVIS, Erica
Minister, British Methodist Episcopal
Church, Guelph

DONKOR, Samuel
Sr. Pastor, All Nations Full Gospel
Church, Toronto

EDWARDS, Haskell G.
Pastor, Seventh-day Adventist Church,
HQ, Markham

FIELDS, Stephen
Incumbent, The Anglican Church of
St. Stephen, Toronto

FRANCIS, Pat
Sr. Pastor, Founder, Deeper Life
Christian Ministries, Mississauga

GRAY, Darryl
Minister, Union United Church,
Montreal

JEMMOTT, Anthony
Incumbent, All Saints Anglican
Church, King City

KAWUKI-MUKASA, Isaac
Congregational Dev't Consultant, The
Anglican Diocese of Toronto

LAWRENCE, Errol A.
Chair/Assoc. Prof., Dept. of Religious
Studies, Canadian U. College, AB

MARKHAM, Jean J. Burke
Minister-in-Charge & Pastor, Peel
Methodist Church, Mississauga

MCNAB, John
Dir. of Pastoral Studies (Ret.), Montreal
Diocesan Theological College

MORRISON, Eva May
Sr. Pastor, Toronto New Covenant
Cathedral/COGOP

SEIVERIGHT, Deloris Devan
Archbishop, Shouters National
Evangelical Spiritual Baptist Faith,
Toronto

WARREN, Brian
Minister/Exec. Dir., Canada in Prayer,
Burlington

WATERMAN, Vincent
Archbishop, St. Philip's African
Orthodox Church of Canada, Sydney

SCIENCE & TECHNOLOGY: Researchers; Engineers; Technicians; Administrators...

BARNES, Leesa
IT Manager/President, BITePRO,
Toronto

BROWNIE, Edward
Biochemistry Research Technologist,
U. of Alberta

CARRENARD, Patrice
Dirigeant d'Entreprise/PDG, VISICOM
MEDIA, Brossard

DADSON SR., Joseph E.
Bio-medical Engineer/President/CEO,
Newsol Technologies, Toronto

FERNANDES, Lester
Geologist (Ret.), COMINCO Ltd.

FRANCOIS, Pierre
Mechanical Engineer/Teacher (Ret.),
Toronto

FRASER, Frank M.
VP Market Development (Ret.),
MDS Nordion, ON

GOODING, Victor E.
Future Technology Development
Specialist, Telesat Canada, Orleans

HAMIS, Ahmed R.
Environmental Coordin., Regional
Municip. of Halton, ON

HERRERA JACKSON, Denise
Consultant/Technical Writer, Farrell
Haynes Assoc., Toronto

IGWEMEZIE, Jude O.
Professional Engineer, CEO, Applied
Rail Research Technologies,
Brampton

KACELENGA, Ray
Principal Engineer, General Dynamics
Canada, Calgary

LORD, Richard M.
Engineer/Immigration Consultant/
Comm'y Organizer, Montreal

MASSIAH, Thomas
Research Chemist (Ret.), Toronto

NDUBUBA, Edward
Co-founder/Dir. of Operations, SS8
Networks Inc., Brampton

OGUNDELE, Gabriel
Sr. Research Scientist, Kinectrics Inc.,
Mississauga

OSAMUSALI, Sylvester
Sr. Nuclear Design Analyst, Ont.
Power Generation, Mississauga

SOUTHWELL, Gracey
Dir., Systems Support and
Operations, Aliant Telecom Broadband
Services, Halifax

SUTTON, Shawn
Dir., Business Planning & Analysis,
Mitel Networks, Gloucester

WILLIAMS, Taly
Environmental Engineer, President,
TM Williams LLC, CA/US

WRITING: Poets; Playwrights; Authors; Storytellers...

AGNANT, Marie-Célie
Écrivaine, Montréal

ALLEN, Lillian
Writer/Poet/Creative Writing Prof.,
Ont. College of Art & Design, Toronto

BADOE, Adwoa
Author, Guelph

bailey, maxine
Manager, Public Affairs, Toronto Int'l
Film Festival

BOYD, George
Playwright/Journalist, Montreal
CHARLES, Bernadette
Poet/Storyteller, Kulanga Production,
Montreal
CLARKE, George Elliott
Prof./Poet/Author/Playwright, Dept. of
English, U of T
COMPTON, Wayde
Writer/Editor, Vancouver
COOPSAMMY, Madeline F.
Writer/Poet, Winnipeg
FOGGO, Cheryl
Writer/Journalist/Film Dir., AB
GALE, Lorena
Actor/Playwright/Dir., Curious Tongue,
Vancouver
GORDON, Kevin
Writer, CA/US
HARRIS, Claire
Author, Calgary
HILL, Lawrence
Writer, c/o Harper Collins, ON
HOLAS, Patricia W.
Creative Dir./Author, Pan-African
Publications, Ottawa
HOPKINSON, Nalo
Author, Toronto
JAILALL, Peter
Teacher/Poet/Storyteller, Mississauga
JOYETTE, Anthony
Painter/Writer, Montreal
KUMSA, Martha Kuwee
Writer, c/o Harper Collins, Toronto
MANLEY, Rachel
Writer, c/o Random House, ON
MORGAN, Dwayne
Exec. Dir./Spoken Word Artist, Up
From the Roots, Toronto
MOTION
Spoken Word Poet/Hip Hop Artist,
Toronto
NYOKA, Gail
Playwright, Toronto
OLLIVIER, Émile
Prof. Éméritus, Écrivain, U. de
Montréal
PHILIP, M. NourbeSe
Poet/Writer, c/o Mercury Press,
Toronto
SADU, Itah
Author/Storyteller, A Different
Booklist, Toronto

SARSFIELD, Mairuth Hodge
Writer, BC
SEARS, Djanet
Writer/Dir./Actor, c/o WCA Film & TV,
Toronto
THOMAS, H. Nigel
Prof./Writer, U., Cité Universitaire, QC
TURENNE, Joujou
Conteuse, Joujou - Amie du Vent,
Montréal

Bibliography

Braithwaite, Rella, Eleanor Joseph. *Some Black Men: Profiles of over 100 Black Men in Canada.* Toronto: The Marlon Press, 1999.

Williams, Dorothy W. *The Road to Now: A History of Blacks in Montreal.* Montreal: Véhicule Press, 1997.

Braithwaite, Rella, Tessa Benn-Ireland. *Some Black Women: Profiles of Black Women in Canada.* Toronto: Black Women and Women of Colour Press, 1993.

Smith, Craig. *Journey: African Canadian History Study Guide.* Yarmouth: C.M.S. Publishing, 2000.

Holas, W.P. *Millennium Minds: 100 Black Canadians.* Ottawa: Pan-African Publications, 2000.

Jamaican-Canadians: A Commitment to Excellence. Toronto: Jamaican Canadian Association, 1987.

Miller, Mark. *Jazz in Canada: Fourteen Lives.* Toronto: University of Toronto Press, 1982.

OTHER:

I found a lot of information on the Internet. Sites which were particularly helpful:

Some Missing Pages: The Black Community in the History of Quebec and Canada.
    URL: *www.qesnrecit.qc.ca/mpages*

Canada Heirloom Series. Government of Canada. URL: *http://collections.ic.gc.ca/heirloom_series/*

Canada Noir. URL: *www.geocities.com/puissant12/CanadaNoir/*

Ontario Black History Online. URL: *http://collections.ic.gc.ca/OBHO/people/peo-cdblist.html*

Canadian Black Heritage in the Third Millennium. URL:
    http://fcis.oise.utoronto.ca/~gpieters/blklinks.html

Feedback

We'd like to know what you think of the first edition of WHO'S WHO IN BLACK CANADA and how we can improve. Please send us a note on the points outlined below or visit us online at: *www.whoswhoinblackcanada.com*

TELL US:

What you liked most and why:_____

_____

_____

What you liked least and why:_____

_____

_____

What you would like to see added: _____

_____

_____

General Comments/Suggestions: _____

_____

_____

NOMINATION FORM

The next edition of WHO'S WHO IN BLACK CANADA will be available in 2005. Help us to identify individuals achieving high levels of success in their professional lives or making a difference in their communities.

Name: _____

Reason for nomination:_____

Tel. No. or e-m address: _____

Your Name:_____

Your Tel. No. or e-m address: _____

Thank You!
WHO'S WHO IN BLACK CANADA
Tel: 416-694-8149;
Fax: 416-694-8920
e-m: info@whoswhoinblackcanada.com

CIBC

CIBC congratulates the 700 individuals who have earned their place in this inaugural publication through their hard work and dedication to their communities.

Black **B**usiness **I**nitiative

Our Mission:

To foster a dynamic and vibrant Black presence within the Nova Scotia Business Community.

Our Goals:

- to help create economic independence for individuals
- to further entrepreneurial development, education, and training in the Black community
- to build partnerships and linkages to the broader business community
- to create and improve access to private and public sector business support
- to improve standards of living and develop pride in communities

BLACK BUSINESS INITIATIVE
Canada Nova Scotia Business Service Centre
1575 Brunswick Street
Halifax, Nova Scotia B3J 2G1
Phone: 902-426-2224
Toll Free: 1-800-668-1010
Fax: 902-426-6530
E-Mail: bbi@cbsc.ic.gc.ca
Web: www.bbi.ns.ca

Encore!

TD Bank Financial Group
is proud to support
Who's Who in Black Canada